The Politics
of the Presidency

The Politics
of the Presidency

Second Edition

Richard A. Watson
University of Missouri-Columbia

Norman C. Thomas
University of Cincinnati

A Division of Congressional Quarterly Inc.
1414 22nd Street N.W., Washington, D.C. 20037

Cover Illustration: Dan Sherbo

Photo Credits: 20, AP/Wide World Photos; 66, UPI/Bettmann; 116, Library of Congress (Wilson, Taft), UPI/Bettmann (Roosevelt), The Bettmann Archive (Eisenhower); 150, AP/Wide World Photos; 198, copyrighted by the White House Historical Association, photograph by the National Geographic Society; 236, Library of Congress; 274, White House Photo; 318, *New York Times,* George Tames; 368, United States Department of Agriculture; 398, AP/Wide World Photos; 440, UPI/Bettmann

Library of Congress Cataloging-in-Publication Data

Watson, Richard Abernathy, 1923-
    The politics of the presidency.

    Bibliography: p.
    Includes index.
    1. Presidents—United States. I. Thomas, Norman C. II. Title.
JK516.W38   1988   353.03' 1   87-15670
ISBN 0-87187-369-9

To Joseph E. Kallenbach
who pointed the way and from whom
we both learned much

Contents

Tables and Figures

Tables

Figures

Preface

The Politics of the Presidency is a comprehensive introductory text on the nation's highest political office. Its theme is the presidency as a protean, or highly changeable, institution. The office varies with the character, personality, and political style of the incumbent as well as with major developments in the society and political system of the United States. We also discuss the presidency as an essentially political office; that is, the chief executive governs more through skilled political leadership than through the assertion of constitutional prerogatives.

The book is organized into three parts. Part One, "The President and the Public," explores the various dimensions of the president's relationship with the American people. The four chapters—on nomination politics, election politics, the kinds of persons who become president, and public politics—show that it is through the relationship between the chief executive and the public that the president first wins the office and then governs the country. Part Two, "The President and the Government," analyzes the presidency within the constitutional system that provides for the separation of powers and the corollary doctrine of checks and balances. The four chapters in Part Two address the development of the presidency and vice presidency and the politics of the president's relations with Congress, the bureaucracy, and the judiciary. Part Three, "The President and Public Policy," examines how presidents formulate and implement domestic, economic, and national security policy.

Throughout the book, we maintain the focus on the protean character of the office by summarizing, in a conclusion to each chapter, the ways each aspect of the presidency has changed over time. The last chapter contains our overall assessment of the protean presidency and analyzes possible reforms of the office.

This revision of *The Politics of the Presidency* benefited from reviews of the first edition, comments from colleagues who used the book, and our own experiences with it in the classroom. In examining all aspects of the American presidency, we drew on scholarly and journalistic analyses, historical and legal materials, and, where appropriate, behavioral and quantitative research. We added a chapter on domestic policy and incorporated findings from many of the excellent studies of the presidency that have been published since our first edition. We also updated the book to cover a wide variety of new topics: the 1984 nomination and election contests, the "rhetorical presidency," new perspectives on the vice presidency, President Reagan's use of the federal courts to carry out his conservative political agenda, Congress's effort to impose fiscal discipline on itself and the president through the Gramm-Rudman-Hollings act, and President Reagan's handling of the Iran-contra affair.

We especially appreciate the assistance of several persons who contributed to this second edition: Professor James Pfiffner of George Mason University, who made many constructive suggestions on its substance; Margaret Seawell Benjaminson, whose fine eye for detail and keen appreciation of a clear and concise writing style enabled us to improve markedly upon the first edition; Noell Sottile, who skillfully guided the manuscript through production; and Joanne Daniels, who oversaw the entire process with a judicious blend of needed prodding and patient tolerance.

We invite readers to write us about the book and would welcome their comments.

Richard A. Watson
Norman C. Thomas

INTRODUCTION

Perspectives on the Protean Presidency

On January 20, 1985, a triumphal Ronald Reagan took the oath of office to begin his second term as president. In a highly successful first term, Reagan instituted major changes in economic policy, reversed a half-century of growth in the domestic programs of the federal government, and restored the military power and international prestige of the United States, which had declined steadily since the end of the Vietnam War in 1973. By 1982, inflation was under control; in late 1983, decisive U.S. military action ended an oppressive left-wing dictatorship in the Caribbean country of Grenada; and throughout 1984, the economy grew rapidly.

In the 1984 election, Reagan scored a historic landslide reelection victory. The Republican party retained control of the Senate (although dropping from fifty-five to fifty-three seats) and gained fourteen seats in the House. The election affirmed the American public's support for the president, and many analysts interpreted it as confirmation of the permanence of the "Reagan revolution." Pundits described Reagan as the "Teflon president"— neither criticism nor the consequences of unfavorable developments would stick to him. To many observers, Reagan seemed to be the most successful president since Franklin D. Roosevelt. He would, they believed, set a new standard of performance against which future presidents would be measured.

Reagan's principal goals for his second term included overhauling the federal tax system, further reducing the role of the federal government in domestic programs, and increasing the nation's security through enhanced military strength and development of a technologically advanced missile defense system. In short, he planned to consolidate and make permanent his revolution.

As Reagan began his new term, his objectives appeared to be within reach. The opposition Democrats, demoralized after their crushing election defeat, had no positive alternatives to the Reagan administration's programs. Throughout 1985 and much of 1986 the president enjoyed continued legislative success. He resisted the appeals of congressional Democrats to change his spending priorities or to accept a tax increase as a way of reducing the budget deficit. Also, he prevailed upon members of Congress to approve military aid to the contra rebels in Nicaragua for fiscal year 1987 after they rejected it for 1986. In an action that would give the Supreme Court a strongly conservative cast long after the end of his presidency, Reagan obtained Senate confirmation of Associate Justice William Rehnquist as chief justice of the United States and of Antonin Scalia as Rehnquist's replacement. Perhaps most important in solidifying the Reagan revolution, the president persuaded Congress to enact the sweeping Tax Reform Act of 1986, which closely resembled his initial proposal.

Until late 1986 popular support for President Reagan remained strong. It did so even though the public disapproved of many aspects of his performance—his handling of the federal deficit (which reached a record $220 billion in 1986), of the national debt (which more than doubled under his administration), and of arms negotiations with the Soviet Union. Even missteps and unfavorable political developments—such as failure to make progress toward a Middle East peace settlement and his visit to a German military cemetery where members of the notorious Nazi SS were buried—seemed not to diminish Reagan's popular support. He also enjoyed extraordinary good fortune; the collapse of world oil prices, for example, brought inflation down further. In sum, Reagan's good luck, his immunity to adverse events, and his remarkable ability to establish and maintain rapport with the American people sustained his personal popularity and restored public support for and confidence in the presidency.

In November 1986, however, Reagan's political fortunes took a sharp turn for the worse. In the midterm congressional elections the Democrats captured control of the Senate with a net gain of 8 seats, giving them a margin of 55-45, and picked up 5 House seats, for a 258-177 edge. Shortly after the election, popular support for Reagan began to fall as the public learned the details of a covert operation in which arms were sold to Iran and the profits from the transaction transferred to the Nicaraguan contras. These actions conflicted with established policies on terrorism and with statutory prohibitions against arms sales to Iran and support for the contras. The affair raised serious questions about the conduct and content of the administration's foreign policy and the president's leadership. Reagan and administration spokespersons were unable to provide a full account or convincing explanations of their actions.

As the 100th Congress convened in January 1987, the political spotlight focused on President Reagan's efforts to repair his damaged credibility among political leaders in Washington and abroad and to recover lost popular support. The contrast was striking between the confident president, who throughout his first six years in office had turned in a performance that delighted his supporters, dismayed his critics, and surprised and puzzled analysts, and the seemingly bewildered "lame duck," struggling to rescue what remained of his presidency.

Rapid changes in presidential politics, such as those that occurred between January 1985 and January 1987, are not new to the American political scene—nor are varying interpretations of their meaning. The following sections outline how scholars' conceptions of the presidency have changed since the 1950s. The Introduction next analyzes the basic forces shaping the office and concludes with a discussion of the protean presidency, the perspective on the presidency presented in this book.

Changing Conceptions of the Presidency

Students of the presidency have identified three conceptions of the office: the heroic, the imperial, and the post-imperial presidencies.

The Heroic Presidency

The 1950s and 1960s were the era of what might be termed the "heroic" presidency. Writing about the office in 1960, at the end of Dwight D. Eisenhower's second term, Clinton Rossiter expressed his belief that the American presidency is "one of the few truly successful institutions created by men in their endless quest for the blessings of free government." [1] His book analyzing the power and limitations of the presidency clearly glorifies the office and the "great" presidents who have shaped it—George Washington, Thomas Jefferson, Andrew Jackson, Abraham Lincoln, Theodore Roosevelt, Woodrow Wilson, Franklin D. Roosevelt, and Harry S Truman. Predicting "a long and exciting future for the American Presidency," Rossiter concluded his analysis with a poetic celebration of the institution: [2]

> It is, finally, an office of freedom. The Presidency is a standing reproach to those petty doctrinaires who insist that executive power is inherently undemocratic; for, to the exact contrary, it has been more responsive to the needs and dreams of giant democracy than any other office or institution in the whole mosaic of American life. It is no less a reproach to those easy generalizers who think that Lord Acton had the very last word on the corrupting effects of power; for, again to the contrary, his doctrine finds small confirmation in the history of the Presidency. The vast power of this office has not been "poison," as Henry Adams wrote in scorn; rather, it has elevated often and corrupted never, chiefly because those who held it recognized the true source of the power and were ennobled by the knowledge.[3]

Also appearing in 1960, in its first edition, was Richard E. Neustadt's *Presidential Power: The Politics of Leadership*, considered by many to be the most perceptive analysis of the office ever written. Like Rossiter, Neustadt is a great admirer of the American presidency. He expressed concern, however, that the limitations of the office, especially those stemming from a "government of separated institutions, sharing power," threaten to make the president a clerk rather than a leader.[4] To rectify this situation, Neustadt proposed that presidents pursue personal political power by bargaining with other political actors—members of Congress, bureaucrats, and party leaders, for example—persuading them that "what he wants of them is what their own appraisal of their own responsibilities requires them to do in their interest not his." [5] Neustadt's analysis of three modern presidents—Franklin Roosevelt, Truman, and Eisenhower—convinced him that FDR's temperament and understanding of political power enabled him to be by far the most successful: "No modern President has been more nearly master in the White House." [6] Toward the end of the book Neustadt made a sweeping statement that epitomizes his glorification of the office:

> The contributions that a President can make to government are indispensable. Assuming that he knows what power is and wants it, those contributions cannot help but be forthcoming in some measure as by-products of his search for personal influence. In a relative but real sense one can say of a President what Eisenhower's first Secretary of Defense once said of General Motors: what is good for the country is good for the President and vice versa.[7]

In 1965, during the administration of Lyndon B. Johnson, still another study appeared celebrating the heroic American presidency—James MacGregor Burns's *Presidential Government: The Crucible of Leadership.* Analyzing the performance of the presidency in history, Burns chose Alexander Hamilton as his model. Although not a president, Hamilton was an influential member of the Washington administration who "succeeded in 'tuning government high,' so high that Washington's administration stands as one of the truly creative presidencies in American history." [8] Burns's analysis of the characteristics of a Hamiltonian president (he includes in this group Washington, Lincoln, and the two Roosevelts) parallels that espoused by Neustadt: they are heroic leaders who build a loyal, personal political organization and expediently use their reputations, prestige, patronage, power, and political friendships, as well as tactics of co-opting and disorganizing the opposition party leadership, to achieve the results they want.[9] Unlike Neustadt, however, who made no mention of the ends for which presidential power is to be used, Burns examined the performance of the presidency to determine whether it has served the basic values of American society. His conclusion affirms the concept of the heroic president:

> For in presidential government Americans have established one of the most powerful political institutions in the free world. They have fashioned, sometimes unwittingly, a weapon that has served them well in the long struggle for freedom and equality at home and in the search for stable and democratic politics abroad. They have grasped the uses of power, and as Harold Laski said, great power makes great leadership possible.[10]

Although these three important presidential scholars of the 1950s and 1960s differed in some respects, for the most part they agreed on the existence and value of a heroic institution. Writing in 1970, Thomas E. Cronin labeled this perspective the "textbook presidency" because it was adopted not only by presidential scholars but also by writers of general American government textbooks of the era, who described the presidency in glowing terms. Underlying their conception of the office was a common assumption: the national government should be the leader in solving the problems of an increasingly interdependent world and of U.S. domestic society as well. The authors of these books on the presidency were political liberals who viewed the office as the only institution in the political system that has the vision of the needs of all Americans (including the disadvantaged) and has a nation-wide constituency providing the political support to meet those needs.

Cronin went on to note that conditions in the late 1960s, in particular the inability of President Johnson to end the Vietnam War, were beginning to tarnish the heroic image of the presidency.[11] As the following section indicates, the 1970s did indeed usher in a radically different version of the nation's highest office.

The Imperial Presidency

Studies appearing between 1970 and 1975 characterized the office as an "imperial presidency," a term coined by Arthur Schlesinger, Jr. (who served in John F. Kennedy's White House) in his 1973 book by that name. In a similar analysis of the presidency in 1970, George Reedy, a former White House aide under President Johnson, described the office as "the American monarchy." The thesis of Reedy's book, *The Twilight of the Presidency,* is that, far from ennobling its occupants, the presidential office creates "an environment in which men cannot function in any kind of a decent and human relationship to the people whom they are supposed to lead."[12] At fault is a presidential "court" composed of sycophants who tell the president what he wants to hear and who thereby isolate him from the harsh facts of political life. Denied the presence of peer pressure and of people who will tell him when he is wrong, the president exaggerates his own importance and competence.

Schlesinger's study benefited not only from the insights gained from the Vietnam War but also from the Watergate scandal. He discovered the origins of the imperial presidency in the field of foreign policy, "from the capture by the Presidency of the most vital of national decisions, the decision to go to war."[13] Tracing the presidents' arrogation of the war power from Congress, with which the Founders intended it be shared, Schlesinger saw the trend becoming more pronounced after World War II, and especially after the ascension of Lyndon Johnson and Richard Nixon to the White House. During the Nixon administration, presidential imperialism spread into the domestic sphere as the president employed a variety of measures to deal with those who opposed him: impounding funds appropriated by Congress, dismantling the Office of Economic Opportunity without congressional authorization, making excessive claims of executive privilege to withhold vital information from Congress, and using a special investigation unit to conduct illegal surveillance of U.S. citizens. In fact, Schlesinger described the Nixon presidency not only as "imperial" but also as "plebiscitary," a concept borrowed from Napoleon and, more recently, from former French president Charles de Gaulle. When a plebiscitary leader is elected, "he personifies the majority and all resistance to his will is undemocratic," at least until the time of the next election. [14]

In 1975, the year after Nixon had been forced to resign, Sen. Walter F. Mondale (D-Minn.) analyzed the contemporary presidency in his book *The Accountability of Power: Toward a Responsible Presidency*. He stated that Vietnam burst "the bubble of Presidential ascendancy and omniscience" and that Watergate initiated "a wholesale decline in Americans' belief in the viability and honesty of their governmental institutions." [15] Mondale blamed the imperial presidency not only on the occupants of that office but on others as well, including Congress, which regularly voted appropriations for U.S. military involvement in Vietnam, and the American people, who knew what their taxes were paying for.

The message of presidency analysts writing in the first half of the 1970s was, therefore, precisely the opposite of those who wrote about the office in the 1950s and 1960s. As William Andrews describes the transformation, "Hallowed Be the Presidency" became "Deliver Us from Presidents." [16] The radical change in viewpoint cannot be attributed to a different type of analyst. Reedy, Schlesinger, and Mondale shared the same political philosophy as those who examined the presidency in the earlier period: they were liberals. Over time these writers came to appreciate that the vast powers of the presidency, which could be used for good purposes (ameliorating domestic social and economic problems and winning World War II), also could be used for bad ones (waging a futile, costly conflict in Southeast Asia and launching an all-out attack on political "enemies" that led to the abuses of Watergate). Just when it seemed, however, that presidential scholars agreed upon the true nature of the presidency, a new conception of the office began to emerge.

The Post-Imperial Presidency

In 1978, three years after Senator Mondale's book was published, Fred Greenstein noted a change in the contemporary American presidency. Observing the rapid turnover in presidents (from 1961 to 1978, five chief executives had served, three of them since 1974), Greenstein suggested that such a short tenure in office has required the chief executive

> to have a hurried approach to the making of policy, . . . to engage in activities that are politically risky: simply to win office he needs to raise aspirations about what he will be able to contribute to the nation; once in office, the difficulty of meeting those aspirations opens up the temptation to cut corners—for example, to rush legislation through Congress and leave considerations of political implementation for later on.[17]

Greenstein went on to outline "the intractable political environment of the post-imperial presidency," which includes a Congress whose leaders cannot serve as "effective intermediaries between their Congress and the president"; a weakened party system over which the president is no longer chief; aggressive media that initially idealize new presidents and then "quickly search out their warts"; and a presidential bureaucracy that "has expanded to the point where the president is victimized rather than helped by members of a staff whom he cannot begin to supervise." [18] He also noted the "presidency-curbing legislation" passed by Congress in the 1970s. New laws required the president to consult Congress "in every possible instance" before committing troops to combat and to report to Congress all executive agreements made with foreign powers; limited the power of the president to reorganize executive departments and to impound funds appropriated by Congress; and made the appointment of the director and deputy directors of the Office of Management and Budget subject to Senate confirmation. Greenstein's analysis illustrates that the presidency of the late 1970s was hardly an imperial one.

In 1980 British journalist Godfrey Hodgson presented similar conclusions about the office in *All Things to All Men: The False Promise of the American Presidency*. In Hodgson's view, presidents are isolated from other elements of the U.S. political system through which they could make the system work: the bureaucracy, Congress, their own political party, the media, and even the American people. Presidents also face social and economic problems so difficult and complex that they "have little chance of making any real progress in the direction of solving them within their first term of office. Moreover, they have virtually no hope of making *visible* progress toward solving them in time to have a positive effect on their own prospects of being reelected." [19] As Hodgson summarized the situation, "Never has so powerful a leader been so impotent to do what he wants to do, what he is pledged to do, what he is expected to do, and what he knows he must do." [20]

The presidency of the last half of the 1970s bore little resemblance to the imperial presidency of the first half of that decade. Some observers, like Hodgson, thought the office was "impotent"; others, like Cronin, asked whether it was "imperiled." [21] Cronin maintained that the experiences of the post-imperial presidency led many political liberals, who had feared the office in the mid-1970s, to conclude that Congress was incapable of leading the nation's affairs and to call for a resurgent and vigorous presidency. Indeed, part of Ronald Reagan's appeal to the voters in the 1980 election was a pledge to restore the strength of the office.

The Reagan presidency has been characterized in various ways. In 1983 Richard Nathan noted approvingly the successful establishment under Reagan of the "administrative presidency strategy," first attempted by Nixon. [22] (This strategy uses administrative rather than legislative means to accomplish presidential policy objectives whenever it is possible to do so.)

As others pointed out, however, this was accomplished at the cost of politicizing the federal bureaucracy and weakening the civil service by increasing the number of policy-sensitive positions filled by political appointees instead of career civil servants.[23] In 1984 Bert Rockman suggested, in his thought-provoking book, *The Leadership Question,* that answers lay not only in more "presidentialism" (efforts to strengthen presidential leadership), but also in "making the whole of government more effective."[24] A year later Theodore J. Lowi argued that a plebiscitary presidency, entailing a direct relationship between the president and the American people, had been developing since 1933 and had come to maturity under Reagan. The result, Lowi asserted, is the pathological growth of big government and the eclipse of Congress and of the political party system.[25] In contrast, in a 1986 study, Rockman favorably described the plebiscitary presidency: along with institutional restraints, it is the answer to the problem of presidential accountability.[26]

This review of changes in attitudes toward the presidency raises the question, why have conceptions of the office varied so widely over a comparatively short period? This question in turn, leads to a more basic one: what are the forces that shape the American presidency?

Basic Forces Shaping the Presidency

All students of the office are aware that many forces affect the presidency, but they tend to emphasize different ones as the most important. The following discussion groups the various influences into three principal categories: the type of person who occupies the office, the nature of the office itself, and the external environment in which the presidency operates.

The Type of Person Occupying the Office

The presidential scholars of the 1950s and 1960s essentially agreed on the type of person who should occupy the office. Rossiter's "great" presidents, Neustadt's skilled manipulators of personal political power, and Burns's chief executives who operated under the Hamiltonian model were all activists who stretched the powers of the office to the fullest extent in their leadership at home and abroad. These three analysts revered Franklin Roosevelt and would have been pleased to have someone like him in office all the time.

These scholars had far less use, however, for the more passive Dwight Eisenhower. Rossiter judged him severely because of his failure to provide visible leadership on important domestic issues such as education and racial integration. He concluded that "Ike" was "a good president but far from a great one."[27] Neustadt and Burns regarded Ike no more favorably. Neustadt concluded that "personal advantage had no place among his aims" and that he was "a hero seeking national unity" who came to the presidency "to crown a reputation, not to make one."[28] Burns cited a poll of U.S. historians that placed Eisenhower toward the bottom of the "average" category of president, and he had no quarrel with that evaluation.[29] In the 1980s, however, Fred Greenstein sparked a revisionist interpretation of Eisenhower's leadership. Greenstein argued that although Ike maintained a statesmanlike public posture throughout his presidency, he shrewdly concealed a self-conscious style of effective political leadership.[30]

With the advent of the imperial presidencies of Johnson and Nixon, scholars became more sensitive to the harmful effect strong, assertive chief executives might have on the office if they pursued the wrong course of action. As Reedy put it, "President Johnson and most of his close advisers interpreted the election result [the 1964 landslide victory of Johnson over Goldwater] as a mandate from the people not only to carry on the policies of the Johnson administration but any other policies that might come to mind." [31] Reedy even complimented Republican president Eisenhower for being a "symbol of legitimacy, continuity and morality" and suggested that perhaps the American people "were right in elevating these qualities to a position higher than the manipulative skill that resolves problems." [32] Reedy called attention to the crucial effect of the president's personal qualities on the conduct of the office: "In the White House, character and personality are extremely important because there are no limitations which govern a man's conduct. Restraint must come from within the presidential soul and prudence from within the presidential mind." [33]

It remained, however, for another student of the presidency, James David Barber, to develop a more systematic approach to the study of presidential character. In his pioneering 1972 book, *The Presidential Character: Predicting Performance in the White House,* Barber added a new dimension to the study of the office—the classification of presidents by type. (Chapter 3 will examine his major ideas in detail.) According to Barber, one can distinguish both between active and passive chief executives (by how much energy they put into the office) and between positive and negative ones (by whether they enjoy being president or serve only out of compulsion or a sense of duty). Citing Johnson and Nixon as examples of active-negative presidents, Barber pointed out the unfortunate characteristics of that type: it comprises driven, rigid individuals who have trouble managing their aggressions and who continue to pursue policies even when the policies have failed (hence, the long, unsuccessful U.S. military effort in Vietnam). Particularly impressive was Barber's 1972 prediction that should Nixon feel a threat to his power and sense of accomplishment, he might pursue an inflexible course of action, which is precisely what he later did when confronted with the incidents that came to be known as "Watergate."

The Nature of the Presidential Office

George Reedy was one of the first presidential scholars to demonstrate a sensitivity to the influence of the office on the incumbent. Although he appreciated the importance of individual personality in the presidency (as mentioned in the preceding section), he was also acutely aware of the reverse relationship. In the foreword of *Twilight of the Presidency* he observed, "The factor that I have missed in most of the works on the presidency I have read is the impact of the institution on the individuals." In the first chapter, "The American Monarchy," Reedy explained how the atmosphere of the "court," consisting of the king and his overly deferential White House aides, dulls the political sensitivities of even the most skilled politicians. As an illustration he cited Lyndon Johnson. As president, Johnson proposed a merger of the departments of Commerce and Labor, thus antagonizing business people and labor leaders alike. Neither group wanted the agency with which it had carefully forged close ties to be merged with the one associated with its traditional opponents. Reedy suggested that Johnson would never have made such a mistake when he was majority leader of the Senate because in that capacity he was forced to "touch base" with peers and a variety of groups who sensitized him to political realities. Reedy also pointed out that other astute public figures made major political blunders when they became president: Woodrow Wilson's clumsy treatment of the Senate over the Versailles Treaty following World War I; Roosevelt's ill-fated attempt to "pack" the Supreme Court in 1937; and Truman's inept handling of the spy scare in the late 1940s. Reedy attributed these incidents to the political isolation from reality that all presidents face.

Bruce Buchanan expanded on this thesis in his 1978 study, *The Presidential Experience: What the Office Does to the Man.* He analyzed the "psychological environment of the presidency" and its effect on the incumbents and their behavior in office. In Buchanan's view, the necessity to play a variety of roles exposes the president to constant psychological pressures, which result in behavior harmful to himself and the conduct of the office. Like Reedy, he believed the president's "symbolic" role of embodying the nation's values makes those around him excessively deferential, causing presidents to make bad decisions. A second consequence of such deference is the incumbent's overidentification with the presidency, which creates "an unhealthy link, in the minds of citizens, between the fate of the presidency and his fate as a person." [34] Buchanan also held that the symbolic role of the presidency and the president's position as "policy advocate" (selling his programs) leads to unrealistic expectations, which the president cannot fulfill. As a result, the president tends to misrepresent his accomplishments (taking credit he does not deserve and unjustly blaming others) and to lie to the public and even to himself. In addition, the policy advocate role exposes the president to constant opposition from others, causing personal frustration, which he vents by arrogating the powers of the other branches. Finally, the roles of "conflict mediator" and "crisis manager" place excessive and often contradictory demands on the president. The strain of this conflict diminishes his physical and psychological energy and, consequently, the effectiveness of his performance.

Schlesinger's *Imperial Presidency* also stressed the importance of the office in shaping the conduct of the president. He focused not on its political isolation or psychological environment, however, but on its broad, ambiguous constitutional powers. Schlesinger contended that these powers, especially in the field of foreign policy, enable presidents to exercise extraordinary control over the nation's affairs, such as the power to wage war unilaterally.

Richard Pious's 1979 study, *The American Presidency*, also emphasized the constitutional powers of the office. He discounted the importance of political factors—election results, party lineups in Congress, the mobilization of public opinion—on the president's ability to exercise power effectively. Rather, he argued "that the key to an understanding of presidential power is to concentrate on the constitutional authority that the president asserts unilaterally through various rules of constitutional construction and interpretation, in order to resolve crises or important issues facing the nation." [35] Pious's view directly contradicts Neustadt's position that the key to presidential power lies within the personality of the president.

The External Environment of the Presidency

While some presidential scholars stress the influence of the incumbent's personality on the office, and others the influence of the office on the incumbent, yet a third school contends that the most important forces affecting the presidency lie outside the institution. A key force in the external environment of the president is the group of political actors with whom he must deal in the process of governing. Among scholars of the heroic presidency, Neustadt paid the most attention to this group. In *Presidential Power* he named "five sets of constituents" who demand aid and service from the president: executive officials, Congress, the president's partisans, U.S. citizens in general, and persons abroad who are affected by U.S. policies.[36] Neustadt described these five constituencies collectively as the "Washingtonians"—a term that includes not only members of Congress and the administration but also "governors of states, military commanders in the field, leading politicians in both parties, representatives of private organizations, newsmen of assorted types and sizes, foreign diplomats (and principals abroad)," all of whom are "inveterate observers of the president." [37] The president shares the governing of the country with this broad array of individuals and groups and must persuade them to do what he wants not only for his sake but for theirs as well.

Analysts of the imperial presidency painted a much different picture of the effect of other political actors on the office. Rather than viewing them as a powerful counterbalance to the chief executive, as did Neustadt, presidential scholars of the first half of the 1970s saw them essentially as weak institutions that isolated the president from reality and failed to check his actions effectively. After analyzing the influence of Congress, members of the executive branch, political parties, and the media, Reedy concluded that only the media keep the president in touch with reality. Schlesinger and Mondale came to a similar conclusion but contended that even the media was subject to exploitation by the president, especially through his ability to command the resources of television for prime-time speeches on subjects of his choosing.

In their studies of the post-imperial presidency, Greenstein and Hodgson also maintained that the political actors with whom the president must work are more important than either the personality of the president or the nature of the office itself. Unlike the analysts of the imperial presidency, however, they considered these political actors neither weak nor ineffective. Rather, as Greenstein wrote, in the era of the post-imperial presidency these external forces are "intractable"; they "are more amorphous, less responsive to their own leadership or any other, and are therefore less well-suited for presidential coalition-building." [38] In a similar vein, Hodgson argued that these institutions do not serve as "connecting rods or gears" through which presidential power can be transmitted to the wheels of the political system.[39] Both Lowi and Rockman, writing in the mid-1980s, found the pluralistic pattern of American politics based on powerful interest groups to be the most important environmental constraint on presidents.

External elements in addition to political actors affect the presidency. One is the social and economic problems he faces while in office. Although Hodgson contended that a president has little chance of making any real progress toward solving difficult problems, at least in his first term, the nation's experience under the early years of the Reagan presidency calls into question the accuracy of that sweeping statement. Certainly, external events and conditions greatly influence a president's agenda and may impose constraints on his action, but purposeful and effective leadership can help the country manage, if not control, them.

Another external factor affecting the presidency is the general mood of the country. As Cronin pointed out: "President Carter would doubtless like to provide leadership of the Roosevelt and Kennedy kind but he doesn't have the appropriate climate of expectations. There is neither the trauma of a depression nor the crusading spirit of a world war, nor the buoyant national optimism of the early 1960s." [40] Barber placed the major emphasis of his study on the character of the president but also recognized that the chief executive has to deal with a "climate of expectations." [41] He explained that the American people look for different things at different times in their president: sometimes they seek "reassurance, a feeling that things will be all right, that the president will take care" of them; at other times they demand a "sense of progress and action," wanting the president to "do something to direct the nation's course"; at still other times they need a sense of "legitimacy" from the president, the feeling that he "should be above politics," that "he should have a right to his place and a rightful way of acting in it." [42] In this way the public mood and climate of expectations shape presidential performance. Observers of the office should recognize, however, that the president can, in turn, influence the popular mood by his rhetoric, attitude, and approach to the task of governing. (See Chapter 4.) Again, Reagan provides a good illustration of one who, for much of his presidency, successfully understood and shaped the popular mood.

A Comprehensive Approach: The Protean Presidency

It is inaccurate to describe the presidency as either "heroic," "imperial," "post-imperial," or "imperiled." Such characterizations fall short because they depict the presidency at only one point in time and thereby imply that the condition is a permanent one—they mistake a snapshot for a portrait. The rapidity with which conceptions of the office have changed over the past quarter-century testifies to the error in this approach.

If any single label is an appropriate description of the presidency, it is "protean." Like Proteus, the sea god of Greek mythology who could change his appearance at will, the presidency is exceedingly *variable,* capable of assuming different shapes and forms. On the political stage presidents are protean actors, playing many roles in the governing system as circumstances demand.*

The presidency is exceedingly variable for several reasons. First, in no other public office do the personality, character, and political style of the incumbent make as much difference as in the presidency. Moreover, as the linchpin of the entire U.S. political system, the presidency is greatly affected by changes that occur anywhere in that system—whether in the formal political structure (Congress, the executive branch, the courts), in the informal political institutions (political parties and interest groups), in society at large, in the mass media, or in conditions surrounding substantive issues, particularly national security and the economy. The president must contend with all of these influences. Furthermore, although the Constitution and

---

*The analogy can be carried further. Proteus knew all things, past, present and future, but disliked telling what he knew. Those who wanted to consult him had to surprise and bind him. The god then tried to avoid answering by assuming all sorts of shapes—that of a lion, a serpent, a bear, a tree, fire, or water—but if the captor held him fast, Proteus at last returned to his proper shape, gave the wished-for answer, and plunged into the sea. Members of Congress, executive branch officials, and representatives of the media who constantly seek information from often evasive presidents may best appreciate this analogy. There is considerable irony in the myth of Proteus and the changing versions of the Iran-contra affair that President Reagan and other administration officials offered in late 1986 and early 1987.

historical precedents give structure to the office, the powers of the presidency are so vast and vague that incumbents have great latitude in shaping the office to their particular desires.

The presidency is not only a highly *changeable* institution but also an essentially *political* one. Although on occasion, especially in times of crisis, presidents rule by asserting their constitutional prerogatives, they usually are forced to govern by political maneuvering, by trying to convince and persuade the many participants in the political process. During the Iranian hostage crisis, for example, Jimmy Carter invoked a number of constitutional prerogatives, but they did not help him handle the problems of the domestic economy or alter the perceived decline of U.S. power and prestige in the world—conditions that contributed substantially to his defeat in the 1980 election. Moreover, the changes that occurred in the first year of the Reagan administration resulted not from the president's exercising constitutional prerogatives but from his successful maneuvering with executive officials, members of Congress, political party and interest group leaders, representatives of the media, and the American public itself.

This perception of the presidency—as a changeable (protean) and political office—explains its appearance over time as heroic, imperial, post-imperial, and imperiled. It has assumed all these forms, and still could assume others. The approach of this book therefore offers students of the presidency a new and comprehensive approach to studying the nation's highest office.

Notes

1. Clinton Rossiter, *The American Presidency,* rev. ed. (New York: Harcourt, Brace, 1960), 15.
2. Ibid., 237.
3. Ibid., 260-261.
4. Richard E. Neustadt, *Presidential Power: The Politics of Leadership* (New York: Wiley, 1960), 33.
5. Ibid., 46.
6. Ibid., 161.
7. Ibid., 185.
8. James MacGregor Burns, *Presidential Government: The Crucible of Leadership* (Boston: Houghton Mifflin, 1965), 28.
9. Ibid., 113-114.
10. Ibid., 351.
11. Thomas E. Cronin, "The Textbook Presidency" (Paper delivered at the annual meeting of the American Political Science Association, Los Angeles, September 8-12, 1970).
12. George Reedy, *The Twilight of the Presidency* (New York: New American Library, 1970), x.

13. Arthur M. Schlesinger, Jr., *The Imperial Presidency* (Boston: Houghton Mifflin, 1973), ix.
14. Ibid., 254.
15. Walter F. Mondale, *The Accountability of Power: Toward a Responsible Presidency* (New York: David McKay, 1975), 4.
16. William G. Andrews, "The Presidency, Congress, and Constitutional Theory," in *The Presidency in Contemporary Context*, ed. Norman C. Thomas (New York: Dodd, Mead, 1973), 13, 17.
17. Fred I. Greenstein, "Change and Continuity in the Modern Presidency," in *The New American Political System*, ed. Anthony King (Washington, D.C.: American Enterprise Institute, 1978), 65.
18. Ibid., 70-75.
19. Godfrey Hodgson, *All Things to All Men: The False Promise of the American Presidency* (New York: Simon and Schuster, 1980), 225.
20. Ibid., 13.
21. Thomas E. Cronin, "An Imperiled Presidency?" in *The Post-Imperial Presidency*, ed. Vincent Davis (New Brunswick, N.J.: Transaction Books, 1980).
22. Richard P. Nathan, *The Administrative Presidency* (New York: Wiley, 1983).
23. Chester A. Newland, "A Mid-Term Appraisal—The Reagan Presidency: Limited Government and Political Administration," *Public Administration Review* 43 (January/February 1983): 1-21; and Edie N. Goldenberg, "The Permanent Government in an Era of Retrenchment and Redirection," in *The Reagan Presidency and the Governing of America*, ed. Lester M. Salamon and Michael S. Lund (Washington, D.C.: Urban Institute Press, 1984), 381-404.
24. Bert A. Rockman, *The Leadership Question: The Presidency and the American Political System* (New York: Praeger, 1984), 236.
25. Theodore J. Lowi, *The Personal Presidency: Power Invested, Promise Unfulfilled* (Ithaca, N.Y.: Cornell University Press, 1985).
26. Bert A. Rockman, "The Modern Presidency and Theories of Accountability: Old Wine *and* Old Bottles" (Paper delivered at the annual meeting of the American Political Science Association, Washington, D.C., August 28-31, 1986), 35-39.
27. Rossiter, *The American Presidency*, 178.
28. Neustadt, *Presidential Power*, 163, 167.
29. Burns, *Presidential Government*, 80.
30. Fred I. Greenstein, *The Hidden-Hand Presidency: Eisenhower as Leader* (New York: Basic Books, 1982).
31. Reedy, *Twilight of the Presidency*, 66.
32. Ibid., 60.
33. Ibid., 20.
34. Bruce Buchanan, *The Presidential Experience: What the Office Does to the Man* (Englewood Cliffs, N.J.: Prentice-Hall, 1978), 61.
35. Richard M. Pious, *The American Presidency* (New York: Basic Books, 1979), 16.
36. Neustadt, *Presidential Power*, 7.

37. Ibid., 58.
38. Greenstein, "Change and Continuity," 73.
39. Hodgson, *All Things to All Men,* 79.
40. Cronin, "An Imperiled Presidency?" 143.
41. James David Barber, *The Presidential Character: Predicting Performance in the White House* (Englewood Cliffs, N.J.: Prentice-Hall, 1972), 8.
42. Ibid., 9.

Selected Readings

Burns, James MacGregor. *Presidential Government: The Crucible of Leadership.* Boston: Houghton Mifflin, 1965.

Corwin, Edward S. *The President: Office and Powers.* 5th ed. New York: New York University Press, 1984.

Heclo, Hugh, and Lester M. Salamon, eds. *The Illusion of Presidential Government.* Boulder: Westview, 1981.

Kallenbach, Joseph E. *The American Chief Executive.* New York: Harper and Row, 1966.

Lowi, Theodore J. *The Personal President: Power Invested, Promise Unfulfilled.* Ithaca, N.Y.: Cornell University Press, 1985.

Nelson, Michael, ed. *The Presidency and the Political System.* 2d ed. Washington, D.C.: CQ Press, 1988.

Neustadt, Richard E. *Presidential Power: The Politics of Leadership From FDR to Carter.* New York: Wiley, 1980.

Rockman, Bert A. *The Leadership Question: The Presidency and the American Political System.* New York: Praeger, 1984.

Rossiter, Clinton. *The American Presidency.* rev. ed. New York: Harcourt, Brace, 1960.

Wildavsky, Aaron, ed. *Perspectives on the Presidency.* Boston: Little, Brown, 1975.

PART ONE

The President and the Public

The president's relationship with the American public is vital to his performance in office. In fact, to *become* chief executive in the first place, he must wage a vigorous electoral campaign aimed at the American people and emerge victorious over his political rivals.[1] Then, having won the office, he must continue to woo the public between elections to win support for his policies.

Political pollster Patrick Caddell understood this. The month after Jimmy Carter won the 1976 presidential election, Caddell remarked in a memorandum to the president-elect that governing with public approval requires a continuous political campaign. In addition, if the president wishes to stay in office beyond his first term (as most do), he must go back to the people in the next electoral campaign to have his tenure extended, then continue to seek their support for the policies he favors in his second term.

Part One explores various aspects of the president's relationship with the American people. The first two chapters, "Nomination Politics" and "Election Politics," treat the two principal phases of the electoral process. These two phases not only lengthen the selection process but also require candidates to wage two separate types of political campaigns. The rules for the nomination and for the election are quite different. Moreover, campaign strategies and techniques must be tailored for the two distinct stages of the presidential battle. Finally, the participants in the two contests are not the same: Hugh Heclo coined the term *selectorate* to describe those who help choose presidential candidates in the nomination process, in contrast to the *electorate,* who vote in the general election.[2]

The third chapter, "What Manner of Person?" shifts from the process by which presidents are chosen to the results of that process, that is, to the kinds of persons who have served in the office over the past two centuries. Included are analyses of the political and social backgrounds of the thirty-nine presidents from George Washington to Ronald Reagan and the ways in which those backgrounds have changed over the years. The chapter concludes with a discussion of the psychological characteristics of U.S. chief executives and how those characteristics affect their performance in office.

The fourth and final chapter in Part One, "Public Politics," focuses on the president's relationship with the American people between elections as he seeks to win public support for his policies. It analyzes the attitudes Americans have toward the presidency and the techniques chief executives use to manipulate those attitudes to enhance their personal popularity. Also discussed are the president's relations with interest groups, the mass media, and members of his own political party.

Notes

1. Exceptions to this rule occur when the president dies, resigns, is permanently disabled, or is impeached and convicted, and the vice president or some other public official succeeds to the office. These situations are discussed in Chapter 5.
2. Hugh Heclo, "Presidential and Prime Ministerial Selection," in *Perspectives on Presidential Selection,* ed. Donald R. Matthews (Washington, D.C.: Brookings, 1973), 25.

Amidst flags and cheering delegates, the Democratic national convention concludes July 19, 1984. Walter Mondale won the presidential slot, and Geraldine Ferraro became the first woman to be nominated for the vice presidency.

CHAPTER ONE

Nomination Politics

The contest for the U.S. presidency is the most significant democratic election in the world. In no other country do so many voters cast their ballot directly for a single officeholder. Nowhere else does a single political campaign last as long and involve as many people or the expenditure of so much money. No other electoral contest receives as much coverage from the mass media. By any standard, a U.S. presidential contest is the World Series of electoral politics.

Complicating the problem for presidential aspirants and their supporters is that candidates must survive two separate tests of political strength. First, they must win their party's nomination (as discussed in this chapter). Then, they must emerge victorious over the other candidates in the general election. (See Chapter 2.)

The characteristic nomination and election phases of the presidential contest have developed over the course of U.S. political history. The Founders never contemplated this separation in the procedure they devised for choosing the chief executive. Major developments in the young nation, however, soon divided the selection process into two parts. Moreover, after the process was divided, changes continued to occur in both nomination and election procedures.

This chapter first describes the development of the nomination process, from the establishment of the congressional caucus in 1796 until the national convention system was instituted in the 1830s and expanded in the 1840s. Next, it explains the current nomination rules. The following two sections examine the dynamics of the presidential nomination campaign and the naming of the candidates and their running mates by the national conventions of the two major parties.

Evolution of the Nomination Process

During the nation's first seven years, from 1789 to 1796, there was no separate procedure for nominating the president. The system operated as the Founders intended: members of the political elite from the various states, acting through the mechanism of the electoral college (see Chapter 2), chose George Washington to lead the country in 1789 and again in 1792. Persons with diverse political views agreed that the nation's wartime hero was a "patriot king" who would rule in the interest of all the people.

In Congress, however, no such political consensus prevailed. In 1790 Alexander Hamilton, the first secretary of the treasury in the Washington administration, presented an economic program that would establish a national bank and a tariff to protect U.S. manufacturers and merchants from foreign competition. Thomas Jefferson, then secretary of state, and James Madison, a member of Congress, opposed the program on the grounds that it benefited only mercantile interests and not the nation's farmers, for whom they had great admiration. Subsequently, Jefferson and Madison also differed with Hamilton on the Jay Treaty, negotiated with England in 1794. Under its terms the British agreed, among other things, to withdraw troops from forts in the Northwest. The treaty failed, however, to satisfy two other grievances of concern to Jefferson and Madison: the lack of compensation for slaves carried away by British soldiers during the Revolution and the impressment into the British Navy of U.S. sailors from U.S. ships seized by the British for trading with the French (who were at war with Britain).

Out of these controversies over domestic and foreign policy emerged an important institution not provided for by the U.S. Constitution—political parties. The Federalist party had formed by the early 1790s with Hamilton acting as the principal initiator of policies in Congress and Washington as the popular leader who could rally support for such policies. Federalists soon were running for Congress and, once in office, voting for Hamilton's programs.[1] Jefferson's resignation from the Washington administration in 1793 and Madison's congressional disputes with Hamilton paved the way for a rival political party, the Republicans.[2] By the mid-1790s cohesive pro- and antiadministration blocs were voting against each other in Congress, and congressional candidates were being identified as Republicans as well as Federalists.[3] George Washington's retirement at the end of his second term in 1797 created an opening for party politics, which then spread from Congress to the presidency.

The creation of political parties in the United States thus ended the brief period in which the political elite of the day selected the president. From then on, party politics would determine the nation's chief executive. This development required the parties to devise some means of choosing candidates to run under their party name, a process known as *nomination*. In 1796 the Federalists chose their candidate, John Adams, through consultation among their prominent leaders. The Republicans turned to their party members in Congress, who nominated Thomas Jefferson as their standard-bearer. Four years later the Federalists followed suit, and the congressional caucus became the nominating mechanism for both parties.

Congressional Caucuses

The congressional caucus was quite practical in this early stage of party development. Because members of Congress were already assembled in the nation's capital, they faced no transportation problems. Moreover, the nominating task was manageable among so few members. They also were quite knowledgeable about potential presidential candidates from all parts of the new country and so were logical agents for choosing candidates for the presidency with its nationwide constituency.

The congressional caucus had serious defects, however. First, it violated the separation-of-powers principle of the Constitution, because members of the legislative body played a key role in choosing the president. Second, the caucus failed to represent areas in which the party had lost the previous congressional election. In addition, interested and informed citizens who participated in grass-roots party activities (especially campaigns) took no part in the deliberations of the congressional caucus.

In time these flaws undermined the congressional caucus system. The Federalists were the first to be affected. As their political fortunes waned, the size of the party's congressional delegation declined so much that it was no longer a viable and representative body. The party was forced to turn to alternative nominating devices. In 1808 and 1812 the Federalists gathered in what one political scientist calls "primitive national conventions," meetings of state delegates closed to persons not specifically invited (only about half the states were represented).[4] In 1816, the party held no organized caucus or convention; instead, it chose its nominee by common consent.[5] The 1816 presidential election was the last contested by the Federalists. The party had lost public support because of internal divisions, failure to organize grass-roots interests, and the pro-British attitude of many of its leaders during the War of 1812.

The Republicans had a quite different experience with the congressional caucus. Between 1800 and 1820 the party nominated three Virginians who had previously served as secretary of state—Thomas Jefferson in 1800 and 1804, James Madison in 1808 and 1812, and James Monroe in 1816 and 1820. However, when the Republican congressional caucus attempted in 1824 to nominate Secretary of the Treasury William Crawford (even though he was from Georgia, he was Virginian by birth), three-fourths of the Republican members of Congress boycotted the meeting.

Eventually, five candidates were nominated (principally by state legislatures) for president in 1824, including Andrew Jackson, who was proposed by the Tennessee legislature. In the election Jackson won more popular votes than any other candidate, but no candidate received a majority of the electoral votes; as a result, the election was thrown into the House of Representatives.

The House, however, did not choose Jackson but awarded the presidency to John Quincy Adams (also a former secretary of state). Adams had benefited from a political deal with Henry Clay, one of the five nominees, who threw his House support to Adams in return for being named secretary of state. This unfortunate combination of circumstances discredited the congressional caucus (by then known as "King Caucus") as a means of nominating presidential candidates.

In 1828 responsibility for presidential nominations was vested entirely in the states, where legislatures and conventions chose "favorite sons" such as Jackson and Adams as candidates. Although the congressional caucus was too centralized to represent the state and local party units, the individual states were too decentralized to select a national official. Some device was needed that would represent party elements thoughout the country and at the same time facilitate the nomination of a common candidate.

National Party Conventions

The nomination method that emerged to meet these needs was a genuine national party convention composed of delegates from all the states. A minor party, the Anti-Masons, pioneered the way in 1831 by convening such an assembly. The National Republicans called a similar convention the following year.[6] (Like the Anti-Masons, the National Republicans had no appreciable representation in Congress and thus could not have used the congressional caucus even if they had wanted to.) The Democratic-Republicans, under President Andrew Jackson (elected in 1828), also held a convention in 1832. Jackson viewed the convention as an ideal way of securing the vice-presidential nomination for his handpicked candidate, Martin Van Buren.

Since the early 1840s, major political parties have nominated their presidential and vice-presidential candidates by holding national conventions. Since the early 1850s, national committees have called the presidential nominating conventions into session, and conventions have adopted a platform.[7] As will be discussed later, today's parties retain in modified form two of the basic features of the early conventions: the allocation of delegates to states primarily on the basis of their representation in Congress (senators plus House members), and the selection of delegates by each state.

Although today's nominating conventions resemble those that developed almost 150 years ago, the entire nomination process has undergone drastic change, especially since 1968. The remainder of this chapter focuses first on the formal rules governing the nomination of candidates and then on the dynamics of the campaign by which such candidates are chosen.

Current Nomination Rules

The rules that govern any political contest are important. Rules both prescribe behavior in political contests and influence election outcomes. By determining the strategies and tactics that participants adopt to improve their chances of winning, rules shape the nominating process. Yet they are shaped by the process as well. As people seek advantage for their particular interests, rules become the focus of struggles for change. The prevailing rules are seldom neutral: they inevitably favor certain individuals and interests over others—sometimes by design, sometimes not.

Since the late 1960s the rules of the presidential nomination contest have become especially important. They are highly complicated because they come from a variety of sources—100 state political parties and 50 legislatures, the national political parties, and the Congress. (Sometimes individuals also turn to the courts to interpret provisions of these regulations and to reconcile conflicts among them.) In addition, the rules have been changed so drastically and so often, particularly in the Democratic party, that it is difficult for candidates and their supporters to keep up with the changes. These changes have created confusion and uncertainty for many participants and have favored those who somehow manage to puzzle their way through the welter of rules. Indeed, some persons contend that Sen. George McGovern won the 1972 Democratic nomination partly because of his close association with the changes made in the nomination rules of that year. (As discussed later in this chapter, McGovern originally chaired the commission that helped bring about changes in the 1972 nomination contest.)

Many rules govern the different stages of the nomination process. The following three sections examine the rules for apportioning convention delegates among the states, selecting delegates within the states, and financing nomination campaigns. A section later in the chapter addresses regulations for the proceedings of the national convention.

Allocating National Convention Delegates

A presidential candidate starts out with a well-defined goal: to win a majority of the votes at the party's national convention in order to be nominated for the presidency. In 1984, the Republican nominee had to win 1,118 votes out of 2,235; the Democratic nominee, 1,967 out of 3,933.

Although the numbers of their convention votes differ, both parties use the same general formulas to decide how many votes each state is entitled to cast at the convention. The parties take into account the size of a state's congressional delegation or its population in determining its basic vote allocation, and its record in supporting the party's candidates in recent years in allocating extra or "bonus" votes to each state. The methods that parties use to determine these bonus votes benefit some states at the expense of others.

The Republican party is interested in a state's recent voting record not only for the presidential nominee but also for governors, senators, and representatives; however, it does not take into account the *size* of the popular vote for these officials, simply whether or not they win. The smaller states, especially those in which the Republican party dominates the nonpresidential elections, therefore have a disproportionate influence in the GOP convention. For example, a state with a small population that has elected a large number of Republican officials, such as Utah, is benefited, even though its small size means that it can cast relatively few popular votes for Republican candidates for president. A large two-party state such as New York, however, is disadvantaged. Democratic candidates may win elections for governor, senator, or representative, which costs the state Republican party bonus votes at the convention; and the large number of popular votes the state has cast over the years for Republican candidates for president is not taken into account, only whether the Republican candidate carried the state.

In contrast, the Democratic party focuses on a state's voting record in recent presidential elections, not gubernatorial, senatorial, or congressional ones; moreover, it is concerned with the total number of popular votes cast for its presidential candidates. A populous two-party state such as New York is advantaged by that system. Its size means that it will cast a large number of popular votes for the Democratic presidential candidate whether that person carries the state or not, and it does not matter that Democratic candidates lose nonpresidential elections. However, a small state in which the Democrats are dominant, such as Rhode Island, is disadvantaged. Even if recent Democratic presidential candidates carried the state they did not win a large number of popular votes, and Democratic victories in nonpresidential elections earn the state no bonus votes.

Selecting Delegates

State delegates to the national conventions of both parties are chosen by one of three methods. The first is selection by *party leaders,* such as members of the state central committee, the party chairperson, or the governor (if the party controls that office). The second is choice by a *state convention* composed of persons themselves elected at caucuses and conventions held in smaller geographical areas, such as precincts, wards, counties, and congressional districts. The third is direct election by the voters themselves in *presidential primaries.* States often combine methods, using a primary to elect district delegates but allowing their state committees to choose "at-large" delegates (those representing the whole state).

Traditionally, persons active in party affairs, public and party officials referred to as "professionals," dominated the selection of delegates. This was only natural under the first method, in which party officials formally appoint the delegates. Professionals also dominated under the second system because they manipulated the caucuses and conventions into choosing themselves and their loyal supporters as delegates. Moreover, professionals ran successfully as delegates in presidential primaries, and because many states did not require them to vote at the national convention for the candidate favored by rank-and-file voters in the primary, delegates were free to vote their own presidential preferences instead.

Between 1968 and 1980, however, there was a definite trend away from control by party professionals and toward increased participation by rank-and-file voters. In 1968 only seventeen states chose delegates by a presidential primary; in 1980, thirty-one did. Meanwhile, the proportion of total national convention delegates chosen in primaries climbed from 38 percent to 72 percent. In the process, the primary replaced the state convention system as the dominant method for choosing delegates to the national convention.

Many of the new primary laws passed between 1968 and 1980 also increased the influence of rank-and-file voters over their party's ultimate choice for president. States encouraged delegates chosen in primaries to indicate which candidate they personally supported for president so that voters could predict how their delegates would vote at the national convention. Some states also permitted voters themselves to indicate their personal preference for president and legally bound the delegates to support the preferred candidates for one or more ballots at the convention. Moreover, under many of the new state laws, a presidential candidate's name was placed on the ballot if his or her candidacy was recognized by the national news media. A candidate who wanted to be removed from the race had to file an affidavit swearing that he or she was not a candidate in any state that presidential year. This system prevented candidates from choosing which state primaries they would enter, thus allowing voters to pass judgment on a broader range of potential nominees than would otherwise have been available to them.

The trend toward greater influence for rank-and-file voters turned around between 1980 and 1984 as six jurisdictions abandoned the primary in favor of the caucus-convention for selecting delegates to the national convention. As a result, the proportion of delegates chosen by state presidential primaries declined from 72 percent to 54 percent.

By 1984 the system that emerged for choosing delegates to the national convention was thus a "mixed" one, with twenty-three states and the District of Columbia using primaries and twenty-seven states using caucus-conventions. As Figure 1-1 indicates, there were some regional variations in the use of the two methods: western states generally preferred caucus-conventions; northeastern states, primaries; and the midwestern and southern states were fairly evenly divided between the two methods.

In addition to the passage of laws by state legislatures, the national political parties themselves have taken action to reform the process for selecting delegates to the national conventions.

Democrats. The vast changes the Democratic party made in its procedures after 1968 can be traced to that year's convention in Chicago. It was an assembly marked by acrimonious debates within the convention hall over the Vietnam War and by bloody battles outside the convention arena between war protestors and the police. The 1968 delegates were concerned

Figure 1-1 Delegate Selection Methods by State and Region, 1984

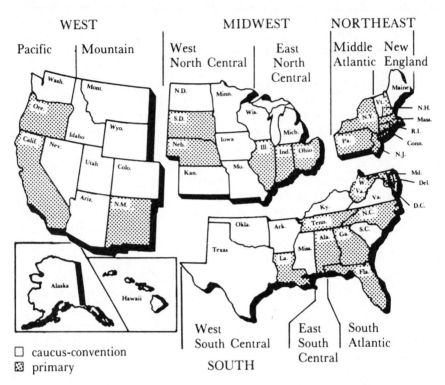

Source: *Congressional Quarterly Weekly Report*, June 2, 1984, 1317, and June 16, 1984, 1443.

that much of the chaos of that convention occurred because the regular party organization was impervious to the will of rank-and-file Democrats. (Sen. Hubert Humphrey won the nomination without entering a single presidential primary, because party leaders favoring him dominated the delegations of the caucus-convention states.) The delegates consequently adopted a resolution requiring state parties to give "all Democrats a full, meaningful, and timely opportunity to participate" in the selection of delegates. Not long after, the Democratic National Committee established a commission chaired by Sen. George McGovern of South Dakota to assist state parties in meeting that requirement. This action established a pattern: following the 1972 convention a new commission, this time under the leadership of Baltimore councilwoman Barbara Mikulski, continued the effort to change the delegate selection process. After the 1976 national convention, the party organized still a third commission, chaired by Morley Winograd (state chairperson of the Michigan Democratic party). In each case the commission recommended changes in rules affecting the selection of convention delegates for the next convention;

most of these were adopted by the Democratic National Committee and ultimately by the Democratic national convention.

For the most part, the battle lines in this series of rules changes were drawn between party professionals and political "amateurs," persons not traditionally active in party affairs but who became involved because of an interest in a particular candidate or issue. The amateurs won the struggle to open up the selection process when the McGovern Commission recommended that states remove restrictive voter registration laws so that non-Democrats and unaffiliated voters could become party members. At the same time, the control of traditional party leaders over caucuses and conventions was reduced by regulations that forbade them to serve automatically as ex officio delegates and by requirements for written party rules, adequate public notice of meetings, and the elimination of proxy voting.

A second issue that plagued all three party commissions was the representation of particular groups within state delegations to the national convention. The amateurs scored an initial victory when the McGovern Commission recommended that minority groups, women, and young people (those aged eighteen to thirty) be represented in state delegations "in reasonable relationship to the groups' presence in the state." This recommendation led many states to adopt a quota system when they chose their delegates to the 1972 convention. Other minority groups, however, such as those of Italian and Polish descent, who had traditionally supported the party, questioned why they had not been included in the quotas. Other Democrats opposed the idea of quotas altogether because the quotas determined the results of the political process rather than merely the opportunity to participate in it—the traditional American concept of political equality. The Mikulski Commission did adopt the latter concept by eliminating the quotas in favor of more inclusive "affirmative action plans," whereby each state party undertook to encourage "minorities, Native Americans, women, and other traditionally underrepresented groups to participate and to be represented in the delegate selection process and all party affairs." The idea of quotas surfaced again, however, as professionals and amateurs battled over representation at the 1980 convention. This time each achieved a victory: the professionals won an increase in the size of state delegations by 10 percent to permit selection of state party and elected officials; the amateurs won the adoption of a rule requiring that state delegations comprise equal numbers of men and women.

A third major problem for all three party commissions was the division of state delegation votes among the various contending candidates. The McGovern Commission recommended that states abolish the "winner-take-all" primaries—whereby the candidate who received simply a plurality of the popular vote was awarded all the delegates—in favor of a provision for the "fair representation of minority views on presidential candidates." California, however, refused to follow this recommendation (the commission only "urged" rather than "required" the action). At the 1972 convention, McGovern himself received all 271 votes of the California delegates, although he had beaten Humphrey in the primary by only 45 to 39 percent of the popular vote. The irony of that development led the Democrats to abolish statewide winner-take-all contests in 1976, so that candidates winning at least 15 percent of the votes in presidential primaries and caucus-convention meetings would receive their proportional share of a state's delegate votes. For the 1980 nomination, Democrats extended the proportional representation principle to district contests. The minimum cutoff figure for candidates entitled to delegate votes was determined by dividing the number of district delegates by 100. (In a district with five delegates, for example, the cutoff would be 20 percent.) In no case, however, was the cutoff figure to be higher than 25 percent, regardless of the number of delegates elected in a district.

The battle over rules for the selection of delegates to Democratic national conventions continued in the 1980s. The Democratic National Committee again appointed a commission—this one chaired by Governor James B. Hunt, Jr., of North Carolina—to develop rules for the 1984 nomination contest. This time party professionals were determined to establish rules that would give them a greater role in the nomination process and also facilitate the selection of "their" kind of candidate rather than an "outsider" like McGovern or Jimmy Carter. They clearly prevailed over the political amateurs in the changes proposed by the Hunt Commission and later adopted by the national committee and the 1984 convention. A bloc of "super-delegates" composed of party and elected officials (constituting some 14 percent of the convention votes) was created; state officials and Democratic members of the House and Senate were responsible for choosing these superdelegates (typically themselves), who were to go to the 1984 convention uncommitted. Another change also favored the states, particularly populous ones, by allowing them to use once again the winner-take-all principle in district contests and thereby reward a front-runner with a large bloc of delegate votes.[8] Finally, the new rules abolished a provision that bound all delegates to the 1980 national convention to vote on the first ballot for the candidate to whom they were linked in the state's delegate selection process. (The vital part this provision played in the 1980 convention is discussed in the section on rules and politics under "The National Convention.") The 1984 delegates were therefore legally free to vote as they desired at that year's convention.

Because unsuccessful Democratic candidates Gary Hart and Jesse Jackson were dissatisfied with the 1984 rules (which, they said, favored Walter Mondale) the national convention created the Fairness Commission to study their complaints and to possibly reduce the role of party and elected officials in the 1988 nomination process. However, members of the new commission, chaired by Donald L. Fowler of South Carolina, followed the lead of Democratic national chairperson Paul G. Kirk, Jr., in developing rules they hope will build a consensus behind a candidate long before the 1988 national convention is held. As a result, only minor changes will be made in the 1984 rules. In fact, the commission did not reduce but actually increased the number of superdelegates from about 550 to some 650, which means that all the Democratic governors, all the members of the Democratic National Committee, and 80 percent of the Democratic members of Congress will have delegate seats at the 1988 convention. The Fairness Commission also relaxed the 1984 rule that restricted participation in the nomination process to Democrats only, so that states such as Wisconsin and Montana can conduct "open" primaries in 1988 with the approval of the national party. The only concession to the major critics of the 1984 rules was a change lowering the proportion of votes a candidate must receive in a primary or caucus to qualify for delegates from 20 to 15 percent. In early March 1986, the Democratic National Committee approved the recommendations of the Fairness Commission, which means that for the first time in a generation Democrats will be operating under essentially the same rules for two consecutive nomination contests.

Republicans. The Republican party also has made some changes in its delegate selection process even though its leaders did not face the pressures for reform that the Democratic leaders faced. A committee chaired by Rosemary Ginn, a Missouri member of the national committee, recommended proposals that were implemented in the choosing of delegates to the 1976 convention. Included were provisions, similar to those of the McGovern Commission, that reduced the influence of traditional party leaders by eliminating them as ex officio delegates, that regularized the nomination process by informing citizens how to participate in it, and that increased participation by opening the primaries and the state conventions to all qualified citizens.

At the same time, the Republican party has not attempted to regulate selection of national convention delegates nearly as extensively as has the Democratic party. The 1972 Republican national convention turned down recommendations of the Ginn Committee to include in future conventions persons under twenty-five years of age in "numerical equity to their voting strength in a state" and to have one man, one woman, one person under twenty-five, and one member of a minority group on each of the convention's principal committees. In 1975 the Republican National Committee refused to adopt the recommendation of a new committee chaired by Rep. William Steiger of Wisconsin that all states be required to have their affirmative action plans approved by the national committee. Nor have the Republicans moved to abolish winner-take-all primaries, like the one in California. Thus the national Republican party has been much less willing than its Democratic counterpart to intervene in state decisions on the selection of delegates to the national convention.

Effect of Changes in Delegate Selection Rules

The rules changes made from 1968 to 1980 had a profound effect on the choosing of presidential nominees, particularly for the Democratic party. The proliferation of primaries and the deliberate lessening of the influence of party leaders in caucus-convention states made these leaders far less influential in the nomination process. Such professionals, who traditionally used their skills to select persons considered electable and loyal to the party (such as Humphrey), were largely replaced by political amateurs who supported "issue-oriented" and "antiestablishment" candidates for the presidency (such as McGovern and Carter).

Democratic rules designed to increase the representation of traditionally disadvantaged groups in the nomination process also brought the intended results. Women in particular benefited. In 1968, before the Democratic reforms, they constituted only 13 percent of the delegates of the Democratic convention. In 1972 that figure nearly tripled to 38 percent and, after a slight decline to 33 percent in 1976, rose to 50 percent in 1980 and 1984 as a consequence of the party's decision to require that both sexes be equally represented at the Democratic national convention.

Finally, rules changes ending the winner-take-all primary in favor of a proportional division of states' convention votes made victories in states such as California less important than they used to be. Although George McGovern owed his convention victory in 1972 to the 271 votes he won from that state, Jimmy Carter won his party's nomination both in 1976 and in 1980 without winning California. (Governor Jerry Brown carried the state in 1976; Kennedy carried it in 1980.) The proportional rule also encouraged candidates to participate in state primaries they did not expect to win, because they had a chance to receive some convention votes rather than being shut out completely, as had occurred in winner-take-all contests.

The 1984 rules favored by the party professionals also brought about the desired effects. Walter Mondale—the candidate they preferred—benefited by the new rules. He received an overwhelming share of the votes at the national convention from the superdelegates and did very well in states that used the winner-take-all principle in district contests to allocate delegates. He also won a greater number of votes in states that used caucuses to select their delegates than did Gary Hart or Jesse Jackson (recall that more states adopted this method in 1984). As a result, Mondale prevailed at the convention, even though his two rivals received a combined share of 55 percent of the votes cast in the primaries.

Financing Presidential Nomination Campaigns

Historically, restrictions on contributions to presidential campaigns have not worked. The federal government passed legislation in 1907 forbidding corporations to contribute money to presidential nominations and elections, but corporations easily circumvented the law by paying executives extra compensation, which they and their families subsequently contributed in their own, not the company, name. The 1947 Taft-Hartley Act prohibited contributions by labor unions, but unions, too, evaded the restrictions by forming political action committees (PACS) to solicit voluntary donations from members and to spend the funds in the committee's name. Finally, the Hatch Act of 1940 (which limited individual contributions to a federal candidate to $5,000) and a federal tax law that imposed progressive tax rates on contributions of more than $3,000 to a single committee both proved ineffective because numerous committees were formed for a single candidate, and each committee was entitled to accept a $5,000 contribution.

The move for campaign reform began with President John F. Kennedy, who was sensitive to the advantages wealth gave a candidate.[9] He appointed the Commission on Campaign Costs, which issued a report in 1962 proposing public reporting of campaign expenditures, tax incentives for contributors, and matching funds for presidential candidates. Nothing came of the proposals during the 1960s, but they laid the groundwork for the wave of reform that swept the country in the 1970s. In 1971 and again in 1974 Congress passed legislation affecting campaign financing. In January 1976, however, in *Buckley v. Valeo* (424 U.S. 1), the Supreme Court ruled certain provisions of the legislation unconstitutional; later that year Congress responded by enacting still further regulations governing the use of money in federal elections. Finally, in 1979 Congress added more amendments to the campaign finance legislation.

A variety of regulations therefore govern the financial conduct of presidential campaigns. The following sections discuss the major ones affecting the nomination process. (Some of the provisions also apply to the general election campaign, which is treated in Chapter 2.)

Disclosure of Information.   Presidential candidates and committees are required to provide full information on the financing of their campaigns. They must report the names of all contributors who give $200 or more and itemize expenses of $200 or more. This information is filed with the Federal Election Commission (FEC), the agency responsible for administering the campaign legislation. The FEC is a bipartisan body of six members nominated by the president and confirmed by the Senate.

Limits on Contributions.   Individuals are limited to contributions of $1,000 to a presidential candidate for each election (the nomination and general election are considered separate contests), $5,000 to a political action committee (one that contributes to more than one candidate), $20,000 to the national committee of a political party, and a total contribution of no more than $25,000 a year. Presidential candidates are free to spend an unlimited amount of their own money and their immediate family's money on their campaigns, but if they accept public financing, their contributions to their own campaign are limited to $50,000 per election.

Limits on Spending. Candidates may spend as much as they wish on presidential campaigns unless they accept public financing, in which case limitations apply. For the 1984 presidential campaign, limits for the nomination process included a national ceiling of $20.2 million plus 20 percent for fund-raising costs—a total of $24.4 million. In addition, each state imposes spending limitations based on its population. In 1984, California had the highest spending limit, $5.4 million; the lowest figure, which applied to a number of small states, was $404,000.

Independent Campaign Expenditures. There is no limitation on independent campaign expenditures, that is, those made by individuals or political committees advocating the defeat or election of a candidate but not made in conjunction with the candidate's campaign. However, individuals or committees making such expenditures in amounts of more than $250 must file a report with the FEC and must state, under penalty of perjury, that the expenditure was not made in collusion with the candidate.

Public Financing. Candidates for the presidential nomination who are able to raise $100,000 in individual contributions, with at least $5,000 collected in twenty different states, receive federal matching funds equal to the total amount of their contributions of $250 or less. (By checking a box on their federal income tax forms, taxpayers authorize the federal government to set aside $1.00 of their tax payments for public financing of campaigns.) In 1984, $10.1 million in federal matching funds was available to each candidate for the nomination process. The federal government also provided the Democratic and Republican parties up to $6 million to finance their nominating conventions.

Like the alteration in delegate selection rules, campaign finance legislation has had a significant effect on presidential nominations. The sources and techniques for raising funds have radically changed. Rather than depending upon a few "fat cats" to finance their campaigns (in 1968 insurance executive W. Clement Stone gave $2.8 million to Richard Nixon's campaign), candidates now raise funds from a large number of small individual contributors, primarily through direct mail solicitation.[10] Public funds also make it possible for persons who formerly could not afford to mount a nomination campaign to do so. Sen. Fred Harris had to abandon a presidential bid in 1972 because he could not raise money from large contributors; but with federal matching funds available, he was able to run in 1976. Moreover, even single-issue Right to Life candidate Ellen McCormack, was able to qualify for federal funds that year. At the same time, the new method of raising funds from a large number of individuals and thereby qualifying for federal matching money means that candidates tend to start their campaigns earlier than they formerly did. Finally, as election specialist Herbert Alexander suggests, public funding also helps "free each candidate's personal organization from the party hierarchy." [11]

The Nomination Campaign

The nomination campaign is a long, winnowing process in which each of the two major parties chooses from a large pool of potential candidates the one person who will represent the party in the general election. As political scientist Austin Ranney points out, the nomination phase is more important than the election stage of the campaign, because "the parties' nominating processes eliminate far more presidential possibilities than do the voters' electing processes." [12]

There are several important differences between the campaign for the nomination and the campaign preceding the general election. A nomination campaign is much less structured than a general election campaign. Rather than contending with one known opponent representing the other major political party, aspirants for their party's nomination typically do not know how many opponents they will face or who they will be. In contrast to the general election's short, definite campaign period (from Labor Day in early September to election day in early November), the nomination campaign is long and indefinite, starting when candidates begin their quest for the presidency. Unlike the general election campaign, which occurs in all fifty states simultaneously, the nomination campaign takes place in stages. Finally, presidential nominees can use their party label to attract votes and count on party leaders to work in their campaign, but candidates for their party's nomination must develop other types of political appeals to attract the support of the "selectorate" and a personal organization to work on their behalf.

The highly unstructured nature of the presidential nominating process causes great uncertainties for candidates in planning and conducting the campaign. A further complication is that most first-time candidates must organize a nationwide political campaign, a task that, by comparison, dwarfs the effort of winning a Senate seat or governorship in even the largest states. As the following discussion indicates, important decisions have to be made all along the road to the party's nomination.

Early Maneuvering

Although the formal nomination process does not start until the beginning of the election year (since 1976, with the Iowa caucuses), political maneuvering takes place long before that time. A few day after the 1972 presidential election, for example, Jimmy Carter's staff laid out a plan for winning the 1976 Democratic nomination. Shortly after vice-presidential candidate Walter Mondale lost the 1980 election, he began his quest for the 1984 Democratic presidential nomination.

Journalist Arthur Hadley calls this political interval between the election of one president and the first primary before the next presidential election "the invisible primary." [13] By this he means that a political contest occurs during this time that has many of the characteristics of the actual state primaries. The major difference between the two types of primary is that the invisible one takes place behind the scenes as far as the general public is concerned, whereas American voters are very conscious of the regular primaries.

The invisible primary is a testing ground for the would-be president to determine whether his candidacy is viable. One factor that Hadley emphasizes is a psychological one: is the candidate willing to undergo the grueling process needed to win, characterized by extended absences from home, long hours on the campaign trail, and short, sometimes sleepless nights? Vice President Walter Mondale, an early casualty of the period preceding the 1976 election, withdrew from the race in November 1974 with the following statement: "I found I did not have the overwhelming desire to be President which is essential for the kind of campaign that is required. I don't think anyone should be President who is not willing to go through fire." [14]

An important task for the presidential candidate at this stage is the assembling of a staff to plan the campaign strategy and of what Hadley calls a "constituency," a larger group of workers who are willing to do the advance work necessary to organize states for the upcoming primary and caucus-convention contests. Recent Democratic party nominees benefited from having dedicated supporters who began their organizational activities very early. A full one and one-half years before the Wisconsin primary in April 1972, a young McGovern staff member, Eugene Pokorny, began to build a base of operation there;[15] in early 1975 a Carter staffer, Tim Kraft, began putting together a Carter organization for the Iowa precinct caucuses to be held in January 1976;[16] and in 1979 Terry Turner was made director of Carter's field operations in Iowa for the 1980 election.

Perhaps the most important factor in this early phase is how would-be candidates fare with the media. As columnist Russell Baker notes, the members of the media are the "great mentioner," the source of name recognition and favorable publicity. Candidates who are ignored because reporters and commentators do not regard them as serious contenders find it almost impossible to emerge as viable presidential possibilities. Adverse comments can also seriously damage a candidacy: in his quest for the 1980 Democratic nomination, Jerry Brown was portrayed by the media as a "spacey," "far-out" politician whose ideas, rhetoric, and lifestyle disqualified him for the presidency. In that same contest, Edward Kennedy's 1979 interview with CBS commentator Roger Mudd turned out to be a disaster because the senator seemed unable to give an adequate explanation of his actions in the accidental drowning of a young woman, Mary Jo Kopechne, in

1969; of his strained relationship with his wife, Joan, and his alleged affairs with other women; and of why he wanted to be president and how his policies and political views differed from those of President Carter. Many observers concluded that the Massachusetts senator never recovered from that interview, which occurred before his official presidential campaign even began.

In contrast, candidates who tend to do well in the invisible primary exploit the advantages provided by the media. Early in his 1976 campaign Carter's staff recommended that he cultivate important political columnists and editors, such as *New York Times* columnist Tom Wicker and *Washington Post* chairperson Katharine Graham, by making favorable comments on their articles and columns and, if possible, by scheduling visits with them. Some candidates enhance their presence in the print media through magazine articles or books published either earlier in their careers or during the nomination campaign itself; examples include Kennedy's *Profiles in Courage*, Nixon's *Six Crises*, and Carter's *Why Not The Best?* They also use television and radio, appearing regularly on shows such as "Meet the Press." They may even use a syndicated radio program or news column of their own, as Ronald Reagan did to advance his political views and, indirectly, his candidacy.

People with presidential ambitions typically take additional steps to enhance their prospects with leaders of their party as well as with the public. In anticipation of the 1972 election, Edmund Muskie, Hubert Humphrey's running mate in 1968, began accepting speaking engagements outside his home state of Maine soon after he and Humphrey were defeated. Looking toward the 1976 election, Jimmy Carter assumed the position of coordinator of the 1974 Democratic congressional campaign, a job that took him to thirty states, where he had the opportunity to get acquainted with Democratic leaders. A trip abroad may also keep candidates in the news and, if they have not had much experience in foreign affairs, help to counteract the charge that they are not knowledgeable in this vital area that consumes so much of the U.S. president's time.

Another key aspect of the invisible primary is the raising of funds necessary for the nomination campaign. As previously explained, the new finance legislation, which favors raising money in small amounts from many individuals, requires candidates to get an early start in soliciting funds. In fact, financial maneuvering may precede the candidate's own personal campaign. In January 1977, with $1 million he had left over from his 1976 campaign, Ronald Reagan established a political action committee called the Citizens for the Republic. In 1978 the organization contributed more than $600,000 to four hundred Republican candidates in federal, state, and local elections, but the remainder of its total expenditure of $4.5 million went to pay operating expenses and traveling costs for Reagan, who served as the principal speaker at political gatherings for the GOP candidates. Thus Reagan himself was the major beneficiary of the Citizens for the Republic: he ingratiated himself with the Republican candidates who received contributions from the organization and gained valuable contacts with Republican party supporters as well as the list of political contributors to the Citizens for the Republic, who were natural targets for his own fund raising for the 1980 presidential campaign. Walter Mondale established a PAC, Committee for the Future of America, that raised $24 million and contributed to more than two hundred House, Senate, and gubernatorial candidates in 1982.

As the presidential election year approaches, campaign fund raising moves into high gear. During the last three months of 1979, seven candidates each raised more than $1 million: Republicans John Connally, Reagan, George Bush, and Robert Dole and Democrats Kennedy, Carter, and Brown. Ultimately, six of the seven received federal matching funds (Connally chose to finance his campaign from private sources alone), as did Republican candidates John Anderson, Howard Baker, and Philip Crane, and Democratic long shot Lyndon LaRouche. Financing for the 1984 contest got off to an even earlier start: during the first three months of 1983, Mondale raised more than $2 million; Reubin Askew, $800,000; Gary Hart, $465,000; Alan Cranston, $440,000; and Ernest Hollings, almost $250,000.

In recent years presidential candidates have also found it wise to enter prenomination "popularity" contests held in some states, even though such contests have no legal effect on the composition of the state delegation to the national convention. The Carter forces packed a Jefferson-Jackson Day fundraising dinner held in Iowa in October 1975 and, consequently, won the straw poll taken there. Four years later members of Carter's staff worked hard to get his supporters elected as delegates to the Florida Democratic state convention held in November 1979; as a result, he clearly defeated Senator Kennedy in a straw vote taken at the convention. At the same time, Ronald Reagan was scoring a triumph over his Republican opponents in a comparable poll taken at the Republican state convention in Florida. Such popularity contests started earlier for the 1984 race: in January 1983, native son Cranston won a preferential poll at a Democratic party state convention in California; in April of that year, Mondale came out first in a similar poll conducted at a party convention in Kennedy's home state of Massachusetts. The following June, Cranston also scored victories in straw polls in Wisconsin and Alabama, and Mondale won in Maine in October.

The early phase of the 1984 contest took on a new dimension when both the AFL-CIO, with its 14 million members and 98 affiliated unions, and the National Education Association (NEA), the nation's largest individual labor union with 1.7 million members, endorsed Mondale as the Democratic candidate before the official state contests. Shortly thereafter, the National Organization of Women (NOW) endorsed Mondale as well.

The early phase of the nomination campaign, which political scientist Donald Matthews refers to as "the emergence of presidential possibilities," serves as a testing period for would-be candidates, especially those in the party out of office.[17] (In the party in power, the incumbent president is typically the front-running candidate to succeed himself.) Some drop out before the official campaign begins, as did Democratic senator Walter Mondale in 1975 and Republican senator Lowell Weicker in 1979. Others establish themselves as leaders in the public opinion polls taken at the beginning of the year and go on to win their party's nomination. As Table 1-1 shows, this was the prevailing pattern from 1936 through 1968. In two recent instances, however, the front-runner was ultimately replaced by a dark horse—McGovern, who was preferred by only 3 percent of the Democrats in January 1972, and Carter, the choice of only 4 percent in January 1976. Leaders in the polls therefore cannot afford to relax after achieving early popularity: the final choice of the nominee depends on presidential primaries as well as on caucus-convention contests.

Targeting the Nomination Campaign

Developments since 1968 have increased the number of state contests in which candidates participate. Primary laws in some states automatically place nationally recognized candidates on the ballot, thus forcing them to participate in contests they may prefer to bypass. The proportional representation feature of the 1980 national Democratic party rules and similar provisions in some Republican state contests encourage candidates to enter races they do not expect to win, because they receive some delegate votes even when they lose. Moreover, the selectorate expects candidates to show they have political support in all parts of the country. As a result, in 1980 both Jimmy Carter and Edward Kennedy were on the ballot in thirty-four of the thirty-five Democratic preference primaries (ignoring only Michigan, where the primary results were not binding, and delegates were chosen in separate caucuses). Republican George Bush entered all thirty-four of the GOP preference primaries, and Ronald Reagan entered thirty-two (he was not on the ballot in Puerto Rico and the District of Columbia). In 1984, Mondale and Hart entered all twenty-five primaries, and Jackson, twenty-four (he was not on the ballot in Puerto Rico).

A candidate's name may appear on a state ballot, but that does not mean he or she will wage an all-out campaign in that state. Limitations of time and energy prevent active campaigning in every state. The allocation of money also becomes a major problem. Not only is there an overall restriction on spending (a total of $24.4 million in 1984 for those accepting public financing), but spending limits also apply in each state. Such considerations require presidential candidates to establish priorities among the large number of primaries and caucus-convention contests. The primaries, in particular, are important, because they determine more than half of the delegates to the national conventions. Moreover, candidates are much more likely to campaign personally and spend more money in states that hold primaries than in those that have caucus-conventions.[18]

Table 1-1   Leading Presidential Candidates and Nominees, 1936-1984

Year	Leading candidate at beginning of election year [a]	Nominee
Party in power		
1936 (D)	Roosevelt	Roosevelt
1940 (D)	Roosevelt	Roosevelt
1944 (D)	Roosevelt	Roosevelt
1948 (D)	Truman	Truman
1952 (D)	Truman	Stevenson
1956 (R)	Eisenhower	Eisenhower
1960 (R)	Nixon	Nixon
1964 (D)	Johnson	Johnson
1968 (D)	Johnson	Humphrey
1972 (R)	Nixon	Nixon
1976 (R)	Ford [b]	Ford
1980 (D)	Carter [c]	Carter
1984 (R)	Reagan [d]	Reagan
Party out of power		
1936 (R)	Landon	Landon
1940 (R)	—	Willkie
1944 (R)	Dewey	Dewey
1948 (R)	Dewey-Taft	Dewey
1952 (R)	Eisenhower-Taft	Eisenhower
1956 (D)	Stevenson	Stevenson
1960 (D)	Kennedy	Kennedy
1964 (R)	—	Goldwater
1968 (R)	Nixon	Nixon
1972 (D)	Muskie	McGovern
1976 (D)	Humphrey [b]	Carter
1980 (R)	— [c]	Reagan
1984 (D)	Mondale [d]	Mondale

Source: Donald Matthews, "Presidential Nominations: Process and Outcomes," in *Choosing the President,* ed. James David Barber (Englewood Cliffs, N.J.: Prentice-Hall, 1974), 54.

[a] Dash (—) indicates that no single candidate led in the polls.

[b] The 1976 information was taken from the January Gallup poll.

[c] Carter led Kennedy in all Gallup polls conducted after the seizure of the hostages by Iran in November 1979. In a February 1980 Gallup poll listing eight candidates, 34 percent of Republican voters named Reagan as their first choice and 32 percent chose Ford; however, when the choice was narrowed to those two candidates, 56 percent preferred Ford and 40 percent, Reagan.

[d] Since President Reagan was unopposed for the Republican nomination, no preference poll was taken. A Gallup poll in mid-February 1984 showed, however, that 86 percent of Republicans approved the president's performance in office. The Gallup poll indicating Mondale to be the leading candidate among Democrats was taken in mid-November 1983.

Candidates take a number of factors into account when deciding which primaries they should emphasize in their nomination campaigns. One is the date of the primary. The earliest contest, traditionally New Hampshire, usually attracts most of the major contenders because it is the first test of popular sentiment of rank-and-file voters. Although the number of New Hampshire delegates is small (in 1984, 22 of 3,933 Democratic delegates, and 22 of 2,235 Republicans), it focuses immediate attention on the winner, as it did on John Kennedy in 1960 and Carter in 1976. Even if a candidate loses in New Hampshire but draws a greater percentage of the vote than expected, the media may interpret the results as a "moral" victory, a judgment that benefited Eugene McCarthy in 1968 and George McGovern in 1972. (It should be pointed out, however, that the media have not generally followed that practice in more recent nomination contests.)

New Hampshire appeals to presidential candidates for another reason: its small area and population make campaigning there manageable. Only about 20,000 Democrats were registered in 1976, and the Carter organization stated that it contacted about 95 percent of them.[19] The state was therefore ideal for the former governor in the early stages of the nomination contest: he had not yet acquired substantial financial resources for media expenditures, and his contingent of Georgia volunteers could conduct an effective door-to-door campaign.

Other primaries provide a late indication of voter preference. The California primary, for example, traditionally occurs near the end of the primary season. If the earlier primaries have not produced a clear favorite, the Golden State can determine who the party's nominee will be. Both Goldwater in 1964 and McGovern in 1972 owed their ultimate selection to their primary victories in California, which projected them as "winners" shortly before delegates throughout the country went to the national convention. The rules of the nomination contest also make California an attractive target for presidential candidates. It has the largest number of state delegates at each of the party conventions and, for Republicans, a winner-take-all provision that delivers those delegates in a solid bloc to the winner of the primary.

Other considerations besides timing and delegate strength affect candidates' decisions about where to concentrate campaign efforts. Naturally, they try to choose states where they think they have the best chance of winning. In 1976 and again in 1980 the Carter forces concentrated major efforts in his native South. In 1976 Henry Jackson chose Massachusetts and New York as special targets because both states contained many Catholics, Jews, and labor union members with whom the Washington senator felt he had close political ties. In 1980 Walter Mondale selected Pennsylvania and Illinois for the same reasons. Morris Udall in 1976, John Anderson in 1980, and Gary Hart in 1984 focused on Massachusetts and Wisconsin because they expected to do well in the liberal academic communities concentrated in those states. The two Republican contenders in 1976, Gerald Ford and Ronald Reagan, worked hard in their home states of Michigan and California to advance their candidacies, as did 1980 Democratic candidates Jimmy Carter in Georgia and Edward Kennedy in Massachusetts.

At times, however, candidates may deliberately choose to contest primaries that are not considered advantageous to them to demonstrate that they have a broader appeal than is generally recognized. John Kennedy went into the West Virginia primary in 1960 to prove that a Catholic could win in a state in which the population was 95 percent Protestant. In 1976 Jimmy Carter chose the Pennsylvania primary to show that a southern Baptist could do well in a northern industrial state with a large Catholic population. Both risks proved to be good ones that greatly advanced the Kennedy and Carter candidacies.

A major problem for candidates is properly managing a primary they clearly expect to lose. Many contenders have found that the most successful approach is to convince the public and particularly the media that they are not contesting the primary, so that a loss is not considered a genuine defeat. George McGovern successfully pursued that ploy in the Florida primary in 1972, as did Ronald Reagan in Wisconsin in 1976. This strategy also enables candidates to save their resources for more promising primaries.

Most important, candidates must avoid raising false expectations during the nomination campaign. In 1976, shortly before the New Hampshire primary, the Reagan staff released the results of a public opinion poll showing him to be ahead of Ford. When the California governor lost that primary by a single percentage point, the media interpreted the results as a serious defeat for him and a major victory for Ford. In 1980 John Connally decided to focus on the South Carolina primary as the one that would establish his candidacy; when he lost to Reagan there, the Texas governor was forced to withdraw from the race altogether.

Even though since 1972 primaries usually have been more consequential in nomination campaigns than caucus-convention contests, in some instances caucus-conventions become crucial. Since 1976 the Iowa caucuses have taken on major importance because they are the first test of the candidates' political strength, and the media therefore attach great significance to an Iowa victory.[20] In 1976 Jimmy Carter's successful campaign in Iowa established him as the Democratic pack leader; in 1980 his victory over Senator Kennedy in that state gave him a psychological edge in the New Hampshire primary a month later.

Caucus-convention states also become important if no clear victor emerges in the presidential primaries. In 1976 both Gerald Ford and Ronald Reagan diligently pursued delegates chosen in Republican party caucuses and conventions, especially in the period immediately preceding the Republican convention. In the end, Ford owed his nomination to the previously uncommitted delegations, such as Mississippi, that cast their ballots at the national convention in his favor.

Manipulating Political Appeals

No candidate in the nomination campaign has the option of using the party label against opponents in the same way that he or she can in the general election. However, a president seeking renomination and facing possible challenges can emphasize that he is presently the representative of his party. He can suggest that persons who challenge him for the nomination are casting doubts on the good judgment of the party, which nominated him four years previously, and that a challenge would divide the party in the upcoming general election. The president can even intimate that attacks on him are in effect attacks on the country itself. President Carter and his spokespersons employed all these tactics in his 1980 contest with his major opponent, Senator Kennedy.

In contrast, the challenger of an incumbent president must make the challenge appear legitimate. Several ways are possible. One is to suggest that the incumbent president is not providing the leadership the nation requires. Another is to intimate that the president is such a weak candidate that he will take the party and its congressional, state, and local candidates down to defeat in November. A third is to avow that the president has not kept the promises he made in his previous campaign and that he has strayed from the traditional policies of his party. Senator Kennedy used all these appeals in his unsuccessful attempt to wrest the 1980 Democratic nomination from President Carter.

In a nomination campaign, the incumbent president also can use the powers of his office to great advantage. In a speech early in the 1980 campaign Senator Kennedy charged that the Carter administration's offer of $7 million to relieve starvation in Cambodia was woefully inadequate; two hours later the president called in television camera crews to announce that $69 million would be given to combat famine and to resettle Cambodian refugees in Thailand. The president also invited Democratic leaders to the White House, and their acceptance was considered an endorsement of Carter's renomination. Aware of Carter's power to approve or disapprove federal grants to states and cities, almost five hundred mayors, governors, and members of Congress attended these meetings to demonstrate their support for his candidacy. As the campaign progressed, the president continued to use the prerogatives of his office. The Sunday before the Iowa caucuses, he appeared on "Meet the Press" and announced that he would insist that U.S. athletes boycott the summer Olympics unless the Soviet Union withdrew its troops from Afghanistan. On the eve of the New Hampshire primary the president invited the U.S. Olympic hockey team to the White House for a televised congratulatory ceremony for its victory over the Soviet team. On the morning of the Wisconsin and Kansas primaries, Carter made a public announcement of a "positive step" toward the release of the hostages in Iran.

The incumbent president therefore has a clear advantage in a nomination campaign. He not only can invoke the symbol of party unity; he can also manipulate events to benefit his candidacy. Incumbency is particularly advantageous if foreign crises occur during the campaign period, for Americans tend to "rally 'round the flag," and hence their president, as they initially did in 1980 for Carter when Americans were taken hostage in Iran. A review of U.S. history clearly shows the superior campaign position of the incumbent: Franklin Pierce was the last president who actively sought his party's renomination and failed to obtain it; James Buchanan won the Democratic nomination from him in 1856.

Presidential candidates in the party out of power face an entirely different campaign situation. Although none of them has the problem of how legitimately to challenge an incumbent president, they do experience other difficulties. Typically, many candidates vie for their party's nomination, and each aspirant must find a way to distinguish himself from his opponents. (Table 1-2 presents information on the range of persons who sought or were considered to be principal candidates for the 1984 Democratic nomination.) A further complication is that the range of political views of the selectorate in the nomination campaign is narrower than that of the electorate in the general election: most Republicans participating in the nomination process are conservative; most Democrats, liberal.

The limited range of the selectorate's views creates problems for those who try to advance their candidacy by taking stands on the issues. A candidate who departs from the standard positions runs the risk of alienating a large number of party members; yet one who does not do so remains indistinguishable from the other candidates. Thus it was difficult for Democratic voters in 1984 to differentiate among the policy positions of liberal candidates Mondale, Cranston, and McGovern. The same was true in 1980 for Republicans attempting to distinguish among the political views of conservative candidates Reagan, Crane, Dole, and Connally. In contrast, Republican representative John Anderson in 1980 took policy positions very different from those of conservative Republicans. (He favored, for example, gun control, the Equal Rights Amendment, the imposition of an import fee on gasoline to discourage consumption, and the public funding of abortions.) As a result, he alienated many Republican voters and had to drop out of the Republican race and run as an independent candidate.

Denied the use of a party label, and facing the problems associated with taking stands on issues, candidates develop other types of political appeals in nomination campaigns. Most important is the projection of a personal image that reflects their most attractive attributes. In 1980 Senator Kennedy, for example, pictured himself as a strong leader who could handle the nation's mounting economic and foreign policy problems. Four years earlier Jimmy Carter sought to take advantage of the nation's distrust of public officials after the Vietnam War and Watergate by creating the image of an honest person and promising to make the government as "truthful, capable, and filled with love as the American people." Thus candidates seek to link their personal characteristics with the perceived needs of the times.

Another important technique used in nomination campaigns is to project oneself as a "winner." This appeal usually is adopted by candidates who do well in the early nomination contests. Confident after his victory over Reagan in the 1980 Iowa caucuses, Bush suddenly announced that his campaign had momentum, or what he referred to as "Big Mo." Unfortunately for Bush, Big Mo lasted only until the New Hampshire primary, which Reagan clearly won. Similarly, in the 1984 Democratic contest Walter Mondale asserted his invincibility after his decisive victory in Iowa; one week later, however, he was upset by Gary Hart in New Hampshire.

Presidential nomination campaigns, therefore, are characterized more by the manipulation of personal images and claims of winner status than by a discussion of the issues. Contributing greatly to this situation is the influence of the media in the nomination process.

Communicating Political Appeals

In 1984, 18 million voters participated in the Democratic primaries. The need to communicate with this vast number of people means that candidates must turn to the mass media. During the 1980 campaign the major candidates depended mainly on short television commercials to carry their messages. Jimmy Carter's advertisements stressed his character: one showed the president with his family and concluded with the statement, "Husband, Father, President. He's done these three jobs with distinction." Edward Kennedy's commercials carried a leadership theme: they focused on the senator looking forceful in Senate hearings and walking through enthusiastic crowds. In 1984, advertisements took a more negative tone: one for Mondale showed a blinking red telephone on the president's desk, raising the fear that Hart could not be entrusted with the "most awesome, powerful responsibility in the world." Hart countered with a political commercial that showed a burning fuse, as a voice suggested that Mondale would risk another Vietnam in Central America by leaving U.S. troops there and by "using our sons as bargaining chips."

Candidate debates became important in the 1980 GOP nomination contest. Reagan refused to participate in the initial, nationally televised one held in Iowa on the grounds that such verbal encounters would destroy party unity; George Bush did well in the debate (he quoted Yogi Berra's classic remark in alleging that Carter had made the "wrong mistake" in imposing an embargo on grain shipments to the Soviet Union), and went on to win the caucuses there. Reagan then switched tactics, engaging in two debates in New Hampshire. In the second one, originally scheduled to include only Reagan

Table 1-2 Major Candidates for 1984 Democratic Nomination

Candidate	Background	Political views[a]	Assets	Liabilities
Reubin Askew	Lawyer, former governor of Florida, born Sept. 11, 1928	Most conservative Democratic candidate; generally opposes abortion and domestic-content legislation	Moderate southerner	Not well known in national politics
Alan Cranston	Journalist, senator from California, born June 19, 1914	Very liberal; emphasizes nuclear freeze and domestic-content legislation; highly critical of "Reaganomics"	First Democratic candidate publicly to announce for the presidency; did well in early straw polls in California, Wisconsin, and Alabama	Oldest Democratic candidate and regarded as too liberal by some Democrats
John Glenn	Astronaut, senator from Ohio, born July 18, 1921	"Centrist" candidate; emphasizes values and morality rather than specific issues	Well known as senator because of his astronaut fame; considered by many to have the best chance of defeating President Reagan	Started quest for presidency late, poor organization, not a good speaker
Gary Hart	Lawyer, senator from Colorado, born Nov. 28, 1936	Emphasizes "new" ideas and approaches to society's problems; critical of excessive expenditures on expensive weapons systems, favors arms control and a mutually verifiable nuclear freeze	Experience as campaign manager of George McGovern in 1972; appeals to young people, many independents, some Republicans	Seen by some as a "loner" in the Senate; did not do well in early state straw polls or in public opinion polls

Jesse Jackson	Minister, civil rights activist, born Oct. 8, 1941	Very liberal on economic and social issues; highly critical of U.S. policy in the Middle East as favoring Israel over Arab nations	Best speaker among Democratic candidates; has great appeal to young blacks	Lack of experience in public office; considered too radical by many moderate Democrats
Ernest Hollings	Lawyer, senator from South Carolina, born Jan. 1, 1922	No clear pattern to his political views; a hawk on national defense but opposes MX missile and B-1 bomber; favors government programs on food stamps and school lunches but opposes those for urban transit and urban redevelopment	Moderate southern candidate who proposed alternative to President Reagan's 1983 budget	Not well known nationally and disadvantaged by southern association with Jimmy Carter
George McGovern	Professor, former senator from South Dakota, 1972 Democratic presidential nominee, born July 19, 1922	Very liberal on economic and social issues; opposes U.S. intervention in Central America	Experienced in presidential campaigns and popular among liberals	Associated with major Democratic defeat in 1972 and late entry into race
Walter Mondale	Lawyer, former senator and vice president, born Jan. 5, 1928	Political protégé of Hubert Humphrey; very liberal on both economic and social issues; favors domestic content legislation and a nuclear freeze	Best organized and financed democratic candidate, favored by organized labor	Not dynamic speaker, poor on television, not favored generally by younger voters and independents

a Refers to views compared with other Democrats, not the general population.

and Bush, the California governor outmaneuvered his opponent by suggesting that the debate be opened to other candidates; when Bush insisted on sticking to the terms of the original two-person encounter, he came across as selfish to the other Republican contenders and to many voters as well. Reagan won the New Hampshire primary and also prevailed in Illinois, where he did well in a multicandidate debate, which included Illinoisan John Anderson.

The Democratic candidates held about a dozen debates in 1984, but none was as crucial as the Reagan-Bush New Hampshire debate of 1980. One problem, particularly early in the nomination campaign, was the large number of candidates (eight in the debate before the Iowa caucus); it was difficult for viewers to keep straight which candidate said what. Nonetheless, these verbal encounters, called "media events" [21] by one scholar, did enable the candidates to confront one another with interesting questions. In Iowa, Hart asked Mondale to indicate a single, major domestic issue on which he disagreed with the AFL-CIO; in Atlanta, Mondale challenged Hart to spell out the substance of his "new ideas," making his point by using the famous line from the Wendy's commercial, "Where's the beef?"

More important, however, than candidate commercials or debates in campaign communications is the coverage of the nomination process by representatives of the media. Particularly influential are nationally syndicated newspaper columnists, such as David Broder, Jack Germond, and Jules Witcover; many people, including writers for local newspapers, take their cues about the candidates and the nomination contest itself from these media "heavies." (One observer refers to this tendency as "pack journalism." [22]) Principal network newscasters, such as Dan Rather, Peter Jennings, and Tom Brokaw, also have played an important role in recent nomination campaigns, since television evening news is the main source of political information for most voters.

As political scientist Thomas Patterson maintains, the mass media focus primarily on the presidential "game"—who is winning and losing, campaign strategy and logistics, and appearances and "hoopla." [23] Thus the chances of the contestants are calculated and their candidacies assessed by the extent to which they surpass or fall short of the media's predictions. The media also attempt to analyze the strategies of the candidates and how successful they are likely to be. Television in particular concentrates its attention on candidate appearances and crowd reactions to such appearances, as it tries to convey the visually exciting aspects of the campaign.[24] Patterson contends that the media devote far less coverage to what he calls the "substance" of the campaign—discussion of issues and policies, the traits and records of the candidates, and endorsements by political leaders.

The media downplay political issues and policies in nomination campaigns for several reasons. As previously discussed, it is difficult to focus effectively on issues when a number of candidates in a nomination contest hold very similar views. Moreover, today's nomination campaigns are so long that candidates' speeches become, from the media's point of view, "unnewsworthy," as the contenders repeat their stands on the issues again and again. Finally, many media representatives assume that most voters are not interested in the issues; in any event, it is difficult to present issues in depth—especially on television, where the average evening news story lasts only a little longer than one minute.

Patterson points out that the media are, however, interested in two kinds of issues.[25] One is the "clear-cut" issue, in which candidates take diametrically opposed stands on a matter of public policy. This opposition creates controversy, on which the media thrive. The other is "campaign" issues, those that involve errors of judgment by candidates, such as Jimmy Carter's remark in 1976 about the desirability of preserving the "ethnic purity" of city neighborhoods. A graphic illustration of the media's preoccupation with campaign issues rather than policy issues is Roger Mudd's previously mentioned interview with Edward Kennedy: it concentrated primarily on Mary Jo Kopechne's death at Chappaquiddick and barely touched on Kennedy's voting record on issues in his seventeen years in the Senate.

The media also devote little attention to how candidates have done in prior public offices. Before the state caucuses and primaries begin, commentators give some coverage to the candidates' records, but that interest declines when the presidential "game" begins. Only when a hiatus occurs in the primary campaign do the media generally return to an examination of the record. In April 1980, for example, during the three weeks between the Wisconsin and the Pennsylvania primaries, the media suddenly began producing detailed comparisons of Reagan's campaign statements and his actual performance as the governor of California.

Thus the media shape the nature of the nomination campaign. They tend to focus attention on the game aspects of the early contests, particularly those in Iowa and New Hampshire. According to Patterson, they typically employ a winner-take-all principle that gives virtually all the publicity, regardless of how narrow the victory or the number of popular votes involved, to the victorious candidate in a state contest. In the 1976 Iowa caucuses Carter's winning of about 14,000 voters, 28 percent of the 50,000 cast (he actually trailed the "uncommitted" group), was interpreted by Roger Mudd as making the Georgia governor a "clear winner" and as opening the "ground between himself and the rest of the so-called pack." [26] At times, however, the media may provide greater coverage to the runner-up: after winning a mere 16 percent of the votes in the Iowa caucuses in 1984, Hart received as much publicity as Mondale, who captured three times as many votes.[27]

Campaign Workers

Although the mass media play a major role in communicating political appeals to the selectorate, interpersonal contacts remain an important element in nomination campaigns. This is particularly true in states that use caucus-conventions to choose their delegates to the national convention. In those states people do not merely go into a voting booth to cast their ballots; rather, they must participate often in lengthy meetings and sometimes in confrontations with supporters of other candidates. A series of meetings usually takes place throughout the state political system until a state convention chooses the national convention delegates. Many people are unwilling to commit that much time and effort to the nomination process unless campaign workers contact them personally.

As the campaign progresses, a candidate must expand the previously mentioned "constituency" that developed in the early, prenomination stage of the process. In the past, candidates often turned to political professionals to sponsor and organize their campaign, as Hubert Humphrey did in 1968. The endorsement of party professionals, however, does not always ensure the nomination. In 1972, for example, the early endorsement of Sen. Edmund Muskie by a number of Democratic party and public officials did not prevent the party from ultimately choosing George McGovern, a candidate with whom many professionals were uncomfortable. In 1976, an "outsider," Jimmy Carter, won the Democratic nomination, even though he had virtually no initial support from his fellow governors or other members of the Democratic political establishment. Among Republicans, Sen. Barry Goldwater won the 1964 nomination despite the opposition of many party leaders and public officials.

Probably the only candidate today who is in a position to line up the support of party professionals is an incumbent president, for he can use his influence over the dispensation of federal grants as political leverage against his opponents. Even this weapon is not always successful, however. Mayor Jane Byrne of Chicago (successor to the most powerful political boss of recent times, Richard Daley) endorsed Senator Kennedy, not President Carter, in the 1980 Democratic contest. Moreover, even when an incumbent president does receive the political blessing of a key political figure, it may not be decisive: Carter lost the New York primary in 1980 to Kennedy even though the president was endorsed by Mayor Edward Koch of New York City.

Today's candidates generally build their personal organization from political amateurs who offer support because they agree with a candidate's stands on the issues or are attracted to his or her personality or political style. Amateurs constituted the base for the Goldwater movement in 1964, for Eugene McCarthy's "Children's Crusade" in 1968, for McGovern's "guerrilla army" in 1972, and for the conservative constituency of Reagan in 1976 and again in 1980. Political scientist Jeane Kirkpatrick refers to such activists as a "new presidential elite." [28] Usually members of the upper middle class, such people have neither experience in nor loyalty to traditional party organizations. As Kirkpatrick contends, they typically take a keen interest in the intellectual and moral aspects of politics and use their verbal skills to great advantage in nomination politics.

At times, members of interest groups also endorse presidential candidates and furnish campaign workers for them. Some major labor unions participated actively in the 1980 Democratic contest. Edward Kennedy drew support from the International Association of Machinists and Aerospace Workers, and the National Education Association worked hard on President Carter's behalf. Both the AFL-CIO and the NEA endorsed Walter Mondale before the 1984 formal nomination process began and then played an important part in helping him secure the Democratic nomination.

Campaign Finance

Presidential candidates since the 1970s have started raising funds for their campaigns before the actual state contests begin. This solicitation of funds continues during the official campaign period itself. Candidates who do not do well in the first few primaries, however, tend to drop out of the race early on. One reason for their doing so is that, under the campaign finance law, federal matching funds must be cut off within thirty days if a candidate obtains less than 10 percent of the votes in two consecutive primaries. Even candidates who do not depend on matching funds may decide that a contest is hopeless; John Connally withdrew from the Republican race in early March 1980 after losing the South Carolina Republican primary to Reagan. (By that time the former Texas governor had spent $11 million of privately raised money and had won only one convention delegate.) Even candidates who score some successes in primaries may nonetheless develop financial problems if their opponents are doing even better. In 1980 Senator Kennedy found that President Carter was outspending him in virtually every state, including his home state of Massachusetts (New Hampshire was one exception). That same year, Bush was forced to take out a bank loan of $2.8 million after losing to Reagan in several primaries.

Candidates must decide not only how to raise funds but also how to spend them. The overall spending limits for the entire campaign ($17.6 million in 1980 and $24.4 million in 1984), as well as expenditure limits in each state, require that money be carefully allocated. Because they want to win in initial primaries and caucuses, candidates are inclined to spend heavily in the very early stage of the campaign. By February 26, 1980, the date of the New Hampshire primary, Reagan had spent two-thirds of his allowable limit for the entire campaign consisting of thirty-four Republican primaries.[29] Figure 1-2 shows that Mondale expended a major portion of his funds before the delegate selection process began in February 1984, while Hart's spending was more in proportion to the number of delegates at stake.

Summary of Developments in Recent Nomination Campaigns

As the elements of campaigning, discussed in the preceding sections, suggest, presidential nomination campaigns are highly complex operations that call for a variety of specialists. Pollsters help candidates assess their nomination

Figure 1-2 Cumulative Proportions of Each Democratic Candidate's Total Expenditures and Delegates Apportioned over Time, 1983-1984 (Percent)

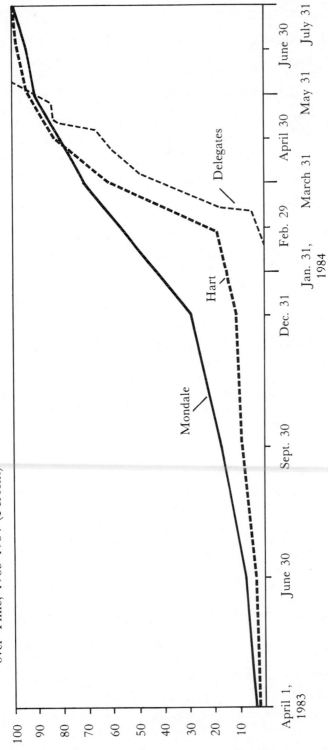

Source: Gary R. Orren, "The Nomination Process: Vicissitudes of Candidate Selection," in *The Elections of 1984*, ed. Michael Nelson (Washington, D.C.: CQ Press, 1985), 48.

Note: Excludes fund-raising expenditures.

prospects and provide vital feedback on the reactions of voters to the candidates and their campaigns, on the issues that people are thinking about, and on the attitudes of social and economic groups about such issues. Media consultants help candidates develop a favorable image, write their speeches, and plan their television appearances. Direct-mail specialists help raise money and get out the vote. Since the 1952 presidential election, candidates have turned more and more to political consultants to organize these diverse operations, to develop strategy, and to manage the overall campaign.

Since the late 1960s control over the fate of presidential candidates has passed from a relatively few party professionals to rank-and-file voters. The attitudes of these voters evolve during the course of the nomination contest, in large part because of the influence of the media. In the early stages of the contest the media help determine who the viable candidates are; then, once the state primaries and caucuses begin, they label the "winners" and "losers," often, thereby, influencing the results of future state contests, for voters gravitate toward the winners and desert the losers. Periodic public opinion polls reflect the presidential preferences of U.S. voters, as do the results of state primaries and caucuses.

Moreover, the attitudes of voters, the media, the polls, and the state contest results influence one another. Candidates who receive favorable treatment from the media tend to do well in the primaries, and their showing there, in turn, raises their standings in the polls. Favorable polls impress representatives of the media as well as political activists and many rank-and-file voters, leading to more victories for the poll leaders in both nonprimary and primary contests. The result of this reinforcement process is that by the time the delegates gather for their party's national convention, one candidate usually has emerged. This candidate has received the most extensive and the most favorable media coverage, has led in the polls, and has won more primary and caucus-convention contests than any other candidate.[30] However, one more hurdle remains for the front-runner to cross—the party's national convention.

The National Convention

The national convention is important to presidential candidates for two reasons. First, whatever may have happened before, the actual nomination occurs at the convention. Second, the convention provides opportunities for candidates to strengthen their chances to win the general election the following November.

Rules and Politics of the Proceedings

Several decisions that precede the balloting for the nomination can affect significantly both the choice of nominee and the outcome of the general election. Sometimes the location of the convention is important. (The party's national committee officially makes this decision: for the party out of power, the national committee chairperson has the greatest say in the matter; for the party in power, the U.S. president does.) The welcoming speech of Illinois governor Adlai Stevenson to the Democratic delegates assembled in Chicago in 1952 is credited with influencing their decision to nominate him that year. In 1968 the confrontation in Chicago between protestors and Mayor Daley's police contributed to Hubert Humphrey's defeat in the general election.

Also important are the struggles between rival slates of delegates from states where the process of selecting delegates was disputed. At the 1952 Republican convention, the Credentials Committee awarded Robert Taft a majority of the delegates in several southern states, but this decision was overturned on the floor of the convention in favor of the ultimate nominee, Dwight Eisenhower. At the 1972 Democratic convention, there were eighty-two separate challenges involving thirty states and more than 40 percent of the delegates; most of the disputes stemmed from alleged violations of the McGovern Commission guidelines. Eventually, all but two were settled by the Credentials Committee; these went to the convention floor and were resolved in Senator McGovern's favor. He was awarded all of California's delegate votes even though, as previously noted, he won only 45 percent of that state's primary vote. Another dispute led to a convention decision to seat the delegation favoring the senator, not the regular Illinois delegation linked with Mayor Daley of Chicago on the grounds that the latter did not contain an adequate representation of youth, women, and minorities and was chosen through improper processes.

Fights over rules of convention proceedings sometimes take on great significance. One such battle occurred at the 1976 Republican convention when the Reagan forces moved to amend the rules so as to require candidates to name their vice-presidential choice before the balloting on presidential candidates; they hoped thereby to force Ford to name a running mate and thus risk the loss of supporters who would be disappointed with his decision. (Before the convention Reagan had chosen liberal-to-moderate Pennsylvania senator Richard Schweiker as his vice president, a move calculated to bring him needed support from uncommitted delegates in large eastern states such as New York and Pennsylvania.) The defeat of that amendment helped pave the way for President Ford's victory on the first ballot that year. In 1980 Edward Kennedy's forces attempted to persuade the Democratic convention delegates to vote down a rule, first proposed by the Winograd Commission and later adopted by the Democratic National Committee, that required delegates to vote on the first ballot for a presidential candidate to whom they were pledged in their home state's primary or caucus-convention. When the convention upheld the rule, the Massachusetts senator knew he had no chance of winning the Democratic nomination, for more than a majority of the delegates were pledged to Carter. Kennedy immediately withdrew his candidacy on the very first night of the convention.

Writing and adopting the party platform entails other important convention decisions. Although critics traditionally have ridiculed the platforms for containing promises the party does not intend to keep, presidents of both parties have used their influence to enact the promises into law.[31] Moreover, many delegates and party leaders take them seriously.[32] In 1948 some of the delegates to the Democratic convention felt that the platform was too liberal on civil rights; twenty years later the Democrats bitterly debated the Vietnam plank of the platform. Republicans also have experienced major conflicts over their party platform: in 1964 the conservative Goldwater forces, which controlled that convention, refused to make any concessions to party moderates, such as governors Nelson Rockefeller of New York and George Romney of Michigan, on civil rights and political extremism.

One of the problems of platform fights is that the intraparty conflict may influence the general election campaign. Some southerners formed a third party in 1948 (the States' Rights party headed by South Carolina governor J. Strom Thurmond), which actually carried four southern states—Alabama, Louisiana, Mississippi, and South Carolina. Republican governors Rockefeller and Romney did little to help Goldwater in 1964, and many Democrats opposed to the proadministration plank on Vietnam in the party's 1968 platform did not rouse themselves in the general election campaign that year.

Because of the possibility of splitting the party in the fall campaign, presidential candidates and their supporters sometimes decide not to fight their major rivals over the platform. After defeating Ronald Reagan for the 1976 Republican nomination, President Ford allowed the views of the California governor to prevail on several major provisions of the platform, including advocating a "moral" foreign policy (in contrast to detente, the policy the Ford administration had pursued with the Soviet Union). In 1980 President Carter followed a similar procedure in permitting the Kennedy forces to add to the Democratic platform a provision for a $12-billion, antirecession job program. In 1984 Mondale allowed Hart to add a plank spelling out the conditions under which a Democratic president would use U.S. forces abroad and Jackson to add one providing for "affirmative action goals and timetables and other verifiable measurements."

Credentials contests, the adoption of rules of procedure, and the writing of the party platform are tests of strength for the candidates and often determine who will prevail in the most important decision of the convention— the balloting for president, which typically takes place on the third day of the proceedings. In the interim, preparations are made for the roll call vote. Presidential hopefuls frequently call on caucuses of state delegations and sometimes contact individual delegates for their support. Polls are taken of delegates so that candidates know how many votes they can count on and from whom they may pick up additional support. In 1960 Edward Kennedy retained contacts with the Wyoming delegates he had worked with the previous spring and was in their midst when his brother won the nomination on the first ballot.[33] Also in 1960, Richard Nixon arranged to have his picture taken with each delegate at the Republican convention.[34]

The strategy a candidate employs in the balloting depends on the amount of delegate support he has. If he is the front-runner, as President Ford asserted he was in 1976, he concentrates on holding the votes he has been promised and on picking up any additional votes needed to win a majority on the initial ballot. The candidate and his workers use the bandwagon technique to achieve this goal—that is, they argue that since he will win the nomination anyway, delegation chairpersons or individual members who are politically smart will come out at that time for his candidacy rather than wait until the matter has already been settled. The candidate, the workers imply, will remember early support in the future when he is in a position to do political favors. Franklin Roosevelt did so quite specifically after he was elected in 1932: he determined whether a person seeking a political position had backed him "before Chicago" (where the convention had been held).

Candidates with less delegate support attempt to counter the bandwagon technique with their own strategies. They try to create the impression that the nomination is still uncertain, as the Reagan forces did at the 1976 Republican convention. At times, they may encourage delegates who do not support them to cast their ballots for favorite sons or other minor candidates; their objective is to hold down the vote for the front-runner on the first roll call. Candidates also attempt to forge alliances to stop the leader. They may agree, for example, that at some time during the balloting, those who fall behind in the voting will throw their support to others. The difficulty with making such an arrangement is that minor candidates frequently have greater differences among themselves than they have with the leader. The only alliance that conceivably might have stopped Richard Nixon at the 1968 Republican convention would have been one between Nelson Rockefeller and Ronald Reagan. However, given their divergent views on vital issues of the day, and Rockefeller's failure to support Goldwater in 1964 (Reagan had made the best speech of that campaign on Goldwater's behalf), the two governors were hardly a compatible political combination.

The leader, along with other candidates, offers various enticements in bargaining with possible political supporters. Some people are interested in persuading the party to take a particular stand on the platform. Others have more tangible concerns: senators or governors may seek the candidate's support in their own campaigns; other political leaders may be looking toward a cabinet post. Although a presidential candidate himself may refuse to make such commitments so that he can go before his party and the electorate as a "free" man beholden to no one, his supporters do not hesitate to make promises. One delegate to the 1960 convention claimed to be the nineteenth person to whom the Kennedy forces had offered the vice presidency.[35]

A definite trend in recent conventions is early victory for the candidate who arrives at the convention with the greatest number of pledged delegates. In the twenty conventions the two major parties have held since World War II, only two nominees—Thomas Dewey in 1948 and Adlai Stevenson in 1952—failed to win a majority of the convention votes on the first ballot. Thus, the convention has become a body that typically legitimizes the decision on the presidential nominee that has already been made by the time the delegates gather to choose a candidate officially.

The selection of the vice-presidential nominee is the final decision of the convention. Although in theory the delegates make the choice, as a matter of political custom they allow presidential nominees to pick their own running mates. On rare occasions nominees may decide against expressing their preferences and permit the convention to make an open choice, as Adlai Stevenson did in 1956. The typical presidential nominee, however, confers with leaders whose judgment he trusts, and, when he makes the decision, the word is passed on to the delegates. Even though some delegates may resist a particular vice-presidential candidate, nominees generally get their way. In 1940 Franklin Roosevelt threatened to refuse the presidential nomination unless Henry Wallace were chosen as his vice president. In 1960 John Kennedy insisted on Lyndon Johnson as his running mate over the objections of some liberal members of the party, including his brother Robert. In effect, the vice president is the first political appointment of the winning presidential nominee.

Various considerations underlie the choice of a vice-presidential candidate. Parties traditionally attempt to balance the ticket—that is, to select a person who differs in certain ways from the presidential nominee. For example, the two candidates may come from separate parts of the country. Over the years, the Democratic party often has chosen southerners to run with presidential nominees who were typically from other, two-party areas; the Kennedy-Johnson ticket in 1960 was such a combination. In 1976, when a southerner, Jimmy Carter, won the Democratic presidential contest for the first time since before the Civil War, the process worked in reverse; he chose Walter Mondale from the northern state of Minnesota as his running mate. In 1972 George McGovern originally chose Sen. Thomas Eagleton as his running mate, because the Missourian possessed certain characteristics the South Dakotan lacked: affiliation with the Roman Catholic church, ties to organized labor, and previous residence in a large city (St. Louis). In 1980 Ronald Reagan chose George Bush (whom he reportedly did not much admire personally) in order to win the support of moderates in the Republican party. In 1984 Mondale selected as his running mate Rep. Geraldine Ferraro of New York, who not only complemented the ticket geographically but also was the first woman and first Italian-American to serve as a major party candidate in a presidential contest. The ticket is balanced in these ways to broaden its appeal and thereby strengthen the party's chances in the general election.

Some presidential nominees, however, at least consider how the vice-presidential candidate will perform in office. The trend toward assigning important responsibilities to the second in command has led some candidates to choose running mates with whom they feel they can work effectively. (See Chapter 5.) This was the main reason Carter chose Walter Mondale over other northern liberal senators he had interviewed for the position, including Edmund Muskie of Maine, Frank Church of Idaho, John Glenn of Ohio, and Adlai Stevenson III of Illinois. The possibility of succession also has led presidents to choose the running mate who seems most able to assume the duties of the nation's highest office. John Kennedy reportedly chose Lyndon Johnson not only because he balanced the Democratic ticket in 1960 but also because Kennedy considered the Texan to be the most capable leader among his rivals for the presidential nomination.

Whatever the considerations that prompt the choice of a running mate, there is no doubt that presidential nominees often make the decision too quickly, and frequently without complete knowledge of the candidate's background. A notable example is McGovern's choice of Eagleton in 1972. McGovern and his staff met the morning after his nomination (many of them having had only two- or three-hours' sleep), and by five o'clock that afternoon they finally settled on Eagleton. The Missourian accepted the nomination after several other persons had either turned it down, could not be contacted, or were vetoed by key McGovern supporters. During that time no one turned up the information on Eagleton's history of mental illness, which ultimately led McGovern to force him off the ticket.

After the vice-presidential candidate is chosen, the final night of the convention proceedings is given over to acceptance speeches. On this occasion the presidential nominee tries to reunite the candidates and various party elements that have confronted one another during the long preconvention campaign and the hectic days of the convention. Major party figures usually come to the convention stage and pledge their support for the winner in the upcoming campaign. At times, however, personal feelings run too high and wounds fail to heal sufficiently for a show of party unity. In 1964, for example, important members of the liberal wing of the Republican party did not support the GOP standard-bearer, Barry Goldwater; and in 1968 many McCarthyites among Democrats (including McCarthy himself) refused to endorse the chosen nominee, Hubert Humphrey, at least immediately. In 1972 prominent Democratic leaders, including George Meany of the AFL-CIO, did not support McGovern. Senator Kennedy and many of his followers did not enthusiastically endorse President Carter on the final night of the 1980 Democratic convention. Thus, the convention does not always achieve one of its main objectives: to rally the party faithful for the general election battle.

Recent Changes in Conventions

The principal activities of today's national conventions are the same as those developed one and a half centuries ago: devising the rules of procedure, adopting platforms, and, most important, nominating presidential and vice-presidential candidates. Recent developments, however, particularly since the mid-1960s, have radically changed the character of party conventions.

The most basic change is the way political power is organized and exercised at the convention. In the past, to win their party's nomination, presidential candidates were forced to negotiate with party leaders, particularly with those who chaired state delegations (often governors).[36] Today, however, candidates' personal organizations dominate the convention proceedings and contact individual delegates directly rather than working through the leaders who chair state delegations. Thus the growth in importance of candidate (rather than party) organizations, which has occurred in presidential nomination campaigns, has carried over into the national convention itself.

The character of convention delegates also changed in the late 1960s and 1970s. Students of those conventions have identified a basic split in both parties between amateur and professional delegates; the former are motivated primarily by candidates' stands on the issues, the latter by their ability to unite the party and win in November.[37] In the 1980s, however, the distinction between the two types of delegates has blurred as former amateurs share power with professionals and take on many of the latter's characteristics. Two political scientists call these people the "new professionals." [38]

Also becoming more prominent are delegate caucuses that transcend state boundaries, such as those organized by women, blacks, and Chicanos. In some instances these groups take the leadership in platform fights, as women did at the 1976 Republican convention over the ratification of the Equal Rights Amendment (ERA) and at the 1980 Democratic convention over the use of Medicaid funds for abortions and the denial of financial and technical campaign support to candidates not supporting ERA. Also surfacing as power blocs are those organized by interest groups: the AFL-CIO had 405 delegates and the National Education Association 302 delegates at the 1980 Democratic convention.[39]

Finally, technological developments have affected recent nominating conventions. Sophisticated electronic equipment enables centralized candidate organizations to communicate directly with their organizers and with individual delegates on the crowded convention floor. Even more important is the mass media's thorough and immediate coverage of convention proceedings. Such coverage has forced the parties to stage proceedings in a way that appeals to a nationwide audience; visually important events must be scheduled to take advantage of prime-time viewing. The media's close attention also has made it difficult for the parties to carry on delicate negotiations. As columnist David Broder has pointed out, not since 1952 (when, he suggests, television "took over" the convention hall) has either major party used more than one ballot to nominate its presidential candidate. He attributes this consequence to the party members' inability "to take the time for the slow and sometimes secretive bargaining that in the past allowed their national conventions to function successfully as coalition-building institutions." [40] Some observers of the 1980 Republican convention believe that one reason the GOP failed to consummate the "dream ticket" of Reagan and Ford was the media's relentless pressure to cover and thereby even to shape the delicate negotiations surrounding that important decision.

Conclusion

If the presidential institution can best be described as *protean*, so can the nomination process through which presidential candidates are chosen. Over the years, significant changes have occurred in the procedure for selecting the persons who represent the major parties in the general election contest. Initially, party leaders in the Congress used congressional caucuses to designate their nominees. Then, for a brief period, the parties turned to state legislatures and conventions to propose favorite-son candidates before moving to a new institution, the national convention, to choose their presidential candidates. Although this method prevails today, the advent of presidential primaries has altered it greatly. Thus, the presidential nomination process has been progressively democratized as the participants have changed from party elites to the general public itself. Through primaries, the public indirectly affects the process by helping determine the composition of the national convention that officially names the presidential candidate.

The changes that occurred from the early days of the nation's history until the mid-1960s, nearly two centuries, were gradual; those that have occurred since then have been abrupt. From 1968 to 1980, what political scientist Bryon Shafer calls a "quiet revolution" took place in the process by which the parties (especially the Democrats) chose their presidential candidates.[41] Alterations in the rules of the game transferred the choice of candidates from caucus-conventions dominated by public and party officials to popular primaries in which an increasing number of rank-and-file voters chose delegates for the national convention who were pledged to support specific presidential candidates. In addition, the private financing of nomination campaigns by large contributors gave way to a system of government subsidies that match the donations of small donors. New political elites also emerged: political amateurs and members of the media replaced professionals, such as governors, senators, House members, and state party leaders, as the most influential people in the nomination of presidential candidates. Moreover, as Shafer points out, the new political elites spoke for a white-collar electorate in contrast to the blue-collar rank-and-file voters, represented mainly by the professionals.[42]

The 1980s have witnessed a "counterrevolution" in nomination politics. Between 1980 and 1984, six states abandoned presidential primaries in favor of caucus-conventions.[43] Consequently, the proportion of national convention delegates chosen in primaries fell from almost three-fourths to slightly more than half. Professionals were brought back into the nomination process in the form of superdelegates, constituting one of seven delegates at the 1984 Democratic national convention. In the battle over the 1988 rules, the professionals once more prevailed over the amateurs, as the number of superdelegates was increased.

The result of this revolution and counterrevolution—created by two decades of continual reform in the Democratic party—is a mixed nomination system. It incorporates the selection of delegates by both the primary and caucus-convention methods. The participants include professionals representing blue-collar constituents, such as organized labor, as well as amateurs, who speak largely for white-collar constituents. Indeed, the 1984 nomination process reflected these differences: Mondale generally was favored by party professionals, Democratic loyalists, blue-collar workers, and older people; and Hart, by amateurs, political independents, white-collar workers, and younger voters. The protean presidential nomination system reflects alterations in the rules of the game as well as the significant political changes that resulted from those alterations.

Notes

1. William Chambers, *Political Parties in a New Nation: The American Experience, 1776-1809* (New York: Oxford University Press, 1963), chap. 2.
2. In the early 1820s the Republican party became known as the Democratic-Republicans and in 1840 was officially designated as the Democratic party (Paul David, Ralph Goldman, and Richard Bain, *The Politics of National Party Conventions* [New York: Vintage, 1964], chap. 3).
3. Joseph Charles, *The Origins of the American Party System* (New York: Harper Torch, 1956), 83-94.
4. Gerald Pomper, *Nominating the President: The Politics of Convention Choice* (New York: Norton, 1966), 17.
5. David, Goldman, and Bain, *Politics of National Party Conventions*, 50.
6. The National Republican party was soon to give way to the Whigs, with many Whig supporters joining the Republican party when it was formed in the 1850s (ibid., 57-59).
7. Ibid., 61.
8. Some states used another variant in 1984, the "winner-take-more" principle, whereby the leading candidate in a district received a "bonus" delegate, and

the remainder of the delegates were divided among the candidates in proportion to the votes they received.

9. Herbert E. Alexander, *Financing Politics: Money, Elections and Political Reform*, 2d ed. (Washington, D.C.: CQ Press, 1980), 27.
10. Although political action committees can help finance nomination campaigns, their contributions are not matched by federal funds as are those of individuals.
11. Alexander, *Financing Politics*, 98.
12. Austin Ranney, "Changing the Rules of the Nominating Game," in *Choosing the President*, ed. James David Barber (Englewood Cliffs, N.J.: Prentice-Hall, 1974), 71.
13. Arthur Hadley, *The Invisible Primary* (Englewood Cliffs, N.J.: Prentice-Hall, 1976).
14. Jules Witcover, "Sen. Mondale Won't Seek Presidential Nomination," *Washington Post*, November 22, 1974, A1.
15. Theodore H. White, *The Making of the President, 1972* (New York: Bantam, 1973), 127.
16. Martin Schram, *Running for President 1976: The Carter Campaign* (New York: Stein and Day, 1977), 8.
17. Donald Matthews, "Presidential Nominations: Process and Outcomes," in *Race for the Presidency: The Media and the Nominating Process*, ed. James David Barber (Englewood Cliffs, N.J.: Prentice-Hall, 1978), 39.
18. John Aldrich, *Before the Convention: A Theory of Presidential Nomination Campaigns* (Chicago: University of Chicago Press, 1980), 70.
19. Schram, *Running for President*, 20.
20. Former senator Howard Baker noted that this development has made the Iowa caucuses the "functional equivalent of a primary" (Lou Cannon and William Peterson, "GOP," in *The Pursuit of the Presidency*, ed. Richard Harwood [New York: Berkeley, 1980], 129).
21. Michael W. Traugott, "The Media and the Nominating Process," in *Before Nomination: Our Primary Problems*, ed. George Grassmuck (Washington, D.C.: American Enterprise Institute, 1985), 111-112.
22. Timothy Crouse, *The Boys on the Bus* (New York: Ballentine Books, 1972).
23. Thomas Patterson, *The Mass Media Election: How Americans Choose Their President* (New York: Praeger, 1980), chap. 3.
24. Television reporters refer to coverage of candidates arriving at and departing from airports as "here he comes, there he goes" stories.
25. Patterson, *Mass Media Election*, chap. 4.
26. Ibid., 44.
27. William C. Adams, "Media Coverage of Campaign '84: A Preliminary Report," *Public Opinion*, April-May, 1984, 10-11, cited in Gary R. Orren, "The Nomination Process: Vicissitudes of Candidate Selection," in *The Elections of 1984*, ed. Michael Nelson (Washington, D.C.: CQ Press, 1985), 53.
28. Jeane Kirkpatrick, *The New Presidential Elite: Men and Women in National Politics* (New York: Russell Sage Foundation and the Twentieth Century Fund, 1976).
29. Cannon and Peterson, "GOP," 128.

30. Recent exceptions to that trend, when two candidates ended the preconvention period fairly even in those respects, are: Ford and Reagan in 1976, McGovern and Humphrey in 1972, and Mondale and Hart in 1984.
31. Gerald Pomper and Susan Lederman, *Elections in America: Control and Influence in Democratic Politics,* 2d ed. (New York: Longman, 1980), chap. 8.
32. Judith Parris, *The Convention Problem: Issues in Reform of Presidential Nominating Procedures* (Washington, D.C.: Brookings, 1972), 110.
33. Theodore H. White, *The Making of the President, 1960* (New York: Pocket Books, 1961), 203.
34. Nelson Polsby and Aaron Wildavsky, *Presidential Elections: Strategies of American Electoral Politics* (New York: Scribners, 1964), 82.
35. Ibid., 4th ed. (1976), 144.
36. Robert Peabody, Norman Ornstein, and David Rohde, "The United States Senate as a Presidential Incubator: Many Are Called but Few Are Chosen," *Political Science Quarterly* (Summer 1976): 248.
37. Robert Robach, "Amateurs and Professionals: Delegates to the 1972 Republican National Convention," *Journal of Politics* (May 1975): 436-469; John Soule and Wilma McGrath, "A Comparative Study of Presidential Nominations: The Democrats, 1968 and 1972," *American Journal of Political Science* (August 1975): 501-517; Robert Nakamura, "Beyond Purism and Professionalism: Styles of Convention Delegate Followership," *American Journal of Political Science* (May 1980): 207-232.
38. William Crotty and John S. Jackson III, *Presidential Primaries and Nominations* (Washington, D.C.: CQ Press, 1985), 122.
39. Michael Malbin, "The Conventions, Platforms, and Issue Activists," in *The American Elections of 1980,* ed. Austin Ranney (Washington, D.C.: American Enterprise Institute, 1981), 128.
40. David Broder, "Political Reporters in Presidential Politics," in *Inside the System,* ed. Charles Peters and John Rothchild, 2d ed. (New York: Praeger, 1973), 7.
41. Bryon E. Shafer, *Quiet Revolution: The Struggle for the Democratic Party and the Shaping of Post-Reform Politics* (New York: Russell Sage Foundation, 1983).
42. Ibid., 524.
43. Although information on the 1988 presidential contest is incomplete at this time (May 1987), it appears that there will be a movement back toward more state primaries in 1988.

Selected Readings

Aldrich, John. *Before the Convention: A Theory of Presidential Nomination Campaigns.* Chicago: University of Chicago Press, 1980.
Alexander, Herbert E. *Financing Politics: Money, Elections and Political Reform.* 3d ed. Washington, D.C.: CQ Press, 1984.

Crotty, William, and John S. Jackson III. *Presidential Primaries and Nominations*. Washington, D.C.: CQ Press, 1985.

Crouse, Timothy. *The Boys on the Bus*. New York: Ballentine Books, 1972.

Grassmuck, George, ed. *Before Nomination: Our Primary Problems*. Washington, D.C.: American Enterprise Institute, 1985.

Hadley, Arthur. *The Invisible Primary*. Englewood Cliffs, N.J.: Prentice-Hall, 1976.

Patterson, Thomas. *The Mass Media Election: How Americans Choose Their President*. New York: Praeger, 1980.

Shafer, Bryon E. *Quiet Revolution: The Struggle for the Democratic Party and the Shaping of Post-Reform Politics*. New York: Russell Sage Foundation, 1983.

Presidential candidates Sen. John F. Kennedy and Vice President Richard Nixon shake hands before their first—and the first ever—nationally televised debate, September 26, 1960.

CHAPTER TWO

Election Politics

As the quest for the presidency shifts from the nomination to the election phase, candidates face new political problems. The rules change, because the electoral college and the campaign finance legislation pertaining to general elections shape the way the fall campaign will be waged. New political appeals must be developed for this new stage of the campaign, now essentially a one-on-one contest, pitting the nominees of the two major parties against each other (although, on occasion, a strong third-party candidate may run). The audience of the campaign increases greatly—about twice as many people vote in the general election as participate in the nomination process. Candidates and staff members therefore must decide how they can win the support of these new voters as well as appeal to persons generally identifying with the other party who backed losing candidates in the nomination process. A further complication is the length of the campaign: this new, expanded phase of the presidential contest is compressed into a mere ten weeks, roughly Labor Day to election day.

The first section of this chapter traces the evolution of the electoral college system and explains how it and recent campaign finance laws affect the general election campaign. The next section analyzes the campaign in the same framework as was used in Chapter 1 for the nomination contest: its early stages and targeting efforts, the kinds of political appeals that are directed toward the electorate, the communication of these appeals through the media and campaign workers, and the sources and types of expenditures. The following sections of the chapter focus on the factors that affect voting in presidential elections and analyze consequences of that voting.

Rules of the Election Contest

The two major rules affecting the general election are (1) the constitutional requirement that the electoral college choose the president and (2) campaign finance laws. They help to determine how and where the fall campaign will be conducted.

The Electoral College

The method of selecting the president was among the most difficult problems the delegates to the Constitutional Convention faced.[1] A variety of plans were proposed, the two most important being selection by the Congress and direct election by the people. The first, derived from the practice in most states of the legislature's choosing the governor, had the backing of a number of delegates, including Roger Sherman of Connecticut. It was eventually discarded because of fear of legislative supremacy and also because the delegates could not choose between state-unit voting, which favored the small states, and joint action of the two chambers, which benefited the large states with their greater voting power in the House of Representatives. Three of the most influential members of the convention—James Madison of Virginia and James Wilson and Gouverneur Morris of Pennsylvania—supported direct popular election, but it was considered too democratic by most delegates. As George Mason of Virginia put it, "It would be as unnatural to refer the choice of a proper magistrate to the people as it would to refer a trial of colors to a blind man."

Having decided against both popular election and selection by legislative bodies, the delegates proceeded to adopt an entirely new plan put forth by one of their own committees. The proposal, which some historians believe was based on a method used in Maryland to elect state senators, specified that each state legislature could choose electors, by whatever means it desired, equal to its total number of senators and representatives in Congress but that none of the electors could be members of Congress or hold other national office.[2] The individual electors would assemble at a fixed time in their respective state capitals and cast two votes each for president. These votes were then to be transmitted to Washington, D.C., where they would be opened and counted during a joint session of Congress. Whoever received the largest number of electoral votes would be declared president, provided a majority (one more than half) had been obtained; if no candidate received a majority, the House of Representatives, voting by states (one state delegation, one vote), would choose the president from among the five candidates receiving the highest number of electoral votes. After the president was chosen, the person with the next highest number of electoral votes would be declared vice president. If two or more contenders received an equal number of electoral votes, the Senate would choose the vice president from among them.

This complicated procedure reflected values and assumptions about human nature enunciated in *The Federalist Papers*. (The particular selection, Number 68, is attributed to Alexander Hamilton, whose views were somewhat more elitist than those of the majority of the delegates to the

Constitutional Convention.) The Founders felt that the average person did not have the ability to make sound judgments about the qualifications of the presidential candidates and that this crucial decision therefore should be left to a small group of electors—a political elite who would have both the information and the wisdom necessary to choose the best persons for the nation's two highest offices. Because the electors could not be national officeholders with connections to the president, they could approach their task without bias; because they assembled separately in their respective state capitals rather than as a single body, there would be less chance of their being corrupted or exposed to popular unrest. Moreover, since they were convened for a single purpose and would be dissolved when their task was completed, the possibility of tampering with them in advance or rewarding them with future favors was eliminated.

Philosophy shaped the presidential selection process adopted by the delegates, but so did a recognition of political factors. One student of the subject suggests that some of the delegates did not expect the electors to be entirely insulated from popular preferences.[3] They anticipated that each state's electors would cast one vote for a "native son," a locally popular political figure, and the other for a "continental character," an individual with a national reputation that members of the political elite would be aware of, even though the person might not be well known to the average citizen. (Evidence for this assumption is provided by Article II, Section 1, of the Constitution, which states that at least one of the two persons for whom an elector votes must not be an inhabitant of the elector's state.) The Founders also expected that after George Washington's presidency, the electoral votes would be so widely distributed that few candidates would receive a majority, and, therefore, most elections (Mason estimated about nineteen out of twenty) would ultimately be decided by the House of Representatives. The electors would thus serve to "screen" (or, in today's terms, "nominate") the candidates, and the House would choose (elect) the president from among them. The conflict between large and small states, which was settled by the Connecticut Compromise on the composition of the Senate and House, also arose in the plan the delegates worked out for the selection of the chief executive. In the initial vote by the electors, the large states had the advantage, because the number of each state's votes reflected the size of its House delegation. If no candidate got a majority, the small states were favored in the second selection, because the contingent vote was by states, not by the number of representatives.

As was true of so many issues decided by the Founders, the method of selecting the president was a compromise. In addition to resolving the large-state/small-state conflict, the electoral college device took into account the attitudes of the advocates of states' rights by allowing the state legislatures to decide how the electors should be chosen. It also held open, for those who favored letting the people choose the president, the possibility of the electors' actually reflecting the popular vote for the president in their state. As political scientist John Roche has pointed out, the intermediate elector scheme gave "everybody a piece of the cake"; he also notes, however, that "the future was left to cope with the problem of what to do with this Rube Goldberg mechanism." [4]

Events soon nullified both the philosophical and political assumptions underlying the Founders' vision of the electoral college and forced them to cope with the "Rube Goldberg mechanism." The formation and organization of political parties in the 1790s proceeded so quickly that by the election of 1800, the electors no longer served as independent persons exercising their own judgments on candidates' capabilities; instead, they acted as agents of political parties and the general public. In 1800, the Republican party was so disciplined that all Republican electors cast their two votes for Thomas Jefferson and Aaron Burr. Although it was generally understood that Jefferson was the Republican candidate for president and Burr the candidate for vice president, the Constitution provided no means for the electors to make that distinction on their ballots. The result was a tie in electoral votes; neither won a majority, and the matter was handed to the House of Representatives for a final decision. Ironically, the Federalists, despite their major defeat in the congressional elections of 1800, still controlled the lame-duck Congress (which did not expire until March 1801) and therefore were in a position to help decide which Republican would serve as president and which as vice president. At the urging of Alexander Hamilton, who disagreed with Jefferson on policy matters but distrusted Burr personally, some of the Federalist representatives eventually cast blank ballots, which permitted the Republican legislators to choose Jefferson as president on the thirty-sixth ballot.

One result of this bizarre chain of events was the ratification in 1804 of the Twelfth Amendment, stipulating that electors cast separate ballots for president and vice president. The amendment also provides that if no presidential candidate receives a majority of the electoral votes, the House of Representatives, balloting by states, will select the president by majority vote from among the three (instead of five) candidates who receive the highest number of electoral votes. If no vice-presidential candidate receives a majority of electoral votes, similar procedures are to be used by the Senate in choosing between the two persons with the highest number of electoral ballots.

Other changes in the selection of the president followed; however, they did not come by way of constitutional amendments but as political developments that fit within the legal framework of the electoral college. Thus, state legislators, who were granted the power to determine how electors should be chosen, began giving this right to the general electorate. By 1832 all states except South Carolina had done so.

Another matter left to the discretion of the states—how their electoral votes would be counted—soon underwent change. States initially were inclined to divide the vote by congressional districts; the candidate who won the plurality (that is, more votes than anyone else) of the popular votes in each district received its electoral vote, and the remaining two electoral votes (representing the two Senate seats) were awarded to the statewide popular winner. However, legislatures soon began to adopt the "unit" or "general-ticket" rule, whereby all the state's electoral votes went to the candidate who received the plurality of the statewide popular vote. Two political consider-ations prompted this decision. The state's majority party benefited because it did not have to award any electoral votes to a minority party that might be successful in individual congressional districts. Also, this system maximized the influence of the state in the presidential election by permitting it to throw all its electoral votes to one candidate. Once some states adopted this procedure, others, wanting to maintain their influence on the presidential contest, felt they had to follow. As a result, by 1836 the district plan had van-ished, and the unit system had taken its place. (Since then, a few states have used the district plan, most recently Maine.)

Another political development of the era changed the nature of the presidential election contest: the elimination of property qualifications for voting. By the early 1840s white manhood suffrage was virtually complete in the United States. The increasing democratization of U.S. political life is reflected, therefore, in the procedure for choosing the most important public official. Yet, the formal provisions of the electoral college remain the same to-day as they were in 1804, when the Twelfth Amendment was adopted.

Today these formal provisions provide a strange system for choosing the chief executive. Although most Americans view the system as a popular election, it really is not. When voters mark their ballots for a presidential can-didate, the vote is actually cast for the electors who are linked with that candidate. In mid-December the state electors associated with the winning candidate (party faithfuls who are chosen in primaries, at conventions, or by state committees) meet in their state capitals to vote. (About one-third of the states attempt by law to bind the electors to vote for the popular-vote winner, but there is some question whether such laws are constitutional.) The results of the electoral balloting are transmitted to Washington, D.C.; on the following January 6 they are counted, and the presiding officer of the Senate, who is the incumbent vice president, announces the outcome before a joint session of the Congress. If, as usually happens, one candidate receives a majority of the electoral votes, the vice president officially declares that candidate to be president, a procedure that occasionally has created some ironic moments. In January 1961, Richard Nixon declared his opponent, John Kennedy, to be president; eight years later another vice president, Hubert Humphrey, declared his opponent, this time Richard Nixon, to be the chief executive.

The electoral college system as it operates today is considered by many students of presidential elections to be not only strange but also grossly unfair; some even consider it dangerous. The final chapter of the book assesses the arguments for and against the electoral college; this section examines only the effects the present arrangements have on campaign strategies.

Under the electoral college system, election results are decided state by state. All the states except Maine use the unit or general-ticket system, which means that all the electoral votes of a state go to the candidate who wins a mere plurality of its popular votes. Thus, in effect, there are fifty separate presidential contests with a "winner-take-all" principle that puts a premium on a popular vote victory in each state, no matter how small the margin of that victory may be.

A built-in bias in the electoral college works to the advantage of certain states over others. The present system benefits the very small and the very large states. The small states have the advantage of what political scientist Lawrence Longley calls the "constant two" votes, that is, the two electoral votes, representing the two senators, that all states receive, regardless of size.[5] This arrangement—the constant two, plus the additional vote for their House member—means that the smallest states control three electoral votes, even though their population alone might entitle them to just one or two votes. The very large states have an even greater advantage; they benefit from the unit or general-ticket system because all their electoral votes are awarded to their popular-vote winner. Thus in 1984 the popular-vote winner in California (Ronald Reagan) received 47 electoral votes, almost 18 percent of the total 270 electoral votes required for election.[6] (See Figure 2-1 for an illustration of the size of the states based on their number of electoral votes for the 1984 election, which reflect changes occasioned by the 1980 census.)

Longley also shows that residency in the very small and the very large states of the Far West and, to a lesser extent, the East is an advantage for some ethnic groups. Voters who are concentrated in urban areas, both central cities and the suburbs, also benefit. In general, however, blacks are not among the ethnic groups who benefit by the rules of the system because the rules put the South, where many blacks live, at a disadvantage. (The South contains a disproportionate number of medium-sized states—those with from four to fourteen electoral votes. Medium-sized states offer candidates neither a great many electoral votes, as the big states do, nor a proportionately large number of electoral votes, as the small states do.)

Finally, the electoral college benefits certain kinds of candidates. These include not only those of the two major parties, who are in a position to win enough popular votes in a state to be awarded its electoral votes, but also third party candidates, who have a regional appeal sufficient to win some states. At a disadvantage, however, are third party candidates without that regional appeal. In 1948, Dixiecrat presidential candidate Strom Thurmond carried four states with a total of thirty-nine electoral votes, even though he won only about 2.4 percent of the national popular vote; that same year the Progressive party candidate, Henry Wallace, with the same percentage of the nationwide vote, did not carry any state and thus received no electoral votes at all.[7]

Figure 2-1 State Size by Number of Electoral Votes, 1984

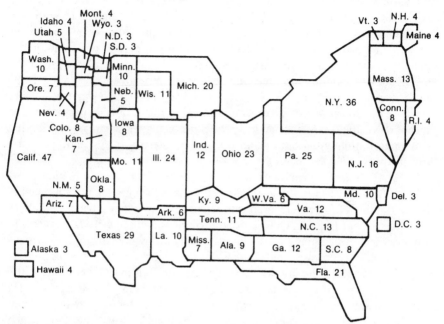

Source: Adapted from Stephen Wayne, *The Road to the White House: The Politics of Presidential Elections* (New York: St. Martin's Press, 1980), 14.

Note: To win, a candidate must receive 270 electoral votes.

Rules Affecting Campaign Finance

The legal provisions for financing the general election differ considerably from those governing presidential nominations. For the general election, complete public financing is provided to nominees of the major parties (those that won 25 percent or more of the popular vote in the last presidential election). In the 1984 presidential election, the federal government gave each candidate $40.4 million and each national committee, $6.9 million. But to be eligible for that money, nominees must agree not to accept other contributions to their campaign. Candidates of minor parties (those that won between 5 and 25 percent of the vote in the previous election) receive partial public financing. Candidates of parties ineligible for public financing (those that won less than 5 percent of the vote in the previous election) can be partially reimbursed after the current election if they receive at least 5 percent of that vote.

Two provisions of the campaign finance law permit the major party candidates to benefit from campaign expenditures besides those they make themselves from public funds. As is true of the nomination process, there is no limitation on independent campaign expenditures, that is, those made by individuals or political committees that advocate the defeat or election of a presidential candidate but that are not made in conjunction with the candidate's own campaign. (Again, however, such individuals and committees must file reports with the Federal Election Commission and must state under penalty of perjury that the expenditure was not made in collusion with the candidate.) In addition, an amendment to the campaign finance law enacted in 1979 permits state and local party organizations to spend money for any purpose except campaign advertising and the hiring of outside personnel; this means that they can engage in grass-roots activities such as distributing campaign buttons, stickers, and yard signs, registering voters, and transporting them to the polls to vote.

Thus, like the provisions for financing presidential nomination campaigns, those governing the general election have brought significant changes in the funding of fall presidential campaigns. The two major party candidates no longer need to depend on wealthy contributors and other private sources to finance their campaigns. (They may still benefit, however, from the independent expenditures of such sources as well as from grass-roots activities by state and local parties.) The law also has the effect of limiting and equalizing the expenditures made by the two major party candidates, which is a distinct advantage for the Democrats because, historically, Republican presidential candidates have spent more than their opponents.[8] (See Table 2-1, which shows that, except for 1948, the Republican presidential candidate outspent his Democratic opponent in every election from 1940 through 1972, the last contest before the enactment of the campaign finance law providing public funding.) Finally, the law benefits the candidates of the two major parties, who receive full public financing of their general election campaigns, in contrast to minor party candidates, who are entitled to only partial financing, if any at all.

The General Election Campaign

Traditionally, U.S. presidential campaigns have begun on Labor Day, but individual candidates are free to choose other times, depending on the political circumstances. Gerald Ford, seeking to reorganize his forces after a bruising battle with challenger Ronald Reagan at the 1976 Republican national convention, waited until a week after Labor Day to launch his fall campaign. In contrast, Ronald Reagan, with the Republican nomination locked up in both 1980 and 1984, hit the campaign trail early to counteract the favorable publicity generated by the Democratic national conventions of those two years. Thus the conditions under which candidates themselves win their party's nomination, plus the circumstances surrounding their opponent's choice, shape decisions on the beginning of the fall campaign.

Table 2-1 Cost of Presidential General Elections, 1940-1972 (Dollars in Millions)

	Republican		Democratic	
Year	Expenditure	Candidate	Expenditure	Candidate
1940	3.45	Willkie	2.78	F. Roosevelt*
1944	2.83	Dewey	2.17	F. Roosevelt*
1948	2.13	Dewey	2.74	Truman*
1952	6.61	Eisenhower*	5.03	Stevenson
1956	7.78	Eisenhower*	5.11	Stevenson
1960	10.13	Nixon	9.80	Kennedy*
1964	16.03	Goldwater	8.76	Johnson*
1968	25.40	Nixon*	11.59	Humphrey
1972	61.40	Nixon*	30.00	McGovern

Source: Excerpted from Herbert E. Alexander, *Financing Politics: Money, Elections and Political Reform* (Washington, D.C.: CQ Press, 1976), Table 2.1, 20.

Note: Asterisk (*) indicates winner.

Candidates also pay close attention to the locality of the first speech of the official campaign. Jimmy Carter chose two sites in his native South: in 1976, Warm Springs, Georgia (a city in his home state in which President Franklin Roosevelt died), and in 1980, Tuscumbia, Alabama. In 1980 Ronald Reagan selected Ellis Island in New York City harbor (the port of arrival for millions of immigrants seeking a new life in the United States), and in 1984, his original political base of Orange County, California.

Targeting the Campaign

As in the nomination process, presidential candidates must decide in which states they will focus their efforts in the fall campaign.[9] The decision is harder at this stage because the general election takes place simultaneously in all fifty states rather than in stages, and campaign efforts must be concentrated into a much shorter period of time than is available for the nomination campaign. Moreover, in the general election, unlike the nomination process, there are no legal limits on the amount of money presidential candidates can spend in individual states; they therefore have a freer hand in their choices, but those choices become more difficult.

By far the most important consideration in targeting the fall campaign is the electoral college. The candidate's goal is clear: to win the presidency, he or she must win a majority—270—of the 538 electoral votes. This fact places a premium on carrying those states with the largest number of electoral votes. In 1984, twelve of the largest states—California, New York, Texas, Pennsylvania, Illinois, Ohio, Florida, Michigan, New Jersey, North Carolina, Massachusetts, and either Georgia, Virginia, or Indiana (each has 12 electoral vótes)—together had a total of 279 votes, enough to elect even a candidate who lost the thirty-eight other states. Naturally, candidates from both major political parties concentrate their personal visits on the largest states.

Another element that affects candidates' decisions on where to campaign is the political situation in a particular state; that is, whether the state generally goes to one party's candidate or whether it swings back and forth from one election to the next. Distinctly one-party states are likely to be slighted by both of the major party candidates. The party in control does not think it is necessary to waste time there. (In 1968 Nixon did not visit or spend money in Kansas; as one campaign aide, Robert Ellsworth, said of his home state, "If you have to worry about Kansas, you don't have a campaign anyway." [10]) In contrast, the opposition party is likely to think it futile to exert much effort in what is obviously enemy territory.[11] The "swing" states naturally draw the greatest attention from presidential candidates of both parties.

Since 1968, both major political parties have developed areas where their presidential candidates usually are successful. The Republicans have been strongest in the West; the Democrats have been strongest in the Northeast. The once-solid Democratic South has varied from election to election. The South was vital to the Democratic electoral strategies of Kennedy in 1960 and Carter in 1976 and helped to put both men in the White House. In contrast, Humphrey in 1968 and McGovern in 1972 wrote off the region, and the election results reflected this decision: Humphrey carried only Texas (considered by some political observers to be a western rather than a truly southern state), and McGovern did not win any states in the South.[12] Since 1968, however, Republican candidates have thought it worthwhile to contest the southern states, and Reagan even managed to defeat native son Jimmy Carter there in 1980. (The president carried only his home state of Georgia in that region and two border states, Maryland and West Virginia.) In 1984 Walter Mondale initially campaigned in a number of states in the South, but when it became apparent that he was not doing well there, he concentrated his efforts in Texas because of its twenty-nine electoral votes and large Mexican-American population, which has traditionally voted Democratic.

The regions that have been crucial in recent presidential contests are the Middle Atlantic states (New York, Pennsylvania, and New Jersey) and the Middle West states of Ohio, Michigan, Illinois, and Missouri. Together this tier of seven highly industrial states controlled 155 electoral votes in the 1984 election. They also tend to be highly competitive, which means that campaign efforts there can be very important in deciding which candidate prevails.

The most systematic plan in targeting a presidential campaign was developed for Jimmy Carter in 1976 by Hamilton Jordan. He assigned points to each state, using three criteria. The first was its number of electoral votes. The second was its Democratic potential based on the number of Democratic officeholders in the state and how well McGovern had done there in 1972. The third was how concerted a campaign was needed in a particular state, taking into account how well Carter had done in the preconvention period, how much time or resources he had previously expended in the state, and how close to Ford he was in the polls. Each campaigner was allocated points as well: for example, a day's campaigning by Carter was worth seven points; by Mondale, five points; and by a Carter child, one point. Jordan then assigned campaigners to states so that scheduling points were matched with those developed under the political-importance formula.[13]

Manipulating Political Appeals

Party Label. Political party labels, unimportant in the nomination process, become a focal point in general election campaigns. Given the Democrats' status as the majority party since the days of Franklin Roosevelt, it is natural that Democratic candidates throughout the years have emphasized their party affiliation and linked their opponents with the minority Republican party. In 1960 John Kennedy stressed that he "stood" with Woodrow Wilson, Franklin Roosevelt, and Harry Truman, whereas his opponent, Richard Nixon, "stood" with McKinley, Taft, Harding, Landon, and Dewey. (Significantly, Kennedy did not mention popular Republican presidents such as Abraham Lincoln, Theodore Roosevelt, or Dwight Eisenhower.) Twenty years later Jimmy Carter pursued a similar strategy, emphasizing that he represented the party of Franklin Roosevelt, Harry Truman, John Kennedy, and Lyndon Johnson (leading Ronald Reagan to quip that the only Democratic president Carter was not talking about was himself). In 1984 Walter Mondale sought to link his candidacy with Harry Truman, who, like Mondale, was counted out of the race by pollsters. In one appearance, Mondale held up the famous erroneous headline of the Chicago *Tribune,* "Dewey Defeats Truman."

Over the years, Republican presidential candidates have devised tactics to counteract the partisan advantage enjoyed by their Democratic opponents. One is to advise the voters to ignore party labels and vote for the "best man." Richard Nixon used this approach in his 1960 campaign, urging Americans to cast their ballots for the person who had experience in foreign affairs, who had stood up to Soviet leader Nikita Khrushchev and bested him in a "kitchen debate" in Moscow. (The informal exchange over the comparative worth of communist and capitalist economic systems took place at a kitchen display at a fair in Moscow.) Another tactic is to suggest that the Democratic presidential candidate does not represent the views of the rank-and-file members of the party. In 1972 Nixon charged that the Democratic convention had rejected the historic principles of that party and implored, "To those millions who have been driven out of their home in the Democratic party, we say come home." Another ploy open to Republican presidential candidates is to associate themselves with past Democratic presidents. In 1976 Gerald Ford tied his candidacy to that of former Democratic chief executive Harry Truman, who, as an underdog incumbent, struggled successfully for the same goal as Ford: election to the office in his own right, not merely by succession. Four years later Ronald Reagan linked his desire for major changes in U.S. society with the New Deal, Fair Deal, and New Frontier administrations of Roosevelt, Truman, and Kennedy. In 1984 he participated in anniversary ceremonies for Roosevelt and Truman and held receptions at the White House in honor of Hubert Humphrey and former senator Henry Jackson.[14]

Whether a candidate represents the majority or the minority party, it is important that prominent political figures in the party support his campaign. In 1964 Barry Goldwater's candidacy suffered (although it is unlikely that he could have won the presidency in any event) because leading Republicans dissociated themselves from the party's presidential nominee and conducted independent campaigns of their own. Sen. Eugene McCarthy's lukewarm and belated endorsement of Hubert Humphrey in the last stages of the 1968 campaign did little to help Humphrey avert his narrow defeat that year. And in 1972 large numbers of Democratic candidates for Congress and state offices deliberately dissociated themselves from the McGovern-Shriver ticket.

Incumbency.   Incumbent presidents who are running for reelection start out with certain advantages in the electoral contest. They are typically better known to the voters than their opponents, who must strive to narrow the recognition gap between the two candidates. The incumbent president frequently assumes the role of statesman, too busy with the affairs of the nation to participate in a demeaning, partisan campaign. Describing the 1972 contest between George McGovern and President Nixon, one journalist remarked, "Around the White House, it bordered on treason to call Nixon a candidate." [15] In 1976 Gerald Ford followed his advisers' recommendation by conducting the early stages of the campaign from the White House Rose Garden—gathering presidential publicity by receiving visitors, signing or vetoing bills, and calling press conferences to make announcements.

While the incumbent is operating above the partisan fray, others are free to make political attacks on the opposition. Frequently, the vice-presidential candidates assume that role, as Humphrey did for the Democrats in 1964 and Robert Dole did for the Republicans in 1976.[16] Or the president's supporters may develop an entire team to carry on the effort. In 1972 the Committee to Reelect the President (note that Nixon's name did not even appear in the title of the committee) organized a special surrogate's office to schedule the campaign appearances of thirty-five White House aides, cabinet members, senators, representatives, mayors, and Republican party officials.

The incumbent president is also in a position to use the prerogatives of the office to good advantage during the election campaign. In 1976 President

Ford suddenly recommended legislation to expand the national park system and to reduce the amount of down payments for mortgages guaranteed by the Federal Housing Administration. The president also can disburse forms of political "patronage" available to the nation's chief executive. In 1980 President Carter announced his support for water projects in Kentucky and Tennessee that he had previously opposed, offered the steel industry protection against foreign imports, approved financial aid to enable residents of Love Canal (the polluted area near Niagara Falls, New York) to move away from that region, and announced federally subsidized loans for drought-stricken farms. Even Chicago—whose mayor, Jane Byrne, supported Edward Kennedy in the primary fight—received its share of national government "goodies," which prompted Byrne to declare that while diamonds are still a girl's best friend, federal grants are next best. In 1984 President Reagan provided assistance to U.S. farmers by allowing the Soviet Union to purchase an extra 10 million metric tons of grain and by changing credit arrangements to grant greater relief to farmers who were heavily in debt.

Incumbent presidents can also use their office to publicize important events in foreign and military policy. During 1972 President Nixon visited both Communist China and the Soviet Union, gathering extensive media coverage in the process. In the spring of 1984, President Reagan went to China; in June of that year he journeyed to the Normandy beaches to lead the fortieth anniversary commemoration of the Allied invasion of France in World War II, an occasion attended by veterans and their families.

Candidate Image. Because the public focuses so much attention in a presidential campaign on the candidates themselves, the personality and character that the aspirants project are particularly important. Each campaign organization strives to create a composite image of the most attractive attributes of its candidate. Although the image necessarily deviates from reality, it must still reflect enough of the essential characteristics of the candidate to be believable. One effective tactic is to take a potential flaw and convert it into an asset. Thus, the somewhat elderly Dwight Eisenhower (he was aged sixty-six at the time of his second campaign in 1956) was pictured as a benevolent father (or even grandfather) whose mature judgment was needed to lead the nation in times of stress.[17] In contrast, the youthful John Kennedy, who was aged forty-three when he ran for the presidency in 1960, was characterized as a man of "vigor" who would make the United States "feel young again" after the Eisenhower years.

Presidential candidates frequently take their opponents' images into account when shaping their own. In 1976 Gerald Ford portrayed himself as a man of maturity and experience to counteract Jimmy Carter's emphasis on being a "new face" and an outsider to the Washington scene. Four years later as the incumbent president, Carter tried to come across as a deliberate and moderate person who could be trusted to maintain his calm in a crisis, in contrast to his supposedly impetuous and irresponsible opponent, Ronald Reagan. Reagan, in turn, presented himself as a decisive leader who could overcome the nation's problems, as opposed to Carter, depicted as an uncertain, vascillating person overwhelmed by the burdens of the presidency and inclined to blame the country's difficulties on the "spirit of malaise" of the American people themselves.

Besides molding their own images to balance those of their opponents, candidates also can directly attack the images of the opposition to put them in a bad light. In 1976, for example, Gerald Ford described Jimmy Carter as follows: "He wavers, he wanders, he wiggles, he waffles." He also charged that his opponent had a strange way of changing his accent: "In California he tried to sound like Cesar Chavez; in Chicago, like Mayor Daley; in New York, like Ralph Nader; in Washington, like George Meany; then he comes to the farm belt and he becomes a little old peanut farmer." During the second debate, after Ford stated that Eastern Europe was not under Soviet domination, Carter countered that the president must have been "brainwashed" when he went to Poland. (Carter was thereby comparing Ford with George Romney, the former Michigan governor whose nomination campaign collapsed in 1968 after he said he had been brainwashed by the military in the course of a trip to Vietnam.) The Georgian also said that during the second debate Ford had shown "very vividly the absence of good judgment, good sense, and knowledge" expected of a president. In 1980 Carter suggested that a Reagan presidency would divide Americans "black from white, Jew from Christian, North from South, rural from urban" and could "well lead our nation to war." Reagan, in turn, impugned Carter's honesty, saying that the president's promise that he would never lie to Americans reminded him of a quotation from Ralph Waldo Emerson, "The more he talked of his honor, the more we counted our spoons." In 1984, Walter Mondale was accused of being overly gloomy about the country and its prospects—"Whine on harvest moon," as Vice President Bush liked to put it. Mondale and Geraldine Ferraro, in turn, attacked President Reagan for being the most "disengaged" president in recent history, one who lacked the knowledge necessary to govern the nation.

Social Groups.   Fairly early in life many Americans begin to think of themselves as members of individual ethnic, geographic, or religious groups. As they get older, they also begin to identify with groups associated with their occupations and to consider themselves as businesspeople or farmers or members of labor unions. Sometimes people relate politically to groups to which they do not belong. A well-to-do white liberal, for example, who sympathizes with the underdog in society may favor programs that benefit poor blacks. Responses to groups can also be negative: a self-made businessperson may have an unfavorable image of labor unions or social welfare organizations.

Presidential candidates take these group attitudes into account in devising campaign appeals. Since the days of Franklin Roosevelt, the Democratic party has aimed its campaigns at certain groups thought to be particularly susceptible to its political overtures: among these are southerners, blacks, members of ethnic groups, organized labor, Catholics, Jews, intellectuals, and big-city "bosses" and their political supporters (hence the quip that the Democratic party has more wings than a boardinghouse chicken). At the same time, the Democrats usually have tried to depict the Republicans as the party of "big business" and the rich.

Republican candidates have used explicit group appeals less often in their presidential campaigns. In fact, in 1964 Senator Goldwater conducted an antigroup campaign. The Republican candidate seemed to go out of his way to antagonize particular blocs, speaking in Knoxville against the Tennessee Valley Authority (TVA); in retirement communities such as St. Petersburg, Florida, against Social Security; and in Charleston, West Virginia, near the heart of Appalachia, against the Johnson administration's War on Poverty. (In writing off such groups as "minorities," Goldwater ignored the fact that an aggregation of minorities makes up a majority.) In 1968 Richard Nixon tried a different approach, aiming his campaign at the "forgotten Americans who did not break the law, but did pay taxes, go to work, school, church, and love their country." He thereby sought to establish a negative association between the Democrats and groups he considered to be outside the American mainstream, such as welfare recipients, atheists, and war protestors.

Some recent Republican presidential candidates, however, have been more inclined to seek the support of groups that traditionally have been sympathetic to the Democratic party. In 1972 the Committee to Reelect the President (Nixon) turned out campaign buttons for almost thirty nationalities, provided copy for ethnic newspapers and radio stations, and made special appeals to Catholics, Jews, blacks, and Mexican-Americans. In his 1980 presidential campaign Reagan appealed to union members by pointing out that he had been president of a labor union for six terms; courted the Polish vote by meeting on Labor Day with Stanislaw Walesa, father of the leader of the strike against the Polish government; and wooed blacks by arguing that their high unemployment rate was caused by the sluggish state of the economy. Four years later the Reagan campaign set aside an "ethnic week" to court groups such as Polish-Americans and Italian-Americans (recall that the Democratic vice-presidential candidate, Geraldine Ferraro, was the first person of Italian background to run for such a high office). Reagan also tried to appeal to Jews by criticizing Mondale for not repudiating Jesse Jackson's anti-Semitic remarks.

Two other groups took on a special significance in both 1980 and 1984. Women were thought to be anti-Reagan because of his promilitary stance and his opposition to social programs and the Equal Rights Amendment.

Democrats played on such fears by portraying Reagan as "trigger-happy" and as insensitive to the needs of economic and social underdogs; the Republicans tried to assure women that he was a man of peace who looked to the private sector and state and local governments for financial assistance to the disadvantaged. The Republicans also appealed to fundamentalist Christians, particularly in the South, by advocating prayer in the public schools and by opposing abortion; Democrats tried to counter such appeals by arguing that prayers should be said in church and the home (not in school), and that the government also had no right to interfere with a woman's private decision whether or not to carry a pregnancy to term.

Another group of voters emerged in 1984 as a particular target for both political parties—young voters. Traditionally Democratic in their sympathies, college-age youth were wooed by Republican appeals of job opportunities in an expanding economy and love of country. The Democrats responded by appealing to the idealism of young people to help those less fortunate than themselves and to their concern about the dangers of nuclear war. As a result, both parties' candidates made many campaign appearances on college campuses (Mondale gave one of his best speeches at George Washington University), with both supporters and hecklers typically in attendance.

Issues and Events.   Over the years, both major political parties have been associated with certain broad issues in American life. Democratic presidential candidates usually emphasize economic issues: by doing so they can link the Great Depression to the Republican president, Herbert Hoover, who was in office at the time, and they can draw on the voters' traditional preference of Democrats over Republicans to handle the economy. In contrast, Republican candidates focus more on foreign policy issues because Democratic presidents were in power at the start of World War I, World War II, and both the Korean and Vietnamese conflicts. As a result, many voters conclude that Republicans are better able to keep the peace than Democrats.

Circumstances surrounding particular elections can lead to changes in the traditional politics. In 1980 the poor economic record of the Carter administration led Ronald Reagan to focus on that issue; four years later, this time as the incumbent president, Reagan continued to emphasize the economy, because inflation and interest rates had fallen since he took office. In 1980 President Carter concentrated on foreign policy so that he could raise fears about Reagan's reliability in keeping the nation out of nuclear war. In 1984 Mondale pointed out that President Reagan was the first U.S. chief executive in the atomic era who had not met with a foreign chief of state to advance negotiations on an arms treaty.

Although candidates address major issues in U.S. society, they frequently do so only in very general terms. The party out of power often used a catchy slogan to link the party in power with unfortunate political events. In 1952, for example, the Republicans branded the Democrats with "Korea, corruption, and communism." The party in power responds in the same way, as when the Democrats defended their record in 1952 by telling the voters, "You never had it so good." In 1976 the situation was reversed; Democrats talked about Watergate, inflation, unemployment, and President Ford's pardon of Richard Nixon. (Carter refused to attack Ford on the issue, but his vice-presidential candidate, Walter Mondale, did.) President Ford asserted that his administration had cut inflation by half, brought peace to the nation ("Not a single American is fighting or dying"), and restored faith, confidence, and trust in the presidency. In 1980, as in 1952, the Republicans attacked the Democratic incumbent: Ronald Reagan blamed President Carter for the nation's mounting economic problems and for allowing the United States to fall far behind the Soviet Union in military preparedness. At the same time the Democratic president pointed with pride to the signing of the Egyptian-Israeli accord, the ratification of the Panama Canal Treaty, and the development of an energy program.

This general sort of attack and defense characterizes most presidential campaigns. The party out of power blames all the ills of American life on the administration; the party in power maintains that all of the nation's blessings have resulted from its leadership. The candidate in the most difficult position is the nonincumbent nominee of the party in power, such as Nixon in 1960 and Humphrey in 1968. Both served as vice president in administrations whose policies they did not fully endorse. Nixon, for instance, did not believe Eisenhower was doing enough in space exploration and national defense. Humphrey opposed the bombing of North Vietnam when it was initiated in 1965. Yet each hesitated to criticize an administration in which he had served. Humphrey's inability to dissociate himself from the Johnson administration's Vietnam policy is considered one of the main reasons for his defeat in 1968.[18]

While addressing political issues only in very general terms, presidential candidates typically make few concrete proposals for dealing with such issues.[19] In 1960 Kennedy urged that he be given the chance to "get the nation moving again," but he was very vague about what, specifically, he would do to move the nation forward. Nixon was even more indefinite in 1968; he refused to spell out his plans for dealing with the most important U.S. political issue, Vietnam. His excuse was that doing so might jeopardize the Paris peace talks then being held.

In some presidential campaigns, however, candidates have made specific suggestions for dealing with issues. In 1972 George McGovern proposed that the defense budget be cut by 30 percent; and early in his campaign he advocated that everyone, regardless of need, be given a $1,000 grant by the government. In 1980 Reagan advocated the passage of the Kemp-Roth tax plan, which called for reducing taxes 10 percent each year over a period of three years. In 1984 Mondale unveiled a plan that called for cuts in defense, health, and agricultural expenditures and tax increases for upper-income earners and corporations so that by 1989 the budget deficit could be reduced by two-thirds.

In manipulating political appeals, candidates usually attempt to develop an all-encompassing theme that will give the voters an overall impression of the campaign. Sometimes the theme focuses on the candidates themselves, as did Humphrey's slogan, "He's a man you can trust," the Carter-Mondale phrase, "Tested and trustworthy," and Reagan's 1984 motto, "Leadership that's working." Or it may be essentially an appeal to a broad group, such as Nixon's "Forgotten Americans" who did not break the law but did pay their taxes, go to work, school, and church, and love their country. At other times the theme is directed at issues and political events ("Korea, corruption, and communism" or "peace and prosperity") or takes the form of a general call for action, such as Kennedy's "We've got to get the nation moving again"; McGovern's "Come home, America"; Carter's promise to make the government as "truthful, capable, and filled with love as the American people"; and Reagan's 1980 invitation to a "new beginning." Once the theme is established, candidates try, by constant repetition, to get the electorate to respond emotionally to it. Their success in doing so depends, however, on another important aspect of presidential campaigns: how political appeals are communicated to the American voter.

Communicating with the Public

Because the electorate is twice as large as the selectorate and the campaign period for the election is much shorter than for the nomination, presidential candidates place even more emphasis on the mass media during this latter stage of the process. Advertising expenses are one measure of that emphasis: in the 1984 campaign, for example, Ronald Reagan and Walter Mondale each spent more than half of the $40 million subsidy from the federal government on television, radio, and print advertisements, with the lion's share spent on political commercials. Of these three types of media, television is by far the most important. It takes much less effort to watch than to read, particularly since viewing can be combined with other activities but reading cannot.[20] In addition, people are more inclined to believe what they see on television than what they read in the newspapers or hear on the radio. As a result, since 1952, television has been the chief source of campaign information for most Americans.

Over the years presidential candidates have employed several television formats. In 1968 Richard Nixon used sixty-second spot announcements during popular programs such as Rowan and Martin's "Laugh-in." The Republicans also staged appearances of Nixon before panels of citizens who asked questions that he could appear to answer spontaneously. (Nixon's advisers carefully screened both the panels and the questions to avoid possible embarrassment or surprise.)

In the 1972 campaign, the candidates adopted new formats for their televised political communications. Although spot commercials remained popular, (one of Nixon's, for example, showed a hand sweeping away toy soldiers and miniature ships and planes to symbolize McGovern's proposed cuts in defense), five-minute commercial advertisements became more common. McGovern chose still longer programs consisting of his addresses on Vietnam and the issue of corruption. Semidocumentary formats, such as a candidate's discussing issues with ordinary citizens, were used as well. McGovern was filmed interacting with workers and owners of small businesses, and Nixon's trips to China and the Soviet Union were dramatized for television viewers.

In 1976 President Ford employed the medium more imaginatively than did Carter. The president held an informal television interview, for example, with television personality and former baseball player Joe Garagiola, who tossed him some "gopher-ball" questions: "How many foreign leaders have you met with, Mr. President?" to which Ford modestly replied, "One hundred and twenty-four, Joe." In the last stages of the campaign, the Ford forces also broadcast short television interviews with voters in Georgia who described Carter as "wishy-washy." Carter concentrated on short commercials in which he looked directly into the camera and talked about various issues, so as to counteract Ford's portrayal of him and to present himself as a strong, positive leader with specific programs.

During the 1980 campaign the television advertisements varied in length from thirty seconds to thirty minutes, but most were short spot messages designed to reach peak audiences. The Carter television commercials appeared in three separate stages: the first showed the candidate being presidential, meeting with foreign dignitaries and working late at night in the Oval Office; the second consisted of interviews with people "in the street" saying that Reagan "scared" them; the third showed Carter being praised by prominent party figures, such as Lady Bird Johnson and Edward Kennedy, and by rank-and-file Democrats—a farmer, a steelworker, and a worker in a rubber factory. Most of the Reagan television advertisements featured the candidate himself, whom the Republicans considered to be a superb communicator, looking straight into the camera. They stressed three themes: Reagan's record as governor of California; his stand on issues, especially the economy; and a recitation of the record of President Carter, illustrated with graphs of rising consumer prices.

In 1984 the Republicans aired a nostalgic, half-hour film of President Reagan riding his horse, walking on a hilltop with Nancy, speaking at the Normandy beaches, and taking the oath of office. Most of the Republican commercials, however, were thirty-second ones. The most famous, "It's morning again in America," showed the sun shining on San Francisco Bay, people hurrying to and from work, and a bride and groom kissing at a wedding while a mellifluous voice asked, "Why would we ever want to go back to where we were less than four short years ago?" The Democrats relied entirely on thirty-second spot commercials. One showed a roller coaster climbing its tracks suggesting what will happen tomorrow as a result of record U.S. deficits), with a voice intoning, "If you're thinking of voting for Ronald Reagan in 1984, think of what will happen in 1985." Another, positive commercial pictured a warm, dynamic Walter Mondale talking to a group of students, urging them to "stretch their minds" and to live their dreams, telling them he wanted to help them be what they wanted to be.

In four elections, televised debates between presidential candidates became the most important communication source of the campaign.[21] The first occurred in 1960 between Richard Nixon, at that time Eisenhower's vice president, and Sen. John Kennedy. In the first of four debates, Nixon's somewhat uncertain manner and his physical appearance (he had not fully recovered from a recent illness and television accentuated his heavy beard) was contrasted with Kennedy's confident demeanor and bright, alert image (he wore a blue shirt and dark suit that showed up well against the television studio background rather than fading into it as Nixon's light-colored clothes did). Also, unlike Nixon, Kennedy had prepared thoroughly for the debates. As a result, viewers perceived a victory for the young Massachusetts senator.[22] Contributing to that perception was that people had not expected Kennedy to best Nixon, who had gained political prominence in part because of his debating skills in previous campaigns. From that point on, Kennedy's campaign assumed more enthusiasm, and the senator himself credited the debate for his eventual close victory over the vice president.

In 1976, presidential debates again played a major part in the campaign. In this case it was the second of those debates between President Ford and Jimmy Carter that proved crucial. In that debate, Ford stated that he did not consider countries of Eastern Europe (in particular, Yugoslavia, Romania, and Poland) to be under Soviet domination. To make matters worse, the president refused to change his answer even after the startled questioner (a newspaper reporter) gave him the opportunity to do so; in fact, it was not until several days after the debate that the president's staff finally persuaded him to retract his statement. Many political observers considered that gaffe to be the turning point of the contest, the one that ended the dramatic decline in public support for Carter (and the increased support for Ford) that had characterized the previous month of the campaign.

In 1980 the presidential debates became more complicated. The sponsors of the debate, the League of Women Voters, originally extended an invitation to debate not only to President Carter and Ronald Reagan but also to independent candidate John Anderson, whose standing in the public opinion polls exceeded the 15-percent cutoff point established by the League. Carter refused to participate on the grounds that the debate would legitimize the Anderson candidacy, which he asserted was strictly a "creation of the media." In contrast, Reagan, who perceived that Anderson would draw more votes away from Carter than from himself, accepted the League's invitation and criticized Carter for refusing to debate. Ultimately, just a week before election day (when Anderson's public support had fallen below 15 percent), a single debate was held between the two major party candidates. Although both men looked and handled themselves well and neither made a serious mistake, most observers concluded that Reagan won the debate on style rather than substance. Carter aides congratulated themselves that the president had kept the focus of the debate on Reagan rather than on his own presidential record, but the tactic apparently backfired. On the one hand, many viewers thought Carter was too aggressive in his accusations; on the other, they felt reassured by Reagan's responses and were convinced that he would not be a trigger-happy president if elected to the office.[23]

In 1984 the Mondale forces requested six separate presidential debates and a format in which the candidates could ask each other questions. The Reagan organization refused that request, and the sides ultimately agreed to two debates between Mondale and Reagan and one between the vice-presidential candidates, Bush and Ferraro. In all three, members of the media would ask the questions. The first presidential debate turned out to be a clear victory for the challenger, Mondale, who projected himself as calm, bright, and confident, while the president appeared confused, inarticulate, and in his summation, to have lost his train of thought altogether. When the president at one point repeated the line from his 1980 debate with Carter "there you go again," Mondale turned pointedly to Reagan and asked, "Remember the last time you said that?" and then answered the question himself: "You said it when President Carter said you were going to cut Medicare. . . .and what did you do right after the election? You went out and tried to cut $20 billion out of Medicare." The debate sent shock waves through the Republican camp not only because the media and most observers (even Reagan supporters) agreed that the president had been defeated decisively, but also because the debate raised the issue of whether his age had slowed him down and made him incapable of handling the demands of the office for the next four years. The second debate, however, ended with a far different result: Reagan prevailed on style, appearing more relaxed and coherent (although he again rambled in his closing remarks). Most important, the president defused the age issue when, in response to a question on the matter, he replied that he did not intend "to exploit my opponent's youth and inexperience," a clever retort that drew a broad smile even from Mondale.

Besides political commercials and debates, a third source of communication in presidential campaigns is the coverage provided by representatives of the mass media themselves, both the broadcast (television and radio) and print (newspapers and magazines) media. These representatives are not nearly as important in general election campaigns, however, as they are in the nomination stage. By the time of the fall election, the campaign is much more structured. The contest essentially is down to two candidates, who by then are fairly well known to the electorate; in addition, the voters at this stage associate the candidates with their respective parties and evaluate them on that basis. Moreover, the candidates have more money to spend on campaign communications than they did in the nomination process; and debates, if they are held, are more focused (typically between only two candidates) and reach a wider audience than any that occurred in the nomination campaign.

The media's coverage of the election campaign is similar to that in the nomination stage. Reporters and commentators pay great attention to the election "game," that is, which party candidate is leading in the public opinion polls and by how much, and to the "hoopla"—campaign rallies and the like. The media also tend to focus on "campaign issues" rather than policy issues, such as Jimmy Carter's remark in the 1976 campaign that he "lusted after women in his heart" and Ford's comment about Eastern Europe. In 1980 the media played up Jimmy Carter's personal attacks on Ronald Reagan and on Reagan's contention that the literal, biblical interpretation of creation should be taught equally with the theory of evolution. In 1984 the media zeroed in on the financial affairs of Geraldine Ferraro and her husband.

Patterson's study of the 1976 election contest does indicate, however, that the voters became more aware of the candidates' positions on policy issues as the campaign progressed.[24] He attributes some of that increase to their familiarity with the policy tendencies of the Democratic and Republican parties. His analysis also shows that newspaper coverage of policy issues increased voters' awareness of them, particularly for voters who previously had not been highly interested in policy issues. In contrast, the short, superficial coverage of the issues by network news did not raise voters' awareness of the issues. More recent campaign studies, however, do not show the superiority of the print media. In their analysis of the 1980 campaign, Robinson and Sheehan conclude that the broadcast networks covered the issues at least as well as the wire services.[25] Moreover, Patterson and Davis found in their study of the 1984 campaign that only 4 of 114 newspaper articles they analyzed mentioned Mondale's charge that Reagan's tax cuts benefited the rich, and none mentioned his progressive tax plan.[26]

Thus, despite the dominance of television in recent presidential contests, the other media continue to play a role in campaigns. Newspapers not only cover the issues in more detail than television but also are free to endorse candidates.[27] The print media are also available for advertisements stressing visual effects. In 1960 the Democrats used pictures of John Kennedy and his attractive wife, Jacqueline, in many of their promotions. In 1976 the Republicans printed full-page advertisements comparing the cover of *Newsweek* magazine that featured President Ford with the cover of *Playboy* magazine that carried the controversial interview with Carter (in which he confessed that he "lusted after women in his heart").

Radio also plays a role in presidential campaigns. It is less expensive than television and can be used in ways that television cannot, such as broadcasting to commuting drivers, as President Ford did in a series of early morning chats during the 1976 campaign. There is also the distinct possibility that a particular candidate will come across better on radio, a reason suggested for President Nixon's using the medium more often than television for his speeches during the 1972 campaign. Moreover, some radio networks, such as National Public Radio, cover presidential campaigns in much greater depth than does television.

The formats available in the various media therefore make it possible for candidates to emphasize different types of appeals and to reach disparate groups. Nimmo distinguishes between two major types of audiences.[28] The first consists of the politically concerned and interested, who use the print media as well as television and radio to obtain information on presidential campaigns. The second comprises less politically involved voters who must be reached through television and sometimes through radio, particularly by means of spot announcements, such as those used by Richard Nixon during his 1968 campaign.

Campaign Organization and Workers

Although the mass media reach more people in the general election campaign than in the nomination contest (more money is spent in a shorter period of time, and some voters become politically interested only after the parties nominate their respective candidates), not everyone personally follows the election campaign, especially in print and on the radio. These voters depend on those who do follow it to pass along information, such as the candidates' stands on the issues. (Of course, the transmitters often alter the messages in keeping with their own views and biases.) Beyond that, personal contacts are particularly important in persuading many people to make the most basic political decision: whether or not to vote at all. Sometimes citizens' apathy can be overcome only by the dogged determination of persons who see that others register to vote and have transportation to the polls.

Presidential candidates typically start the general election campaign with a core of people who, in effect, constitute their personal organization. If there has been a spirited nomination battle, the principal organizers of the campaign shift their attention to the general election. John Kennedy put his brother Robert in charge of his 1960 campaign against Richard Nixon, and Hamilton Jordan continued as the head of Jimmy Carter's 1976 fall campaign. Others who worked for the candidate in the primary and caucus-convention states also usually are available for the election campaign. Incumbent presidents frequently assign key members of their administration to work on the fall campaign. In 1972 Richard Nixon initially put his attorney general, John Mitchell, in charge of the Committee to Reelect the President and transferred other persons in the White House office to assignments on the committee. Three important figures in the Carter administration, Robert Strauss, Hamilton Jordan, and Gerald Rafshoon, played significant roles in the 1980 campaign.

Because the electorate for the general campaign is so much broader than the selectorate, which participates in the nomination phase, presidential candidates must increase their number of supporters in the fall to include people who had not been involved previously. One potential source of new recruits is political rivals who had sought the nomination themselves. In 1972 George McGovern asked Hubert Humphrey to campaign for him; Humphrey did so out of personal friendship and party loyalty. In 1984 both Gary Hart and Jesse Jackson worked hard on Mondale's behalf in the fall campaign. In 1976 Ford and Reagan supporters co-chaired the general election campaign in many states.[29] In many instances, however, personal loyalties and commitments to issues are so strong that it is not possible to recruit those who supported the other candidates for the nomination. In 1968 the Humphrey organization was not able to persuade many of Eugene McCarthy's supporters to work in the general election campaign after McCarthy lost the presidential nomination. In 1980 many people who backed Edward Kennedy's unsuccessful bid for the Democratic nomination did not work for President Carter in the fall campaign; nor in 1984 did many of Gary Hart's supporters campaign for Mondale.

Persons associated with the regular party organization are another potential source of campaign workers. Termed "organizational loyalists" by John Kessel, these are the people who owe their allegiance to the party instead of a particular presidential candidate or set of political issues.[30] Because of such loyalties, they are often willing to work in the fall campaign for whichever candidate wins their party's nomination, no matter what their personal feelings about the nominee may be. At the same time, because they are pragmatic and not ideological, party loyalists may not work hard for a presidential candidate who they think is a loser and who will hurt the candidacies of party representatives seeking other political offices. Many Republicans took this attitude toward Goldwater in 1964, as did some Democratic leaders toward Humphrey in 1968, McGovern in 1972, and Mondale in 1984.

State and local political parties are another potential source of workers for the presidential general election campaign. For several reasons, however, problems traditionally have arisen in persuading these organizations to work for the presidential candidates. First, state and local races are more important than the presidential contest to local leaders, particularly those in patronage positions. Second, national, state, and local organizations compete for the same resources, such as visits by candidates and financial donations. Finally, the campaign finance legislation passed in the early 1970s, providing public funds for presidential campaigns, prohibited state and local parties from spending money on such campaigns.

The 1979 amendment to the campaign finance legislation, however, permitted state and local party organizations to spend money in presidential campaigns for any purpose except campaign advertising and hiring outside personnel. This legislation enabled both parties in 1980 to develop grass-roots support for their presidential campaigns, although the Republicans clearly outdid the Democrats. Early in the fall campaign Reagan met with Republican members of Congress on the steps of the Capitol to symbolize cooperation among all elements of the party in electing Republicans to public office. As election day approached, the GOP stated that it had half a million Reagan volunteers ringing doorbells and another 400,000 staffing telephone banks on his behalf.

Democratic presidential candidates have generally benefited from another major source of campaign workers: those provided by organized labor. In 1968 the AFL-CIO said it had registered 4.6 million voters, printed and distributed more than 100 million pamphlets, operated telephone banks in 638 localities, sent out 70,000 house-to-house canvassers, and provided almost 100,000 volunteers on election day to transport people to the polls.[31] This effort was extended on Hubert Humphrey's behalf and is credited with winning the votes of a large number of workers who initially planned to vote for George Wallace.

In contrast, the antipathy of George Meany and other AFL-CIO leaders toward George McGovern caused the organization to remain neutral in the 1972 presidential race and to concentrate its efforts instead toward helping Democrats win House seats and state and local offices. In 1976 the AFL-CIO returned to its traditional policy of supporting Democratic presidential candidates and played an important role in registering its members and their families and in transporting them to the polls to vote for Jimmy Carter. In 1980, although some of its principal leaders backed Senator Kennedy in the Democratic nomination struggle, labor generally did support President Carter; the National Education Association was especially active on his behalf. In 1984, except for the Teamsters, who backed Reagan, labor unions were united on behalf of Walter Mondale.

One distinctive feature of the 1984 campaign was the extent to which both political parties sought to register new voters. Initially, observers thought that the Democrats would benefit most from this effort by registering traditionally low-voting groups such as blacks, Hispanics, and the poor. Their registration effort ran into difficulties, however, because of rivalries among organizations attempting to register the same people and the reluctance of some political organizations to add new voters who would later share in deciding which candidates would prevail in Democratic primary contests for various offices. Moreover, the Republican party launched an all-out drive of its own to counteract the rival party's effort. Republicans registered a large number of white southerners, with the assistance of fundamentalist ministers, and selected key states, such as California, Texas, and Florida, for special registration drives.

Campaign Finance

Since 1976, campaign reform legislation has significantly influenced general election campaigns. In 1976 both Ford and Carter accepted federal matching funds ($21.8 million each that year) and were therefore restricted to that figure for the entire campaign (plus another $3.2 million that each national committee could spend on behalf of its presidential candidate). As a result, both sides had to conduct more restricted campaigns than they did in 1972, when the Republicans spent $61 million and the Democrats $30 million. The public subsidy provided equally to both candidates meant that Ford had to forgo the traditional Republican advantage in campaign funds. As the incumbent president, however, he received a great deal of free publicity, and his Rose Garden strategy enabled him to reserve his financial resources for the last ten days of the campaign, in which he spent $4 million on television and radio broadcasting, primarily in airing the television commercials with Joe Garagiola. All told, both candidates spent about half of their total campaign outlay on the mass media, particularly television, and therefore had limited funds available for organizing their grass-roots campaigns. Largely missing from the 1976 contest were fund-raising activities and the buttons, bumper stickers, and yard signs, used extensively in previous elections (recall that under the law then in effect state and local parties could not assist the presidential campaign by spending money for such purposes).

The 1980 campaign brought new developments in campaign finance. The two major party candidates accepted public financing, and each spent about $18 million of the $29.4 million in federal funds on the mass media, which again meant that they had limited funds available for grass-roots activities. In 1980, however, the law permitted state and local parties to make expenditures for such activities. Figures provided by the Federal Election Commission show that Republican state and local committees spent $15 million on grass-roots efforts on Reagan's behalf compared with $5 million spent by Democratic organizations for Carter.

Also of increased importance in the 1980 campaign were the actions of independent groups in support of Reagan. In the summer of 1980 several organizations announced plans to spend up to $70 million on media efforts for the Republican candidate. A citizens' interest group, Common Cause, together with the Federal Election Commission and the Carter-Mondale Presidential Committee, legally challenged such expenditures on the grounds that the groups were not truly autonomous since some of their leaders had been closely associated with Reagan in past political campaigns. Although these challenges were unsuccessful, they did impede the fund-raising efforts of the independent groups and forced them to cut back on their original plans. Eventually, independent organizations spent approximately $10.6 million on Reagan's behalf. Although much less than originally anticipated, these expenditures were nonetheless significant: independent groups were estimated to have spent only $28,000 for President Carter, about one-quarter of 1 percent of the amount spent for Reagan.[32]

In 1984 both presidential candidates again spent a major portion of their federal funds ($40.4 million plus $6.9 million for the national committee) on the mass media. Both parties also expended considerable sums of money on voter registration efforts. The Republicans funneled much more money to state parties to assist in the campaign than the Democrats did.

Both the rules of the game and the campaign strategies and resources developed by the opposing candidates shape the outcome of presidential campaigns. The campaign, however, is only one influence on the way people vote.

Voting in Presidential Elections

Long-term political dispositions that voters begin to acquire early in life, such as party affiliation and social group loyalties, affect how they vote in presidential elections. So do short-term forces, such as the particular candidates and issues involved in specific elections. Over the years, however, these individual factors have exerted varying degrees of influence in different elections.

Party Affiliation

Analyses of presidential elections in the 1950s by one group of researchers at the University of Michigan indicate that the single most important determinant of voting at that time was the party affiliation of the voter.[33] This general psychological attachment, shaped by family and social groups, tended to intensify with age. For the average person looking for guidance on how to vote amid the complexities of personalities, issues, and events of the 1950s, the party label of the candidates was the most important reference point. In this era—which voting analyst Philip Converse refers to as the "Steady State" period[34]—partisanship was also fairly constant. When asked, about 45 percent of Americans in 1952 and 1956 said they thought of themselves as Democrats; about 28 percent, as Republicans. When asked to classify themselves further as "strong" or "weak" partisans, both Republicans and Democrats tended to divide equally between those two categories. Independents in 1952 and 1956 averaged about 23 percent of the electorate.

In the mid- to late 1960s, however, partisan affiliation in the United States began to change. (See Table 2-2.) In 1964, party affiliation among the voters rose about 5 percent for the Democrats but fell about 3 percent for the Republicans; the independents' share of the electorate also declined slightly. Beginning with the 1968 election, the number of independents began to increase, primarily at the expense of the Democrats, until they constituted one-third of the electorate in 1972. Even those voters who stayed with the Democrats were more inclined than formerly to say they were weak rather

Table 2-2   Party Identification, 1952-1984 (Percent)

Party	1952	1956	1960	1964	1968	1972	1976	1980	1984
Strong Democrat	22	21	21	26	20	15	15	17	17
Weak Democrat	25	23	25	25	25	25	25	23	20
Total	47	44	46	51	45	40	40	40	37
Strong Republican	14	14	13	13	14	13	9	9	13
Weak Republican	13	15	14	11	10	10	14	14	15
Total	27	29	27	24	24	23	23	23	28
Independent	22	24	25	23	30	35	36	34	34

Source: The University of Michigan Center for Political Studies.

than strong party members. Moreover, after 1968, more people identified themselves as independents than as Republicans.

Another indication of the declining importance of political party identification in presidential elections is the increase in recent years in the number of "switchers," that is, people who vote for one party's candidate in one presidential election and for another party's candidate in the following election. Analyses of presidential voting from 1940 to 1960 show that approximately one-eighth to one-fifth of the electorate switched from one election to the next.[35] From 1968 to 1980 the proportion ranged from one-fifth to one-third.[36] A similar phenomenon has occurred in split-ticket voting, that is, voting for candidates of more than one party in the same election. In 1952 of the Americans who voted, some 13 percent cast a split ticket in presidential-House races; by 1972, 30 percent did. The number of split-ticket voters declined to 26 percent in 1976, rose to 35 percent in 1980, and declined to 25 percent in 1984.[37] Still more significant, even voters who identify with one of the major parties have increasingly displayed partisan disloyalty by switching and ticket splitting.

Thus, independence from political parties, whether measured by voters' expressed attitudes toward the parties themselves or by reports of their actual behavior in the voting booth, has increased in recent years in the United States. This rise in independents is not, however, spread evenly across the voting population.[38] It has occurred primarily among young people, particularly those who entered the electorate in 1964 or later. New voters who came of age since that time are much more likely to be political independents than are voters of earlier political generations.

Independents in the United States not only have grown dramatically in numbers but also have changed in character. In the 1950s, independents tended to be less knowledgeable about political issues and candidates and to participate less in the political process than partisans.[39] Since the early 1960s, however, they have shown themselves to be just as knowledgeable about political matters as Democrats and Republicans.[40] Furthermore, although not as likely to vote as are party identifiers, independents do participate at least as much as partisans in other political activities, such as writing to political officials and voting on referendums. Thus, nonpartisanship, rather than general political disinterest, characterizes many of the younger independents, particularly those with a college education. A new type of independent seems to have joined the ranks of nonpartisans prevalent in the 1950s.

Observers of voting behavior have suggested several possible reasons for the decline in partisanship among U.S. voters. One is the decreased transfer of partisanship from one generation to the next; beginning in the late 1960s younger groups became less likely than earlier generations to retain their family partisan affiliation.[41] Two political "shock" periods, as Converse calls them, also weakened partisan loyalties.[42] The first, which began in 1965 and stemmed from the Vietnam War and racial unrest, affected voters of all ages, Democrats somewhat more than Republicans. The second, which began in 1972 and was precipitated by Watergate and the disclosure that led to Vice President Spiro Agnew's resignation, had a distinct impact on older Republicans.

As shown in Table 2-2, however, the decline in partisanship reached its peak in 1972. The proportion of independents did not change in the three presidential elections after that. The trend away from party affiliation therefore appears to have stopped. Moreover, in the mid-1980s the number of voters identifying with the Republican party has increased while the number identifying with the Democratic party has decreased.

Social Groups and Social Class

Analysts of the presidential elections of 1940 and of 1948 found that a fairly close association existed between voters' social group membership and social status and their support for one of the two major parties.[43] Democrats received most of their support from southerners, blacks, Catholics, and people with limited education, lower incomes, and a working-class background. Republican candidates were supported by northerners, whites, Protestants, and people with more education, higher incomes, and a professional or business background.

Table 2-3 shows how various groups voted in presidential elections from 1952 through 1984. The support of many groups for their traditional party's candidates declined over the thirty-two-year period. Especially noticeable for the Republicans was their loss of votes from white-collar workers and Protestants. The most significant drop for the Democrats came in the southern vote in the 1968 and 1972 elections. The party regained this vote in 1976, however, when Jimmy Carter, of Georgia, headed the ticket (only to lose it again in 1980 and 1984). The only group that significantly increased its support for its traditional party candidate over the thirty-two-year period

Table 2-3   Group Voting Patterns in Presidential Elections, 1952-1984 (Percent)

| | 1952 | | 1956 | | 1960 | | 1964 | |
	Stevenson	Eisenhower	Stevenson	Eisenhower	Kennedy	Nixon	Johnson	Goldwater
Group								
Sex								
male	47	53	45	55	52	48	60	40
female	42	58	39	61	49	51	62	38
Race								
white	43	57	41	59	49	51	59	41
nonwhite	79	21	61	39	68	32	94	6
Education								
college	34	66	31	69	39	61	52	48
high school	45	55	42	58	52	48	62	38
grade school	52	48	50	50	55	45	66	34
Occupation								
professional,								
business	36	64	32	68	42	58	54	46
white collar	40	60	37	63	48	52	57	43
manual	55	45	50	50	60	40	71	29
Age								
under 30	51	49	43	57	54	45	64	36
30-49	47	53	45	55	54	46	63	37
50 and								
older	39	61	39	61	46	54	59	41
Religion								
Protestant	37	63	37	63	38	62	55	45
Catholic	56	44	51	49	78	22	76	24
Region								
East	45	55	40	60	53	47	68	32
Midwest	42	58	41	59	48	52	61	39
South	51	49	49	51	51	49	52	48
West	42	58	43	57	49	51	60	40
Members of								
labor union								
families	61	39	57	43	65	35	73	27
National	44.6	55.4	42.2	57.8	50.1	49.9	61.3	38.7

Source: Excerpted from *Gallup Report,* November 1984, 8, 9.

was nonwhites, who have been more firmly in the Democratic camp since 1964 than they were in 1952.

Table 2-3 also shows that the circumstances of particular elections can greatly alter group voting tendencies. In 1964, when the very conservative

Table 2-3 (Continued)

	1968			1972		1976		1980			1984	
Humphrey	Nixon	Wallace	McGovern	Nixon	Carter	Ford	Carter	Reagan	Anderson	Mondale	Reagan
41	43	16	37	63	53	45	38	53	7	36	64
45	43	12	38	62	48	51	44	49	6	45	55
38	47	15	32	68	46	52	36	56	7	34	66
85	12	3	87	13	85	15	86	10	2	87	13
37	54	9	37	63	42	55	35	53	10	39	61
42	43	15	34	66	54	46	43	51	5	43	57
52	33	15	49	51	58	41	54	42	3	51	49
34	56	10	31	69	42	56	33	55	10	34	66
41	47	12	36	64	50	48	40	51	9	47	53
50	35	15	43	57	58	41	48	46	5	46	54
47	38	15	48	52	53	45	47	41	11	40	60
44	41	15	33	67	48	49	38	52	8	40	60
41	47	12	36	64	52	48	41	54	4	41	59
35	49	16	30	70	46	53	39	54	6	39	61
59	33	8	48	52	57	42	46	47	6	39	61
50	43	7	42	58	51	47	43	47	9	46	54
44	47	9	40	60	48	50	41	51	7	42	58
31	36	33	29	71	54	45	44	52	3	37	63
44	49	7	41	59	46	51	35	54	9	40	60
56	29	15	46	54	63	36	50	43	5	52	48
43.0	43.4	13.6	38	62	50	48	41	51	7	41	59

Barry Goldwater was the Republican standard-bearer, all the groups, including those that typically support the GOP, voted for the Democratic candidate, Lyndon Johnson. In 1972, when the very liberal George McGovern ran on the Democratic ticket, all the groups that usually sympathize with that party, except for nonwhites, voted for the Republican candidate, Richard Nixon. In 1984, when Mondale, a traditional, New Deal Democrat, ran against the highly popular Republican president, Ronald Reagan, the Democrats won the overwhelming support only of nonwhites and, by a narrow margin, persons with a grade school education and members of labor unions.

Table 2-3 also makes clear how much additional group support Reagan picked up in 1984 compared with 1980. In every category, a greater percentage of voters supported Reagan after four years as president than when he first ran for the office. The increases were particularly pronounced among voters under age thirty (19 percent), Catholics (14 percent), and males, professional and business people, and southerners (11 percent each).[44]

Party identification and group affiliation, therefore, have not meant as much in recent presidential voting as they once did. Other forces, such as candidates, issues, events, and presidential performance are now more important in the political world of the American voter.

Candidates

The precise influence of candidates on the outcome of elections is difficult to determine. It is much easier for observers of the process to focus on the specific qualities of a particular candidate, such as Eisenhower's personal warmth, Kennedy's youth and Catholicism, and Johnson's expansive style, than it is to compare candidates systematically over a series of elections.[45]

Recognizing these limitations, scholars nonetheless have made some overall comparisons of voters' reactions to candidates from 1952 through 1980. Each presidential year, the Michigan Center for Political Studies asked people whether there was anything about each of the major candidates that would make them want to vote for or against that person. The total number of favorable and unfavorable comments were then tabulated for each candidate; the more numerous the favorable comments about a candidate, the more positive the score. The overall scores, positive and negative, of the two major party candidates were compared with one another to determine the relative appeal of the nominees in each election year. (See Figure 2-2.)

Two significant findings are revealed in Figure 2-2. One is the variability of voters' attitudes toward the candidates over the course of the eight presidential elections. The differences in candidate appeal were much less pronounced in 1952, 1960, 1968, 1976, and 1980 than they were in 1956, 1964, and 1972. The second finding is that except for 1964 and 1976, voters evaluated the Republican candidate more favorably than the Democratic candidate. Although it is not noteworthy that Dwight Eisenhower was more popular than Adlai Stevenson in 1956 and that Richard Nixon received a more favorable rating from the voters than George McGovern in 1972, it is somewhat surprising to find that Nixon was evaluated higher by the voters than John Kennedy in 1960.

Figure 2-2. Appeal of Democratic and Republican Candidates for President, 1952-1980

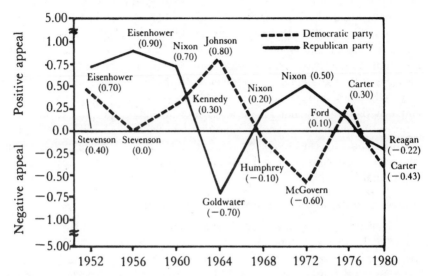

Sources: Arthur Miller and Warren Miller, "Partisanship and Performance: Rational Choice in the 1975 Presidential Election" (Paper delivered at the annual meeting of the American Political Science Association, Washington, D.C., September 1-4, 1977), 90. The 1980 data are from Arthur Miller, "Policy and Performance Voting in the 1980 Election" (Paper delivered at the annual meeting of the American Political Science Association, New York, September 3-6, 1981), Figure 1. (All data are based on the American National Election Studies conducted by the Center for Political Studies, University of Michigan.)

Note: The numbers 5.00 and −5.00 are the greatest possible positive and negative scores, because 5 is the maximum number of comments that were tabulated over the election series. The number shown with each candidate's name is his composite score.

Herbert Asher has suggested possible reasons Republican candidates usually have been more popular than their Democratic opponents since 1952.[46] One is that the Democratic party draws support from a broader variety of groups than the Republican party does, so it is more difficult for the Democratic nominee to please all the elements of the party. Another possible explanation is that since Republicans have been the minority party, they have to be particularly careful to nominate very attractive candidates. Finally, the nature of the times has favored Republican candidates. In 1952 and 1968 the incumbent Democratic party was faced with defending the Korean and Vietnam wars; such hostilities were either over or virtually over when the Republicans were the incumbent party in 1956 and 1972. In 1980 the Democratic administration was beset with the Iranian crisis and also with high inflation caused by rising oil prices.

The Michigan survey suggests that voters' attitudes toward candidates stem from diverse sources: candidates' party affiliations, their stands on issues, perceptions of how they managed or would manage the government, and their personality and character traits. To focus more particularly on personal qualities alone, in the 1984 study, the Michigan group asked respondents to evaluate Reagan and Mondale on twelve specific traits, which they combined into four summary measures: leadership (commands respect, is inspiring, provides strong leadership); competence (is hard-working, intelligent, and knowledgeable); integrity (is decent, is moral, sets a good example); and empathy (is compassionate, is kind, "really cares about people like you"). In contrast to some expectations, Reagan was favored over Mondale on only two of those four measures, leadership and integrity (Mondale prevailed on competence and empathy); and only on leadership was the president's margin substantial.[47]

Issues, Events, and Presidential Performance

Michigan researchers in the 1950s suggested that issues influence a voter's choice only if three conditions are present.[48] First, the voter must be aware that an issue or a number of issues exist. Second, issues must be of some personal concern to the voter. Third, the voter must perceive that one party better represents his or her own thinking on the issues than the other party does.

When these three conditions were applied to U.S. voters in the 1952 and 1956 presidential elections, researchers found that these criteria existed for relatively few voters. About one-third of the respondents were not aware of *any* of the sixteen principal issues about which they were questioned. Even the two-thirds who were aware of one or more issues frequently were not personally concerned about them. Finally, a number of those who were aware and concerned about issues were not able to perceive differences between the two parties' positions on them. The conclusion of the analysis was that issues *potentially* determined the choice of, at the most, only one-third of the electorate. (The proportion who *actually* voted as they did because of issues could have been, and probably was, even less.)

Studies of political attitudes in the 1960s[49] and early 1970s[50] show that issues had become more important to voters. In this period the number and types of issues of which voters were aware increased. Voters during the Eisenhower years had exhibited some interest in traditional domestic matters (welfare, labor-management relationships) and in a few foreign policy issues (the threat of communism, the atomic bomb); beginning with the 1964 election, however, voters' interests broadened to include concerns such as civil rights and Vietnam. Vietnam in particular remained a prominent consideration in the 1968 and 1972 contests and was joined by new matters such as crime, disorder, and juvenile delinquency (sometimes referred to collectively along with race problems as the "social issue").

The connection between voters' own attitudes on issues and their perceptions of where the parties stand on them has grown closer since the early 1960s. Gerald Pomper's analysis of voters' attitudes on issues from 1956 through 1972 shows that beginning with the 1964 presidential election, attitudes became more aligned with partisan identification.[51] Democrats were more likely to express the "liberal" position on economic, civil rights, and foreign policy issues than were Republicans. Also, voters in the 1960s perceived more clearly than voters in the 1950s the differences between the general approaches the two parties take on issues. During this decade a consensus developed that the Democratic party takes a liberal stand, and the Republican party, a conservative one. With these developments, the potential for voting on the basis of issues has increased in recent years. Correlations of voters' attitudes on issues with the way they voted in presidential elections in the 1960s as compared with the 1950s also show that this potential for issue voting was converted into actuality.

Recent analyses also reveal a change in the way the American people think about politics. When voters in the 1950s were asked to indicate what they liked or disliked about the candidates and the parties, only about one in ten responded in ideological terms by linking his or her attitudes on such matters to political issues or by mentioning such general concepts as "liberal" or "conservative" to describe differences between candidates and parties. Far more people made references to group benefits—such as Democrats helping the worker, Republicans helping business—or to the nature of the times, linking Democrats to foreign wars and Republicans to economic downturns and depressions. More than one-fifth of the voters in the 1950s gave replies that had no issue content at all, such as "I just like Democrats better than Republicans" or "Ike's my man." In the 1960s and early 1970s, however, the number of "ideologues" increased considerably, to as much as one-third of the electorate in 1972, for example.[52] Particularly noticeable was a movement away from the perception of politics primarily from the vantage point of group benefits and toward a broader view of issues and general political ideas.

In addition to this broadening of the conceptualization of politics, voters increasingly related political issues to one another as liberal or conservative. Studies of the electorate in the 1950s showed that voters were inconsistent in this respect; that is, people who took the "liberal" position that government should take an active role in providing welfare for the needy did not necessarily think it should assume a similar role in encouraging racial integration in the schools.[53] Nor were voters' attitudes on either of these domestic matters related to their opinions on the foreign policy issue of what stand the U.S. government should take toward the threat of communism in the world. Beginning with the 1964 election, however, voters attitudes were more often correlated, showing consistency among domestic issues as well as between domestic and foreign issues.[54]

Many observers assumed that the decline in social unrest, produced by the U.S. involvement in Vietnam and the racial tensions of the late 1960s and early 1970s, would mean a return to a less ideological and issue-related presidential election in 1976. A study of that election by political scientists Arthur Miller and Warren Miller indicates, however, that this did not occur.[55] Using the same criteria that were used to discern the development of ideological thinking in the earlier period—voters' liberal and conservative attitudes on issues, their perceptions of party differences on such matters, and a correlation among their attitudes on issues— Miller and Miller concluded that ideological thinking declined only slightly between 1972 and 1976. Economic matters were much more important to the electorate in 1976 than social or cultural issues; Democrats were particularly concerned over the rise in unemployment before the election. Because many people believed that the Democratic party would do a better job than the Republican party in dealing with unemployment, and because Carter emphasized economic issues over noneconomic ones in his campaign, many voters distinguished between the two parties and their respective candidates on economic grounds. As Miller and Miller stated, the results of the 1976 election ultimately turned on "incumbent performance [Ford's] versus partisan ideology [Democratic]."

Analysis of the 1980 election shows that economic issues were again more important to the electorate that year than were social and cultural issues, with inflation being the most important concern for many voters. Arthur Miller attributes President Carter's defeat primarily to voter dissatisfaction with his performance in office, particularly his inability to deal with the economy and, to a lesser extent, with a perceived decline in U.S. prestige in the world.[56] Warren Miller, too, sees dissatisfaction with the incumbent's performance in office as an important element in his defeat but also believes that many people voted for Reagan because they agreed with his conservative policies.[57] Other analysts also conclude that dissatisfaction with Carter's performance in office and evaluations of the policy stands of the two major candidates were reasons for Reagan's victory, but dissatisfaction with Carter was somewhat more important than ideological considerations.[58]

The economy was again on the minds of the U.S. electorate in 1984 and was a major reason for President Reagan's overwhelming victory over Mondale. The voters were generally more satisfied with their family's financial situation and with national economic conditions than they were in 1980, and they credited President Reagan with bringing about those positive changes. In fact, there was an optimistic feeling about the general state of the nation, which again was attributed to the president's leadership. As in 1980, the performance of the incumbent significantly influenced the voting decisions of the electorate, but in 1984, the incumbent's performance was the primary reason for *retaining* rather than *removing* the president from office. Moreover, Mondale's vice presidency in the Carter administration allowed the electorate to compare the performance of the present administration with the previous one, rather than choosing between the incumbent and an unfamiliar and untested challenger.[59]

The electorate also evaluated the candidates' policy positions differently in the 1984 and the 1980 elections. In 1980, voters generally approved of Reagan's conservative policies, but in 1984, voters were actually closer to the liberal views of Mondale on desired policy *changes* than they were to the conservative views of the president (especially on cutting defense spending, increasing government aid to women, and avoiding involvement in Central America).[60] At the same time, the electorate was in general agreement with the *current* policies of the Reagan administration.[61] Between 1980 and 1984 it seems that the Reagan administration shifted government policies in the direction of increasing spending for defense and reducing domestic programs, and by 1984 the electorate had decided that the shift had gone far enough and should not be continued.

Many forces, therefore, influence voting behavior in presidential elections. Over the years the two major parties have developed different characteristics, and voters associate candidates with those characteristics. Democratic candidates have been favorably regarded for their party affiliation, their attitudes toward social groups, and their stands on domestic issues. In contrast, Republican ones have benefited from their positions on foreign policy issues, their party philosophy, their perceived ability to manage the government, and a generally favorable assessment of them as candidates.

Consequences of Presidential Elections

The most immediate and most obvious consequence of a presidential election is the voters' choice of a leader of the country and of the executive branch in particular for the succeeding term of office. As the following discussion indicates, however, presidential elections have broader political effects as well.

Effect on the Political Party System

Campbell and his associates have categorized presidential elections according to three clusters of electoral factors.[62] A *maintaining election* is one in which the long-term partisan orientation of the electorate keeps the traditional majority party in power (since 1932, the Democrats). The majority party candidate wins primarily because the people vote according to their traditional party loyalties. Short-term forces, such as candidates and issues, are present, but instead of determining which party wins, they contribute to the size of the majority party's victory. When they favor that party, as they did in 1964 when Goldwater was the Republican nominee, the vote margin separating the two major candidates is larger than usual. If short-term forces are in balance, as they were in 1948, the vote division approximates the proportion of voters who identify with the two parties.

A *deviating election* occurs when short-term forces benefit the minority party and override the long-term partisan preferences of the electorate. An especially appealing candidate or an outstanding issue, event, or type of presidential performance allows the minority party candidate to win with the support of some majority party members, independents, and a good share of new voters. The electorate does not, however, change its basic party preferences. Examples of deviating elections are those of 1952, 1956, 1968, and 1972: they were won by the Republican candidates, Eisenhower and Nixon, but the commitment of many voters to the majority party—the Democrats—was unaltered.[63]

An election that brings about major political change is a *realigning election*. These elections entail a major realignment of electoral support among blocs of voters who switch their traditional party affiliation. An unusually large number of new voters may also enter the electoral arena and cast their ballots disproportionately for one party's candidate. Unlike the deviating election, the effects of the realigning election persist in durable loyalties to the advantaged party. Political historians usually include five elections in the realigning category: 1800, 1828, 1860, 1896, and 1932.

Immediately after the 1980 election, many observers concluded that the decisive Reagan victory (51 percent of the popular vote to 41 percent for Carter), plus the unexpected Republican capture of the Senate and gain of thirty-three seats in the House of Representatives, four governorships, and more than two hundred state legislative seats, meant that 1980 was a realigning election. Moreover social groups that traditionally vote Democratic—including Catholics, blue-collar workers, and voters with no college education—cast their ballots for the Republican nominee, which gave further credence to the contention that the liberal New Deal era in U.S. politics was over and a new Republican majority had finally been formed.[64] When President Reagan embarked successfully on a series of major policy changes, and when by mid-1981 the percentage of voters declaring themselves to be Republicans equaled that of Democrats, some observers became even more convinced that a party realignment had taken place.

Subsequent events, however, indicated that the 1980 election was not a realigning one. As President Reagan began to have problems with the Congress and the economy took a downturn, the number of voters identifying with the Republican party declined, and those declaring themselves to be Democrats rose again until the gap between the two major parties approached its traditional 5-3 ratio. In the 1982 elections the Democrats picked up 26 seats in the House of Representatives, a net gain of 7 governorships, and some 160 additional seats in state legislatures, showing that many Democrats had not permanently deserted their traditional party.

The results of the 1984 presidential election, in which President Reagan captured 59 percent of the popular vote (compared with Mondale's 41 percent) and the electoral votes of forty-nine states (Mondale carried only his home state of Minnesota and the District of Columbia), raised the issue of whether the 1984 election was a realigning one. Several developments were evident in the middle of the 1980s that one would expect to find if a realignment of significant magnitude were occurring: younger voters and newly registered ones tended to be Republicans; many traditional Democrats were deserting the party because they agreed more with the Republicans on issues such as economic growth and opportunity, the necessity of building up the national defense, and social concerns (prayer in the public school, abortion, busing); and the number of political independents appeared to have leveled off or even declined.[65]

Other developments of the mid-1980s, however, did *not* point in the direction of a realigning election. Although President Reagan, himself, won by a large margin in the 1984 election, the Republican party actually lost two seats in the Senate, and the fourteen seats it picked up in the House of Representatives did not compensate for the twenty-six it lost in the 1982 elections. Moreover, despite the presidential landslide, Democrats still controlled thirty-four of the nation's fifty governorships and both houses of the legislature in twenty-eight states, compared with eleven for the Republicans. In late 1985, a Gallup poll found that the Democrats were on the rise again; 40 percent of the American public identified with that party compared with 33 percent who said they were Republicans.[66] Finally, in the 1986 congressional elections, the Democrats unexpectedly picked up 8 seats in the Senate to gain control of that body by a margin of 55 to 45 and added 5 seats in the House of Representatives to increase their numerical superiority over the Republicans to 258-177.

If either the 1980 or 1984 election is compared with the previous realigning elections (1800, 1828, 1860, 1896, and 1932), some major differences appear. The new majority party that emerged in each of these five earlier elections captured not only the presidency but also both houses of Congress (not just the Senate). With the exception of the first instance the emerging party controlled the House of Representatives in the session preceding the key presidential election (the Republicans did not do that in either 1978 or 1982). Moreover, two years after the presidential race, the new majority party maintained control of both houses of the Congress in what one writer calls "cementing" elections.[67] In contrast, the Republicans in 1982 failed to capture the House of Representatives and in 1986 lost both the Senate and the House to the Democrats. Finally, voting participation generally increased in past realigning elections, but participation in the 1980 election declined from the 1976 contest; and despite the registration efforts of both parties in 1984, voter turnout rose by less than 1 percent that year.

What actually has occurred since the the late 1960s is what Kevin Phillips terms a "split-level" realignment.[68] The Republican party has become the dominant party in presidential elections, capturing four of the last five contests, three of them (1972, 1980, and 1984) by substantial margins.

Meanwhile, the Democrats are clearly the majority party in the House of Representatives (the Republicans last controlled that body in the 1953-1955 session). Since 1980 only the Senate can properly be termed a "two-party" institution.

Other analysts, such as Walter Dean Burnham, prefer to characterize the recent era as one of party "decomposition" or "dealignment." [69] Traditional loyalties of the American public to political parties have declined greatly, and therefore the party affiliation of candidates is no longer the principal factor in voting decisions, as it once was. Instead, short-term forces, such as the candidates themselves, issues, events, and incumbent performance, shape how people cast their ballots. As a result, voters switch their votes in presidential elections from one party's candidate to another and split their ballots for different party candidates running for separate offices in the same election. As Burnham explains, "Electoral disaggregation carried beyond a certain point would, after all, make critical realignment in the classical sense impossible." [70]

In early 1987, the state of U.S. politics appears to be closer to dealignment than to realignment. Recent elections have not constituted a general realignment, as that term has traditionally been used; the Republicans have failed to capture control of both houses of the Congress (along with the presidency), and the prospect of that occurring in the near future seems unlikely. Moreover, while the Republicans were losing eight Senate seats in 1986, they picked up an equal number of governorships from the Democrats, indicating that voters were splitting their ballots, focusing more on evaluations of individual candidates than demonstrating a renewed loyalty to the Democratic party.

The present electoral volatility in U.S. politics significantly influences the president's ability to act as an effective leader of his political party and of the national government in general, topics subsequent chapters of this book will examine. Presidential elections also affect another important matter, which will be explored in Part Three, namely, the making of public policy in the U.S. political system.

Effect on Policy Making

The strongest conceivable influence voters in presidential elections could exercise on policy making in the United States would be to send to the winning candidate a clear message that identified the issues they felt were most important and that defined specific policies the candidate should follow in dealing with those issues. Such a message is called a *mandate*—a set of instructions to the new president on how to govern the nation. As Pomper suggests, the theory of a mandate "has been particularly associated with the Labour party of Great Britain, although it is supported in other nations as well." [71]

For many reasons presidential elections may not meet the requirements of a mandate. As discussed in preceding sections, issues often have little to do with a voter's choice of candidate. Some people vote according to traditional loyalties—they simply choose the candidate who represents the political party with which they identify. Others base their decision on the personal qualities of the competing presidential candidates; they vote for the candidate whose qualities they like or for the opponent of a candidate they dislike (the "lesser of the two evils").

Even when voters choose a candidate because of issues, the election may not produce a mandate. Voters differ on the particular issues they are interested in: some may be concerned over the state of the domestic economy; others, the U.S. position in the world community. Thus, a candidate may garner a plurality of the votes cast by issue-conscious voters, without any single issue having majority support. Moreover, it is one thing for voters to be interested in an issue and quite another for them to be able to suggest specific policies to deal with that issue. Finally, individual policies favored by voters may conflict with one another. Voters may favor, for example, increased government expenditures for national defense but also support a tax cut and a balanced budget. If it proves to be impossible to carry out all these policies simultaneously (as was true during Reagan's presidency), the electorate may provide no clear message on which policy has the highest priority.

The failure of a presidential election to produce a mandate does not mean that it has no implications for public policy making in the United States. As one observer explains, elections are in effect a "retrospective" judgment on the performance of the incumbent officeholder.[72] When voters reelect the officeholder, they are showing their general satisfaction with the way his administration has been handling the principal issues facing the country. Voters may also use this evaluation of past performance to indicate their expectations of a president's future performance.[73] In 1984, for example, people who voted for President Reagan approved of the way he had handled major problems (especially the economy) and assumed he would continue to handle those problems successfully in the next four years. Yet they gave little guidance on the specific policies the administration should follow. As discussed in a preceding section, on several major issues the electorate more often agreed with Mondale than with Reagan. Moreover, in the 1984 campaign the president made few specific promises about how he would address the major issue of the economy (the budget deficit), except to say that he would raise taxes only as a "last resort." Thus, a vote to keep a president in office is primarily a favorable judgment both on his past performance and on the prospects of achieving particular *outcomes* (such as a prosperous economy); it is not an assessment of the *means*, that is, the specific policies, necessary to reach those outcomes.

In retrospective voting, the voters oust an administration from office primarily because they are so dissatisfied with its past performance and so pessimistic about its future performance that they are willing to give the winning opponent the opportunity to do a better job. Beyond this message, however, a presidential election offers a new president little guidance. The electorate indicates the general *goal* that it wants the president to achieve rather than the policies he should follow to reach that goal. In the 1968 election the voters did not instruct Richard Nixon to follow any particular course of action in extricating the nation from Vietnam, but they did give him the message that he should somehow reach that goal. The electoral message also may suggest that the new president should not continue to follow the policies of his predecessor on the issue. It may also indicate the *general direction* of the public policies the newly elected president should pursue. For example, Warren Miller feels that the 1980 presidential election not only constituted a negative assessment of the performance of President Carter in office but also expressed a general preference for more conservative policies on government spending and on the scope of government services and support for a major reduction in federal income taxes, among other matters. Miller makes it clear, however, that the election did not provide a mandate for President Reagan's specific positions on each issue.[74]

Aside from the question of what policy directions (if any) presidential elections offer successful candidates, presidents themselves frequently interpret the election results as a mandate to pursue policies that they personally favor. As presidential advisor George Reedy put it, "President Johnson and most of his close advisors interpreted the election result [the 1964 landslide victory of Johnson over Goldwater] as a mandate from the people not only to carry on the policies of the Johnson administration but any other policies that might come to mind." [75] The same tendency applies when the candidate of the party out of power wins an election. When Ronald Reagan assumed the presidency after his victory over Jimmy Carter in 1980, he claimed a mandate from the people to embark on a broad range of conservative policies, some of which—such as reduced rates of government expenditures on health, education, and environmental protection and opposition to the Equal Rights Amendment and abortion—ran counter to voters' preferences.

The indefinite guidance the electorate offers the winner of presidential elections gives the president great freedom in initiating public policies. In recent years new presidents often have sought to have enacted the pledges made in their party platforms.[76] Moreover both Lyndon Johnson and Richard Nixon acted on more than half of the promises they made in campaign speeches in 1964 and 1968,[77] as did Dwight Eisenhower and John Kennedy on the promises they made in their 1952 and 1960 campaigns.[78] A positive relationship does exist, therefore, between what presidential candidates say they will do if elected and the policies they actually follow after they assume office, whether or not the electorate supports them for that reason.

At the same time, U.S. presidents must strive to keep their policies in line with the preferences of the voters. If their new policies go further than their electoral supporters intended, or even if the admittedly favored policies do not turn out to be successful, presidents face the possibility of being ousted from office at the next election. As political scientist V. O. Key points out, "Governments must worry, not about the meaning of past elections, but about their fate at future elections." This means that "the electorate can exert a prospective influence if not control" over government policy.[79]

The type of presidential election has some bearing on the policies enacted after the election. Maintaining elections not only keep the majority party in power but typically result in the continuation of its policies, which have met the general approval of the electorate. Deviating elections provide the opportunity for some change in policies but not a radical departure from the past. The Eisenhower administration, for example, slowed down and modified some of the policies of previous Democratic administrations, but it did not try to repeal the New Deal. Realigning elections (or eras) typically result in major changes in public policy. An analysis of the statutes enacted from 1789 to 1968 shows that those passed in the period immediately following a realigning election departed most from policies of the past.[80]

Conclusion

The rules governing the election of presidential candidates have undergone far less change than those that apply to their nomination. The general-ticket system, whereby all the electoral votes of a state go to the candidate who receives a plurality of its popular votes, has prevailed since the 1830s despite frequent attempts to alter it. (The concluding chapter will analyze these attempts.) Recent changes in rules governing the financing of presidential elections provide for full public funding of the campaigns of the two major-party candidates, but these changes do not appear to have influenced the general election process as much as the new rules for the partial financing of nomination contests have affected the nomination process.

The protean nature of the general election process is reflected in the *conduct* of presidential campaigns. What journalist Sidney Blumenthal calls the "permanent campaign" is dominated by political consultants who have replaced traditional political party leaders as the main link between candidates and voters.[81] Contributing to this development is the use of television, which enables candidates to communicate directly with the American public rather than depending on persons associated with the party organization to do it for them. These developments have changed the ways the American people evaluate presidential candidates. Rather than judging candidates primarily by their party affiliation (and perceptions of how the respective parties treat certain social groups), as used to be the case, voters today judge candidates on other grounds—their personal characteristics (particularly those revealed by television), their stands on issues, their association with the events of the day, and their relationship to the performance of the incumbent administration.

The result is a volatile selection process influenced by short-term forces rather than the long-term ones of the past.

Of late, however, the national political parties have been attempting a comeback that would give them more influence both in presidential races and in contests for congressional, state, and local offices.[82] The Republican party acted first by adopting new technology, such as direct mail, to build a large base of small contributors and to provide financial and other campaign assistance to Republican candidates throughout the political system. More recently the Democratic national organization has begun using some of the same techniques. In 1984 both national parties also undertook major efforts to register new voters. As A. James Reichley suggests, the two parties "now seem to be developing an increased commitment to a clearly defined ideology." [83] Although today's parties may never achieve the prominence they once enjoyed in political campaigns, their influence in future campaigns may well be greater than it has been in recent decades.

Notes

1. Max Farrand, *The Framing of the Constitution of the United States* (New Haven: Yale University Press, 1913), 160.
2. Neal Peirce, *The People's President: The Electoral College in American History and the Direct-Vote Alternative* (New York: Simon and Schuster, 1968), 430.
3. Lucius Wilmerding, *The Electoral College* (New Brunswick, N.J.: Rutgers University Press, 1958), chap. 8.
4. John Roche, "The Founding Fathers: A Reform Caucus in Action," *American Political Science Review* (December 1961): 811.
5. Lawrence Longley, "Minorities and the 1980 Electoral College" (Paper delivered at the annual meeting of the American Political Science Association, Washington, D.C., August 28-31, 1980).
6. The 270 electoral votes constitute a majority of the total number of 538. The number *538* is the total of 435 electoral votes representing members of the House of Representatives, 100 representing the senators from the fifty states, and 3 representing the District of Columbia.
7. Wallace, however, may have affected the results of the Truman-Dewey contest in some states; Wallace's winning 8 percent of the popular vote in New York State probably drained enough votes away from Truman to allow Dewey to defeat him by about 1 percent of the popular vote.
8. Although presidential candidates are free to refuse public funds, none has done so, perhaps because of the difficulty of raising money under the limitations on contributions from individuals and political action committees. Candidates may also think that the American public favors the use of public rather than private funds in the presidential general election.

9. Although campaign activities are carried in the national media, local media give special publicity to the candidate and thus affect the immediate audience. Moreover, some voters are flattered by the fact that a candidate takes the time and effort to come to their locality to campaign.

10. Lewis Chester, Godfrey Hodgson, and Bruce Page, *The American Melodrama: The Presidential Campaign of 1968* (New York: Viking, 1969), 620.

11. Presidential candidates sometimes, however, venture into states thought to belong politically to their opponents. In 1976 Jimmy Carter made some trips into normally Republican areas to put Ford on the defensive, therefore forcing him to spend time and money in states he expected to carry (Martin Schram, *Running for President 1976: The Carter Campaign* [New York: Stein and Day, 1977], 247). Carter in 1980 and Mondale in 1984 also visited California, in part to require Ronald Reagan to use some resources to protect his home state.

12. John Kessel reports the comment made during the 1972 campaign that "McGovern could not carry the South with Robert E. Lee as his running-mate and Bear Bryant as his campaign manager" (John Kessel, "Strategy for November," in *Choosing the President,* ed. James D. Barber [Englewood Cliffs, N.J.: Prentice-Hall, 1974], 109).

13. This carefully thought-out plan is to be contrasted with the pledge Richard Nixon made at the 1960 Republican national convention to visit all fifty states personally. In the closing days of the campaign, Nixon took precious time to fly to Alaska, which he had not previously visited, while his opponent, John Kennedy, was barnstorming through heavily populated Illinois, New Jersey, New York, and the New England states.

14. Thomas Cronin, "The Presidential Election of 1984," in *Election 84: Landslide without a Mandate,* ed. Ellis Sandoz and Cecil Crabb, Jr. (New York: Mentor, 1985), 49.

15. Timothy Crouse, *The Boys on the Bus* (New York: Ballentine Books, 1972), 257.

16. One of the interesting features of the 1980 campaign was that President Carter did *not* use Vice President Mondale much in that way; instead, the president launched frequent personal attacks on Ronald Reagan himself while for the most part Mondale played the role of the "happy warrior" in the campaign.

17. In 1980 the Republicans handled the potential problem of an even older Ronald Reagan, who was almost seventy at the time of the fall campaign, in a very different way: he was depicted as an unusually vigorous man for one his age. This image was helped considerably by Reagan's full head of hair, as contrasted to Eisenhower's bald pate.

18. A variant of this problem occurred in 1984 for Walter Mondale. Although he was not the incumbent vice president, he did hold that office from 1976 to 1980 under Carter and was associated with the policies of that administration, some of which he did not agree with (placing an embargo on grain shipments to the Soviet Union, for example).

19. One political scientist calls "position issues" those that "involve advocacy of governmental action from a set of alternatives," in contrast to "valence

issues," which "merely involve linking of the parties with some condition that is positively or negatively valued by the electorate" (Donald Stokes, "Special Models of Party Competition," in *Elections in the Political Order,* ed. Angus Campbell, Philip Converse, Warren Miller, and Donald Stokes [New York: Wiley, 1966], 170-171).

20. Marshall McLuhan, *Understanding Media: The Extensions of Man* (New York: McGraw-Hill, 1964), chap. 1.

21. A problem in holding presidential debates is a provision of the Federal Communications Act of 1934 requiring the networks to provide equal time to *all* candidates, including those of minor parties. In 1960 Congress temporarily suspended the provisions of the act to allow the Nixon-Kennedy debates. In 1976, 1980, and 1984 the debates were sponsored and paid for by the League of Women Voters. The networks supposedly covered them as "news events," a legal fiction that was exposed when the first Carter-Ford debate in 1976 was interrupted for twenty-eight minutes until an audio failure could be repaired.

22. This was especially true of people who watched the first Nixon-Kennedy debate on television. Those who heard that same debate on the radio, however, thought the two candidates came out about equally (Theodore White, *The Making of the President, 1960* [New York: Pocket Books, 1961], 348).

23. In addition, Albert Hunt suggests that Reagan convinced many viewers of the debate that he was sufficiently smart to go head-to-head with the president and not crumble. President Carter, however, did not meet the greater expectations the viewers had of his debate performance, namely, that he explain why things had not gone very well in the previous four years and how he would do better in a second term (Albert Hunt, "The Campaign and the Issues," in *The American Elections of 1980,* ed. Austin Ranney [Washington, D.C.: American Enterprise Institute, 1981], 170-171).

24. Thomas Patterson, *The Mass Media Election: How Americans Choose Their President* (New York: Praeger, 1980), chap. 13.

25. Michael Robinson and Margaret Sheehan, *Over the Wire and on TV: CBS and UPI in Campaign '80* (New York: Russell Sage Foundation, 1983), 166.

26. Thomas Patterson and Richard Davis, "The Media Campaign: Struggle for the Agenda," in *The Elections of 1984,* ed. Michael Nelson (Washington, D.C.: CQ Press, 1985), 116.

27. Over the years endorsements have clearly favored the Republican candidate, except in 1964, when the press favored Johnson over Goldwater. As a group, newspaper owners and editors, who decide on endorsements, tend to be conservative, possibly because much of their advertising revenue comes from large corporations. Political reporters, by contrast, are widely perceived to be liberal.

28. Dan Nimmo, *The Political Persuaders: The Techniques of Modern Political Campaigns* (Englewood Cliffs, N.J.: Prentice-Hall, 1970), 117-118.

29. Jonathan Moore and Janet Fraser, *Campaign for President: The Managers Look at 1976* (Cambridge, Mass.: Ballinger, 1977), 133.

30. John Kessel, "Strategy for November," in *Choosing the President,* ed. James D. Barber (Englewood Cliffs, N.J.: Prentice-Hall, 1974), 179.

31. Theodore White, *The Making of the President, 1968* (New York: Bantam, 1969), 453-454.
32. Herbert E. Alexander, *Financing the 1980 Election* (Lexington, Mass.: D.C. Heath, 1983), 387.
33. Angus Campbell, Philip Converse, Warren Miller, and Donald Stokes, *The American Voter*, abr. ed. (New York: Wiley, 1964).
34. Philip Converse, *The Dynamics of Party Support: Cohort-Analyzing Party Identification* (Beverly Hills: Sage, 1976), 34.
35. V. O. Key, *The Responsible Electorate: Rationality in Presidential Voting* (Cambridge, Mass.: Belknap Press, 1966).
36. Based on data provided by the Center for Political Studies.
37. One possible reason for the high percentage of ticket splitting between presidential and House races in 1980 was the presence of independent John Anderson in the presidential contest that year. In most states Anderson's supporters did not have the option of voting for an independent House candidate.
38. Norman Nie, Sidney Verba, and John Petrocik, *The Changing American Voter* (Cambridge, Mass.: Harvard University Press, 1979), chap. 4.
39. Campbell et al., *The American Voter*, 83-85.
40. Gerald Pomper, *Voter's Choice: Varieties of American Electoral Behavior* (New York: Dodd, Mead, 1975), chap. 2.
41. Nie, Verba, and Petrocik, *Changing American Voter*, 70-72.
42. Converse, *Dynamics of Party Support*, chap. 4.
43. For the 1940 election, Paul Lazarsfeld, Bernard Berelson, and Hazel Gaudt, *The People's Choice* (New York: Columbia University Press, 1944); for the 1948 election, Paul Lazarsfeld, Bernard Berelson, and William McPhee, *Voting* (Chicago: University of Chicago Press, 1954).
44. It should be pointed out that one reason for the Reagan increases was the absence in 1984 of a third party candidate, such as John Anderson, to drain off votes. This factor also contributed to Mondale's winning a greater percentage of votes than Carter did among several groups, although only that of white-collar workers exceeded 5 percent.
45. Warren Miller and Teresa Levitin, *Leadership and Change: The New Politics and the American Electorate* (Cambridge, Mass.: Winthrop, 1976), 42.
46. Herbert Asher, *Presidential Elections and American Politics: Voters, Candidates and Campaigns since 1952* (Homewood, Ill.: Dorsey, 1976), chap. 5.
47. J. Merrill Shanks and Warren Miller, "Policy Direction and Performance Evaluation: Complementary Explanations of the Reagan Elections" (Paper delivered at the annual meeting of the American Political Science Association, New Orleans, August 29-September 1, 1985), 60, 69.
48. Campbell et al., *The American Voter*, chap. 7.
49. Pomper, *Voter's Choice*.
50. Nie, Verba, and Petrocik, *The Changing American Voter*.
51. Pomper, *Voter's Choice*, chap. 8.
52. Nie, Verba, and Petrocik, *The Changing American Voter*, chap. 7.
53. Philip Converse, "The Nature of Belief Systems in Mass Publics," in *Ideology and Discontent*, ed. David Apter (New York: Free Press, 1964).

54. Norman Nie and Kristi Anderson, "Mass Belief Systems Revisited: Political Change and Attitude Structure," *The Journal of Politics* (August 1974): 540-591.

55. Arthur Miller and Warren Miller, "Partisanship and Performance: Rational Choice in the 1976 Presidential Election" (Paper delivered at the annual meeting of the American Political Science Association, Washington, D.C., September 1-4, 1977).

56. Arthur Miller, "Policy and Performance Voting in the 1980 Election" (Paper delivered at the annual meeting of the American Political Science Association, New York, September 3-6, 1981).

57. Warren Miller, "Policy Directions and Presidential Leadership:'Alternative Interpretations of the 1980 Presidential Election" (Paper delivered at the annual meeting of the American Political Science Association, New York, September 3-6, 1981).

58. Paul Abramson, John Aldrich, and David Rohde, *Change and Continuity in the 1980 Elections* (Washington, D.C.: CQ Press, 1982).

59. Martin Wattenberg, "The Hollow Realignment: Partisan Change in a Candidate-Centered Era" (Paper delivered at the annual meeting of the American Political Science Association, New Orleans, August 29-September 1, 1985).

60. Abramson, Aldrich, and Rohde, *Change and Continuity in the 1984 Elections,* rev. ed. (Washington, D.C.: CQ Press, 1987), chap. 6.

61. Shanks and Miller, "Policy Direction and Performance Evaluation."

62. Campbell et al., *The American Voter,* chap. 16.

63. Analysts refer to an election following a deviating period as a *reinstating* one, because it reinstates the usual majority party. Examples are the 1960 and 1976 elections, when the Democrats returned to power after the two Eisenhower and the two Nixon victories. A reinstating election, therefore, is like a maintaining one in that long-term partisan factors determine the result.

64. See Kevin Phillips, *The Emerging Republican Majority* (New Rochelle, N.Y.: Arlington House, 1969).

65. Thomas Cavanaugh and James Sundquist, "The New Two-Party System" in *The New Direction in American Politics,* ed. John Chubb and Paul Peterson (Washington, D.C.: Brookings, 1985), chap. 2.

66. *The Gallup Report,* October-November 1985, 42-44.

67. Wattenberg, "The Hollow Realignment," 4.

68. This term is used in Phillips's biweekly newsletter, *The American Political Report* (January 11, 1985), as cited in Abramson, Aldrich, and Rohde, *Change and Continuity in the 1984 Elections,* 287.

69. Walter Dean Burnham, *Critical Elections and the Mainsprings of American Politics* (New York: Norton, 1970), chap. 5.

70. Ibid., 91-92.

71. Gerald Pomper, with Susan Lederman, *Elections in America: Control and Influence in Democratic Politics,* 2d ed. (New York: Longman, 1980), 212.

72. V. O. Key, Jr., *The Responsible Electorate: Rationality in Presidential Voting* (Cambridge, Mass.: Belknap Press, 1966).

73. Anthony Downs, *An Economic Theory of Democracy* (New York: Harper and Row, 1957); and Morris Fiorina, *Retrospective Voting in American*

National Elections (New Haven: Yale University Press, 1981).
74. Miller, "Policy Directions and Presidential Leadership."
75. George Reedy, *The Twilight of the Presidency* (New York: New American Library, 1970), 66.
76. Pomper, *Elections in America,* chap. 8.
77. Fred Grogan, "Candidate Promise and Presidential Performance" (Paper delivered at the annual meeting of the Midwest Political Science Association, Chicago, April 21-23, 1977).
78. Arnold John Muller, "Public Policy and the Presidential Election Process: A Study of Promise and Performance" (Ph.D. diss., University of Missouri-Columbia, 1986).
79. Key, *The Responsible Electorate,* 77.
80. Benjamin Ginsberg, "Elections and Public Policy," *American Political Science Review* (March 1976): 41-49.
81. Sidney Blumenthal, ed., *The Permanent Campaign* (Boston: Beacon Press, 1980).
82. A. James Reichley, "The Rise of National Parties" in *New Direction in American Politics,* ed. Chubb and Peterson.
83. Ibid., 196.

Selected Readings

Abramson, Paul, John Aldrich, and David Rohde. *Change and Continuity in the 1980 Elections.* Washington, D.C.: CQ Press, 1982.
_____. *Change and Continuity in the 1984 Elections.* Rev. ed. Washington, D.C.: CQ Press, 1987.
Campbell, Angus, Philip Converse, Warren Miller, and Donald Stokes. *The American Voter.* abr. ed. New York: Wiley, 1964.
Chubb, John, and Paul Peterson. *The New Direction in American Politics.* Washington, D.C.: Brookings, 1985.
Key, V. O., Jr. *The Responsible Electorate: Rationality in Presidential Voting.* Cambridge, Mass.: Belknap Press, 1966.
Miller, Warren, and Teresa Levitin. *Leadership and Change: The New Politics and the American Electorate.* Cambridge, Mass.: Winthrop, 1976.
Nelson, Michael, ed. *The Elections of 1984.* Washington, D.C.: CQ Press, 1985.
Nie, Norman, Sidney Verba, and John Petrocik. *The Changing American Voter.* Cambridge Mass.: Harvard University Press, 1979.
Pomper, Gerald, with Susan Lederman. *Elections in America: Control and Influence in Democratic Politics.* 2d ed. New York: Longman, 1980.
Ranney, Austin, ed. *The American Elections of 1980.* Washington, D.C.: American Enterprise Institute, 1981.
Robinson, Michael, and Margaret Sheehan. *Over the Wire and on TV: CBS and UPI in Campaign '80.* New York: Russell Sage Foundation, 1983.

These chief executives exemplify the four presidential personality types defined by political scientist James David Barber: Wilson, *active-negative;* Taft, *passive-positive;* Franklin Roosevelt, *active-positive;* Eisenhower, *passive-negative.*

CHAPTER THREE

What Manner of Person?

This chapter turns from consideration of the process by which presidents are chosen to the results of that process—the kinds of persons who have served in the office over the past two centuries. The first section discusses the minimum legal qualifications for the presidency. The second analyzes the political backgrounds of U.S. presidents, the kinds of public offices they held before becoming chief executive, the trends in such officeholding, and the reasons for the trends. The third section examines the social backgrounds of American presidents; the fourth, their psychological characteristics.

Legal Qualifications for the Presidency

Few persons seeking the presidency need concern themselves about their legal eligibility to hold the office. The qualifications set forth in Article II, Section 1, of the Constitution are minimal. One need only satisfy three requirements. One must be a "natural-born citizen," at least thirty-five years of age, and a resident of the United States for at least fourteen years.

Of the three requirements, the first poses the most interesting legal questions. According to scholar Charles Gordon, it is clear that "native-born" citizens, that is, those born in the United States, are eligible to serve in the presidential office.[1] It is also certain that individuals who become citizens through the process of naturalization (such as former secretary of state Henry Kissinger, who was born in Germany) do not meet the constitutional requirement of being natural-born. Eligibility is in doubt, however, for persons *born abroad of American citizens.* Included in this category in recent years have been two prominently mentioned presidential candidates. Former Republican governor George Romney of Michigan, an early contender in the 1968 race, was born in a Mormon colony in

Mexico.[2] Former Massachusetts governor Christian Herter, born of American parents studying art in France, was a potential candidate first in 1952 and again in 1960 following service as secretary of state in the latter years of Dwight D. Eisenhower's administration.

Neither the Romney nor the Herter candidacies materialized, so there is no definitive answer whether persons born abroad of American parents are eligible to serve as president. Legal scholars differ on the subject. Gordon maintains that the Founders intended to ensure full citizenship rights to such persons, including the right to be president.[3] In contrast, Isidor Blum believes that the framers of the Constitution used the term *natural-born* synonymously with *native-born,* which would exclude all individuals not born in the United States.[4] Without a constitutional amendment clearing up the ambiguity, or a definitive judicial decision on the issue, the question of presidential eligibility for persons born abroad of American citizens remains unanswered. The issue is probably academic, however: as Edward Corwin argued, should the American people actually elect such a person to the presidency, it is highly improbable that any other constitutional agency would venture to challenge their decision.[5] Moreover, as Gordon points out, the Supreme Court might well avoid ruling on the issue by holding that it involves a "political question" over which the Court has no authority.

The two other presidential qualifications present only minor legal problems. One question is whether the age requirement of thirty-five applies to the time a person is chosen by the electors in mid-December or to January 20, when the official term begins. (State courts have favored the latter interpretation when construing analogous provisions of state constitutions.) Another question is the definition of the fourteen-year residency requirement. It could be interpreted to mean the period immediately preceding a person's assumption of the presidential office. Herbert Hoover would not have met that interpretation of the requirement, however, and his title to the office was not challenged.

The constitutional qualifications for the presidency therefore raise some interesting legal questions. From a practical standpoint, however, they have little effect on who is entitled to serve in the office. Even if the courts were to rule on these matters and take the strictest interpretations possible, relatively few persons would be disqualified for the presidential office.[6] The overwhelming proportion of candidates seeking the presidency are born in the United States, are considerably older than thirty-five, and have resided in this country for at least fourteen years, including the period immediately preceding their assumption of the office. Informal qualifications rather than legal ones have determined who has served in the presidency throughout U.S. history. As the following sections indicate, however, the nature of those informal qualifications changes over time, as political leaders and voters take different kinds of experiences into account in assessing who they think would make a good president.

Political Backgrounds of U.S. Presidents

Although the thirty-nine persons who served in the presidency from Washington to Reagan have come from diverse backgrounds, most have one experience in common: previous service in a civilian governmental office.[7] The only exceptions to this rule are three career military officers, Zachary Taylor, Ulysses S. Grant, and Dwight Eisenhower, whose heroic exploits in the Mexican War, Civil War, and World War II, respectively, thrust them suddenly into the vortex of presidential politics. Not only did these three presidents lack experience in civilian office, but as professional military men they had not even been involved in partisan activities. Taylor, elected as the Whig candidate in 1848, had never voted before in a presidential election and had no party affiliation.[8] Grant, the Republican party candidate elected in 1868, had voted for James Buchanan, the Democratic standard-bearer in 1856, and had political views that have been described as "obscure." [9] Even more perplexing for party leaders was Dwight Eisenhower, the Republican party candidate in 1952 and 1956, whom a number of liberal Democratic leaders had tried to draft for their party's nomination in 1948.[10]

Early Career Patterns

Most U.S. chief executives served a long apprenticeship in public office before reaching the presidency, usually beginning their careers at lower levels of the political system when they were in their twenties or thirties. Some, such as Andrew Johnson and Calvin Coolidge, began their public careers as city aldermen or councilmen. Others were first elected to county offices: John Adams was a highway surveyor, Harry S Truman a member of the county court (an administrative, not a judicial, position). Some presidents, including Andrew Jackson, James Buchanan, Grover Cleveland, William McKinley, and William Howard Taft, entered the public service as prosecuting or district attorney; others, such as Rutherford B. Hayes and Benjamin Harrison, served as city solicitor or attorney. Several chief executives, Thomas Jefferson, Abraham Lincoln, Theodore Roosevelt, and Franklin D. Roosevelt among them, began their public careers as state legislators.

The typical career pattern for the above presidents was to move up the political ladder by winning offices representing progressively larger constituencies. Those who started in city or county offices tended to go on to the state legislature, and state legislators often broadened their political horizons to include statewide offices, such as secretary of state, attorney general, lieutenant governor, or governor. Approximately two-thirds of the presidents served in either the House of Representatives or the Senate or both. Indeed, some chief executives came to the presidency after holding a wide variety of offices: Martin Van Buren, for example, began as a county surrogate, moved on to the New York State senate, became state attorney general and then governor; he raised his sights to the federal government, where he served as a senator, secretary of state, minister to Great Britain, and vice president before being elected president in 1836.[11]

Although most American presidents held public office from an early age until they were elected to the presidency in their fifties or early sixties, other chief executives, in addition to the three military heroes, did not follow this pattern. Woodrow Wilson spent most of his adult life as a professor of government and later as president of Princeton University; in 1910, at age fifty-four, he was elected governor of New Jersey, just two years before he won the presidency. Ronald Reagan was primarily a radio, movie, and television performer until his fifties, when he became active in national politics in the 1964 presidential campaign on behalf of Barry Goldwater. In 1966 he was elected to the first of two terms as governor of California; in 1980 he was elected president. Neither William Howard Taft nor Herbert Hoover held any elective office before being chosen as president. After serving as an attorney and later a judge in county, state, and federal governments, Taft became governor general of the Philippines and secretary of war. Hoover chaired the Commission for Relief in Belgium, and, after the United States entered the war, was U.S. food administrator with broad authority over the prices, production, and distribution of food; he later served as secretary of commerce in the Harding and Coolidge administrations. Nor have all the presidents reached the nation's highest office on the typical schedule: Teddy Roosevelt and John Kennedy were still in their early forties; James Buchanan was in his middle sixties; and William Henry Harrison and Ronald Reagan were in their late sixties when elected to the office.

American presidents thus have followed a variety of political routes on their way to the White House. The offices they held immediately before the presidency, however, have been relatively limited.

Last Political Office before the Presidency

Over the course of the nation's development, presidents usually have come to the White House directly from high public office. (See Table 3-1.) Typical positions include the vice presidency, appointive executive office, state governorships, and Senate seats. Yet, from one era to the next in U.S. political history, particular circumstances as well as general changes in American politics have favored one office over another as a stepping stone to the presidency.

The office most often held immediately before the presidency is that of vice president. Thirteen of the thirty-nine presidents followed this pattern. Of that thirteen, however, nine moved into the nation's highest political office as a result of the death or resignation of the incumbent rather than by winning that position on their own.[12] Only John Adams, Thomas Jefferson, and Martin Van Buren ran for and won the presidency while still vice president. Richard Nixon was also a vice president but did not move directly to the presidency. He was nominated in 1960 while serving as Eisenhower's vice president but was defeated in the 1960 presidential contest by John Kennedy. Not until 1968, after an unsuccessful attempt to win the California governorship in 1962 and a period of practicing law in New York City, was he ultimately elected president.[13]

Twelve persons—including four generals, Washington, Taylor, Grant, and Eisenhower—served in appointive federal office before becoming president. Six of those holding civilian offices came from foreign affairs positions: James Madison, James Monroe, and John Quincy Adams served as secretary of state; Taft was secretary of war; and William Henry Harrison and Buchanan held diplomatic posts. The two other presidents who previously served in appointive civilian federal office were Franklin Pierce (U.S. district attorney for New Hampshire) and Hoover (secretary of commerce). This career pattern, however, is distinctly a product of the political past: of the former federal appointees, only Taft and Hoover and two military figures, Grant and Eisenhower, served as president since the Civil War.

The office from which persons most often have moved to the presidency since the Civil War is a governorship. Of the eight chief executives who were governors, only one, James K. Polk, served before the Civil War. The period in which former governors most often became president was 1876-1932, from the election of Hayes to the election of Franklin Roosevelt. (During that time, Cleveland, McKinley, and Wilson were elected.) After FDR died in 1944, more than thirty years passed before another governor won the presidency: Jimmy Carter was elected in 1976 and Reagan in 1980 (although neither held the position of governor at the time of their election).

The final source of presidents has been the Congress: five were members of the Senate—Andrew Jackson, James Garfield, Benjamin Harrison, Warren Harding, and John Kennedy—and one, Abraham Lincoln, was a member of the House of Representatives. (Lincoln served as a one-term representative in the 1840s and lost to Stephen A. Douglas in his bid for a Senate seat in 1858, two years before being elected president.) Although the time span in which senators became president is broad, the office was particularly important as a recruiting ground for chief executives in the period from FDR's death until Carter's election. Kennedy is the only person to have gone directly to the presidency from the Senate in that era; but Harry Truman, Lyndon Johnson, and Richard Nixon served in the Senate before moving to the vice presidency and then becoming president. Moreover, two losing presidential candidates since 1960, Barry Goldwater in 1964 and George McGovern in 1972, were senators at the time of their nomination, and Vice President Hubert Humphrey, the unsuccessful Democratic presidential candidate in 1968, was a prominent senator before being chosen by Lyndon Johnson as his running mate in 1964. Walter Mondale was also a senator when he was tapped for the vice presidency by Jimmy Carter in 1976.

Several factors have increased the importance of the Senate as a recruiting ground for presidents. The focus of American politics has tended to

Table 3-1   Last Political Office Held by U.S. Presidents before the Presidency

Office	President	Year became president
Vice president		
Succeeded to presidency[a]	Tyler (W. H. Harrison)	1841
	Fillmore (Taylor)	1850
	Johnson, A. (Lincoln)	1865
	Arthur (Garfield)	1881
	Roosevelt, T. (McKinley)	1901
	Coolidge (Harding)	1923
	Truman (F. Roosevelt)	1945
	Johnson, L. (Kennedy)	1963
	Ford (Nixon)	1974
Won presidency in own right	Adams, J.	1797
	Jefferson	1801
	Van Buren	1837
	Nixon	1969
Appointive federal office		
Military position	Washington (commander in chief)	1789
	Taylor (general)	1849
	Grant (general)	1869
	Eisenhower (supreme commander of NATO)	1953
Civilian position	Madison (secretary of state)	1809
	Monroe (secretary of state)	1817
	Adams, J. Q. (secretary of state)	1825
	Harrison, W. H. (minister to Colombia)	1841
	Pierce (U.S. district attorney for N.H.)	1853
	Buchanan (minister to Great Britain)	1857
	Taft (secretary of war)	1909
	Hoover (secretary of commerce)	1929
Governor	Polk (Tenn.)	1845

[a] Name in parentheses is the president from whom the vice president succeeded to office.

Table 3-1   (Continued)

Office	President	Year became president
Governor	Hayes (Ohio)	1877
	Cleveland (N.Y.)	1885
	McKinley (Ohio)	1897
	Wilson (N.J.)	1913
	Roosevelt, F. (N.Y.)	1933
	Carter (Ga.)	1977
	Reagan (Calif.)	1981
Congress		
Senate	Jackson (Tenn.)	1829
	Garfield (Ohio)	1881
	Harrison, B. (Ind.)	1889
	Harding (Ohio)	1921
	Kennedy (Mass.)	1961
House of Representatives	Lincoln (Ill.)	1861

shift away from the state capitals to Washington, D.C., and senators have taken greater advantage of the national news media concentrated there than have members of the House or the Supreme Court.[14] Also, senators increasingly have associated themselves with major public policies, a development that provides them great political visibility. Beyond this, the nation's greater involvement in foreign affairs since World War II naturally has placed the Senate in the public eye because of the influential role the upper chamber of Congress plays in the conduct of relations with other countries. Moreover, the six-year term of senators enables them to try for the presidency without giving up their legislative seat: of the senators who ran for the presidency in this century, only Barry Goldwater lost his place in the upper chamber because of his candidacy.[15]

Recent developments have made the vice presidency à better position from which to seek the nation's highest office. As discussed in Chapter 1, since the 1960s presidential candidates have given more consideration to how a potential vice-presidential running mate will perform in office. Moreover, chief executives have begun to assign their vice presidents duties that are more meaningful and that increase their exposure to party leaders and the general public. Eisenhower, for instance, virtually turned over to Nixon the job of political campaigning and forging ties with Republican party professionals around the nation. Johnson permitted Humphrey to continue to cultivate the friendships he had long enjoyed with Democratic chieftains. Each of these vice presidents also traveled widely abroad as representatives of the United States and received the publicity that naturally attends such globe-trotting on the nation's behalf. As a result, both men achieved what no vice president has done since Martin Van Buren in 1836: they were nominated as their party's presidential candidate while serving in the nation's number two position. Although both were subsequently defeated in the general election (Nixon by Kennedy and Humphrey by Nixon), both races were extremely close, sufficiently so that the vice presidency now can be viewed as a potential steppingstone to the nation's highest political office.[16]

Governors no longer hold as crucial a position in the presidential selection process as they did when, as heads of state delegations, they negotiated at the national convention with their peers to choose the party's nominee (who frequently turned out to be a governor). Another handicap facing recent governors who aspire to the presidency is that only those from states with large cities that serve as communications centers for the nation, such as New York, Los Angeles, and Chicago, receive as much publicity as national officials in Washington, D.C. In addition, governors have no responsibilities of consequence in foreign affairs and frequently do not appear well-versed in such matters. They also are more tied to their home states (particularly when the state legislature is in session) than are senators and vice presidents, who are expected to move freely about the country. Finally, many governors serve short stints in office—in some cases because of legal limitations on their tenure, in others because they fail to meet public expectations that they will solve major domestic problems without increasing taxes. They therefore find it difficult to become sufficiently well known to be viable presidential candidates. All these factors have worked in recent years to the disadvantage of governors seeking the presidency.

Carter's election in 1976 and Reagan's bid for the nomination that year and election in 1980 indicate, however, that governors possess some advantages as candidates, particularly if they are *not* occupying that office at the time they seek the presidency. Both men were free to devote themselves full-time to the demanding task of winning the nomination, an opportunity not available to senators with heavy legislative duties who sought the presidency in both of those years (for example, Democrats Frank Church and Henry Jackson in 1976 and Republicans Howard Baker and Robert Dole in 1980). Both Carter and Reagan also benefited from the recent anti-Washington mood of the voters, which has made them receptive to candidates who had not served in a national office. Citizen concern with the burgeoning costs of government and the problems of controlling the federal bureaucracy (the subject of Chapter 7) could continue to make governors attractive presidential candidates: they can claim valuable executive experience in managing large public enterprises and thousands of state government employees in contrast to a senator's essentially legislative duties and management of a small personal staff. Finally, the decline in the public's concern over foreign affairs compared with the domestic economy in recent years may counteract the advantages senators held over governors as presidential candidates before the Vietnam War ended.

It is probable that the offices of vice president, senator, and governor will continue to be principal recruiting grounds for presidential candidates.[17] The same is not true, however, of appointive federal positions. The attainment of such positions fails to demonstrate that the appointees are capable of winning broad support in an important electoral contest. Moreover, cabinet officials carry other kinds of political liabilities: they have short tenures based entirely upon the pleasure of the president, and they have lost much of their power and prestige in recent years to members of the White House staff.[18] In addition, presidents tend not to appoint to important executive positions persons with an independent political following that might threaten the chief executive's own popularity. (President Kennedy, for example, decided not to appoint Adlai Stevenson as his secretary of state.) No cabinet official since Hoover has moved directly to the presidency—strong evidence of the barriers federal appointees face when considering a bid for the presidency.

Social Backgrounds of U.S. Presidents

Although there is no single indicator of social status upon which all Americans would agree, occupation is probably the most important criterion for social ranking in the United States.[19] Moreover, the occupation of a person's father provides a reasonably accurate picture of his or her class origins. By analyzing such origins, one can determine the extent to which family background has provided U.S. presidents social advantage. Family origins also indicate whether presidents have had political advantage, that is, whether they come from families whose other members occupied important political positions.

Family Origins

Four American families alone produced eight American presidents (one-fifth of the total).[20] Included were John Adams and his son John Quincy Adams; James Madison and Zachary Taylor, who had grandparents in common; William Henry Harrison and his grandson Benjamin Harrison; and the cousins Theodore and Franklin Roosevelt. Other presidents from politically prominent families include John Tyler and Franklin Pierce, whose fathers were governors of Virginia and New Hampshire, respectively; William Howard Taft, the son of a secretary of war, attorney general, and ambassador to Austria and Russia; and John Kennedy, whose father chaired the Securities and Exchange Commission and was ambassador to Great Britain.

Besides the family political tradition, these twelve presidents also came from a high social class; most of their fathers were wealthy farmers and planters, businessmen, or professionals. The same was true of other chief executives who came from a similar social background but whose fathers did not hold high political office. George Washington, Thomas Jefferson, and James Monroe were sons of wealthy farmers who held lesser political offices: the fathers of Washington and Jefferson were county sheriff and state legislator, respectively, and Monroe's father was a circuit judge. The fathers of three presidents were ministers: Chester A. Arthur (Episcopalian), Grover Cleveland (Presbyterian), and Woodrow Wilson (Presbyterian). Although these sons of clergymen may not have been as economically and politically advantaged as the sons of wealthier men, their family origin must be considered upper class if social prestige is taken into account. The same is true of Warren Harding, whose father was a country doctor. Thus, nineteen presidents were from politically or socially prominent families (including those whose fathers were professional men)—almost half of those who have served in the White House.

The remaining chief executives came from diverse backgrounds. Those most socially disadvantaged were Andrew Johnson, whose father held a variety of jobs including janitor and porter in an inn, and four other presidents who were born in log cabins—Millard Fillmore and James Buchanan, sons of poor dirt farmers, Abraham Lincoln, whose father worked at both farming and carpentry, and James Garfield, the son of a canal construction worker.[21] Three more recent presidents—Eisenhower, Nixon, and Reagan—were the sons of poor men who tried numerous jobs without much success. Eisenhower's father was a mechanic in a creamery for a time; Nixon's father was a streetcar conductor in Columbus, Ohio, before moving to California; and Reagan's father worked on and off as a shoe salesman. Three other chief executives— Jackson, Hayes, and Hoover—were born after the death of their fathers and were raised by relatives who were better off than their own parents. (The fathers of Jackson and Hayes were dirt farmers; Hoover's father was a blacksmith.)

The remaining presidents were born into middle-class families. Van Buren's father kept a tavern and Coolidge's, a store. Polk, Grant, and McKinley were sons of a surveyor, a tanner, and an ironmonger, respectively. The fathers of three recent presidents—Truman, Johnson, and Carter— combined farming with dealing in livestock, real estate, and peanuts, respectively. Gerald Ford was adopted and raised by his mother's second husband, who was in the paint and lumber business. (Ford, born Leslie King, Jr., was also given his stepfather's name.)

Although presidents have come from diverse backgrounds, those with upper-class origins have been the most prevalent. (Table 3-2 summarizes this information.) The most noticeable pattern appears in the earliest stage of U.S. political history, from the administrations of Washington through John

Quincy Adams, who was elected in 1824. All six chief executives who served during this period came from socially, and in many cases politically, prominent families. This was also the period during which presidential candidates were nominated by congressional caucus.

After both political parties adopted the national nominating convention in the early 1830s, the picture changed. Although some presidents from prominent families continued to serve in office (John Tyler and Zachary Taylor, for example), others from a much different background began to make it to the White House. The five presidents who came from the humblest origins—Fillmore, Buchanan, Lincoln, Johnson, and Garfield—are concentrated in the period 1850-1880. No generalizations can be made, however, about twentieth-century presidents, who come from distinctly upper-class families (the two Roosevelts, Taft, and Kennedy) as well as working-class ones (Eisenhower, Nixon, and Reagan).

Ethnic and Religious Background

Whereas the family occupational origins of U.S. presidents have been relatively diverse, their ethnic backgrounds have been comparatively similar. Of the thirty-nine persons who have occupied the White House, thirty-four have had ancestors who came from some part of the British Isles—England, Scotland, Ireland, or Wales. In some instances, their heritages are a mixture of these nationalities—Scotch-Irish or English-Scotch-Irish. Of the five other presidents, three—Van Buren and the two Roosevelts—were of Dutch ancestry. Two other chief executives, Hoover and Eisenhower, trace their roots to Switzerland and Germany, respectively. Thus, all American presidents have had a European lineage, and even more specifically, a northern and western one; none has come from southern or eastern Europe.

Although Article VI of the U.S. Constitution specifically outlaws a religious test for any national office, including the presidency, only one president, John Kennedy, a Roman Catholic, has not been of the Protestant faith. Moreover, within that broad category, the Episcopalian, Presbyterian, and Unitarian churches have been overrepresented in relation to the size of their national membership. Although some presidents have belonged to the Methodist and Baptist churches, the large memberships of these two religious groups have been underrepresented in the presidency. No Lutheran or Mormon has ever been elected to the White House.

The presidents' ethnic backgrounds reflect the nation's historical experience with groups migrating to the United States. Immigrants generally have been forced to start at the bottom of the economic ladder and over the years to work up to the higher-status occupations. Because immigrants from the British Isles arrived first in this country, they have been the most socially advantaged throughout the nation's history. The same has been true in the political arena. Members of the newer immigrant groups have been initially successful in winning office at the lower levels of the political system (that is,

Table 3-2   Social Backgrounds of U.S. Presidents, by Father's
Occupation

Class and occupation	President	Year became president
Upper class		
Prosperous farmers and planters	Washington	1789
	Adams, J.	1797
	Jefferson	1801
	Madison	1809
	Monroe	1817
	Adams, J. Q.	1825
	Harrison, W. H.	1841
	Tyler	1841
Professionals		
Ministers	Arthur (Episcopalian)	1881
	Cleveland (Presbyterian)	1885, 1893
	Wilson (Presbyterian)	1913
Other	Pierce (general)	1853
	Harrison, B. (lieutenant colonel)	1889
	Taft (lawyer)	1909
	Harding (physician)	1921
Prosperous businessmen	Roosevelt, T.	1901
	Roosevelt, F.	1933
	Kennedy	1961
Civil servants	Taylor (collector of internal revenue)	1849

cities and counties), where their fellow ethnics have been geographically concentrated. Only recently have many people from eastern and southern Europe been able to win the statewide offices of governor or senator, from which U.S. presidents typically have been recruited. As more and more of the newer immigrants become governors and senators, a larger pool of such candidates will be created, a development that in time probably will be reflected in the nomination and election of more non-British chief executives.

The religious backgrounds of U.S. presidents are linked to other factors. Most immigrants from the British Isles, particularly the English and Scottish,

Table 3-2 (Continued)

Class and occupation	President	Year became president
Middle class		
Small businessmen	Van Buren (tavern owner)	1837
	Coolidge (storekeeper)	1923
	Ford (owner of lumber and paint business)	1974
Small landowners	Truman	1945
	Johnson, L.	1963
	Carter	1977
Tradesmen	Polk (surveyor)	1845
	Grant (tanner)	1869
	McKinley (ironmonger)	1897
Working class		
Dirt Farmers	Jackson	1829
	Fillmore	1850
	Buchanan	1857
	Hayes	1877
	Lincoln	1861
Other	Johnson, A. (janitor-porter)	1865
	Garfield (canal worker)	1881
	Hoover (blacksmith)	1829
	Eisenhower (mechanic)	1953
	Nixon (streetcar conductor)	1969
	Reagan (shoe salesman)	1981

belong to Protestant churches. The disproportionate number of Episcopalian, Presbyterian, and Unitarian presidents indicates that members of these denominations tend to come from the upper social strata of American society, from which so many presidents have been recruited. The underrepresentation of Baptists and Methodists and the complete absence of Mormons in the presidency have to do with their regional distribution. In recent years, few presidents have come from the South, where many Baptists and Methodists live;[22] and none has come from the Mountain states, where Mormons are concentrated.

Geographic Origins

U.S. presidents have come from a number of regions of the nation.[23] In the early years, they were recruited primarily from the South: of the first five chief executives—Washington, Adams, Jefferson, Madison, and Monroe—only Adams was not from Virginia. In the period before and immediately after the Civil War, more presidents came from border states: Jackson, Polk, and Johnson, for example, were from Tennessee; Taylor was from Kentucky. After the Civil War the Midwest increasingly became a source of chief executives: three successive presidents, Grant, Hayes, and Garfield, traced their roots to Ohio, as did McKinley, Taft, and Harding. Another major recruiting ground, the Northeast, has furnished chief executives throughout the nation's history, from the election of John Adams in 1796 until John Kennedy's victory in 1960. Of the thirteen chief executives who came from this most populous region of the country, six were from New York (Van Buren, Fillmore, Arthur, Cleveland, and the two Roosevelts), and four were from Massachusetts (the two Adamses, Coolidge, and Kennedy).

Thus, U.S. presidents have come disproportionately from certain states. Five states—New York, Ohio, Virginia, Massachusetts, and Tennessee—have furnished twenty-four of the thirty-nine chief executives. Thirty-four states have yet to see one of their residents make it to the White House. The western region of the United States has been particularly underrepresented: no president has been chosen from a mountain state, and only Nixon and Reagan have been from the Pacific Coast area (Nixon grew up and spent his pre-Washington years in California, and Reagan spent his years in the entertainment business there).

The geographic origins of U.S. chief executives reflect both the history and the procedures of presidential politics. Many early incumbents were recruited from Virginia because of that state's size and its political prominence and because, under the congressional caucus system of choosing candidates, the Republican party nominated successively three native sons—Jefferson, Madison, and Monroe. With the demise of the congressional caucus and the adoption of the national convention, the process broadened to include candidates from other parts of the country. Before the Civil War, party leaders tried to bridge the division between the northern and southern states over slavery by choosing candidates from border states. When the trauma of the Civil War subsided, those leaders turned increasingly to the Midwest and Northeast, the two regions that contained large, competitive two-party states such as Ohio and New York. Candidates from these states possessed certain political advantages. They frequently occupied a governor's post, considered to be a good training ground for the presidency, and headed the state delegation to the nominating convention in which "favorite-son" candidacies had an advantage. Nominating conventions often chose candidates from the large states under the assumption that voters in such states would support their favorite-son candidate in the general election and thereby deliver a large bloc of electoral votes to that party's presidential aspirant.

Recent presidential contests indicate, however, that the regional origins of the candidate are no longer as important as they once were. Jimmy Carter, a resident of the medium-size, politically noncompetitive state of Georgia, managed to overcome these traditional handicaps to become the first president from the South since before the Civil War. Moreover, two recently defeated candidates, Republican Barry Goldwater in 1964 and Democrat George McGovern in 1972, were identified with small states, Arizona and South Dakota, respectively. The diminished importance of regional origin may well be a result of a broader phenomenon: the increasing nationalization of presidential politics whereby candidates are evaluated by their roles in events and issues that transcend the concerns of particular states or regions.

Occupation

Although the family occupational backgrounds of the presidents are fairly broad, their own careers have been much less diverse.[24] Twenty-four of the thirty-nine chief executives practiced law at some time in their lives. Occupations of other presidents include the military (William Henry Harrison, Taylor, Grant, and Eisenhower), education (Wilson and Lyndon Johnson), journalism (Harding and Kennedy), engineering (Hoover), and entertainment (Reagan). Two presidents were gentleman farmers (Washington and Madison), and Carter combined farming with his family peanut business after abandoning his career as a Navy engineer to return home to Georgia when his father died. Two presidents who pursued less prestigious careers before entering public life were Truman, who, in addition to trying his hand at farming, was a timekeeper on a railroad, and Andrew Johnson, who was a tailor.

It is not particularly surprising that so many presidents were lawyers, since that profession is closely linked with a political career. As political scientist Donald Matthews points out, lawyers are the "high priests" of American politics for several reasons.[25] Law is a prestigious occupation entailing interpersonal negotiation and conciliation as well as verbal and argumentative faculties, skills that are of great value in the give-and-take of the political process. Moreover, many people go into the law because they consider it a natural preparation for public life. (As Woodrow Wilson put it: "The profession I chose was politics; the profession I entered was law. I entered the one because I thought it would lead to the other.") The law is also, as Max Weber describes it, a "dispensable" profession; because it does not change as much as other professional fields, such as medicine and engineering, lawyers who leave public life can return to the practice of law fairly easily.[26]

Although the law is a natural profession for future presidents, in recent years fewer chief executives have come from that occupation. Of the eight who have served as president since World War II, only two (Nixon and Ford) were lawyers; Truman, Eisenhower, Kennedy, Johnson, Carter, and Reagan came from a wide variety of other occupational backgrounds. As increasing numbers of people from nonlegal backgrounds (business and teaching in particular) become senators and governors, the positions from which today's presidents often are recruited, still more presidents without legal training may occupy the White House.

Education

Most U.S. presidents have been well educated. Only nine of the thirty-nine did not have any formal instruction at a college or university. Moreover, the trend has been toward more college-trained chief executives. Of the sixteen who have occupied the presidency in this century, only one, Harry Truman, did not attend an institution of higher learning.[27]

The universities and colleges presidents attended are among the most highly regarded in the nation. The country's most prestigious institution, Harvard, leads the list with five chief executives as alumni—the two Adamses, the two Roosevelts, and Kennedy. Alma maters of other presidents include major private universities such as Princeton (Madison and Wilson), Yale (Taft), Stanford (Hoover), and a wide variety of prestigious, smaller private colleges, such as Allegheny (McKinley), Amherst (Coolidge), Bowdoin (Pierce), Dickinson (Buchanan), Hampden-Sidney (William Henry Harrison), Kenyon (Hayes), Union College (Arthur), and Williams (Garfield). Although less prevalent than private institutions, well-known, public universities also figure among the alma maters of the presidents: Miami of Ohio (Benjamin Harrison), the University of Michigan (Ford), the University of North Carolina (Polk), William and Mary (Jefferson, Monroe, and Tyler), and two service academies, Annapolis (Carter) and West Point (Grant and Eisenhower).

The fact that so many presidents attended prestigious institutions of higher learning probably has less to do with their career aspirations than with either parental guidance, in upper-class families, or the desire of many presidents from a modest social background to improve their economic and social positions through education. (A classic example of the latter phenomenon was James Garfield, the son of a canal construction worker who died when Garfield was two; Garfield managed, after a long struggle for education, to graduate from Williams College and then become principal of a church school before being admitted to the bar and eventually going into politics.) More presidents attended private rather than public educational institutions because private schools were established earlier, particularly in the northeastern states (such as New York and Massachusetts, which have produced a total of ten presidents) and the midwestern states (such as Ohio, which has produced six presidents). Several recent presidents, including Eisenhower, Johnson, Ford, and Carter, attended public institutions, a trend that may become more pronounced in the future. The selection of more presidents from states in which public universities are more prevalent than private ones (such as the western states) would contribute to this trend.

Summary of Social Characteristics

The typical American president has been a Protestant (generally from a high-status denomination), born of a relatively prosperous family, whose ancestors came to the United States from the British Isles. The presidents themselves (including those from modest backgrounds) generally have been well educated at prestigious private institutions, and many have practiced law before entering public life. Their backgrounds are quite similar to those of two other groups of national political elites, justices of the U.S. Supreme Court and U.S. senators.[28]

Such a background is not, however, a prerequisite for the presidency, as recent chief executives prove. John Kennedy was a Roman Catholic, and other recent chief executives were from Protestant denominations not considered to be upper class. Eisenhower's parents were Mennonites; Reagan adopted his mother's Protestant denomination, Christian (his father was a Catholic); and the parents of Truman, Johnson, and Carter were Baptists. Truman attended no college at all, and Lyndon Johnson, Nixon, and Reagan were students at three relatively unknown ones (Southwest State Teachers College, Whittier College, and Eureka College, respectively). Moreover, six recent presidents—Truman, Eisenhower, Kennedy, Johnson, Carter, and Reagan—never practiced law.

The backgrounds of persons who have made it to the White House in recent years differ considerably from those of their predecessors. As members of traditionally disadvantaged groups—blacks, women, immigrants from Mexico, eastern and southern Europe, and the Far East—rise through the hierarchy of political offices, the backgrounds of presidents may differ still more.

Psychological Characteristics of U.S. Presidents

It is admittedly difficult to analyze the psychological characteristics of individuals. As Fred Greenstein points out, psychologists view personality as a complex phenomenon, involving diverse factors such as how people adapt to the world around them by screening reality (cognition), how they express their feelings (affect), and how they relate to others (identification).[29] Moreover, personality is "inferred" rather than directly observed: it is a construct introduced by the analyst to account for the regularities in a person's behavior. For these reasons, examinations of psychological characteristics are much more uncertain and subjective than are examinations of political and social backgrounds.

Despite these problems, political scientists and historians in recent years have tried to use psychological concepts to help explain why political figures behave as they do, a field of study that has come to be known as *psychobiography*. Several presidents, including Woodrow Wilson, Richard Nixon, and Lyndon Johnson have been the subjects of such biographies.[30] These studies tend to concentrate on the childhood experiences of the subjects, particularly their relationships with their fathers and mothers, and how such experiences shaped their perceptions of themselves, their sense of or lack of self-confidence, and their psychological needs.

Two political scientists, Erwin Hargrove and James David Barber, have gone a step further and categorized several presidents by their general approach to the office.[31] Both distinguish, for example, between presidents of "action" and presidents of "restraint." "Active" presidents attempt to use fully the potential powers of the presidency and invest a great deal of personal energy in the job. In contrast, "passive" presidents (those of "restraint") do not have the inclination or ability to exercise political power and devote less time and effort to being president.

Barber also distinguishes between the "positive" and "negative" dimensions of their performance. Positive presidents enjoy political life and derive a great deal of personal satisfaction from serving in the office. Negative presidents do not experience pleasure from being president but serve out of compulsion or a sense of duty to their country.

In addition to the effects of childhood experiences, psychobiographies also examine other aspects of presidents' personalities. Some have assessed individuals' political values or ideology: Hargrove singles out their beliefs about public policy and the proper behavior of a political leader; Barber stresses what he calls their "world view," conceptions of "social causality, human nature, and the central moral conflicts of their time." [32] Both Hargrove and Barber also consider features of political "style." Hargrove emphasizes what he terms "mental traits," that is, qualities of mind and temperament. Barber includes three types of political roles required of a president: how he uses *rhetoric* to speak directly or through the media to large audiences; how he handles *personal relations*, face-to-face encounters with other politicans and members of private groups; and how he does his *homework*, his method of organizing the endless flow of details that come to his desk for decisions.

Although all these matters are important to understanding a president's personality and political style, Barber emphasizes as most important the early childhood experiences that shape a person's "character," his "basic stance" toward life and the presidency. That stance includes how active or inactive he is and whether he gives the impression that he enjoys or does not enjoy political life. Using these criteria, Barber develops four character patterns familiar in psychological research: active-positive, active-negative, passive-positive, and passive-negative. The following discussion analyzes recent presidents within these four categories.

Active-Positive

Active-positive presidents vigorously exercise political power and appear to have fun doing so. Their major goal is to improve the conditions of life for U.S. citizens, using government to accomplish that result. Thus active-positive chief executives exert leadership over Congress, chart new directions in public policy, and take actions that stretch the powers of the presidency.

Active-positive presidents have a fundamental sense of confidence in themselves and in their ability to achieve success in life. Although they often have only limited success in their early political careers, they demonstrate a capacity for personal growth as they ascend the political ladder to higher office. Included as part of that growth is a sense of political vision about what the country needs at the time they are in office, along with the ability to transmit that vision to others with whom they are associated in public life.

Active-positive presidents are goal-oriented, but they are also flexible in their pursuit of those goals. If a particular policy or course of action does not appear to be working, they are willing to change it or to abandon it altogether rather than suffer a costly political defeat. Active-positive chief executives tend to be pragmatic, willing to compromise to achieve their ends. They also appreciate the necessity of conflict in politics and are willing to try to understand and to deal with their political opponents.

Barber categorizes several recent presidents as active-positive. Included in the initial edition of his book are Franklin Roosevelt, Harry Truman, and John Kennedy. In his 1977 second edition he added Gerald Ford and Jimmy Carter. Of these five incumbents, Roosevelt probably best exemplifies the basic psychological traits of an active-positive president.

Born in 1882, the only child of wealthy parents of Dutch background, *Franklin Roosevelt* grew up on the family estate in the Hudson River Valley in New York State and did not go to school until he was fourteen. Doted over by a mother who kept him in dresses until he was five years old and by a father, much older than his mother, who introduced him to the joys of ice-boating and sailing, Roosevelt had a childhood that could be described only as serene and secure. He was the object of great affection from his family and friends and responded with a trust and love for others.

Roosevelt's education was what one would expect of a family with a patrician tradition. He went to a prep school (Groton) whose headmaster, Endicott Peabody, instilled in him "manly Christian character" and an upper-class sense of social responsibility for the less privileged in society. He then went to Harvard, where he was editor in chief of the school newspaper, the *Harvard Crimson,* and to Columbia law school. In 1907 he joined a conservative New York law firm.

Bored with the law, Roosevelt announced to his fellow law clerks that he intended to go into politics, following a career path similar to that of another Roosevelt—his much-admired cousin Theodore. He intended to become a New York legislator, assistant secretary of the navy, governor of New York, and, if luck shone on him, president of the United States. By 1910 he had reached the first office, and in 1913, at age thirty-one, he accepted Teddy's old job as assistant secretary of the Navy, in which capacity he served for seven years. After an unsuccessful race as the Democratic vice-presidential candidate in 1920 and a tragic bout with polio, which he contracted in 1921, he eventually followed his political schedule, becoming governor of New York in 1929 and president in 1933.

Roosevelt's political life was one of action, but he had no consistent political philosophy beyond the sense of responsibility for the disadvantaged he had acquired at Groton. He was pragmatic and willing to experiment with new courses of action. His view of the presidency also paralleled that of his cousin Teddy: it is preeminently a place of moral leadership.

Roosevelt left a legacy of action and innovation unmatched by any other chief executive. When he came into office in March 1933, business failures were legion, 12 million Americans were unemployed, banks all over the country were closed or doing business under restrictions, and the American people had lost confidence in their leaders as well as in themselves. Counseling the nation in his inaugural address that "we have nothing to fear but fear itself," the new chief executive moved into action: a four-day bank holiday was declared, and an emergency banking bill was prepared within a day's time. During his first one hundred days in office, the nation witnessed a social and economic revolution in the form of Roosevelt's New Deal. Congress adopted a series of far-reaching government programs insuring bank deposits, providing crop payments for farmers, establishing codes of fair competition for industry, granting labor the right to organize, providing relief and jobs for the unemployed, and creating the Tennessee Valley Authority (a government corporation) to develop that region. With these measures and other programs that followed (Social Security, public housing, unemployment compensation, and the like), Roosevelt established the concept of the "positive state" in America—a government that had the obligation to take the leadership in providing for the welfare of all the people.

Roosevelt did not ignore relations with other countries. Soon after he took office he extended diplomatic recognition to the Soviet Union, embarked on a Good Neighbor policy toward South America, and pushed through the Reciprocal Trade Program, which lowered tariffs with other nations. In his second term, FDR began the slow and difficult task of preparing the nation for its eventual entry into World War II by funneling aid to the Allies, trading fifty "over-age" destroyers to Britain for naval and air bases in the British West Indies, Argentia (Newfoundland), and Bermuda, and obtaining the passage of the nation's first peacetime draft. As FDR himself put it, after Pearl Harbor "Dr. New Deal" became "Dr. Win-the-War," taking over the economic control of the war effort granted him by Congress and establishing the victorious strategy of concentrating on defeating Germany before Japan. Also while the hostilities were still going on, he took the leadership in setting up the United Nations. (Unfortunately, he died before he could see the organization established in 1945.)

Roosevelt was an innovator whose actions shaped the presidential office itself. He was not only an effective legislative leader but also a skilled administrator responsible for a thorough reorganization of the executive branch, including the creation of the Executive Office of the President (examined in Chapter 7). Most important, FDR was the most effective molder of public opinion the nation has ever known. He pioneered the use of "fireside chats" over radio to explain his actions to the people. In addition, he raised the presidential press conference to new heights as a tool of public persuasion. As a man who could take idealistic goals, reduce them to manageable and practical programs, and then sell them to Congress and the American people, Roosevelt has no peer.

Despite this record of achievement, Roosevelt made some mistakes, particularly after his sweeping electoral victory in 1936. He was unsuccessful in defeating several incumbent southern members of Congress in the Democratic primaries in 1938 (discussed further in Chapter 5). Moreover, when he tried to expand the size of the Supreme Court to add persons who shared his views, the public and Congress reacted against his "court packing" plan (discussed further in Chapter 8). Thus, active-positive presidents in their zeal sometimes underestimate the force of custom and public expectations about what is proper and improper in the realm of American politics.

Active-Negative

According to Barber, active-negative presidents also invest a great deal of energy in being president, but unlike their active-positive counterparts, they do not appear to derive enjoyment from serving in the office. Rather than exercising political power for the benefit of the citizenry, active-negative chief executives seem to seek power for its own sake. There is a compulsiveness to their behavior, as if they are driven to pursue a political career rather than doing it because the career gives them pleasure.

Active-negative presidents have a poor self-image and lack a sense of self-confidence, traits caused by painful childhood experiences. In fact, they seek power and domination over others as compensation for their own lack of self-esteem. They often achieve considerable success in life, including political success, but their triumphs bring them no real sense of satisfaction. Instead, they feel compelled to seek still further accomplishment.

Active-negative presidents seek definite political goals and tend to be single-minded in the pursuit of such goals. Although they are sometimes willing to compromise in order to achieve success, particularly the attainment of a political office, once in office—especially the presidency, from which there are no further political steps to climb—they often begin to believe that the policies they favor are morally right and vital to the nation's interest. In such circumstances active-negative presidents are unwilling to compromise with opponents they come to think of as their mortal enemies. Once embarked upon a policy that they believe is a matter of high principle, they continue to pursue that course of action, even if it obviously is not working. Active-negative presidents therefore tend to be their own worst enemies and to contribute ultimately to their own political failure.

The presidents Barber regards as active-negative in their political orientation include Woodrow Wilson, Herbert Hoover, Lyndon Johnson, and Richard Nixon. The following discussion of Wilson's career illustrates many of the classic features of an active-negative character.[33]

Born in Staunton, Virginia, the son of a Presbyterian minister with a large congregation, *Woodrow Wilson* had the benefit of a rich intellectual background. However, he was slow to learn: he was nine years old before he learned his alphabet and eleven before he could read. He was also frail and wore glasses, in marked contrast to his father, a tall handsome man with a commanding physical presence. Young Wilson was loved, but he was also dominated by a father who expected much of him and ridiculed him when he did not live up to his father's expectations. Surrounded early in life by girls and intimidated by the rough play of boys, the child retreated to the protection provided by his mother, a quiet, gentle woman.

At sixteen Wilson went off to Davidson College, a small Presbyterian school in North Carolina. He experienced homesickness, his health failed, and he returned home and stayed there for more than a year until he entered Princeton at eighteen. There his shyness initially prevented his acquiring many friends, but by his sophomore year he found a niche for himself: he organized the Liberal Debating Club, wrote its constitution, and became its most prominent member. Eventually, like Roosevelt, he went on to become the editor of his school paper, the *Princetonian.* He also wrote an outstanding paper on cabinet government in the United States, which was published by the *International Review,* then edited by his enemy-to-be, Henry Cabot Lodge.

Later Wilson attended the University of Virginia Law School but withdrew and, after practicing for only one year in Atlanta, returned to school to attend Johns Hopkins University, from which he received a doctorate in political science. Continuing his scholarly career, he taught at Bryn Mawr College in Pennsylvania and at Wesleyan College in Connecticut, where he was also a successful football coach. He then returned to Princeton, where he became one of the outstanding lecturers on the campus. Eventually, he became president of Princeton.

Wilson made an auspicious start as president of Princeton by taking the leadership in developing a new curriculum, reorganizing academic departments, and modifying its tutorial system. He met his first defeat, however, when he tried to abolish the traditional undergraduate eating clubs and replace them with residential quadrangles. He subsequently got into a bitter struggle with Andrew West, the dean of the graduate school, over the development of a graduate center; when Wilson refused to compromise on that issue, he lost the argument. At this point he decided to abandon academic life for a public one; in 1908, he won the governorship of New Jersey, and from that post he went to the presidency five years later.

Unlike Roosevelt, Wilson suffered from insecurity, which biographers Alexander and Juliette George attribute primarily to the overwhelming domination of his father, whom he could not please but would not oppose.[34] As a result, he directed his hostility toward male figures, such as West and Lodge, who became his mortal enemies. Robert Tucker has suggested an alternative psychological explanation of Wilson's behavior—that he is a classic example of a "neurotic personality," one who forms an "idealized image" of himself to compensate for insecurity about his personal significance.[35] When Wilson began to think of that idealized image as the person he really was, he inevitably fell short of his own expectations, became dissatisfied with himself, and became hostile toward others who also refused to see him in idealized terms. Whatever the particular cause, Wilson's sense of personal inadequacy resulted in an unwillingness to compromise and a compulsion to work, coupled with dissatisfaction with his considerable achievements.

Wilson's values and world view reflected his Calvinistic background. He believed that God ordained him to be president of the United States and that his own causes were those of the Almighty. His political philosophy was a kind of Jeffersonian faith in smallness (the government should regulate large corporations) and in the innate wisdom of the common people. Wilson viewed the presidency as an office of unlimited potential and wished to convert it into a kind of prime ministership similar to that of the British, whose political and social institutions he so much admired.

Wilson used various techniques to implement his prime-minister concept of the presidency. A skilled public speaker, he was the first president since John Adams to go before the Congress in person to give his State of the Union message. He held frequent meetings with legislative leaders both at the White House and at the President's Room, seldom used before, in the Capitol. Like Jefferson, he was a powerful party chief who worked through congressional leaders and the Democratic caucus to influence legislative decisions. He also did not hesitate to take his case to the people: on one occasion, when representatives of special interests made concerted efforts to defeat a low-tariff bill he favored, Wilson made a public statement decrying the fact that "the people at large should have no lobby and be voiceless in these matters, while great bodies of astute men seek to create an artificial opinion and to overcome the interests of the public for their private profit." [36]

These techniques were highly successful as Wilson took the leadership in both domestic and foreign affairs. In his first term in office he pushed through a vast program of economic reform that lowered tariffs, raised taxes for the wealthy, created a central banking system, regulated unfair trade practices, provided low-interest loans to farmers, and established an eight-hour day for railroad employees. When the United States became involved in World War I during his second term, rather than prosecute it through unilateral executive action, Wilson went to the Congress and obtained authority to control the economic as well as the military aspects of the war. He thus was granted the power to allocate food and fuel, to license trade with the enemy, to censor the mail, to regulate the foreign language press of the country, and to operate railroads, water transportation systems, and telegraph and telephone facilities. At the end of the war he made a triumphant trip to Europe, where he assumed the leading role in the writing of the Versailles peace treaty.

Eventually, however, Wilson's sense of moral righteousness and his unwillingness to compromise caused his downfall. Conceiving the League of Nations as his contribution to a practical implementation of the teachings of Jesus Christ, he adamantly refused to accept any reservations proposed by the Senate for the League of Nations Covenant of the Treaty of Versailles. In the process he played into the hands of his archenemy, Henry Cabot Lodge, who calculated that Wilson's intransigence and personal hatred of him would be so intense that the president would reject all compromises. In the end Lodge proved to be right: spurning the advice of his wife and of close friends, such as Colonel Edward House, Wilson avowed it "better a thousand times to go down fighting than to dip your colors to dishonorable compromise." A trip to win popular support for the League ended in failure; as a result, the country whose leaders proposed the League of Nations ended up not belonging to the organization at all. Active-negative presidents can pursue courses of action that adversely affect not only their own political causes but the fortunes of the nation as well.

Passive-Positive

Passive-positive presidents are not in politics to seek power either for the betterment of the American people or to compensate for their own sense of inadequacy. Rather, they choose politics because they are, in Barber's terms, "political lovers." [37] This love is a two-way process. They genuinely enjoy people and want to help them, not by means of imaginative policies or programs, but by doing small favors, sympathizing with them, and boosting their morale. In return, passive-positive presidents seek affection from their constituents, the feeling that they are wanted and loved.

Barber suggests that passive-positive presidents have a low sense of self-esteem combined with a superficial optimism about life. They tend to place too much faith in the essential goodness of their fellow human beings and are frequently taken advantage of by people who abuse that trust. As a result, passive-positive presidents often end up disappointed and disillusioned with the world of politics.

Passive-positive individuals are "other-directed," that is, they let others set their goals in life for them. Because they tend not to have goals of their own, they find it difficult to make decisions, particularly when they receive conflicting advice. Moreover, knowing that decisions inevitably hurt some people and create hard feelings toward the person responsible, passive-positive presidents tend to postpone decision making, thereby leaving the affairs of state to drift.

In his first edition Barber used two twentieth-century presidents to illustrate passive-positive chief executives: William Howard Taft, who preceded Wilson in office, and Warren Harding, Wilson's successor. In his most recent revision, he described a third such president—Ronald Reagan.[38]

William Howard Taft well represents the passive-positive personality. Like Roosevelt and Wilson, Taft had a doting mother who showered him with love. His father, seventeen years older than his mother, was a lawyer who was given to making preachments on discipline (but who was not inclined to follow his own advice, at least as far as the young Taft was concerned). Taft's boyhood was a pleasant one; unlike Wilson, he liked physical combat and engaged in an occasional fight. Most of all, though, he was a friendly lad with a perennial smile and sunny disposition.

Taft's romance with life continued when he left home to attend Yale University. There he was taken into the exclusive Skull and Bones Club and was considered to be the most popular boy in the school. Although his father considered his extensive social life to be inconsistent with high scholarship, Taft graduated second in a class of 132. Afterwards, he attended the University of Cincinnati Law School.

Back home in southern Ohio, Taft served a short stint as a reporter covering the courts and then began a career in law and politics that eventually resulted in his being appointed a state, and later a federal, judge. He enjoyed being a referee more than an advocate in legal proceedings and set a goal for himself of appointment to the U.S. Supreme Court. However, his ambitious wife, Nellie, whom he dearly loved, steered his career away from the judiciary toward active politics.

In 1901 Taft complied with President McKinley's request to head a commission to govern the Philippines. In 1904, McKinley's successor, Theodore Roosevelt, called Taft home to be secretary of war. In that post he served as a diplomatic trouble-shooter and domestic peacemaker for the president. Taft fell under the president's spell and, at Roosevelt's urging, allowed himself to be nominated for the presidency in 1908, when Roosevelt retired from the office.

Taft had an engaging personality and found it difficult to say no to anyone, including his ambitious wife and a wide host of friends. Most of all in life, he wanted approval and love. Although he flirted with the Progressive ideas of his hero, Roosevelt, at heart Taft was a conservative with a great admiration for existing institutions and a fear of radicals and militants. He needed order and reason in his life and found them in the law. In contrast to Roosevelt, who argued that he could take any action not expressly forbidden by the Constitution or the laws, Taft held that the president possessed only those powers specifically delegated to him from those two sources. (See Chapter 8 for a more extensive discussion of this matter.)

When Roosevelt left for a trip to Africa in 1909, all was well between him and the new president. However, Taft soon began to disappoint his mentor. After making tariff reductions his first objective, he finally signed a bill giving generous concessions to domestic producers. He also was unable to arbitrate a fight between Gifford Pinchot, the conservation-minded chief of the Forest Service, and Pinchot's boss, Richard Ballinger, secretary of the interior, whom Pinchot accused of giving away public lands to private profiteers. Respecting the authority of the superior officer, Taft ultimately accepted Pinchot's resignation.

These and other incidents led Roosevelt and the Progressive wing of the Republican party to conclude that Taft was not the man to whom they could entrust their leadership. He, in turn, was horrified when Roosevelt proposed that the voters had the right to overturn judicial decisions. Roosevelt opposed Taft for the Republican nomination in 1912, and, when Taft became the nominee, Roosevelt ran against him on the Progressive ticket. The resulting split in the Republican party helped put Woodrow Wilson into the White House.

After he left the presidency, Taft was appointed to the post he had wanted all along: the chief justice of the United States. He worked harder and longer in that position than he ever did as president. In the structured judicial environment, removed from the pressures of the political arena, Taft found peace with his first love, the law.

Passive-Negative

Passive-negative presidents combine two characteristics one would *not* expect to find in the person who attains the nation's highest office: an unwillingness to invest much energy in that office and a lack of pleasure in serving.

Why then are such persons in politics at all? Barber explains that they are there because they think it is their civic duty. They serve in political life not because it gives them enjoyment but rather because they believe it is something they *ought to do.*

Passive-negative presidents have a fundamental sense of uselessness and compensate for that feeling by dutifully agreeing to work on behalf of their fellow citizens. They frequently achieve success in nonpolitical roles in society but lack the experience and inclination to perform effectively as political leaders.

Passive-negative presidents tend to dislike the conflicts that are part of political life. In the face of conflict, they are inclined to withdraw, frequently letting others do political battle for them. They stress vague principles and elements of "fair play" as a way of dealing with disagreements in political life.

Barber uses two presidents to exemplify passive-negative chief executives: Calvin Coolidge, who was elevated to the presidency in 1923 when Warren Harding died in office, and Dwight Eisenhower, the military hero of the 1940s who became president in 1953.

Dwight Eisenhower typifies the passive-negative president. Unlike Roosevelt, Wilson, or Taft, he was not born of a rich or prominent family; his father was a creamery mechanic. When Ike was six, his father moved the family of eight from Texas to Abilene, Kansas, where they lived in a house of only eight hundred square feet. Ike enjoyed physical activities, particularly sports, and seems to have been influenced primarily by his mother, a woman with a fundamentalist religious background who managed with some success to calm the boy's considerable temper.

The family's meager resources would not permit Eisenhower to go to an Ivy League college, but he won admission to West Point (after being turned down at Annapolis because he was too old) with the primary aim of continuing the athletic career he had begun in high school. Unfortunately, he injured his knee badly in a football game and was forced to give up not only that sport but baseball, track, and boxing as well. After that incident he fell into despondency and his grades suffered. He graduated sixty-first in a class of 164, hardly an indication of the prominence he would achieve in the nation's military establishment.

Eisenhower subsequently redeemed himself in the army, graduating first in a class of 275 from the Command and General Staff school and then serving on Gen. Douglas MacArthur's staff in the Philippines. Shortly after the attack on Pearl Harbor, he was assigned to the War Plans Division with the job of preparing a blueprint for the cross-channel invasion of Europe. In that capacity he came to the attention of Army Chief of Staff George Marshall, and at Marshall's suggestion President Roosevelt placed him in command of the invasion of Africa and eventually of the victorious Allied forces in Europe.

As the nation's principal war hero, Eisenhower in 1948 was subjected to pressures by many people to run for president, including some Democrats who were disillusioned with Truman. He declared, however, that he had no interest in a political career and instead became army chief of staff and then president of Columbia University, a position for which he was ill-suited. In 1950, against his wishes, he accepted President Truman's request to become supreme commander of the North Atlantic Treaty Organization. Persuaded by Republican politicians to run for president in 1952, he won easily over the Democratic candidate, Adlai Stevenson.

Eisenhower's main personal assets were an extremely pleasant personality that radiated optimism, an exceptional organizational ability, and the facility to persuade people with differing viewpoints to work together. He was not highly ambitious and accepted positions not for his personal aggrandizement but out of a deep sense of duty to his country. His primary values were a belief in individualism and voluntary action and a marked dislike for the coercion of big government. His conception of himself as president was that of a nonpartisan leader bringing unity to the nation.

Eisenhower's performance in office reflected his background and values. He refused to play the role of party leader, assigning that task to his vice president, Richard Nixon. He sought both to make Congress a coequal branch of government, rather than the inferior institution he felt it had become under Roosevelt and Truman, and to return to the states the powers that the national government had assumed. As an administrator of the executive branch, Eisenhower implemented methods he had learned in the military: an extensive delegation of authority to others and a rigid chain of command.

In keeping with his conservative political philosophy and passive conception of the presidency, Eisenhower did not attempt new ventures in public policy. Yet he made no effort to turn back the clock by eliminating the major features of Democratic rule of the previous twenty years. He moved cautiously within the established framework, proposing an increase in Social Security benefits, eliminating segregation in the nation's capital, and increasing the country's military commitments around the world.

Summary of Psychological Characteristics

In summary, active-positive, active-negative, passive-positive, and passive-negative are Barber's conceptions of the different types of twentieth-century presidents. (See Table 3-3.) As stated at the outset of this discussion, however, analyses of an individual's psychological characteristics are imprecise and subjective, and other scholars have raised serious questions about how accurately Barber has classified several presidents, including Eisenhower, Ford, Carter, and Reagan. (The last chapter of the book examines this matter in detail.)

Although Barber primarily emphasizes a president's character in influencing his performance in office, he does take other factors into account. He points, for example, to the connection between the "climate of expectations" and the kind of person who is chosen as president.[39] At times the American people demand a "sense of progress and action" and so turn to activists such as Roosevelt and Wilson to direct the nation. At other times, they want "reassurance," a feeling that things will be all right, or a sense of "legitimacy," a belief that the office is occupied by a person who properly represents the nation's ideals; in such circumstances they may prefer a passive chief executive, such as Taft or Eisenhower. There is also a rough cyclical pattern to presidential types: activists inherit problems that passive chief executives ignore, and passive presidents slow down the excesses of the activists.

How a president performs in office depends, therefore, not only on his own personal preferences but also on public expectations of his performance. Further, as Barber notes, a president is also affected by the "power situation" he faces—his relationships with major interest groups, his own and the opposition political party, the courts, and Congress.[40] He must also deal with

Table 3-3 Barber's Categorization of Twentieth-Century Presidents

Energy directed toward the presidency	Attitude toward the presidency	
	Positive	Negative
Active	F. D. Roosevelt, Truman, Kennedy, Ford, Carter	Wilson, Hoover, Johnson, Nixon
Passive	Taft, Harding, Reagan	Coolidge, Eisenhower

Source: James David Barber, *The Presidential Character,* 3d ed. (Englewood Cliffs, N.J.: Prentice-Hall, 1985).

Note: Barber's analysis includes all twentieth-century presidents except McKinley, who was assassinated in 1901, and his successor, Theodore Roosevelt, who served until 1909, when Taft became president.

opposition forces from within the executive branch itself. (These matters are explored in subsequent chapters of the book.)

Conclusion

For many reasons, the kinds of people who have served in the presidential office have changed since Washington's day. One reason is the nature of the selection process itself. Initially, congressional caucuses that nominated presidential candidates tended to choose persons from socially (and often politically) advantaged families. When national conventions replaced that system, persons from a broad variety of social backgrounds emerged as nominees for the nation's highest office. The conventions' traditional choice of favorite sons from large, politically competitive states, in turn, has occurred less often in recent years as the results of presidential primaries, rather than deliberations among the delegates themselves, have determined who the parties would select as their nominees. The increasing demands of protracted nomination campaigns have also given an advantage to candidates not occupying any political office at the time they began their campaign.

Developments initiated by presidents themselves also have affected the kinds of persons who serve in the office. Recent presidents have assigned their vice presidents important responsibilities more often than earlier presidents did; vice presidents, therefore, have a better chance of themselves becoming serious presidential candidates. In contrast, because recent presidents have not chosen prominent political figures for their cabinet and usually treat White House staff members as more important than the department heads, the cabinet is no longer a training ground for the presidency.

Broad currents in American society also have contributed to the changing, or protean, backgrounds of U.S. presidents. The nationalization of American politics and the greater focus on foreign affairs, along with the increased importance of television coverage, especially in Washington, D.C., have given greater visibility to senators as potential presidential candidates. Fewer lawyers hold senate seats and governorships from which presidents typically are recruited; a legal background, therefore, is no longer as common in a presidential aspirant as it once was. Moreover, the trend toward attendance at public colleges and universities, especially in western states, means that a private-school background also is less common among today's chief executives.

Trends in the psychological characteristics of the presidents are not as clear, however, as trends in their political and social backgrounds. Barber's classification of presidents in this century is fairly evenly divided between positive and negative chief executives. His categorization does include considerably more active than passive presidents, particularly since Roosevelt's inauguration in 1933: only Eisenhower and Reagan have been designated as passive among the nine chief executives who have served since that time.[41]

Notes

1. Charles Gordon, "Who Can Be President of the United States: The Unresolved Enigma," *Maryland Law Review* (Winter 1968): 1-32.
2. Romney dropped out of the race early in 1968 after being unable to cope with constant pressure from the media to explain his views on Vietnam.
3. Gordon, "Who Can Be President."
4. Isidor Blum, "Is Governor Romney Eligible to Be President?" *New York Law Journal* (October 17, 1968).
5. Edward S. Corwin, *The President: Office and Powers,* 5th ed. (New York: New York University Press, 1984), 39.
6. Julian Bond was only twenty-eight when he was nominated for the vice presidency at the 1968 Democratic convention by the supporters of Eugene McCarthy, but it was a tactical move rather than a serious one (Lewis Chester, Godfrey Hodgson, and Bruce Page, *An American Melodrama: The Presidential Campaign of 1968* [New York: Viking, 1969], 590). Bond withdrew his name because he failed to meet the age requirement of thirty-five. Vice-presidential candidates must meet the qualifications of the presidency to be eligible to succeed to that office.
7. There have been forty presidencies to date but only thirty-nine presidents because Grover Cleveland served two nonconsecutive terms, 1885-1889 and 1893-1897.
8. Hugh Montgomery-Massingberd, ed., *Burke's Presidential Families of the U.S.A.* (London: Burke's Peerage, 1975), 250.

9. Ibid., 320.
10. Robert Donovan, *Conflict and Crisis: The Presidency of Harry S Truman, 1945-48* (New York: Praeger, 1977), chap. 40.
11. Van Buren's presidential aspirations did not end when he was defeated for reelection in 1840; he was an unsuccessful candidate for the Democratic nomination in 1844 and ran as the nominee of the Free Soil party in 1848 (Rexford Tugwell, *How They Became President* [New York: Simon and Schuster, 1968], 100).
12. In this century, Theodore Roosevelt, Calvin Coolidge, Harry Truman, and Lyndon Johnson were subsequently elected president on their own; Gerald Ford was nominated but not reelected.
13. Walter Mondale, who served as vice president under Jimmy Carter, went into the private practice of law after their defeat in the 1980 contest; four years later he succeeded in winning the Democratic presidential nomination but was soundly defeated in the general election by incumbent Ronald Reagan.
14. Nelson Polsby, *Congress and the Presidency,* 3d ed. (Englewood Cliffs, N.J.: Prentice-Hall, 1976), 99-102.
15. William Keech and Donald Matthews, *The Party's Choice* (Washington, D.C.: Brookings, 1976), 23.
16. At the time of this writing (spring 1987), Vice President George Bush is considered the leading candidate for the 1988 Republican presidential nomination.
17. Some major presidential candidates in recent years have come from the House of Representatives, including Democrat Morris Udall in 1976 and Republican John Anderson in 1980. House members, however, face a much more difficult problem in gaining political visibility than do prominent members of the Senate.
18. Donald Matthews, "Presidential Nominations: Process and Outcomes," in *Choosing the President,* James David Barber, ed. (Englewood Cliffs, N.J.: Prentice-Hall, 1974), 49.
19. Donald Matthews, *The Social Background of Political Decision Makers* (New York: Random House, 1954), 23.
20. Sidney Hyman, *The American President* (New York: Harper, 1954), 221.
21. Ibid, 222.
22. The South was the major source of the country's very early presidents, but they came primarily from upper-class denominations.
23. The frame of reference here is where presidents spent their important adult years, not necessarily where they were born. Woodrow Wilson, for example, was born in Virginia, but he spent his prepresidential years in academia and politics primarily in New Jersey.
24. *Occupation* and *career* here mean those not associated with public life. Some chief executives, however, spent virtually all their lives in politics. For example, Lyndon Johnson taught school for only one year before becoming an assistant to a member of the House, and John Kennedy was a journalist for even less time before running for the House of Representatives.
25. Matthews, *Social Background,* 30.
26. Max Weber, "Politics as a Vocation," in *Max Weber: Essays in Sociology,* ed.

H. H. Gerth and C. W. Mills (New York: Oxford University Press, 1946), 85.

27. Truman did attend night classes at the Kansas City Law School, but it was a proprietary institution not then affiliated with a university. (It is now part of the Law School of the University of Missouri-Kansas City.)

28. John Schmidhauser, "The Justices of the Supreme Court," *Midwest Journal of Political Science* (February 1959): 1-57; Donald Matthews, *U.S. Senators and Their World* (New York: Vintage, 1960).

29. Fred Greenstein, *Personality and Politics: Problems of Evidence, Inference and Conceptualization* (New York: Norton, 1975), 3.

30. Alexander George and Juliette George, *Woodrow Wilson and Colonel House: A Personality Study* (New York: John Day, 1956); Bruce Mazlish, *In Search of Nixon: A Psychohistorical Inquiry* (Baltimore: Pelican, 1973); Doris Kearns, *Lyndon Johnson and the American Dream* (New York: Harper and Row, 1976).

31. Erwin Hargrove, *Presidential Leadership: Personality and Political Style* (New York: Macmillan, 1966); James David Barber, *The Presidential Character: Predicting Performance in the White House* (Englewood Cliffs, N.J.: Prentice-Hall, 1972).

32. Barber, *Presidential Character*, 7-8.

33. We considered choosing Richard Nixon as our example of an active-negative president but decided on Wilson because there have been better psychological studies of him than of Nixon or of any other U.S. president.

34. George and George, *Woodrow Wilson and Colonel House.*

35. Robert Tucker, "The Georges' Wilson Reexamined: An Essay on Psychobiography," *American Political Science Review* (June 1977): 606-618.

36. Arthur S. Link, ed., *The Papers of Woodrow Wilson* (Princeton, N.J.: Princeton University Press, 1978), 27:473.

37. Barber, *Presidential Character*, 174.

38. James David Barber, *The Presidential Character: Predicting Performance in the White House*, 3d ed. (Englewood Cliffs, N.J.: Prentice-Hall, 1985).

39. Ibid., 6-7.

40. Ibid.

41. As previously noted, serious questions arose over how accurately Barber has assessed these two presidents. The final chapter analyzes this matter.

Selected Readings

Barber, James David. *The Presidential Character.* 3d ed. Englewood Cliffs, N.J.: Prentice-Hall, 1985.

George, Alexander, and Juliette George. *Woodrow Wilson and Colonel House: A Personality Study.* New York: John Day, 1956.

Greenstein, Fred. *Personality and Politics: Problems of Evidence, Inference and Conceptualization.* New York: Norton, 1975.

Hargrove, Erwin. *Presidential Leadership: Personality and Political Style.* New York: Macmillan, 1966.

Hyman, Sidney. *The American President.* New York: Harper and Row, 1954.

Kearns, Doris. *Lyndon Johnson and the American Dream.* New York: Harper and Row, 1976.

Mazlich, Bruce. *In Search of Nixon: A Psychohistorical Inquiry.* Baltimore: Pelican, 1973.

Tugwell, Rexford. *How They Became President.* New York: Simon and Schuster, 1968.

Setting a democratic tone for his presidency, President Jimmy Carter walks with his wife, Rosalynn, down Pennsylvania Avenue from the U.S Capitol to the White House in his inaugural parade, January 20, 1977.

CHAPTER FOUR

Public Politics

Students of the presidency long have identified the chief executive's relationship with the American public as a major factor in the governing of the nation. Writing at the turn of the century, Henry Jones Ford concluded that "the only power which can ... define issues in such a way that public opinion can pass upon them decisively, is that which emanates from presidential authority." [1] Eight years later, Woodrow Wilson echoed that sentiment: "His is the only national voice in affairs. Let him once win the admiration and confidence of the country; and no other single force can withstand him; no combination of forces will easily overpower him." [2] Nor has that situation changed in recent years. Sidney Hyman maintains that the use of public opinion distinguishes "strong" and "weak" presidents: "The strong ones knew how to weave and guide that opinion into the machinery of government so that *the work of the presidency could proceed under the sanction of law.* The weak ones, lacking that talent, were limited in their work to what was funneled to them *by the men outside the presidency who actually commanded public opinion or at least congressional opinion.*" [3] Richard Neustadt further explains that "Washingtonians" (those who share with the president the governing of the nation, such as members of Congress and the administration, state governors, military commanders, party politicians, journalists, and foreign diplomats) evaluate the president's "public prestige," that is, "his standing with the public outside Washington," before deciding whether to follow his lead on policy matters. [4]

The president must be able, therefore, to influence public opinion if he is to take the leadership in initiating public policies and in persuading other public officials to support his policies. In the process, the chief executive must woo the American public between elections just as he does as a candidate during the election period.

Like an election campaign, the courtship of the voters that takes place between elections must take account of public attitudes. In other words, the

151

minds of American citizens are not blank pieces of paper on which the president's efforts to win their support are written. Rather, citizens have political attitudes in general, and toward the presidency in particular, that affect the way they view the incumbent. The key to securing their support is for the president to trigger these predispositions to obtain as favorable a response as possible to his efforts to govern the nation.

This chapter begins with a general analysis of public attitudes toward the presidency and then considers the ways chief executives try to win the support of the American people. The third principal section examines a key influence in the between-elections campaign: the relationship between the president and the media. The fourth section analyzes the president's relationships with one particular segment of the broader American public—members of his own political party.

Public Attitudes toward the Presidency

David Easton explains that citizens' basic political attitudes extend toward three major components of a political system: the political community, the regime, and the authorities.[5] The political community is the broadest geographical unit in which citizens permit political officials to make binding decisions that affect their lives. In the modern world the political community is the nation-state, such as the United States. The regime, or what some political scientists call the "rules of the game," includes the functions, procedures, and structures of government set forth in a formal constitution as well as informal agreements and understandings about what is proper and improper in the realm of politics. The third component Easton refers to is the authorities, the public officials who occupy the vital positions in the governmental structure. Attitudes toward these three elements of a political system determine just how much support the people give their political leaders. If these attitudes are sufficiently strong and positive, the public may follow its leaders even if it does not like the particular incumbent or the policies he or she advocates.

To a considerable extent, public attitudes focus on the president in each of these three areas. Like the British monarch, the U.S. chief executive is the symbol, the personification, of the nation and the state. It is the president who inspires feelings of loyalty and patriotism, particularly in times of crisis when he becomes the rallying point for national efforts. Thus, both political friends and foes of Franklin D. Roosevelt turned to him for leadership when the Japanese attacked Pearl Harbor in December 1941.

Even though the United States is a democratic nation, the presidency is surrounded with the trappings of ceremony and pomp. As Joseph Kallenbach points out, the inauguration of a president bears certain resemblance to the coronation of a king, complete with the taking of an oath in the presence of the notables and "the hailing by the multitudes." [6] Ceremonial aspects of the office include the display of the presidential seal, the playing of "Hail to the Chief" when the president arrives at an event, and many traditional duties, such as visiting other nations and entertaining foreign heads of state when they visit Washington, D.C., lighting the Christmas tree on the White House lawn, and dedicating special weeks to a host of good causes. All such activities emphasize the role the chief executive plays in embodying the nation, its government, and its ideals.

Beyond the basic beliefs about the nation, the rules of the game, and government leaders—sometimes referred to as matters of "political culture"—the public also has views toward the day-to-day operation of the political system, in particular, the important issues of the day and the policies the government should follow in dealing with those issues. In addition, voters react to the personalities of candidates for office. They may also identify with particular groups, such as political parties or social, economic, or geographical divisions in the population; and they shape their attitudes on issues and candidates accordingly. These views, which are generally assumed to be less stable and enduring than beliefs about the political culture, are often described as matters of "public opinion."

The president is linked in people's thinking to these matters as well. As the nation's leading political figure, he is expected to develop and help put into effect controversial policies that are binding on the entire populace. People respond favorably or unfavorably to his particular personality and political style and to the events that occur while he is in office. They also assess the president by the way he relates to particular groups—theirs or the opposite political party, as well as social (religious, ethnic, racial), economic (business, labor), and geographical (southern, western) divisions of the population.

Thus, numerous and diverse attitudes affect public opinion toward the president. At times, people may see him as the embodiment of the nation; on other occasions they may link him with a particular issue or policy they favor or oppose. The following sections analyze the ways both children and adults view the president and the factors that affect their thinking about him.

Attitudes of Children

Three major studies, conducted during the Eisenhower and Kennedy administrations, of the political attitudes of white, urban, middle-class children aged seven through thirteen all showed the importance of the president in the child's political world.[7] Along with the local mayor and police officers, to children the president is the most visible political official. In fact, David Easton and Jack Dennis state that the president is "a towering, glittering mountain peak for the younger child, easy to single out from the whole range of authority."[8] Only later, as a teenager, does the individual become aware that the president shares the running of the government with Congress and the Supreme Court. Thus, in the *cognitive* (knowing) world of the young child, the president personifies the government.

These early studies also underscored the *affective* (emotional) dimension of children's attitudes toward the president. Not only are they aware of the importance of the president, but they also think of him as a "good" person who cares about people, wants to help them, and wants to "get things done." For the young child the president is both powerful and "benevolent"; only when the child grows older does he or she view the president less favorably.

Researchers offered a variety of explanations for the favorable attitudes of young children. Some of the children's opinions are related to their parents' political attitudes. Parents who view the president favorably pass on these views to their children; those who do not, often tend to suppress their unfavorable views for fear of undermining the child's respect for authority. Another reason is that children's favorable attitudes toward other authority figures, particularly their fathers, carry over into their respect for the president, who becomes a kind of family figure "writ large." A third explanation for children's favorable views is the child's sense of "vulnerability"; because they view the president as a powerful figure who can vitally affect their lives, they want to believe the president is a good person who will protect rather than threaten them.

Scholars also agreed that children distinguish between the person temporarily occupying the office and the presidency itself. They therefore can respect the institution without respecting the incumbent. It was also assumed that this favorable attitude of children toward the president carries over into their adult years, providing a solid basis of support for the entire U.S. political system.

The essential agreement of the above findings suggested that children's attitudes are universal. Subsequent inquiries indicate, however, that this is clearly not the case. A study of poor children in Kentucky, conducted during the Johnson administration, showed them to be much less favorably disposed toward the president, regarding him as less honest, less hard working, less caring, and less knowledgeable than had the urban middle-class children of previous studies.[9] In fact, about one-quarter of the Kentucky children viewed him as "not a good person," a finding that led the authors to characterize the president for these children as the "malevolent" (rather than the "benevolent") leader.

The Kentucky findings differed in other ways from those of earlier studies. Although they did not view the president as benevolent, the rural Kentucky children did not grow more critical of the chief executive as they became older. Moreover, their attitude toward the president was not related to how they viewed their own father: children with absent fathers were *more favorably inclined* toward the president than were those whose fathers lived with the family. The authors speculated that this occurred because the negative attitudes of Kentucky males toward government therefore were not transmitted to the children from whom they were separated.

The authors of the Kentucky study concluded that "children's views of politics may be a culturally bound phenomenon." [10] Subsequent inquiries indicated that such views may also be shaped by salient political events. After revelations of the Watergate scandal, two researchers interviewed the same kind of children who had been interviewed in 1962 and found that the interval had made a real difference in the way children viewed the president.[11] Those in the mid-1970s were much less likely to idealize the chief executive than were their counterparts in the early 1960s. They also did not assign the president as important a role in running the country or in making its laws as did the children who were asked about such matters in 1962. As the authors of the study explained it, "Just as the President in early 1974 had come to occupy a smaller place in the hearts of this country's young persons, he held a smaller place in their minds as well." [12]

Fred Greenstein also did follow-up studies, in 1969-1970 and in 1973, to determine whether children's attitudes toward the president had changed since the Eisenhower years.[13] He found that despite the Vietnam War, the 1969-1970 respondents were generally positive toward the president, although this was much less true of black children. Children interviewed during the 1973 Watergate hearings, however, had a much less idealized view of the president and were much more sensitive to the possibility that the president might place himself above the law. He concluded that children had been much more insulated from the political turmoil of the 1960s than they were from the Watergate scandal of the 1970s.

Two studies of upper-middle-class children in the Boston surburbs also demonstrate the way political events affect children's attitudes toward the president.[14] Those interviewed in late 1973 no longer had an idealized view of the president; in fact, he was to them a malevolent rather than a benevolent figure. At the same time, they still regarded him as a powerful leader. By early 1975, when the second round of interviews was conducted, some of the extremely negative feelings revealed in 1973 had moderated, but children's views of the president were still closer to those of 1973 than the ones of the early 1960s.

Finally, a 1976 study of poor children in Kentucky (similar to those interviewed in the mid-1960s) shows how political events shape their attitudes toward the president.[15] Interestingly enough, children interviewed in late 1974 were not more negative toward the presidency as an institution, but they were very negative toward former president Nixon. (They rated Gerald Ford, who was president at the time of the study, much higher than Nixon.) At the same time, their views of the president's knowledge, compared with the 1966 study, had not changed: the children definitely did not like Nixon, but they did not think he was ignorant. The 1976 study also revealed that the Kentucky children's opinion of Nixon depended on their partisan affiliation:

Democrats viewed Nixon the least favorably, independents and Republicans progressively less so.

Thus, children's attitudes depend on their social and economic backgrounds as well as on the geographical area in which they live. They also respond to salient political events, such as Watergate. Moreover, differences exist between their affective and cognitive views of the president: they may dislike a president but still think he is an important and powerful political leader. They also distinguish between the personal qualities of a president and his performance in office. Finally, because children as a group do not necessarily regard all presidents favorably, no base of presidential support automatically carries over into their adult years. Rather, as following sections will indicate, presidents must struggle to win support from American citizens.

Attitudes of Adults

Although the president does not dominate the political world of adults the way he does that of young children, he still is by far the most visible person in the American political system. Greenstein cites a 1969-1970 survey in which young adults were asked to name the person holding various political offices at the national level.[16] Ninety-eight percent correctly named the president; the vice president was the next best-known official, identified by 87 percent of those questioned. In contrast, the third most visible person, a senator from their own state, was correctly identified by 57 percent of the respondents, and only 39 percent knew the name of the House member from their district.

The president is not only well known but also generally respected and admired. Findings of the Survey Research Center at the University of Michigan in the mid-1960s indicated that of all the occupations in the United States, including "famous doctor," "president of a large corporation like General Motors," "bishop or other church official," "Supreme Court justice," and "senator," more than half the adults named the president as the most respected. Moreover, Gallup polls since 1948 show that when Americans are asked to name the man, living anywhere in the world, whom they most admire, the president of the United States is almost always their first choice.[17] The First Lady usually heads the list of most admired women.

Greenstein finds several reasons for the president's high standing with the American public.[18] As with children, the president is a "cognitive aid" that links adults to government and politics. He also serves as an outlet for feelings: "The detailed preoccupation of the media with the president's hobbies and social activities has become an American equivalent of the more ceremonial displays of symbolic activity associated elsewhere with monarchs." [19] The president is a symbol of national unity as well as of stability and predictability.

Another survey also revealed more favorable attitudes toward the "generalized abstract" president than toward a specific incumbent.[20] Most persons surveyed agreed that the president "stands for our country" and that they sleep better when a president they trust is watching over the country. They also tended to believe that the president should be given a chance to work out his policies before he is criticized and that even if the president were wrong, once he has committed the nation to action, he should be supported. Most respondents also believed that in time of crisis in domestic or foreign affairs, all citizens should rally to support the president.

Some citizens, however, were more likely to be highly supportive of the president than were others. These include citizens who are older, who belong to a more conservative religious denomination, who have little formal education, who identify with the lower or working class, who have a low-prestige occupation, and who are black and female. Specific psychological traits were associated with persons providing high presidential support—in particular, personal inflexibility and authoritarianism. Persons who favorably evaluated the entire American political system also were likely to be highly supportive of the president.

The authors of this survey speculated that citizens' support for the president may decline over time as the U.S. population becomes younger, less associated with fundamental religions, better educated, and more psychologically flexible. Should this happen, presidents will be forced to depend less on general, long-term support from the citizenry and more on short-term responses to contemporary events. As the following discussion indicates, such responses are indeed an important aspect of citizens' attitudes toward the American president.

Public attitudes relate not only to the presidency as an institution but also to a particular occupant of the office. Since the end of World War II, the Gallup organization periodically has polled a cross-section of Americans on whether they approve or disapprove of the way the president is handling his job. The emphasis of the question, and therefore the response, is not on the personal qualities of the president but on his performance in office.

A study by John Mueller, based on his analysis of the answers to that Gallup question from 1946 to 1970, shows that all the presidents of that period, except for Dwight Eisenhower, declined in popularity over the course of their term in office.[21] They typically start with a high level of support, as the public accords them a measure of trust that they will do well in the job. As presidents undertake various actions, however, they antagonize more and more groups. Mueller explains that a "coalition of minorities" forms as different minorities respond unfavorably to different presidential decisions, as businesses did when President Kennedy forced them to roll back a steel price rise in 1962, and as southerners did when he sent federal officials to the South to enforce integration. Various groups become unhappy with the president for different reasons, but the result is a progressive decline in the president's popularity.[22] In addition to this overall downward trend, public opinion on the presidency is affected by certain kinds of events. A downturn in the economy, particularly if it increases the rate of unemployment, harms presidential popularity. (A decrease in unemployment, however, does not improve the president's popularity.) International events can affect public opinion either way. On the one hand, a dramatic event, involving national and presidential prestige, may inspire Americans to "rally round the flag" and support their chief executive. They do so even if things turn out badly, as they did at the Bay of Pigs in 1961 when the U.S. effort to help ex-Cuban forces invade the island and overthrow Fidel Castro ended in a fiasco. On the other hand, wars, such as those in Korea and Vietnam, ultimately harm the president's popularity, as the conflict drags on and casualties mount.

Finally, the party affiliation of adults in the United States affects their opinion of the president's performance. Those who identify with the party not in power start out with much less support for the president than do members of his own party. In addition, those in the "out-party" are more easily alienated by his policies or by unfavorable events; they also tend to become antagonistic again sooner after the temporary favorable effect of an international crisis. As a result, presidents enjoy far less support at the end of their term from out-party identifiers than from "in-party" identifiers.

Subsequent studies confirm some of Mueller's major findings. Samuel Kernell determined that at the outset of a presidential term the chief executive's prestige is generally high, as the public offers him the opportunity to establish successful relationships with other public officials with whom he governs the nation.[23] Like Mueller, he found that international "rally" events tend to increase the president's popularity, whereas long-term wars, like Korea and Vietnam, cost the chief executive public support. Jong Lee also found that foreign policy events influence presidential support, with wars and military crises affecting that support for an average duration of five months.[24] However, George Edward's analysis of potential rally events from 1953 to 1980 showed that some, such as the ending of the Vietnam War and U.S. military action against the Soviet Union in Cuba, substantially increased the president's approval rate, while others, such as the ending of the Korean War and military action against Cuba at the Bay of Pigs, did not.[25] He concludes that events that generate sudden increases in presidential popularity are "highly idiosyncratic and do not seem to significantly differ from other events that were not followed by significant surges in presidential approval." [26]

Studies confirm that economic factors affect presidential popularity. In addition to the rate of unemployment, the rate of inflation also influences the public attitude toward the president.[27] Edwards found that in assessing President Carter, Democrats were strongly affected by unemployment statistics while Republicans were more concerned with inflation.[28] Finally, another analyst has determined that increases in both unemployment and inflation affect the public's perception that things are getting worse economically and thus tend to lower the president's popularity.[29]

Scholars have challenged Mueller's theory that the coalition of minorities causes a steady, long-term decline in presidents' popularity. James Stimson[30] suggests that rather than being steady, the decline is cyclical, reaching a low point the third year of a president's term and then rising again in the fourth year as the president who is seeking reelection manipulates events to his advantage.[31] The president who does not stand for reelection also benefits in his fourth year in office because, as he is retiring, his motives are less open to cynical interpretation. Stimson attributes the decline in the president's popularity not primarily to his alienating various groups but to the public's becoming disillusioned with presidential performance, as unrealistic expectations about what the chief executive can accomplish fail to be fulfilled. He suggests that the less well-informed segments of the American public are most likely to harbor such expectations.

Kernell, too, maintains that events rather than time in office affect a president's prestige.[32] Moreover, it is not presidents' decisions that determine their popularity, as the coalition-of-minorities factor suggests; rather, presidents are judged by real events and conditions that occur during their administration. They are also held accountable by the American public for what they *do not* do: if a president does not attempt to deal with a major problem, such as the energy crisis, and it persists, his popularity will decline.

Figure 4-1 shows results of the Gallup poll on President Reagan's performance in his first six years in office. His initial approval rate of 51 percent was low (Jimmy Carter's, in contrast, was 66 percent), but it rose to a high of 68 percent following the unsuccessful attempt on his life by John Hinckley, Jr., in late March 1981. His popularity began to decline in mid-1981 and continued to do so as the economy worsened, reaching its lowest point in early 1983. Then the economy began to improve, and so did President Reagan's approval rate, which increased steadily in 1983 and ended on a high note late that year following the invasion of Grenada. His approval rate remained constant during the first half of 1984 and then rose at the time of the summer Olympics and the fall election campaign. Most unusual was that President Reagan's ratings remained high during the first year of his second term—President Eisenhower's average approval rate fell from 64 percent in 1956, the year in which he was reelected, to 54 percent in 1957; President Nixon's declined from 58 percent in his reelection year of 1972 to 43 percent in 1973. President Reagan's ratings remained high during most of the second year of his second term before plummeting by 16 percent after the revelation of the Iran-contra affair, the largest single decline in the history of Gallup surveys on presidential approval ratings.

Edwards emphasizes that the public judges presidents by their *policies*. As he puts it, "Evidently the public evaluates the president more on the basis of how it thinks the government is performing on economic policy than how it thinks the economy itself is performing." [33] Moreover, people assess economic policy by how it affects the entire nation, not just their personal situation. He finds a similar pattern in public judgments of presidents' handling of war,

Figure 4-1 Approval Ratings of President Reagan's Performance, 1981-1986 (Percent)

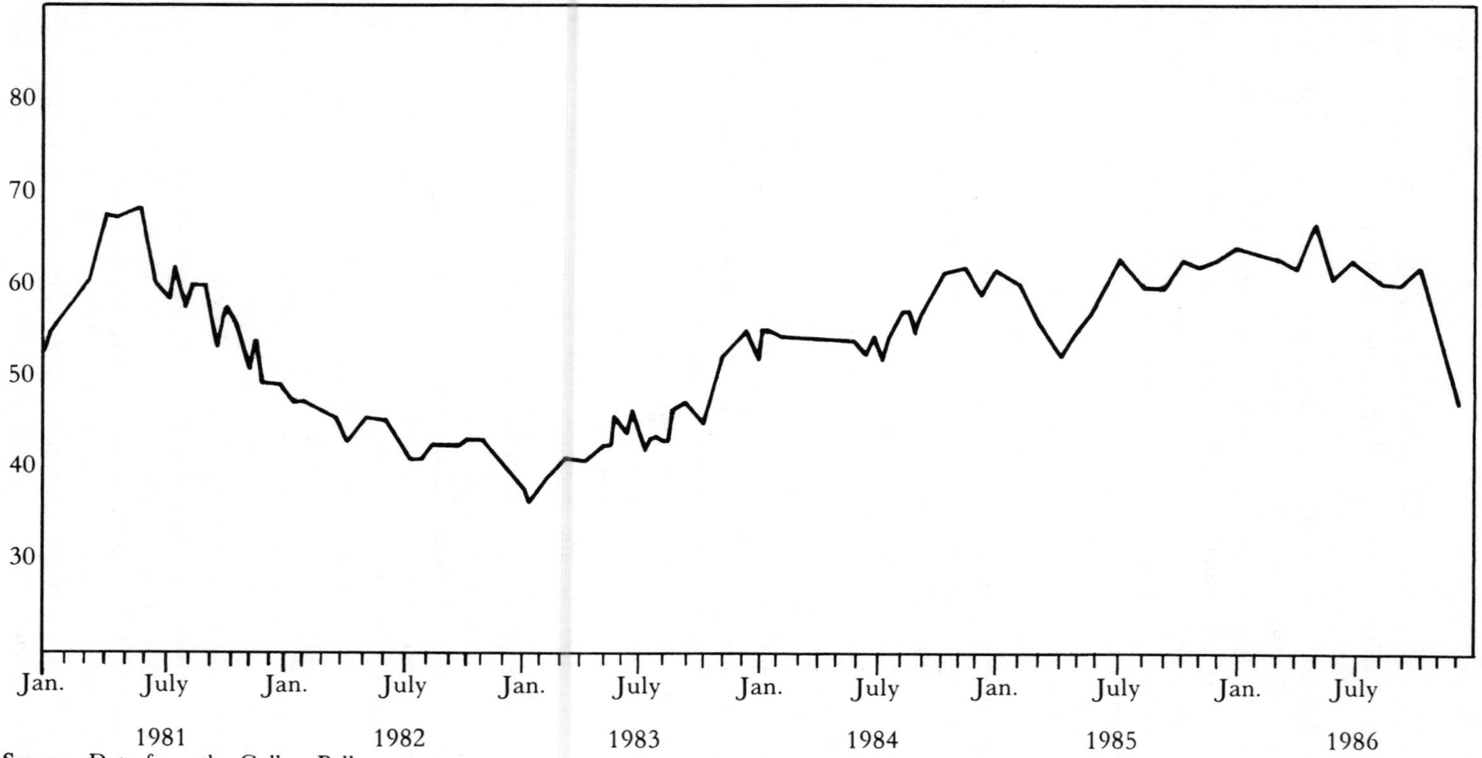

Source: Data from the Gallup Poll.

with the nation's welfare rather than an individual's own experience being most important.

It is not just events that determine how a president is regarded but how the public *perceives those events.* This, in turn, depends on how the news is reported by the mass media. If there is a discrepancy between the balance of good and bad news and the way the president was regarded before the reporting of that news, his popularity will move in the direction of that discrepancy.[34] It has also been determined that a relationship exists between the amount of television news time accorded the president, as well as the portion of "positive" coverage he received, and how he is viewed by the public.[35] "Negative" coverage also affects his opinion ratings.[36] A similar connection exists between the number of nationwide radio or television broadcasts a president himself makes and the amount of support he receives from the American public.[37]

Thus, public views toward the presidents reflect long-term attitudes on the presidency as an institution as well as short-term responses to particular incumbents based on international and domestic events, the state of the economy, policies of the president, news reports on events, and the president's own use of the media. The next section analyzes how chief executives use such influences to enhance their popularity with the American public.

Shaping Perceptions of the President

Presidents direct their appeals to different kinds of audiences. One is the general public; another is special segments of that public, represented primarily by interest groups.

Appealing to the Public

Americans' attitudes toward the president are most likely to be favorable when they link him with the nation, with the constitutional system, and with the presidential office as an institution. Chief executives therefore seek to present themselves in those terms, that is, to personalize the American political system and to embody American ideals.

Presidents use several techniques to create that image. One is to emphasize the ceremonial aspects of the office. This entails, among other things, displaying the presidential seal and having the band strike up "Hail to the Chief" when he appears in public. Chief executives also tap the patriotic sentiments of the American people by staging events on the nation's major holidays. On his first Fourth of July in the White House, for example, Ronald Reagan held a picnic complete with a gigantic fireworks display. Five years later, he helped commemorate the restoration of the Statue of Liberty, again on the Fourth of July. Presidents may link themselves with worthwhile causes by dedicating a new hospital, dam, or library; Gerald Ford, for example, dedicated a new library in Pekin, Illinois, the hometown of another famous Republican leader, the late senator Everett Dirksen of Illinois.

Trips also emphasize the president's role as head of state. This is particularly true of foreign travel, since the chief executive is then seen as the representative of the United States and of all the American people. Eisenhower visited eleven foreign countries, Kennedy toured Europe with his wife, and Nixon made a historic visit to mainland China as well as to the Soviet Union and the Middle East. Early in his term, Jimmy Carter went to Great Britain to meet with leaders of the major western industrial nations. Ronald Reagan attended a conference in Canada with officials of the same nations during his first year in office and later in his first term visited China, the Normandy beaches of France, and his family's ancestral home in Ireland.[38]

To a lesser extent, domestic trips also enhance the image of the president as a national leader. As Louis Koenig points out, George Washington initiated a "Grand Tour" of two-months' duration by visiting the South in 1791.[39] Modern presidents have continued Washington's tradition, frequently dispensing patronage to states and localities along the way. Such trips also enable presidents to escape for a time the political infighting of the nation's capital and to reassure themselves that the popularity they enjoyed on the campaign trail has not disappeared. The trip that Jimmy Carter and his family took by paddleboat down the Mississippi in the summer of 1979 served such a purpose, as he found the adulation of the crowds a needed tonic to his political woes, including a contemplated upcoming nomination battle with his major rival, Sen. Edward Kennedy of Massachusetts. Travel to special locations highlights particular themes. In 1985, for example, Ronald Reagan kicked off his tax reform proposal in Williamsburg, Virginia, calling it the "new American Revolution." [40]

Not all presidential trips turn out well, however. Woodrow Wilson's ill-fated attempt to take his case for the Versailles peace treaty to the American people ended in failure. He collapsed near the end of his tour and was disabled for a long period. Moreover, the American people failed to respond to his pleas, and some historians have concluded that not a single senator's vote was changed by this difficult journey. In the first year of his second term, Reagan scheduled a visit to a cemetery at Bitburg, West Germany, to symbolize reconciliation between the United States and that country. However, because the cemetery contained graves of officers of the Waffen S.S., the military arm of Hitler's elite corps, many people criticized Reagan for appearing to honor an organization responsible for the mass killings of the Holocaust. Despite the passage of a resolution by the House of Representatives urging him to cancel the trip to the cemetery, the president went anyway, to the consternation of many of his political supporters and advisers.

A president's involvement in crises may also improve his standing with the American people. As previously indicated, this is particularly true of military crises, when the chief executive stands to benefit from the rally-round-the-flag phenomenon. What is most important is that the president appear to be decisive, as Kennedy did in the Cuban missile crisis and Ford did in the *Mayaguez* incident with Cambodia after the Vietnam War. To a lesser extent, the same principle applies to domestic crises; most Americans admired Reagan's tough stand in firing the air traffic controllers when they illegally struck in the summer of 1981. Presidents win the public's favor when they play the role of the strong leader defending the interests of the nation from foreign or domestic threats.

Unlike basic attitudes of political culture, which link the chief executive with the country, the constitutional system, and the presidential office, attitudes relating him to less stable matters of public opinion are much more likely to be unfavorable. People may respect the presidency as an institution but may not like the personality or political style of the current incumbent. They may agree with the broad, general rules of the game and the basic values that the president embodies but disagree with positions he takes on controversial issues of public policy. They may also feel that the president is unsympathetic with certain economic, social, or political groups with which they themselves identify or that he is partial to groups that they oppose. Presidents must take these factors into account when they attempt to shape public attitudes that link them with the day-to-day operation of the American political system.

One tactic that presidents employ is to try to create a favorable impression of themselves as individuals. This approach frequently takes the form of emphasizing their "down-to-earth" qualities, the traits that make them "ordinary" persons. When Gerald Ford first succeeded to the presidency, much was made of the fact that he cooked his own breakfast. At his swearing-in ceremony, Jimmy Carter wore a dark business suit rather than the traditional morning coat, then walked down Pennsylvania Avenue to the White House rather than riding at the head of the inaugural parade as his predecessors had done. He also participated in a radio call-in show and visited a New England community for a mock town meeting, staying overnight with a family who had supported his presidential campaign. Ronald Reagan saw to it that he was frequently photographed in informal Western attire, often astride his favorite horse or chopping wood on his ranch.

Presidents also like to be pictured as family men, surrounded by an adoring wife and respectful children. Frequently, however, these persons influence the president's views and undertake public activities to help them. Eleanor Roosevelt served as her husband's social conscience, and Betty Ford's somewhat liberal views on social issues supplemented the more traditional ones of her more conservative spouse. Sometimes the president's children become politically involved: Jimmy Carter sent his son Chip to Buffalo to offer advice on how to deal with a massive snow storm, and the young Carter was also part of a delegation to try to persuade Arab nations to accept the Israeli-Egyptian peace agreement.

Perhaps the president's most difficult task in fostering favorable public attitudes is assuaging opposition to his stands on public policy issues, many of which are highly controversial. One method chief executives employ in dealing with this difficult problem is to sensitize themselves to public views. This requires a close reading of the results of public opinion polls periodically conducted by organizations such as Gallup, Harris, and Roper. Recent presidents have even hired their own pollsters (such as Patrick Caddell for Jimmy Carter and Richard Wirthlin for Ronald Reagan) to probe public attitudes more deeply on issues in which the chief executives are particularly interested. Although presidents may not choose to follow the sentiments of a majority of Americans, a knowledge of public attitudes may be helpful: Jimmy Carter used polls to measure how effectively he was getting his message across to the public, and Ronald Reagan uses them to determine when the mood of the country is amenable to his proposals.[41]

Presidents also attempt to foster favorable public attitudes toward themselves by staging ceremonies connected with the enactment of public policies they perceive to be popular with the American people. Lyndon Johnson signed the Elementary and Secondary Education Act of 1965 at the one-room schoolhouse in Stonewall, Texas, where his own education had begun; and he held a ceremony for the Medicare Act of 1965 in Independence, Missouri, hometown of former president Harry Truman, who first proposed a government health insurance program. Jimmy Carter went to New York City to sign the 1978 law providing federal loan guarantees to that financially distressed city. And in 1981 Ronald Reagan staged a nationally televised ceremony from his ranch in southern California, where he signed into law his program of budget and tax cuts.

Communicating with Interest Groups

Presidents know that the general public is not greatly concerned with many issues of public policy; they therefore concentrate their efforts on particular segments of the population, typically interest groups, that do have a vital interest in specific issues. For example, presidents give major addresses on business to the convention of the National Association of Manufacturers or the Chamber of Commerce of the United States, and on labor relations to a meeting of the AFL-CIO. Because it is impossible for the president to address all important groups personally, chief executives often dispatch emissaries, such as cabinet officers involved in an issue, to speak on behalf of them and their programs.

Beyond a concern with current matters of public policy, however, presidents also attempt to convince members of groups that they are sympathetic to the problems their members face. Often, chief executives pay particular attention to those groups that help them get elected. (They thus attempt to convert their electoral coalition into one that helps them govern.) Democratic presidents tend to focus on labor unions and organizations of blacks; Republicans concentrate on business and professional organizations.

At the same time, presidents know that as the leader of the nation, they are supposed to represent all the people, not just those who supported their election. Tradition provides that chief executives appear before prominent interest groups, even those that are politically opposed to them. Richard Nixon addressed the annual convention of the AFL-CIO, and Ronald Reagan went before an assembly of the National Association for the Advancement of Colored People.

Presidential concern with winning the political support of particular groups is reflected in the development of White House liaisons with such groups. Harry Truman used David Niles, formerly on Franklin Roosevelt's staff, as a liaison with minority groups.[42] Lyndon Johnson designated persons in his White House to establish relationships with Jews, Catholics, and other groups. Joseph Pika identifies eight population groups represented in the Nixon, Ford, Carter, and Reagan administrations: business, labor, Jews, consumers, blacks, women, Hispanics, and the elderly.[43]

The Office of Public Liaison is yet a further step. First conceived in the Nixon administration and consolidated in one unit under Gerald Ford when William Baroody, Jr., was made public liaison chief, the office has continued to be a part of the White House office in subsequent administrations. Jimmy Carter initially planned to cut back its staff but according to a key aide, Stuart Eizenstat, later realized its potential for selling policies involving interest groups.[44] The Office of Public Liaison also was important in promoting the economic policies of the Reagan administration.[45]

Thus, the official representation of interest groups in the White House office has become institutionalized in the administrations of both political parties. Persons who serve in the office play two potential roles in the political process. One is to articulate the demands of interest groups, a role emphasized by Margaret (Midge) Costanza, first public liaison chief under Jimmy Carter. An ardent feminist, Costanza supported the use of federal funds for abortion even though the president held a contrary position on that issue. The other role is to rally the support of interest groups in support of the president's programs, a task assumed by Ann Wexler, who followed Costanza as head of the office in the Carter administration. There is little doubt, however, that the office exists primarily to further the president's desires rather than those of interest groups: Costanza was removed from her position, but Wexler received high praise from her Democratic colleagues, Republican successors, and press observers.[46]

Thus, presidents attempt to shape the attitudes of the general public as well as those of interest groups to garner favor and support.[47] Their success in that endeavor depends to a considerable extent upon the ability to communicate their appeals through the media, the subject of the following section.

The President and the Media

Historically, the most important medium linking the president to the American public has been the press. In the early years of the Republic there was a partisan press similar to that which prevails in many European countries today. During the Washington administration the *Gazette of the United States* was established as the party organ of the Federalists; the Republicans, under the leadership of Jefferson, established a rival paper, the *National Gazette,* which became a major critic of President Washington. Later, when Jefferson himself became president, still another paper, the *National Intelligencer,* came to be the voice of his administration. The partisan press reached its peak during the presidency of Andrew Jackson when federal officeholders were expected to subscribe to the administration organ, the *Washington Globe,* which was financed in great part by revenues derived from the printing of official government notices.[48]

The partisan press began to decline during the presidency of Abraham Lincoln. The establishment of the Government Printing Office in 1860 destroyed the printing-contract patronage that had supported former administration organs; in addition, Lincoln felt that tying himself to one newspaper would limit his relationships with others.[49] Other developments also contributed to the demise of the partisan press. One was the invention of the telegraph, which led to the formation of wire services. Wire service information, distributed to all parts of the country, tended to be standardized and politically neutral to avoid antagonizing the diverse readerships of the various subscribing newspapers. Another development was the increased use of the press for advertising, which provided newspapers with a secure financial base independent of the support of presidential administrations. As Michael Grossman and Martha Kumar have observed, by the end of the nineteenth century "news about the White House was transmitted to the public by independent, nonpartisan news organizations," a feature that continues to affect relationships between the president and the press today.[50]

In this century, two new media, radio in the 1920s and television in the 1950s, emerged to take their place along with the press as channels between the chief executive and the American people. Today a great variety of media outlets covers the words and actions of the U.S. president.

The Presidential Media

The media covering the presidency differ not only in their physical format (print media being newspapers and magazines; broadcast media, radio and television), but also in the way they deal with executive branch developments and in their target audience. Moreover, they vary greatly in how important they are to the chief executive and his programs.

Diplomats and Negotiators.   Most influential are what Grossman and

Kumar term the "diplomats" and "negotiators," a select group of journalists whom the president recognizes as especially important in carrying his message to various publics and in determining how he will fare with other representatives of the media.[51] The diplomats include columnists, elite reporters, and the anchorpersons of the broadcast media. The negotiators include the bureau chiefs and other executives of the media.

Columnists deal in matters of opinion rather than merely in factual developments affecting the presidency. As Grossman and Kumar explain, "They are guaranteed space, they have no assigned topics, they are freed from the pressure of breaking news stories at deadline, and they have the opportunity to introduce their own perspectives into their stories." [52] In recent years George Will has epitomized this sort of columnist. Similar in nature are elite reporters who cover current developments affecting the presidency but who also interpret the news, that is, explain why certain events have occurred and the effect these events will have on the president's program and the governing of the country. Some elite reporters eventually acquire a column of their own, as have James Reston and Tom Wicker of the *New York Times*. Moreover, in some cases a single individual fills both roles simultaneously: David Broder not only has his own syndicated column but also covers major stories as the chief political reporter of the *Washington Post*.

Syndicated columnists and elite reporters are important to the president because of the audiences they reach, which include not only prestigious persons outside government (such as business and labor leaders, lobbyists, and academics), but also top officials in government itself (such as members of Congress, members of the bureaucracy, judges, governors, and mayors). They offer important views on the political feasibility of a president's proposed programs and on the effects they will have on various segments of the population. Some also become specialists in particular areas of public policy: Robert Novak, for example, is recognized as an authority on the defense establishment.

Television anchorpersons, such as Dan Rather, Peter Jennings, and Tom Brokaw, are important to the president because of the size of the audience they reach. Since far more people watch television than read newspapers, the information the ordinary citizen receives about the presidency depends on what these anchorpersons choose to include in the nightly broadcasts. In addition, such broadcasters also participate in documentaries and news analysis programs that convey definite views on matters of great importance to the president and the nation. A special program of former anchorperson Walter Cronkite on the Vietnam War appeared shortly after the Tet offensive in 1968 and is credited with convincing many Americans that the U.S. military effort there was a failure.

Bureau chiefs and other media executives are important to the president for several reasons. First, they help determine within their own news organization which stories will be covered and how they will be handled.

They also negotiate with the White House over the provisions of air time to carry presidential messages as well as the physical coverage of presidential events. Finally, they advise the administration on which of their reporters should be issued White House press passes and who should be represented in "pools" that travel with the chief executive to cover significant events.

The Washington Reporters.   Although less important to the chief executive than the diplomats and negotiators, the regular Washington reporters play a key role in conveying important information about the president and his policies to many audiences. Grossman and Kumar refer to them as "Milton's army" ("They also serve who only stand and wait") because they spend a great deal of time waiting around the White House to see if any of the daily events will merit coverage.[53] Although they have this feature in common, they differ on the kind of presidential news they cover and the way they cover it. The organization to which they belong also determines how much prestige they have with the president and with their fellow reporters.

Scholars who have studied Washington reporters agree that those who work for the *New York Times* and *Washington Post* are considered the most influential.[54] Their influence stems from their audience: they are the reporters most widely read by the Washington "elite"—public officials, important persons in the private sector, and Washington reporters themselves. Thus, important people, including the president and members of his staff, find out what is going on in Washington and communicate with one another through the *Times* and the *Post*. In addition, these papers serve as a reference point for other reporters, who tend to regard the stories that appear in these two newspapers as the most relevant and reliable sources of information on the national government. As Stephen Hess notes, these publications (particularly the *Times*) also influence decisions on which news stories will be carried on network television broadcasts.[55]

Reporters for the three major television networks also loom large in the presidential media because they determine what news the general American public receives about the president and his programs. Also contributing to the importance of television is that viewers tend to believe what they see on television; that is, it determines reality for them. At the same time, this medium has serious limitations in conveying vital information about the presidency. Because of the extremely short time devoted to most important stories (about seventy-five seconds on the average), and the necessity of emphasizing events that are visually exciting, in-depth reporting and analysis usually are missing from most television broadcasts.[56]

Also important to American presidents are the nation's two major newsweeklies, *Time* and *Newsweek*. They bring national news to a broad readership throughout the country, and their reporters benefit from having weekly rather than daily deadlines and from combining their efforts into a single, in-depth account. Particularly important to U.S. presidents is the possibility of being pictured on the cover of these magazines and, consequently, the possibility of favorable coverage of the event for which they were pictured.

Also significant are the reporters for the wire services—Associated Press (AP) and United Press International (UPI). Somewhat less consequential today than they were before the development of network television, they nonetheless provide presidential coverage for newspapers across the country that subscribe to their services. Wire service reporters appear as prominent participants in presidential press conferences and as members of pools covering presidential trips and other important events. Their stories, however, constitute "hard news" rather than analysis and focus on the official and personal activities of the president—what Grossman and Kumar refer to as "body-watching." [57] Because they often prepare several stories a day for client newspapers with different deadlines and must cater to the diverse interests of this broad clientele, they have little opportunity for in-depth or interpretative reporting.[58]

This combination of Washington reporters constitutes the "inner circle" or "inner ring" of the presidential media. Beyond lie many other national reporters who are employed by a wide variety of news organizations, differing in degree of importance to the chief executive. Included are those who write high-quality, in-depth pieces for the *Wall Street Journal*—a weekday publication available throughout the United States, with a large daily circulation[59]—and those who write for *U.S. News & World Report,* a weekly news magazine somewhat less prestigious than *Time* or *Newsweek,* but traditionally one that has appealed to many members of the business community as well as to public officials who regard it as more "objective" than the two other, more critical magazines. Other journalists work for elite publications with specialized readerships, such as *Business Week, Congressional Quarterly,* the *National Journal,* and the *New Republic;* for large, regional, daily newspapers, such as the *Los Angeles Times, Baltimore Sun,* and *Chicago Tribune;* and for the chains, such as Knight-Ridder or Scripps-Howard, that provide service to many newspapers. Finally, there are the reporters who provide coverage for radio stations around the country (including those that belong to commercial networks as well as those affiliated with the National Public Radio system) and photographers who provide a pictorial record of the presidency.

These, then, are the highly diverse components of the presidential media (presented in tabular form in Table 4-1). The following section analyzes the means by which the president deals with the various elements of that media.

Presidential Channels of Communication

Because of the diverse media interested in the presidency, the chief executive and members of his administration use different techniques and channels of communication to manage the flow of information about the president. These

Table 4-1   Presidential Media, in Order of Importance to the President

Diplomats	Negotiators
1. Syndicated columnists (for example, Will)	1. Bureau chiefs
2. Elite reporters (for example, Broder) (Both provide in-depth analysis and opinions on presidential politics and policy with specialization of subject matter; have an elite audience of leaders in public and private sectors; frequently appear on TV talk shows such as "Washington Week in Review," "Meet the Press.")	2. Other media executives (Both determine how stories on the president will be covered and handled; decide on air time for presidential speeches and events; advise administration on persons to be issued White House passes and included in travel pools.)
3. Television anchorpersons (for example, Rather) (Reach large audiences on nightly news broadcasts; also sometimes do documentaries with in-depth analysis.)	

Washington Reporters
Inner Circle

1. Reporters for *New York Times* and *Washington Post*
   (Convey important information to Washington elite; serve as reference point for other reporters; influence decisions as to stories to be included on network television broadcasts.)
2. Reporters for major television networks
   (Reach large audiences but time constraints usually make coverage superficial.)
3. Reporters for *Time* and *Newsweek*.
   (In-depth weekly analysis often involving several reporters; picture on cover important to president.)
4. Wire services (Associated Press, United Press International)
   (Provide "hard news" coverage of presidential activities for many newspapers requiring tight deadlines; participate in presidential press conferences and in trip pools.)

Outer Circle

1. Reporters for *Wall Street Journal* and *U.S. News & World Report*
   (Slightly less prestigious than reporters for *New York Times, Washington Post, Time,* and *Newsweek,* but excellent in-depth analysis.)
2. Reporters of elite publications with specialized readership (for example, *Business Week, Congressional Quarterly, National Journal*)
3. Reporters for large regional dailies (for example, *Los Angeles Times*)
4. Reporters for chains (for example, Knight-Ridder, Scripps-Howard)
5. Reporters for radio stations
6. Photographers

Sources: Authors' interpretations based on Michael Baruch Grossman and Martha Joynt Kumar, *Portraying the President: The White House and the News Media* (Baltimore: Johns Hopkins University Press, 1981); Stephen Hess, *The Washington Reporters* (Washington, D.C.: Brookings, 1981); Leon Sigal, *Reporters and Officials* (Lexington, Mass.: D.C. Heath, 1973).

vary from formal communications provided to all members of the presidential media to special arrangements through which information is given to select segments of the media. In addition, the nature of communications varies. Some statements may be quoted verbatim and attributed to the president or to one of the top officials in his administration. Other statements are "not for direct quotation," which means that the source may be named but the remarks must be paraphrased. Still others are for "background only," that is, the information may be reported but not attributed to a source. Finally, "off-the-record" information is provided only for the reporter's general knowledge and understanding and is not to be reported in any form.[60] Moreover, as the following discussion indicates, different individuals and units within the executive branch serve as channels to members of the presidential media.

The Press Secretary. The most important person in the executive branch for day-to-day contact with the presidential media is the press secretary. He holds two daily briefings in which he tries to satisfy the insatiable desires of members of the media for news about the president and his administration.[61] At such briefings the secretary typically provides routine information on executive branch appointments and resignations, on presidential actions and policies, and on scheduling matters—the persons visiting the president that day, his list of meetings and travel plans. In addition, the press secretary often holds private meetings with select reporters to provide background information to help explain why the president is doing what he is and how he hopes to deal with a particular problem or program.

Grossman and Kumar describe the secretary as "the manager of the message," a job encompassing several roles.[62] First, he is a conduit who transmits news and messages from the president and principal executive officials to the news organizations; the secretary also provides feedback to the president on what is going on in the press, primarily through a daily news summary. He performs an important staff role in coordinating the wide range of publicity activities of the entire executive branch, ensuring that officials and their press secretaries send the same, not contradictory, messages about the president and his programs. In addition, he is expected to play some part in matters of public policy, advising the president of the best time to release information, who should release it, to whom it should go, and what form it should take.

The press secretary also serves as an agent who must work with three separate constituencies: the president, members of the White House staff, and representatives of the media. Although members of the staff supposedly are working in the interest of the president, at times some of them try to use the media to serve their personal ambitions and policy goals; it is the press secretary's job to prevent their doing so in a manner detrimental to the chief executive and his concerns and priorities. Also, the press secretary is an intermediary between the members of the media on the one hand and both the president and members of the White House staff on the other, sometimes convincing the former that their demands are unreasonable, and on other occasions ensuring that the president or White House staff members are sensitive to the legitimate needs of media representatives.

Having to serve these three constituencies makes the press secretary's job a very difficult one. The most important constituent is the president. The secretary can perform well only if he has continuous access to and the confidence of the president so that members of the media may assume he is speaking for the chief executive. If the president tries to be his own press secretary, as M. L. Stein suggests was true of Lyndon Johnson, even such a capable and influential person as Bill Moyers will not succeed in managing the message.[63] Even if the secretary has good personal relations with the president, he cannot be effective if he is not well regarded by members of the senior White House staff. (Grossman and Kumar maintain that both Ronald Ziegler under Nixon and Ronald Nessen under Ford had this problem.)

Students of the subject generally rate three press secretaries as the most successful. Stephen Early, who served with Franklin Roosevelt, provided authoritative and accurate information, and many reporters considered him less likely to try to mislead them than was Roosevelt. Early also benefited from the fact that his tenure preceded the rise of a potent White House staff; he therefore did not have to deal with this constituency, which has provided problems for more recent press secretaries. James Hagerty, who worked with Eisenhower, was perhaps the most successful of all the secretaries: Ike kept him informed on everything that was going on in the White House, and Hagerty did a marvelous job of keeping the media well informed during the periods when Eisenhower was ill (particularly at the time of his heart attack in 1955). Finally, Jody Powell is the best example of a recent press secretary who performed effectively. His long friendship with Jimmy Carter enabled him to have exceptionally good access to the president; he got along well with the other members of the "Georgia Mafia" [64] (particularly Hamilton Jordan) who served on the Carter White House staff; and his easy charm and keen sense of humor made him popular with representatives of the media.

The Presidential Press Conference.   Beginning with the administration of Woodrow Wilson, presidents have held press conferences to try to influence public opinion and to gauge what is in the public mind as revealed by the questions put to them by reporters from all parts of the country. Over the years, however, each president has used the institution in his own way.[65] Warren G. Harding, Calvin Coolidge, and Herbert Hoover required that questions be submitted in advance. (This practice began when Harding, unprepared for a question about a treaty, gave an erroneous and damaging interpretation of it.) Beginning with Franklin Roosevelt, presidents have permitted spontaneous questioning. The risks of this practice have been minimized in recent years by having members of the president's staff draw up a list of questions likely to be asked by reporters, together with suggested answers and supporting information. (In 1982, President Reagan began holding full-scale mock news conferences.)[66] Presidents have also benefited from the use of "planted" questions, that is, those suggested by members of the president's staff to receptive reporters and then posed to a prepared chief executive. Presidents can always refuse to answer certain questions on the grounds that the subject matter is too sensitive for public discussion at the time of the press conference. Ronald Reagan, for instance, frequently refused to comment on actions the government might take on foreign and military matters.

The success of a press conference depends on the skills of the president. Harry Truman, who enjoyed the give-and-take of exchanges with the reporters, nonetheless performed poorly in formal encounters: he tended to answer questions quickly rather than thoughtfully, and he was unable to envision just how his words would look in print or how they might be interpreted. Dwight Eisenhower also came across badly. Not only did he have trouble expressing himself clearly and grammatically, but he also displayed meager knowledge about many vital issues of the day.[67] At times, Ronald Reagan made factual errors in responding to reporters' questions.

In contrast, Franklin Roosevelt and John Kennedy were masters of the press conference. The former had a seen sense of what was newsworthy and even suggested reporters' headlines to them. He also prepared members of the press for actions he took on controversial problems by educating them initially with confidential background information; consequently, reporters tended to support Roosevelt's ultimate decisions because they understood his reasoning. Kennedy, who served a brief stint as a newspaperman and enjoyed the company of reporters, used his press conferences to great advantage; his ability to field difficult questions impressed not only the members of the press but also the American public, who viewed the proceedings on live television. Although Jimmy Carter was not as effective as either Roosevelt or Kennedy, his overall performance in press conferences also was considered successful; he came across as calm, well prepared, frank, and articulate.

Despite differences among presidents on how well they handle the press conference, there are some similarities in its use by all chief executives, such as scheduling. Since the advent of television, press conferences have been held less frequently.[68] Presidents also are less likely to schedule such conferences during periods of international involvement, especially when major policy options are being weighed. After an important decision has been made (such as entering the Korean War or invading Cambodia), a president may schedule a conference to present the nation with a *fait accompli*. Also, the president's standing in the polls affects the scheduling of press conferences.[69] They are more likely to be held when that standing is on the decline rather than on the upswing, perhaps because presidents wish to use the conference to

Table 4-2   Presidential News Conferences with White House Correspondents, 1929-1984

President	Average per month	Total number
Hoover (1929-1933)	5.6	268
Roosevelt (1933-1945)	6.9	998
Truman (1945-1953)	3.4	334
Eisenhower (1953-1961)	2.0	193
Kennedy (1961-1963)	1.9	64
Johnson (1963-1969)	2.2	135
Nixon (1969-1974)	0.5	37
Ford (1974-1977)	1.3	39
Carter (1977-1981)	0.8	59
Reagan (1981-1984)	0.5	26

Sources: Samuel Kernell, *Going Public: New Strategies of Presidential Leadership* (Washington, D.C.: CQ Press, 1986), 69. His data for Hoover, Carter, and Reagan are from *Public Papers of the Presidents of the United States*, various vols. (Washington, D.C.: Government Printing Office). Data for the others were taken from Michael Baruch Grossman and Martha Joynt Kumar, *Portraying the President: The White House and the News Media* (Baltimore: Johns Hopkins University Press, 1981), 245.

try to improve their image with the public but choose not to "rock the boat" when things are going well.

Most persons who have studied or been involved in the press conference have concluded that it serves primarily the interests of the president rather than the media. As George Reedy, press secretary to Lyndon Johnson, has pointed out, a president rarely receives an unexpected question on an important issue in a press conference, and even if he did, he could respond with a witty or a noncommittal remark.[70] Grossman and Kumar summarize the president's advantage as follows: "The President decides when to hold a conference, how much notice reporters will be given, who will ask the questions, and what the answers will be."[71]

Despite these advantages, presidents are holding fewer press conferences. (See Table 4-2.) Chief executives prefer other means of communication with representatives of the media as well as with the American people.

Other Presidential Channels of Communication.   In some instances presidents may want to communicate directly with the American people without having their remarks filtered by reporters or columnists. Although he held relatively few press conferences, Richard Nixon appeared more often on prime-time television during his first eighteen months in office than did presidents Eisenhower, Kennedy, and Johnson combined during their first eighteen months. One of the advantages of this approach is that the president is not required to answer searching questions from the press as he is in conferences.[72] The television networks carrying the presidential messages tried to compensate for their inability to question the chief executive directly by having reporters and columnists analyze his remarks immediately after the speech. When some of that analysis turned out to be very critical in the view of the Nixon administration, its officials complained to network executives about this "instant analysis," and the practice was discontinued for a time.

Even presidents who enjoy and do well in regular press conferences like to use other means of communicating directly with the American people. Franklin Roosevelt made effective use of radio for his famous "fireside chats," a technique that enabled him to create the feeling that he was coming directly into American homes and speaking personally to each of his millions of listeners. Jimmy Carter used the same approach in his first television address to the nation; seated before an open hearth and wearing a cardigan sweater, the new president sought to project an image of informality and to underscore his concern with the nation's energy crisis.

Presidents also try to establish special relationships with particular segments of the presidential media. Often singled out for attention are the media diplomats and negotiators—the principal columnists, reporters, and media executives who influence the attitudes of elites toward the president and his programs. After his inaugural ball John Kennedy stopped by Joseph Alsop's home; a few days later he went to Walter Lippmann's home; later he had dinner at the home of Rowland Evans. In his first few weeks in office Lyndon Johnson conferred with Lippmann at the journalist's home. Jimmy Carter invited small groups of elite columnists, reporters, and their spouses to a series of dinners at the White House.

Presidents also establish ties with members of the media who are not a part of the regular Washington group. President Kennedy invited editors and owners of regional newspapers to White House conferences at which he discussed major public policy issues. President Nixon held briefings with select newspaper owners and editors from around the country and had on hand key officials, such as Henry Kissinger, to discuss foreign policy problems and decisions. Nixon, Ford, and Carter all mailed speeches and articles of current interest to news organizations throughout the nation. The Reagan administration incorporated local television reporters into the ongoing routines of White House media relations.[73]

Presidents also use other special techniques in dealing with the media. One is to grant exclusive interviews and stories to select representatives of the media with the hope that they will return the favor by treating the chief executive and his programs favorably in their publications. John Kennedy, at a White House party, told his close friend Ben Bradlee of the Soviet's release of Francis Gary Powers (pilot of the U-2 spy plane shot down over Russia in 1959), enabling the *Washington Post* to have a two-hour "beat" on the rest of the press.[74] Presidents also sometimes "leak" information to create stories that discredit persons with whom they have differences. Kennedy provided a complete account of the Cuban missile crisis to two reporters who were also friends, Charles Bartlett and Stewart Alsop. The resulting article that appeared in the *Saturday Evening Post* included, at the president's insistence, the comment of a highly placed official that United Nations Ambassador Adlai Stevenson "wanted a Munich" (where British Prime Minister Neville Chamberlain capitulated to Adolf Hitler's 1938 annexation of part of Czechoslovakia).[75] Leaks can also be used as a "trial balloon": a possible course of action is reported for the purpose of testing public response to it; if the response is very negative, the president can then decide not to proceed as planned and be spared the embarrassment associated with abandoning a policy to which he was publicly committed.

In managing his relationship with the media, the president must take into account his particular strengths and weaknesses. Called "the Great Communicator," Ronald Reagan benefited greatly from his previous professional experience in radio, films, and television. He rivaled Franklin Roosevelt in his skill at delivering a prepared speech. To take advantage of those skills, the president frequently addressed the nation on prime-time television and used a series of Saturday radio broadcasts to justify his administration and its policies.

The administration also avoided or restricted its use of other media formats that President Reagan did not handle as well as prepared speeches, specifically those that required the president to give spontaneous answers to questions. The president did not participate in call-in shows and seldom invited reporters to the White House for informal, on-the-record question and answer sessions. Also, President Reagan would not answer impromptu questions from reporters at photo sessions, and he held fewer press conferences than President Carter or many of his predecessors. Particularly in his first term, many of the press conferences were aired during the day rather than during prime-time hours in the evening when a larger audience would be watching.

Relations between the president and the media also depend on other factors. The persons managing the relationship can make a difference. In his first administration, President Reagan benefited greatly from the skill and experience of White House staff members David Gergen, James A. Baker III, and Michael Deaver who carefully managed his media and public image. Their absence was keenly felt in his second term when those images were not nearly so favorable. The nature and timing of events also influence how the media and the American people view the president. The potentially damaging effects of the bombing of the Marine barracks in Lebanon in late 1983 were mitigated by stories, shortly following, on the successful invasion of Grenada. In contrast, there was no comparable development in late 1986: the story on the Iran arms shipment was followed immediately by another damaging one on the alleged diversion of profits from the arms sale to assist the contras in Central America. Moreover, the complexity and long-term nature of the Iran-contra affair meant that media and public attention focused on the matter for a protracted time as one revelation after another was released.

The Historical Relationship between the President and the Media

Presidents often have viewed the press unfavorably. George Washington, whom journalists treated rather well, initially was inclined not to run for a second term because of what he considered a critical press.[76] He also is reported to have inserted an attack on the press in his Farewell Address, which Hamilton struck from a later draft.[77] Thomas Jefferson once expressed the sentiment that if he had to decide "whether we should have a government without newspapers or newspapers without government," he would prefer the latter; however, after being attacked by the Federalist press, he complained that "even the least informed of the people have learned that nothing in a newspaper is to be believed." A century and a half later Harry Truman expressed his reservations about the press in a letter to a friend: "I really look with commiseration over the great body of my fellow citizens who, reading newspapers, live and die in the belief that they have known something of what has been passing in the world in their time." [78] Even John Kennedy, who was generally sympathetic to the media, confessed that after some time in office his treatment by the press was such that he "was reading more and enjoying it less."

The members of the media, in turn, often have criticized the way presidents have handled their media relations. Typically, chief executives are accused of "managing" the news and, as their terms in office progress, of becoming increasingly "isolated" from the representatives of the media and from the American people. Some, such as Lyndon Johnson and Richard Nixon, also were charged with deliberately lying to both the media and the public.

There is little question that to some extent a built-in conflict exists between the president and the media. Chief executives often want to suppress information they feel will endanger the nation's security or put their administrations in a bad light. Members of the media, in turn, are eager for news, however sensitive it may be, and have an interest in criticizing the president and his associates as a means of stimulating public interest and thereby creating a demand for their services.

Despite such potential conflicts, a basis of cooperation exists between presidents and the press.[79] Quite simply, they are mutually dependent: neither presidents nor the press can perform their job without the assistance of the other. The president must be able to communicate with the public through the media, and the media must receive the cooperation of the president if they are to cover the most important official in the national government and give the American people an accurate assessment of his activities.

Grossman and Kumar's analysis of recent media coverage of the president shows that, for the most part, coverage has been favorable.[80] A survey of the stories on the president that appeared in *Time* magazine and the *New York Times* from 1953 to 1978 and on the CBS "Evening News" from 1968 to 1978 indicated that there were more positive than negative ones. Moreover, pictures, particularly those appearing in newspapers, tended to be favorable even when they accompanied a negative story. The analysis did show a rise in the number of unfavorable stories during the Vietnam and Watergate periods but also revealed that after 1974 the treatment of the president became more favorable again. However, a recent analysis of the CBS "Evening News" from 1968 to 1985 found that in eleven of the seventeen years studied, the president received more negative than positive coverage; in addition, negative stories became more numerous with each year of a president's term as well as from one administration to the next.[81]

While the particular relationship that exists between the media and the president naturally depends on who is serving in the office, their general relationship goes through certain predictable phases.[82] The first, which Grossman and Kumar call "alliance," is a period of great cooperation. Both parties agree on which items are newsworthy; these include information on the new people in the administration and its proposed goals and policies. The media are willing to serve as conduits for the messages the president wants to send the American people. In turn, the presidency is "open" during this period; reporters are likely "to have their phone calls answered, to be granted interviews, and to get information that has not been specifically restricted." [83]

The second phase is called "competition." The two parties do not agree on what constitutes news—the president wants to concentrate on picturing members of his administration as part of a happy team, committed to common goals and policies; the media focus on conflicts among personalities in the administration and controversies over policies.[84] The open presidency of the first phase gives way to one characterized by manipulation, in which the president restricts access to himself and the members of his administration. He typically courts the favor of certain elite journalists and may even try to ingratiate himself with reporters and columnists who have not treated him well in the past. Presidents also may go on the attack, trying to have individual reporters fired or reassigned, and may openly criticize the media as a whole. Reporters respond in various ways: some become a "friend of the court," ingratiating themselves with the chief executive in return for favors; others take on the role of "adversary," using a combative style in their relationships with the president; still others become "historian-observers and institutional analysts," interpreting administration policies and personalities in terms of the mood of the times and examining the entire executive process by which policies are formulated and implemented.

The third and final phase of presidential-media relationships is "detachment." The president turns over much of the management of the news to surrogates. He appears before the media only in settings that are favorable to him, particularly if he is running for reelection, and he carefully schedules his appearances to coincide with major events. He also gives increased emphasis to contacts with members of the regional press and with interest groups. The media, in turn, engage in more investigative reporting, seek information from sources other than the White House, and participate in joint ventures with other reporters in their own news organization.

Today both the president and the media possess valuable advantages in dealing with each other.[85] As previously noted, the chief executive virtually establishes the news agenda and, particularly on foreign trips, not only selects the news that will be reported about particular events but also determines what those events will be. He decides what format to use in conveying his message (prime-time television, for example, rather than a press conference), can plant questions and leak information to sympathetic media representatives, and can withhold information, particularly about foreign and military affairs, so as to conceal mistakes of his administration. The media, for its part, can lessen its dependence on the president for news by broadening its network of contacts in the executive branch, can do "detective" work by using documentary sources to find out what is actually happening, can compel presidents to release information through questioning at news conferences as well as with the assistance of the Congress and occasionally the use of the Freedom of Information Act, and can insist that reporters of their choice be admitted to the press room, to news conferences, and to daily briefing sessions.

The president benefits from the services of many people in the executive branch who deal with the media, but the media also have their own share of resources. Today, a large number of reporters cover the White House, most of them well educated.[86] To an increasing extent, they benefit from specialized expertise in substantive areas such as law, science, welfare, and defense policy. As Grossman and Rourke have observed, "If it is credible to speak of an imperial presidency as a shorthand description of the growth of executive power in American society, it may be no less plausible to think of the emerging citadels of power in the American press as an imperial media. The outcome of this imperial media, and consequences for the governance of American democracy, are as yet far from clear."[87]

The next section shifts the focus from the president as a representative of all the American people to his responsibility to a particular segment of the public—the members of his own political party.

The President and His Political Party

Initially, the Founders were opposed to political parties. The early leaders regarded them as a potentially divisive influence in a young nation struggling against disruptive forces of geographical and economic rivalries. They viewed the president as a nonpartisan "patriot king" (epitomized by

George Washington) who would rule in the interests of all the people. However, as discussed in Chapter 1, domestic and foreign policy issues soon gave rise to the creation of rival political parties: the Federalists, led by Washington and Hamilton, and the Republicans founded by Jefferson and James Madison. By the mid-1790s the two groups were voting against each other in Congress and fielding rival candidates in congressional elections. When the still-popular George Washington retired at the end of his second term in 1796, the party competition spread to presidential contests as well.

No person better illustrates this basic change in political attitudes than Thomas Jefferson. In 1789 he declared that "if I could not go to heaven but with a party, I would not go there at all." Within a few years, however, he helped found a political party and in 1800 was elected as that party's first president. He then took firm control of the party and used it as a means of governing the nation. As James MacGregor Burns points out, Jefferson took an active role in a variety of political endeavors:[88]

> He personally drafted bills and had them introduced in Congress; saw to it that the men he wanted took the leadership posts in Congress by holding out promises of advancement; made the Speaker and the floor leader of the House his personal lieutenants; changed the leadership as he saw fit; used Ways and Means and other committees as instruments of presidential control; and dominated the Republican Caucus in the House.

No president since that time has been as powerful a party leader as Jefferson (although Andrew Jackson and Woodrow Wilson also became strong figures in their party). Today, public officials and party leaders and activists want the president to be the chief of the party that helped to put him in the White House. The president's role as partisan leader involves him in all the major political activities of his party. He is expected to play some part in the election contests for other offices. As party chief, he also is responsible for identifying problems and formulating programs to deal with them. Finally, the president must organize and manage the government so it will implement his programs.

The President and Electoral Activities

The president naturally is more involved with the electoral activities of his own office than with those of other elective offices. If a president decides to seek reelection, the renomination is usually his for the asking; he dominates every aspect of the convention—location, choice of major officers, party platform, and selection of his running mate—and makes strategic decisions about the general election campaign. The chief executive may choose, for example, to have little to do with congressional candidates of his own party running in a presidential election year, a strategy that Richard Nixon followed in 1972 in his quest to win support from traditionally Democratic voters.

U.S. presidents also have come to play an important part in midterm congressional elections. Even Dwight Eisenhower, who did not enjoy playing the role of partisan leader, gave some forty speeches in the 1954 campaign. President Kennedy took an active part in the 1962 congressional elections until the Cuban missile crisis forced him to cancel speaking engagements and return to Washington. Although Lyndon Johnson did not go on the campaign trail in 1966 (in part because the Vietnam War had made him so unpopular that many congressional candidates preferred that he stay away), the pattern of presidential involvement was restored and even expanded by Richard Nixon in 1970 when he traveled to twenty states in behalf of Republican candidates. His successor, Gerald Ford, visited eighteen in 1974 to try to help members of Congress and governors running on the Republican ticket. In 1978 Jimmy Carter campaigned for thirty-three House candidates as he took to the trail along with Vice President Mondale, the First Lady, and members of the Carter family. Although many Republican congressional candidates in states hard hit by the recession did not want President Reagan's assistance in 1982, he did campaign for forty of them and gave a nationally televised speech for the Republicans on the eve of the election. In 1986, the president campaigned and raised money for all fifteen Republican senatorial incumbents who were originally elected with him in 1980, pleading with voters to continue Republican control of the Senate during his last two years in office.

A popular president who decides to campaign in the midterm elections has the difficult decision of determining which candidates he will work for. Should he concentrate on crucial competitive contests, or should he also assist close political friends who seem to be in no appreciable danger of being defeated but who seek his assistance anyway? Should he campaign in favor of important party figures even though they voted against him on major legislative measures? If the president does not, and an ignored person wins anyway, he or she may retaliate with even less support in the future; moreover, if his party's candidate loses, the opposition replacement may be even more opposed to the president's programs.

Because of such unattractive possibilities, a president may be tempted to try to pick his party's nominees for Senate and House seats. However, this is seldom done. A study by William Riker and William Bast of congressional nominations from 1943 to 1960 indicated that of the approximately 1,200 nominations during this period, presidents endorsed candidates in only 39 instances. (Since two of these were subsequent endorsements of candidates endorsed earlier, only 37 endorsements were involved.)[89] The presidents' candidates managed to win both the party's nomination and the subsequent general election in only 17 cases. Even such a popular president as Franklin Roosevelt had limited success in his 1938 foray into congressional nominations: of his 12 endorsees that year, only 6 prevailed in both the nomination and general election contests.

Riker and Bast attribute this limited presidential involvement in congressional nomination contests to the long tradition of such contests being exclusively the business of the state or district the member of Congress represents. If there is local opposition, the president who gambles on intervention only to have his protégé lose in a primary fight risks a decline in political prestige and also the enmity of the winning candidate. For these reasons, presidents typically avoid overt involvement in spirited nomination contests.

If the battle lines in a congressional nomination have not been drawn, however, a president can influence the selection of congressional candidates by taking early action in support of prospective contenders. President Kennedy, for example, encouraged Joseph Tydings, Jr., of Maryland, to seek a seat in Congress; and President Nixon persuaded some ten Republican members of the House to give up their seats to run for the Senate, where they would be more important to him politically.[90] Thus, chief executives attempt to build a base of support in Congress by personally recruiting candidates who share their views on public policy. Presidents also work discreetly behind the scenes through sympathetic state and local political leaders to interest people in running and may use their influence to funnel needed funds to candidates whom they favor.

A president's involvement in congressional general elections is much safer politically than his entrance into nominations: he cannot be accused of meddling in interparty affairs, and his endorsed candidates need only win one electoral contest, not two (the nomination *and* the election). Still, there are limits to what a president can accomplish, especially in elections for the House of Representatives. For one thing, the sheer number of contests (435 every two years) precludes his participation in many of them. For another, there is good evidence that the off-year House elections are primarily local, not national, events. Scholars who have examined off-year congressional elections report the same basic finding: how people vote has more to do with their evaluations of the congressional candidates than with their assessment of the president.[91] Moreover, incumbency is a valuable asset for congressional candidates; they benefit from previous campaign experience, close relationships with voters, greater knowledge of issues, and superior financial resources, which give them a considerable advantage over their opponents.[92] Presidents who attempt to campaign against sitting members of Congress therefore face almost insurmountable odds.

This is not to say that presidents play no role at all in congressional elections. Analysis of eight such elections indicates that the share of the congressional vote won by House candidates of the president's party depended on the condition of the national economy and the president's standing in public opinion polls at the time of the elections.[93] A study of midterm congressional elections between 1946 and 1966 shows that voting in midterm elections tends to be *negative;* that is, those who disapprove of the president's performance in office are more likely to cast their ballot in such elections than those who approve of his performance.[94] Gary Jacobson contends that the president's role in congressional elections is essentially an indirect one: the state of the economy and the president's ratings in the public opinion polls influence the caliber of candidates who run in congressional elections. If, for example, these are not favorable, the opposition party will be able to field an unusually large proportion of formidable challengers with well-financed campaigns, and the president's party in Congress will lose a considerable number of seats.[95]

Senatorial midterm elections offer a somewhat more encouraging opportunity for presidents who wish to influence the results of such contests. At most, 34 seats are up for contention, so the chief executive can concentrate his efforts in a way that is not possible when 435 seats are at stake. A study of the 1974 Senate elections showed that party identification principally determines how voters cast their ballots; presidents therefore can try to influence voting decisions by emphasizing their role as party leader.

Although sitting senators are in the same position as House members in being able to bring their name to the attention of constituents,[96] incumbency is not as advantageous for a senator as it is for a House member, because senatorial challengers are much more visible to the electorate than are those who run against House incumbents. (The Senate, being more prestigious than the House, attracts more able candidates; voters in a state have only one Senate contest to watch; and Senate challengers find it easier to raise money than House challengers do, which enables senatorial candidates to make greater use of television in their campaigns, thus further adding to their visibility.) Popular presidents are thus in a better position to help persons who challenge incumbent senators of the opposite party, perhaps even increasing their visibility by publicly associating themselves with the challengers.

The results of Senate elections since the early 1960s reflect the combined effect of these factors. In 1962, when John Kennedy was president, his party lost five seats in the House but picked up two in the Senate; in 1974, when Gerald Ford succeeded to the presidency after the forced resignation of Richard Nixon, Republicans lost forty-eight House seats but only five Senate seats. (See Table 4-3 for information on how the president's party has fared in off-year elections for the House and Senate since 1942.)

Other considerations besides electoral ones deter presidents from playing the role of party leader on all occasions. One is that voting in the U.S. Congress does not follow strictly partisan lines. (Chapter 6 will examine this matter further.) President Eisenhower was dependent on votes from Democratic members of Congress for many of his programs, particularly in foreign policy. Presidents Kennedy and Johnson also received crucial Republican support on civil rights legislation as a result of the efforts of Everett Dirksen, the Republican floor leader in the Senate. Dirksen also defended Johnson's Vietnam policies more vigorously than did many Democrats. In such

Table 4-3   Gains and Losses of President's Party in House and Senate Off-Year Elections, 1942-1986

Year	President	President's party	Change in House seats	Change in Senate seats
1942	Roosevelt	Democratic	−50	−8
1946	Truman	Democratic	−54	−11
1950	Truman	Democratic	−29	−5
1954	Eisenhower	Republican	−18	−1
1958	Eisenhower	Republican	−47	−12
1962	Kennedy	Democratic	−5	+2
1966	Johnson	Democratic	−48	−4
1970	Nixon	Republican	−12	+1
1974	Ford	Republican	−48	−5
1978	Carter	Democratic	−16	−3
1982	Reagan	Republican	−27	+1
1986	Reagan	Republican	−5	−8

Sources: *Statistical Abstract of the United States* (Washington, D.C.: Government Printing Office, 1986), 247. Data for 1986 are from *Congressional Quarterly Weekly Report,* November 8, 1986, 2803.

Note: Data represent the difference between the number of seats held by the president's party in present and preceding Congresses.

circumstances, it was hardly surprising that neither Democratic president expended any genuine effort to get Dirksen defeated in Illinois. Richard Nixon treated some of his Democratic supporters the same way: his attorney general, Richard Kleindienst, told Mississippians in the 1972 campaign that if he lived there, he would vote for Democratic senator James Eastland. When many southern Democrats voted in 1981 for Ronald Reagan's program of budget and tax cuts, the Republican president said publicly that he did not see how he could oppose them in the 1982 congressional elections.

For other reasons as well some presidents play down their activities in midterm elections. If their party's candidates do not do well, the election may be interpreted as a repudiation of their administration. Campaign rhetoric can be taken personally by members of the opposition party, making it more difficult for the president to win their future support for his legislative program. The chief executive also may be concerned that too much time spent on the campaign trail will create the impression in people's minds that he is not exerting enough effort on the more important duties of his office. Finally, campaigning may detract from his image as the leader of all the American people.

Presidents resort to certain tactics to offset these disadvantages. One is to schedule foreign visits (during which he is seen as representative of the entire nation) to coincide with congressional elections. Richard Nixon, for example, visited the Middle East and Mediterranean areas in early October 1970. Another tactic is to make use of the vice president. Spiro Agnew campaigned longer and in more states in 1970 than Nixon did, and it was he rather than the president who attacked the opposition candidates in personal terms.[97] This practice allowed Nixon to take the "high road" in the congressional campaign by stressing issues rather than personalities.

The above factors, together with the decline in the importance of political parties in recent years, makes the president's role in midterm elections difficult. Roger Brown concludes that when presidents "have been persuaded to shoulder part of the campaign burden, their efforts have been directed towards influencing the composition of the next Congress and fostering goodwill on the part of the congressional party."[98] Michael McConachie's analysis of the effects of presidents' participation in midterm campaigns shows that such participation does improve the electoral record of congressional candidates for whom they campaign; these candidates tend to support legislative proposals of the president more than do members of Congress of his party for whom he does not campaign. Both of these effects, however, are very limited.[99] McConachie concludes that to conduct a successful midterm campaign, the president should strive to campaign vigorously throughout all regions of the country; work and cooperate with national, state, and local party leaders; set realistic goals for the midterm election (a House seat gain, for example, has occurred only once, 1934, in this century); and choose candidates to assist and areas to visit that will make him look good.[100]

The limitations of the effects of presidential participation in congressional elections were graphically illustrated by President Reagan's experiences in 1982 and 1986. Despite his best campaign efforts—and in 1986, his great personal popularity—the Republican party lost twenty-seven House seats in 1982 and eight Senate seats in 1986 to the Democrats.

The President and Party Programs

One area of partisan activity that the president clearly dominates is the preparation of party programs for dealing with major national problems. An incumbent president seeking reelection has the greatest influence in the writing of the party platform at the national convention. He also has the opportunity to identify party issues and programs during the course of the presidential campaign. He may choose to emphasize certain parts of the platform, ignore others, or even take stands at variance with those contained in the document.

Traditionally, students of American politics have concluded that party platforms and presidential campaign speeches are not to be taken seriously. (The former are for candidates to "run" on, not to "stand" on; the latter are merely rhetoric and do not constitute commitments on the candidate's part.) Recent studies have called into question, however, these somewhat cynical views. As noted in Chapter 1, Gerald Pomper's analysis of the platforms of the Republican and Democratic parties from 1944 through 1978 revealed that presidents took the pledges seriously and that they worked with the Congress or issued executive orders to enact most of their campaign commitments.[101] Similarly, Fred Grogan found that both Lyndon Johnson and Richard Nixon acted on more than half of the promises they made in campaign speeches in 1964 and 1968, respectively.[102] Arnold Muller's analysis of the campaign pledges of Dwight Eisenhower and John Kennedy determined that each of them took action on about three-fourths of his promises.[103] And Jeff Fishel's study of the pledges and actions of Kennedy, Johnson, Nixon, Carter, and Reagan concluded that these five presidents acted on some two-thirds of their campaign promises.[104]

Partisan Influences in Organizing and Managing the Government

The extent to which presidential programs actually are implemented depends to a considerable degree on the president's influence over the party within the government. This group comprises officials in the legislative and executive branches who are either elected under a partisan label or appointed primarily because of their party activities or because it is expected that they will implement party views on public policy matters.

The president's control over his party in the Congress is distinctly limited. He has little to do with its composition, since most senators and representatives are elected independently of him. Moreover, he has comparatively little influence over the organization of his party in Congress. Although Thomas Jefferson determined who his party's leaders would be, for the most part American chief executives have been chary of interfering with the right of Congress to choose its own people. Dwight Eisenhower was forced to work with Senate Republican leader William Knowland, whose views on foreign policy were quite different from his own. During part of John Kennedy's administration, the Democratic Speaker of the House was John McCormack, a political rival from Kennedy's home state.

The president has more influence over the party in the executive branch. (Chapter 7 will examine further the president's relations with the executive branch.) The only other elected official, the vice president, is to be used or not as the president sees fit. In addition, the chief executive can make appointments to policy-making posts that both reward individuals for their service to the party and permit them to influence the administration of government programs. In particular, his closest political advisers on the White House staff constitute what is, in effect, the president's personal party: persons who have labored in his presidential campaign continue to protect his interests and promote his policies after they assume top governmental posts in his administration.[105]

Conclusion

The president's relationship with the American people between elections has undergone significant changes in recent years. Kernell contends that whereas a president used to promote his programs primarily by negotiating with other political elites in the Congress and executive branch, today he increasingly chooses to "go public"; that is, he resorts to "promoting himself and his policies in Washington by appealing to the American public for support." [106] He does this by means of public addresses, public appearances, and political travel. James Ceaser and his associates make the same point. Referring to this development as "the rise of the rhetorical presidency," they argue that "presidential speech and action increasingly reflect the opinion that speaking *is* governing. Speeches are written to become the events to which people react no less than the 'real' events themselves." [107]

A variety of factors have contributed to this development. The mass media—first radio, and more recently television—have enabled the president to communicate directly with the American people and to reach the public instantaneously. Moreover, the tactics of the campaign have influenced the governing process: Washington "outsiders" such as Jimmy Carter and Ronald Reagan are disposed to use the same approaches in governing as they used in winning the nomination and the election. As Ceaser and his associates explain, "So formative has the campaign become of our tastes for oratory and of our conception of leadership that presidential speech and governing have come more and more to imitate the model of the campaign." [108] They also contend that beginning with Woodrow Wilson, the president himself has changed his view of leadership: he now employs "oratory to create an active public opinion that, if necessary, will pressure the Congress into accepting his program." [109] Kernell sees this development as a somewhat more recent one, a practice the president increasingly uses because the elites with whom he formerly bargained over his programs are more numerous, fragmented, and politically independent than they were in the recent past.[110]

Although these new developments undoubtedly have affected the presidency, the fact remains that public opinion cannot be transformed directly into public policy. If the president wants to see his programs adopted and implemented, he must use the powers and institutional arrangements of his own office, and he must work with the Congress, the executive branch, and the courts to accomplish his purposes.

Notes

1. Henry Jones Ford, *The Rise and Growth of American Politics: A Sketch of Constitutional Development* (New York: Macmillan, 1900), 283.
2. Woodrow Wilson, *Constitutional Government in the United States* (New York: Columbia University Press, 1908, 1961), 68.
3. Sidney Hyman, *The American President* (New York: Harper and Row, 1954), 66. Hyman's italics.
4. Richard Neustadt, *Presidential Power: The Politics of Leadership from FDR to Carter*, rev. ed. (New York: Wiley, 1980), 69.
5. David Easton, *A Systems Analysis of Political Life* (New York: Wiley, 1965), chaps. 10-13.
6. Joseph Kallenbach, *The American Chief Executive: The Presidency and the Governorship* (New York: Harper and Row, 1966), 275.
7. Fred Greenstein, *Children and Politics* (New Haven: Yale University Press, 1965); Robert Hess and Judith Torney, *The Development of Political Attitudes in Children* (Chicago: Aldine, 1967); David Easton and Jack Dennis, *Children in the Political System: Origins of Political Legitimacy* (New York: McGraw-Hill, 1969).
8. Easton and Dennis, *Children in the Political System*, 206-207.
9. Dean Jaros, Herbert Hirsch, and Frederick J. Fleron, Jr., "The Malevolent Leader: Political Socialization in an American Subculture," *American Political Science Review* (June 1968): 564-575.
10. Ibid., 575.
11. Jack Dennis and Carol Webster, "Children's Images of the President and Government in 1962 and 1974," *American Politics Quarterly* (October 1975): 386-405.
12. Ibid., 398.
13. Fred Greenstein, "What the President Means to Americans: Presidential Choice between Elections," in *Choosing the President,* ed. James David Barber (Englewood Cliffs, N.J.: Prentice-Hall, 1974).
14. Christopher Arterton, "The Impact of Watergate on Children's Attitudes towards Political Authority," *Political Science Quarterly* (June 1974): 269-288; Christopher Arterton, "Watergate and Children's Attitudes towards Political Authority Revisited," *Political Science Quarterly* (Fall 1975): 477-496.
15. Dean Jaros and John Shoemaker, "The Malevolent Unindicted Co-conspirator: Watergate and Appalachian Youth," *American Politics Quarterly* (October 1976): 483-505.
16. Greenstein, "What the President Means to Americans," 125.
17. Two notable exceptions were Harry Truman in 1951 at the time of the Korean War and Richard Nixon in 1973 in the midst of the Watergate scandal. In each instance, however, the president was ranked third: Truman behind two war heroes, Dwight Eisenhower and Douglas MacArthur, and Nixon behind Secretary of State Henry Kissinger and evangelist Billy Graham.
18. Greenstein, "What the President Means to Americans," 144-147.

19. Ibid., 144.
20. Samuel Kernell, Peter Sperlich, and Aaron Wildavsky, "Public Support for Presidents," in *Perspectives on the Presidency*, ed. Aaron Wildavsky (Boston: Little, Brown, 1975), 148-181.
21. John Mueller, *War, Presidents and Public Opinion* (New York: Wiley, 1973).
22. As indicated above, President Eisenhower's popularity remained high during his stay in office. Mueller attributes this development to a variety of reasons, including Ike's personal appeal, the credit he received for the ending of the Korean War, his "amateur" status (as contrasted to being considered a "professional" politician), which allowed him to appear "above the battle," and the fact that he made few changes in domestic policy and so did not antagonize groups as much as other presidents.
23. Samuel Kernell, "Explaining Presidential Popularity," *American Political Science Review* (June 1978): 506-522.
24. Jong Lee, "Rallying around the Flag: Foreign Policy Events and Presidential Popularity," *Presidential Studies Quarterly* (Fall 1977): 252-256.
25. George C. Edwards III, *The Public Presidency: The Pursuit of Popular Support* (New York: St. Martin's Press, 1983), 239-247.
26. Ibid., 247.
27. Henry Kenski, "The Impact of Economic Conditions on Presidential Popularity," *Journal of Politics* (August 1977): 764-773; Kristen Monroe, "Economic Influences on Presidential Popularity," *Public Opinion Quarterly* (Fall 1978): 360-369.
28. Edwards, *The Public Presidency*, 235.
29. Robert Shapiro, "Politics and the Federal Reserve," *Public Interest* (Winter 1982): 119-139.
30. James Stimson, "Public Support for American Presidents: A Cyclical Model," *Public Opinion Quarterly* (Spring 1976): 1-21.
31. Another possible reason the incumbent president's performance ratings tend to rise in the fourth year is that when potential political opponents begin to appear on the scene, citizens compare the president with these flesh-and-blood persons rather than with an abstract ideal of a chief executive.
32. Kernell, "Explaining Presidential Popularity."
33. Edwards, *The Public Presidency*, 233.
34. Richard Brody and Benjamin Page, "The Impact of Events on Presidential Popularity: The Johnson and Nixon Administrations," in *Perspectives on the Presidency*, ed. Wildavsky.
35. Donald Singleton, "The Role of Broadcasting in Presidential Popularity: An Exploration in Presidential Power" (Paper delivered at the 1976 annual meeting of the International Communication Association).
36. Fred Smoller, "The Six-O'Clock Presidency: Patterns of Network Coverage of the President," *Presidential Studies Quarterly* (Winter 1986): 42-43.
37. Timothy Haight and Richard Brody, "The Mass Media and Presidential Popularity: Presidential Broadcasting and News in the Nixon Administration," *Communications Research* (Spring 1977): 41-60.
38. Foreign trips have other side benefits as well. Not only are they flattering to the people of the visited country, but they also appeal to ethnic groups at

home with family ties to those nations (Irish-Americans, Italian-Americans, French-Americans, and the like).

39. Louis Koenig, *The Chief Executive,* rev. ed. (New York: Harcourt, Brace and World, 1968), 188.

40. Samuel Kernell, *Going Public: New Strategies of Presidential Leadership* (Washington, D.C.: CQ Press, 1986), 93.

41. Edwards, *The Public Presidency,* 16-17.

42. Stephen Hess, *Organizing the Presidency* (Washington, D.C.: Brookings, 1976), 47.

43. Joseph A. Pika, "Interest Groups and the Executive: Presidential Intervention," in *Interest Group Politics,* ed. Allan J. Cigler and Burdett A. Loomis (Washington, D.C.: CQ Press, 1983), 318.

44. Martha Joynt Kumar and Michael Baruch Grossman, "Political Communications from the White House: The Interest Group Connection," *Presidential Studies Quarterly* (Winter 1986): 97.

45. Ibid., 98.

46. Ibid.

47. In some instances, however, presidents attack special interest groups. John Kennedy publicly castigated the steel companies when, contrary to what he understood to be an understanding with them, they raised steel prices in 1962. During his presidency Jimmy Carter publicly criticized oil companies, as well as doctors and lawyers, for being unduly concerned with their own financial interests rather than those of society in general. Such actions usually reflect a president's unhappiness with the attitudes of particular groups toward his policies but may also be calculated to curry the favor of members of the general public, who themselves resent the attitudes of groups they feel are too rich and powerful.

48. James Pollard, *The Presidents and the Press* (New York: Macmillan, 1947), chap. 1.

49. William Rivers, *The Opinion-Makers* (Boston: Beacon Press, 1967), 7.

50. Michael Baruch Grossman and Martha Joynt Kumar, *Portraying the President: The White House and the News Media* (Baltimore: Johns Hopkins University Press, 1981), 19.

51. Ibid., chap. 8.

52. Ibid., 209, 210.

53. Ibid., chap. 3. The quotation is from John Milton, "On His Blindness."

54. Ibid.; Stephen Hess, *The Washington Reporters* (Washington, D.C.: Brookings, 1981), chap. 2; Leon Segal, *Reporters and Officials* (Lexington, Mass.: D.C. Heath, 1973), chap. 1.

55. Hess, *The Washington Reporters,* 31.

56. There are, of course, some notable exceptions to this rule. The "MacNeil-Lehrer Report," broadcast nightly by the Public Broadcasting Service (PBS), examines two or three topics in depth for one hour; ABC's "Nightline" looks at one topic for one-half hour. NBC's "Agronsky and Company" pits columnists of opposite political views (liberal Carl Rowan and conservative James J. Kilpatrick, for example) against each other in discussion of controversial topics; PBS's "Washington Week in Review" uses major political reporters, such as Hedrick Smith of the *New York Times* and

Haynes Johnson of the *Washington Post,* to analyze the significant news developments of the previous week.

57. Grossman and Kumar, *Portraying the President,* 43.

58. William Rivers quotes one reporter as complaining that writing for a wire service "is like having a thousand mothers-in-law" (*The Opinion-Makers,* 28).

59. Stephen Hess includes the *Wall Street Journal* with the *New York Times* and *Washington Post* (and the now-defunct *Washington Star*) in his inner ring of news media, but his own statistics show that considerably fewer Washington reporters read the *Journal* than either the *Times* or *Post* (*The Washington Reporters,* p. 25).

60. Rivers, *The Opinion-Makers,* 37.

61. The reporters who come to the 9:15 a.m. briefing are from organizations that can afford to assign more than one person to the White House; a broader group of reporters attends the noon briefing (Stephen Hess, *The Government-Press Connection: Press Officers and Their Offices* [Washington, D.C.: Brookings, 1984], 73).

62. Grossman and Kumar, *Portraying the President.* chap. 5.

63. M. L. Stein, *When Presidents Meet the Press* (New York: Julian Messner, 1969), 166.

64. This term was given to a group of persons from Georgia who had been closely associated with Jimmy Carter during his entire political career. A similar group who served with John Kennedy was known as the "Irish Mafia."

65. Elmer Cornwell, *Presidential Leadership of Public Opinion* (Bloomington: Indiana University Press, 1965), chaps. 2-8.

66. Edwards, *The Public Presidency,* 114.

67. Fred Greenstein suggests that on some occasions Eisenhower did this deliberately to avoid providing information he preferred to withhold (*The Hidden-Hand Presidency: Eisenhower as Leader* [New York: Basic Books, 1982], 66-70).

68. William Lammers, "Presidential Press Conference Schedules: Who Hides and When?" *Political Science Quarterly* (Spring 1981): 261-278.

69. Jarol Manheim and William Lammers, "The News Conference and Presidential Leadership of Public Opinion: Does the Tail Wag the Dog?" *Presidential Studies Quarterly* (Spring 1981): 177-188.

70. George Reedy, *The Twilight of the Presidency* (New York: New American Library, 1970), 164.

71. Grossman and Kumar, *Portraying the President,* 244.

72. There is general agreement that Ronald Reagan does far better in delivering prepared messages on television or radio than he does in responding to reporters' questions at press conferences.

73. Kernell, *Going Public,* 74.

74. Tom Wicker, "On Press," *Book Digest Magazine,* March 1978, 34-65.

75. David Halberstam, *The Best and the Brightest* (New York: Random House, 1972), 28.

76. Pollard, *The Presidents and the Press,* 14.

77. Max Kampelman, "Congress, the Media and the Press," in *Congress against*

the President, ed. Harvey Mansfield (New York: Academy of Political Science, 1975), 92.

78. Ibid., 95-96.
79. Grossman and Kumar, *Portraying the President,* chap. 1.
80. Ibid., chap. 10.
81. Smoller, "The Six O'Clock Presidency." It should be noted that Smoller's analysis is based on transcripts of the CBS broadcasts, while Grossman and Kumar used films of the broadcasts.
82. Grossman and Kumar, *Portraying the President,* chap. 11.
83. Ibid., 178.
84. This tendency first became apparent during the second year of the Reagan administration when reporters began to ask him more embarrassing questions (for instance, why he did not set an example by making more generous donations to private charities). They also appeared not to take seriously the president's statement that members of his administration were one big happy family.
85. Michael Grossman and Francis Rourke, "The Media and the Presidency: An Exchange Analysis," *Political Science Quarterly* (Fall 1976): 455-470.
86. Stephen Hess showed that in 1978, 73 percent were college graduates and 33 percent had graduate degrees (*Washington Reporters,* 83); Leo Rosten reported that in 1936, 51 percent were college graduates, and 6 percent had an advanced academic degree (*The Washington Correspondents* [New York: Harcourt, Brace, 1937], 159-60).
87. Grossman and Rourke, "The Media and the Presidency: An Exchange Analysis," 470.
88. James MacGregor Burns, *The Deadlock of Democracy: Four-Party Politics in America* (Englewood Cliffs, N.J.: Prentice-Hall, 1963), 36.
89. William Riker and William Bast, "Presidential Action in Congressional Nominations," in *The Presidency,* ed. Aaron Wildavsky (Boston: Little, Brown, 1969).
90. Most of them were unsuccessful in their Senate bid. However, President Nixon appointed some to ambassadorships to compensate for their giving up their House seat.
91. Thomas Mann presents his findings on the 1974 elections in *Unsafe at Any Margin: Interpreting Congressional Elections* (Washington, D.C.: American Enterprise Institute, 1978), 92; Lyn Ragsdale presents her findings on the 1978 elections in "The Fiction of Congressional Elections as Presidential Events," *American Politics Quarterly* (October 1980): 375-398.
92. David Leuthold, *Electioneering in a Democracy: Campaigns for Congress* (New York: Wiley, 1968).
93. Edward Tufte, "Determinants of the Outcomes of Midterm Congressional Elections," *American Political Science Review* (September 1975): 812-826.
94. Samuel Kernell, "Presidential Popularity and Negative Voting: An Alternative Explanation of the Midterm Decline of the Presidential Party, *American Political Science Review* (March 1977): 44-66.
95. Gary Jacobson, *The Politics of Congressional Elections* (Boston: Little, Brown, 1983), 138 ff.
96. David Mayhew, *Congress: The Electoral Connection* (New Haven: Yale

University Press, 1974).

97. Nixon let the vice president handle the sticky job of criticizing Republican senator Charles Goodell of New York, who voted against the president on a number of key issues, such as Vietnam. Agnew even helped raise money for the victorious Conservative party candidate, James Buckley.

98. Roger Brown, "Presidents as Midterm Campaigners," in *Presidents and Their Parties: Leadership or Neglect?* ed. Robert Harmel (New York: Praeger, 1984), 146.

99. Michael McConachie, "Presidential Campaigning for Congressional Candidates in Midterm Elections, 1962-1982" (Ph.D. diss., University of Missouri-Columbia, 1985), chap. 6.

100. Ibid., 202.

101. Gerald Pomper with Susan Lederman, *Elections in America: Control and Influence in Democratic Politics,* 2d ed. (New York: Longman, 1980), chap. 8.

102. Fred Grogan, "Candidate Premises and Presidential Performance" (Paper delivered at the annual meeting of the Midwest Political Science Association, Chicago, April 21-23, 1977).

103. Arnold Muller, "Public Policy and the Presidential Election Process: A Study of Promise and Performance" (Ph.D. diss., University of Missouri-Columbia, 1986), 351.

104. Jeff Fishel, *Presidents and Promises: From Campaign Pledge to Presidential Performance* (Washington, D.C.: CQ Press, 1985), 38.

105. Lester Seligman, "The Presidential Office and the President as Party Leader," *Law and Contemporary Problems* (Autumn 1956): 724-734.

106. Kernell, *Going Public,* 1.

107. James Ceaser, Glen Thurow, Jeffrey Tulis, and Joseph Bessette, "The Rise of the Rhetorical Presidency," *Political Studies Quarterly* (Spring 1981): 159.

108. Ibid., 167.

109. Ibid., 163.

110. Kernell, *Going Public,* esp. chap. 2.

Selected Readings

Burns, James MacGregor. *The Deadlock of Democracy: Four-Party Politics in America.* Englewood Cliffs, N.J.: Prentice-Hall, 1963.

Cornwell, Elmer. *Presidential Leadership of Public Opinion.* Bloomington: Indiana University Press, 1965.

Edwards, George C., III. *The Public Presidency: The Pursuit of Popular Support.* New York: St. Martin's Press, 1983.

Fishel, Jeff. *Presidents and Promises: From Campaign Pledge to Presidential Performance.* Washington, D.C.: CQ Press, 1985.

Grossman, Michael Baruch, and Martha Joynt Kumar. *Portraying the President: The White House and the News Media.* Baltimore: Johns Hopkins University Press, 1981.

Harmel, Robert, ed. *Presidents and Their Parties: Leadership or Neglect?* New York: Praeger, 1984.
Hess, Stephen. *The Washington Reporters.* Washington, D.C.: Brookings, 1981.
Kernell, Samuel. *Going Public: New Strategies of Presidential Leadership.* Washington, D.C.: CQ Press, 1986.
Mueller, John. *War, Presidents and Public Opinion.* New York: Wiley, 1973.

PART TWO

The President and the Government

In working with the government to have his programs and policies adopted and implemented, the president is confronted with a basic fact of the American political system: the separation-of-powers principle vests authority not only in the executive branch but in the legislative and judicial branches as well. He therefore must work with officials in these two other branches who are in a position to facilitate, supplement, modify, or nullify his proposals and actions. Moreover, he does not have complete control even over the executive branch, which he supposedly heads. The presidential office itself provides the means by which the president can attempt to accomplish his purposes, but how he uses the broad and indefinite powers and institutions of that office depends to a considerable extent on his own values and style of operation.

Part Two opens with Chapter 5, which examines the development of the presidency and traces the changes in the nation's highest office resulting from both outside forces and the actions of strong presidents. Also analyzed are the constitutional provisions for the continuity of presidential leadership should the incumbent become unable to govern.

Chapter 6 treats the president's relationship with the U.S. Congress, his major constitutional rival, symbolically located at the other end of Pennsylvania Avenue. It analyzes the reasons for the typical disagreements that occur between the president and the Congress as well as the formal powers and informal means he has for attempting to resolve those differences. This chapter also addresses the actual influence the president is able to exert over congressional legislation and the principal sources of that influence.

Chapter 7 focuses on the president's association with members of the executive branch. It analyzes the reasons he has so much difficulty controlling government employees who are supposed to be his subordinates. Among these reasons are the sheer size and complexity of the executive bureaucracy; conflicting loyalties its members feel to their own agencies, congressional committees, and outside interest groups; and the influence Congress possesses over the structure of the executive branch, the provision and allocation of money expended by its officials, and the appointment and removal of the men and women who occupy the major positions in the federal bureaucracy.

Chapter 8, the last chapter in Part Two, examines the president's relationship with the judicial branch of government. It examines the primary means by which he can influence the federal courts—his power to appoint its members; to help set the agenda of the appellate courts through the actions of his appointee, the solicitor general of the United States; to participate with Congress in legislation affecting the federal courts; and to exercise discretion over the enforcement of the decisions of those courts. The chapter concludes with an analysis of the ways the federal courts, especially the Supreme Court, influence the actions of the president.

The White House stands as a symbol to the United States and the world of a unique political office.

CHAPTER FIVE

The Presidential and Vice-Presidential Offices

This chapter focuses on the presidential institution itself, the general nature of the office common to each presidency, despite differences among individual incumbents. The establishment of the presidency by the Founders was an act of political creativity that resulted in a unique form of executive government. Yet, as the following discussion indicates, the office has changed over time as events and the responses of incumbents to those events have shaped and reshaped the presidency. Moreover, the office possesses the capacity not only for growth but also for continuity. Provisions exist for terminating the president's tenure before the expiration of his term; there are also stipulations about how a successor to the president is to be chosen to fill the vacancy in the office. Included in the discussion is an analysis of the establishment, development, and current status of the office of the immediate successor to the president—the vice president of the United States.

The Establishment of the Presidency

The establishment of the U.S. presidency reflects the early Americans' previous experiences with executive power. The colonists' initial contact with executive power came in the form of decrees issued by the King of England and the actions of governors sent by the mother country to the individual colonies. Some of these executives had pursued a policy of minimal interference in colonial matters (termed by British statesman Edmund Burke as one of "salutary neglect"); but after the French and Indian War, George III began to exercise far greater control over American affairs. Dissatisfied with the inability of some of the colonies to provide adequate military forces during the encounter with the French, the British decided to use their own troops to provide order in the colonies and to make the residents bear their share of the financial burden of the military, along with the debt the London government had incurred in the course of fighting the war. Further, the colonists would be required to provide funds from which royal governors would be paid. The presence of British troops and the enactment of new taxes, designed to enable the colonies to meet their new financial responsibilities, became major grievances, which ultimately led the colonists to revolt against the mother country. This experience led the colonists to associate executive power with the arbitrary decisions of George III and the royal emissaries he sent to America to enforce his decrees.

This distaste for executive power was mirrored in the political institutions that Americans created to govern themselves after the Revolution. The Articles of Confederation provided for a national legislative body with a single house in which each state had an equal vote. There was no provision at all for independent executive and judicial branches. In most of the states, also, the legislature was the dominant branch. Governors typically served one-year terms, had strict limitations on their eligibility, and were elected by the legislature.

In time, however, a reaction set in against this type of legislative democracy. Attempts to administer laws through ad hoc committees, councils, or conventions proved to be unsuccessful; and it was ultimately necessary for Congress to create permanent departments of diplomacy, war, and finance and to appoint eminent men, such as Robert Livingston, John Jay, and Robert Morris, to head their activities.[1] The British occupation of New York required that state to develop a strong governorship free of legislative dominance in order to handle its military and civilian affairs. In Massachusetts the voters adopted a constitution that included a popularly elected governor (eligible to succeed himself) with substantial powers, including that of vetoing legislative acts.

Thus, as the Founders gathered for the Constitutional Convention in 1787, disparate experiences led them to have ambivalent feelings about executive power. On the one hand, under the British they had seen how such power could be used to further tyranny. On the other, they also had learned that a legislature alone could not effectively carry on the day-to-day activities of government. The result was that those who met in Philadelphia were convinced that the new government required some kind of separate executive branch, but they were not agreed on what the nature and power of the executive should be.

There was even some question of establishing a monarchy: as John Jay put it in a letter to George Washington, "Shall we have a king?" Of the fifty-five delegates at the Constitutional Convention, however, only Alexander Hamilton seemed willing to consider seriously the British model, which he deemed the "best in the world." Others either opposed it on principle or recognized, as John Dickinson of Delaware put it, that a monarchy was "out of the question." The Americans' experience as colonists under George III and colonial governors sent as emissaries of the king had created a climate of opinion that excluded any kind of monarchy.

There were, however, other American models to consider—the state governorships of the day. For the most part, these were weak offices overshadowed by state legislatures; but New York and Massachusetts, the two exceptions, both provided for independent governors vested with important political powers. That the governors of these two states served effectively without endangering political freedom convinced many of the delegates that a strong chief executive accountable to the people was not to be equated with a tyrannical king or colonial governor.

Two disparate concepts concerning the nature and powers of the national executive emerged.[2] One was the idea of a "weak" executive whose primary function would be to put into effect the will of the legislature. To this end, a plural executive would be established, or, if only one man headed the branch, a strong council would share his powers and hold him in check. The Congress would choose the chief executive for a limited term; moreover, he could not be reappointed immediately and would even be subject to removal by the legislative body during his term of office. The powers of the executive would be limited and in essence delegated to him by Congress, which would also make appointments to the executive branch and hold the authority to make treaties and declare war. This concept of the office provided for no executive veto of laws passed by the Congress.

At the other extreme was the idea of a "strong" executive, independent of the Congress and responsible for important functions in the new government. Under this concept a single chief executive, chosen by some means other than legislative appointment, would have no limit placed on his tenure. If he were to be removable at all, it would be only for definite, enumerated reasons, and then only after impeachment and conviction by a judicial body or the legislature. His powers would be derived from the Constitution and not be subject to legislative interference. He would appoint judicial and diplomatic officials and participate in the execution of foreign affairs, including the making of treaties. He would have a veto over legislation passed by Congress, a power that he would exercise either alone or in conjunction with the judiciary. Finally, either there would be no executive council at all, or, if one did exist, it would be merely an advisory body whose actions would not bind the chief executive.

In the initial stages of the Convention, it appeared that the delegates would create an essentially weak executive. The New Jersey Plan called for a plural executive chosen by Congress; members would be eligible for a single term and be removable by the national legislative body on application of the majority of the executives of the states. Federal officials would be empowered to execute federal laws and to direct, but not take command of, military operations. The Virginia Plan provided for an executive (it was vague whether the executive was to be single or plural) chosen by the Congress and with no right to hold a second term. The powers were limited to executing national laws and implementing rights vested in Congress. Thus, neither of the two major plans envisioned a strong chief executive.

In the course of the convention's deliberations, however, the office was strengthened. A decision made early by the Committee of the Whole to provide for a single executive was a major victory for the friends of a strong presidency. Subsequent convention decisions—aided by the key Committees on Detail and on Style, with James Wilson an important figure in the former and Gouverneur Morris in the latter—eventually led to an independent chief executive with considerable political powers.

The presidency created by the convention resembles in many respects the model of a strong executive. The president is chosen by some method other than legislative appointment (electoral college), is eligible to succeed himself, and can be removed only for specific causes (treason, bribery, high crimes, and misdemeanors), and then only upon the bringing of an impeachment charge by the House of Representatives and conviction by vote of two-thirds of the members of the Senate. He is not dependent on the Congress for his authority; rather, specific powers are granted to him by the Constitution. In addition, as a result of the efforts of Gouverneur Morris, he is given broad, undefined authority by the opening sentence of Article II: "The executive power shall be vested in a President of the United States of America."

At the same time, the president does not enjoy all the prerogatives of the strong-executive model. Although he has the veto power, it is not absolute, since his action can be overridden by a two-thirds vote in each of the two houses of Congress. Moreover, his appointment power is subject to the approval of the Senate, as is his authority to negotiate treaties. Thus, although the Founders did not create a council that shares all the chief executive's powers, they did grant the upper chamber a check on certain presidential actions.

Why did the convention move from an essentially weak concept of the executive to a final version that more closely fits the strong-executive model? (See Table 5-1 for a summary of the two models and the final decision by the convention.) Individual delegates certainly played a part in the outcome. The efforts of Pennsylvanians Wilson (a strong advocate of a single chief executive) and Morris (who had also helped create the strong New York governorship), Rufus King and Elbridge Gerry of Massachusetts, Charles Pinckney and John Rutledge of South Carolina, and Hamilton of New York, among others, helped shape the convention's decisions all along the way. George Washington, too, was a key figure in the process even though he never spoke about the issue personally. Pierce Butler, a delegate from South Carolina, described Washington's contribution in a letter written after the convention completed its deliberations: "Nor ... do I believe that they [the president's powers] would have been so great had not many members cast their eyes toward George Washington as president, and shaped their ideas of the powers to be given to the president by their opinions of his virtue." [3]

Table 5-1 Models of Executive Considered by the Constitutional Convention

Elements of executive	Weak-executive model	Strong-executive model	Decision by convention
Relation to Congress	To put into effect will of Congress	Powers independent of Congress	Powers independent of Congress but with checks and balances
Number of executive	Plural or single individual checked by council	Single individual with no council or only advisory one	Single individual with Senate advisory on some matters
Method of choosing	By Congress	By means other than congressional selection	Electoral college
Tenure	Limited term; not immediately renewable	No limitation	Unlimited
Method of removal	By Congress during term of office	Only for definite, enumerated reasons after impeachment and conviction by judicial body or Congress	For treason, bribery, high crimes and misdemeanors, by impeachment by majority of House and conviction by two-thirds of Senate
Scope and source of powers	Limited powers delegated by Congress	Broad powers from constitution, not subject to congressional interference	Broad powers delegated by Constitution
Appointment and foreign policy and war-making powers	None—province of Congress	Would appoint judicial and diplomatic officials and participate in foreign policy and war-making powers, including making of treaties	Appoints executive and judicial officials with consent of Senate; shares foreign policy and war-making powers with Congress; Senate must approve treaties negotiated by president
Veto	None	Veto over legislation passed by Congress, exercised alone or with judiciary	Qualified veto, may be overridden by two-thirds vote of House and Senate.

Source: Joseph E. Kallenbach, *The American Chief Executive* (New York: Harper and Row, 1966), chap. 2.

Other factors also played a role in the final decision. Because the powers of the Congress were increased as compared with those of the legislature under the Articles of Confederation, some delegates came to the opinion that a strong executive was needed to counterbalance the new legislative body. Joseph Kallenbach also points out that during the course of the proceedings, an alliance probably formed between the supporters of a strong chief executive and the delegates from the small states, an alliance that furthered the interests of both groups.[4] Evidence of a coalition is particularly noticeable in the recommendations of the Committee on Postponed Matters and Unfinished Business to grant the president and Senate joint responsibilities in the appointment of executive officials and the making of treaties and to have the Senate, rather than the Supreme Court, be the trial body in impeachment cases. Both the president and the small states benefit from the electoral college arrangement: the president is selected initially by a process that does not involve the Congress directly, but if no candidate receives an electoral majority, the House, voting by state rather than by individual member, chooses the chief executive.

Controversy over the executive continued after the convention adjourned. George Mason of Virginia, one of the delegates who refused to sign the Constitution, charged that the provisions relating to the presidency would prove to be a device for an "elective monarch"; this sentiment was shared by Luther Martin of Maryland, who also refused to sign the document. Moreover, the ratifying conventions of some states proposed that the first Congress initiate amendments restricting the president's eligibility for reelection as well as limiting certain of his powers. Congress declined, however, to act on any of these proposed amendments. Washington's presence in the highest office in the land undoubtedly helped to allay fears over the possible abuse of executive power.

Certain amendments of the Constitution change the executive article somewhat: the Twelfth, on the choosing of the president and vice president; the Twentieth, pertaining to the beginning of their term; the Twenty-second, which limits the tenure of the chief executive; and the Twenty-fifth, about presidential disability and succession. Nevertheless, the essential constitutional framework of the presidential office remains as it was created almost two centuries ago. Most of the vast changes in the presidency since that time have arisen not from formal legal alterations in its structure but from informal political customs and precedents.

The Development of the Presidency

One of the dominant trends in American political life has been the growth of the presidency. The legislative and judicial branches of the national government have also increased in power and influence over the years, but not at the same pace as the executive.

Although the trend has been in the direction of a more powerful presidency, growth has not been constant. The office occupied by Grant from 1869 to 1877 was not as potent as that of Lincoln from 1861 to 1865. Conditions in American society, the people's reactions to these conditions, and the personal qualities of particular incumbents have affected the functions and influence of the presidency.

Factors Affecting the Development of the Presidency

In defending a single executive in *Federalist* No. 70, Alexander Hamilton emphasized what he termed "energy" as a desirable characteristic of good government. He went on to suggest that energy was particularly associated with the executive, as compared with the legislative body. As he put it: "Decision, activity, secrecy, and dispatch will generally characterize the proceedings of one man in a much more eminent degree than the proceedings of any greater number; and in proportion as the number is increased, these qualities will be diminished." [5]

More than any other single factor, this axiom of human behavior, so clearly enunciated by Hamilton, explains the growth of presidential power and influence. The need for "decision, activity, secrecy, and dispatch" has become increasingly necessary to a leading power in an interdependent world. If military action is contemplated, the president as commander in chief of the armed forces has a crucial role to play in decisions on committing American troops. (Chapter 11 further examines the president's role in national security.) As noted in the Introduction, historian Arthur Schlesinger, Jr., contends it was the capture of "the most vital of national decisions, the decision to go to war," that led to the "imperial" presidency, an office that appropriated powers the Constitution and historical practice had reserved in Congress.[6]

Even without military action, the president plays a dominant part in foreign affairs in general. A number of powers make his voice the crucial one in foreign affairs; these include the negotiation of treaties, which require senatorial approval, and of executive agreements, which do not; the initiation as well as the breaking off of diplomatic relations with foreign governments; and the choosing of representatives abroad. Moreover, as in military matters, diplomacy requires a certain amount of secrecy. The late British scholar Harold Laski suggested that international diplomatic negotiations, like a proposal of marriage, "must be made in private, even if the engagement is later discussed in public." [7]

The president's role in crises, however, is not confined to military and foreign affairs. To an increasing extent the American people have demanded that the national government "do something" about economic depressions, social problems such as race relations, the plight of the cities, and other pressing concerns. Once again, such expectations have enhanced the influence of the presidency, for a president can move swiftly and forcefully to help counteract mass unemployment, send troops to assist in integrating the schools, or deal with major riots such as those that occurred in some American cities in the late 1960s. Thus, the presidency has grown in power and influence as the American people have accepted the concept of the "positive state," that is, one in which the government, particularly the national government, plays a principal role in meeting (and, it is hoped, even preventing) the many crises of a complex society.

Hamilton's conviction that a large assembly of men has trouble taking decisive action has been borne out by the experience of the U.S. Congress. As he suggested, the problem becomes greater as the number is increased; this is precisely what happened as the number of senators and representatives grew from 26 and 65, respectively, in the first Congress to 100 and 435 today. The present American political system makes it especially difficult for legislators to move quickly on problems. The variety of viewpoints represented by members of Congress from different kinds of constituencies in a large and diverse country prevents the national legislature from making the rapid decisions that are called for in a crisis. Also contributing to congressional sluggishness have been its rules as well as the way power has been greatly decentralized within the two chambers. (Chapter 6 will examine this topic further.) Because the Congress often cannot, or will not, act decisively when the occasion demands, people turn to the president to do so.

Hamilton may not have foreseen another development that has led to the expansion of presidential power and influence: the democratization of the selection process for chief executive. (Given his distrust of the common man, he certainly would have disapproved of this change.) As previously indicated, the shift from choice by elites in the various states to a national popularity contest has given the president a nationwide constituency that no other officeholder (except his political inferior, the vice president) can claim. As a result, he is the most visible figure in American politics and the one official from whom the public expects action and leadership. As Kallenbach suggests, because the president is accountable at the ballot box to the American people as a whole, he can claim them as his following and as support for his policies.[8]

All these conditions have contributed to the natural growth of the presidency, uninhibited by the constitutional provisions pertaining to the office. The indefinite phraseology of the opening sentence of Article II of the Constitution—"The executive power shall be vested in a President of the United States"—has been, in effect, a grant of broad authority for bold and innovative ventures. Supplementing this general grant of presidential power are other clauses—for instance, "He shall take care that the laws be faithfully executed"—on which presidents can draw for legal justification of their actions. Woodrow Wilson may have exaggerated the situation somewhat when he asserted in 1908, five years before he occupied the presidency himself, that the chief executive "is at liberty, both in law and conscience, to be as big a man as he can," but few students of the presidency would deny the great potential of the office.[9]

Wilson's observations point up still another major factor in the development of the presidency: the important part that individual presidents have played in the process. Neither the legal potential of the office nor the natural conditions conducive to increased presidential power in themselves guarantee decisive actions. The crises that both James Buchanan and Abraham Lincoln faced were virtually identical. Buchanan, however, took the position that he was powerless to prevent the secession of the Southern states from the Union, whereas Lincoln took bold steps to try to counter it.

Individual Presidents and the Development of the Office

Persons who have contributed significantly to the growth of the presidency leave an office that is more powerful than the one they inherited. In turn, they establish procedures and customs that their successors tend to follow. As presidential scholar Edward Corwin explains, "Precedents established by a forceful or politically successful personality in the office are available to less gifted successors, and permanently so because of the difficulty with which the Constitution is amended." [10]

It is naturally a matter of judgment as to which of the presidents have met these criteria. Corwin's own analysis focuses on seven presidents: George Washington, Thomas Jefferson, Andrew Jackson, Abraham Lincoln, Theodore Roosevelt, Woodrow Wilson, and Franklin Roosevelt.[11] Clinton Rossiter selects the same seven and adds Harry Truman.[12] Finally, as is shown on Table 5-2, three separate polls of historians, evaluating the leadership skills of all the presidents, rate highest Corwin's original seven chief executives. The following discussion therefore focuses on these seven presidents, about whose contributions scholars agree.

George Washington. Because George Washington was the first person to occupy the presidency, whatever he did established precedents for his successors. He himself clearly recognized his situation; soon after his inauguration he expressed the opinion that "many things which appear of little importance in themselves . . . may have great and durable consequences from their having been established at the commencement of a new general government." [13] With this thought in mind, Washington soon turned to his group of department heads for advice on political matters. (In doing so, he expanded his constitutional right to gather their individual opinions, in writing, on subjects relating to the duties of their offices; the expansion encompassed soliciting their oral judgments as a group on any matter he put before them.) By forcing Secretary of State Edmund Randolph to resign because of his failure to back the administration's foreign policy, Washington established the precedent that department heads should support the president's policies.

Table 5-2 Rankings by Historians of U.S. Presidents

Schlesinger, 1948 (N = 55)	Schlesinger, 1962 (N = 75)	Murray-Blessing, 1982 (N = 846)
Great	**Great**	**Great**
Lincoln	Lincoln	Lincoln
Washington	Washington	F. Roosevelt
F. Roosevelt	F. Roosevelt	Washington
Wilson	Wilson	Jefferson
Jefferson	Jefferson	
Jackson		**Near great**
		T. Roosevelt
	Near great	Wilson
	Jackson	Jackson
Near great	T. Roosevelt	Truman
T. Roosevelt	Polk	
Cleveland	Truman	**Above average**
J. Adams	J. Adams	J. Adams
Polk	Cleveland	L. Johnson
		Eisenhower
		Polk
		Kennedy
Average	**Average**	Madison
J. Q. Adams	Madison	Monroe
Monroe	J. Q. Adams	J. Q. Adams
Hayes	Hayes	Cleveland
Madison	McKinley	
Van Buren	Taft	**Average**
Taft	Van Buren	McKinley
Arthur	Monroe	Taft
McKinley	Hoover	Van Buren
A. Johnson	B. Harrison	Hoover
Hoover	Arthur	Hayes
B. Harrison	Eisenhower	Arthur
	A. Johnson	Ford
		Carter
		B. Harrison
Below average	**Below average**	**Below average**
Tyler	Taylor	Taylor
Coolidge	Tyler	Tyler
Fillmore	Fillmore	Fillmore
Taylor	Coolidge	Coolidge
Buchanan	Pierce	Pierce
Pierce	Buchanan	
		Failure
		A. Johnson
		Buchanan
Failure	**Failure**	Nixon
Grant	Grant	Grant
Harding	Harding	Harding

Source: The results of all three polls appear in Robert Murray and Tim Blessing, "The Presidential Performance Study: A Progress Report," *Journal of American History* (December 1983): 540, 541. The 1948 poll by Arthur Schlesinger, Sr., first appeared in *Life*, November 1, 1948, 65; his 1962 poll first appeared in *New York Times Magazine*, July 29, 1962, 12, 13.

The Washington administration also saw the rise of legislative leadership by the executive. The broad economic program created and steered through the Congress by Secretary of the Treasury Alexander Hamilton paved the way for the close liaison with Congress established by subsequent executive department heads. Although the initiatives in this case were more the product of Hamilton than of Washington, the latter lent his prestige and political support to the efforts, thus providing an example that subsequent presidents would follow in influencing public policies.

In foreign policy Washington moved quickly to establish the prerogatives of the president. He received Edmond Charles ("Citizen") Genêt as an emissary from the new French government, setting the precedent that the president has the right to receive ambassadors and to grant diplomatic recognition to foreign countries. When he sought the Senate's advice on treaty negotiations with certain Indian tribes, and the Senate delayed by referring the matter to committee, Washington stalked out of the chamber in anger, vowing never again to bring such a matter to the Senate. Since that date, no president has sought that body's counsel on the negotiation of a treaty, despite the constitutional instruction that he "shall make such treaties with its advice." [14] When the House of Representatives demanded that he present papers pertaining to the negotiation of the Jay Treaty, he refused to do so on the grounds that the Constitution granted the lower chamber of Congress no authority in such matters.

It is difficult to overemphasize the importance of Washington to the existence of the new government struggling to achieve legitimacy among a divided people, many of them suspicious of the Constitution and of a presidential office that Patrick Henry said "squinted toward monarchy." On occasion, Washington lent his great prestige to the maintenance of "law and order" in the new republic, as he did in the Whiskey Rebellion when he sent troops against the farmers of western Pennsylvania who threatened to rebel at paying an excise tax on liquor. (On the approach of the military force, the rebels dispersed.) Yet Washington's temperate approach to public affairs was demonstrated vividly in the same incident when he pardoned two of the ringleaders of the rebellion who were convicted of treason. With all his initiatives in conducting domestic and foreign affairs and in asserting and protecting the prerogatives of the executive branch, Washington's presidency was, as Rossiter suggests, "nothing if not painfully constitutional." [15] At a turbulent time in the life of a new nation, when conditions were ripe for the kind of monarchical rule that prevailed in most countries of the world, this was an astonishing achievement.

Thomas Jefferson. As Corwin observes, "What we encounter in Jefferson for the first time is a president who is primarily a party leader, only secondarily chief executive." [16] Using the Republican party members in the Congress as his medium, he proceeded to dominate the political affairs of the legislature. His control extended to decisions of the party caucus (which, unlike today's counterpart, did exercise significant powers over legislation) and to the appointment and removal of standing committee members, as well as party officials in the Congress. So potent was his leadership that he pushed the drastic Embargo Act of 1807 through both houses in one day. Nor was his control restricted to crises. It is a testament to Jefferson's domination that he did not veto a single piece of legislation: no law he seriously opposed was reported out of the Congress during his eight years in office.

Jefferson also epitomized the president who stretches the powers of the office when the occasion demands it. When Napoleon unexpectedly offered French lands (the Louisiana Purchase) for a minimal price, he put Jefferson in a quandary: as a believer in a strict construction of the powers of the national government, Jefferson doubted the constitutionality of acquiring foreign territory (in fact, he favored a constitutional amendment on the matter), yet he was torn by fears of losing the chance to consummate such a favorable agreement. Putting aside his constitutional qualms, Jefferson chose direct action. More than one president since that time has decided to act in response to political rather than legal considerations.

Andrew Jackson.   Jefferson exercised political leadership by working through his party organization in Congress; Andrew Jackson became a strong president by asserting his independence of the legislative branch. In fact, his administration was characterized by conflicts with Congress. In a battle over the national bank (supported by the legislature but opposed by Jackson) the president forced the secretary of the treasury to resign so that he could place a friend, Roger Taney, in office for the purpose of withdrawing funds from the national institution and depositing them in state banks. (The Senate censured him for his action, but he was later successful in having the censure motion lifted.) Similar conflicts also developed over opposition to his nominations. The Senate turned down Martin Van Buren as ambassador to the Court of St. James; it also refused to sanction Roger Taney's appointment to the Supreme Court on three separate occasions. (Jackson, however, was to have his revenge: Taney ultimately became chief justice and in that capacity swore in Van Buren as president.) The full range of Jackson's disputes with the Congress is reflected in his use of the veto: he exercised it on no fewer than twelve occasions, the first president to use it to any significant degree.

Jackson did not recoil from other kinds of political conflicts. He asserted his independence of the judicial branch by taking the position that the president has as much right as the Supreme Court to judge the constitutionality of legislation. Moreover, when John Marshall issued a ruling with which Jackson disagreed, he invited the chief justice to enforce it himself. He also acted decisively to protect the rights of the national government against the states: when South Carolina threatened to secede from the Union if a high tariff law were enforced, Jackson issued a proclamation declaring the action treasonous and pushed a bill through Congress giving him the power to use force to prevent it. (No other state joined South Carolina, and its officials backed down.)

Jackson's vigorous actions in defiance of other branches and levels of government were possible because he was the first president with a popular constituency. Chosen not by a congressional caucus but by a national convention reflecting grass-roots party support, Jackson considered himself the "tribune of the people." When he had disagreements with members of Congress, he appealed over their heads to the population at large for support of his policies; to keep control of his administration, he instituted the "spoils system" (so named for the idea "to the victor belong the spoils") to reward his political friends and punish his enemies. Jackson was a key figure in transforming the presidency from a somewhat elitist office to a popular one.

Abraham Lincoln. The nineteenth-century presidency reached the zenith of its powers during the wartime administration of Abraham Lincoln. Alfred Kelly and Winfred Harbison consider the eleven-week period from the outbreak of hostilities at Fort Sumter, South Carolina, on April 12, 1861, until the new president called the Congress into special session the following July 4 as a time of "quasi-presidential dictatorship." [17] During those momentous weeks Lincoln authorized a series of drastic actions: he called up the militia and volunteers, blockaded Southern ports, expanded the army and navy beyond the limits set by statute, pledged the credit of the United States without congressional authority to do so, closed the mails to "treasonous" correspondence, arrested persons suspected of disloyalty, and suspended the writ of *habeas corpus* in areas around the nation's capital. Admitting that most of these matters lay within the jurisdiction of the Congress rather than the presidency, Lincoln took the position that they were done because of popular demand and public necessity, and with the trust "that Congress would readily ratify them." Thus, he deliberately chose not to call the national legislature into special session until he was ready to do so, and then he presented it with *faits accomplis*.

Although Lincoln's presidency was most dramatic in those early days of hostilities, he continued to exercise firm control over the war during the entire time he was in the White House. He did not hesitate to control the mails and newspapers, to confiscate property of persons suspected of impeding the conduct of the war, and even to try civilians in military courts in areas in which the regular courts were open. To justify such actions, he appealed to military necessity, asserting that the "commander in chief" clause and the "shall take care" clause (that the laws be faithfully executed) combined to create a "war power" for the president that was virtually unlimited. Lincoln's success in defending that position is demonstrated by the fact that neither the Congress nor the courts placed any significant limits on his actions.

Theodore Roosevelt. An internal domestic crisis shaped Lincoln's presidency in the middle of the nineteenth century; Theodore Roosevelt's presidency was vitally affected by the emergence of the United States as a world power at the beginning of the twentieth. Concerned over the rise of Japan as a threat to American interests in the Pacific, Roosevelt sought and obtained a major role in negotiating the Portsmouth Treaty, which terminated the Russo-Japanese War of 1905. In the Western hemisphere he pursued a policy of intervening in the affairs of neighbors to the south when such intervention might further what he perceived to be the national interests of the United States. Troops were sent to Santo Domingo, in the Dominican Republic, and to Cuba for this reason. Even more blatant was Roosevelt's role in fomenting the rebellion of Panama against Colombia so that the United States could acquire rights to build a canal. An avowed nationalist with the desire to expand U.S. influence in international affairs, Roosevelt ordered the navy around the world as a demonstration of American military might. When Congress balked at the expense, he countered that there were sufficient funds to get the navy halfway there; if the lawmakers wanted the fleet back home, they would have to provide the money for the return trip.

Roosevelt also responded vigorously to the other important development of his era: the rapid industrialization of American life. He had charges pressed against corporations that violated antitrust laws, and he pushed legislation through Congress that gave the Interstate Commerce Commission power to lower railroad rates. When coal mine operators in Colorado refused to agree to arbitration of a dispute with their workers, Roosevelt threatened to have army troops seize the mines and administer them as a receiver for the government. He thus became the first American chief executive to intervene in a labor dispute who did *not* take management's side. Beyond this, Roosevelt championed major reclamation and conservation projects, as well as meat inspection and pure food and drug laws.

Perhaps most important, Roosevelt did much to popularize the presidency after a third of a century of lackluster leaders. (Of the eight men who served from Lincoln through McKinley, only Grover Cleveland is considered to be at all significant.) A dynamic personality, an attractive family, and love of the public spotlight enabled Roosevelt "to put the presidency on the front page of every newspaper in America." [18] Considering himself (as did Jackson) the "tribune of the people" and seeing the office as a "bully pulpit" from which the incumbent should set the tone of American life, Roosevelt was the first president to provide meeting rooms for the members of the press and to hold informal news conferences to link the presidency with the people.

Woodrow Wilson and Franklin Roosevelt. The principal contributions of these two twentieth-century presidents were discussed in Chapter 3. Both pushed through the Congress major domestic programs; they also served as commander in chief during World Wars I and II, respectively, not only directing the armed forces but also managing the wartime economy and rallying the American people to the war effort. Each also was an innovator in the use of the presidential office. Implementing his prime-minister concept of the presidency, Wilson personally delivered his State of the Union message to the Congress and effectively played the role of the chief of his political party by working through congressional leaders and the Democratic caucus to influence the passage of his legislative program. Roosevelt took the leadership in reorganizing the executive branch and used his superb communications skills to reach the American public in "fireside chats" on radio and to charm and manipulate members of the print media in his press conferences.[19]

Thus, a variety of influences have contributed to the development of the American presidency: the demands of foreign and domestic events, the inability and unwillingness of Congress to assume leadership, and the actions of strong chief executives who established precedents for their successors to draw on. Moreover, the American public has come to expect all U.S. chief executives to exhibit initiative in meeting the many problems of American society. In the process, the office has become more and more complex and demanding. The kinds of varied responsibilities that contemporary presidents face, as well as the methods they use to discharge those responsibilities, are examined in succeeding chapters. First, however, this chapter will turn to another major aspect of the presidential office: the circumstances that terminate the incumbency of a president before the expiration of his term and the provisions for filling the vacancy with a successor.

Terminating Presidential Tenure

Four distinct circumstances can result in a president's tenure in office being ended before the expiration of his term. Three of them—impeachment and conviction, resignation, and death—are permanent in that the affected president does not return to office. The fourth circumstance, disability (sometimes called "inability"), can also be permanent but in some situations may be only temporary, with a removed chief executive once again resuming the duties of his office.

Impeachment and Conviction

Under Article II, Section 4, of the Constitution, the president (along with the vice president and any civil officer of the United States) can be removed from office by impeachment for and conviction of "treason, bribery, or other high crimes and misdemeanors." The House of Representatives is empowered to impeach, that is, to bring accusations or charges against the president; a majority vote of the House members present is sufficient for an impeachment. Should that occur, the Senate then sits as a body to try the case, but to convict the chief executive, two-thirds of the Senators present must vote to do so.

Over the years, procedures have been developed to handle the distinct impeachment and conviction phases of the process. Resolutions seeking impeachment are referred to one of the House committees (usually the Judiciary Committee), which investigates and reports to the entire House. If the committee finds that the evidence of an impeachable offense justifies a trial, it recommends that one or more "articles of impeachment" be adopted. (Impeachable offenses are discussed later in this section.) After debate, the House votes on such articles (it is also free to amend them); a majority vote in favor of adopting one or more of the articles constitutes an impeachment. "Managers" are then chosen (either by the body itself or by its Speaker) to present the case to the Senate. The members of the Senate act as a trial body, and the chief justice of the Supreme Court presides over proceedings that involve the president. The president is represented by counsel and may appear before the Senate if he chooses to do so. After the evidence and arguments are heard, the Senate votes on each article separately; if a two-thirds vote is obtained on any of them, the president is thereby convicted and removed from office on pronouncement of the chief justice.

Although a number of impeachment resolutions against U.S. presidents have been introduced in the House of Representatives over the years, only twice did that body formally authorize an investigation of grounds for impeachment.[20] The first took place in 1868 against Andrew Johnson. The second occurred more than a century later in 1974 against Richard Nixon.

Impeachment of Andrew Johnson.   Johnson, a Tennessee Democrat who was the only member of the U.S. Senate from a seceding state to remain loyal to the Union, was placed on the Republican ticket by Abraham Lincoln in the campaign of 1864. After the president was assassinated in 1865 and Johnson the presidency, he soon found himself in direct conflict with congressional Republicans over the reconstruction of the South. Johnson favored a conciliatory policy that provided for the readmission of the South into the Union after obvious steps such as the nullification of the secession, the repudiation of Confederate state debts, and the abolition of slavery had been taken. Many of the Republican members of Congress, particularly those associated with the Radical wing of the party, demanded much more, including the creation of a Freedmen's Bureau to protect former slaves from whites and to provide them with education and other services. They also favored legislation guaranteeing the civil rights of Negroes and the creation of military governments in the South to oversee Reconstruction. Federal jobs also became a bone of contention between Johnson and the Republicans: the president fired many executive officeholders during and after the election campaign of 1866, and the Congress responded with the Tenure of Office Act of 1867, forbidding the removal of officers appointed with the consent of the Senate unless the Senate concurred in the removal.

The battle between Johnson and congressional Republicans initially took the form of presidential vetoes of Reconstruction legislation followed by Congress's overriding the vetoes. In late February 1868, however, the president dismissed Secretary of War Edwin Stanton, an ally of the Radical Republicans, without senatorial approval, declaring the Tenure of Office Act to be an unconstitutional limitation on his removal power. Within a day the House passed a resolution on impeachment and referred it to the Committee on Reconstruction, headed by Radical Republican leader Thaddeus Stevens of Pennsylvania. The next day the committee reported an impeachment resolution, and two days later the whole House concurred with the committee's action in a 126-49 straight party-line vote.

The House drew up eleven articles of impeachment (the main one based on the removal of Stanton in violation of the Tenure of Office Act) and appointed managers to argue the charges before the Senate. The trial began on March 30, 1868, with the chief justice of the United States, Salmon Chase, presiding. On May 11 the Senate took its first vote on the Eleventh Article (a summary of many of the charges in the previous articles), which ended with a vote of 35-19, one vote short of the two-thirds needed to convict. The Radicals maneuvered a ten-day adjournment to try to line up more votes for Johnson's conviction, but when the senators reassembled and voted on two other articles, the same vote prevailed and the president was spared removal from office.[21] Writing in 1973, historian Michael Benedict concluded that the Johnson incident demonstrated that impeachment is "a dull blade, and the end result is that the only effective recourse against a president who ignores the will of Congress or exceeds his powers is democratic removal at the polls." [22]

Investigation of Richard Nixon. Within a year after Benedict's conclusion appeared in print, the nation was faced with its second major impeachment case involving the president of the United States. The incident arose as a result of the infamous Watergate scandal in which officials of the Nixon administration were implicated in a variety of wrongdoings: breaking into the Democratic National Committee headquarters in the apartment complex of the Watergate Hotel in Washington, D.C.; other wire taps and burglaries conducted by a special unit within the White House known as the "plumbers" (so called for their assignment to plug the alleged "leaks" of information important to the nation's security); sabotage and "dirty tricks" directed against the campaigns of leading presidential candidates in 1972; improper solicitation of, and failure to report, money raised by the finance committee to reelect the president; and compiling an "enemies list" of persons inimical to the Nixon administration who were to be "screwed" (as White House counsel John Dean inelegantly put it) by the Internal Revenue Service (IRS) and other government agencies. A special prosecutor, Harvard law professor Archibald Cox, was appointed by Attorney General Elliott Richardson to investigate these incidents; and when Cox refused to obey an order of President Nixon to cease attempting to obtain tapes, notes, and memoranda of presidential conversations pertaining to possible criminal activities of administrative officials, the president ordered Richardson to discharge Cox. Richardson refused to do so and instead resigned, as did Deputy Attorney General William Ruckelshaus, who had temporarily succeeded to the top law-enforcement post when Richardson vacated it. (Solicitor General Robert Bork then became acting attorney general and fired Cox.) This series of dramatic events, tabbed the "Saturday Night Massacre" (for Saturday, October 20, 1973, when the events took place), set off a storm of public protest and led to the introduction of resolutions signed by eighty-four representatives calling for the impeachment of the president or for an investigation of impeachment procedures. Speaker Carl Albert immediately referred such resolutions to the House Judiciary Committee for investigation.

In the months ahead the committee, comprising twenty-one Democrats and seventeen Republicans, meticulously gathered evidence on various aspects of the president's activities. When it subpoenaed forty-two tapes of conversations between Nixon and his advisers, he refused to surrender them, arguing that because of their confidential nature they were protected from disclosure by the doctrine of executive privilege. The president did provide the committee with a 1,300-page, edited transcript of the taped conversations, but the committee subsequently informed him that the transcript did not comply with its subpoena. Ultimately, however, the committee got a windfall of evidence when federal district judge John Sirica, who was presiding over a criminal proceeding against administrative officials for alleged Watergate violations, ruled that the committee was entitled to have the report of the grand jury in the case as well as related material dealing with the president's possible involvement in Watergate matters. The committee also heard testimony from key administration officials. The result was thirty-eight volumes of materials, which the committee made available to the House and Senate for their consideration.

The Judiciary Committee also struggled with a number of legal problems on matters of both procedure and substance. It debated whether to allow the president's attorney—James St. Clair, a Boston trial lawyer—to sit in on the committee's hearing, examine and submit evidence, and present and cross-examine witnesses. The members also argued over what was meant by the constitutional language of "high crimes and misdemeanors," the kinds of violations that constitute impeachable offenses. Did the language refer only to criminal offenses, or were presidential actions that entailed abuse of power and violations of the public trust also high crimes and misdemeanors? Finally, members differed on how specific the articles of impeachment must be, whether they had to contain names, dates, and places to support charges of presidential wrongdoing. The committee ultimately settled these matters by according St. Clair the desired privileges, by including violations of both criminal offenses (specifically those relating to the obstruction of justice) and abuses of power in its articles of impeachment, and by allowing detailed information supporting the charges against the president to be included in its report and summary of evidence rather than in the articles of impeachment themselves.

For six days in late July 1974, the committee debated Nixon's fate before a nationwide television audience as pro- and anti-impeachment members of Congress analyzed the evidence, voiced the arguments for and against Nixon's removal from office, and devised the specific articles of impeachment that should be recommended to the whole House for consideration. Ultimately, all twenty-one Democrats and six of the committee's Republican members voted in favor of the first article, accusing the president of obstructing justice in connection with the cover-up of the Watergate break-in. A second article, charging Nixon with abusing the powers of his office by attempting to use improperly such organizations as the IRS and the Federal Bureau of Investigation (FBI), was supported by the same bipartisan coalition plus one more vote from Rep. Robert McClory of Illinois, the second-ranking Republican on the committee. A third article, involving contempt of Congress based upon the president's refusal to turn over tapes subpoenaed by the committee, passed by a narrower margin: 21-17. Two other articles, one relating to the secret bombing of Cambodia and the other based on Nixon's tax payments and improvements on his private properties, each failed to pass by a 12-26 vote. With the completion of the work of the Judiciary Committee, the entire House set aside the last two weeks of August 1974 for debate on the possible impeachment of Richard Nixon.

Dramatic events intervened, however, which made the House debate and subsequent impeachment actions unnecessary. On Monday, August 5, 1974, President Nixon made a public statement about tapes he was furnishing to Judge Sirica as a result of a Supreme Court decision, *United States v. Richard Nixon*,[23] handed down the day the Judiciary Committee began its televised debates; the Court ruled that the president had to turn over certain tapes of presidential conversations pertinent to the Watergate case. (This case is discussed further in Chapter 8.) Nixon stated that the tapes revealed that he had known of the Watergate incident six days after it occurred and that he had ordered the FBI called off the case because the men involved had connections with the Committee to Reelect the President. This disclosure of vital information that the president had kept from the American public, the House Judiciary Committee, and even his own attorney set off a wave of anger, particularly among the ten Republican members of the Judiciary Committee who had supported him during that body's debate less than two weeks before. All ten soon indicated that they would now vote for impeachment.

In five tense days in early August, events moved to a climax. Republican senators Barry Goldwater and Hugh Scott and House Minority Leader John Rhodes visited the White House on Wednesday, August 7, to inform the president that his support had eroded so badly in both chambers that he would most certainly be impeached and convicted. The next morning, August 8, Nixon told Vice President Gerald Ford of his intent to resign, and that evening (six years to the day from his 1968 nomination acceptance speech) he went before the nation's largest television audience—some 120 million—to inform the American people. At noon on Friday, August 9, Ford was sworn in as the thirty-seventh president of the United States, while Richard Nixon returned with his family to his home in San Clemente, California, once more a private citizen.

Impeachable Offenses and Judicial Review.   Thus, in the nation's almost two centuries of existence, only two presidents have been seriously threatened with removal from office through impeachment and conviction, and in neither case did that full procedure take place. As a result, there remain two unanswered questions about the process. One is what constitutes an "impeachable offense." The other is whether the impeachment and conviction procedure is subject to judicial review.

There have been widely differing views on what kinds of offenses give rise to the impeachment procedure. The British jurist William Blackstone provided the narrowest interpretation: impeachment, he stated, "is a prosecution of the already known and established law," meaning a violation of existing criminal law. At the other extreme is the view expressed in 1970 by Gerald Ford, then a member of the House, who in the process of proposing the impeachment of Supreme Court Justice William Douglas, asserted that an impeachable offense is "whatever the majority of the House of Representatives considers it to be at a given moment in history; conviction results from whatever offense or offenses two-thirds of the other body [the Senate] considers to be sufficiently serious to require the removal." [24] More specifically, however, the question has focused on whether any other offense besides a criminal one is impeachable. Two legal scholars who have analyzed the issue in recent years—Raoul Berger and Charles Black—reach the same conclusion: impeachable offenses include not only crimes but official abuse of power, that is, violation of the public trust. [25] As Black terms it, impeachable offenses are those "which are obviously wrong . . . and which so threaten the order of political society as to make pestilent and dangerous the continuance in power of their perpetrator." [26] Black also makes the point that not only are some impeachable offenses not crimes (for example, the use of the tax system to harass opponents) but also not all crimes constitute impeachable offenses (for example, a president's obstructing justice by actively assisting "a young White House intern in concealing the latter's possession of three ounces of marijuana"). [27]

But while Berger and Black agree that an impeachable offense includes noncriminal acts, they disagree on whether the impeachment and conviction procedure is subject to judicial review. Berger takes the position that it is, because such a review "is required to protect the other branches from Congress' arbitrary will" and also because it is "hardly likely" that the Framers "would reject a crucial check at the nerve center of the separation of powers." [28] Black, however, finds nothing in the Constitution that gives the Supreme Court either original or appellate jurisdiction over impeachment cases, and he points to the absurdity of a situation that would allow the Court (perhaps in a 5-4 decision) to put a president back into office after he had been impeached by a majority of the House and convicted by a two-thirds vote in the Senate.[29]

Resignation

Many presidents since George Washington may have considered resignation from office, but Richard Nixon, under great pressures from political friends and foes alike, is the only chief executive who actually exercised that option. Just before the 1916 election, however, Woodrow Wilson suggested in a letter to Secretary of State Robert Lansing that if he were defeated for reelection, he would appoint his Republican opponent Charles Evans Hughes to Lansing's position; then he and his vice president, Thomas Marshall, would resign, and under the presidential succession law then in effect, Hughes would become president immediately rather than having to wait four months until his elected term was scheduled to begin. Fortunately for Wilson, and for Marshall (who was not consulted on the matter), a Democratic election victory rendered the procedure unnecessary. Four years later, immediately after Warren Harding's victory over James Cox, when William Jennings Bryan asked Wilson to appoint Harding secretary of state and then resign along with Marshall, "the proposal was greeted with icy silence." [30] After the Republicans won the 1946 congressional elections, Sen. J. William Fulbright of Arkansas proposed that President Harry Truman appoint Republican senator Arthur Vandenberg of Michigan as secretary of state and then resign.[31] According to Truman's daughter, Margaret, however, "Dad ignored this bit of idiocy." [32]

Death

The most prevalent circumstance that has terminated the tenure of American presidents has been death in office. Eight chief executives have suffered this fate, four of them by violence of assassination—Abraham Lincoln, James Garfield, William McKinley, and John Kennedy.[33] The other four—William Harrison, Zachary Taylor, Warren Harding, and Franklin Roosevelt—died of natural causes. Thus, of the thirty-nine presidents (recall that Grover Cleveland served two terms, with Benjamin Harrison's presidency intervening between them), eight—about one in five—could not finish their term of office.

Disability

A fourth circumstance that can lead to either a temporary or permanent termination of a tenure is disability (also called "inability"). Article II,

Section 1, of the Constitution specifically provides that in case of the inability of the president "to discharge the duties of the said office, the same shall devolve on the Vice President." However, this terse language leaves a number of questions unanswered: (1) What exactly, constitutes presidential disability—physical illness, mental illness, any disability that prevents his carrying out his duties? (2) Who, exactly, determines whether disability exists—the president himself, the vice president, Congress, the Supreme Court? (3) What is it that the vice president succeeds to—the powers and duties of the office or the office itself? If it is the latter, how can the president retrieve his office if he recovers from his disability? (4) Who is it that decides if and when the president has recovered from his disability—the president himself or the vice president who has taken over? If there is disagreement between the two, how is that resolved and by whom?

On several occasions presidents have been disabled (see Table 5-3) and, because there were no definite answers to these questions, political leaders have had to improvise means of dealing with the immediate problem. On two occasions the results were most unfortunate. After being shot by an assassin, President Garfield was confined to bed for 80 days before he died. During that time he was able to fulfill only one official act (signing an extradition paper), yet Vice President Chester A. Arthur declined to take any action to replace Garfield, for two reasons. First, he was outside the president's inner circle, since he was from the opposite political faction of the Republican party (Arthur was a "Stalwart," a conservative Republican; Garfield was a "Half-Breed," a more moderate Republican). Second, some of the members of the president's cabinet thought that it would be legally impossible for Garfield ever to get the office back once Arthur had assumed it.

Even more serious was Woodrow Wilson's incapacity for 280 days following a stroke, which he suffered on a speaking tour to win support for the League of Nations. During this long period, when the Versailles peace treaty was before the Senate, the nation was demobilizing after the war, and the economy was in a state of transition, the president was completely shielded from contact with everyone except his wife and physician. Vice President Thomas Marshall (like Chester Arthur) hesitated to act, and the overtures of Secretary of State Robert Lansing to persuade Marshall to take over the affairs of the nation were successfully opposed by close political friends of the president.

The nation once again faced the problem of presidential disability when Dwight Eisenhower had a heart attack in 1955, an ileitis attack and operation in 1956, and a mild stroke in 1957. Although only the first incident was serious (and kept him totally removed from public affairs for only four days), the concern raised by the issue prompted Eisenhower, Kennedy, and Johnson to make agreements with their vice presidents—Nixon, Johnson, and Humphrey, respectively—that provided for handling

Table 5-3 Major Instances of Presidential Disability

President	Duration of disability
William Henry Harrison	7 days before his death
Zachary Taylor	5 days before his death
James A. Garfield	80 days before his death
William McKinley	8 days before his death
Woodrow Wilson	280 days from his stroke until he resumed cabinet meetings
Warren G. Harding	4 days before his death
Dwight D. Eisenhower	143 days from his heart attack until his announced recovery

Source: Richard Hansen, *The Year We Had No President* (Lincoln: University of Nebraska Press, 1962), 1.

Note: Does not include short periods of disability such as the nine and one-half hours Lincoln was unconscious before he died or the some twenty hours during which Reagan was incapacitated following the attempt on his life.

the problem.[34] Congress also made inquiries into the issue. Eventually the Twenty-fifth Amendment, which addresses most issues pertaining to disability, was ratified in 1967.

Specifically, the amendment provides that either the president himself or the vice president and a majority of the cabinet (or some other body designated by Congress) can declare that the president is unable to discharge the powers and duties of his office, in which case the vice president becomes *acting* president (not president). This procedure was applied for the first time on July 13, 1985, when President Reagan transferred his powers to Vice President Bush just before receiving anesthesia for an operation to remove a malignant tumor from the president's lower intestine.[35] The president can also declare when his disability is over and resume the powers and duties of the office (as President Reagan did as soon as he awoke eight hours later from the operation); however, if the vice president and cabinet (or other body designated by Congress) disagree with the president's judgment, Congress ultimately decides this issue. The amendment therefore treats the second, third, and fourth problems concerning disability and leaves only the first (what constitutes disability) completely unanswered. Perhaps that issue is unanswerable, and one should accept the definition of the leading scholar on the issue, Ruth Silva, that disability "covers all cases in which the president is, in fact, unable to exercise a power that the public interest requires to be exercised."[36]

Thus, a president's tenure can be terminated by impeachment and conviction, resignation, death, or disability.[37] As discussed in the following section, provisions also exist for automatically filling presidential vacancies so that the continuity of the office is preserved.

Presidential Succession

Although Americans take for granted the vice president's succession to the office upon the death of the president, many political systems do not provide machinery that determines in advance who will become the leader of the nation if something happens to the incumbent. When Joseph Stalin suddenly died of a heart attack in March 1953, a power struggle ensued in the Soviet Union before Nikita Khrushchev eventually took over sole leadership of the nation. For more than twenty-five years of Communist control of China, speculation continued about who would become the political leader upon Mao Tse-tung's death. The succession to power thus can be a major problem in totalitarian societies, but even democratic nations do not always take account of the issue: in Great Britain, for example, no official is designated to succeed immediately to the prime ministership.

In contrast, the United States Constitution provides for presidential succession, a continuity of the presidential office if it is either permanently or temporarily vacant. Article II, Section 1 (as amended by Section 1 of the Twenty-fifth Amendment), provides for the vice president to take over if a presidency is terminated because of impeachment and conviction, resignation, death, or disability. In addition, Section 3 of the Twentieth Amendment makes a similar provision in the event that a president-elect dies before taking office,[38] a president is not chosen, or one has failed to qualify for the office at the beginning of the term. These constitutional sections also empower Congress to provide by law who will succeed to the office or act as president if there is no vice president available or qualified to fill the presidential office.

On three occasions Congress has enacted legislation to provide for presidential succession in the event of a double vacancy. A 1792 law tapped the legislative leadership by placing in line for the presidency first the president pro tempore of the Senate, then the Speaker of the House of Representatives; it also provided that if the double vacancy occurred in the first two years and seven months of the presidential term, Congress was required to call a special election to choose a new president and vice president. In 1886 Congress switched to the cabinet as a preferable source of presidential talent, beginning with the secretary of state, on down the line in chronological order of the establishment of the executive departments. This law was somewhat unclear on the matter of a special election, but one student of the subject, John Feerick, concludes that its probable intention was "to let Congress decide whether or not to have a special presidential election under the circumstances."[39] Finally, in 1947, at the behest of President Truman (who argued that it was better to have an elected than an appointed official as president and that he ought not to be able to choose his successor by naming a secretary of state), Congress went back to the legislative leaders as first in the line of succession. This time, however, Congress provided that the Speaker of the House precede the president pro tempore of the Senate, who, in turn, is to be followed by members of the cabinet; there is no provision at all for a special election under this most recent succession law.[40]

The same amendment that provides for presidential disability, the Twenty-fifth, also contains provisions that affect executive succession. Section 2 states that if there is a vacancy in the vice presidency, the president shall nominate a vice president, who must be confirmed by a majority vote of both houses of Congress. This procedure was invoked twice within ten months— first in October 1973, when Vice President Agnew resigned (after having been fined for federal income tax evasion) and President Nixon chose Gerald Ford as vice president, and later by Ford himself when he succeeded to the presidency after Nixon's resignation and then nominated Nelson Rockefeller as his vice president. This constitutional procedure not only permits the person ultimately selected as vice president to take over the duties of that office but also puts him, rather than the Speaker of the House, first in line for the presidency.[41] By providing machinery to rectify a double vacancy, the Twenty-fifth Amendment thus makes it less likely that presidential succession will ever reach the legislative leadership of the two houses of Congress.

Because no person besides the vice president has ever succeeded to the presidency, and because this situation is even more likely to prevail since the adoption of the Twenty-fifth Amendment, it is all the more important that one understand that office as well.

The Vice Presidency

No office in the American political system has been the object of as much derogation and derision as the vice presidency. It has been associated with some of the more memorable quotations in American politics, many of them provided by persons who occupied the office themselves. Its first incumbent, John Adams, complained to his wife that "my country has in its wisdom contrived for me the most insignificant office that ever the invention of man contrived or his imagination conceived." Thomas Marshall, who served with Woodrow Wilson for eight years, said the vice president "is like a man in a cataleptic state: he cannot speak; he cannot move; he suffers no pain; and yet he is perfectly conscious of everything that is going on about him." One vice president under Franklin Roosevelt, John Nance Garner, opined that the office "isn't worth a pitcher of warm spit"; another, Harry Truman, said that all the vice presidents in history "were about as useful as a cow's fifth teat." Nor were such opinions restricted to vice presidents themselves; political humorist Finley Peter Dunne, writing under the pen name of "Mr. Dooley," an Irish politician, explained that the office "isn't a crime exactly. Ye can't be sint to jail f'r it, but it's a kind of disgrace. It's like writin' anonymous letters."

Such comments raise some basic questions about the vice presidency. What kind of office did the Founders intend to create? Has it changed over the years, and, if so, in what ways? What roles does the vice president play in the American political system today?

Establishment of the Vice Presidency

The delegates at the Constitutional Convention devoted very little attention to the office of the vice president. There is even some disagreement over the reasons for the creation of the office. Irving Williams suggests that the Founders were most concerned with providing a successor in case something happened to the president.[42] He contends that the delegates adopted a plan first proposed by Alexander Hamilton, which made the office of vice president like that of a lieutenant-governor in most states (in Pennsylvania he was actually called the vice president): he would preside over the Senate and take over as chief executive if something happened to the incumbent. However, Arthur Schlesinger, Jr., attributes the creation of the vice presidency not to the issue of succession but rather to the "mode of election" of the president.[43] He argues that the delegates were concerned that if the presidential electors of the various states voted for only one person, local feelings would incline them to designate a candidate from their own state. Therefore, the delegates required that the electors each cast two ballots, one of which would be for a person not from their own state. The idea was that this system would lead to the selection of a *national* president, someone who was well regarded throughout the country. The vice president would also be a major political leader since he would be the person who received the second highest number of electoral votes.

Although some delegates to the Constitutional Convention were uneasy about the vice-presidential office that was created (there was particular concern that having the vice president preside over the Senate would enable his political superior, the president, to destroy the independence of the legislature), the vice presidency did not become an issue in the battle over the ratification of the Constitution. It was discussed in only three of the states, and none of the state conventions proposed an amendment to the Constitution affecting the vice-presidential office.[44] The *Federalist Papers* virtually ignored the issue, devoting only two paragraphs to it in a total of eighty-five essays.[45]

Development of the Vice Presidency

The first two vice presidents—John Adams and Thomas Jefferson—were influential political figures. The former did not merely preside over the Senate as an impartial officer; as Williams explains, Adams "conceived the office as a place to exercise the function of majority leader and thus was for all practical purposes a member of the Senate."[46] In the process Adams presented the agenda, intervened in debate, gave his opinion on matters, and "exercised his right of the casting the tie vote more than any other future vice president would." [47] After serving as vice president for eight years, Federalist Adams himself was elected president in 1796, and the electoral system that year made his partisan rival, Republican Thomas Jefferson, his vice president. The rivalry between the two did not end when the constitutional system placed them in the same administration. When Adams asked Jefferson to serve as a special emissary to France to try to bring about better relations with that country's new revolutionary government, the vice president refused on the grounds that such a responsibility was beyond the duties of his office (and also because Jefferson did not want to lighten his political opponent's burdens). While serving as the vice president, Jefferson also provided information to his Republican party lieutenants on how best to attack Adams in the upcoming election of 1800, a contest in which he would defeat Adams for the presidency.

In the nation's early experience, therefore, the vice presidency attracted capable persons who did not think it necessary to cooperate with the president with whom they served. However, the bizarre Jefferson-Burr deadlock in 1800 (discussed in Chapter 2) led to the adoption in 1804 of the Twelfth Amendment, which stipulated that the electors cast separate votes for president and vice president. The effect of this change in the "mode of election" was immediate. No longer perceived as an office occupied by the second most popular political leader in the nation, the vice presidency quickly became, for the most part, a dumping ground for a succession of nonentities who, although loyal to the president, played no important role in the American political system. [48] Throughout the remainder of the nineteenth century, many of the vice presidents were actually older than the presidents with whom they served, and the vice-presidential office was often vacant. Moreover, vice presidents usually were not renominated to that office, and even those that succeeded to the presidency (Tyler, Fillmore, Johnson, and Arthur) were not chosen by their party for another presidential term.

At the turn of the century the vice presidency became more politically visible, when the popular Teddy Roosevelt agreed to go on the Republican ticket in 1900 with William McKinley. Although Roosevelt did so very reluctantly (he had no real alternative since Republican Boss Thomas Platt of New York made it clear that he would use his influence to prevent Roosevelt's renomination as governor of that state), the ambitious vice president immediately began to maneuver for the Republican presidential nomination in 1904 and suddenly succeeded to that office in 1901 when McKinley was assassinated. Unlike the pattern of the 1800s, however, Roosevelt was renominated and reelected in his own right in 1904. The same was true of Calvin Coolidge, who succeeded to the presidency on the death of Warren Harding in 1923 and was nominated in his own right and elected in 1924. [49]

Thus, vice presidents became more important in the early years of the twentieth century but only if they succeeded to the presidency. The vice-presidential office itself remained insignificant. Thomas Marshall did preside over the cabinet when Woodrow Wilson was at Versailles working on the peace treaty, and Warren Harding made Coolidge a regular member of the cabinet. That practice ceased, however, when Coolidge's vice president, Charles Dawes, refused to attend cabinet meetings because he considered it wrong in principle. It remained for Franklin Roosevelt to make something of the vice presidency office (just as he did the presidency). When Roosevelt insisted on having Henry Wallace as his running mate in 1940 and then proceeded to assign Wallace important responsibilities, the character of today's vice presidency began to emerge.

Roles Assumed by Recent Vice Presidents

Although not all vice presidents who have served since 1940 have been given important duties by their presidents, there has been a definite trend in that direction. As Paul David suggests, once functions, duties, and prerogatives of the vice presidency are in place, "withdrawal through action by the president becomes more difficult than their initial establishment." [50] As a result, vice presidents have come to play a variety of roles in the American political system.

The oldest role, and the only one formally rooted in the Constitution, is that of participating in the activities of Congress, specifically as presiding officer of the Senate with the right to vote in cases of a tie. Particularly in recent years, however, that has been the least important responsibility of vice presidents. They typically do not spend much time presiding over Senate deliberations; rather, that task usually falls to freshmen senators from the majority party. (It was not Lyndon Johnson who was in the chair on November 22, 1963, when President Kennedy was assassinated but his brother, Edward Kennedy of Massachusetts, at that time the youngest member of the Senate.) Nor is the casting of votes in case of a tie in the Senate a significant power: Donald Young notes that such votes occur rarely more than once a year. [51]

Beyond their formal participation in Senate proceedings, vice presidents sometimes can be influential from behind the scenes in behalf of the president's legislative program, particularly if they themselves have formerly served in Congress. John Nance Garner, a former Speaker of the House of Representatives, played an important role in persuading many of his former colleagues to vote for bills proposed by President Franklin Roosevelt in his first term of office. Hubert Humphrey and Walter Mondale, both former senators from Minnesota, worked effectively in the upper chamber in behalf of legislation favored by their chief executives, Lyndon Johnson and Jimmy Carter. Vice presidents must be careful, however, not to overreach in their attempts to influence their former colleagues, because the latter typically think of them as representatives of the rival executive branch of government. When Senate Majority Leader Mike Mansfield proposed in 1961 that his immediate predecessor, Lyndon Johnson, at that time vice president, preside over the Senate Democratic Caucus, the proposal was deeply resented by the Democratic senators and quickly withdrawn.

The vice-presidential role that has grown most in importance in recent years is that of assisting the president in his administrative responsibilities. Since the days of Franklin Roosevelt, vice presidents have sat in on cabinet sessions and have often also presided over cabinet sessions in the absence of the president. Moreover, the National Security Act of 1947 made the vice president a statutory member of the National Security Council (examined further in Chapter 11) so that he is privy to the sessions of that body dealing with matters of foreign and military policy. When the president is not available for its meetings, the vice president usually presides in his place.

In recent years presidents also have used their vice presidents to coordinate administrative agencies involved in particular projects. Both Richard Nixon and Lyndon Johnson, as vice presidents, were placed in charge of efforts to prevent discrimination against minority groups; Hubert Humphrey was assigned the responsibility of helping to provide employment to needy youths in the nation's cities; and Spiro Agnew was designated as the administration's liaison with governors and mayors. Presidents consider the interests and backgrounds of their vice presidents in determining how best to use their talents in administrative positions. (Humphrey, for example, had been mayor of Minneapolis; Agnew, a county executive in Baltimore and governor of Maryland.)

As is true of their legislative role, however, there are limitations on the part vice presidents can assume in the executive branch of the government. During World War II, Franklin Roosevelt assigned the responsibility of coordinating activities relating to the war effort to Henry Wallace, who had previously served as FDR's secretary of agriculture. (Wallace's posts included the chairmanship of the Economic Defense Board, the Supply Priorities and Allocation Board, and the Board of Economic Warfare.) Eventually, this attempt to make the vice president a kind of "super secretary" over regular department secretaries ended in failure, for Wallace got into squabbles with these officials (who naturally resented having the vice president interposed between them and the president) as well as with some conservative members of Congress who distrusted him and his ideas. The same fate befell Vice President Nelson Rockefeller when President Ford placed him in charge of the Domestic Council, a group assigned the task of taking the leadership in developing domestic programs.

Henry Wallace did initiate a role that has occupied a great deal of the time of subsequent vice presidents: emissary of the president to foreign countries. FDR sent Wallace on fact-finding trips to China, Mexico, and the Soviet Union. Over the years, vice presidents have served as the "eyes and ears" of the president for developments abroad and have represented the United States in the absence of the president himself. Nixon visited fifty-four countries in his eight years as vice president.[52] Lyndon Johnson also undertook some important missions for John Kennedy: conferring with leaders in Vietnam, Taiwan, Thailand, India, and Pakistan over the possibility of the United States making a major commitment of troops to Vietnam, calming West Germans after the Soviet Union erected the Berlin Wall, and notifying the governments of Greece, Turkey, Cypress, and Iran of reductions in the amount of foreign aid they were receiving from the United States.[53] Walter Mondale was sent to Canada and Mexico to talk over a variety of difficult problems with these U.S. neighbors. At times, vice presidents also have assumed operational assignments relating to foreign and military affairs: Reagan asked George Bush to chair his administration's "crisis management" team, a group responsible for coordinating and controlling federal resources in responding to emergencies.

Vice presidents have undertaken a variety of assignments pertaining to the president's relationships with the American public. Especially prominent has been their participation in political party activities, including campaigns in off-year elections. In fact, some vice presidents, especially Richard Nixon (for Dwight Eisenhower) and Spiro Agnew (for Nixon), have assumed the role of what Arthur Schlesinger, Jr., has termed "political hit men," savaging members of the opposition.[54] In recent years presidents have used their vice presidents also as liaisons with particular social groups: Agnew was assigned the responsibility of trying to woo blue-collar workers, and Mondale worked closely with farmers and members of labor unions. Nixon also used Agnew to attack the national television news media; the vice president dutifully read speeches prepared by the president's speech writers lashing out against the liberal "Eastern Establishment" press, a "small and unelected elite" concentrated in the "geographical and intellectual confines of Washington, D.C., or New York City."

A recent student of the office, Paul Light, maintains that "after two hundred years as errand-boys, political hitmen, professional mourners, and incidental White House Commissioners, vice presidents can now lay claim to regular access to the president and the opportunity to give advice on major decisions."[55] Vice presidents, he points out, now have staff resources that provide them the time and energy required to advise the president, physical proximity in the White House to the president, and regular meetings with him, which allow the vice president to compete for the president's attention. Another student of the subject, Joel Goldstein, notes that recent vice presidents have become general advisers of the presidents with whom they serve. He attributes this development to the fact that chief executives (rather than party leaders) now choose their running mates and therefore have an opportunity to select persons with compatible views and agreeable personalities to whom they can assign duties that will be helpful to the conduct of the presidency.[56] Goldstein states also that the expanded activities of the presidency exert a "gravitational pull" that "has drawn the second officer into the executive orbit." [57]

As Light contends, there is a difference between a vice president's being able to render *advice* to the president on major public policy decisions and his actually exerting *influence* over those decisions. Both Nelson Rockefeller and Walter Mondale possessed the inclination and resources to advise Gerald Ford and Jimmy Carter, respectively. Yet Mondale was much more influential than Rockefeller because, among other reasons, he enjoyed better political relations with Carter's White House staff than Rockefeller did with Ford's, and Carter was much more persuadable on policy matters than Ford was.

The clear trend in recent years is for the vice president to be a more important political figure than was true in the past. Although George Bush was Ronald Reagan's principal rival for the 1980 Republican presidential nomination, and at one time he differed sharply with Reagan on major policy matters, the president nonetheless assigned the vice president important responsibilities. (During the nomination campaign, for example, Bush referred to "supply side" economics as "voodoo" economics.) In addition to chairing the crisis-management team, Bush also was placed in charge of the Task Force on Regulatory Relief, designed to free businesses from what President Reagan considered to be excessive government interference in the private sector of the economy.

Although the vice president has emerged as a more important political figure in recent years, in the final analysis he is subject entirely to the wishes of the president, who chooses him and then decides which responsibilities he will be assigned. The political fortunes of the vice president are tied closely to those of the president, and the second in command is sometimes required to walk a fine line between independence of the chief executive and disloyalty to him. Hubert Humphrey faced that problem over the Vietnam War in 1968 when he sought to succeed Lyndon Johnson as president; George Bush found himself in a similar situation over the Iran-contra affair as he looked forward to becoming the Republican presidential nominee in 1988, when President Reagan would be ineligible to run.

Conclusion

The presidency, a unique American institution created by the Constitutional Convention, has undergone vast changes over the years. The broad, indefinite powers granted to the chief executive have given incumbents considerable latitude to shape the office to meet the necessities of their day as well as their own conceptions of the role the president should play in the American political system. Moreover, initiatives undertaken by presidents who were strong leaders often have become precedents, which their successors have followed, even though they themselves may not have intended to be so venturesome.

The vice presidency has been less of a protean office than has the presidency. Throughout most of the nation's history, it has been an insignificant institution, populated by mediocre persons who were assigned few, if any, important duties. In recent years, however, persons of considerable talent have been willing and able to serve as vice president and fully expect to be given significant responsibilities, such as advising the president on major public policy decisions. Moreover, vice presidents are now provided the staff resources and access to the president to enable that advice to be heard.

Along with major changes in the presidency has come a continuity in the office that enables its responsibilities to be carried forward should something happen to the incumbent. The impeachment proceedings that led to the resignation of President Nixon demonstrate that means exist for making a peaceful transfer of political power in the nation's highest office. The Twenty-fifth Amendment has also done much to provide continuity to the office by removing many of the uncertainties surrounding presidential disability and by creating a designated procedure to fill a vacancy in the vice-presidential office.

Notes

1. C. C. Thach, Jr., *The Creation of the Presidency, 1775-1789: A Study in Constitutional History* (Baltimore: Johns Hopkins University Press, 1922), chap. 3.
2. Joseph Kallenbach, *The American Chief Executive: The Presidency and the Governorship* (New York: Harper and Row, 1966), chap. 2.
3. In Douglas Southall Freeman, *Patriot and President,* vol. 6 of *George Washington* (New York: Scribner's, 1943), 117; cited in Louis Koenig, *The Chief Executive,* 4th ed. (New York: Harcourt Brace Jovanovich, 1981), 29.
4. Kallenbach, *The American Chief Executive,* chap. 2.
5. *The Federalist Papers,* ed. Clinton Rossiter (New York: New American Library, 1961), 424.
6. Arthur M. Schlesinger, Jr., *The Imperial Presidency* (Boston: Houghton Mifflin, 1973), ix.
7. Harold Laski, *The American Presidency: An Interpretation* (New York: Harper and Brothers, 1940), 172.
8. Kallenbach, *The American Chief Executive,* 243.
9. Woodrow Wilson, *Constitutional Government in the United States* (New York: Columbia University Press, 1908), 70.
10. Edward Corwin, *The President: Office and Powers,* 4th ed. (New York: New York University Press, 1957), 30.
11. Ibid., chap. 1.
12. Clinton Rossiter, *The American Presidency,* rev. ed. (New York: Harcourt, Brace, 1960), chaps. 3, 5.

13. Leonard White, *The Federalists: A Study in Administrative History* (New York: Macmillan, 1967), 99.
14. As a matter of political strategy presidents now often seek the advice of influential individual senators. Woodrow Wilson's failure to consult with prominent Republican senators about the Treaty of Versailles is reputed to have contributed to his failure to get it approved.
15. Rossiter, *The American Presidency*, 91.
16. Corwin, *The President: Office and Powers*, 20.
17. Alfred Kelly and Winfred Harbison, *The American Constitution: Its Origins and Development*, 4th ed. (New York: Norton, 1970), 424.
18. Rossiter, *The American Presidency*, 102.
19. Richard Nixon also undertook a number of major changes in the office, including impounding funds appropriated by Congress, making excessive claims of executive privilege, dismantling the Office of Economic Opportunity, and conducting improper surveillance of American citizens. However, as will be discussed in subsequent chapters, these actions were nullified by the Congress or the courts or not followed by his successors. His administration is therefore not included here because these changes were only temporary.
20. The House actually impeached twelve other public officials (primarily federal judges), and the Senate ultimately convicted four of them. The most recent case involved U.S. District Judge Harry E. Claiborne of Nevada. On July 22, 1986, the House voted unanimously to impeach him, and on October 9, the Senate removed Claiborne from office after convicting him of "high crimes and misdemeanors" related to his 1984 conviction for tax fraud.
21. The key figure in the vote was Edmund Ross of Kansas, who, although a Radical Republican and under tremendous pressure to vote for conviction, voted not guilty. Six other Republican senators joined Ross in saving President Johnson.
22. Michael Benedict, *The Impeachment and Trial of Andrew Johnson* (New York: Norton, 1973), 180.
23. 418 U.S. 683 (1974).
24. That statement came back to haunt Ford four years later when he was serving as vice president and President Nixon's impeachment was under consideration. Ford tried to distinguish the two cases by pointing out that federal judges serve during "good behavior" while the Constitution does not use that language to apply to presidents.
25. Raoul Berger, *Impeachment: The Constitutional Problems* (Cambridge, Mass.: Harvard University Press, 1973); Charles Black, Jr., *Impeachment: A Handbook* (New Haven: Yale University Press, 1974).
26. Black, *Impeachment: A Handbook*, 39-40.
27. Ibid., 316.
28. Berger, *Impeachment: The Constitutional Problems*, 119.
29. Black, *Impeachment: A Handbook*, chap. 4.
30. Rossiter, *The American Presidency*, 210.
31. While there was no person then serving as vice president to complicate the matter, Truman would have been giving up more than two years of his term rather than only a few months.

32. Margaret Truman, *Harry S Truman* (New York: William Morrow, 1973), 322.

33. In addition, six other presidents were victims of unsuccessful assassination attempts—Jackson, Theodore Roosevelt, Franklin Roosevelt, Truman, Ford (on two occasions), and Reagan. The assault on Teddy Roosevelt occurred in October 1912 after he was president and while he was campaigning for reelection as the Progressive party candidate (the assailant feared he would win); the attempt on Franklin Roosevelt's life took place after he was elected for the first time but before he was inaugurated.

34. Richard Hansen refers to such agreements as "stopgaps" (Richard Hansen, *The Year We Had No President* [Lincoln: University of Nebraska Press, 1952], chap. 5).

35. Fortunately, no major problem of disability occurred when President Reagan was shot on March 30, 1981. Although he was unconscious for more than two hours while undergoing surgery, he recovered quickly and the following day was able to meet with his senior aides and sign a bill dealing with dairy price supports.

36. Ruth Silva, "Presidential Succession and Disability," *Law and Contemporary Problems* (Autumn 1956): 646-663.

37. It should also be noted that the Twenty-second Amendment places a limitation on the number of terms a president can serve. Under its provisions, no person can be elected to the office more than twice; moreover, if he has served more than two years of a term to which someone else was originally elected, then he can be elected only once. Thus, the longest a person can serve in the office is ten years. There have been suggestions over the years that the amendment be repealed, most recently by Republican leaders, such as Rep. Guy Vander Jagt of Michigan, who would like to see President Reagan run for a third term. Others, however, have proposed that the president be limited to a single, six-year term. (The concluding chapter of the volume will examine both of these proposals).

38. There is some question as to when a person becomes president-elect: when the popular votes are counted and the results are known; when the electors cast their ballots in their respective state capitols; or when the electoral ballots are counted and the outcome is announced by the incumbent vice president before a joint session of Congress. Fortunately, no incident has yet occurred to raise that legal issue.

39. John Feerick, *From Falling Hands: The Story of Presidential Succession* (New York: Fordham University Press, 1965), 146.

40. The afternoon President Reagan was shot, Secretary of State Alexander Haig, when asked who was making decisions for the government, mistakenly stated that "constitutionally, gentlemen, you have the president, the vice president and the secretary of state."

41. On sixteen occasions before the enactment of the Twenty-fifth Amendment, the vice-presidential office was vacant: eight vice presidents succeeded to the presidency, seven died, and one resigned.

42. Irving Williams, *The Rise of the Vice Presidency* (Washington, D.C.: Public Affairs Press, 1956), chap. 2.

43. Arthur M. Schlesinger, Jr., *The Imperial Presidency* (New York: Popular Library, 1973), 481-485.

44. Williams, *The Rise of the Vice Presidency,* chap. 2.

45. Schlesinger, *The Imperial Presidency* (Popular Library ed.), 483.

46. Williams, *The Rise of the Vice Presidency,* 23.

47. Ibid.

48. There were two major exceptions to the rule. John Calhoun, a national political figure who served under both John Quincy Adams and Andrew Jackson, battled with both presidents and ultimately resigned during Jackson's first term to accept a Senate seat. For his second term, Jackson chose Martin Van Buren, a skillful New York politician who had previously served as his secretary of state; Jackson also helped Van Buren get nominated and elected as president in his own right in 1836.

49. As indicated in Chapter 3, this pattern has continued in more recent years, as Truman, Johnson, and Ford were all nominated in their own right, and the former two elected to the presidency.

50. Paul David, "The Vice Presidency: Its Institutional Evolution and Contemporary Status," *Journal of Politics* (November 1967): 721.

51. Donald Young, *American Roulette: The History and Dilemma of the Vice Presidency* (New York: Viking, 1974), 379. The vice president can also affect the deliberations of the Senate by ruling on important procedural motions, as Vice President Mondale did in 1977 when he declared certain amendments to a controversial natural gas bill to be out of order, a tactic that ended a filibuster against the bill. Opportunities to exercise this power rarely occur.

52. Ibid., 261.

53. David, "The Vice Presidency," 737-738.

54. Schlesinger, *The Imperial Presidency* (Popular Library ed.), 475.

55. Paul Light, *Vice Presidential Power: Advice and Influence in the White House* (Baltimore: Johns Hopkins University Press, 1984), 1.

56. Joel Goldstein, *The Modern American Vice Presidency: The Transformation of a Political Institution* (Princeton, N.J.: Princeton University Press, 1982), 301-305.

57. Ibid., 306.

Selected Readings

Black, Charles, Jr. *Impeachment: A Handbook.* New Haven: Yale University Press, 1974.

Corwin, Edward. *The President: Office and Powers.* 4th ed. New York: New York University Press, 1957.

Feerick, John. *From Falling Hands: The Story of Presidential Succession.* New York: Fordham University Press, 1965.

Goldstein, Joel. *The Modern American Vice-Presidency: The Transformation of a Political Institution.* Princeton: Princeton University Press, 1982.

Kallenbach, Joseph. *The American Chief Executive: The Presidency and the*

Governorship. New York: Harper and Row, 1966.

Light, Paul. *Vice-Presidential Power: Advice and Influence in the White House*. Baltimore: Johns Hopkins University Press, 1984.

Rossiter, Clinton. *The American Presidency*. rev. ed. New York: Harcourt, Brace, 1960.

Schlesinger, Arthur, Jr. *The Imperial Presidency*. New York: Popular Library, 1973.

As congressional legislators look on, President Lyndon B. Johnson signs the Civil Rights Bill, April 11, 1964. Johnson worked successfully with Congress to enact his Great Society legislation in 1964 and 1965.

CHAPTER SIX

Congressional Politics

In January 1986, two journalists who closely follow Congress and the presidency observed that "at the height of his popularity and backed by an awesome electoral mandate, President Ronald Reagan finds himself confronted by an increasingly defiant Congress." They suggested that the "struggle between Reagan and Congress could be a formula for stalemate." [1] For much of the year, however, President Reagan appeared to be more than holding his own in his relations with Congress. Foremost among his legislative achievements in 1986 was the enactment of the most comprehensive reform of the federal income tax since its establishment in 1913. He also prevailed, albeit narrowly, with his proposals to sell sophisticated arms to Saudi Arabia and to provide aid to the Nicaraguan contras, and he resisted intense congressional efforts to modify his budgetary priorities. Reagan's continued effectiveness in dealing with Congress was much in doubt when the 100th Congress convened in January 1987, owing to the capture of the Senate by the opposition Democrats in the 1986 congressional elections and the effect of the Iranian arms affair on his popular support and his reputation as a persuasive leader. Reagan's pattern of generally positive relations with Congress, at least until late 1986, contrasts with the experience of his three immediate predecessors. To understand how he avoided becoming locked into no-win struggles as his predecessors had, one must examine the politics of presidential-congressional relations and the ways in which modern presidents have managed them.

Modern presidents usually discover, upon taking office, that the skills and techniques of leadership that enabled them to capture their party's nomination and win the election are not identical with those needed to sustain their popularity. Whereas nomination and electoral politics require the ability to raise money, to build an organization composed of professionals (public relations experts, market researchers, and party politicians), to project an attractive and engaging image, and to sense the concerns of the public, the

237

politics of governing—that is, legislating and administering—require talents that will move a complex and often cumbersome government to "get things done." These talents include persuasion, personal and organizational leadership, and managerial skill. Ronald Reagan appears to be an exception in that to a considerable extent he possesses both sets of talents.

Americans tend to judge presidents primarily by their performance in office. A principal criterion of evaluation is the president's ability to persuade Congress to pass his legislative program. Other national political leaders expect the president to develop legislative proposals that will achieve the goals of his administration. The public and members of the news media expect the president to steer those proposals through Congress. Unwillingness or inability to meet these expectations usually results in loss of presidential popularity and assessments of ineffectiveness or failure. Even presidents who are philosophically opposed to an active federal government, as Dwight D. Eisenhower was, find themselves unable to resist the pressures to provide legislative leadership. Pressing national problems seem to demand presidential attention, and the president feels compelled to take action to solve them. Most solutions require congressional approval, which has not, however, always been forthcoming.

This chapter examines the president's relations with Congress. It begins by tracing the development of his legislative role in the twentieth century and then shifts to an analysis of the constitutional relationship between the president and Congress. It follows with a discussion of the president's formal legislative powers and a description of the means by which he attempts to influence Congress. It then analyzes the basis of the president's support in Congress. Finally, the chapter explores how the president's influence on Congress can be evaluated.

Development of the President's Legislative Role

The Constitution, in Article I, Section 8, gives Congress "all the legislative powers herein granted." Quite clearly, the Framers expected that Congress would have primary responsibility for formulating national policy and that the president's legislative role would be limited. Until the twentieth century most presidents did limit their involvement in the congressional process. Even Thomas Jefferson and Abraham Lincoln, who were most inclined to try to lead Congress, encountered strong opposition, and their activism did not alter the pattern of congressional supremacy.[2]

Early in the twentieth century, under the leadership of Theodore Roosevelt and Woodrow Wilson, the presidency acquired a greatly expanded legislative role as the national government responded to the problems of industrialization and urbanization. Roosevelt worked closely with congressional leaders and sent several messages to Congress that defined a legislative program. He saw it as the duty of the president to "take a very active interest in getting the right kind of legislation." [3] Wilson, who as a political science professor had argued that strong presidential leadership of Congress was needed if the nation was to cope with its growing problems, actively participated in the legislative process.[4] He took the lead in defining the goals of his program, he helped formulate bills, he reinstated the practice abandoned since 1796 of personally delivering the State of the Union message to Congress, he used members of his cabinet to build congressional support for his bills, and he personally lobbied for some of his key measures such as the Federal Reserve Act and the Clayton Antitrust Act.

The next major expansion of the president's legislative role occurred under Franklin D. Roosevelt. Taking office in 1933 when the economy was mired in the depths of the Great Depression, FDR called Congress into a special session that lasted for one hundred days. During that period the new president proposed and Congress passed legislation designed to meet the economic crisis. The banking system was overhauled, a program of industrial self-government under the National Recovery Administration was authorized, farm income was buttressed through passage of the Agricultural Adjustment Act, financial markets were regulated under the Truth in Securities Act, and a program of comprehensive development of one of the nation's most depressed areas was instituted through creation of the Tennessee Valley Authority.

During the remainder of his first term FDR continued to submit and Congress to pass a series of measures designed to help farmers, industrial workers, and individual citizens. The legislation promoted soil conservation and restricted excess agricultural production, it guaranteed labor the right to organize and bargain collectively, and it established a system of social insurance to protect people against the loss of work due to economic slowdowns, physical disability, or old age. Administrative agencies were established to implement many of these New Deal statutes.

FDR's principal mode of operation was to send to Congress messages that analyzed a problem and outlined his proposed solution. Often the messages were accompanied or followed by a draft bill. He then assigned aides to monitor the bills and lobby for their passage. Coordination of his legislative program was accomplished through a clearance process administered by the Bureau of the Budget.[5] FDR made extensive use of the veto as a means of bending Congress to his will by threatening to veto legislation that failed to meet his demands. He also used the veto to prevent passage of legislation he regarded as unwise or contrary to his purposes. His major contribution was to establish firmly the expectation that the president would be actively involved at all stages of the legislative process by submitting a legislative program to Congress, working for its passage, and coordinating its implementation.

FDR's two immediate successors, Harry S Truman and Dwight Eisenhower, institutionalized the president's legislative role by creating structures and processes to assist in carrying it out on a regular, systematic basis.[6] This was accomplished by the Bureau of the Budget and by members of the White House staff. By the mid-1960s it appeared to some observers that the presidency had come to dominate the legislative process. Writing in 1965, Samuel P. Huntington remarked that "the congressional role in legislation has largely been reduced to delay and amendment." Such tasks as initiative in formulating legislation, assignment of legislative priorities, generation of support for legislation, and determination of the final content of legislation had "shifted to the executive branch," which, in Huntington's view, had gained "at the expense of Congress."[7] Others have argued, however, that although congressional and presidential roles in the legislative process have changed substantially, Congress remains a vitally important participant. The president's program is critical in determining the congressional agenda, but Congress is constantly modifying and altering policy through appropriations, amendments, and renewals of statutory authorizations.[8]

Moreover, Congress and the president are not engaged in a zero-sum game in which the power of one necessarily decreases as the power of the other increases. In an absolute sense, since 1933 Congress has increased its power as an instrument of government by vastly expanding the subjects on which it has legislated. During that time, however, the power of Congress as an innovator of public policy has declined relative to that of the president. In three brief periods of legislative activity—1933-1937, 1964-1965, and 1981—activist presidents (FDR, Johnson, and Reagan) led responsive Congresses in the adoption of major changes in domestic policy. Congress also responded to presidential leadership in establishing the role of the United States in world affairs during and immediately following World War II.

Nevertheless, there have also been periods in which Congress substantially increased its authority vis-à-vis the president. During the 1970s, for example, Congress expanded its control over the executive branch through increased use of the legislative veto (see Chapter 7), curbed presidential use of military force abroad through passage of the War Powers Resolution of 1973 (see Chapter 11), and strengthened its ability to determine the amount of federal spending through establishment of the congressional budget process (see Chapter 10).

Congress did not move in the 1970s, however, to diminish the president's legislative role. Congress still depends on the president to develop, submit, and lobby for the passage of a legislative program, and it has not tried to displace the president as the primary source of its agenda.

The always-present potential for presidential leadership of Congress became dramatically evident in 1981 when Ronald Reagan took office following the landslide Republican victory in the 1980 elections. Reagan quickly took command of conservative congressional majorities, which passed his taxing and spending proposals and sharply altered the course that domestic social and economic policy had been following since the 1930s.[9] But

Reagan's period of dominance was short-lived as congressional critics of his policies regrouped in 1982 and have since attacked deficits in the range of $100-200 billion in his 1983-1987 budgets. Reagan discovered, as had Roosevelt in 1938 and Lyndon B. Johnson in 1966, that congressional approval of a president's program is not automatic. Congressional support must be cultivated and maintained, and when the conditions that created it change, it can rapidly disappear. Without such support, presidents face frustration and ineffectuality.

The Presidential-Congressional Relationship

There is an inherent tension between Congress and the presidency, yet cooperation between the two institutions is necessary if the government is to act in a significant way. The Constitution creates institutional competition through the separation of powers, but it also mandates a sharing of powers among the branches of government. Joint action by the president and Congress is required to authorize programs, appropriate money to pay for them, and levy taxes to provide the funds. Neither branch can achieve its goals or operate the government without the participation of the other.

The Separation of Powers

James Madison's *Federalist* No. 51 makes it clear that the Framers had contemplated presidential-congressional conflict:

> To what expedient ... shall we finally resort, for maintaining in practice the necessary partition of power among the several departments, as laid down in the constitution? The only answer that can be given is ... by so contriving the interior structure of the government as its several constituent parts may, by their mutual relations, be the means of keeping each other in their proper places....
>
> In order to lay a due foundation for that separate and distinct exercise of the different powers of the government, which to a certain extent is admitted on all hands to be essential to the preservation of liberty, it is evident that each department should have a will of its own....
>
> But the great security against a gradual concentration of the several powers in the same department consists in giving to those who administer each department the necessary constitutional means and personal motives to resist the encroachments of the others.... Ambition must be made to counteract ambition. The interests of the man must be connected with the constitutional rights of the place.[10]

Since 1789, the task of governing the United States has been to overcome the constitutional dispersion of power among competing institutions. The most important division of power, from the standpoint of making and implementing national policies, is that between the president and Congress. The pattern of the presidential-congressional relationship has not been static. According to Lawrence C. Dodd, a cyclical pattern of power aggrandizement by Congress or the presidency and resurgence by the other institution has operated from the outset of government under the Constitution.[11] In the nineteenth century the institutional surges and declines oscillated evenly within well-defined boundaries and returned at the end of each cycle to the balance envisioned in the Constitution. The economic, social, and technological transformations occurring during the twentieth century, however, created problems and conditions that called increasingly for executive rather than legislative decision making. The presidency could act more quickly, more decisively, and more consistently than Congress, which has had difficulty ascertaining its institutional will and coherently pursuing its goals.

In consequence, presidential surges have resulted in permanent expansions of executive power and presidential aggrandizements, such as Lyndon Johnson's use of the war powers to involve the United States in the Vietnam War (see Chapter 11) or Richard Nixon's sweeping claims of executive privilege and his extensive impoundments of appropriated funds (see Chapter 7). Although Congress managed to reassert its constitutional authority during the 1970s,[12] the cycle turned again in the 1980s toward increased reliance on presidential power. The nation found that it needed presidential leadership to deal with difficult problems such as severe inflation, economic interdependence, renewed Soviet expansionism, and international terrorism.

Sources of Presidential-Congressional Conflict

Forces promoting conflict are always present in the presidential-congressional relationship. In addition to institutional competition born of the separation of powers, conflict stems from the difference in the constituencies of the members of Congress and the president and from the fragmentation of power within Congress. The 535 members of Congress represent constituencies that vary in geographical area, population, economic structure, and social composition. Each congressional constituency is but a part of the nation. Every member of Congress depends for reelection on constituency-based political forces. Thus, different members speak for different economic, social, and geographical interests, and all members are necessarily somewhat parochial at times in their policy orientations. Consequently, claims by certain members to be acting in behalf of the national interest must be judged in the context of their constituency interests.

Since congressional parties lack the power to command the votes of their members, there is no institutional basis for any of the elected party leaders of either house to speak on its behalf. The only way in which the national interest emerges in Congress is through bargaining between members and blocs of members responsive to particular interests. This practice results in the formation of temporary majority coalitions to pass specific measures. Congressional policy making is thus deliberate, incremental or piecemeal, and reactive. Congress is often unable to maintain consistency in its actions in different policy areas and cohesiveness within areas. Speed, efficiency, consistency, and cohesiveness are usually lacking, except in a crisis.

In contrast, the president's constituency is the entire nation. The president alone can speak authoritatively in behalf of the national interest. He also can claim to be acting for various inarticulate and unorganized interests who are not adequately represented in Congress. He can resist the claims and demands of well-organized particular interests by posing as the champion of the national interest. The difficulty that Congress encounters in determining and speaking for the national interest and the ease with which the president may do so stem from their differing constituencies and are a continuing source of tension between them.

The inability of Congress to match the decisiveness, cohesion, and consistency of the presidency as a national policy-making institution is also a product of the fragmented structure of its internal authority. Widely recognized are the weakness of congressional parties, the limited power of party leaders, the absence of party discipline in congressional voting, the presence of strong committees and subcommittees, and the ambitions of individual members to enhance their reelection chances and to advance to higher office.[13]

Former presidential aide and later Secretary of Health, Education and Welfare Joseph Califano has charged that Congress lacks institutional will.[14] An internally fragmented Congress that is lacking will is not without power, but it tends to be a negative and restraining force on the presidency. Also, Congress is usually more comfortable with distributive policies and programs, which provide benefits on a widespread basis, than with redistributive policies, which change the allocation of wealth and power in society.

According to Randall Ripley and to Roger Davidson and Walter Oleszek, Congress, as presently constituted, values the function of "representation" over that of "lawmaking." [15] By this they mean that it is responsive primarily to constituency interests and to well-organized interest groups. The presidency, in contrast, might be said to stress the lawmaking function whereby electoral mandates are translated into policies that are adopted by congressional coalitions. If Congress is to become an institutional decision maker that participates equally with the presidency in translating electoral mandates into law, it will need to reduce its internal fragmentation and develop an internal structure of authority that can provide consistency and cohesiveness to its actions, legitimately define the national interest, and act decisively and comprehensively not only during crises but also in ordinary times.

Patterns of Presidential-Congressional Policy Making

As noted previously, there is a constitutional imperative for cooperation between the two institutions: Congress has the legislative powers of the government, and its approval is necessary for any kind of executive action. Within the boundaries set by the Constitution and by political conditions, four patterns of relationship are possible between the presidency and Congress in making national policy: presidential domination, congressional domination, joint program development, and stalemate.[16] All but joint program development involve substantial conflict. All but stalemate result in final legislative action. In the presidential domination pattern, the presidency serves as the principal source of initiation for legislative proposals and plays the major role in shaping the details of legislation. Under congressional domination, Congress is the primary initiator and it shapes the details. In the joint program development model both Congress and the presidency share in initiating and shaping legislation. In the stalemate model, either branch may initiate proposals and both may be involved in shaping legislative details, but no action results because neither side is willing to compromise.

The patterns vary according to issues and presidential leadership styles. Presidential domination tends to prevail in the areas of foreign and military policy and when presidents attach high priorities to specific pieces of legislation, as Lyndon Johnson did in 1964-1965 with his Great Society program.[17] Congressional domination was the prevailing pattern in the 1970s, when Congress passed major legislation on the environment, consumer protection, and occupational safety; and it has always prevailed on public works. The presidency and Congress have tended to cooperate extensively on economic development legislation and tax policy. Stalemate characterized much of the energy legislation proposed by presidents in the 1970s, as well as proposals for construction of a supersonic transport and welfare reform bills. Occasionally, a proposal may be stalemated for years and then move rapidly to passage as conditions change or a new president takes office, as was the case with medicare.

Presidential leadership style is related to the pattern of congressional relations with the presidency. An activist president who is committed to an extensive legislative program, such as FDR or Lyndon Johnson, is normally comfortable with the presidential domination pattern, whereas a president who is more restrained and less active, such as Dwight Eisenhower or Gerald R. Ford, may be inclined toward the cooperation of joint program development or may accept considerable congressional program development. Ronald Reagan, an activist with a conservative agenda that does not require extensive new legislation, has adopted varied patterns in his relations with Congress. To achieve his primary goals of reducing the role of the federal government and strengthening the armed forces, he has opted for presidential domination. On issues of less importance to him, such as farm policy and social security financing, he has been willing to share responsibility with Congress. When he has sharply disagreed with Congress, as he did over reducing the federal budget deficit, he has been willing to settle for a stalemate, but on no matters of consequence has he accepted congressional domination.

Since FDR, no president has sought a stalemate with Congress, although such a condition has developed on occasion. Stalemates tend to occur more often when Congress and the presidency are controlled by different political parties than when one party is in power in both branches. A necessary condition for stalemate is a sharp division of opinion between the president and the congressional majority. During the Nixon and Ford administrations presidential-congressional relations were stalemated over several key bills as two conservative Republican presidents quarreled with liberal Democratic Congresses about presidential prerogatives and spending priorities. From 1982 to 1986, President Reagan and Congress were stalemated for several months each year over his proposed budgets for the next fiscal year. Their disagreements focused on how to reduce projected deficits of $100-200 billion. Key Republican leaders in the Senate joined their Democratic counterparts in the House of Representatives in pressing the president to ease his opposition to cuts in defense spending and to selective tax increases. He insisted that the only means of reducing the deficits was through deep cuts in spending for domestic programs, which most members of Congress were reluctant to do. The outcomes were generally unsatisfactory to both sides: large deficits with small reductions in spending and no major tax increases.

The President's Legislative Powers

The president has two sets of tools at his disposal for the accomplishment of his legislative goals: (1) the formal powers vested in him by the Constitution and by statute and (2) the informal resources inherent in his office. He uses both sets of tools simultaneously and in conjunction with each other. In the interest of analytical clarity, however, this chapter will examine them separately.

The Constitution provides for the president's legislative role. Specifically, in Article II, Section 3, it authorizes him to call Congress into special session, and it requires him "from time to time to give the Congress information on the state of the Union, and to recommend to their consideration such measures as he shall judge necessary and expedient." Most important, Article I, Section 7, makes the president a direct participant in the legislative process by providing for his approval or disapproval of "every bill" and "every order, resolution, or vote to which the concurrence of the Senate and House may be necessary." These formal legislative powers are augmented by statutory delegations of authority to the president and to administrative agencies and by implied powers derived from the general grant of executive power in Article II. These delegated and implied powers serve as the basis for presidential legislation through the issuance of executive orders (examined in Chapter 7).

Special Sessions

The president's power to call Congress into special session is less important today than it has been in the past. The principal reason for the reduced significance of special sessions is the tendency of Congress, since the 1930s, to remain in session for much of the year, taking periodic short recesses. The expansion in governmental activity, the complexity of the appropriations process, and the change from indefinite to specific term authorizations of federal programs have so increased the congressional workload that early adjournments have all but disappeared. When Congress was not in almost continuous session, the president could call it back to Washington to consider specific proposals. Calling a special session had the effect of placing responsibility for action on Congress.

Perhaps the most effective modern use of the power to call Congress into session was made by FDR in March 1933 shortly after his inauguration. The special session met for one hundred days and enacted the first stage of the New Deal program of economic recovery and social reform statutes. A dramatic exercise of the special session power occurred in July 1948, when President Harry Truman called the Republican-controlled Congress back to Washington from its summer recess to give it the opportunity to enact several key planks in the party's 1948 platform.[18] When Congress failed to act, as Truman had anticipated, he made that inaction a key theme in his successful reelection campaign.

Messages

Although contemporary presidents have not gained much leverage over Congress by controlling its sessions, they derive substantial power by virtue of their constitutional duty to report to Congress on the state of the nation and to recommend legislation that they deem necessary. Since the Budget and Accounting Act of 1921 and the Employment Act of 1946, Congress has required that the president annually submit messages to it that explain and justify his budget and that report on the condition of the economy. The State of the Union message, the budget message, and the economic report have enabled presidents since Truman to set the congressional agenda by laying before Congress a comprehensive legislative program. These mandatory messages announce the president's goals and priorities along with his assessment of the nation's problems, and they are also an attempt to bring the force of public opinion to bear upon Congress. Special messages emphasizing specific problems and proposing bills to deal with them complete the definition of the president's program. (Chapter 9 examines the development of that program.)

Although individual members of Congress introduce a multitude of bills independently of the president, his program dominates the congressional agenda. Congress, the public, and the federal bureaucracy expect the president to take the initiative in the legislative process. In the twentieth century, members of Congress have come "almost routinely to demand that the president—not their own leaders—develop new policies and programs" to deal with the complex problems the nation faces.[19]

The Veto Power

The Constitution establishes a major legislative role for the president by requiring his approval of measures passed by Congress (Article I, Section 7, paragraph 2). Within ten days (Sundays excepted) after a bill or joint resolution is presented to the president, he must either: (1) sign it into law; (2) disapprove or veto it and return it to the house of Congress in which it originated along with a message explaining his action; or (3) take no action on it, in which case it becomes law without his signature at the end of ten days. If Congress adjourns within that ten-day period and the president does not sign a measure awaiting his action, then it does not become law. In this instance the president exercises a "pocket veto." The president's action is final because adjournment prevents a measure from being returned to Congress for reconsideration and a possible override.

The veto is the president's ultimate legislative weapon in that it gives him the weight of two-thirds of the members of each house of Congress. In his classic treatise *Congressional Government,* Woodrow Wilson noted the importance of the veto even at a time when Congress dominated the national government: "For in the exercise of his power of veto, which is, of course, beyond all comparison, his most formidable prerogative, the President acts not as the executive but as a third branch of the legislature." [20] But Wilson did not foresee that modern presidents would employ the veto as a significant instrument of policy control over Congress. Charles L. Black, Jr., argues that the Framers of the Constitution intended that the veto be used sparingly and then only to protect the presidency from unconstitutional congressional encroachments. To support his interpretation, Black notes that the first six presidents employed the veto for that limited purpose. [21]

Louis Fisher rejects Black's narrow interpretation of the veto as not well founded and points out that both Washington and Madison vetoed bills on other than constitutional grounds. [22] In addition, Alexander Hamilton in *Federalist* No. 73 provides clear indication that the Framers contemplated broad, substantive use of the veto:

> [The veto] not only serves as a shield to the Executive, but it furnishes an additional security against the enaction of improper laws. It establishes a salutary check upon the legislative body calculated to guard the community against the effects of faction, precipitancy, or any impulse unfriendly to the public good, which may happen to influence a majority of that body.
>
> ... The primary inducement to conferring the power in question upon the Executive is to enable him to defend himself; the secondary one is to increase the chances of the community against the passing of bad laws through haste, inadvertence, or design. [23]

Fisher also has argued that the Framers did not anticipate such developments as the growth of governmental activity, the rise of political parties, and the attachment of "riders" (unrelated amendments) to appropriations bills; hence one should not give much weight to arguments that the veto is used excessively.[24]

President Jackson adopted a broad interpretation of the veto power as giving him the right to reject legislation on the basis of its wisdom, merit, or equity as well as on constitutional grounds.[25] This "tribunative" view of the veto has been espoused by modern presidents (since 1933), some of whom have used it extensively.

Table 6-1 reveals a much more extensive use of the veto by Presidents Roosevelt, Truman, and Eisenhower than by presidents who have served since 1960. In part this may reflect widespread acceptance of the social and economic reforms of the New Deal and the expanded international role of the United States. Presidents and Congress possibly have had somewhat fewer and less sharp disagreements over policy in the past twenty-seven years. However, the intensity of congressional-presidential conflict over the Vietnam War, over spending priorities and budget deficits, and over foreign policy issues such as aid to the Nicaraguan contras suggests that a more likely explanation is a decline in the popularity of the veto. Extensive use of the veto may be regarded as a sign of the president's inability to persuade Congress by less drastic means. The less frequent use of the veto after 1960 also corresponds with the development of systematic congressional liaison as well as a decline in the number of private bills subject to a veto.

Table 6-1 also shows that from 1961 through 1984, Democratic presidents, whose party controlled the Senate from 1961 through 1980 and the House during the entire period, vetoed fewer bills than the Republicans, who faced opposition majorities most of the time. President Reagan, operating with a Republican majority in the Senate, vetoed fifty-seven bills during his first six years in office. Neither Kennedy nor Johnson had any of their vetoes overridden, in contrast to overrides of seven Nixon, twelve Ford, two Carter, and four Reagan vetoes. (Congress overrode two more Reagan vetoes in 1987.) With the exception of the Ford administration, vetoes have been infrequent since 1960 in comparison with the 1933-1960 period.

The effect of the veto power on policy is both negative and positive. It is negative by nature; once used, it signifies an impasse between the president and Congress, and policy is unchanged. Sometimes a president finds that the veto is his most viable means of communicating his intentions to Congress. Ford's sixty-six vetoes, for example, were his way of conveying his social and economic policy preferences to a liberal Democratic Congress. The positive aspect of the veto lies in its use as a bargaining tool to shape legislation. By threatening to exercise his veto, the president can define the limits of his willingness to compromise with Congress. He can state in advance what he will and will not accept and thus reduce the likelihood of a showdown over a bill. Selective and sensitive use of the threat to veto can be a means of avoiding or of reconciling conflict with Congress.

Presidents do not veto bills on the basis of purely subjective judgments or

Table 6-1 Presidential Vetoes of Bills, 1933-1984

President	Regular vetoes	Pocket vetoes	Total	Number of vetoes overridden	Percentage of vetoes overridden
FDR (1933-1945)	372	263	635	9	1.4
Truman (1945-1953)	180	70	250	12	4.8
Eisenhower (1953-1961)	73	108	181	2	1.1
Kennedy (1961-1963)	12	9	21	0	0
Johnson (1963-1969)	16	14	30	0	0
Nixon (1969-1974)	26	17	43	7	16.3
Ford (1974-1977)	48	18	66	12	18.2
Carter (1977-1981)	13	18	31	2	6.5
Reagan (1981-1984)[a]	18	21	39	4	10.3

Source: U.S. Senate Library, *Presidential Vetoes, 1977-1984* (Washington, D.C.: Government Printing Office, 1985), ix.

[a] According to *Congressional Quarterly Weekly Report*, by the end of 1986 Reagan's veto total increased to 57—31 regular and 26 pocket vetoes.

random advice. Rather, they rely on a systematic procedure, begun during Franklin Roosevelt's administration, for the analysis of enrolled bills (those that have passed both houses of Congress) once they are "received" (that is, once they have arrived at the White House).[26]

The Legislative Reference Division of the Office of Management and Budget (OMB) immediately solicits reactions to a measure from the pertinent departments and agencies and from the budget examiners in the OMB program divisions that have jurisdiction over the bill. Recommendations and supportive rationales for presidential action on the legislation are due from the agencies and examiners within forty-eight hours. Legislative Reference collates the materials and prepares for the president a memorandum that summarizes the features of the legislation, reviews agency reactions, and states OMB's recommendations.

One study of presidential disposition of enrolled bill recommendations during the Nixon-Ford administration found that a presumptive bias exists in favor of enrolled bills. A favorable OMB recommendation almost ensures that the president will sign a bill. A negative recommendation, however, is more of a danger signal, and the president and his staff will examine closely the recommendation of the "lead" agency in the federal bureaucracy. When OMB and the lead agency disagree, the president is likely to sign the bill. OMB disapproval carries more weight, however, than disapproval by the lead agency. (See Table 6-2.)

The White House staff does not act independently on enrolled bills; rather, it bases its advice on the positions of the Office of Management and

Table 6-2   OMB and Lead Agency Recommendations and Presidential Action on Enrolled Bills, January 1969-June 1976

Pattern of advice	Approval by president (%)
OMB approval/lead agency approval	96
OMB approval/lead agency disapproval	95
OMB disapproval/lead agency approval	65
OMB disapproval/lead agency disapproval	35

Source: Stephen J. Wayne, Richard L. Cole, and James F. C. Hyde, "Advising the President on Enrolled Legislation," *Political Science Quarterly* 94 (Summer 1979): 310.

Budget and the lead agency. The goals of Nixon and Ford, two Republican presidents facing an opposition Congress, were "to rule and win." [27] That they withstood more than three-fourths of the efforts of Congress to override their vetoes indicates that they were quite successful. The enrolled bill process was an important advisory mechanism in their exercise of the veto power.

The President's Legislative Influence

In 1960 Richard Neustadt startled students of the presidency when, in his now celebrated treatise *Presidential Power*, he asserted that the formal powers of the president amounted to little more than a clerkship. The Constitution, Neustadt argued, placed the president in a position of merely providing services to other participants in national politics. "Presidential power," Neustadt declared, "is the power to persuade." [28] As the preceding examination of the president's formal legislative powers suggests, this is largely the case in his relations with Congress. It is not enough for the president to present his legislative program to Congress; he must also persuade congressional majorities to enact each statutory component of that program. To do so, the president employs mostly informal rather than formal methods of influence. These informal legislative tools can be used to exert pressure on Congress both indirectly and directly.

Indirect Influence

The principal means by which a president can seek to influence Congress indirectly are through appeals to the public and by enlisting the support of interest groups. Popular appeals are likely to be most effective when there is evidence of substantial public support for the president's position and when Congress is reluctant to follow his lead. In such circumstances, a careful presidential appeal can generate pressure that causes Congress to act. The tactic is less likely to succeed when public opinion is divided and when there is substantial opposition to the president's position. Presidents are also more likely to use popular appeals successfully in a crisis that appears to require congressional action.

There is at least one major limitation to presidential appeals for popular support. The president can antagonize Congress by too frequently "going over its head" to the people. In doing so he attacks, directly or by implication, the wisdom and the motives of Congress and its members. Presidents have found that selective use of popular appeals can be effective, but indiscriminate use of the device is likely to be counterproductive over time.

Obtaining and marshaling the support of interest groups has become increasingly important to presidents in their efforts to apply leverage on Congress. Since the mid-1960s interest groups have grown in number and in the scope of their efforts to shape national policy. The proliferation of interest groups and the intensification of their activities stem in part from the declining role of parties as mechanisms for linking public opinion with public policy and in part from the increased participation of citizens in national policy politics.

Interest groups, which have become the major vehicle for such participation, take an active part in policy making through informal alliances with congressional committees and administrative agencies.[29] Presidents find it helpful, if not necessary, to obtain the backing of interest groups before moving on major legislation, and the national officers and federal relations directors of important groups are often consulted in the process of formulating such legislation. Interest group representatives are regularly appointed to presidential advisory bodies such as commissions and task forces and they serve on advisory councils to administrative agencies. (Presidential liaison with interest groups is examined in Chapter 9.)

Direct Influence

Presidents use two informal tools in their direct efforts to persuade members of Congress. They may grant or withhold services and amenities that they have at their disposal as rewards for support or sanctions for lack of it, and they have opportunities to benefit from their involvement in the legislative process. Presidents vary greatly in their skills at exploiting these resources.

Services and Amenities. Presidents often gain leverage with members of Congress by bestowing or denying favors. Such favors may be given directly to an individual member or to important persons in his or her constituency, or the favor may be of benefit to the constituency itself.[30] Favors given as rewards to individual members include: appointments with the president and other high-ranking officials; letters or telephone calls from the president expressing thanks for support on key bills; campaign assistance in the form of cash contributions from the national committee, a presidential visit to the constituency, or a presidential endorsement; the opportunity to announce the award of federal grants to recipients in the constituency; invitations to be present at bill-signing ceremonies, to attend White House social functions, and to accompany the president on trips; and White House memorabilia such as pens, cufflinks, and photographs. Favors for influential congressional constituents include: appointments; appearances by administration officials at organizational meetings; invitations to social functions; mailings on important occasions such as anniversaries; memorabilia; and VIP treatment such as White House mess privileges. To some extent all members of Congress share in such benefits, but the president's supporters have more ready access to them and feel more comfortable asking for them.

The most important constituency-related rewards are jobs and projects. There are jobs at all levels of the federal government that are exempt from the Civil Service and are filled by appointment. Congressional recommendations by members of the president's party greatly influence the selection of U.S. district court judges, U.S. attorneys, U.S. marshalls, customs collectors for ports of entry, and a variety of lesser positions. Patronage is not an unalloyed advantage to the president, however, as disappointed job-seekers inevitably are resentful. Projects include military installations; research and administrative facilities; public works such as buildings, dams, and navigational improvements to rivers and harbors; government contracts with local firms; grants to local governments and educational institutions; and the deposit of federal funds in banks. Presidential control over projects is, of course, exercised through the bureaucracy, and it is limited by previous decisions that have produced the current pattern of governmental activities. In other words, some benefits will necessarily go to constituencies of the president's congressional opponents.

Involvement in the Legislative Process.   The president can use his involvement in the legislative process advantageously, but to do so requires knowledge and skill, which are the product of his political background, experience, and leadership style. To turn his participation in the legislative process to his advantage, the president should have knowledge of Congress and the Washington community, a sense of timing, a willingness to consult with congressional leaders and to give them notice in advance of major actions, sensitivity to the institutional prerogatives of Congress and to the personal and political needs of its members, and a balance between firmness and flexibility in resolving differences with Congress.

No president has ever possessed all of these skills, nor is one likely to do so. By most accounts, however, Lyndon Johnson exhibited more of them than did other recent presidents and made the most effective use of his involvement in the legislative process. Johnson believed that constant, intense attention by the president and his administration was necessary to move his legislative program through Congress.[31] Johnson's success in persuading Congress to enact his Great Society bills in 1964 and 1965 makes his approach to Congress a good example for study. (To avoid misleading the reader, it should be noted that Johnson's legislative triumphs were aided in no small measure by factors for which he could not claim full credit, including sizable partisan and ideological support in Congress and popular support for him and his legislative program.)

According to George C. Edwards, Johnson grounded his legislative strategy in intimate knowledge of Congress as an institution and of its key members.[32] He knew whom to approach on various issues and how to approach them. Johnson also placed considerable emphasis on proper timing. He waited to send bills to Congress until the moment seemed right for maximizing support and minimizing opposition. He sent bills singly rather than in a package so that opposition would not develop automatically around several measures at once. In addition, Johnson took care to consult with key senators and representatives in formulating legislation, often involving them in drafting bills. Just before sending a bill to Congress, Johnson and his top aides would hold a briefing for congressional leaders in which they explained its features. He also gave key senators notice of major appointments that required senatorial confirmation. Another feature of Johnson's congressional strategy was to make cabinet members responsible for the success of legislation in their areas and to use the cabinet to help coordinate administration liaison with Congress. Finally, when crucial votes were approaching on Capitol Hill, Johnson made intense personal appeals to key members whose votes served as cues for others and to members who were identified as uncommitted or wavering.

The Johnson approach to congressional relations, however, by no means guarantees the success of a president's program. Johnson lost much of his touch with Congress as he became increasingly involved in foreign policy matters and as the momentum of the Great Society gave way to the unpopularity of the Vietnam War. The loss of forty-eight Democratic seats in the House of Representatives in the 1966 congressional elections also adversely affected Johnson's ability to push bills through Congress.

Like Johnson, President Ford also had intimate knowledge of Congress, and he worked diligently to maintain good relations with its leaders, but his success was limited. In contrast, Richard Nixon disdained personal efforts to court Congress, yet he enjoyed considerable legislative success early in his administration. His relations with Congress did not turn sour until he challenged the Democratic majority directly by impounding appropriated funds and by asserting a sweeping doctrine of executive privilege under which administration officials refused to provide information to congressional committees.

Still, it seems manifest that the Johnson approach entailing detailed knowledge of Congress, respect for its constitutional prerogatives, and sensitivity to the personal and constituency needs of its members can only increase the president's influence. If the president is able to create a friendly climate on Capitol Hill, one that is not hostile to him personally and in which his proposals are received with an open mind, then his prospects for success will be greatly enhanced. President Carter's inability to create such a climate is often cited as a reason for the limited success of some of his key legislative goals, such as welfare reform and a comprehensive energy conservation program. In contrast, President Reagan's congenial demeanor and relaxed style helped establish within Congress an attitude toward his legislative program that was generally positive and not openly hostile. Reagan's ability to create a friendly climate in his congressional relations appears to have been an important factor in the passage of tax reform legislation in 1986. Several times during the 99th Congress the tax bill seemed doomed, only to be resurrected as members responded to presidential appeals for an equitable tax system.

Modes of Presidential-Congressional Relations

In their relations with Congress, presidents have different modes or patterns of behavior that they can follow: bargaining, arm-twisting, confrontation, and detachment. Bargaining is the predominant mode of presidential-congressional relations. Occasionally, the president bargains directly with members of Congress whose support is regarded as essential to the passage of a bill. In May 1981, for example, the Reagan administration agreed to revive a costly program to support the price of sugar in exchange for the votes of four Democratic representatives from Louisiana on a comprehensive budget reduction bill.[33]

Presidents usually try to avoid such explicit bargains because they have limited resources available to trade, and the desire among members for these resources is keen.[34] Moreover, Congress is so large and congressional power so decentralized that it is not possible for presidents to bargain extensively over most bills. In some instances the president may be unable or unwilling to bargain. Fortunately, much presidential-congressional bargaining is implicit. Rather than a quid pro quo exchange of favors for votes, implicit bargaining involves generalized trading in which tacit exchanges of support and favors occur.

If bargaining does not result in the approval of presidential legislative proposals, presidents may resort to stronger methods such as arm-twisting, which involves intense, even extraordinary, pressure and threats. In one sense, arm-twisting is an intensified extension of bargaining, but it entails something more, a direct threat of punishment or retaliation if the member's opposition continues. To illustrate, in 1969 during a Senate battle over the antiballistic missile (ABM), Kansas Republican James Pearson, an ABM opponent, was informed that his state might lose Pentagon contracts if the ABM failed and that the Department of Agriculture had withdrawn support for a rural job development bill that he favored.[35]

The most frequent practitioner of arm-twisting among modern presidents was Lyndon Johnson. When more gentle efforts at persuasion failed or when a member previously supportive opposed him on an important issue, Johnson resorted to such tactics as deliberate embarrassment, threats, and reprisals. On occasion, when President Carter was opposed by Democratic members, he threatened them with the loss of projects for their constituencies, but he was less consistent than Johnson in taking reprisals. In contrast, President Eisenhower was most reluctant to pressure Congress. Arm-twisting is understandably an unpopular presidential tactic and, if used frequently, can create resentment and hostility. Still, judicious demonstration that there are costs associated with sustained opposition or desertion by normal supporters will strengthen a president's bargaining position.

Presidents who are unable to gain support for their key proposals through bargaining and arm-twisting have two additional methods of dealing with Congress: confrontation and detachment. Confrontation might consist of appeals to the public, direct challenges to congressional authority, assertion of presidential prerogative, or similar tactics. President Nixon confronted Congress often and more sharply than any modern president. Disdaining the role of legislative coalition builder, Nixon saw himself instead as deserving of congressional support by virtue of his election mandate and his constitutional position as chief executive. Between 1971 and 1973, for example, he challenged congressional spending decisions that were at variance with his budget proposals by impounding, or refusing to spend, more than $30 billion that Congress had appropriated. As noted previously, Nixon also asserted a sweeping doctrine of executive privilege that denied Congress the authority to question thousands of executive branch officials and to obtain access to routine documentary information.

President Carter appeared ready to confront Congress in 1977 and again in 1979 when he passionately appealed to the public for support of his energy program, but he withdrew from the battle before it was fully joined. President Reagan challenged congressional opposition to his 1983-1987 budget proposals, occasionally taking to the stump to defend them, but he avoided debilitating confrontations by accepting higher domestic spending than he requested and by tolerating large deficits.

There are occasions when easing presidential pressures on Congress may be productive. President Carter's energy legislation, which passed in modified form as separate bills in 1978, 1979, and 1980, demonstrates that a willingness to compromise after an intense effort can result in partial success. Also, ending the attempt to pass legislation that has little or no chance, such as Carter's welfare reform proposals in 1977 and 1979, enables an administration to concentrate its energies on other bills with greater chance of success.

A strategy of confrontation is unlikely to result in sustained congressional responsiveness to presidential initiatives. Congress has constitutional prerogatives and constituency bases of support that enable it to resist presidential domination. The imperatives for cooperation between the two branches are so great that most presidents try to avoid confrontations with Congress and enter them only when the constitutional integrity of the presidency is at issue.

The need for cooperation also works against detachment as a presidential strategy for dealing with Congress. Detachment is feasible only if the president has little or no disposition toward positive governmental action. Given the scope and magnitude of that activity, it is highly unlikely that any president today could largely leave Congress to its own initiatives. Even President Eisenhower, perhaps the most passive of modern presidents and the one most deferential to Congress, recognized the importance of good relations with it by establishing an office of congressional relations in the White House.

Organizing Congressional Liaison

The Eisenhower liaison office formalized presidential relations with Congress. Under the direction of presidential assistant Bryce Harlow, the liaison staff provided information to members of Congress, helped Republicans with constituency-related matters, and lobbied for presidential proposals through explanation and low-key persuasion. During the Kennedy and Johnson administrations, the congressional liaison staff, under presidential assistant Lawrence F. O'Brien, actively asserted itself on behalf of presidential proposals. The staff was deeply involved in the formulation of the president's legislative program, and it furnished a congressional perspective to the process. It also worked closely with departmental and agency legislative personnel in the preparation of legislative proposals, and it coordinated bureaucratic lobbying with its own efforts.

By the end of the Johnson administration the congressional liaison operation had expanded from the rudimentary efforts under Eisenhower to establish a friendly climate on Capitol Hill to a complex set of activities that now includes intensive lobbying, intelligence gathering, representation, and coordination of executive branch legislative activity. Lobbying involves efforts, through persuasion and use of formal powers, to form congressional coalitions to enact the president's program. Intelligence gathering is the acquisition and evaluation of information about Congress for the White House. It is of special importance in determining the prospects for passing specific bills. Representation entails acting as spokesperson for the president's position to members of Congress as well as presenting congressional views within the White House. Coordination of executive branch relations with Congress ranges from monitoring and tracking bills, to collaborating with departmental liaison offices, to controlling departmental staff appointments.

The basic structure of the congressional liaison staff has remained intact since the Kennedy administration. Operational staff, who maintain daily contact with members of Congress, are assigned to the House or the Senate.

The Senate staff deals primarily with members whom they know personally or with whom they have some reason for developing a working relationship, such as ideological compatability or regional background. House liaison staff are assigned to work with members on a geographical basis. Under Kennedy, for example, three staff members were assigned to work with urban and eastern Democrats, southern Democrats, and nonurban and western Democrats.[36] Presidents Nixon and Ford assigned a staff member to work with southern Democrats in addition to making geographical assignments among Republicans. Nixon, Ford, and Carter were unsuccessful in their attempts to organize liaison staff contacts according to substantive issues.[37] Issue-based assignments fail, apparently, because of the uneven flow of work related to issues and because there is too much opportunity for certain problems and members to be neglected. Although the Carter administration abandoned issue-based organization of congressional liaison, it did not return to the geographical system. Rather, it based staff assignments for both houses on prior personal knowledge or contact. Staff assignments in the Reagan liaison office have followed the traditional pattern. The size of the congressional liaison office has varied from six persons under Eisenhower to twenty under Nixon; thirteen were serving in the Reagan office at the start of the administration.[38]

Presidential liaison with Congress is now thoroughly institutionalized. The organizational structure of the staff is fairly well fixed (assignments on the basis of the two houses of Congress with geographical subdivision within each house), its activities and tactics are accepted by Congress, and the services it provides to Congress and the president have become routine. The liaison operation is expected to dispense favors and conduct presidential bargaining with Congress. Congressional leaders expect to share in presidential legislative policy making, and members of Congress know that the president will use the liaison office to push his legislative program.

The President and Legislation

If all presidents approach Congress with the same formal powers and informal tools of influence and operate through well-established institutional arrangements, what accounts for the success or failure of their legislative efforts? Studies have identified at least five factors that affect the president's ability to achieve his legislative goals: his partisan and ideological support in Congress, his popular support, his style in dealing with Congress, cyclical trends in presidential-congressional relations, and the content of his program. It is not possible to assess the relative importance of each factor, but all of them have come into play since 1933, when FDR inaugurated the modern legislative presidency. (The first four factors will be examined here; the fifth in Chapter 9.)

Congressional Support

The president's support in Congress depends heavily on the size and cohesiveness of his party's strength there. It is manifest that a president whose party controls both houses of Congress enjoys certain advantages by virtue of party loyalty that are not available to a president faced with a Congress controlled by the opposition party. Since 1932, Democratic presidents have had to deal with an opposition Congress only in 1947-1948, whereas Republican occupants of the White House have confronted full opposition control in all years except 1953-1954 and 1981-1986. (See Table 6-3.)

Edwards has shown that from 1961 to 1983, three Democratic and three Republican presidents consistently received strong support on roll call votes from the congressional members of their parties.[39] This was the case on four measures of presidential support among individual members of Congress.[40] Edwards and other scholars have found that congressional members of the president's party have tended to support him more strongly on foreign policy legislation than on domestic policy issues, such as civil rights and social welfare. Partisan support for the president on domestic policy is apparently depressed by constituency pressures, as is frequently the case with southern Democrats under Democratic presidents, and is also lowered when the president's proposals conflict with the usual policy stance of the party.

Interestingly, partisan support for presidents in Congress, at least in recent decades, apparently owes little to the storied effect of presidential coattails. Edwards has pointed out that the ability of presidents to transfer their electoral appeal to congressional candidates of their parties declined steadily from 1952 to 1976.[41] Even in 1964, when President Johnson won a landslide victory over Republican Barry Goldwater and the Democrats gained thirty-eight seats in Congress, the measurable coattail effect was weak. Edwards attributes this decline to increased split-ticket voting, the reduced competitiveness of House seats, and the electoral success of incumbents since 1952. The consequences of the reduced coattail effect are the loss of presidential leverage with Congress and greater difficulty for presidents in winning congressional approval of key legislative proposals.

Because the president cannot rely on full support from the members of his party, he must obtain support from some members of the opposition. (This is imperative when the opposition controls one or both houses of Congress.) Several factors other than party membership influence congressional voting decisions, thus making it necessary for the president to seek bipartisan support. These include constituency pressures, state and regional loyalty, ideological orientations, and the influence of interest groups.[42] On many occasions, presidents have received crucial support from the opposition. President Eisenhower, for example, successfully sought Democratic votes on foreign policy matters; Republicans contributed sizable pluralities to the enactment of civil rights legislation in the 1960s; conservative Democrats mainly from the South often supported the domestic policy proposals of

Table 6-3 Partisan Control of the Presidency and Congress, 1933-1988

Dates	Presidency	Congress
1933-1946	Democratic	Democratic
1947-1948	Democratic	Republican
1949-1952	Democratic	Democratic
1953-1954	Republican	Republican
1955-1960	Republican	Democratic
1961-1968	Democratic	Democratic
1969-1976	Republican	Democratic
1977-1980	Democratic	Democratic
1981-1986	Republican	Divided: House-Dem., Senate-Rep.
1987-1988	Republican	Democrat

Presidents Nixon and Ford; and conservative Democrats in the House were essential to President Reagan's 1981 legislative victories and to the passage of aid to the Nicaraguan contras in 1986.

Congressional support for the president is built, then, primarily on his fellow partisans and stems from the policy objectives they share with him and from their sense of party loyalty. Party affiliation is not by itself, however, a sufficient basis for the enactment of the president's legislative program. Constituency, regional, and ideological pressures reduce the number of partisan backers, and the president must try to attract support from members of the opposition party on the basis of their ideological orientations and their constituency and regional interests.

Popular Support

According to Neustadt, the president's prestige, or popular support, affects congressional response to his policies. It has been widely observed that a highly popular president enjoys substantial leeway in dealing with Congress, whereas a president whose popularity is low or falling sharply is likely to encounter considerable resistance. Edwards suggests two explanations for the relationship between presidential popularity and congressional support for his program.[43] The first holds that members of Congress believe that one of their functions is to discover and reflect public opinion. They further believe that the public expects them to cooperate with the president and to enact the major elements of his legislative program. Therefore, they increase or decrease their support for the president's program in accordance with fluctuations in public support for him.

The second explanation is an incentive model. It holds that members of

Congress, when deciding whether to support or oppose the president, consider their own reelection prospects. They believe that the voters in their constituencies will react to their positions on the president's program. Thus, they tend to support, or at least to refrain from openly opposing, the program of a highly popular president and to oppose or otherwise demonstrate their independence from an unpopular one. In the last year of the Carter presidency, for example, several congressional Democrats sought to disassociate themselves from the president and his program because of his low approval in national polls. Similarly, in Ronald Reagan's second year in office many congressional Republicans and Democrats who had fully supported the president's 1981 economic legislation expressed reservations about his 1983 budget as his popularity declined sharply. However, during the first two years of Reagan's second term when his popularity ratings were consistently high, Democrats in Congress avoided challenging his opposition to a tax increase as a means of reducing the budget deficit, and they supported his drive for "revenue neutral" tax reform.

Edwards has demonstrated, through an analysis of the relationship between presidential popularity as measured by Gallup polls and presidential support on congressional roll calls from 1953 to 1976, that members of Congress act on the basis of the president's popular support.[44] Among House members there was a .5 correlation between presidential popularity and presidential support in the period under study; among Senators the correlation was .4. Further analysis showed that the relationship between presidential popularity and congressional support for the president was largely a function of partisanship. (See Table 6-4.)

To determine the effect of the president's party on the relationship, Edwards examined it during Democratic and Republican administrations. (See Table 6-5.) His data revealed that congressional Democrats were very responsive to presidential popularity among Democrats during both Democratic and Republican administrations. However, congressional Republicans responded to presidential popularity among their fellow partisans only during

Table 6-4   Correlations between Presidential Popularity among Partisans in the Public and Presidential Support among Partisans in Congress, 1953-1975

	Democrats	Republicans
House	.86	.75
Senate	.86	.83

Source: George C. Edwards III, *Presidential Influence in Congress* (San Francisco: Freeman, 1980), 93, 94.

Table 6-5 Correlations between Presidential Popularity among Partisans in the Public and Presidential Support among Partisans in Congress in Democratic and Republican Administrations, 1953-1976

	Republican administrations (1953-1960, 1969-1976)		Democratic administrations (1961-1968)	
	Democrats	Republicans	Democrats	Republicans
House	.51	.31	.84	−.56
Senate	.44	.76	.76	−.57

Source: George C. Edwards III, *Presidential Influence in Congress* (San Francisco: Freeman, 1980), 97, 98.

Republican administrations. Edwards explains that this apparent exception to the hypothesized relationship is due to the responsiveness of congressional Republicans to the more highly partisan nature of their public supporters than is the case for Democratic members of Congress.[45] When he controlled for the partisan element among Republicans in the electorate, the negative correlations became positive (that is, a positive relationship emerged between support for Democratic presidents among congressional Republicans and among Republican voters).[46]

Although presidential popularity is clearly related to congressional support for the president's legislative program and can be used as a tool of influence, it cannot be easily manipulated. There are factors, such as the erosion of popular support over time and the condition of the economy, over which the president has no control.[47] What the president can do is to take advantage of his popularity when it is high to influence congressional opinion, as Lyndon Johnson did in 1964-1965 and Ronald Reagan did in 1981 and, to a lesser extent, in 1985 and 1986 until it fell sharply because of the Iranian arms affair. (The full impact of the affair on Reagan's popular support was not apparent as of this writing in May 1987.) He can also attempt to appeal to the public beyond party lines for support.[48] To the extent that he succeeds in building popular support, he can help to strengthen his support in Congress, if his style in dealing with Congress enables him to exploit it.

Presidential Style and Legislative Skills

The president's style in dealing with Congress has long been considered an important determinant of his legislative success. Presidential style in congressional relations encompasses the degree to which the president is accessible to members of Congress, his interactions with and sensitivity to the members, and the extent of his involvement in the legislative process.[49]

Modern presidents have varied greatly in their accessibility to members of Congress. Johnson and Ford, for example, were usually available to members and leaders alike without great difficulty, whereas Nixon was remote and inaccessible most of the time. Kennedy and Reagan frequently sought contact through telephone calls. Although accessibility on demand is not feasible because of the pressures on the president's time, it enhances the president's congressional support if members know they can reach him on matters of great importance to them. Accessibility to congressional leaders of both parties is particularly important if the president is to work effectively with Congress.

The president's interactions with and sensitivity to members of Congress are related to his accessibility. Presidents who are easily accessible tend to be relaxed and open with members of Congress and sensitive to their personal needs as well as to institutional prerogatives. Johnson, Ford, Kennedy, and Reagan had relaxed and congenial relations with most members of Congress, whereas Eisenhower and Carter tended to be uncomfortable with many of them, and Nixon was ill at ease in most of his contacts with congressional members. Eisenhower and Carter regarded it as unseemly for the president to mingle with legislators as "one of the boys."

It is not clear how much a president's interpersonal relations influence his congressional support, but they are a distinctive part of his style and affect the disposition of leaders and members toward him personally. If nothing else, presidential popularity with members of Congress, such as Gerald Ford enjoyed, can improve relations even when there are sharp differences over issues. If the president has strained personal relations with many representatives and senators, as did Jimmy Carter, sustained congressional support will be difficult to achieve even when the president's party has a majority and many members share his goals.

The extent of presidential involvement in the legislative process is a key element of his style in congressional relations. Johnson, Ford, Kennedy, and Reagan all maintained a close interest in the course of legislation, and Johnson even actively directed its progress on occasion. In contrast, Nixon, Eisenhower, and Carter were more detached and had less interest in the building of congressional coalitions. Although it is not essential for the president to be a skilled legislative tactician, an open highly involved approach to Congress will serve a president better than a remote, detached posture.

Presidential legislative skills, as discussed earlier in this chapter, appear to be related to style. An open, involved style such as Johnson's is associated with a high level of skills. This is only natural since presidents who care little for congressional involvement and for direct efforts to persuade Congress, such as Eisenhower or Nixon, are unlikely to possess extensive legislative skills. However, Edwards has shown, through an empirical analysis of congressional support for recent presidents, that only a modest relationship exists between a president's legislative skills and congressional support for his program.[50] He argues that presidential legislative skills are effective at the margins of congressional coalition building and not at the core. Other factors over which the president has little control—such as public opinion, the alignment of political and social forces, economic and social conditions, and long-term trends in the political system—are more important as determinants of congressional decisions. "Presidential legislative skills," Edwards maintains, "are more useful in exploiting discrete opportunities than in creating broad possibilities for policy change." [51] Edwards's conclusion that the president is weakly positioned to lead Congress is supported by careful analysis, but it runs counter to much of the conventional wisdom of scholars and journalists. If nothing else, his analyses should caution observers of the presidency against uncritical acceptance of personalized explanations of presidential success in Congress and encourage the search for other influences.

Cyclical Trends

Long-term cyclical fluctuations in presidential and congressional power also appear to affect the fate of specific presidential programs.[52] The inauguration of FDR in 1933 marked the beginning of a period of presidential ascendancy that lasted until Richard Nixon became enmeshed in the Watergate scandal. During that time Congress made extensive delegations of power to the president and to executive branch agencies, presidents assumed responsibility for legislative leadership, Congress acquiesced in presidential domination of foreign and military policy, and the public looked to the presidency more than to Congress to solve the nation's problems.[53] The president and Congress clashed often during that period, but the dominant trend was one of presidential aggrandizement. When conflict occurred, Congress usually took defensive stands against presidential assertiveness.

In 1973 a Congress jealous of what it perceived to be its constitutional prerogatives, angry over the protracted "presidential war" in Vietnam, and locked in battle with President Nixon over impoundment and executive privilege moved to reassert itself. Seizing the opportunity afforded by Nixon's preoccupation with Watergate, Congress enacted the War Powers Resolution of 1973, the Budget and Impoundment Control Act of 1974, and the National Emergencies Act of 1976.[54] These statutes were the major elements in a congressional resurgence that restrained presidential power. In 1974 the House Judiciary Committee approved three impeachment charges against President Nixon, who resigned on August 8 before the House could act on them. Nixon's two immediate successors, Gerald Ford and Jimmy Carter, had to deal with a resurgent Congress intent on curbing the uses of presidential power and retaining the constitutional parity with the president that it regained, at least partially, in the 1970s. Increased skepticism of claims for presidential prerogative, careful scrutiny of presidential proposals, demands for more extensive consultation of congressional leaders by the White

House, and more exacting senatorial confirmation hearings on presidential appointments were the hallmarks of the recent period of congressional resurgence, which appears to have ended in 1981.

During the Reagan presidency Congress has been more willing to accept presidential policy leadership and less assertive in insisting on its institutional prerogatives. The presidential-congressional relationship has not, however, returned to the conditions that prevailed under the "imperial presidency." President Reagan has had friendly relations with Congress despite sharp differences over policy (such as the budget deficit) and over presidential powers (such as impoundments and deferrals of appropriated funds). The changed relationship appears to be due to congressional and public preference for strong presidential leadership and growing disenchantment with the scaled down presidencies of Ford and Carter, and to Reagan's leadership style and his effectiveness as a communicator.

The President's Effect on Congress

What overall impact does the president have on Congress? How can one judge presidential effectiveness with Congress? Analysts have sought answers to these questions through the use of aggregate measures based on recorded votes in Congress: presidential support scores, discussed previously in this chapter, and presidential box scores, based on the number and percentage of presidential legislative requests that are enacted into law. (Both measures are calculated by Congressional Quarterly, but the box scores were discontinued in 1975.) To further refine the support scores one can separate members by party and subdivide Democrats into northerners and southerners.[55] Analysts also have refined the scores by classifying bills by domestic and foreign policy proposals.[56] Such aggregate measures provide an overall picture of presidential effectiveness, but they leave a great many questions unanswered. For example, how controversial were a president's proposals? What potential effect did his proposals have on the economy and society? Did he risk much or little by making them? Did the successful bills require a major effort at coalition building, and, if so, what was the partisan and regional composition of the coalitions?

A comparison of congressional support for Presidents Johnson, Carter, and Reagan suggests the limitations of aggregate measures. (See Table 6-6.) According to most assessments, Johnson's legislative accomplishments—the social programs of the Great Society—outstripped those of all modern presidents since FDR in their significance. Carter's legislative record, in sharp contrast, is marked by frustration and limited achievement of major goals. Reagan, after a highly successful first year and difficulty thereafter, generally is regarded as standing close to Johnson in his ability to lead Congress.[57] Yet, data based on congressional roll calls indicate that differences between the three performances are slight. The data also show that Carter

Table 6-6 Congressional Support for Presidents Johnson, Carter, and Reagan (Percent)

	Johnson	Carter	Reagan[a]
House of Representatives			
Democrats	68	65	37
Northern	76	69	31
Southern	52	55	50
Republicans	42	39	67
Senate			
Democrats	60	67	45
Northern	67	70	42
Southern	44	61	56
Republicans	52	47	76

Source: George C. Edwards III, "Presidential Legislative Skills: At the Core or at the Margin?" (Paper delivered at the annual meeting of the Midwest Political Science Association, Chicago, April 9-12, 1986), 43-48.

[a]Data for Reagan are for 1981-1983.

enjoyed approximately the same level of support in the House and Senate as did Johnson and Reagan (from 1981 to 1984). They show that Carter actually did substantially better among southern Democratic senators than Johnson and that Reagan enjoyed more support from Senators of his own party than either Carter or Johnson. According to Edwards's interpretation of the data, there is little relationship between presidential legislative skills and measurable support for public policies.[58]

The data also suggest that measurement of presidential impact on Congress requires qualitative as well as quantitative assessments. For example, Randall Ripley reports that in 1977 President Carter made forty-three recommendations to Congress. At the end of the year Congress had approved twenty-one, rejected four, and left eighteen pending. Carter's first year was only moderately successful compared with the first-year performances of Wilson in 1913, FDR in 1933, and Reagan in 1981, or with Johnson in his second year, 1965.[59] Several of Carter's key proposals—a comprehensive energy program and welfare reform—were not enacted.

Even though Congress subsequently enacted several of Carter's principal requests, such as the Panama Canal Treaty and the establishment of the Departments of Energy and Education, the prevailing assessment of his legislative accomplishments is quite negative.[60] Why was this the case when, judged by standard quantitative measures of his achievements, he ranked with most modern presidents? The answer seems to be that most assessments of presidential legislative records are based on qualitative evaluations of the substance of the measures that are enacted and the president's management of his congressional relations. If the statutes that are passed are thought to be of limited or moderate importance, if they fall short of the president's announced goals, or if they fail to provide satisfactory solutions to the problems they were designed to address, then the president is likely to be judged harshly. Procedurally, if the president appears to be inept or disinterested in his handling of congressional relations, his critics will probably find fault with his legislative performance. Carter was found lacking on both substantive and procedural grounds, whereas Johnson and Reagan were not.

Why was Carter unsuccessful with Congress, particularly in comparison with Reagan (assuming that one accepts that judgment)? A combination of the factors discussed in this chapter provide an explanation. First, the congressional climate was more favorable to Reagan than to Carter. When Carter took office Congress was in a period of cyclical assertiveness that required it to challenge and closely examine major presidential proposals. Four years later Congress, impressed by Ronald Reagan's electoral triumph, looked to him to provide it with leadership and direction. It appeared to recognize the limits of its institutional capacity to provide comprehensive alternatives to the president's program.

A second factor that helps to account for the disparity in the legislative success of Carter and Reagan is their contrasting agendas. (Agenda development will be examined in Chapter 9.) Carter presented Congress with a lengthy agenda that included several comprehensive proposals. Moreover, he neglected to indicate to Congress which proposals had the highest priority. To have asked for so much, so soon, in times that were not particularly ripe for congressional action almost guaranteed that little would be accomplished. In contrast, Reagan presented Congress with a limited agenda—the budget and economic policy—and assigned it the highest priority. As Charles Jones puts it, Reagan established "a new context for congressional choice," a "consolidative agenda" in which new social programs were not even proposed.[61] Even though Reagan encountered substantial congressional resistance after 1981, congressional action remained within the boundaries of his consolidative agenda.

Alternatively, it can be argued in defense of Carter that although he may have attempted too much, he would not have been any more successful had he tried to accomplish less. Also, expectations may account for the differing evaluations. Carter's lengthy agenda raised numerous expectations, several of which were not met; as a result, he was judged ineffective. In contrast, Reagan's limited agenda raised fewer expectations, most of which were met; and he was perceived to be effective.

A third factor that distinguishes the Carter and Reagan legislative records is the leadership style and techniques used in dealing with Congress. Carter tended to cast proposals in moralistic tones that frequently alienated members of Congress. Also, he demonstrated little sensitivity to the institutional norms of Congress or to its members' sense of constitutional prerogatives. He expressed disdain for bargaining with congressional leaders and impatience with the preference of most members of Congress for incremental as opposed to comprehensive policies. Another stylistic aspect of Carter's leadership that proved disconcerting to his supporters in Congress was his tendency to shift positions quickly and without consultation. This difficulty was compounded by a legislative liaison operation that often lacked coordination of White House and departmental lobbying efforts.

Reagan approached Congress as a communicator president, a style Jones describes as "consistent with the classic separation of powers model of presidential-congressional relations." [62] Under this model the presidency is separate from but not independent of Congress. The president and his staff consult Congress regularly and extensively and engage willingly in direct negotiations; bargaining is the normal mode of business. The essential feature of this model is the maintenance of open channels of communication as a means of achieving political understanding between the two branches. Reagan has been able to use the politics of communication to his advantage. He has clearly defined his goals in terms of conservative ideology and consistently, but not inflexibly, pursued them. He has manifested respect for the institutional prerogatives of Congress while articulating and advancing those of the presidency. And he has established an effective working relationship with the Republican party organizations in Congress.[63]

The contrasting experiences of Carter and Reagan in their relations with Congress provide few new lessons. Both found, or at least should have found, that success is not automatic. It requires consultation before and during legislative consideration and a willingness to negotiate and bargain with Congress. Coordination of legislative proposals between the White House and the departments and agencies is essential. More important, cooperation between the president and congressional leaders and between the institutional presidency and Congress is mandatory. The constitutional separation of powers does not allow the two branches to operate independently of each other; rather, it requires that they exercise their shared powers jointly.

Conclusion

The president's relationship with Congress takes place within the framework of the constitutional separation of powers. That framework ensures conflict while requiring cooperation. This has been true during the two hundred years that the republic has operated under the Constitution. The Framers of the Constitution sought to prevent tyranny by establishing a balance between executive and legislative power. However, the concept of balance entails a static relationship, whereas the relationship that has existed between the president and Congress has been continually in flux. First one branch has expanded its authority; then the second branch has reasserted its prerogatives, recaptured lost powers, and acquired new ones.

The cycle of institutional aggrandizement, decline, and resurgence reflects certain strengths and weaknesses in the presidency and Congress and their respective abilities to respond to social forces, economic conditions, and political change. For most of the nineteenth century Congress was ascendant. The demands placed on the government were few, and its role was limited. Congress easily mastered the major issues that arose in national politics, such as the tariff and territorial expansion, although it grappled unsuccessfully with the problem of slavery. Strong presidents were in office during periods of external threat (1801-1808), social change (1829-1836), territorial expansion (1845-1849), and civil war (1861-1865). Through their actions, Thomas Jefferson, Andrew Jackson, James K. Polk, and Abraham Lincoln enhanced the powers of the presidency and demonstrated its leadership potential. But Congress always reasserted itself quickly.

The twentieth century brought industrialization and urbanization, with a host of accompanying problems and a revolution in transportation and communications. The major institutional strengths of Congress—its deliberateness, its sensitivity to local and regional interests, and its resistance to the centralization of political authority—which had been primarily responsible for its former ascendancy, became weaknesses in the context of the twentieth century. The executive branch under the leadership of the president was better able to respond to the needs of a rapidly changing society. Congress enacted legislation that authorized new governmental functions, established administrative agencies to perform them, and delegated extensive discretionary powers to the president and other executive branch officials. In addition, Congress greatly expanded the presidential office. Under the leadership of activist presidents such as the two Roosevelts, Wilson, Truman, Kennedy, Johnson, and Nixon, the presidency became the principal centralizing force in American politics. The orientation of the presidency toward its national constituency and the weakness of American political parties made the presidency an effective if not ideal instrument for providing policy leadership and coordination.

Eventually, however, extensive reliance on presidential power to solve national problems and protect national interests resulted in the abuse of that power. The eight-year involvement of the United States in the Vietnam War (1965-1973), the protracted conflict between President Nixon and Congress over issues such as impoundment and executive privilege, and the Watergate affair led to a congressional resurgence. Most members of Congress, supported by the arguments of scholars and journalists, realized that presidential power was subject to misuse and concluded that the presidency had become too powerful. Congress moved rapidly, in the period 1972-1974, to curb the presidency. It passed the War Powers Resolution, established the congressional budget process, restricted impoundment, strengthened its oversight of the bureaucracy, expanded its use of the legislative veto, and buttressed its staff capability through such actions as the establishment of the Congressional Budget Office. Most dramatically, it began impeachment proceedings against President Nixon, which ended in his resignation. Nixon's immediate successors, Presidents Ford and Carter, found that Congress frequently resisted their suggestions and asserted its independence.

There is little doubt that the congressional resurgence of the 1970s brought a much-needed restoration of the constitutional balance between Congress and the presidency. The nation, and especially its leaders, recognized the dangers of excessive reliance on a strong presidency. However, the institutional conditions that contributed to the growth of the presidency and the expansion of presidential power in the first place—the local orientation of Congress and the endemic weakness of American political parties—remained largely unchanged. Congress did little to enhance its ability to provide policy leadership independently of the president or to integrate its decisions in pursuit of broad national goals. Popular disenchantment with the lack of focus and direction that resulted from the limitation of the presidency without a concomitant increase in the capacity of Congress to govern quickly manifested itself. In the 1980 election, voters responded to Ronald Reagan's promise to provide positive, purposeful leadership in the White House. Initially, Congress acted as if it welcomed the return of the strong presidency, and Reagan enjoyed a series of legislative triumphs in 1981. Reagan's congressional coalition lacked stability, however, and by mid-1982 he and Congress began what would become a series of protracted annual disagreements over the budget deficit and related economic issues. Reagan enjoyed additional legislative successes, such as the 1986 Tax Reform Act, and congenial relations with Congress, but he did not repeat the spectacular performance of his first year in office.

Although the need for presidential-congressional cooperation is clear, there are few ways of obtaining it other than through consultation involving persuasion and bargaining. The president cannot command congressional approval of his proposals any more than Congress can direct him in the exercise of his constitutional powers. The threat of governmental stalemate is always present, and more often than not policy is an unsatisfactory compromise of presidential and various congressional viewpoints.

Clearly, the presidential-congressional relationship is a dynamic one. It varies according to external events and conditions, cycles of presidential and congressional assertiveness, and the leadership skills and styles of individual presidents. The changes that occur in the relationship, as between the 1970s and 1980s and the presidencies of Jimmy Carter and Ronald Reagan, exemplify the protean character of the presidency. As the United States moves through its third century, the relationship between the president and Congress will be characterized by the stability provided by the Constitution as well as by adaptations to social, economic, and political change.

Notes

1. Richard E. Cohen and Dick Kirschten, "An Era of Deadlock," *National Journal,* January 18, 1986, 126.
2. Stephen J. Wayne, *The Legislative Presidency* (New York: Harper and Row, 1978), 8-12.
3. Theodore Roosevelt, *Autobiography* (New York: Macmillan, 1913), 292.
4. Woodrow Wilson, *Constitutional Government in the United States* (New York: Columbia University Press, 1908, 1961).
5. Richard E. Neustadt, "The Presidency and Legislation: The Growth of Central Clearance," *American Political Science Review* (September 1954): 641-670.
6. Richard E. Neustadt, "The Presidency and Legislation: Planning the President's Program," *American Political Science Review* (December 1955): 980-1018; Wayne, *The Legislative Presidency;* Larry Berman, *The Office of Management and Budget and the Presidency* (Princeton, N.J.: Princeton University Press, 1979).
7. Samuel P. Huntington, "Congressional Responses to the Twentieth Century," in *The Congress and America's Future,* ed. David B. Truman (Englewood Cliffs, N.J.: Prentice-Hall, 1965), 23.
8. Ronald C. Moe and Steven C. Teel, "Congress as Policy-Maker: A Necessary Reappraisal," *Political Science Quarterly* (Fall 1970): 443-470; John R. Johannes, *Policy Innovation in Congress* (Morristown, N.J.: General Learning Press, 1972); Gary Orfield, *Congressional Power: Congress and Social Change* (New York: Harcourt Brace Jovanovich, 1975).
9. In the Senate the Republicans had a 53-47 majority. In the House, the 192 Republicans, who voted together on the key elements of President Reagan's economic legislation in a remarkable display of cohesion, were joined by a sizable block of conservative southern Democrats called the "Boll Weevils." In both chambers, Republicans and conservatives maintained voting cohesion that provided the majorities to enact the Reagan program.
10. Alexander Hamilton, John Jay, and James Madison, *The Federalist* (New York: Modern Library, 1938), 335-337.
11. Lawrence C. Dodd, "Congress and the Quest for Power," in *Congress Reconsidered,* ed. Lawrence C. Dodd and Bruce I. Oppenheimer (New York: Praeger, 1977), 298-302.
12. James L. Sundquist, *The Decline and Resurgence of Congress* (Washington, D.C.: Brookings, 1981).
13. Roger H. Davidson and Walter J. Oleszek, *Congress and Its Members,* 2d ed. (Washington, D.C.: CQ Press, 1985), chaps. 3-6; David R. Mayhew, *Congress: The Electoral Connection* (New Haven: Yale University Press, 1974); Morris P. Fiorina, *Congress: Keystone of the Washington Establishment* (New Haven: Yale University Press, 1977).
14. Joseph A. Califano, *A Presidential Nation* (New York: Norton, 1975), chap. 3.
15. Randall B. Ripley, *Congress: Process and Policy,* 3d ed. (New York: Norton, 1983), 18-19; Davidson and Oleszek, *Congress and Its Members,* chap. 1.

16. Ripley, *Congress: Process and Policy,* 28-31.
17. The key components of the Great Society were the Economic Opportunity Act of 1964, which launched a "war on poverty," the Civil Rights Act of 1964, the Voting Rights Act of 1965, the Elementary and Secondary Education Act of 1965, and the Medicare Act of 1965.
18. Joseph E. Kallenbach, *The American Chief Executive* (New York: Harper and Row, 1966), 327-328.
19. Sundquist, *Decline and Resurgence of Congress,* 143.
20. Woodrow Wilson, *Congressional Government* (New York: Meridian, 1956), 53.
21. Charles L. Black, Jr., "Some Thoughts on the Veto," *Law and Contemporary Problems* (Spring 1976): 87, 90.
22. Louis Fisher, *Constitutional Conflicts between Congress and the President* (Princeton, N.J.: Princeton University Press, 1985), 142-144.
23. Hamilton, Jay, and Madison, *The Federalist,* 476-477.
24. Louis Fisher, *The Constitution between Friends* (New York: St. Martin's Press, 1978), 84-85.
25. Kallenbach, *The American Chief Executive,* 354.
26. Stephen J. Wayne, Richard L. Cole, and James F. C. Hyde, Jr., "Advising the President on Enrolled Legislation," *Political Science Quarterly* (Summer 1979): 303-318.
27. Ibid., 316.
28. Richard E. Neustadt, *Presidential Power: The Politics of Leadership* (New York: Wiley, 1960), 10.
29. Theodore J. Lowi, *The End of Liberalism,* 2d ed. (New York: Norton, 1979); Randall B. Ripley and Grace A. Franklin, *Congress, the Bureaucracy, and Public Policy,* 3d ed. (Homewood, Ill.: Dorsey Press, 1984).
30. Joseph A. Pika, "White House Office of Congressional Relations: A Longitudinal Analysis" (Paper delivered at the annual meeting of the Midwest Political Science Association, Chicago, April 20-22, 1978).
31. Lyndon B. Johnson, *The Vantage Point* (New York: Holt, Rinehart and Winston, 1971), 448; Doris Kearns, *Lyndon Johnson and the American Dream* (New York: Harper and Row, 1976), 226.
32. George C. Edwards III, *Presidential Influence in Congress* (San Francisco: Freeman, 1980), 117-120.
33. Laurence L. Barrett, *Gambling With History: Reagan in the White House* (Garden City, N.Y.: Doubleday, 1983), 334.
34. Edwards, *Presidential Influence in Congress,* 131.
35. Ibid., 142.
36. Pika, "White House Office of Congressional Relations," 9.
37. Ibid., 10; Eric L. Davis, "Legislative Liaison in the Carter Administration," *Political Science Quarterly* (Summer 1979): 289.
38. Eric L. Davis, "Congressional Liaison: The People and the Institutions," in *Both Ends of the Avenue,* ed. Anthony King (Washington, D.C.: American Enterprise Institute, 1983), 67.
39. George C. Edwards III, "Presidential Legislative Skills: At the Core or at the Margin?" (Paper delivered at the annual meeting of the Midwest Political

Science Association, Chicago, April 9-12, 1986).

40. Edwards has developed four indexes, which are percentages of support for roll call votes on which the president has taken a stand: (1) overall support on all votes on which the president has taken a stand; (2) support that was not unanimous on votes on which the winning side fell below 80 percent; (3) support on the single most important vote on each bill; and (4) key votes selected by Congressional Quarterly as being highly significant. The four indexes range from broad to relatively exclusive (there are, on average, only ten key votes a year in the House and nine in the Senate). (Ibid., 11-12; George C. Edwards III, "Measuring Presidential Success in Congress: Alternative Approaches," *Journal of Politics* [May 1985]: 667-685.)

    It should be noted that use of Congressional Quarterly's presidential support scores is controversial. Anita Pritchard argues that the scores are crude instruments that at best "measure the level of agreement between congressional members and the president on the issues on which the president takes a public stand." She maintains that the scores do not measure support for the president or his influence on congressional voting. (Anita Pritchard, "An Evaluation of *CQ* Presidential Support Scores: The Relationship between Presidential Election Results and Congressional Voting Decisions," *American Journal of Political Science* [May 1986]: 493-494.)

41. Edwards, *Presidential Influence in Congress*, 71-78.

42. John W. Kingdon, *Congressmen's Voting Decisions*, 2d ed. (New York: Harper and Row, 1981); Aage R. Clausen, *How Congressmen Decide* (New York: St. Martin's Press, 1973).

43. Edwards, *Presidential Influence in Congress*, 89-90.

44. Ibid., 90-100.

45. George C. Edwards, "Presidential Influence in the House: Presidential Prestige as a Source of Presidential Power," *American Political Science Review* (March 1976): 112.

46. Edwards, *Presidential Influence in Congress*, 97.

47. John E. Mueller, *War, Presidents and Public Opinion* (New York: Wiley, 1973).

48. Samuel Kernell, *Going Public: New Strategies of Presidential Leadership* (Washington, D.C.: CQ Press, 1986), chap. 1.

49. Wayne, *The Legislative Presidency*, 166.

50. Edwards, *Presidential Influence in Congress*, 188-192; Edwards, "Presidential Legislative Skills."

51. Edwards, "Presidential Legislative Skills," 40.

52. Dodd, "Congress and the Quest for Power."

53. Arthur M. Schlesinger, Jr., *The Imperial Presidency* (Boston: Houghton Mifflin, 1973).

54. Thomas E. Cronin, "A Resurgent Congress and the Imperial Presidency," *Political Science Quarterly* (Summer 1980): 209-238.

55. Edwards, *Presidential Influence in Congress*, chap. 3.

56. Aaron Wildavsky, "The Two Presidencies," *Transaction*, vol. 4, 1966, 7-14; Lance T. LeLoup and Steven A. Shull, "Congress versus the Executive," *Social Science Quarterly* (March 1979): 704-719.

57. Charles O. Jones, "A New President, a Different Congress, a Maturing

Agenda," in *The Reagan Presidency and the Governing of America*, ed. Lester M. Salamon and Michael S. Lund (Washington, D.C.: Urban Institute Press, 1984), 261-287.
58. Edwards, "Presidential Legislative Skills."
59. Randall B. Ripley, "Carter and Congress," in *The Presidency: Studies in Policy Making*, ed. Steven A. Shull and Lance T. LeLoup (Brunswick, Ohio: King's Court Communications, 1979), 65-82.
60. Ripley, "Carter and Congress"; Davis, "Congressional Liaison."
61. Jones, "A New President," 285.
62. Ibid.
63. Ibid., 286.

Selected Readings

Dodd, Lawrence C., and Richard L. Schott. *Congress and the Administrative State.* New York: Wiley, 1979.
Edwards, George C., III. *Presidential Influence in Congress.* San Francisco: Freeman, 1980.
Fisher, Louis. *President and Congress.* New York: The Free Press, 1972.
―――. *The Politics of Shared Power: Congress and the Executive.* 2d ed. Washington, D.C.: CQ Press, 1987.
―――. *Constitutional Conflicts between Congress and the President.* Princeton: Princeton University Press, 1985.
King, Anthony, ed. *Both Ends of the Avenue.* Washington, D.C.: American Enterprise Institute, 1983.
Lepawsky, Albert, ed. *The Prospect for Presidential-Congressional Government.* Berkeley: University of California, Institute of Governmental Studies, 1977.
Ripley, Randall B., and Grace A. Franklin. *Congress, the Bureaucracy, and Public Policy.* 3d ed. Homewood, Ill.: Dorsey Press, 1984.
Sundquist, James L. *The Decline and Resurgence of Congress.* Washington, D.C.: Brookings, 1981.
Wayne, Stephen J. *The Legislative Presidency.* New York: Harper and Row, 1978.

The Old Executive Office Building, located just west of the White House, is home to many of the agencies that compose the Executive Office of the President, including the White House staff and the National Security Council.

CHAPTER SEVEN

Executive Politics

One of the most common descriptions of the president's tasks is "chief executive." In U.S. political life the president is held responsible for the operation of the government. When government fails to meet popular expectations, the president is judged to be at fault. Indeed, when President Jimmy Carter explained his administration's failure to fill some of its key campaign promises by saying that he had learned there were certain things that government cannot do, his critics suggested that it was time to replace him with someone who could make government work. Yet, all modern presidents have encountered difficulties in their efforts to direct the executive branch. For example, Franklin D. Roosevelt complained about the independence of the navy; John F. Kennedy lamented the inertia of the State Department; Richard Nixon railed against disloyal bureaucrats in various domestic program agencies; and Ronald Reagan made his campaign attack on an overgrown federal bureaucracy one of the enduring themes of his presidency. Richard Rose, who has studied the president as a manager, has remarked that the "president's title of chief executive is a misnomer; he can more accurately be described as a nonexecutive chief." [1] The essence of Rose's argument is that even within the executive branch the president's powers of command are limited and that his success as an administrator depends heavily on his ability to win the trust of others.

This chapter examines the president's responsibilities as chief executive and the factors that affect his administrative performance. It opens with a discussion of the president's executive role and an examination of that role's constitutional, legal, and administrative foundations. Then it explores his relationships with the executive branch and with the cabinet. Having established that the president's powers of command over the units of the executive branch are limited, the chapter analyzes the formal powers and managerial tools that modern presidents have available to them in discharging their administrative duties.

The President as Executive

The president's executive role is grounded in Article II of the Constitution. In ambiguous language the Constitution vests "the executive power" in the president and directs him to "take care that the laws be faithfully executed." He may also "require the opinion, in writing, of the principal officer in each of the executive departments" and "grant reprieves and pardons." He derives substantial power from his designation as "commander-in-chief of the army and navy." Modern presidents have tended to interpret these constitutional provisions broadly and have derived from them substantial additional powers. In addition to their constitutionally based powers, presidents have received extensive delegations of statutory authority from Congress.

There is an apparent paradox in, on the one hand, the president's position as head of a vast and complex military and civilian bureaucracy and his considerable formal legal powers and, on the other hand, his limited ability to direct that bureaucracy toward the achievement of his policy objectives and program goals. One may better understand that paradox by considering the constitutional relationship of the presidency to the legislative and judicial branches of government and the nature of the federal bureaucracy and the president's relationship to it.

As discussed in Chapter 6, the Constitution not only created the executive branch (with the president as head); it also established legislative and judicial branches and prescribed a sharing of powers among those separate governmental institutions. The president is dependent on congressional cooperation to carry out his executive responsibilities. Only Congress can authorize governmental programs, establish administrative agencies to implement the programs, and appropriate funds to finance them. However, presidents find that congressional cooperation is often not easily obtained since they and the members of Congress have different constituency and institutional perspectives.

There are also occasions when the exercise of presidential power must be approved by the judiciary. A notable instance of judicial disapproval of executive action involved President Harry S Truman's seizure of the steel mills in 1952 in order to forestall a strike during the Korean War.[2] The points to be made here are that presidential power is not self-executing and that it is subject to restraint. Presidents require the cooperation of Congress and the judiciary but frequently find themselves in conflict with these other branches of government.

Although the federal bureaucracy is the bulk of the executive branch, and the accomplishment of governmental objectives depends largely on its performance, it must be recognized as the creation of the legislative branch. In establishing federal departments and agencies, Congress responds not only to presidential requests, but also to demands and pressures from constituency forces, interest groups, and the general public. The result is that the structure of the federal bureaucracy is not hierarchical; rather, it tends to reflect the political fragmentation and committee jurisdiction of Congress. The president does not look down upon subordinate administrative units from a position at the apex of a pyramid of authority. Instead, he confronts a complex and confusing array of departments and agencies with varying degrees of independence from him.

Arthur Miller argues that checks on presidential power come more from the "entrenched bureaucracy" than from Congress.[3] Bureaucratic units are staffed principally by career civil servants who constitute a permanent government. They respond to demands from interest groups and to direction from congressional committees as well as to presidential leadership. Most modern presidents have entered office believing, or soon became convinced, that they cannot take the support and loyalty of the bureaucracy for granted but must constantly strive to acquire them.[4]

Moreover, the vastness and scope of the federal bureaucracy, as measured by expenditures or numbers of employees, further contribute to the difficulty of the president's executive role. (Contrary to the assertions of politicians and journalists, bureaucratic size and scope are not necessarily prima facie evidence of *presidential* power.) The task of defining objectives and coordinating their achievement grew increasingly difficult for presidents from 1933 through 1980 as the functions of the federal government expanded. Attempting to do so while adhering to democratic procedures and without resort to authoritarian or extralegal methods provided an even greater challenge.

The president's task as the nation's chief executive (Rose's objections to the term notwithstanding) is much more, then, than issuing commands. Nor is the job mainly that of finding ways to bring a disorganized and unruly bureaucracy under his operational control. Rather, he must secure congressional cooperation while suppressing natural tendencies toward conflict with the legislative branch, and he must give direction to the bureaucracy so that it will work with him in accomplishing his administration's goals.

The President and the Executive Branch

Ideally, presidents should use the White House staff and other units of the Executive Office of the President to help them define their objectives, convert them into operating programs, allocate resources to the agencies that administer the programs, and coordinate the implementation of programs within the federal government and among federal, state, and local governments. Department managers should direct the work of the career civil servants, coordinate the operations of their component bureaus, and develop and maintain linkages with other federal departments and agencies and with state and local governments. Presidents quickly discover, however, that the reality of their relations with the federal bureaucracy bears little resemblance to the idealized vision just described. For example, Joseph Califano, a former presidential aide and cabinet officer, has observed that "smaller federal agencies and numerous bureaus within large departments respond to presidential leadership only in the minds of the most naive students of government administration." [5]

According to Thomas E. Cronin, there are "presidentialist" and "departmentalist" views of presidential-departmental relations.[6] The essence of the presidentialist view is that since presidents are held accountable for the performance of the bureaucracy, they must be given sufficient powers and management tools to control it. Presidentialists put a high premium on loyalty to the president and to his goals and react with hostility and mistrust when bureaucratic loyalty appears to be less than wholehearted. The departmentalist perspective holds that the president's objectives can best be achieved if the bureaucracy is granted a considerable degree of independence. Presidents and their staffs should refrain from exerting control over the operations of departments and agencies and focus on the definition of broad policy objectives and on problems of coordination. Departmentalists regard loyalty as a reciprocal relationship and argue that successful governmental performance depends on presidential support of the bureaucracy as well as on bureaucratic loyalty to the president.

The tension between the White House and the bureaucracy that is reflected in these contrasting views has been present in every modern administration. It exists, at least in part, because of what Hugh Heclo has identified as the distinction between "political leadership in the bureaucracy" and "bureaucratic power." [7] The direction and effectiveness of the political leadership that the president provides are heavily dependent on the personality, leadership style, and values of the president as well as on external events and conditions.

In contrast, bureaucratic power is relatively permanent and does not depend on personalities and transitory political and environmental factors. It is a power that belongs to the career civil servants who compose the permanent government. The loyalties of these bureaucrats are to their professional norms, their agencies, and the programs they operate. Their power derives from the advice, information, and compliance that they can give or withhold from the president and other political executives. Governmental performance, Heclo suggests, "can be thought of as the product of political leadership times bureaucratic power." [8]

At least five general factors contribute to bureaucratic power and shape the pattern of presidential-bureaucratic relations: the size, complexity, and dispersion of the executive branch; bureaucratic inertia and momentum; the personnel of the executive branch; the legal position of the executive branch; and the susceptibility of executive branch units to external political influence. Major consequences of the interaction of these factors are presidential frustration and a pattern of policy making that often is sharply at odds with the norm of democratic accountability.

Size, Complexity, and Dispersion
of the Executive Branch

The enormous expansion in the scope of federal government activities since 1933 has tremendously increased the size of the executive branch. The number of agencies and the programs they administer, however they are counted, have multiplied manifold. The size of the budget and the number of federal employees indicate the magnitude of the operation. By early 1987 the proposed 1988 budget had grown to $1 trillion, and there were more than 2.7 million civilian and 2.5 million military employees. The domestic activities of the federal government reached into every community in the nation and touched the lives of individuals from birth to death. Considerations of national security extended U.S. military and foreign policy activities around the world. It is hardly surprising, then, that providing leadership and direction to the federal bureaucracy is a difficult task. It would be so even if the president could command prompt and unquestioning obedience from subservient departments and agencies.

The multiplicity of agencies and programs creates an additional obstacle to effective political leadership in the executive branch. The complexity that results from overlapping jurisdictions leads to duplication of efforts and complicates the president's job. It places a premium on coordination by the presidency. Usually the president does not deal with individual administrative units when he defines his goals for a policy area, but with many. In outdoor recreation, for example, the Forest Service (a unit of the Agriculture Department), the National Park Service (a unit of the Interior Department), and the Army Corps of Engineers all maintain facilities for public use. Or consider the use of land owned by the federal government. Policies of the Forest Service and the Interior Department's Bureau of Land Management are sometimes in sharp conflict. A legendary struggle within the bureaucracy is that waged between the Corps of Engineers and the Bureau of Reclamation of the Interior Department. Several presidents tried in vain to yoke the two agencies in common pursuit of a water resources development policy.[9]

An indication of the complexity of federal activities in education came to light between 1977 and 1979 as the Carter administration tried to establish a Department of Education. Using the U.S. Office of Education, an agency in the Department of Health, Education and Welfare (HEW), as the base for the new department, the administration tried to incorporate the education activities of other federal agencies. Although some consolidation was accomplished, such as the transfer of the Defense Department's overseas schools for military dependents, many significant activities remained outside the new department, including the health education activities of the new Department of Health and Human Services, the veterans' education programs of the Veterans Administration, the Department of Agriculture's Graduate School, and the research training programs of the National Science Foundation.

Bureaucratic complexity also stems from the interdependence of many federal activities. It has become increasingly apparent that policy goals in one area are affected by objectives in other areas. The difficult trade-off between energy and environmental policies, which was acutely experienced in the 1970s, illustrates policy interdependence. Efforts to conserve energy and reduce foreign oil imports were often at variance with attempts to reduce air and water pollution. At times the Department of Energy and the Environmental Protection Agency appeared to be working at cross purposes—for example, substitution of coal for oil lessened dependence on imported oil but increased problems of maintaining air quality. Housing policy decisions also illustrate interdependence. The impact of these decisions on inflation, unemployment, the environment, and racial segregation need to be considered. Programs that may help to increase the stock of low- or middle-income housing may have undesirable consequences elsewhere.

The great size of the federal bureaucracy further frustrates presidential efforts at direction and control because its activities are so widely dispersed. Presidents, their aides, and their principal political appointees are at the center of government. The people who operate programs, deliver services to individuals, and regulate the conduct of businesses and other organizations are at the periphery. These people, almost all of whom are civil servants, were there when the president and his staff took office, and they will be there after the political executives have departed. They know their programs and the pitfalls involved in administering them. They control the resources, human and material, that are needed to implement programs successfully. Their position, at the point of delivery "where programs meet people," is the source of much of their power.[10]

Bureaucratic Inertia and Momentum

The executive branch, like all large bureaucracies, is difficult to manage because of bureaucratic inertia. It is hard to get a new government activity started, and, once it is under way, it is even more difficult to stop or significantly change the activity. Francis Rourke cites a "celebrated law of bureaucratic inertia," which holds that "bureaucracies at rest tend to stay at rest and bureaucracies in motion tend to stay in motion."[11] Rourke attributes bureaucratic inertia to organizational routines—prescribed operating procedures that have worked successfully in the past. Another important factor contributing to bureaucratic inertia is the support of interest groups for programs that benefit them and in which they have material stake.

The aspect of bureaucratic inertia primarily responsible for presidential frustration is the momentum that ongoing programs possess. The degree of that momentum is revealed in the number of activities to which the government is committed by public laws, the amount of money allocated for those activities in annual appropriations, and the number of civil service and military employees who carry out the activities.[12] Nearly 76 percent of President Reagan's proposed 1987 budget constituted "uncontrollable" expenditures that the government was obligated to make. The principal uncontrollable items include interest on the national debt, entitlement programs such as social security, medicare and medicaid, federal retirement and veterans' benefits, and contractual obligations to pay for, among other things, weapons systems and public facilities. Even the "controllable" portion of the budget is highly resistant to cuts because of support from groups that benefit from those expenditures. Presidents can influence the shape of the federal budget, but major changes usually require several years to be implemented. From one year to the next, presidents tend to be limited to incremental changes.

Presidents, however, are often impatient to make changes. They have a fixed term of office in which to accomplish their objectives. The incremental adjustments that are possible through annual budgeting hardly seem adequate given the scope of their objectives and the time available to them. The time perspective of the bureaucracy is much different. Members of the permanent government can afford to be patient. In the budgetary process they fight to maintain their "base," which is their current appropriation, and to add as large an increment to it as possible.[13] Over time, successful pursuit of such a strategy will result in sizable growth, as small annual commitments are transformed into large permanent gains. Bureaucratic momentum thus works to the advantage of the permanent government and acts as a constraint on presidents who try to counter it. President Reagan has tried to overcome the effects of incremental budgeting by a top-down process that restricts total governmental spending and thus forces agencies and their congressional and interest group supporters to accept cuts or limited growth. His efforts have had only limited success.[14] (The reasons will be discussed in Chapter 10.)

The large number of career federal employees also commits the president to maintain ongoing programs. Major reductions in personnel or redirection of their activities are economically and politically costly. People will oppose actions that threaten to deprive them of their jobs or that require them to move, undergo additional training, or reduce their sense of security and importance. Most presidents can make only modest adjustments in the size and mission of the federal work force. President Reagan has been more successful in this regard than other modern presidents, but even his efforts have brought about no large-scale changes.[15] (During Reagan's first three years in office the number of employees in nonpostal, domestic agencies fell by approximately 92,000, but an increase of more than 55,000 civilian employees in the Department of Defense resulted in a net reduction of less than 1 percent.)[16]

Bureaucratic Personnel

Presidents depend on two classes of officials to operate the federal bureaucracy: the seven hundred or so people whom they appoint to leadership positions in the cabinet, subcabinet, agencies, and bureaus, and the approximately seven thousand higher civil servants, most of whom are members of the Senior Executive Service (SES). The characteristics and roles of these political and career executives differ sharply, and the relationships between them have tended to hinder presidential direction of the implementation of policies.

The political executives constitute what Hugh Heclo has called a "government of strangers." [17] Aside from cabinet members, a few key subcabinet appointees, and heads of major independent agencies, they are unknown to the president and to one another.

Selection of cabinet members, especially at the outset of an administration, involves the president directly and has traditionally entailed the attempt to build support for the administration by including representatives of various constituencies in the party and the country. Selection of other political executives is affected by multiple and often conflicting pressures, such as loyalty to the president, party membership, technical competence, the wishes of the cabinet member under whom the appointee will serve, and the demands of congressional members, interest groups, and state and local party leaders.

The process through which presidents recruit people to serve in their administrations is significant as an instrument of control over policy, as a tool of administrative management, and as a key component of presidential relations with Congress, interest groups, and political parties. Consequently, it is a highly political process. Presidents since Eisenhower have used personnel staffs located in the White House to run the appointment process for them. The process has tended to be rather chaotic at the start of a new administration, because of the large number of positions to be filled and uncertainty about how to proceed, but it eventually becomes fairly systematic. Calvin Mackenzie, in a study of the process, concluded that presidential personnel staffs have served modern presidents well. [18]

According to Mackenzie, the essential ingredient for effective recruitment and selection of appointees is active presidential involvement in the process and sustained presidential support for the personnel staff. Ronald Reagan excelled in this regard, whereas Richard Nixon's lack of interest contributed to the difficulties he experienced in using his appointment power to establish effective control over the executive branch. The Reagan administration personnel staff, headed by E. Pendleton James, a professional executive recruiter with previous experience in the Nixon administration, exercised tight control over the recruitment of political executives. Cabinet members were not permitted to conduct independent searches for subcabinet officials, and final approval of subordinate appointments was retained by the White House. Beginning work during the transition period, the White House personnel staff made ideological consistency the primary criterion for appointment. Prospective appointees were carefully screened for policy views, political and personal backgrounds, and, if considered necessary, expertise. Although it took the Reagan administration a long time to get its political executives fully in place, the result has been tighter control over the executive branch and greater cohesion within it than other modern presidents have been able to achieve.[19]

The political executives chosen by the presidential appointment process are often amateurs in the precarious world of Washington politics. They lack the political knowledge and substantive skills needed to provide effective leadership in their jobs. They quickly discover their dependence on career executives and other lower-ranking civil servants for the information and advice that will enable them to serve the president effectively. That support is not obtained without a price, however—loyalty to the agency and support for its programs within the administration, before Congress, and with the public.

By the time most political executives learn their jobs and strike a balance between the often conflicting claims of the White House and the permanent government, they will have left their positions. It is generally conceded that it takes from twelve to eighteen months for political executives to master their jobs, but their average tenure is only two years. The high rate of turnover among them makes it difficult to develop teamwork within departments and agencies. Cabinet secretaries are continually adapting to new subordinates, and persons on the same hierarchical level barely get to know one another. One result is that expectations and roles are in flux, and there are problems of coordination and control.

Political executives in the bureaucracy are in a kind of twilight zone where they look upward to the president for support and direction and downward to the permanent government for support and services. In such a position they are imperfect instruments for presidential control of the bureaucracy. They can best serve the president by winning the trust of the careerists who compose the permanent government, but to do so they find it expedient to maintain a considerable degree of independence from the White House.

Career executives and other civil servants provide the institutional resources, such as political experience, substantive knowledge, and technical competence, required to accomplish an agency's mission. They are aware of political problems that the agency faces and of its political resources. They have established linkages with its clientele and with the congressional committees that oversee it through legislative and appropriations powers. They also have a vested interest in their agencies and their programs. Their loyalties are based on norms of bureaucratic and occupational professionalism. They recognize the legitimacy of the president's position and of the claims of political executives for their support, but they will not hesitate to use their substantial capacity to resist the directives of their political superiors.

In most recent administrations, sharp conflicts have often occurred between the White House and career executives. The reasons for this adversarial relationship lie in behavior patterns and perspectives that are fairly common among career executives. The relatively secure tenure of higher civil servants (as contrasted with the expendability and shorter tenure of political executives) allows them to take a more gradual approach to change. If something cannot be done now, there is always next year or some time later. There is also a strong inclination on the part of career executives to avoid direct confrontation and to pursue their objectives obliquely and by indirection, because such an approach is less likely to generate political opposition. In contrast, political executives tend to pursue their goals quite directly and to see virtue in conflict.

Careerists also try to avoid becoming identified with a political party or a political appointee. The civil servant must remain politically neutral in order to remain a civil servant; hence, he or she is cautious about political involvement. Political executives, many of whom are unfamiliar with the ways of the bureaucracy, often mistake such caution for opposition or disloyalty. This point of view is reinforced by the high value that career executives place on maintaining their relationships with clientele group representatives, congressional members and staff, and individuals outside the Washington community who are involved in or knowledgeable about their agency's programs.

Such relationships, or networks, provide information and support that help the bureaucrats be of service to their political superiors. Involvement in the networks, however, can place a strain on the career executives' relations with their superiors, who often regard civil servants' informal contacts outside the agency as evidence of disloyalty. This perspective, which is especially pronounced among members of the White House staff, is understandable, but it overlooks the importance of such relationships to the services that career executives provide.

Frederick V. Malek, a management specialist who served as deputy director of the Office of Management and Budget (OMB) during the Nixon administration, provides a good example of the White House perspective on the career service.[20] According to Malek, the career service suffers from five major defects: an adversarial attitude toward the political leadership; resistance to change and innovation; inadequate training and development as managers; narrow perspectives because of careers limited to one or two agencies; and poor pay practices on the part of Congress, which usually "caps" upper-level salaries of the career service, thus making it less attractive. Malek did not, however, advocate replacing career executives with political appointees in policy-sensitive positions.[21]

To correct such perceived deficiencies and to increase presidential control over the higher civil service, the Carter administration engineered the passage of the Civil Service Reform Act (CSRA) of 1978. The CSRA established the Senior Executive Service, a professional managerial corps of career civil servants, and made its members eligible for financial bonuses. It also increased the ability of political executives to transfer career officials within and between agencies and to increase the number of noncareerists in SES and lower positions.[22] Another feature of the CSRA, the replacement of the three-person bipartisan Civil Service Commission by the single-headed Office of Personnel Management (OPM), also increased presidential control of the career service. Reagan's first director of OPM, Donald J. Devine, aggressively implemented a partisan style of leadership.[23] It is unclear at this time whether Reagan's successors will use politicization as extensively or as effectively as he has to direct the executive branch.[24] Debate over the issue is certain to continue as future administrations confront the task of controlling the federal bureaucracy.

Legal Arrangements

The legal position of the executive branch is the fourth factor that affects a president's control over the bureaucracy. All departments and agencies are established by Congress and derive their authority to operate from statutes. Moreover, "it is the agency heads, not the president, who have the men, money, material, and legal powers." [25] Presidents do not enter into contracts, initiate projects, or make grants. Their subordinates do so, but not in response to presidential directives. It is true, of course, that presidents act through subordinates, but they do so principally through persuasion because of the nature and source of their legal authority and that of their subordinates.

Although the Constitution charges the president with responsibility for executing the laws, Congress has delegated authority to and imposed duties directly on various administrative officials. In some cases, such as independent regulatory commissions and the Federal Reserve Board, the president has no formal power to direct agency actions or set agency policy. His influence upon these units is based on his budgetary and appointment powers and on his persuasive abilities. For cabinet members, heads of independent agencies, and other political executives with operating authority to whom Congress has directly delegated power, the situation is ambiguous. As chief executive the president, by virtue of the "take care" clause of the Constitution, can command the decisions of his subordinates. In doing so, however, he risks confrontation with Congress and with the clientele groups and individuals affected by the administrative units involved. Also, the Supreme Court long ago ruled that the president may not interfere with the performance of a "purely ministerial" duty that does not involve the exercise of discretion or judgment.[26] Nor may the president prevent the execution of the law by subordinates.

The growth of large-scale public bureaucracy has been accompanied by broad delegations of discretionary authority to administrative officials. Such delegations have been necessary because Congress cannot legislate in sufficient detail to cover all contingencies that may arise. Congress has also made vague and general grants of power because it finds it politically advantageous to shift difficult and potentially unpopular decisions to the bureaucracy. The Supreme Court has approved the delegation of legislative authority to the executive branch with the proviso that the delegations be accompanied by clear statutory guidelines.[27] However, the Court's insistence on statutory standards has seldom been followed by Congress or by the judiciary.[28] The standards that the Court has approved have often tended to be vague and unspecific, such as "just and reasonable rates," "excess profits," and "the public interest, convenience, and necessity." In spite of judicial review of the fairness of administrative procedures and judicial reference to the legislative history of statutes as found in congressional committee hearings and reports and floor debates in Congress, administrative officials retain substantial discretionary authority that complicates the president's task of controlling the bureaucracy.

Susceptibility to External Influence

It is often observed that the federal bureaucracy is highly susceptible to external influence and pressure. A primary reason for this susceptibility to forces outside of individual departments, agencies, and bureaus is the inability of American political parties to provide administrative units with political support and to link party programs with the pursuit of presidential policy goals.

In contrast to "the government" in parliamentary democracies such as the United Kingdom or Canada, American presidential administrations are not integrated by ties of party loyalty and commitment to a party program. Administrations lack internal policy cohesiveness and depend on the president's personal leadership to hold them together. In the face of external criticism and pressure, executive branch units are unable to find much support within the administration. Demands on the president are extensive, his attention span is limited, and he tends to conserve his political resources for high-priority objectives.

If presidential support for an agency is lacking, the agency must look elsewhere for help in maintaining its authority, funding, and personnel. It looks to the public for support, especially among the individuals and groups who are affected by its programs, and it looks to Congress, particularly to the committees or subcommittees with jurisdiction over its legislative authorizations and its appropriations.

The regulations that agencies promulgate and enforce, or the benefits and services that they deliver, provide the basis for the development of enduring ties between them and their clientele groups. An agency without a well-organized clientele is in a precarious position. Clientele groups can publicize an agency's accomplishments and defend it against attack. In exchange, the agency administers its programs with a manifest concern for the interests of the clientele. The agency consults with clientele group officials and with individual notables who are attentive to its activities. Such outsiders are invited to participate in agency decision making. They do so by serving on advisory councils and panels and through informal personal contacts. Agencies seldom perform such acts as the drafting of guidelines and regulations or the award of grants without extensive external participation and consultation. There is also a two-way flow of personnel between agencies and their clientele organizations. These mutually beneficial relations between agencies and their clientele are characteristic of most domestic policy areas in the federal government.

Washington has countless examples of close relationships between administrative agencies and clientele groups. The National Education Association (NEA) and several other education interest groups have provided support and protection to the U.S. Office of Education (now the Department of Education) in exchange for access and information. The NEA led the congressional effort to elevate the Office of Education to departmental status in 1979 and the battle to prevent the abolition of the Department of Education during the Reagan administration. Over the years several Office of Education political executives have found employment with the NEA and other education interest groups after leaving the government. On occasion, those lobbies have helped to recruit or have provided personnel to staff the agency.

Agencies also find it easy and convenient to develop strong ties to the congressional committees or subcommittees with which they deal. Committee members usually receive immediate attention and preferential treatment from agency personnel. Congressional requests for consideration on appointments and grants, suggestions concerning program administration, and inquiries on behalf of constituents are quickly acknowledged. Congressional influence with the agencies strengthens the committee members in their constituencies.[29] Bureaucrats use their connections with congressional committee members to gain favorable budgetary treatment and changes in their statutory authority. Agencies may use their committee ties to obtain more funds than the president has recommended for them or to modify their activities in a way that is not fully in accord with presidential preferences.

The result of agencies' quest for support outside the executive branch, among their clientele and in Congress, is the development of triangular relationships involving an agency, its clientele groups, and congressional committees. These "iron triangles"[30] or "policy subgovernments"[31] are semiautonomous centers of power. They abound in Washington and are a major obstacle to presidential control of the bureaucracy. They are not, however, totally resistant to presidential directives, nor is it in their interest to be so. Agencies frequently need presidential support and attention. Moreover, they often find that their interests coincide with those of the president. Agencies and the president need each other to accomplish their goals. If the true test of a president's power is his power to persuade, one of the best measures of an agency's strength is the degree to which a president must "bargain with it in order to secure its cooperation."[32]

The concept of policy subgovernments, although widely recognized as empirically accurate, is incomplete. The so-called iron triangles are complemented by a myriad of amorphous "issue networks" comprising individuals and groups with knowledge about and a desire to act on particular policy problems.[33] Issue networks differ from policy subgovernments in that they are unstructured and open. People move into and out of them freely and are more likely to be motivated by their positions on issues than by material interests.

Issue networks make policy making more complicated and less predictable. They have differing implications for democratic politics and presidential control of the bureaucracy. On the one hand, they increase the potential involvement of a wide range of experts and policy specialists in governmental problem solving, they provide a technocratic link between Congress and the executive branch, and they give political executives increased room for maneuvering. On the other hand, issue networks make it more difficult for the president to control political executives by reducing his leverage over them, and they are not democratically accountable. In sum, although they may be good for policy making, they are "bad for democratic politics." [34]

The President and the Cabinet

Most modern presidents have come to office determined to make more extensive use of the cabinet as a collective decision-making body than their predecessor did. The public has tended to applaud candidates' pledges that the cabinet will play a major role in their administrations. Yet, with the possible exception of Dwight Eisenhower, presidents have not used their cabinets as vehicles of collective leadership. Moreover, they have experienced strained relationships with many individual cabinet members. This gap between expectation and experience suggests that there is a widespread lack of understanding of the cabinet on the part of the public and most political leaders. According to Thomas Cronin, the cabinet "is simultaneously one of the best known and least understood aspects of our governmental system." [35] In point of fact, the Constitution places executive authority, ultimately, in the president alone. The notion of collective or collegial leadership is incompatible with constitutional reality. The president is not first among equals; he is explicitly "number one," the person in charge. Cabinet members are the president's appointees, and they serve at his pleasure. He has no obligation to consult them as a group or, when he does so, to act according to their wishes. The cabinet has no formal constitutional or legal standing. It exists by custom, and presidents are free to use it as little or as much as they see fit.

The fact that the cabinet has seldom been a high-level decision-making body does not mean that it lacks political significance. It has great symbolic value as a means of representing major social, economic, and political constituencies in the highest councils of the administration. Newly elected presidents try to select cabinet members whose presence will unify those constituencies behind him and his administration. Elevation of an agency to cabinet status signifies the importance the nation places on its activities.

During the Carter administration, for example, the Federal Energy Agency became the nucleus of a new Department of Energy, and the Office of Education provided the core of the Department of Education. Opponents of these moves argued that the federal role in energy and education should be diminished rather than enhanced by the award of cabinet status. President Reagan proposed the abolition of the two new departments as part of his attempt to reduce the activities of the federal government. (Later, he dropped the abolition effort, which had few supporters in Congress, among interest groups, or in the public.)

As noted previously, in selecting cabinet members, presidents have employed criteria such as prior political experience, identification with politically significant groups, and technical expertise. There is no dominant criterion, but Nelson Polsby found in a study of the Nixon and Carter cabinets that presidents tend initially to select cabinets that are broadly representative and whose members can speak for clientele groups and party constituencies. Over time, they tend to choose people "of no independent public standing, with no constituencies of their own." [36] This also appears to have been true of the Reagan administration.

Presidents face constraints in selecting cabinet members. Appointees to head some departments, such as Agriculture, must generally be acceptable to clientele groups. In choosing the secretaries of defense and treasury, presidents give expertise and experience heavy weight. Generalist administrators, however, are often named to head the departments of Commerce, Health and Human Services, Housing and Urban Development, and Transportation.

Presidents often try to use the cabinet as a decision-making body early in their administrations, but most of them eventually abandon the effort. They find that most cabinet members are concerned primarily with issues that affect their departments and with their personal relationships with the president. There is often competition between cabinet members for the president's attention, and personality clashes within the cabinet are not infrequent. Under these circumstances, cabinet meetings are unsatisfactory devices for focused, analytical discussion of major issues. At best they can serve as forums for informal discussion of issues and problems and for the exchange of information. Even President Eisenhower, who genuinely wanted his cabinet to function as a policy review and coordinating body, was unable to use it to formulate policy. The crucial factor limiting the role of the cabinet is the absence of any integrating force within the administration other than the president. The weakness of political parties in the governing process and the president's preeminent constitutional and political position combine to make him the only source of cohesion and policy coordination.

Individual cabinet members experience conflicting pulls of loyalty to the president on the one hand and to the permanent governments within their departments on the other. These conflicting loyalties inhibit the development of an informal sense of unity and common purpose without which the cabinet cannot realize its potential as a formal advisory body and policy-making mechanism.[37]

Although it may be an overstatement to assert that departmental and clientele pressures make cabinet members "natural enemies" of the president,[38] there is an unavoidable tension in their relationship that constitutes a great dilemma for him. No president can function effectively if cabinet members regularly choose departmental over presidential interests. However, cabinet members who display unquestioning responsiveness to the president's desires and are insensitive to the needs and concerns of their departments jeopardize their capacity to implement his policies effectively. Furthermore, cabinet members are not fully in command of their departments. The strongest clientele pressures are applied to the bureaus that administer programs, not to the department heads. It is the operating bureaus, not the departments, that constitute the bureaucratic components of policy subgovernments. Cabinet members deal with subgovernments mainly through persuasion. For this they need access to the president and presidential support. Presidents and presidential aides who fail to give cabinet members support and room to bargain with subgovernments and who expect quick and complete obedience to White House directives almost ensure the ineffectiveness of the cabinet members, as well as their own frustration.

Presidents frequently have developed strong, positive relationships with individual cabinet members and, through them, with their departments, but there is no assurance that this will happen. A personality conflict between the president and a cabinet member or antipathy on the part of the White House staff can prevent such a development. There is a tendency in most administrations for one or two cabinet members to stand out and to develop close ties with the president. Individuals such as Secretary of State John Foster Dulles and Secretary of the Treasury George Humphrey dominated the Eisenhower cabinet, and the advice of Secretary of Defense Robert S. McNamara was highly regarded by Presidents Johnson and Kennedy. Secretary of Labor and later Secretary of the Treasury George Shultz established dominant influence in President Nixon's cabinet, and Secretary of State Henry Kissinger was the preeminent figure in the Ford administration.

Interestingly, the Carter cabinet did not have a standout member who enjoyed a preferred position with the president. This appears to have been due primarily to Carter's heavy reliance on his personal staff, most of whom came to Washington with him from Georgia, and his inability to establish close rapport with cabinet members who had extensive Washington experience and their own supportive constituencies—for example, Secretary of State Cyrus Vance and HEW Secretary Joseph Califano. Also, Carter's top aides were openly and sharply critical of cabinet members who were viewed as too independent.

From 1981 through 1986, no one member of the Reagan administration dominated the cabinet. Secretary of State Alexander Haig attempted to do so at the outset of the administration, but he resigned under pressure from the White House staff after seventeen months in office. Haig's successor at State, George Shultz, and Secretary of Defense Caspar Weinberger often clashed over foreign and military policy, but neither gained a lasting advantage over the other. In Reagan's second term, Attorney General Edwin Meese III, who served as counselor to the president through the first term, and Secretary of the Treasury James A. Baker III, White House chief of staff in the first term, came to dominate legal and social policy issues and international economic affairs, respectively. In Reagan's second term, cabinet members in the president's favor enjoyed considerable leeway to pursue their own agendas, without aggressive interference by the White House staff, provided they did not conflict with the president's ideological precepts.[39]

Whatever the variations in relations between individual presidents and their cabinet members, there has been a tendency for modern presidents to develop close ties with the heads of the departments of State, Defense, Treasury, and Justice. Cronin refers to these as the "inner cabinet" departments because their activities and responsibilities are of the highest priority—national security, the condition of the economy, civil rights, and the administration of justice—and because they cut across the concerns of the public and all members of Congress. These matters tend to dominate the president's time and attention.[40] Thus, inner cabinet members almost always have direct, frequent, and continuing contact with the president.

The heads of the other departments—Agriculture, Commerce, Education, Energy, Health and Human Services, Housing and Urban Development, Interior, Labor, and Transportation—constitute the "outer cabinet."[41] Their departments have more sharply focused activities. Outer cabinet members, subjected to strong clientele and congressional pressures, find themselves acting as advocates for those interests within the administration. Frequently, those pressures conflict with the president's broader priorities. Outer cabinet members also find that they often are regarded suspiciously by White House aides, with whom they have frequent contact because the activities of their departments are not important enough to allow them to claim much of the president's time. Their relative lack of access to the president and their necessary interaction with presidential staffers who tend to distrust them leads to a sense of isolation and frustration. During the Nixon administration, for example, Interior Secretary Walter Hickel complained publicly that he seldom saw the president and lost his job when he wrote and released a letter to that effect. In the Carter administration HEW Secretary Califano experienced great frustration at having to deal primarily with White House staff instead of the president.[42]

Because of the diversity and scope of departmental activities and the particularistic orientations of outer cabinet members, presidents have generally looked to sources other than the cabinet for advice on policy implementation. Since its creation in 1947, the National Security Council (NSC) and its staff have been used extensively by presidents to coordinate the making and execution of foreign and military policy. (See Chapter 11.) In the important areas of economic policy, presidents work closely with the chairperson of the Council of Economic Advisers, the director of the Office of Management and Budget, the secretary of the Treasury, and the chairperson of the Federal Reserve Board. (See Chapter 10.) In the domestic policy areas, which involve primarily the outer cabinet departments, domestic policy staffs and OMB have provided assistance to the president in policy formulation (see Chapter 9), and cabinet committees, interagency committees, and policy councils have been employed to coordinate policy implementation.

Cabinet committees, which are usually appointed on an ad hoc basis to handle specific problems, can focus quickly on them and develop flexible solutions. Their usefulness for long-term monitoring of policy implementation is limited, however, by other demands on their members and by the tendency of their operations to become routine and to lose flexibility. Interagency committees, which operate mostly at the agency and subcabinet levels, may achieve a measure of coordination, but their work is often hampered by competition between agencies and by their lack of status and visibility.

Presidents also have used policy councils to highlight particular problems. Before the Reagan administration, most policy councils other than the NSC were more of symbolic value than operational utility to presidents in their management of the executive branch. In his first term Reagan invested heavily in the cabinet council approach. He established seven councils in addition to the NSC: commerce and trade, economic affairs, energy and natural resources, food and agriculture, human resources, legal policy, and management and administration. Initially, the Reagan councils met frequently, with staff support from their component departments and from the Office of Policy Development in the White House. The councils discussed working papers on issues within each council's jurisdiction. The president chaired the councils and met with them when decisions were about to be made. The secretaries of commerce, treasury, interior, agriculture, and health and human services, the attorney general, and Counselor to the President Edwin Meese chaired working sessions of the respective councils. At those meetings cabinet members and key presidential aides attempted to relate departmental and agency positions to the broader perspectives of the entire administration.

The theory behind the cabinet council system was that issues would move upward through the full cabinet to the president for decision. Over time, as it became apparent that the system was unduly cumbersome, Chief of Staff James Baker and budget director David Stockman circumvented cabinet council recommendations, making them largely irrelevant.[43] By exposing them to presidential concerns and keeping them in contact with the president himself, the system did, however, help to prevent cabinet members and other top agency officials from solely favoring bureaucratic and clientele interests within their departments.

During Reagan's second term, following the movement of Baker and Meese (the architect of the cabinet council system) from the White House to the cabinet and the designation of former treasury secretary Donald Regan as chief of staff, the number of cabinet councils was reduced to two with more clearly defined jurisdictions and lines of authority: the Economic Policy Council and the Domestic Policy Council. Baker, as secretary of the treasury, and Meese, as attorney general, chaired the two new councils. Under the second-term system, designed by Regan, the cabinet councils modulated the flow of issues, at times bottling them up, and acted as a forum for interagency conflict. Most of the important economic policy issues, such as tax reform and budget priorities, were handled outside the system; most other domestic policy in Reagan's second term was "budget driven," that is, policy issues that involved expenditures and were resolved by OMB.[44] The Regan system, which was designed to protect the president politically, allowed the more aggressive cabinet members, such as Baker, Meese, Shultz, and Weinberger, to set the administration's policy tone within the framework of the president's broad ideologically defined agenda.

Presidential Control of the Bureaucracy

George Edwards has identified four major factors that affect policy implementation: communication, resources, bureaucratic structure, and the dispositions of implementing officials.[45] The preceding analysis of presidential relations with the cabinet and the bureaucracy has revealed that presidents encounter obstacles to control of policy implementation in all four of these areas. Presidents are not, however, without resources for this effort. They have substantial powers granted by the Constitution, delegated by Congress, and derived from the nature of their office. The most important are the powers to appoint and remove subordinates, to issue executive orders, and to prepare the annual federal budget and regulate expenditures.

Appointment and Removal

The essential powers for presidential control of the bureaucracy are the powers to appoint and remove subordinate officials. As critical as these powers are to the president's executive responsibilities, however, they are subject to limitation by Congress.[46] The Constitution gives the president broad powers of appointment (Article II, Section 2, paragraph 2), but it makes high-ranking officials subject to senatorial confirmation, and it authorizes Congress to vest the appointment of lower officials in the president, in department heads, or in the courts. Congress determines whether an appointment to a position must be confirmed by the Senate. It can also narrow the president's discretion in making appointments by establishing detailed qualifications for various offices. Also, in establishing the civil service system and extending it to most civilian employees of the federal government,

Congress limited policy-sensitive presidential appointments to a small number of positions. Congress cannot, however, give itself the power to appoint executive officials.[47] Neither can it force the president to make an appointment to a vacant position.[48] The president's appointive powers are constrained also by political considerations and practices, such as senatorial courtesy whereby the president gives the senators of his own party a veto over certain administrative and judicial appointments in the states.

The Senate generally has given presidents considerable leeway in the appointment of top-level political executives, but confirmation is not automatic, and the Senate has used rejections to express disapproval of specific individuals or of particular practices.[49] Since the Watergate scandal of 1972-1974, the Senate has tended to be more careful in examining the backgrounds, qualifications, and relevant policy views of presidential nominees.

The Constitution also empowers the president to make appointments when the Senate is in recess. Such appointments must be confirmed by the end of the Senate's next session, but in the interim the appointee continues to serve. Senators often object to recess appointments to high-level positions because they feel inhibited from thoroughly examining persons who have already begun their duties. Because recent Congresses have remained in session most of the year, however, presidents have had fewer opportunities to make recess appointments.

The removal power is the logical complement of the appointment power. The ability to remove subordinate officials on performance or policy grounds is fundamental to presidential control of the executive branch. Without the removal power, the president cannot be held fully responsible for the actions of his subordinates or for failure of departments and agencies to achieve his objectives. The Constitution is silent, however, concerning the removal of executive officials other than through impeachment, a cumbersome process that is limited to instances of "bribery, treason, and other high crimes and misdemeanors."

Presidents have clashed sharply with Congress over the removal power. In 1834 the Senate censured President Andrew Jackson for removing Secretary of the Treasury William John Duane, who had disobeyed Jackson's orders to remove government deposits from the Bank of the United States. In a vigorous message of protest, Jackson asserted that the removal power had its basis in the Constitution and was beyond the reach of Congress. Eventually, the Senate lifted the censure. The post-Civil War conflict between President Andrew Johnson and Congress over reconstruction policy also involved the removal power. In 1867 Congress passed the Tenure of Office Act over Johnson's veto. That statute authorized all persons appointed with the advice and consent of the Senate to continue to hold office until the president appointed and the Senate confirmed a successor. Johnson's subsequent removal of Secretary of War Edwin Stanton, who had publicly attacked him, led to impeachment proceedings against Johnson. Although Johnson survived the impeachment trial by one vote in the Senate, the issue of the removal power remained unresolved. In 1876 Congress required senatorial consent for the removal of postmasters; but in 1887, after battling with President Grover Cleveland over the suspension of several hundred officials, Congress repealed the Tenure of Office Act.

The Supreme Court dealt directly with the removal power in a decision involving a challenge to President Woodrow Wilson's summary removal of a postmaster.[50] In a sweeping opinion by Chief Justice William Howard Taft (a former president), the Court invalidated the 1876 law. It held that the Constitution gave the president the removal power and that Congress could not place restrictions on its exercise. Nine years later, however, the Court upheld the provisions of the Federal Trade Commission Act, which limited the grounds for removal of its members.[51] President Roosevelt had removed Commissioner William E. Humphrey because of policy differences rather than the statutory grounds of "inefficiency, neglect of duty, or malfeasance in office." The Court ruled that the president's unqualified power of removal is limited to "purely executive offices" and that Congress may prescribe conditions for the removal of officials performing "quasi-legislative" and "quasi-judicial" functions. However, the Court has not clarified fully the meaning of these terms. In addition to placing statutory limits on the removal of certain classes of officials, Congress can restrict the president's removal power by reorganization and program cutbacks, provided such actions do not violate constitutional rights, and it can apply pressure through its investigatory power.[52]

Perhaps the most dramatic recent use of the removal power occurred in August 1981 when President Reagan fired 11,400 striking members of the Professional Air Traffic Controllers Organization. A U.S. Court of Appeals upheld the action, interpreting it as a discharge of the president's obligation to enforce a statute prohibiting strikes by federal employees.[53]

Although there are some statutory and judicial restrictions on the removal power, its precise limits remain somewhat undefined. Moreover, the president may be able through informal means to force officials from office for reasons other than statutory cause. The president can call publicly for an official's resignation, or he may revoke authority he has delegated to an official as a means of indicating displeasure and lack of confidence. In 1975 President Gerald Ford removed Robert Timm as chairperson of the Civil Aeronautics Board on grounds of "incompetence," but allowed him to remain on the board. Timm resigned two months later. The president may also reorganize or abolish an agency (through use of his reorganization powers) as a means of removing an official, as President Eisenhower did with the War Claims Commission.[54]

Executive Orders

Under a strict interpretation of separation of powers, the president has no direct legislative authority. Established practice, however, based on liberal interpretations of the Constitution by presidents and the Supreme Court, has vested substantial authority in him to issue executive orders that have the force of law. From the beginnings of the Republic, presidents have issued orders and directives on the basis of Article II. Most modern presidents have followed Theodore Roosevelt's "stewardship" theory of executive power, which holds that Article II confers on them inherent power to take whatever actions they deem necessary in the national interest unless prohibited from doing so by the Constitution or by law. Executive orders have been a primary means of exercising this broad presidential prerogative power.

It is generally recognized that executive orders must find their authority in the Constitution or in an act of Congress. As noted above, the Supreme Court has upheld delegations of legislative power to the executive branch provided Congress establishes "intelligible" standards to guide administrative officials in the exercise of their authority.[55] In reviewing challenges to statutory delegations, however, the Court has consistently adopted a presumption in favor of statutes authorizing executive action by order or rule.

Executive orders have played a major role in presidential policy making. Presidents have used them in such crucial areas as civil rights, economic stabilization, and national security. In the realm of civil rights President Franklin Roosevelt established a Fair Employment Practices Commission in 1943 to prevent discriminatory hiring by government agencies and military suppliers. In 1948 President Truman ended segregation in the armed forces by executive order. Shortly after taking office, President Kennedy in March 1961 issued a sweeping order creating an Equal Employment Opportunity Commission with broad enforcement orders. President Johnson went even further, requiring by executive order preferential hiring of minorities by government contractors. Following passage of the Civil Rights Act of 1964, presidential orders involving civil rights declined; but before that landmark statute, presidents used executive orders to make policy in a sensitive area in which Congress was unable or unwilling to act.

President Roosevelt established broad precedents for the use of executive orders to achieve economic stability. During World War II he established through executive orders an Office of Price Administration (OPA) and an Office of Economic Stabilization and gave them extensive powers over prices, wages, and profits. The OPA also rationed scarce consumer goods such as meat, butter, sugar, shoes, automobile tires, and gasoline. As the basis for his actions Roosevelt cited his responsibility as president to respond to the "unlimited emergency" created by the war. The Emergency Price Control Act of 1942 provided retroactive statutory endorsement for the establishment of the emergency agencies and the measures implemented by them.

In 1970, in the face of persistent inflation, Congress passed the Economic Stabilization Act, which authorized the president to issue orders that would control wages and prices. It was a sweeping delegation that spelled out few criteria to guide the president's actions. Republican president Richard Nixon's outspoken opposition to economic controls led many observers to conclude that the main purpose of the Democratic Congress in passing the statute was to embarrass him and his party in the 1970 congressional election campaign by giving him strong anti-inflationary tools that he would not use. To the surprise of almost everyone, on August 15, 1971, Nixon issued an executive order imposing a ninety-day freeze on nonagricultural wages and prices and established a Cost of Living Council to administer the controls. A subsequent order, issued on October 15, 1971, extended the controls and established additional machinery to aid in administering them. A legal challenge to the statute, as an unconstitutional delegation of unbridled authority, failed before a U.S. district court.[56] The court found that Congress had considered the statute carefully and concluded that the president needed extensive discretion to deal with inflation. The court decided that the delegation was therefore reasonable, and it stated that experience in administering previous price control statutes, passed in 1942 and 1950, furnished implicit standards for guidance in implementing the 1970 law.

President Reagan used an executive order early in his first term to establish a comprehensive program to oversee the issuance of regulations by departments, agencies, and independent regulatory commissions. The order, which formally implemented Reagan's commitment to administrative deregulation, created the President's Task Force on Regulatory Relief, set up the Office of Information and Regulatory Affairs in OMB, and required that all regulations meet a uniform cost-benefit standard "to the extent permitted by law." [57] OMB used the cost-benefit standard and the paperwork review procedures of the order to substitute market forces for federal regulations, and on occasion it prevented the issuance of proposed regulations.

Presidents have also used executive orders in pursuit of national security. In 1942, for example, President Roosevelt ordered the internment of all persons of Japanese ancestry living in the Pacific coastal states, 70,000 of whom were U.S. citizens. The Supreme Court upheld this massive deprivation of basic civil liberties on the basis of the commander-in-chief clause.[58] During the Korean War, however, the Supreme Court invalidated President Truman's seizure of the steel industry on the grounds that he had not used the machinery established in the Taft-Hartley Act of 1947 to avert a strike.[59]

In another aspect of national security presidents have used executive orders extensively to administer and structure federal intelligence agencies. In 1973 President Nixon overhauled the system for classifying information, and in 1976 President Ford reorganized the intelligence agencies, imposed restrictions on their activities, and established procedures to make them more directly accountable to the president.

From 1932 until 1983 Congress exerted a measure of control over executive lawmaking through use of the legislative veto, a device whereby it added language to certain statutes that enabled it to review and reject executive orders or administrative regulations authorized by the legislation. The legislative veto took various forms. It allowed disapproval by concurrent resolution, or by simple resolution of either house, or by action of a committee of either house. In its most common form, the legislative veto required that the proposed action lie before Congress for a specified period—usually sixty or ninety days—during which either chamber could disapprove it. The president's reorganization authority, which Congress first authorized in 1939, carried such a procedure. Other major statutes that contained a form of legislative veto include the War Powers Resolution of 1973, the Budget and Impoundment Control Act of 1974, the Federal Elections Campaign Act of 1974, and the National Emergencies Act of 1976. In all, more than three hundred statutes provided for some type of legislative veto.

The legislative veto sparked extensive controversy. Its supporters defended it as an effective means of controlling the exercise of delegated legislative power by the executive branch. They contended that it was an appropriate condition for Congress to attach to a delegation of power. Indeed, Edward S. Corwin, one of the nation's most noted constitutional scholars, argued that delegation can be kept from becoming abdication "only by rendering the delegated powers recoverable without the consent of the delegate." [60]

Opponents of the legislative veto asserted that it unconstitutionally violated the separation of powers because it interfered with the president's authority to veto acts of Congress. They also maintained that in the case of vetoes by one house or by a committee, the veto enabled a part of Congress to act for the whole institution. [61] Presidents from Truman through Reagan regarded legislative veto provisions of statutes as unconstitutional, although before taking office Reagan had endorsed the idea of granting to both houses of Congress and the president the authority to veto administrative regulations. These presidents, did not, however, refuse to sign bills containing legislative veto provisions.

The Supreme Court did not confront the constitutionality of the legislative veto until June 1983. At that time, in *Immigration and Naturalization Service v. Chadha*, it held the one-house legislative veto provision of the Immigration and Nationality Act to be unconstitutional on the grounds that it involved "the exercise of legislative power" without "bicameral passage followed by presentment to the President." [62] Two weeks after the *Chadha* decision, the Court affirmed without further comment a U.S. court of appeals decision that a two-house legislative veto provision contravened constitutional provisions for making law. Initial reaction to *Chadha* was that it was not a definitive ruling and that somehow Congress would find a way statutorily to control executive branch lawmaking. [63]

At this writing, more than three years afterward, the Court's ruling appears to have invalidated effectively the use of resolutions by one or both houses of Congress to disapprove of an executive action on the basis of delegated power. Committee vetoes are also invalid, but Congress has continued to include provisions requiring them in appropriations bills, and agencies, such as the National Aeronautics and Space Administration, have continued to comply with them. Arrangements between committees and agencies are not binding, but executive branch officials observe them because Congress can revoke the discretionary authority that it has delegated.[64] In addition to the persistence of de facto committee vetoes, Congress has begun to employ a device that accomplishes the purpose of the legislative veto and is compatible with the *Chadha* ruling—the joint resolution of approval. Instead of providing that an executive action will become effective unless Congress acts to disapprove it by joint resolution, in which case the president may exercise his veto, the resolution of approval requires passage of a joint resolution before an action can be taken.[65] For example, the Reorganization Act Amendments of 1984 provide that a presidentially prepared reorganization plan submitted to Congress cannot take effect unless approved by a joint resolution within ninety days. This places the burden on the president rather than on Congress, and he has only a specific number of days in which to act. In effect, the joint resolution of approval works like a one-house legislative veto: if either house refuses to approve an action, it cannot be taken. The major disadvantage of the joint resolution for Congress is that it requires much time, and extensive use of it would threaten the congressional agenda with legislative gridlock.

Congress has not responded to the *Chadha* decision with a general strategy. It has employed a variety of tactics: informal arrangements, limited use of joint resolutions of approval and disapproval (as was done on foreign arms sales and the export of nuclear materials), and removal of certain matters from agency jurisdiction (as it did by prohibiting the Food and Drug Administration from banning the sale of saccharin).[66] Although the legislative veto, used extensively by Congress during the 1970s to curb executive power, has been sharply limited by the Supreme Court, the underlying rationale for the veto retains considerable vitality, for it enhances congressional control of agency action and expedites the conduct of the administrative process. As Louis Fisher has observed, "In one form or another legislative vetoes will remain an important method for reconciling legislative and executive interests."[67]

Presidents and Money

Presidents have substantial financial powers, delegated by Congress, which they employ in their efforts to control the bureaucracy. The most important of these is budgeting, that is, planning for spending within a specific period of time. Within the federal government, the budget is used to control the amount of spending by departments and agencies. It also establishes the president's spending priorities, sets the timing of program initiatives, and distributes rewards to and imposes sanctions on executive branch units.[68] By controlling the total amount of the budget, the president can attempt to influence the performance of the economy. (See Chapter 10.)

Presidential use of the executive budget is a twentieth-century development. The enormous increase in expenditures during World War I, and the task of managing the sizable national debt that resulted, convinced Congress of the need for an executive budget. The Budget and Accounting Act of 1921 made the president responsible for compiling departmental and agency estimates and for submitting them annually to Congress in the form of a budget. The statute established the Bureau of the Budget (BOB), located in the Treasury Department, to assist the president in assembling and revising the estimates of the departments and agencies. The departments and agencies were prohibited from submitting their requests directly to Congress as they had done previously.

The initial emphasis in the development of the federal budgetary process was on the control of expenditures and the prevention of administrative abuses.[69] The focus of the budget was on objects of expenditure, that is, the personnel, supplies, and equipment needed to operate each agency. During the New Deal period, in the 1930s, the emphasis shifted from control to management. The budget was seen as a means of evaluating and improving administrative performance. The focus of the budget also shifted from objects of expenditure to the work and activities of departments and agencies. The transfer of BOB in 1939 from the Treasury Department to the new Executive Office of the President symbolized the management orientation. BOB was to become the president's management arm. A decade later, upon recommendation of the Hoover Commission, the government adopted a performance budget organized by functions and activities rather than by line items representing objects of expenditure.

The third stage in the development of budgeting is its orientation toward planning. This stage has featured the attempt to link annual budgeting, geared to the appropriations process in Congress, to long-range planning of government objectives. The focus is on the relationship of long-term policy goals to current and future spending decisions. The limited success of the planning orientation is reflected in the rapid arrival and departure of budgeting systems, such as the program planning budgeting system (PPBS) and zero base budgeting (ZBB).[70] The traditional budgeting process, as it had developed by the early 1970s, embodied all three orientations, but it was least effective as a planning device.

The limitations of the executive budget as an aid to presidential decision making stem from the incremental nature of the traditional budgetary process and from restrictions and conditions imposed by Congress. Budgeting is inherently incremental because it is done annually. The budget cycle forces the president and Congress to act according to a timetable that stretches from twenty-two months before the start of the fiscal year (October 1) through the ensuing year. Budgetary decision makers in Congress and the bureaucracy are concerned primarily with how large an increase or decrease will be made in a departmental or agency budget. Departmental and agency officials try to protect their current appropriation, which serves as a base, and add to it a portion of any increase in the total budget.

Congress makes its own budgetary decisions and is not bound to the president's requests. In the 1970s it quarreled bitterly with Presidents Nixon and Ford over spending for domestic programs, and, as noted above, in the 1980s it squared off with President Reagan over the size of the deficits in his proposed budgets. Congress limits total spending through resolutions proposed by the budget committees in each house. Although the Congress's budget total is usually fairly close to the president's budget total, often there are sharp differences between their priorities.

Throughout the budgetary process the congressional and bureaucratic participants focus attention on spending for the forthcoming fiscal year. Pressures are intense, and the political stakes are high. There is little opportunity in such a setting for consideration of long-range objectives and costs or for examining the effects on other government programs of different spending levels for specific activities.

The fiscal stress that the government experienced beginning in the mid-1970s has led to adjustments in the budget process designed to reduce pressures for increased spending and to enhance restraint. Among the major adjustments are norms or targets imposed from the top down, baseline budgeting, and multiyear budgeting. The baseline assumes no changes in budget policy and extrapolates revenue and expenditure trends. Underlying the projections is the message that unless cutbacks are made, future spending and deficits will be excessive.[71] Baseline budgeting reorients the process from increments to cutbacks. Multiyear budgets have also been redirected from plans for growth of programs and expenditures to devices for averting them.[72] These adaptations have not been overly successful, however, and pressures to protect and increase spending remain strong.

In addition to budgeting, presidents have certain discretionary spending powers that increase their leverage over the bureaucracy. They have substantial nonstatutory authority, based on understandings with congressional appropriations committees, to transfer funds within an appropriation and from one program to another. The committees expect to be kept informed of such "reprogramming" actions.[73] Fund transfer authority is essential to sound financial management, but it can be abused to circumvent congressional decisions. In 1970, for example, President Nixon transferred funds to support an extensive unauthorized covert military operation in Cambodia. Nevertheless, Congress has given presidents and certain agencies the authority to spend substantial amounts of money on a confidential basis, the largest and most controversial of which are for intelligence activities.

Presidents also have exercised some measure of expenditure control through the practice of impounding or returning appropriated funds to the treasury. Presidents since Washington routinely have impounded funds as a means of achieving savings when expenditures fall short of appropriations.[74] They have also withheld funds when authorized or directed to do so by Congress for purposes such as establishing contingency reserves or imposing a ceiling on total expenditures. Presidents from FDR through Lyndon Johnson also impounded some of the funds that Congress had added, over their objections, for various programs. Although such actions often drew congressional criticism, they did not lead to confrontation because they occurred infrequently and were generally focused on expenditures for specific programs or projects. Congress itself recognized that circumspect use of impoundments helped its members to resist strong pressures for increased spending.[75]

Impoundment became a major constitutional issue during the Nixon administration. Sweeping impoundments in domestic program areas, especially agriculture, housing, and water pollution control, led to charges that the president arbitrarily and illegally had substituted his spending priorities for those of Congress. What distinguished the Nixon impoundments from those of earlier administrations was their "magnitude, severity, and belligerence." [76] Specifically, the Nixon impoundments differed from those of previous presidents in five ways: they involved larger amounts; some were made in direct violation of explicit congressional instructions to spend the funds; some were designed to terminate entire programs rather than individual projects; some were directed at appropriated funds that had not been included in the president's budget proposals; and Nixon claimed constitutional rather than statutory authority for impoundment.[77] Nixon used impoundments as the primary weapon in a battle with Congress over domestic spending priorities. He did not bargain or negotiate over them but imposed his priorities by fiat.

The results of the Nixon impoundment controversy were lawsuits to compel release of the funds, most of which were decided against the president on statutory grounds, and the Impoundment Control Act of 1974. The Antideficiency Act of 1950 had limited the purposes of impoundments to the establishment of contingency reserves and the saving of money that would otherwise be wasted. The 1974 statute established procedures for congressional review by requiring that the president report all impoundments to Congress. Proposals to rescind appropriated funds, that is, to return them to the treasury, must be approved by both houses within forty-five days. Proposals to defer spending to the next fiscal year could be disapproved by either house.

The Supreme Court's 1983 ruling invalidating the legislative veto affected congressional power to control deferrals. (Since the 1974 legislation called for approval of recisions by both houses, *Chadha* did not invalidate that procedure.) But the only way left for Congress to overturn a deferral is to pass a bill or joint resolution, which is subject to presidential veto. This greatly enhances the president's deferral power. The most effective means available to

Congress to circumvent a possible veto is to attach a rider cancelling the deferral to an appropriation bill that the president feels compelled to sign in order to keep the involved agencies operating. But riders are a cumbersome device. When President Reagan began to defer sizable amounts ($5.4 billion for fiscal 1986) in his second term as a means of reducing spending on programs that he opposed, Congress found itself without a viable means of controlling deferrals.[78] In spring 1986 four House Democrats brought suit to have the president's deferral powers under the 1974 act declared invalid on the grounds that Congress intended to limit rather than extend them. Also, the House added a rider to a supplemental appropriations bill that declared ineffective the relevant provisions of the 1974 legislation. At this writing (May 1987) an acceptable balance between presidential discretion to defer spending and congressional control has not been found.

Presidential Management of the Bureaucracy

In addition to their formal powers, modern presidents have relied on managerial tools in their ongoing efforts to coordinate and direct executive branch operations. Three major tools—staffing, reorganization, and planning—have been employed with mixed results. The limited success of presidential efforts to manage the federal bureaucracy more effectively stems primarily from the political character of the administration of the executive branch. This branch is not a tightly structured hierarchy in which the president is supreme and officials at all levels act in response to directives from above. As noted previously, the president must rely more on persuasion than command to achieve his objectives, and departments and agencies have substantial autonomy. This is not to argue that the public sector is an inhospitable locale for the use of modern management techniques but to suggest that their use is significantly affected by political forces.

Staffing

Beginning with the administration of Franklin Roosevelt, the institutionalized presidency has grown steadily as presidents have turned to staff support as a means of discharging their many roles and of directing the executive branch. The 1937 report of the President's Committee on Administrative Management (known as the Brownlow Committee) took as its central theme the need to provide the president with adequate assistance. The principal contributions of the Brownlow Committee to the development of the institutionalized presidency were the establishment of the Executive Office of the President as a framework for presidential staff units and the transfer of the Bureau of the Budget from the Treasury Department to the Executive Office. Since those developments in 1939, additional staff units have been created (and a few have been abolished), the White House staff has expanded from a few dozen to several hundred, and the importance of the White House staff and other executive office staffs has grown enormously. The trend, from FDR through Nixon, was toward a "personalized and centralized presidency." [79]

Over time, presidential assistants assumed increasing responsibilities for managing the operations of the federal bureaucracy. Under Ford, Carter, and Reagan the progression halted, but the president's reliance on staff remained high, and staff members continued to play key roles that went beyond limited policy advice and supportive services.

In deciding how to organize staff resources, the president confronts three issues. First, does he prefer a hierarchical structure of the White House or a laissez-faire arrangement in which senior aides work independently of each other and have direct access to the president? Second, does the president prefer to make decisions from a few options prepared by trusted sources or from several alternatives prepared by diverse sources and subjected to intense scrutiny in the White House? Finally, what policy staffs does he plan to use, what jurisdictions will the staffs have, and how will they interact with cabinet members and other political executives? [80] The ways in which Presidents Carter and Reagan approached these issues illustrate some of the consequences of presidential staffing choices.

Jimmy Carter took office determined to avoid the pitfalls of the extensively centralized Nixon White House. Consequently, he adopted a "spokes-in-a-wheel" organizational model in which ten assistants had direct access to him. [81] (President Ford used a similar organizational model at the beginning of his presidency but after several months decided the arrangement was unsatisfactory and appointed a chief of staff. Carter, still reacting to Watergate and the Nixon presidency, did not regard Ford's difficulties with a decentralized staff as relevant.) [82] Under Carter no one other than the president himself exercised any coordinating authority. But Carter had a ponderous administrative style, highlighted by a penchant for detail and an exhaustive policy agenda that would have been more suited to a hierarchical model of organization. He would have been more comfortable, and probably more effective, responding to a wide range of policy options prepared by staff units. As it was, he tended to do much of his own staff work and became enmeshed in operational details. With no chief of staff or high-level body to coordinate the flow of issues and access of individuals to the president, the Carter administration lacked a sense of direction with clear priorities. In addition, Carter allowed the staff units for national security, economic, and domestic policy extensive autonomy. The result was an overloaded president and severe policy drift. To his credit, Carter recognized these difficulties and in July 1979, at the midpoint of his third year in office, restructured the White House along hierarchical lines with a chief of staff, Hamilton Jordan, controlling access to him and providing a measure of centralized direction. By that time, however, Carter's popular support and his professional reputation among Washington politicians had eroded substantially.

Ronald Reagan, in contrast to Carter, organized his White House in a manner that supported rather than conflicted with his administrative style. Reagan had a limited, ideologically defined agenda. He had little interest in details and preferred to make decisions from a limited number of options. Neither the hierarchical nor the spokes-in-a-wheel model were well suited to him. Instead, he adopted a modified spokes model in which three, and later four, senior officials had direct access to him and coordinated cabinet committees and policy staffs operating in their areas of responsibility.[83] The policy staffs had limited responsibilities and involvement as Reagan drew on a wide range of officials for advice. The result was an organizational arrangement that imposed presidential discipline on the administration and kept the president informed of major issues and problems and involved him in decisions at critical points. Neither his professional reputation nor his public prestige suffered as a consequence of his staffing pattern. As Colin Campbell aptly put it, "Reagan spared himself from becoming manifestly one of the least engaged presidents in this century by knowing how to organize his White House to maximum effect." [84]

Reagan's adoption of the hierarchical model at the start of his second term, with Donald Regan as chief of staff, had mixed results. Given Regan's lack of interest in policy except to maintain the president's original ideological agenda, the White House staff had limited involvement in shaping new policy initiatives. Instead, as noted above, individual cabinet secretaries assumed a lead role. Under these arrangements President Reagan was even less engaged, except for a few key issues such as tax reform and aid to the contras, than he was in his first term.

The change in White House organization appeared to have worked well for President Reagan until the Iranian arms affair erupted in November 1986. Until then both his popular support and his reputation among other political leaders remained high. As the Iranian affair unfolded, politicians and journalists questioned Reagan's administrative competence and his substantive judgment. The process for making and implementing foreign policy received special scrutiny and criticism (see Chapter 11) as did the role of Chief of Staff Donald Regan. It is doubtful, however, that the adoption of the hierarchical model of staff organization contributed to the Iranian fiasco. If anything, it should have helped to prevent it by compensating for Reagan's lack of attention to details and his detachment from matters of policy.

Unquestionably, staffing is crucial to presidential management of the bureaucracy. The roles of presidential staff in program implementation and of the cabinet in advising the president have varied in recent administrations, but the tendency has been toward reliance on a strong, sizable, and centralized White House staff to protect the political interests of the president, to act as his principal policy advisers, and to direct (as opposed to monitor and coordinate) the implementation of his priorities by the bureaucracy. Critics of this structure argue that it has undercut the advisory potential of the cabinet, narrowed the president's perspective on policy choices, and inhibited effective and responsive bureaucratic performance. Recent experience under Presidents Nixon and Reagan supports this view. Yet, Presidents Ford and Carter both tried a decentralized model of White House staffing and abandoned it in favor of hierarchical arrangements. Unfortunately, there is no proven answer to the question of how a president can most effectively provide leadership to his administration.

Reorganization

It has been almost an article of faith among political leaders and public administration theorists that executive reorganization can increase presidential power over the bureaucracy.[85] Among recent presidents, Lyndon Johnson, Richard Nixon, and especially Jimmy Carter had strong convictions that the performance of the executive branch could be improved and the bureaucracy brought to heel through changes in administrative structure. Indeed, one of the main themes in Carter's 1976 campaign against the government in Washington was the need for reorganization. In his 1979 State of the Union message Carter proclaimed that with congressional help his administration had "begun to reorganize and gain control of the bureaucracy." Yet by most accounts, the results of Carter's reorganization efforts were modest.[86]

Organizational structure and administrative arrangements are significant because they reflect values and priorities and because they affect access to decision makers. The location and status of an administrative unit—as a department, an independent agency, or a component of a department—symbolize the importance of its goals and of the interests it serves. Administrative arrangements can also contribute to or frustrate the achievement of accountability to Congress and the public. Reorganizing, however, does not necessarily result in increased efficiency of operation, greater program effectiveness, and enhanced public accountability. This is true because there is no ideal form for a government agency or a consistent set of prescriptions for organizing the executive branch.

According to Herbert Kaufman, one set of standard prescriptions tends to centralize authority and another tends to disperse it. More important, Kaufman points out, the most profound consequences of organizational change are not in the "engineered realm of efficiency, simplicity, size, and cost of government"; rather, they lie in the areas of "political influence, policy emphasis, and communication of governmental intentions." [87] The creation of a consumer protection agency, for example, would enhance the influence of consumer interests, which currently must look to consumer affairs units located in producer-oriented agencies. The placement of the Occupational Safety and Health Administration in the Department of Labor rather than in the Department of Health, Education and Welfare led to an initial focus of regulations on mechanical rather than on biological hazards in the workplace. Experience has shown that although the rationale for reorganization is couched in the rhetoric of economy and efficiency, the crucial factors in decisions to reorganize are power, policy, and symbolic significance.

In 1939 Congress authorized presidents to propose executive reorganization plans that take effect after sixty days unless disapproved by both houses. When extending that authority in 1949, Congress allowed either house to disapprove such plans. Congress continued to renew the reorganization authority with little change until 1973, when it was allowed to lapse in the conflict with President Nixon over his efforts to centralize control of the executive branch. In 1977 President Carter requested and received renewal of the authority with provision for veto by either house. President Reagan displayed little interest in using the reorganization power to enhance his control of the executive branch. Congress extended the reorganization power in 1984, but in response to the Supreme Court's invalidation of the legislative veto, it required a joint resolution of approval for a plan to take effect.

President Carter's reorganization achievements exceeded those of his immediate predecessors and of his successor but fell far short of the thorough restructuring of the executive branch and reduction in the number of agencies that he had promised in the campaign. Congress passed legislation that established new cabinet departments of Energy and of Education and allowed five reorganization plans to take effect. In contrast to previous presidents who appointed special task forces or study commissions to advise them on executive branch organization, President Carter established a special unit in the Office of Management and Budget, the President's Reorganization Board, to direct the reorganization effort. This approach enabled him to place his own emphasis on reorganization and to incorporate it as an ongoing aspect of his management of the executive branch. The approach lacked, however, the prestige and political support that could be obtained by a blue ribbon panel, and it tended to produce continuous incremental rather than breakthrough change. Also, it was susceptible to influence by individuals and groups with a stake in existing organizational arrangements.

There are both operational and conceptual explanations of the limited success of Carter's reorganization project. Operationally, observers assert, the president and his reorganization staff failed to comprehend the highly political nature of the task.[88] They were unprepared for the jurisdictional conflicts that accompanied congressional consideration of the proposals. Conceptually, the president regarded reorganization as an exercise in management from the bottom up. He lacked a well-conceived, comprehensive strategy that could be defended on political grounds. Most critically, Carter regarded reorganization as a "purpose in itself divorced from policy and program development." [89] For Carter the principal goal of reorganization was the fulfillment of campaign commitments. What was lacking was an understanding of reorganization as a means of redistributing influence and redirecting policy. The Carter experience indicates that reorganization has its uses, but they are more in the realm of policy and politics than of management improvement.

Planning

Aaron Wildavsky defines planning as "current action to secure future consequences." [90] Foresight in anticipating problems and developing solutions to them is the essence of effective planning. One of the hallmarks of successful corporate management has been long-range planning. The federal government, however, has not planned with a high degree of success. Planning is applicable to all major activities of the government—national security, economic affairs, human resources, and natural resources—and the nation has "paid a heavy price" for the government's failure "to take adequate account of the future." [91] In the early 1950s, for example, experts were warning of the eventual depletion of domestic oil sources, yet only after the oil embargo of 1973-1974 did the government begin to develop an energy policy that looked to the future.

The reasons for the limited success of planning by the federal government lie in the nature of the planning process and its relationship to politics. Planning is a rational process. It operates on the assumption that objectives are known and accepted. The task is to select the best means appropriate to the achievement of the desired ends. Planning decisions are made comprehensively, that is, "as if a single mind were supporting a single set of preferences." [92] Conflict and disagreement do not interfere because the planners know what is desired. However, public planning, like all other planning, takes place in an uncertain world. Planners do not have adequate knowledge of the future, and their predictions are often fallible.

In addition to the intellectual limitations of all planning, public planning is limited by politics. Public planners do not have the power to command acceptance of their choices. Public choices are made on the basis of the preferences of individuals and groups through a process of bargaining and compromise. The agreements reached in the process of political decision making determine the objectives of public planners. There is no correct result because political preferences are continually changing. As a consequence, political planners make accommodations to social forces. They shorten their time frames, thus reducing the need for prediction, and offer their plans as proposals or suggestions rather than as directives. The result is that political factors tend to dominate planning, and planning tends to blend with regular political decision making.

Presidents have engaged in long-range planning with only limited success. As noted previously, attempts to combine annual budgeting with comprehensive planning through the program planning budgeting system and zero base budgeting have not succeeded. Introduced throughout the government by President Johnson in 1965, PPBS sought to choose between alternative programs and long-range objectives on the basis of cost-benefit calculations. ZBB, a project of President Carter, compared the effects of alternative funding levels on long-term objectives within a single program. Both approaches entailed comprehensive attempts to relate spending decisions to long-range consequences. Each required extensive amounts of information and analyses that were never integrated with budgetary decisions. Thus, bureau and agency officials did not find it worthwhile to take either process seriously. A fatal defect of both PPBS and ZBB was neglect of the hard political choices involved in the budgetary process. Nor was Congress supportive of either device.

President Nixon introduced a similar technique that focused on the goals of government, management by objectives (MBO), to strengthen presidential oversight of the executive branch. He directed twenty-one departments and agencies to prepare rank-order lists of their principal objectives. After OMB reviewed the lists, the president approved objectives for each reporting unit. These presidential objectives then became the standard for monitoring the performance of the units. MBO differed from the planning process of PPBS and ZBB in that it focused first on immediate objectives, then on intermediate objectives that could be achieved in a fiscal year, and finally on long-term goals.[93] MBO was primarily useful within departments and agencies for routine oversight of agreed-on actions. It helped to spot problems and it facilitated communications between the departments and OMB. What it could not do was aid in the choice between objectives. In this respect it was outside the political process and the central concerns of the president.

MBO lapsed into desuetude under President Carter. Aside from ZBB, Carter's major planning effort was to require agencies to use a multiyear framework in planning their budget requests. The objective was to integrate planning with the budget cycle. Other than to continue multiyear budgeting, President Reagan has shown little interest in planning. He appears to believe that domestic policy planning is socialistic and incompatible with a free-market economy. Foreign and defense policy planning has been more successful than domestic policy planning, and Reagan and future presidents certainly will engage in national security planning. National security policy is often a matter of life or death, and the question of national survival makes planning imperative, whereas domestic policy issues are more diffuse and less compelling. Also, national security planning is not nearly as affected by governmental fragmentation and interest group demands as is domestic policy planning. Still, the large number of domestic programs and the intense pressures to restrict the growth of federal spending suggest that future presidents will turn to planning as a means of rationalizing and coordinating these programs.

Conclusion

Can the president lead the executive branch? It is apparent that although the president has substantial formal powers and managerial resources, he is by no means fully in control of his own branch of the government. His capacity to direct its many departments and agencies in the implementation of his policies is limited by bureaucratic complexity and fragmentation, conflict between the presidency and the bureaucracy, external pressure and influence on the bureaucracy, and the absence of an effective management system within the government.

The continuing attempts of modern presidents to overcome such obstacles provide another illustration of the protean character of the presidency. Efforts to strengthen presidential leadership and management of the executive branch involved three major areas: personnel administration, advice and assistance, and management. The most prominent examples include the creation of the Executive Office of the President in 1939, Lyndon Johnson's enthusiastic endorsement of the program planning budgeting system in 1966, Richard Nixon's centralization of executive authority in an administrative presidency, and Jimmy Carter's reorganization program and endorsement of the Civil Service Reform Act of 1978. The strategy of the Reagan administration, to accomplish policy change through administrative action, indicates that although presidents cannot achieve complete control of the executive branch, they can establish sustained direction of executive branch policy making.

Perhaps the most persistent theme in analyses and studies of the president's executive responsibilities is the need to improve the quality of his subordinates. Conventional wisdom holds that the key to presidential control of the bureaucracy lies in the appointment of top-level political executives who share his goals. In establishing control over the executive branch, President Reagan used to great advantage careful, centralized control of appointments, making ideological compatability with his goals the principal criterion. (He moved away, however, from recommendations of most experts that greater reliance should be placed on senior career officials who can provide continuity and institutional memory to an administration.) Reagan's placement of loyal and ideologically sympathetic persons in sensitive positions and the downgrading of senior careerists appear to have served his purposes well.

The second element of Reagan's administrative strategy involved staffing and decision making. By initially selecting a model of White House organization that was compatible with his personal administrative style and his policy objectives—a modified spokes-in-a-wheel model—and using cabinet councils to coordinate policy, Reagan achieved a higher degree of policy consistency than other recent administrations. He also adapted staffing and decision-making arrangements to changes in personnel and in political and other conditions. His adoption of the chief-of-staff model in his second term appeared to work well, but it failed to prevent the politically damaging Iranian arms scandal.

The major managerial feature of Reagan's administrative strategy was to use the budget to enforce presidential spending priorities on departments and agencies. In the face of strong pressures to reduce spending, Reagan reversed the traditional pattern of budget preparation from the bottom up, in which agencies attempted to protect their bases, and instituted top-down budgeting with presidential and OMB decisions being determinative.[94] Although the durability of centralized budgeting is questionable, it has enabled the president to gain leverage over Congress and the bureaucracy in his attempts to control spending.

The final element in Reagan's administrative strategy was the attempt to accomplish policy change administratively wherever possible. This involved establishing procedures for review of regulations by OMB, diminution of the intensity of regulatory enforcement, and reinterpretation of agency functions and relations with clientele in accordance with the administration's ideology.[95]

The relatively successful administrative presidency of Ronald Reagan should not blind one to the substantial difficulties that the president faces in his role as chief executive. Even a federal government that is no longer expanding its activities is still vast and complex. The triangular policy subgovernments, the issue networks, and the fragmented and parochially oriented Congress present major external obstacles to presidential control and direction. President Reagan overcame these to some extent by virtue of his temperament, leadership style, and perhaps most important, his limited, well-defined agenda, which sought to curtail rather than expand the role of government. Yet, Reagan's detached, "laid back" administrative style was a major factor leading to the most difficult event of his presidency, the Iranian arms scandal. President Reagan's approach to his executive responsibilities should indicate to his successors that effective leadership of the president's own branch is a difficult task at best and that there is no way to accomplish it that will guarantee effectiveness and please everyone involved.

Notes

1. Richard Rose, "Government against Subgovernments: A European Perspective on Washington," in *Presidents and Prime Ministers,* ed. Richard Rose and Ezra N. Suleiman (Washington, D.C.: American Enterprise Institute, 1980), 339.
2. *Youngstown Sheet and Tube Co. v. Sawyer,* 343 U.S. 579 (1952).
3. Arthur S. Miller, *Presidential Power in a Nutshell* (St. Paul, Minn.: West, 1977), 24.
4. James Pfiffner challenges this viewpoint and maintains that presidents tend to overestimate the opposition they will get from the bureaucracy (James P. Pfiffner, "Political Appointees and Career Executives: The Democracy-Bureaucracy Nexus in the Third Century," *Public Administration Review* [January/February 1987]: 57-65). Pfiffner cites evidence from a recent National Academy of Public Administration study that political appointees perceive career executives as responsive and competent. In addition, Francis

Rourke argues that opposition to presidents is as likely to come from political appointees as from career executives (Francis E. Rourke, "The Presidency and the Bureaucracy," in *The Presidency and the Political System,* ed. Michael Nelson [Washington, D.C.: CQ Press, 1984], 359-360).

5. Joseph A. Califano, Jr., *A Presidential Nation* (New York: Norton, 1975), 23.
6. Thomas E. Cronin, *The State of the Presidency,* 2d ed. (Boston: Little, Brown, 1980), 224-227.
7. Hugh Heclo, *A Government of Strangers* (Washington, D.C.: Brookings, 1977), 7.
8. Ibid.
9. Arthur Maas, *Muddy Waters: The Army Corps of Engineers and the Nation's Rivers* (Cambridge: Harvard University Press, 1951).
10. Richard Rose, *Managing Presidential Objectives* (New York: Free Press, 1976), 160.
11. Francis Rourke, *Bureaucracy, Politics, and Public Policy,* 3d ed. (Boston: Little, Brown, 1984), 32.
12. Rose, *Managing Presidential Objectives,* 13-20.
13. Aaron Wildavsky, *The Politics of the Budgetary Process,* 4th ed. (Boston: Little, Brown, 1984).
14. David A. Stockman, *The Triumph of Politics: Why the Reagan Revolution Failed* (New York: Harper and Row, 1986).
15. Stockman, *The Triumph of Politics,* 274-275, 313, 345-346.
16. Edie N. Goldenberg, "The Permanent Government in an Era of Retrenchment and Redirection," in *The Reagan Presidency and the Governing of America,* ed. Lester M. Salamon and Michael S. Lund (Washington, D.C.: Urban Institute Press, 1984), 390.
17. Heclo, *Government of Strangers.*
18. G. Calvin Mackenzie, *The Politics of Presidential Appointments* (New York: Free Press, 1981).
19. Richard P. Nathan, *The Administrative Presidency* (New York: Wiley, 1983), 74-76.
20. Frederick V. Malek, *Washington's Hidden Tragedy* (New York: Free Press, 1978), 95-117.
21. Ibid., 102.
22. Goldenberg, "The Permanent Government," 381-404.
23. Chester A. Newland, "A Midterm Appraisal—The Reagan Presidency, Limited Government and Political Administration," *Public Administration Review* (January/February 1983): 15-16.
24. Charles H. Levine, "The Federal Government in the Year 2000: Administrative Legacies of the Reagan Years," *Public Administration Review* (May/June 1986): 201-204.
25. Harold Seidman and Robert Gilmour, *Politics, Position, and Power: From the Positive to the Regulatory State,* 4th ed. (New York: Norton, 1986), 85.
26. *Kendall v. United States,* 37 U.S. (12 Pet.) 524 (1838).
27. *Panama Refining Co. v. Ryan,* 293 U.S. 338 (1934); *Schechter Poultry Co. v. United States,* 295 U.S. 495 (1935).
28. Louis Fisher, *Constitutional Conflicts between Congress and the President*

(Princeton: Princeton University Press, 1985), 18.

29. Morris P. Fiorina, *Congress: Keystone of the Washington Establishment* (New Haven: Yale University Press, 1977).
30. Rose, *Managing Presidential Objectives,* 16.
31. Randall B. Ripley and Grace A. Franklin, *Congress, the Bureaucracy, and Public Policy,* 3d ed. (Homewood, Ill.: Dorsey Press, 1984).
32. Rourke, *Bureaucracy, Politics, and Public Policy,* 74.
33. Hugh Heclo, "Issue Networks and the Executive Establishment," in *The New American Political System,* ed. Anthony King (Washington, D.C.: American Enterprise Institute, 1979), 102.
34. Ibid., 116-121.
35. Cronin, *State of the Presidency,* 293.
36. Nelson W. Polsby, "Presidential Cabinet-Making: Lessons for the Political System," *Political Science Quarterly* (Spring 1978): 16.
37. Richard F. Fenno, Jr., *The President's Cabinet* (New York: Vintage Books, 1959), 132.
38. David B. Truman, *The Governmental Process* (New York: Knopf, 1951), 406.
39. Ronald Brownstein and Dick Kirschten, "Cabinet Power," *National Journal,* June 28, 1986, 1582-1589.
40. Cronin, *State of the Presidency,* 270-272.
41. Ibid., 282-285.
42. Joseph A. Califano, *Governing America* (New York: Simon and Schuster, 1981).
43. Brownstein and Kirschten, "Cabinet Power," 1583.
44. Ibid., 1588-1589.
45. George C. Edwards III, *Implementing Public Policy* (Washington, D.C.: CQ Press, 1980).
46. Fisher, *Constitutional Conflicts,* chaps. 2, 3.
47. *Buckley v. Valeo,* 421 U.S. 1 (1976).
48. In 1973 President Nixon named Howard J. Phillips acting director of the Office of Economic Opportunity (OEO), an agency that Nixon planned to dismantle. Phillips began to phase out its programs and withhold funds from them. Sen. Harrison A. Williams (D-N.J.) took legal action to force Nixon either to submit Phillips's name to the Senate for confirmation or to stop dismantling OEO. A U.S. court of appeals ruled that Phillips was illegally holding office and enjoined him from further actions (James P. Pfiffner, *The President, the Budget, and Congress: Impoundment and the 1974 Budget Act* [Boulder: Westview, 1974], 116-117).
49. Perhaps the most notable examples are the Senate's rejection of Admiral Lewis Strauss to be secretary of commerce in 1959 and its refusal to confirm the appointment of Leland Olds to serve a third five-year term as chairperson of the Federal Power Commission in 1949. Strauss had incurred the enmity of several senators during his prior service as chairperson of the Atomic Energy Commission. Olds's rejection symbolized senatorial opposition to the oil and natural gas policies of the Truman administration.
50. *Myers v. United States,* 272 U.S. 52 (1926).
51. *Humphrey's Executor v. United States,* 295 U.S. 602 (1935).

52. Fisher, *Constitutional Conflicts between Congress and the President*, 98.
53. Ibid., 94.
54. In 1953 President Eisenhower removed a Truman appointee from the War Claims Commission to make way for a Republican. The official, Weiner, sued, and the Supreme Court eventually ruled that there was no basis for the removal given the "intrinsic judicial character" of the agency (*Weiner v. United States*, 357 U.S. 349 [1958]). Eisenhower had abolished the agency in 1954, however, using his reorganization authority (Kallenbach, *The American Chief Executive*, 404).
55. *J. W. Hampton and Co. v. United States*, 276 U.S. 394 (1928).
56. *Amalgamated Meat Cutters v. Connally*, 337 F. Supp. 737 (1971).
57. George C. Eads and Michael Fix, *Relief or Reform: Reagan's Regulatory Dilemma* (Washington, D.C.: Urban Institute Press, 1984).
58. *Hirabayashi v. United States*, 320 U.S. 581 (1943); *Korematsu v. United States*, 323 U.S. 214 (1944).
59. *Youngstown Sheet and Tube Co. v. Sawyer*, 343 U.S. 579 (1952).
60. Edward S. Corwin, *The President: Office and Powers*, 4th ed. (New York: New York University Press, 1957), 130.
61. Lee H. Watson, "Congress Steps Out: A Look at Congressional Control of the Executive," *California Law Review* (1975): 990.
62. *Immigration and Naturalization Service v. Chadha*, 462 U.S. 919 (1983).
63. Joseph Cooper, "Postscript on the Congressional Veto," *Political Science Quarterly* (Fall 1983): 427-430; Barbara Hinkson Craig, *The Legislative Veto: Congressional Control of Regulation* (Boulder: Westview, 1983), 139-150; Fisher, *Constitutional Conflicts*, 181-183.
64. Louis Fisher, "Judicial Misjudgments about the Lawmaking Process: The Legislative Veto Case," *Public Administration Review* (November/December 1985): 708-709.
65. Ibid., 709-710.
66. Elder Witt, "High Court to Clarify Sweep of Its Legislative Veto Ruling," *Congressional Quarterly Weekly Report*, December 6, 1986, 3025-3026.
67. Fisher, "Judicial Misjudgments," 711.
68. Richard M. Pious, *The American Presidency* (New York: Basic Books, 1979), 256-257.
69. Allen Schick, "The Road to PPB: The Stages of Budget Reform," *Public Administration Review* (December 1966): 243-258.
70. Wildavsky, *The Politics of the Budgetary Process*, chap. 6.
71. Allen Schick, "Macro-Budgetary Adaptations to Fiscal Stress in Industrialized Democracies," *Public Administration Review* (March/April 1986): 129.
72. Ibid., 130.
73. Louis Fisher, *Presidential Spending Power* (Princeton: Princeton University Press, 1979), chap. 4.
74. Ibid., 148.
75. Vivian Vale, "The Obligation to Spend: Presidential Impoundment of Congressional Appropriations," *Political Studies* (1977): 508-532.
76. Fisher, *Constitutional Conflicts*, 236.
77. Pfiffner, *President, Budget, and Congress*, 40-44.

78. Jonathan Rauch, "Power of the Purse," *National Journal*, May 24, 1986, 1261.
79. Stephen Hess, *Organizing the Presidency* (Washington, D.C.: Brookings, 1976), 8.
80. Colin Campbell, *Managing the Presidency: Carter, Reagan, and the Search for Executive Harmony* (Pittsburgh: University of Pittsburgh Press, 1986), 44-45.
81. Ibid., 83-84.
82. James P. Pfiffner, "White House Staff versus the Cabinet: Centripetal and Centrifugal Roles," *Presidential Studies Quarterly* (Fall 1986): 671.
83. Campbell, *Managing the Presidency*, 94-95.
84. Ibid., 112.
85. Peri E. Arnold, "Executive Reorganization and Administrative Theory: The Origin of the Managerial Presidency" (Paper presented at the annual meeting of the American Political Science Association, Washington, September 1986).
86. John R. Dempsey, "Carter Reorganization: A Midterm Appraisal," *Public Administration Review* (January/February 1979): 74-78; John R. Plumlee, "Carter's Major Structural Reorganizations: A Longitudinal Analysis" (Paper delivered at the annual meeting of the Midwest Political Science Association, Chicago, April 1979); Seidman and Gilmour, *Politics, Positions, and Power*, 48; Rochelle L. Stanfield, "At Least It Didn't Cost Much," *National Journal*, June 2, 1979, 917.
87. Herbert Kaufman, "Reflections on Administrative Reorganization," in *Setting National Priorities: The 1978 Budget*, ed. Joseph A. Pechman (Washington, D.C.: Brookings, 1977), 403.
88. Dempsey, "Carter Reorganization," 75.
89. Seidman and Gilmour, *Politics, Position, and Power*, 116.
90. Aaron Wildavsky, *Speaking Truth to Power* (Boston: Little, Brown, 1979), 120.
91. Malek, *Washington's Hidden Tragedy*, 129.
92. Wildavsky, *Speaking Truth to Power*, 129.
93. Rose, *Managing Presidential Objectives*, chap. 6.
94. Allen Schick, "The Budget as an Instrument of Presidential Policy," in *The Reagan Presidency and the Governing of America*, ed. Salamon and Lund, 113.
95. Lester M. Salamon and Alan J. Abramson, "Governance: The Politics of Retrenchment," in *The Reagan Record*, ed. John L. Palmer and Isabell V. Sawhill (Cambridge, Mass.: Ballinger, 1984), 97.

Selected Readings

Berman, Larry. *The Office of Management and Budget and the Presidency, 1921-1979*. Princeton: Princeton University Press, 1979.

Campbell, Colin. *Managing the Presidency: Carter, Reagan, and the Search for Executive Harmony.* Pittsburgh: University of Pittsburgh Press, 1986.

Cronin, Thomas E. *The State of the Presidency.* 2d ed. Boston: Little, Brown, 1980.

Heclo, Hugh. *A Government of Strangers.* Washington, D.C.: Brookings, 1977.

Hess, Stephen. *Organizing the Presidency.* Washington, D.C.: Brookings, 1976.

Lowi, Theodore J. *The End of Liberalism.* 2d ed. New York: Norton, 1979.

McKenzie, G. Calvin. *The Politics of Presidential Appointments.* New York: Free Press, 1981.

Nathan, Richard P. *The Administrative Presidency.* New York: Wiley, 1983.

Redford, Emmette S., and Richard T. McCulley. *White House Operations: The Johnson Presidency.* Austin: University of Texas Press, 1986.

Rourke, Francis E. *Bureaucracy, Politics, and Public Policy.* 3d ed. Boston: Little, Brown, 1984.

Salamon, Lester M., and Michael S. Lund, eds. *The Reagan Presidency and the Governing of America.* Washington, D.C.: Urban Institute Press, 1984.

Seidman, Harold, and Robert S. Gilmour. *Politics, Position, and Power: From the Positive to the Regulatory State.* New York: Oxford University Press, 1986.

President Ronald Reagan escorts Sandra Day O'Connor through the White House Rose Garden. Justice O'Connor was Reagan's first appointee to the Supreme Court and the first woman ever appointed associate justice.

CHAPTER EIGHT

Judicial Politics

The Founders clearly expected the executive and legislative branches to be in perennial conflict with each other, and they deliberately constructed the U.S. constitutional system to accomplish that result; as James Madison explained in *Federalist* 51, "Ambition must be made to counteract ambition." [1] Their intentions toward the relationship between the executive and judicial arms of the government were, however, quite different. Neither John Locke nor Montesquieu, the two political philosophers from whom the Founders drew their ideas on the separation of powers, provided for a separate judicial branch of government. Rather, both considered the power to decide disputes and to enforce the law to be a function of the executive arm of the government. Although the Founders did create a distinct judicial branch, they nonetheless considered its principal function to be similar to that of the executive: both would expound and enforce the law (rather than enact it, as the legislature would). As Alexander Hamilton explained in *Federalist* 78, the major differences between judicial and executive powers were how they would be exercised: the former would depend on "judgment," the latter on "force" or "will." [2]

The Founders also based their expectations about the affinity of the executive and judicial branches on other considerations besides the similarity of the functions they were to perform. As Robert Scigliano points out, they deliberately increased the powers of both branches at the expense of the Congress because they feared that the latter would dominate the political system as it had done under the Articles of Confederation. [3] They therefore granted broad authority to both the executive and the judiciary. Article II of the Constitution states that "the executive power shall be vested in the President of the United States," and Article IV stipulates that "the judicial power of the United States shall be vested in one Supreme Court and in such inferior courts as the Congress may from time to time ordain and establish." In contrast, Article I begins, "All legislative powers *herein granted* shall be vested in a Congress of the United States" (italics added). As a result, to undertake a particular activity, the first two branches need only claim that it is executive or judicial in nature and that it is not forbidden by the Constitution; however, to justify its passing a law, the Congress must point to a specific power listed in Article I, Section 8, or show that such a law is "necessary and proper" for executing one or more of those specific powers.

The Founders were also concerned with protecting the executive and judicial branches against a too-powerful Congress. At one point they considered joining the president and the Supreme Court in a Council of Revision with a veto power over legislation passed by Congress (and by state legislatures). Ultimately, they abandoned that idea for fear it might interfere with the ability of judges objectively to interpret legislation they had helped to influence and because it might lead the Supreme Court to share too much the views of the executive. However, the Founders did guard against Congress's using its power of the purse to intimidate or punish the two other branches by providing that the president's salary could not be changed during his term and judges' salaries could not be lowered while they were in office.

There is also some indication that the Founders wanted and expected the executive and judicial branches to represent social and economic interests different from those represented by members of the House. Unlike House members, who were directly elected by the people, the president was selected by the electoral college, and he, in turn, nominated the members of the Supreme Court, who were then to be approved by the Senate. (Note that the Founders gave the House of Representatives no role in choosing judges.) In addition, the longer term of the president (four years with the possibility of renewal) and of Supreme Court members (life) would make them less subject to public pressures than were members of the House of Representatives with their two-year terms. And because only a few persons would be chosen for the presidency and the Supreme Court, those positions would be far more prestigious than seats in the lower house of the Congress. This, in turn, would have the effect of attracting abler persons to the presidency and the Supreme Court, and since property ownership was considered reflective of natural ability (John Adams and James Madison agreed on this point), such persons would be of economic substance from the upper social class.

All these considerations lead Scigliano to conclude that the Founders intended that the presidency and the Supreme Court "act, for certain purposes, as an informal and limited alliance against Congress and that they have in fact done so." [4] At the same time, he suggests that the Founders left open another basic question that created a major source of potential conflict between the president and the Supreme Court: who has the final power to interpret the Constitution? If, as Hamilton asserted in *Federalist* 78, the Supreme Court does, then it is in a position to nullify actions of the president that the judges consider to be unconstitutional. If each branch, however, is empowered to interpret the Constitution as far as its own duties are concerned—a position taken by Thomas Jefferson—then the president himself is the judge of the constitutionality of his actions and is not subject to judicial control in that respect. As will be discussed subsequently in this chapter, that issue supposedly was settled in the landmark case of *Marbury v. Madison* in favor of the Supreme Court, but as a practical matter it continues to be an issue in the American political system.[5]

This chapter examines the basic relationship between the president and the federal courts. The first section analyzes the most important influence the president exerts over these courts: his power (with the consent of the Senate) to appoint their members. The chapter next explores other means by which the chief executive affects the business of the courts and, finally, examines the reverse situation: how the federal courts, and the Supreme Court in particular, influence the actions of the president.

Presidential Appointment of Federal Judges

The Constitution specifically provides for "one Supreme Court" and "such inferior courts as the Congress may from time to time ordain and establish" (Article III, Section 1). By legislation enacted over the years, Congress has established two types of "inferior" federal courts. The first is the district courts, trial bodies in which federal cases are first heard. The other is the U.S. courts of appeals, sometimes also referred to as "circuit courts," which serve as major appellate tribunals, reviewing principally the civil and criminal decisions in cases initially heard in federal district courts as well as the orders and decisions of federal administrative units, particularly the independent regulatory agencies.[6] Similarly, the Constitution mentions only the method of appointment of Supreme Court judges: they are to be chosen by the president with the advice and consent of the Senate. Congress provides, however, for the same process to be used for staffing the lower federal courts, so the president and the Senate are partners in the appointment process for all federal judges.

Although the formal process for selecting all federal judges is the same—presidential nomination and ultimate appointment with the consent of the Senate—the president's role in federal judicial appointments varies considerably, depending upon the court involved. The following discussion analyzes first the appointments to the two lower federal courts and then the selection of justices to the nation's highest tribunal, the Supreme Court.

Selection of Lower Court Judges

Although the president makes the formal nomination of persons for appointment to the lower federal courts, in fact he usually delegates the responsibility to others. As Harold Chase explains, "If a president takes seriously his legal responsibilities for nominating and appointing federal judges, the search for and screening of candidates requires more time than he can personally give to it." [7] This task typically is assigned to the attorney general, who, in turn, often delegates it to the deputy attorney general and then usually advises the deputy how to proceed. Moreover, if a particular recommendation may cause difficulty with an important senator or with majority party leaders, the president himself may be consulted on the matter.

The executive branch recruitment and screening process for judicial candidates entails several considerations. Justice Department officials frequently turn to members of their own department who they believe have a special knowledge about lawyers in their own states. They also have the Federal Bureau of Investigation check into the professional standing and integrity of prospective candidates. As discussed later in this section, sitting federal judges are often asked for their opinion about candidates, and members of the Standing Committee on Federal Judiciary of the American Bar Association (ABA) also usually are requested to investigate the qualifications of prospective nominees and to make recommendations regarding them.

Just as the attorney general plays a major role in choosing lower federal judges, so do senators of the president's party from the state in which the nominee is to serve (all states have at least one federal district court), or, for courts of appeals judges, the state of his or her residence. As Joseph Harris notes, since the early days of George Washington's administration, an informal rule of "senatorial courtesy" has applied whereby members of the Senate generally will refuse to confirm persons to federal positions who do not have the support of the appropriate senator or senators.[8] (Until 1934 it was sufficient to invoke the rule that the nominee be declared "personally obnoxious" to the senator, but since then the Senate has required that reasons be given for opposition.) Moreover, beginning about 1954, the Senate Judiciary Committee began the practice of circulating a "blue slip" to each senator from the state in which the prospective judge was to serve—including those *not* from the president's party—so they could register their objection to the nominee and delay the nomination by refusing to return the slip to the committee.[9] This combination of informal senatorial practices places senators from the state in which a judge is to serve in a powerful position to influence judicial appointments.

Thus, both the attorney general and a particular senator's help determine who will be chosen. In some instances one party will defer to the other to develop the initial list of prospective nominees. That has been the general practice for most presidential administrations, although the Kennedy administration chose to play a major role in actively recruiting persons for the lower federal bench. Although most senators recruit candidates of their own for the federal courts, some, such as former senators Frank Lausche (D-Ohio) and Harry F. Byrd (D-Va.), have taken the position that it is the president's constitutional job to choose federal judges and that asking him to appoint their candidates would be akin to asking favors for themselves.[10]

If both the attorney general and the concerned senator persist in pushing their own candidates for the federal bench, a stalemate may occur. The senator usually can block the president's nominee by invoking either the senatorial courtesy or blue-slip custom of the upper chamber. The attorney general can advise the president not to fill the vacancy, thereby putting pressure on the senator to do something about the situation or face the problem of a backlog of federal cases in his or her home state. Or the president can wait until the end of the session and make a recess appointment, which does not require immediate senatorial confirmation. Moreover, even though Senate approval for the temporarily appointed judge is required in the next session of Congress, the president may benefit from the fact that in the meantime his person has been a sitting judge, and a good performance may deter the Senate from refusing the confirmation.

What typically occurs with lower federal court appointments is that one party is given the major role in initially recruiting persons for the bench, but the other retains a veto power over those he or she finds unacceptable for the position. On federal district court appointments, the attorney general (and thus the president) usually defers to the wishes of the senator from the state concerned. Few chief executives are willing to risk the loss of a senator's political support over a district court judgeship, since the work of such a tribunal is seldom crucial to his own political goals or programs.

The president is generally more influential in the selection of judges to the U.S. courts of appeals. He takes greater personal interest in them than in district court appointments for two reasons. First, the courts of appeals handle matters more important to him. Their review of actions of the independent regulatory commissions, for example, can affect his overall economic program. Second, courts of appeals judgeships are less numerous and more prestigious and therefore invite the interest of his major political supporters. Furthermore, senators are in a weaker bargaining position on appointments to the courts of appeals. Since these courts encompass several states, the Senate does not accord any senator from a particular state the privilege to name an appointee. By political custom these judgeships are apportioned among the various states involved, but the president and his advisers determine how and in what sequence to do so. As a result, the president's advisers take the initiative in recruiting persons to the U.S. courts of appeals, and the senator from the state in which a candidate resides retains the right to veto the nomination, providing the lawmaker can persuade the rest of the Senate that the prospective judge truly is objectionable.

Although the attorney general and individual senators are chiefly responsible for appointments to the lower federal courts, many other persons and groups also are involved in the selection process. Although, ideally, the "post should seek the person," in reality candidates who aspire to a federal judgeship must take actions to advance their own cause. As Joel Grossman states, "The candidate who does not make at least a minimum effort in his own behalf is likely to remain a private citizen." [11] Candidates must make it clear to persons involved in the appointment process that they desire the position, either by actively seeking it themselves or by having others campaign on their behalf. Candidates help their cause by having been active in past political campaigns, especially those of the president or of the appropriate senator.

Party leaders also are frequently influential in appointments to the lower federal courts. Harold Chase reports that a Justice Department official in a Democratic administration was emphatic that in the making of judicial appointments to the district courts in Illinois the late mayor Richard Daley of Chicago "had to have a seat at the conference table." [12] State party leaders also may become involved if there are no senators in a state from the president's political party or if both senators are from his party but they disagree over the appointment. National political leaders also may become intermediaries in the selection process: President John F. Kennedy used Republican minority leader Everett Dirksen as a liaison between the White House and Republican senators for appointments to the federal bench of persons from the opposition party.

Sitting federal judges often become involved in federal judicial appointments. This most often occurs when they are asked their opinion about a prospective candidate by the attorney general or the American Bar Association committee. At times, however, judges take the initiative either to advance a candidate of their own or to try to prevent the appointment of someone they feel will not make a good judge. Most often the judges involved are those who sit on a federal district court or court of appeals. Supreme Court justices also may interpose themselves into the process for choosing lower federal court judges. Most notorious in that respect was William Howard Taft, who took a keen interest in appointments to those courts while he served as chief justice.[13]

Another participant in the selection process for judges of lower federal courts is the Standing Committee on Federal Judiciary of the American Bar Association. First established in 1946 with the goal of promoting professionally qualified persons for the federal bench, the group had little success in influencing judicial appointments during the administration of Harry S Truman. When Dwight D. Eisenhower came into office in 1953, however, his administration agreed to an arrangement whereby the Department of Justice would ask the committee to evaluate nominees to the federal bench in return for the committee's agreement to stop recommending its own candidates for the federal courts. The committee was most influential during the last two years of the Eisenhower administration, when no one was nominated for a federal judgeship without the committee's approval. As Grossman states, "It was during this period that the committee's right to be consulted on each prospective nomination grew into a virtual veto power." [14]

The committee has continued to be important in federal judicial selection, but it has never regained the virtual veto power it had from 1958 to 1961. Neither the administration of John F. Kennedy nor of Lyndon B. Johnson was as deferential to the committee as the Eisenhower one had been.

Initially, it was thought that Richard Nixon's Justice Department would restore the committee's veto power over nominations to the federal courts, but, as discussed in the following section, serious disagreements between the committee and the Nixon administration over the qualifications of some of his nominees for the Supreme Court damaged the relationship. Alan Neff's assessment of the recent influence of the committee is that it has been "somewhere below the level it reached during the later Eisenhower years and above that of the Nixon years." [15]

Jimmy Carter's administration introduced several new elements into the selection of lower federal court judges. During his campaign for the presidency in June 1976, Carter announced that if elected he would choose all federal judges strictly on the basis of professional competence rather than for personal or political loyalty to him or as a reward for assistance in his campaign. In December of that year the president-elect and his future attorney general, Griffin Bell (himself a former federal court of appeals judge), met with Democratic senator James Eastland of Mississippi, who chaired the Senate Judiciary Committee. Out of that meeting came an agreement that the president would acquire control over nominations for the courts of appeals and, in return, would defer to the right of senators to nominate persons for the federal district courts.

In February 1977 President Carter issued an executive order creating the United States Circuit Judge Nominating Commission; the Department of Justice subsequently issued supplemental instructions to guide its operation. The entire commission, whose members were to be appointed by the president, were divided into thirteen panels, two for the very large fifth and ninth circuits and one for each of the other federal circuits. Each panel had eleven members, including lawyers and laypersons as well as women and minorities, and at least one resident from each state within the circuit. When a vacancy occurred because of the retirement of a sitting judge or the creation of a new judgeship, the appropriate panel was convened to interview potential nominees, and within sixty days it recommended to the president the names of three to five persons for the court of appeals judgeship. President Carter then selected his nominee from that list.

Meanwhile, other developments brought major changes in the selection of federal district judges as well. When Congress passed the 1978 Omnibus Judgeship Act, which created 35 additional circuit judgeships and 117 new district ones, at the insistence of the House of Representatives language was added to the act granting to the president the right to promulgate standards for judicial selection and recommending that he "give due consideration to qualified individuals regardless of race, color, sex, religion, or national origin." Thus, the same emphasis on merit selection and the greater representation of women and minorities that Carter advocated in the selection of courts of appeals judges was extended to the federal district courts. Carter subsequently issued an executive order embodying those principles, and senators from some thirty states voluntarily adopted the use of nominating commissions to recommend candidates for federal district courts.

Senators using such commissions differed on the extent to which they were willing to relinquish their influence over federal district judgeships. Some chose all the commissioners themselves; others permitted members of the House of Representatives from their state as well as state bar associations to name some of the commissioners. Some senators instructed the commissions to transmit their recommendations for district judges directly to the Justice Department and the president without the senator's endorsement; others asked that the commissioners send them the list of recommended persons, and they then narrowed the field to the exact number of judicial vacancies and submitted only those names to President Carter.

One other development during the Carter administration affected the selection of lower court judges: the Senate Judiciary Committee, which came under the chairmanship of Sen. Edward M. Kennedy (D-Mass.) in 1979, changed some of its traditional practices. The senator announced that the committee would no longer allow individual senators to use the blue slip procedure to veto unilaterally particular nominees but would reserve the right to review independently and overrule a senator's failure to return a slip. Moreover, in 1980 the committee refused to confirm Charles Winberry as a federal district judge in North Carolina, despite his having the endorsement of Democratic senator Robert Morgan of that state. (Committee members were not satisfied with Winberry's answers to charges that he acted improperly as counsel in a criminal case and served as a conduit for bribery of a federal judge.) Neff reports that this was the first formal rejection of a district court nominee by the Judiciary Committee in forty-two years.[16]

Experiences during the Carter administration therefore greatly changed the process by which lower court judges are chosen. Individual senators became less influential while the president's role increased. Other persons and groups became significantly involved in federal judicial selection for the first time. Included were members of the House of Representatives and officials of state bar associations, who were permitted by senators in some states to name nominating commissioners for the federal district courts. Moreover, lay-persons, women, and minorities serving on nominating commissions became influential in the selection of federal judges. Finally, as Neff points out, the ABA's Standing Committee on Federal Judiciary lost its exclusive position to speak for the legal community on judicial selection; the Justice Department turned instead to the National Bar Association, a predominantly black lawyers' organization, and the Federation of Women Lawyers to evaluate candidates' commitment to equal justice and to determine whether they held biases against any groups because of race, religion, or sex.[17]

Major changes in the nomination of lower federal court judges also occurred in Ronald Reagan's administration. Sheldon Goldman notes that in Reagan's first term, responsibility in the Justice Department for suggesting prospective judges included not only the attorney general and deputy attorney general but also the assistant attorney general for legal policy and the special counsel for judicial selection.[18] In addition, five persons from the Reagan White House—Chief of Staff James Baker, presidential counselor Edwin Meese, presidential counsel Fred Fielding, and presidential assistants for personnel and for legislative affairs—were, along with four representatives from the Justice Department, made members of a newly created President's Committee on Federal Judicial Selection. The committee did not merely react to the Justice Department's recommendations on prospective judges; it also proposed candidates. Moreover, the president's personnel office conducted investigations of prospective nominees independently of the Justice Department's investigations. Goldman concludes that when Meese eventually became attorney general, "the cooptation of judicial selection by the Reagan White House" was "completed." [19]

As Goldman indicates, the Reagan administration introduced other changes in the nomination of lower federal court judges. His was the first Republican administration in thirty years in which the ABA's Standing Committee on Federal Judiciary was not actively used and consulted in the prenomination stage of judicial selection. The president also abolished the selection commission for appellate judges created by former president Carter, and, as Goldman states, in the process abandoned "the most potentially effective mechanism for expanding the net of possible candidates to include women and racial minorities." [20] Lawrence Baum also suggests that the Carter administration sought to appoint liberals to the lower courts, but in the Reagan administration conservatism on issues such as abortion became an important criterion.[21] Finally, as Robert Carp and Ronald Stidham note, after Republican senator Strom Thurmond of South Carolina became chairperson of the Senate Judiciary Committee in 1981, the reforms initiated by Democratic senator Edward Kennedy were abandoned for the more "traditional" methods of selecting federal judges.[22]

Despite the differences in their appointments of lower federal court judges, Carter and Reagan shared one great advantage: the opportunity to make a large number of appointments to the lower courts. In his four years in office, Carter named 258 persons to these courts; by the end of his sixth year in office, Reagan had chosen some 300. Goldman points out that by the end of his second term, President Reagan will have the opportunity to name a majority of the lower federal judiciary in active service.[23]

Characteristics of Lower Court Judges

All presidents tend to appoint to the lower federal courts persons who have certain qualities in common. One is membership in the legal profession. Although this is not a legal requirement, it is an informal qualification: only lawyers have been appointed to federal judgeships. Moreover, in keeping with the contemporary preparation of lawyers, virtually every judge appointed to the federal bench since the end of World War II has been a graduate of a law school (as contrasted to having served an apprenticeship in a law office, the typical method of studying law in the past). A second characteristic is that most have been active in political party affairs (which is what calls them to the attention of senators and attorneys general) and have held public office, most often one associated with the courts, such as city, county, or state prosecutor, district attorney, or U.S. attorney. Another common trait is that many have held judicial positions: federal district judges quite often have been state judges, and those who sit on the courts of appeals frequently come to that bench from a federal district court.

The president, however, does make a difference in the types of lawyers who are appointed to the lower federal courts. Table 8-1, based upon information developed by Goldman, compares the persons appointed to the federal district courts by Reagan during his first term in office with those chosen by Carter, Ford, Nixon, and Johnson. The differences among Reagan's and Carter's appointees, in addition to party affiliation, are particularly pronounced in their educational and racial backgrounds. The Reagan appointees were more likely to have attended private rather than public undergraduate and law schools than were Carter appointees; about 14 percent of Carter's appointees were blacks, but less than 1 percent of Reagan's were. Thus, as Goldman suggests, differences in the backgrounds of federal district judges mirror to some degree disparities in typical Republican and Democratic voters.[24]

In several respects, however, Reagan and Carter appointees had more in common with each other than they did with appointees of the three previous presidents, Republicans Ford and Nixon and Democrat Johnson. Judges appointed by Reagan and Carter were more likely to have come from another judicial position to a federal district judgeship and to have had more judicial than prosecutory experience than were appointees of Ford, Nixon, and Johnson. (Goldman suggests that a person's judicial position provides a record for determining his or her professional quality and judicial philosophy, matters in which both recent presidents appeared to be particularly interested.) Appointees of these two presidents were also more likely to have been active in their respective parties than were their predecessors. Reagan and Carter also appointed more women. Reagan named a greater percentage of Catholics to the federal district bench than the four other presidents, even slightly more than Johnson; these appointments may reflect Reagan's decision to provide major representation on the district bench of a religious group that has traditionally been Democratic but that voted in record numbers for him. He may also have been influenced by the fact that Catholic doctrine on abortion parallels his own strong views on the subject.

Table 8-2, also based on information provided by Goldman, shows similar comparisons of the appointees to the federal courts of appeals. The differences among the Reagan and Carter judges are again most pronounced in their party, educational, and racial backgrounds. Reagan appointed only Republicans to the appeals courts whereas Carter chose primarily Democrats but some Republicans and independents as well. Reagan's appointees were more likely to have attended an Ivy League undergraduate school but less likely to have gone to an Ivy League law school than were judges chosen by Carter. (More Reagan judges went to other private law schools, however, than did those appointed by Carter.) Reagan chose only one black to the courts of appeals compared with Carter's appointment of nine black judges. Moreover, unlike the situation for district judges, women fared far less well with Reagan than they did with Carter: Reagan chose only one woman as a court of appeals judge; Carter appointed eleven.[25]

Table 8-2 also shows other distinct characteristics of the judges appointed by Reagan. More of them than previous judges had been law professors, a tendency Goldman attributes to the fact that their legal publications enabled the Reagan administration to evaluate their philosophy on the role of the courts in the U.S. political system. The Reagan appointees were also more likely than their predecessors to have had judicial rather than prosecutory experience, which also bore on the administration's desire to analyze the judicial philosophy revealed in their decisions. Finally, the Reagan administration showed the same inclination to appoint a significant number of Catholics to the courts of appeals as it had demonstrated in choosing judges for the district courts.

Effects of Lower Court Appointments

The appointment process and background characteristics of lower federal court judges reflect important political considerations. Presidents are in a position to reward persons who have been active in their political campaigns or in those of important senators. Federal judgeships also present the opportunity for a president to make appointments that are symbolic for religious, racial, or women's groups that want to have more of their members in prestigious positions on the bench. These considerations may, in turn, help to win the loyalty of such groups to the president and to his political party. Thus, judicial appointments, like those to executive posts, are an important form of political patronage.

The question remains, however, whether appointments to lower federal courts affect public issues that come before those courts, that is, whether there are consequences for *policy* as well as personnel in such appointments. One study of decisions made by federal district court judges appointed by eleven presidents from Woodrow Wilson through Gerald Ford found major differences among the judges in the extent to which they rendered "liberal" as contrasted to "conservative" decisions.[26] ("Liberal" decisions were defined as those extending civil rights and civil liberties, upholding legislation that benefits working people and economic underdogs, or favoring motions made in behalf of defendants in criminal cases.) Generally speaking, federal district

Table 8-1 Characteristics of Appointees to District Courts, of Reagan, Carter, Ford, Nixon, and Johnson (Percent)

Characteristic	Reagan appointees[a]	Carter appointees	Ford appointees	Nixon appointees	Johnson appointees
Occupation					
Politics/government	7.8	4.2	21.2	10.6	21.3
Judiciary	40.3	44.6	34.6	28.5	31.1
Large law firm	11.6	14.0	9.7	11.3	2.4
Moderate size firm	25.6	19.8	25.0	27.9	18.9
Solo or small firm	10.8	13.9	9.6	19.0	23.0
Professor of law	2.3	3.0	—	2.8	3.3
Other	1.6	0.5	—	—	—
Undergraduate education					
Public-supported	34.1	57.4	48.1	41.3	38.5
Private (not Ivy League)	49.6	32.7	34.6	38.5	31.1
Ivy League	16.3	9.9	17.3	19.6	16.4
None indicated	—	—	—	0.6	13.9
Law school education					
Public-supported	44.2	50.5	44.2	41.9	40.0
Private (not Ivy League)	47.3	32.2	38.5	36.9	32.5
Ivy League	8.5	17.3	17.3	21.2	27.5
Experience					
Judicial	50.4	54.5	42.3	35.2	34.4
Prosecutory	43.4	38.6	50.0	41.9	45.9
Neither	28.7	28.2	30.8	36.3	33.6

Party					
Democrat	95.0	6.7	8.3	82.1	—
Republican	5.0	93.3	91.7	7.1	100.0
Independent	—	—	—	10.7	—
Past party activism	57.5	60.0	58.3	73.2	58.1
Religious origin or affiliation					
Protestant	60.0	75.6	58.3	60.7	67.7
Catholic	25.0	15.6	33.3	23.2	22.6
Jewish	15.0	8.9	8.3	16.1	9.7
Ethnicity or race					
White	95.0	97.8	100.0	78.6	93.5
Black	5.0	—	—	16.1	3.2
Hispanic	—	2.2	—	3.6	3.2
Asian	—	—	—	1.8	—
Sex					
Male	97.5	100.0	100.0	80.4	96.8
Female	2.5	—	—	19.6	3.2
ABA ratings					
Exceptionally well qualified	27.5	15.6	16.7	16.1	22.6
Well qualified	47.5	57.8	41.7	58.9	41.9
Qualified	20.0	26.7	33.3	25.0	35.5
Not qualified	2.5	—	8.3	—	—
No report requested	2.5	—	—	—	—
Total number of appointees	40	45	12	56	31

Source: Sheldon Goldman, "Reaganizing the Judiciary: The First Term Appointments," *Judicature* (April-May 1985): 324-325.
Note: Dash (—) indicates none.
a Data are for Reagan's first-term appointees.

Table 8-2 Characteristics of Appointees to Courts of Appeals, of Reagan, Carter, Ford, Nixon, and Johnson (Percent)

Characteristic	Reagan appointees[a]	Carter appointees	Ford appointees	Nixon appointees	Johnson appointees
Occupation					
Politics/government	3.2	5.4	8.3	4.4	10.0
Judiciary	61.3	46.4	75.0	53.3	57.5
Large law firm	9.6	10.8	8.3	4.4	5.0
Moderate size firm	9.6	16.1	8.3	22.2	17.5
Solo or small firm	—	5.4	—	6.7	7.5
Professor of law	16.1	14.3	—	2.2	2.5
Other	—	1.8	—	6.7	—
Undergraduate education					
Public-supported	29.0	30.4	50.0	40.0	32.5
Private (not Ivy League)	45.2	50.0	41.7	35.6	40.0
Ivy League	25.8	19.6	8.3	20.0	17.5
None indicated	—	—	—	4.4	10.0
Law school education					
Public-supported	35.5	39.3	50.0	37.8	40.0
Private (not Ivy League)	48.4	19.6	25.0	26.7	32.5
Ivy League	16.1	41.1	25.0	35.6	27.5
Experience					
Judicial	70.9	53.6	75.0	57.8	65.0
Prosecutory	19.3	32.1	25.0	46.7	47.5
Neither	25.8	37.5	25.0	17.8	20.0

Party					
Democrat	3.1	92.6	21.2	7.3	94.3
Republican	96.9	4.9	78.8	92.7	5.7
Independent	—	2.5	—	—	—
Past party activism	61.2	60.9	50.0	48.6	49.2
Religious origin or affiliation					
Protestant	61.2	60.4	73.1	73.2	58.2
Catholic	31.8	27.7	17.3	18.4	31.1
Jewish	6.9	11.9	9.6	8.4	10.7
Ethnicity or race					
White	93.0	78.7	88.5	95.5	93.4
Black	0.8	13.9	5.8	3.4	4.1
Hispanic	5.4	6.9	1.9	1.1	2.5
Asian	0.8	0.5	3.9	—	—
Sex					
Male	90.7	85.6	98.1	99.4	98.4
Female	9.3	14.4	1.9	0.6	1.6
ABA ratings					
Exceptionally well qualified	6.9	4.0	—	5.0	7.4
Well qualified	43.4	47.0	46.1	40.2	40.9
Qualified	49.6	47.5	53.8	54.8	49.2
Not qualified	—	1.5	—	—	2.5
Total number of appointees	129	202	52	179	122

Source: Sheldon Goldman, "Reaganizing the Judiciary: The First Term Appointments," *Judicature* (April-May, 1985): 318-319.

Note: Dash (—) indicates none.

[a] Data are for Reagan's first-term appointees.

judges appointed by Democratic presidents were more likely to render liberal decisions than were district judges appointed by Republican presidents. (Wilson's and Johnson's appointees were the most liberal; Eisenhower's and Nixon's, the most conservative.)

In a similar way, Goldman analyzed decisions of the federal courts of appeals to determine whether there was any association between the backgrounds of the judges and the way they voted on the issues that came before their courts. His first study, which covered the period from 1961 to 1964, showed only one clear pattern: Democratic judges were more likely to vote on the liberal side on cases involving economic issues than were their Republican colleagues.[27] (By "liberal," Goldman means the "underdog" in such cases: labor unions in disputes with management, insured persons against insurance companies, tenants against landlords, debtors against creditors, injured employees against their companies, and the like.) There were no significant cleavages between the judges on the basis of their religious background. A subsequent study by Goldman, covering cases decided by the federal courts of appeals from 1965 to 1971, confirmed the general finding of the earlier study that Democratic judges tended to be more partial to economic underdogs than were Republican judges.[28] In addition, this study revealed an association not shown in the previous one: Catholic judges were somewhat more likely to vote with the liberal side on economic issues than were Protestant judges. A more recent study by Jon Gottschall of voting by courts of appeals judges from July 1, 1983, to December 31, 1984, determined that judges appointed by Democratic presidents Carter, Johnson, and Kennedy were much more likely to vote on the liberal side of issues than were those chosen by Republican presidents Reagan, Ford, and Nixon.[29]

Thus, presidential appointments to the lower federal courts do affect policy. In recent years Democratic presidents have tended to take liberal positions on issues; Republican presidents, conservative positions. When presidents appoint judges from their own political party, the rulings of such judges usually are consistent with the president's philosophy.

As the next section indicates, the politics of the appointment and confirmation of Supreme Court justices is quite different from that of lower federal court judges. Although the individuals and groups involved in choosing both kinds of judges are essentially the same, their relative influence in the two selection processes is not the same.

Selection of Supreme Court Justices

The president clearly dominates the process of selecting members of the Supreme Court. He is vitally interested in the decisions reached by that tribunal since they affect his programs, the operation of the entire political system, and the functioning of U.S. society in general. Because a Supreme Court judgeship is so prestigious, few, if any, lawyers are inclined to turn down the post. Thus, the chief executive has a keen interest in who sits on the

Court and a relatively free hand in choosing its members.

As with lower federal court judges, the attorney general assists the president in identifying and screening potential candidates for the nation's highest court. Because vacancies for the Supreme Court occur so infrequently (one every two years, on average), the president can concentrate his efforts on the appointment in a way that simply is not possible for the numerous appointments made in the federal district and circuit courts. Scigliano estimates that as of mid-1970, presidents had known personally 60 percent of the 134 nominees for the High Court.[30] In some instances, presidents have had close personal relationships with their appointees. Frederick M. Vinson, an old friend of President Truman's, was serving as secretary of the treasury at the time of his appointment. Byron R. White had chaired a national citizens' committee for the election of John Kennedy in 1960. Thurgood Marshall had served as solicitor general for Lyndon Johnson before Johnson appointed him to the Court.

Not all presidents take a vital interest in selecting personal acquaintances for the Court. In such instances it is the attorney general who plays the major role in an appointment, which is ultimately approved by the president. Attorney General Edward Levi, who served in the Ford administration, was the key person in the selection of John Paul Stevens, who had been a colleague of Levi's on the faculty of the University of Chicago Law School. William French Smith took the lead in recruiting Sandra Day O'Connor, President Reagan's first appointee to the Supreme Court.

Individual senators do not play as important a role in the selection of Supreme Court justices as they do for persons chosen to the lower federal courts (especially the district courts). The principal reason for the distinction is that the High Court's geographical jurisdiction encompasses the entire nation, so no senator or group of senators can claim that the appointment is within his or her special province.[31] Presidents will eventually obtain the blessing of the senators of their own party from the state of residence of the nominee (as Reagan did from Republican senator Barry Goldwater for the appointment of O'Connor, both from Arizona), but senators generally are presented with a fait accompli rather than being involved in the recruitment process. A lawmaker would think long and hard about trying to prevent a constituent from having the honor of sitting on the nation's highest tribunal, especially knowing that in the face of opposition the president could then turn to a citizen of another state for the appointment.

Two other groups that play a much smaller role in the selection of Supreme Court justices than in the selection of members of the lower federal courts are candidates and party leaders. The adage "The post should seek the person" is more applicable for positions on the nation's highest tribunal, so lawyers usually do not actively promote their own candidacy.[32] Also, because appointments to the Supreme Court are considered to be above partisan politics, persons such as the national party chairperson do not influence appointments to the same extent as state party leaders influence appointments to the lower federal courts, especially at the district level.

Supreme Court justices themselves are more influential in selecting their colleagues than are their counterparts in lower federal courts. Henry Abraham and Bruce Murphy determined that no fewer than 48 of the 101 persons who sat on the High Court as of 1976 attempted to exert influence in behalf of a candidate or a philosophy of judicial selection.[33] Leading the way were William Howard Taft with eighteen attempts (fourteen were successful) and Harlan F. Stone with nine (five were successful). This influence has been exerted both on behalf of proposed candidates (Chief Justice Warren E. Burger suggested the name of Harry A. Blackmun in 1970, and William Rehnquist endorsed Sandra Day O'Connor in 1981)[34] and against them; the justices have been somewhat more successful in the latter than in the former endeavor. Particularly active have been chief justices of the Supreme Court who want to have as colleagues persons who share their own views (as was true of the conservative Taft). Moreover, even if the chief justice does not take the initiative in providing advice to the president on an appointment, the president may well ask for advice, thinking that the justice knows better than anyone else the specific demands of a judgeship on the Court at that particular time and the kind of person who can best handle such demands.

One group that is often consulted in lower federal court appointments but rarely in those for the Supreme Court is the ABA's Standing Committee on Federal Judiciary. Beginning with the appointment of Justice William J. Brennan, Jr., by President Eisenhower in 1956 and continuing until 1970, the committee was asked to evaluate candidates for the Supreme Court but only *after* the appointment had been publicly announced and transmitted to the Senate Judiciary Committee for action. After the difficulties that led to the rejection of nominees Clement Haynsworth, Jr., and G. Harrold Carswell, the Nixon administration decided to allow the ABA committee to screen candidates before their names were submitted to the Senate Judiciary Committee. The arrangement was to be short-lived, however: one of the first actions of the ABA committee when two vacancies occurred in 1971 was to express serious doubts about the capabilities of President Nixon's two top choices, Mildred Lillie, a California appeals court judge, and Herschel Friday, an Arkansas lawyer. This led Attorney General John Mitchell to withdraw the prescreening privilege of the committee. President Ford restored it, and the committee responded by giving his only nominee to the Supreme Court, John Paul Stevens, a high rating. The committee was not consulted, however, before President Reagan appointed Justice O'Connor.

Thus, the process of recruiting justices to the Supreme Court is controlled by the president with the assistance of the attorney general and sitting Supreme Court justices, particularly the chief justice. The president faces one other obstacle, however, which is far more formidable than obstacles to lower court appointments: the nominee must be confirmed by the *entire*

Senate. Operating through the Judiciary Committee, which hears testimony from interested groups and usually questions the nominee on his or her views, the Senate takes seriously its role of consenting to the appointment of a person to the nation's highest court. An indication of just how seriously the Senate takes this responsibility is that about 20 percent of the nominees to the Court have not been confirmed by the Senate, a much higher proportion than for any other federal office.[35]

Certain factors tend to be linked with the Senate's failure to confirm Supreme Court nominees. Rejections are most likely to occur when the Senate is controlled by the political party opposite that of the president.[36] Moreover, rejections are particularly evident in the last year of a president's term because opposition leaders in the Senate want to hold the position vacant in hopes that the new president will be from their own party. This was at least in part the reason for the Senate's refusal to confirm Lyndon Johnson's nomination of Abe Fortas as chief justice when Earl Warren retired in 1968. When Richard Nixon won the presidential election in 1968 and shortly thereafter appointed his own candidate, Republican Warren Burger as chief justice, the Senate approved the choice.

Certain characteristics of the nominees themselves also are associated with the Senate's failure to confirm.[37] One is involvement with controversial issues of public policy, a situation that often stimulates concerned interest groups to oppose the nomination. All four nominees who failed to win confirmation in this century were opposed by interest groups. John P. Parker, a southern court of appeals judge nominated by Herbert Hoover in 1930, fell victim to the combined opposition of the American Federation of Labor and the National Association for the Advancement of Colored People, which considered his rulings as an appeals judge to be anti-labor and racist. Two Nixon nominees, Haynsworth, a federal court of appeals judge from South Carolina, and Carswell, a federal court of appeals judge from Florida, were rejected within a few months of each other in late 1969 and early 1970. Both were opposed by black and liberal interest groups for their rulings on civil rights cases. (Haynsworth was opposed by labor as well.) In turn, Fortas's nomination for chief justice was bitterly attacked by conservative groups because of his liberal decisions in obscenity cases and suits concerning the rights of the accused in criminal proceedings.[38]

In some instances other considerations are involved. Fortas's acceptance of a legal fee from a family foundation and his advising of President Johnson on political matters were considered by some persons to be unethical activities for a justice of the Supreme Court. Similarly, Haynsworth was criticized for ruling on cases in which he had a personal financial interest. Much of the opposition to Carswell from members of the bar, particularly law professors, stemmed from his lack of professional qualifications, indicated by the mediocrity of his decisions.[39]

Characteristics of Supreme Court Justices

The characteristics of Supreme Court justices reflect the informal qualifications that presidents take into account when appointing them. Scigliano places these qualifications into three categories: professional, representational, and doctrinal.[40]

The *professional* qualifications are similar to those described for lower court judges. Although not required to be lawyers, all 103 justices who have served on the Supreme Court have been attorneys. Not only have they been trained as lawyers; their professional lives have been devoted primarily to the practice or teaching of law. Also, like lower court judges, they have held public office, many associated with the courts, such as prosecutor and district attorney (only 1 of the 103 had not served in public office). An analysis of the occupations of Supreme Court justices at the time of their appointment reveals that they have come principally from four types of positions: twenty-two held federal office in the executive branch; twenty-three were judges of a lower federal court; twenty-two were judges of a state court; and eighteen were attorneys in private practice. Elective officials also have served on the nation's highest bench, including eight U.S. senators, four members of the House of Representatives, and three state governors.

Representational qualifications are the aspects of a nominee's background that are thought to make various groups feel that they have a representative on the Supreme Court. The representational qualification most often considered is the partisan affiliation of the justices, most of whom have been from the same political party as the president who appointed them. Of the 103 appointees to the Court, only 13 were not of the same party as the president who named them. Of these 13, 10 were appointed by Republican presidents (3 by Taft alone); only 3 Democratic presidents selected Republicans for the High Court (Wilson appointed Louis D. Brandeis, Franklin Roosevelt elevated Stone to chief justice, and Truman appointed Harold H. Burton).

Presidents have been interested in other representational qualifications also. Early in the nation's history, geography was a major consideration because various states and sections of the country were thought to be entitled to representation on the Court. This factor has not been of consequence in this century, however, except when President Nixon made clear early in his administration his intention to appoint a southerner. (His unsuccessful nominations of Haynsworth and Carswell failed to achieve that result, but he eventually appointed Lewis Powell, a Democrat from Virginia.) More salient in recent years have been qualifications based on religion, race, and sex. At various times persons have held a "Catholic" seat (Justice Brennan) or a Jewish seat (Justice Fortas). In 1967 Lyndon Johnson appointed Thurgood Marshall, the first black on the Court; and Ronald Reagan pledged in his 1980 presidential campaign that, if elected, he would appoint a woman to one of his first vacancies on the Court, a promise he fulfilled by making Sandra Day O'Connor his first appointee.[41]

Doctrinal qualifications refer to the perception by the president that a nominee shares his own political philosophy and approach to public policy issues. A vivid statement of this consideration was contained in a letter Republican president Theodore Roosevelt sent to his good friend Sen. Henry Cabot Lodge of Massachusetts explaining a nomination:

> The nominal politics of the man [Horace H. Lurton, a Democrat] has nothing to do with his actions on the bench. His real politics are all important. . . . He is right on the Negro question; he is right on the Insular business; he is right about corporations; he is right about labor. On every question that would come before the bench, he has so far shown himself to be in much closer touch with the policies in which you and I believe than even White [Associate Justice Edward D. White] because he has been right about corporations where White has been wrong.[42]

Reagan's choice of O'Connor is a recent example of a nominee's having both representational and doctrinal qualifications. In his meeting with O'Connor as a prospective nominee, the president discussed social and family issues and was reported to be pleased to hear that abortion was personally abhorrent to her; moreover, he found that her political views were generally conservative, like his own. As a state court judge, O'Connor had been inclined to defer to the actions of legislative and executive officials and to favor shifting more responsibilities from the federal to the state courts, positions also consistent with Reagan's judicial philosophy and advocacy of states' rights.

Reagan's choices of William Rehnquist for chief justice and of Antonin Scalia to fill Rehnquist's position as associate justice appear to have been motivated primarily by doctrinal considerations.[43] Rehnquist's fifteen-year record as associate justice demonstrated that of all the justices, he came closest to the president's views in opposing abortion, busing, and affirmative action and in being generally disposed to defer to state and congressional legislation and to executive authority. Scalia's legal writings (he had served on the law school faculties of the Universities of Chicago and Virginia) and his opinions written while he was a judge on the U.S. court of appeals in Washington reveal essentially the same conservative legal philosophy.

As Scigliano explains, however, doctrinal considerations are not always important to presidents, particularly in times of relative political and social calm, or when they feel that the general philosophy of the majority of the justices is similar to their own and is not likely to change in the near future. Moreover, as the following section indicates, even when presidents do try to choose justices who will rule in the way they desire, they are not always successful.

Effects of Supreme Court Appointments

Appointments to the Supreme Court present the same kinds of political advantages for presidents as do those for lower federal courts. In fact, the rewards of High Court appointments are even more significant because of the prestige of the position. Other than the presidency itself, probably no public office is more prized or coveted than that of Supreme Court justice.

Again the question arises: do such appointments have any *policy* consequences? Are actions presidents take while in office more likely to be supported by their own appointees or by justices from their political party than by other members of the Court? An even broader question, are the values that presidents themselves possess more likely to be protected in judicial rulings made by their own appointees or by members of their own party than by the other justices of the Court?

Stuart Nagel sought to answer the first question by examining the decisions in one hundred Supreme Court cases involving the use of presidential power.[44] He found that when justices appointed by the president and those not appointed by him differed in their opinions (68 percent of the time), the president's appointees were more supportive of his actions. Similarly, he found that in 64 percent of comparable cases a greater proportion of justices from the president's own party upheld his use of power than did those from the opposing political party.

Scigliano examines the broader question of whether presidents get what they want and expect from the persons they appoint to the Court, that is, whether their appointees do in fact make decisions that reflect their values.[45] Taking into account presidents' direct and indirect statements about their appointees, as well as assumptions about whether decisions reached by such appointees reflected the views of the president, Scigliano concludes that approximately three-fourths of the justices conformed to the expectations of the chief executive who appointed them. The remaining one-fourth did not. The latter group includes some notable examples.

Shortly after Theodore Roosevelt appointed Oliver Wendell Holmes, Jr., to the Supreme court, Holmes voted on the side of private enterprise and against the administration in a famous antitrust case, *Northern Securities v. United States*, an action that provoked Roosevelt to say he could make "a judge with a stronger backbone out of a banana."[46] Upset by what he considered to be the extreme liberalism of rulings made by Chief Justice Earl Warren and Associate Justice William Brennan, President Eisenhower referred to them as two of the "mistakes" of his presidency.[47]

Scigliano suggests various reasons why one in four justices do not meet the expectations of the presidents who appoint them. One is that the persons appointed simply do not have the values the president thinks they do, possibly because the president does not probe them sufficiently or thinks that because a prospective justice has a certain position on one issue, he or she will hold a comparable view on another. Also, in making Supreme Court appointments, presidents are influenced by considerations other than doctrinal ones. Moreover, some persons can and do change their views over time, and they may do so after they go on the Court, especially if they are influenced by other justices.[48] Finally, justices have a sense of judicial obligation and may rule according to judicial precedents or their understanding of the Constitution rather than on the basis of their own value preferences. Whatever the reason for their actions, justices of the Supreme Court are virtually immune from pressures from the chief executive. There is no more prestigious office to which they can be appointed as a reward for pleasing the president; moreover, since they may hold office for life (no Supreme Court justice has ever been removed from office), there is little chance to punish them for their transgressions.

Despite these limitations, if a president makes the effort to learn the values of prospective nominees, then appoints a person with values like his own, he usually is rewarded with decisions that reflect his views. Analyses by political scientists David Rohde and Harold Spaeth of Supreme Court cases decided in the last eleven terms of the Warren Court (1958-1968) and the first five terms of the Burger Court (1969-1973) revealed three major values underlying the decisions: *freedom* (cases on First Amendment and criminal procedure safeguards), *equality* (cases on political, economic, or racial discrimination), and *New Dealism* (cases on economic activities associated with government regulation).[49] Of the six judges rated as liberal on all three values, four were appointed by liberal Democratic presidents—Roosevelt (William O. Douglas), Kennedy (Arthur Goldberg), and Johnson (Fortas and Marshall); the two other justices (Warren and Brennan) constituted Eisenhower's two "mistakes." Of the seven justices rated as conservative on these three values, six were appointed by conservative Republican presidents—Eisenhower (Charles E. Whittaker and John M. Harlan) and Nixon (Rehnquist, Burger, Powell, and Blackmun), and only one by a liberal Democrat, Franklin Roosevelt (Felix Frankfurter).[50] As Rohde and Spaeth suggest, the Court had a definite liberal cast until the end of the 1968 term, but with the appointment of Chief Justice Burger by President Nixon, the tide began to turn in a conservative direction.[51]

Other Presidential Influences on the Federal Courts

Although the appointment of federal judges is the most important method by which the president affects the courts, he can influence their activities through other means as well. The first is his relationship with the solicitor general, an official Scigliano calls "the lawyer for the executive branch." [52] The second is the president's role in legislation that affects the operation of the Supreme Court. The third is the role the president plays in the enforcement of court decisions.

Role of the Solicitor General in the Appellate Courts

The solicitor general, an official appointed by the president with the consent of the Senate, is the most important individual in setting the agenda of the federal appellate courts. He determines which cases of those the government loses in the federal district courts will be taken to the courts of appeals. Second, of the cases the government loses in the courts of appeals (or, in some instances, district court cases that are directly appealable to the Supreme Court), he decides which to recommend that the High Court hear.[53] The Supreme Court chooses the cases it will hear, and it is more likely to take those proposed by the solicitor general than by other parties, including those who lost to the federal government in the lower courts. (In contrast, the courts of appeals *must* take cases properly appealed to them.) The importance of this role of the solicitor general is reflected in the fact that the federal government has been a party in about half the cases heard in both the federal courts of appeals and the Supreme Court in recent years.

The solicitor general's influence in determining the Supreme Court's agenda is not restricted, however, to cases in which the federal government itself is a party. He also decides whether the government will file an amicus curiae (friend of the court) brief supporting or opposing appeals by other parties to have their cases heard before the High Court. Scigliano's analysis of the 1958-1967 terms indicates that the solicitor general's record in this role was especially impressive: the Court heard 82 percent of the cases supported by the solicitor general, a figure even higher than the 70 percent for the government's own cases. In contrast, the court heard only 7 percent of the cases in which the government was neither a party nor an amicus.[54]

The solicitor general also supervises the writing of briefs that present reasons why cases should be either accepted or rejected by the Supreme Court. Moreover, once the Court decides to accept a case involving the federal government, the "lawyer for the executive branch" decides the position the government should take and the arguments that should be made to support that position. Moreover, the same applies when the government is not a direct party to the suit but an amicus supporting the position of one of the two immediate parties. Thus, as Scigliano points out, "the Solicitor General not only determines whether the executive branch goes to the Supreme Court but what it will say there."[55]

The federal government's amicus role has expanded greatly in recent years. Steven Puro, who analyzed the briefs filed from 1920 through 1973, found that 71 percent occurred in the last twenty years of that period.[56] He concluded that whether by its own initiative or as a result of an invitation from the Supreme Court, the federal government participated as amicus in almost every major domestic question presented before the Court since World War II. Particularly prominent in recent years has been the government's entrance into the controversial issues of civil liberties, civil rights, and the jurisdiction and procedures of the courts.

When the federal government does become involved in a case before the Supreme Court, it is usually successful. Scigliano's analysis of Court opinions chosen at ten-year intervals beginning in 1800 shows that the United States won 62 percent of its litigation there during the nineteenth century and 64 percent during this century.[57] Its record as amicus is even more impressive: Puro found that in the political cases he examined, the federal government supported the winning side in almost 74 percent of its appearanes.[58] A recent analysis by Karen O'Connor of race discrimination employment cases from 1970 to 1981 showed that the government won 70 percent of the cases in which it was a direct party and 81.6 percent of those in which it filed amicus briefs.[59]

Scigliano suggests several reasons why the federal government is so successful in its appearances before the Supreme Court. One is that the solicitor general develops a great deal of expertise in dealing with the Court, since he or members of his staff argue far more cases there than any other party, including any law firm in the country.[60] Also, the solicitor general tends to build up credit with the Court, since he helps its members manage their caseload by holding down the number of government appeals and provides the Court with high-quality briefs. Moreover, as mentioned at the beginning of this chapter, the executive and judicial branches share a common perspective based upon a similar concern with the execution or enforcement of the law. Finally, the justices tend to share the doctrinal attitudes of the presidents who appoint them. As Puro points out, amicus briefs filed by the solicitor general in the 1960s tended to take the liberal side in civil liberties cases (the individual against state and local governments and corporations). That situation changed during the Nixon administration, however, when the federal government increasingly took a conservative position in amicus cases on such issues (with state and local governments and corporations and against the individual), and the Court began to adopt a more conservative position in its rulings.

With the advent of the Reagan administration came a concerted effort to use the solicitor general's office to help implement the president's conservative political agenda. Termed by Elder Witt as Reagan's "other campaign" [61] (one in addition to appointing conservatives to the federal bench), the campaign led by Solicitor General Rex Lee entailed efforts to persuade the Supreme Court to change previous "liberal" rulings on such matters as abortion, prayer in the public schools, busing, affirmative action, the rights of the accused in criminal cases, and federal-state relations. The campaign met with some successes: the Supreme Court permitted city officials in Pawtucket, Rhode Island, to include a religious creche in their holiday display (*Lynch v. Donnelly*), allowed the city of Memphis to use seniority rules in deciding which firefighters to lay off for budgetary reasons, even though recently hired blacks were adversely affected (*Firefighters Local Union No. 1784 v. Stotts*), and permitted the use of evidence gathered by means of a search warrant that the police in good faith thought was valid but that in fact was not (*United States v. Leon*).[62] The campaign also was marked by some failures, however: the High Court struck down Alabama's law permitting a "moment of silence" for classroom prayer (*Wallace v. Jaffree*), upheld regulations of the Internal Revenue Service denying tax-exempt status to private schools that discriminate against minorities (*Bob Jones University v. United States*), and reaffirmed a woman's right to abortion (*Akron v. Akron Center for Reproductive Health*).[63]

With the beginning of Reagan's second term, the campaign on behalf of the president's conservative political agenda took a new turn. In July 1985, Attorney General Edwin Meese in an address before the American Bar Association expanded the administration's policy arguments into a full-fledged constitutional debate.[64] He urged the Supreme Court to abandon its practice of making policy choices on the basis of "what it thinks is fair and decent," rather than on constitutional principle. He urged the justices to adopt a "jurisprudence of original intention," focusing on the text of the Constitution and on what the Founders intended when they wrote the document. Using that as a basis of decision, the attorney general argued that the Court now should rule what was always intended, that the Bill of Rights apply only to the national government, not the states, thus abandoning sixty years of decisions in which it had decided to the contrary.[65]

Meese's speech soon brought a reaction. Justice Brennan attacked the concept of jurisprudence of original intent as "little more than arrogance cloaked as humility," arguing that "it is arrogant to pretend that from our vantage we can gauge accurately the intent of the Framers on application of principle to specific, contemporary questions." Justice Stevens joined the debate on Brennan's side, criticizing in particular Meese's argument that the Bill of Rights should not be applied to the states. Meanwhile, however, Lee's successor as solicitor general, Charles Fried, seemed to adopt Meese's argument of original intent by filing an amicus brief urging the Supreme Court to overrule the *Roe v. Wade*[66] decision providing for a woman's right to abortion on the grounds that "there is no explicit textual warrant in the Constitution for the right to an abortion."

Thus, the solicitor general plays a major role in setting the agenda of the federal appellate courts, determining the legal positions and arguments judges will hear there, and influencing the decisions they will reach. He links the executive and judicial branches by communicating to the Court the policies favored by the executive branch on issues affecting its own operations as well as on social and political issues in which the government is not a direct party. As Puro suggests, by filing amicus briefs in controversial cases involving racial segregation and malapportionment of legislative bodies, the executive branch indicated its willingness to commit its support and resources to help carry out the Court's decisions.

Although the solicitor general operates fairly independently, he is not immune from presidential influence. His appointment parallels that of federal judges.[67] He is sometimes selected primarily by the president himself, as when Truman chose his friend J. Howard McGrath. In other instances, state political figures may determine the choice, as was true of McGrath's successor, Philip Pearlman, who owed his appointment to the support of Maryland Democratic leaders as well as Republican members of the Maryland congressional delegation.

There is, however, a major distinction between the solicitor general and a federal judge: The solicitor general is an employee of the executive, not the judicial, branch and therefore is subject to direction from the attorney general and, on occasion, the president himself. Puro notes that there were frequent contacts between the solicitor general and the president and members of his staff in both the Truman and Eisenhower administrations. Truman recommended that the government appeal the decision in the *Roanoke Rapids* case to the Supreme Court because the government's whole electric power policy was at stake; Eisenhower was involved in suggested changes to the government's brief in *Brown v. Board of Education* and also approved other legal briefs submitted to him for comment.[68] John Ehrlichman maintained that Chief Justice Burger also discussed pending cases with President Nixon.[69]

Finally, the solicitor general is considerably less politically insulated than a federal judge. He does not hold life tenure; the average tenure of a solicitor general is two years. Not only can he be removed from office by the president but he can also be rewarded with a more prestigious position. For example, Stanley Reed and Robert Jackson (who both served under Franklin Roosevelt) and Thurgood Marshall (who was solicitor general under Lyndon Johnson) all were appointed justices of the Supreme Court by the chief executive who had previously chosen them as solicitor general.

President's Role in Legislation Affecting the Supreme Court

Still another means by which the president can affect the actions of the Supreme Court entails not his executive position but his role in the legislative process. The president's authority to propose bills to Congress and to work for their adoption, as well as his power to oppose measures favored by members of Congress and, if necessary, to veto them, means that the president can influence legislation affecting the Court.

Over the years presidents have become involved in the power of Congress to *establish the size of the Supreme Court.* In the latter days of the presidency of John Adams, the lame-duck Congress, still controlled by the Federalists, passed the Judiciary Act of 1801 reducing the number of justices from six to five to prevent the incoming president, Republican Thomas Jefferson, from appointing a replacement for an ailing justice, William Cushing. The following year, however, the Congress—by then under control of the Republicans—repealed the 1801 law and restored the number of justices to six. In 1807 the number of justices was increased to seven to accommodate population growth in Kentucky, Tennessee, and Ohio. Thus, this first attempt to thwart a president from making appointments to the Supreme Court ended in failure: Jefferson went on to name three justices, including one, Thomas Todd, to occupy the new seat. (Cushing himself lived until 1810, and his successor was named by James Madison, not Jefferson.)

Manipulation of the size of the Court so as to affect presidential appointments also occurred in the 1860s. The 1863 Judiciary Act expanding the Court from nine to ten members enabled Abraham Lincoln to appoint Stephen J. Field to the Court, and Field subsequently supported the president on war issues. Shortly thereafter, the Radical Republicans, who controlled the Congress, passed legislation reducing the number of justices to prevent Lincoln's successor, Andrew Johnson, from appointing justices who they feared would rule against the Reconstruction program. Shortly after Ulysses S. Grant was inaugurated in March 1869, the size of the Court was again expanded; this expansion, plus a retirement, enabled Grant to appoint William Strong and Joseph P. Bradley to the Court. Both voted to reconsider a previous Supreme Court decision (*Hepburn v. Griswold*)[70] that had declared unconstitutional the substitution of paper money for gold as legal tender for the payment of contracts; the new decision validated the use of "greenbacks" as legal tender. Thus, the three successive changes in the size of the Court within a period of six years brought the intended results.

In 1937 President Franklin Roosevelt attempted to change the size of the Court. Frustrated by the invalidation of much of the early New Deal (between January 1935 and June 1936 the Court struck down eight separate statutes), Roosevelt asked Congress in early 1937, shortly after his landslide electoral victory in 1936, to pass legislation permitting him to appoint an additional justice (up to six in number) for each sitting member of the Court who failed to retire voluntarily at age seventy. The president sought to cloak his real purpose of liberalizing the Court by contending that the additions were necessary to handle the Court's caseload. Few persons were deceived by the ploy, however, and the proposal stimulated violent opposition from members of the bar, the press, and many of Roosevelt's former political supporters in Congress. Shortly thereafter Justice Owen J. Roberts, who up to that point had been aligned with four conservative colleagues in striking down New Deal legislation, began to vote with the other four justices to uphold the legislation. The unpopularity of the measure, Justice Roberts's mitigating action (some observers tabbed the development "a switch in time saves nine"), and the sudden death of Senate Majority Leader Joseph Robinson of Arkansas, who was leading the fight for the Roosevelt proposal, resulted in Congress's failure to adopt the "court-packing plan." As Justice Robert Jackson described the outcome of the incident, "In politics the black-robed reactionary Justices had won over the master liberal politician of our day. In law the President defeated the recalcitrant Justices in their own Court." [71]

Presidents also can conceivably affect the operation of the Supreme Court by becoming involved in legislative actions of Congress that *remove certain categories of cases from the appellate jurisdiction of the Supreme Court.* The most notorious use of that congressional power occurred in the aftermath of the Civil War. William McCardle, an editor of a Mississippi newspaper, was arrested and held for trial by a military tribunal for criticizing in his editorials the Reconstruction program imposed on the South by military government. He sought a writ of *habeas corpus* in the federal court of appeals, arguing that the Reconstruction Acts, which allowed his arrest and trial by a military tribunal, were unconstitutional. When the court denied the writ, he took advantage of an 1867 law expanding the appellate jurisdiction of the Supreme Court to review denials of such writs and brought his case to the High Court. Concerned that the Supreme Court might use the *McCardle* case[72] to declare the Reconstruction Acts unconstitutional, Congress passed a law repealing the 1867 statute and prohibiting the Court from acting on any appeals then pending. President Johnson, who opposed the Reconstruction program of the Radical Republicans, vetoed the law, but the Congress overrode his veto. The Court then dismissed the McCardle case on which it had already heard arguments but not yet ruled. Although Congress prevailed over President Johnson in that particular instance by overriding his veto, the incident nonetheless illustrates the power of the president to affect the appellate jurisdiction of the Supreme Court through his sharing of the legislative power with the Congress.[73]

Presidents also have been involved in instances in which Congress has enacted legislation that had the effect of *reversing specific rulings of the Supreme Court.* The difference that individual presidents can make in such matters is illustrated by the tidelands oil dispute. In 1951, after the Supreme Court ruled first in 1947 and again in 1950 that the federal government, not the states, owned the three-mile strip of oil-rich, submerged lands off the ocean shores, Congress passed legislation granting ownership of these tidelands to the states. Democratic president Truman successfully vetoed the legislation, however, and the matter became an issue in the 1952 presidential campaign, in which the Republicans promised to restore the lands to the states. They kept their promise when Eisenhower won the election and subsequently approved new legislation passed in 1953 ceding the federal mineral rights in offshore lands to the states.

These then are the major ways in which presidents can become involved with Congress in legislation affecting the Supreme Court.[74] The next section analyzes the influence the president exercises through an important executive function—the enforcement of court decisions.

Enforcement of Court Decisions

Although the federal courts have the authority to hand down decisions on cases within their jurisdiction, in some instances they depend upon the president to enforce them. A classic example of the president's refusal to do so occurred in the administration of Andrew Jackson. On two separate occasions the Supreme Court ruled that Georgia had no authority over Cherokee Indian lands, but the state ignored the Court rulings and ordered the release first of an Indian charged with murder and later of a white missionary imprisoned for refusing to pay a state license fee. In both cases President Jackson, who sympathized with the state of Georgia, did nothing to enforce the Supreme Court rulings. In the second instance he was reputed to have said, "Well, John Marshall [the chief justice] made his decision, now let him enforce it." As discussed in the next section, President Lincoln even refused to enforce a court order directed against a military officer under his direct command.[75]

That decision by Lincoln was, however, an exception to the rule, for chief executives usually have enforced court decisions, even when they would have preferred not to. Immediately after the Supreme Court held in 1952 in *Youngstown Sheet and Tube Co. v. Sawyer*[76] that Truman's seizure of the steel mills was unconstitutional, he ordered them restored to private operation. Nixon complied with the Court's 1974 decision in *United States v. Nixon*[77] that he turn over to the Court tapes of conversations with executive aides, an action that led to disclosures of the president's involvement in the Watergate cover-up, which ultimately forced him to resign his office.

Thus presidents, through their appointment of federal judges and solicitors general, their involvement in congressional legislation affecting the Supreme Court, and their authority to determine whether or not judicial decisions will be enforced, influence the operation of the federal courts. The following section analyzes the reverse situation: the extent to which federal courts affect the way presidents conduct the responsibilities of their office.

Judicial Checks of Presidential Action

The Founders left open the question of who had the final power to interpret the Constitution. If, as Jefferson contended, each branch has the authority to interpret the Constitution as far as its own duties are concerned, then the president, like Congress, is the judge of the constitutionality of his own actions. If, however, the Supreme Court has the right to make the final judgment on such matters through the power of judicial review, then the Court is in a position to check the actions of the president as well as those of Congress. Significantly, it was a political clash between Republican president Thomas Jefferson and a Federalist chief justice of the United States, John Marshall, that led to the case of *Marbury v. Madison*,[78] in which the Court established its power of judicial review.

After the Federalists were defeated in the election of 1800, they labored—in the interval between the election and the inauguration, when the Republicans would assume control of the presidency and the Congress—to retain a Federalist foothold in the one remaining branch still open to them: the judiciary. The lame-duck Congress passed legislation creating several new justiceships of the peace in the District of Columbia. In the waning days of his administration, President Adams appointed Federalists to these new judicial posts (they became known as "midnight" appointments because they were accomplished shortly before that hour on March 3, 1801). In the last-minute rush, however, John Marshall, who was then secretary of state (and at the same time serving also as chief justice of the United States) did not get all the necessary commissions of office signed; included among them was one making William Marbury a justice of the peace in the District of Columbia. The new Republican secretary of state, James Madison, who, along with the new president, Thomas Jefferson, resented the Federalists' attempt to pack the bench, refused to deliver the commission to Marbury or otherwise honor his appointment.

Frustrated in his attempts to obtain his commission, Marbury turned for help to the Supreme Court, over which John Marshall presided as a result of his appointment by President Adams. Marbury asked that the Court issue a writ of mandamus (an order requiring a public official to perform an official duty over which he has no discretion) compelling Madison to deliver the commission. As his authority for the suit, Marbury invoked a provision in the Judiciary Act of 1789 granting the court the power to issue such writs.

Marbury's case presented Chief Justice Marshall with a dilemma.[79] On the one hand, if he and the rest of the Federalist judges on the Court ruled that Marbury was entitled to the commission, his political enemy, President Jefferson, could simply order Madison not to deliver it, which would serve to demonstrate that the judiciary could not enforce its mandates. On the other hand, to rule that Marbury had no right to the commission would seem to justify Jefferson's and Madison's claim that the midnight appointments were improper in the first place.

The chief justice was up to the challenge, however. He ruled that, although Marbury had the right to the commission and a writ of mandamus was the proper remedy to obtain it, the Supreme Court was not the tribunal to issue it. In reaching this conclusion, he reasoned that the original jurisdiction of the Supreme Court is provided for in the Constitution, and Congress cannot add to that jurisdiction. Therefore, the section of the Judiciary Act of 1789 granting the Supreme Court the power to issue writs of mandamus in cases it hears for the first time is unconstitutional and hence unenforceable.

The ruling extricated Marshall from an immediate difficulty; it had other effects as well. It created the possibility that the Federalists on the Court could use this new-found power to check actions of the Republican Congress and president. Most important for the long term, it established the power of the courts to declare acts of public officials invalid.

Crucial as the *Marbury v. Madison* decision was, it did not settle definitely the scope of judicial review. As might be expected, Jefferson took the position that the ruling merely meant that the Court could strike down laws relating to the judicial branch itself (as the Judiciary Act of 1789 did by granting the Supreme Court the right to issue writs of mandamus), but that the Court has no power over matters relating to the two other branches of government because each is the judge of the constitutionality of matters within its own province. More than a half-century later, however, in the case of *Dred Scott v. Sandford*,[80] the Court invalidated Congress's attempt to abolish slavery in the territories, thereby laying to rest Jefferson's argument. Ultimately, the court also declared actions of presidents to be unconstitutional. Before turning to the cases themselves, however, the chapter next will analyze the theories that presidents themselves have espoused on the scope of presidential power.

Theories on the Scope of Presidential Powers

Students of the presidency have identified three major theories of presidential power enunciated by U.S. chief executives. The first and most limited of the three is the "constitutional" theory and is associated with William Howard Taft. As Taft himself put it, "The true view of executive functions . . . as I conceive it is that the President can exercise no power which cannot fairly and reasonably be traced to some specific grant of power or justly implied and included within such grant as proper and necessary." [81]

The second concept of presidential power, known as the "stewardship" theory, is usually associated with Theodore Roosevelt (although Clinton Rossiter actually traces it back to Alexander Hamilton); [82] it provides the president with a broader source of power. In his autobiography, Roosevelt stated the theory as follows:

> Every executive officer . . . was a steward of the people. . . . I declined to adopt the view that what was imperatively necessary for the nation could not be done by the President unless he could find some specific authorization to do it. My belief was that it not only is his right but his duty to do anything that the needs of the nation demanded unless such action was forbidden by the Constitution or the laws.[83]

The third and most expansive concept of presidential power is referred to as the "prerogative" theory and is associated with Franklin Roosevelt. The theory can actually be traced to English political philosopher John Locke, who, in his *Two Treatises of Civil Government*, took the position that the executive has "this power to act according to discretion for the public good, without the prescription of the law and sometimes even against it. . . ." [84] Although Franklin Roosevelt never spelled out his theory in writing, as did Taft and Theodore Roosevelt, the statement he made in a wartime address to Congress in 1942 is most often associated with FDR's concept of presidential power: he threatened that if Congress did not repeal certain provisions of the Emergency Price Control Act that he found objectionable, he would act on his own authority (even though the regulation of prices is normally within the province of the national legislature).

Thus, the three theories enunciate quite different concepts of presidential power. Taft took the position that to act on a matter, the president must be able to point to some specific positive grant of power or one implied from such a power. Theodore Roosevelt's concept was just the opposite: the chief executive can take any needed action unless it is forbidden by the Constitution or the laws. And Franklin Roosevelt's position was that if the circumstances require it, the president in an emergency can act against the provisions of the Constitution and the laws that operate in normal times. (As will be discussed later in this chapter, Abraham Lincoln took the same general position.)

Major Cases Invalidating Presidential Actions

Of the thirty-nine persons who have served as president over the course of the nation's history, only four have been objects of major court decisions invalidating their actions. The first, Abraham Lincoln, was a nineteenth-century chief executive; the three others, Franklin Roosevelt, Harry Truman, and Richard Nixon, are products of the modern presidency.

Abraham Lincoln. Lincoln's conflict with the judiciary stemmed from the conditions surrounding the Civil War. Early in that conflict Lincoln concluded that existing laws and judicial procedures were inadequate for dealing with spying, sabotage, and other acts of disloyalty, and he suspended the traditional writ of *habeas corpus* when he felt that the public safety required it. John Merryman, a Southern sympathizer who was arrested and imprisoned in a military fort for allegedly helping to burn railroad bridges near Baltimore, obtained a writ of *habeas corpus* ordering his release, but the military commander of the fort refused to obey the court order, citing Lincoln's suspension of the writ. Roger Taney, chief justice of the United States, acting as a federal circuit judge, issued a contempt citation against the fort commander and ordered the appearance of Merryman before the circuit court; the commander prevented the court order from being served and refused to surrender his prisoner. Taney then wrote an opinion stating that only the Congress, not the president, can suspend the writ of *habeas corpus* and that Lincoln's actions constituted a usurpation of both legislative and judicial power. Lincoln responded to Taney's opinion in a message to Congress July 14, 1861, in which he enunciated the prerogative theory of presidential power: it is better, he argued, for the president to violate a single law to a limited extent than to have "the government itself go to pieces" because of a failure to suppress the rebellion.

During the remainder of the war many people, including civilians, who were engaged in activities thought to be dangerous to the public safety, were arrested and tried by military commissions. In 1864 Clement Vallandigham, a "copperhead" (a Northerner sympathetic to the Southern cause), appealed to the Supreme Court his conviction for making a public speech denouncing the Lincoln administration for needlessly prolonging the war; but the Court refused to take the case on the grounds that it had no authority to review the proceedings of a military commission. In 1866, a year after Lincoln's death and the end of the war, the Supreme Court finally heard the case of L. P. Milligan, a civilian sentenced to death by a military commission for releasing and arming rebel prisoners for the purpose of invading Indiana. The Court held that the trial of a civilian by a military commission in an area remote from the theater of war violated the Constitution. In so ruling, the Court used language that seemed to reject the prerogative theory of the presidency claimed by Lincoln: "No doctrine, involving more pernicious consequences, was ever invented by the wit of man than that any of its [the Constitution's] provisions can be suspended during any of the great exigencies of government." [85] The majority opinion went on to state that martial law cannot arise from a *threatened* invasion but only an actual one that effectually closes the courts.

Franklin Roosevelt.   President Roosevelt ran into major difficulties with the Supreme Court, which invalidated much of his early New Deal legislation for exceeding the powers of Congress. The Court struck down presidential actions as well, primarily those entailing his administrative powers.

Two cases, *Panama Refining Co. v. Ryan* and *Schechter Poultry Corp. v. United States*, both decided in 1935, related to powers delegated to the president by Congress.[86] The first case involved his statutory authority under the National Industrial Recovery Act to prohibit the transportation in interstate commerce of "hot oil," that is, oil produced or stored in excess of the limitations enforced by states, regulations designed to boost falling prices and to conserve resources. In striking down the provision, the Court ruled that the congressional grant of authority amounted to an unconstitutional delegation of legislative power since the statute set no standard for guidance of the president, no criteria or conditions under which he should act. In the *Schechter* case, which challenged the chief executive's authority under the same statute to promulgate fair codes of competition for industry, the Court invalidated that provision of the act for the same reason: the law set no standards to guide the president, and in Justice Cardozo's opinion, constituted "delegation run riot."

The third major case that invalidated an action taken by President Roosevelt was *Humphrey's Executor v. United States*, also decided in 1935.[87] Acting under what he conceived to be the authority of *Myers v. United States*,[88] which allowed the president to remove executive officials, the president discharged Humphrey from his position on the Federal Trade Commission (FTC). In doing so, FDR frankly admitted that he was not taking this action because of any of the reasons for removal of members that were set forth in the statute creating the FTC ("inefficiency, neglect of duty, or malfeasance in office"), but because of policy differences he had with the commissioner. The Supreme Court ruled that because Humphrey was not in a "purely executive" position and because the FTC exercises quasi-legislative and quasi-judicial functions, Congress had the authority to stipulate the conditions for the removal; therefore, Roosevelt's failure to respect those conditions invalidated his removal of the commissioner.

Harry Truman. President Truman was the subject of only one major case invalidating his actions but it was a landmark one, *Youngstown Sheet and Tube Co. v. Sawyer*.[89] What became known as the "steel-seizure" case grew out of an industry-wide strike during the Korean War by the U.S. Steel Workers of America when the Wage Stabilization Board failed to settle a dispute between the workers and the owners. President Truman ignored the provisions of the Taft-Hartley Law that permitted the president to obtain an injunction postponing for eighty days a strike that threatened the national safety and welfare. Instead, he issued an executive order seizing the steel mills, based on his authority under the Constitution and U.S. law and as commander in chief. He also reported his actions in a special message to Congress, inviting its members to take action on the matter, but the Congress refused. The steel companies protested the seizure as unconstitutional, and the case went to the Supreme Court.

By a 6-3 vote the Court invalidated the president's action. Justice Hugo L. Black, who wrote the majority opinion (five other justices provided lengthy concurring opinions), summarily rejected the theory of executive prerogative and based his decision on the fact that, in its deliberations over the Taft-Hartley Law, Congress had decided against authorizing the president to seize industrial property; thus the chief executive acted against the will of Congress, which amounted to an unconstitutional usurpation of legislative power. The dissenting opinion, written by Chief Justice Vinson, took the position that in times of a national crisis the president must exercise discretionary prerogative power ("those who suggest that this is a case involving extraordinary powers should be mindful that these are extraordinary times"). In addition, the chief justice held that the president's action was supportive of the intention of the national legislators to provide steel for weapons needed in a congressionally supported war in Korea.

Richard Nixon. When Richard Nixon assumed the presidency, he vowed to appoint to the Supreme Court "strict constructionalists" who would not read their own values into the Constitution so as to interfere with the right of public officials (especially police officers) to carry out their duties. During his first term the president appointed four new members to the Court: Chief Justice Warren Burger and Associate Justices Harry A. Blackmun, Lewis Powell, Jr., and William Rehnquist. Ironically, however, Nixon himself became the object of no fewer than five adverse decisions of the Supreme Court, and in some of those decisions his own appointees voted against him.

The first case, *New York Times v. United States*,[90] decided in 1971 not long after the president took office, arose out of the publication by the *New York Times* and the *Washington Post* of the *Pentagon Papers,* an inside account of U.S. involvement in the war in Southeast Asia, prepared by the Department of Defense. Acting under the president's direction, Attorney General John Mitchell sought a court injunction to prevent their publication on the grounds that it would cause grave and irreparable damage to the national security and that it violated a provision of the Espionage Act of 1917 forbidding the communication of defense information harmful to the nation's security. Six of the judges decided that such "prior restraint" was unconstitutional: Justices Black and Douglas held that such restraint violates the First Amendment no matter how great the threat to national security; Justice Brennan could find no threat to national security in this particular instance; and Justices White, Marshall, and Potter Stewart based their decision on the absence of statutory authority for federal courts' issuing prior-restraint injunctions in national security cases. The three dissenters—Justices Burger, Blackmun, and Harlan—felt that the Court had disposed of the case without adequately exploring questions of fact and law and that the courts should be more flexible in handling conflicts between First Amendment freedoms and issues of national security.

In 1972 Nixon lost another argument involving national security. Congress provided in the Omnibus Crime Control and Safe Streets Act of 1968 that the federal government's use of wire taps and electronic surveillance be approved in advance by a judge, who is required to issue a warrant authorizing the surveillance. On the direction of the president, however, the attorney general's office, without obtaining a warrant, ordered surveillance of a person accused of bombing an office of the Central Intelligence Agency in Ann Arbor, Michigan; it claimed that such surveillance was a reasonable exercise of the president's power to protect the national security. The Court, in *United States v. United States District Court for the Eastern District of Michigan*,[91] speaking through one of Nixon's own appointees, Justice Powell, held that warrantless surveillance in a domestic security matter is unconstitutional because it violates a "convergence of First and Fourth Amendment values."

The most damaging decision for the president, *United States v. Nixon,*[92] was handed down in July 1974 and led to his resignation. The case grew out of the Watergate scandal and involved Special Prosecutor Leon Jaworski's attempt to subpoena tapes of sixty-four conversations between the president and his assistants that Jaworski needed in criminal litigation against some of the leading figures in the Nixon administration. The president refused to surrender the tapes, claiming the existence of an executive privilege relating to private conversations between the chief executive and his advisers. In a unanimous opinion written by Chief Justice Warren Burger (Nixon's first appointee to the Court), the Court recognized for the first time the principle of executive privilege as having "constitutional underpinnings." The opinion went on to say, however, that the Court, not the president, is the final judge of the proper use of executive privilege; moreover, in this instance, the general claim of the privilege, when unrelated to military, diplomatic, or national security issues, must give way to the more immediate need for evidence in a criminal case and to the fundamental principles of due process of law and the fair administration of justice.

After Richard Nixon left office, he suffered two more judicial defeats. In *Train v. City of New York*,[93] the Court held that the president's impoundment (refusal to make expenditures) of moneys appropriated by Congress under the Water Pollution Control Act of 1972 was unconstitutional because the statute itself gave him no authority to do so; in so ruling, the Court rejected the president's argument that as chief executive he could impound funds when spending would mean either increased prices or taxes for the American people. In *Nixon v. Administrator, General Services Administration*,[94] the Court upheld the Presidential Recordings and Materials Preservation Act of 1974, placing in federal custody tapes and papers of the Nixon administration; in reaching its decision, the justices weighed the harm done to the individual rights of the former president against the public interest in preserving the Nixon materials and concluded that the latter interest should prevail.

Thus, the federal courts have been willing on some occasions to invalidate presidential actions that exceed constitutional authority. There are also, however, limitations on the willingness of justices to rule against the chief executive.

Limitations on Judicial Checks of Presidential Action

Courts have been very reluctant to strike down actions of the president as unconstitutional; the fact that this has occurred in only eleven major cases in almost two hundred years indicates that judicial checks on the chief executive are exceptions to the rule. This is especially so in times of foreign and military crises. None of the major wartime presidents—Lincoln, Wilson, or Franklin Roosevelt—was seriously impeded by the courts in the prosecution of hostilities. As previously noted, Lincoln ignored the *Merryman* decision, and the *Milligan* one was handed down after the Civil War was over and Lincoln was dead. During the hostilities, the Court upheld the Union blockade of Southern ports on the grounds that Lincoln's action was necessary to deal with the rebellion (the *Prize Cases*).[95] During World War I the "hands-off" policy of the courts continued: convictions under the Espionage and Sedition Acts of persons charged with interfering with the war effort were upheld in cases decided after the war was over (*Schenck v. United States, Abrams v. United States,* and *Pierce v. United States.*)[96] During World War II the Supreme Court upheld the government program relocating Japanese-Americans living on the West Coast to camps in the interior (*Korematsu v. United*

States), and also the trial of German saboteurs by a military commission (*Ex parte Quirin*).[97] Only after the relocation centers were being disbanded did the Supreme Court decide that it was unlawful to detain a loyal U.S. citizen of Japanese background (*Ex parte Endo*).[98] Moreover, in a decision similar to that of the *Milligan* case, the Court ruled that it was unconstitutional for a civilian to be tried by a military commission in Hawaii, but that decision was handed down six months after the hostilities were over (*Duncan v. Kahanamoku*).[99] Thus, when the Court must rule on presidential actions, particularly in times of crisis, it tends to support the chief executive, or it delays making an adverse decision until the crisis is over.

The federal courts have devised another means of avoiding adverse decisions against the president: they simply declare that a particular issue is a "political question" and refuse to rule on the matter. As Witt explains, "The doctrine rests on the separation of powers theory—that the Supreme Court exercises the judicial power and leaves political, or policy, questions to Congress and the president." [100] Delineating between a judicial issue and a political or policy issue is not an easy matter, but the fact that the courts themselves make the distinction allows them to invoke the doctrine when for one reason or another they choose not to invalidate presidential or congressional action. The doctrine is invoked most often in the area of foreign policy. It was first used by the Supreme court in 1829 in an international boundary dispute (*Foster v. Neilson*) and a federal court of appeals used it in 1973 (*Holtzman v. Schlesinger*) to avoid ruling on the constitutionality of U.S. involvement in the war in Cambodia.[101]

Thus, the issue left unresolved by the Founders—whether the Supreme Court or the president has the right to decide whether a president's actions violate the Constitution—in some respects is still unresolved. The doctrine of judicial review has been established and extended on some occasions to apply to presidential actions. The federal courts are reluctant, however, to use this power to check the chief executive, especially during crises. At those times, the courts tend to allow the president to make his own constitutional judgments. Therefore, when presidents are most likely to stretch the powers of their office to deal with what they perceive to be an extraordinary situation, the courts are least likely to intervene to protect the rights of the American people.

Finally, some presidential actions simply cannot be dealt with by the courts at all. The qualities Hamilton identified with the executive—"decision, activity, secrecy and despatch"—are such that the president can present the courts with a fait accompli, which they can do little or nothing about. The most awesome decisions that presidents make, such as those of President Truman to drop the atomic bomb and to send U.S. troops into Korea, do not lend themselves to adjudication and must be dealt with in the political, not the judicial, arena.

Conclusion

Although the president does not have the day-to-day relationship with the federal courts that he has with the Congress and other members of the executive branch, he does possess two powers in particular through which he can significantly influence the activities of the courts. One is the power to appoint the members of all three federal courts—district courts, courts of appeals, and the U.S. Supreme Court. The other is the power to help shape the agenda of the appellate courts through the actions of another of his appointees, the solicitor general of the United States. Moreover, both of these powers have long-term consequences: federal judges (unlike members of the Congress and the political appointees of the executive branch) serve for life, and Supreme Court decisions that the solicitor general helps to determine usually are followed by future justices because of the principle of *stare decisis*.

There appears to be a trend towards greater presidential involvement in the selection of federal judges, even those who serve on the lower federal courts. Both the Carter and Reagan administrations paid particularly close attention to the political philosophy of potential judges. The Carter administration also made a major effort to recruit women and members of minority groups to the lower federal bench, and the Reagan administration placed the first woman on the Supreme Court. Because Congress recently created a large number of new lower court judgeships, both presidents were able to choose an unusually large proportion of the members of those courts.

Recent presidents also have made a greater effort to shape federal court opinions through the actions of the solicitor general. Increasingly, that official is carefully chosen with the expectation that he or she will try to implement the president's political agenda, especially by filing amicus curiae briefs in a broad range of cases.[102] The Reagan administration has attempted to use the federal courts to implement policy goals that it has been unable to accomplish through the regular political process; for example, outlawing abortion and providing for voluntary prayer in the public schools. Solicitor General Charles Fried's effort to persuade the Supreme Court to override its decision permitting abortion, and Attorney General Edwin Meese's call for a return to the jurisprudence of original intent and for the reversal of sixty years of decisions extending the Bill of Rights to the states, are ambitious attempts to establish public policy through the federal courts.

Notes

1. Alexander Hamilton, James Madison, and John Jay, *The Federalist Papers,* ed. Clinton Rossiter (New York: New American Library, 1961), 322.

2. Ibid., 465.
3. Robert Scigliano, *The Supreme Court and the Presidency* (New York: Free Press, 1971), chap. 1.
4. Ibid., vii.
5. *Marbury v. Madison*, 1 Cranch 137 (1803).
6. In addition to the federal courts of general jurisdiction authorized by Article III, special courts handle disputes arising from particular functions of Congress under powers granted by Article I. Included are the U.S. Court of Appeals for the Federal Circuit, the U.S. Court of Military Appeals, territorial courts, U.S. Claims Court, and the U.S. Court of International Trade.
7. Harold Chase, *Federal Judges: The Appointing Process* (Minneapolis: University of Minnesota Press, 1972), 17.
8. Joseph Harris, *The Advice and Consent of the Senate: A Study of the Confirmation of Appointment by the United States Senate* (Berkeley: University of California Press, 1953), 40.
9. Alan Neff, *The United States District Judge Nominating Commissions: Their Members, Procedures, and Candidates* (Chicago: American Judicature Society, 1981), 17-18.
10. Chase, *Federal Judges*, 36.
11. Joel Grossman, *Lawyers and Judges: The ABA and the Politics of Judicial Selection* (New York: Wiley, 1965), 42.
12. Chase, *Federal Judges*, 29.
13. Walter Murphy, "Chief Justice Taft and the Lower Court Bureaucracy: A Study in Judicial Administration," *Journal of Politics* (August 1962): 453-476.
14. Grossman, *Lawyers and Judges*, 73.
15. Neff, *District Judge Nominating Commissions*, 14.
16. Ibid., 43. In some instances, however, senators have withdrawn the names of persons they were sponsoring rather than have the nomination rejected by the Senate. Edward Kennedy, for example, did this when his nomination of Francis X. Morrissey for the federal district court in Massachusetts ran into difficulties because of Morrissey's lack of judicial qualifications.
17. Ibid., 45. At the same time, the committee continued to exert influence over some appointments. President Carter did not appoint to the federal bench some persons proposed by nominating commissions but opposed by the ABA committee on grounds such as their being too old or having insufficient trial experience.
18. Sheldon Goldman, "Reaganizing the Judiciary: The First Term Appointments," *Judicature* (April-May 1985): 315-317.
19. Ibid., 315-316.
20. Ibid., 316.
21. Lawrence Baum, *The Supreme Court*, 2d ed. (Washington, D.C.: CQ Press, 1985), 39.
22. Robert A. Carp and Ronald Stidham, *The Federal Courts* (Washington, D.C.: CQ Press, 1985), 110.
23. Goldman, "Reaganizing the Judiciary," 314. When the Democrats captured control of the Senate in 1987, the Senate Judiciary Committee,

chaired by Joseph Biden (D-Del.), created an all-Democratic unit to investigate and hold hearings on all of President Reagan's judicial nominees before the full committee votes on them.

24. Another difference not shown by the table is the disparity in the financial backgrounds of the Reagan and Carter appointees: more than 20 percent of the Reagan appointees had a net worth of over $1 million; only 4 percent of Carter's did.

25. The financial backgrounds of Reagan appointees to the courts of appeals were also substantial: more than 23 percent of them were millionaires compared with 10 percent of Carter's.

26. See Carp and Stidham, *The Federal Courts,* 117-121, citing Robert A. Carp and C. K. Rowland, *Policymaking and Politics in the Federal District Courts* (Knoxville: University of Tennessee Press, 1983).

27. Sheldon Goldman, "Voting Behavior in the United States Courts of Appeals, 1961-1964," *American Political Science Review* (June 1966): 374-384.

28. Sheldon Goldman, "Voting Behavior in the United States Courts of Appeals Revisited," *American Political Science Review* (June 1975): 491-507.

29. Jon Gottschall, "Reagan Appointments to the United States Courts of Appeals: The Continuation of a Judicial Revolution," *Judicature* (June-July, 1986): 48-54.

30. Scigliano, *The Supreme Court and the Presidency,* 95.

31. Earlier in the nation's history, an informal custom assigned certain states, such as New York, Pennsylvania, and Ohio, the right to have a "seat" on the Supreme Court, but that custom generally has not been applied in this century.

32. There is, however, one major exception to this rule—William Howard Taft. While still president, he appointed Edward White as chief justice, a man of comparatively advanced years (sixty-five), calculating that when White retired, he, Taft, would have an opportunity to move into the position himself. When White died early in President Warren G. Harding's term, Taft mounted a concerted campaign in his own behalf and obtained the coveted position from the new president.

33. Henry Abraham and Bruce Murphy, "The Influence of Sitting and Retired Justices on Presidential Supreme Court Appointments," *Hastings Constitutional Law Quarterly* (1975-1976): 37-63.

34. Baum, *The Supreme Court,* 35.

35. Ibid., 46; Harris, *Advice and Consent of the Senate,* 303.

36. Scigliano, *The Supreme Court and the Presidency,* chap. 4.

37. Henry Abraham, *Justices and Presidents: A Political History of Appointments to the Supreme Court* (New York: Penguin Books, 1974), chap. 2.

38. It should be noted that William Rehnquist's nomination for chief justice in 1986 was attacked by liberal groups because of his alleged insensitivity to the rights of minorities and women. Although he was ultimately confirmed, the thirty-three votes cast against his nomination was the largest number ever cast against a confirmed justice.

39. One of Carswell's supporters, Republican senator Roman Hruska of Nebraska, even tried to defend him on the grounds that there are many

mediocre judges, lawyers, and other people who are entitled to representation on the Court. As Baum suggests, his statement seemed to support the charges of incompetence against Carswell (*The Supreme Court*, 50-51). In any event, the nomination was rejected by a 51-45 vote.

40. Scigliano, *The Supreme Court and the Presidency*, chap. 4.

41. Despite the recent concern with minority representation on the Supreme Court, as John Schmidhauser has pointed out, "The typical Supreme Court justice has generally been white, Protestant (with a penchant for a high social status), usually of ethnic stock originating in the British Isles, and born in comfortable circumstances in an urban or small-town environment" (*Judges and Justices: The Federal Appellate Judiciary* [Boston: Little, Brown, 1979], 96). As indicated in Chapter 3, that description also fits the presidents who have appointed the justices.

42. Henry Cabot Lodge, *Selections from the Correspondence of Theodore Roosevelt and Henry Cabot Lodge, 1884-1918* (New York: Scribner's, 1925), vol. 2, 228, 230-231; cited in Abraham, *Justices and Presidents*, 68. Lodge replied that a Republican with similar views could be found, and he persuaded Roosevelt to nominate William Moody, the attorney general of Massachusetts. Lurton subsequently was appointed by Roosevelt's successor, another Republican president, William Howard Taft.

43. Although Scalia is the first Italian-American to be nominated for the High Court, little was made of that fact at the time of his nomination and confirmation.

44. Stuart Nagel, "Comparing Elected and Appointed Judicial Systems," Sage Professional Papers, No. 64-001 (Beverly Hills: Sage Publications, 1973), 25-26.

45. Scigliano, *The Supreme Court and the Presidency*, chap. 3.

46. *Northern Securities v. United States*, 193 U.S. 197 (1904); Stephen Wasby, *The Supreme Court in the Federal Judiciary System* (New York: Holt, Rinehart and Winston, 1978), 95.

47. Abraham, *Justices and Presidents*, 246.

48. A classic instance of justices changing their views was Thomas Jefferson's appointees to the Court, who came under the great influence of his political enemy, Chief Justice John Marshall (Scigliano, *The Supreme Court and the Presidency*, 127).

49. David Rohde and Harold Spaeth, *Supreme Court Decision Making* (San Francisco: Freeman, 1976), chap. 7.

50. Frankfurter declared himself to be an independent at the time he was appointed to the Court.

51. Rohde and Spaeth, *Supreme Court Decision Making*, 144.

52. Scigliano, *The Supreme Court and the Presidency*, chap. 6.

53. Some regulatory commissions have the statutory authority to decide whether lower court defeats in which they were involved will be appealed to the Supreme Court, but only the Interstate Commerce Commission has made much use of this authority. Moreover, although all agencies have the right to appeal to the attorney general or president if they disagree with the solicitor general's decision not to appeal one of their cases, only rarely has the solicitor general been overruled by these superiors (ibid., chap. 6).

54. Ibid., 176.
55. Ibid., 172.
56. Steven Puro, "The United States as *Amicus Curiae,*" in *Courts, Law and Judicial Processes,* ed. S. Sidney Ulmer (New York: Free Press, 1981), 220-230.
57. Scigliano, *The Supreme Court and the Presidency,* chap. 6.
58. Puro, "The United States as *Amicus Curiae.*"
59. Karen O'Connor, "The *Amicus Curiae* Role of the U.S. Solicitor General in Supreme Court Litigation," *Judicature* (December-January, 1983): 261.
60. This situation is to be contrasted with the paucity of experience the attorney general has before the Court: traditionally, he argues only one case before his term is over. For an interesting account of Robert Kennedy's first appearance before the Court two years after he became attorney general, see Victor Navasky, *Kennedy Justice* (New York: Atheneum, 1980), chap. 6.
61. Elder Witt, *A Different Justice* (Washington, D.C.: Congressional Quarterly Inc., 1986), chaps. 6, 7.
62. *Lynch v. Donnelly,* 79 L. Ed. 2d 604 (1984); *Firefighters Local Union No. 1784 v. Stotts,* 78 L. Ed. 2d 76 (1983); *United States v. Leon,* 78 L. Ed. 2d 720 (1983).
63. *Wallace v. Jaffree,* 80 L. Ed. 2d 178 (1984); *Bob Jones University v. United States, Goldsboro Christian Schools Inc. v. United States,* 76 L. Ed. 2d 157 (1983); *Akron v. Akron Center for Reproductive Health, Akron Center for Reproductive Health v. Akron,* 76 L. Ed. 2d 687 (1983). In the *Bob Jones* case, Solicitor General Lee, however, did not present the administration's side of the case; rather, the Supreme Court appointed William Coleman, Jr., a prominent black attorney who served as secretary of transportation in the Ford administration, to do so.
64. Witt, *A Different Justice,* 135.
65. The Court first ruled in *Gitlow v. New York,* 268 U.S. 652 (1925), that the Fourteenth Amendment extended the free speech guarantee of the First Amendment to the states as well as the federal government. Since then it has extended other features of the Bill of Rights to the states.
66. *Roe v. Wade,* 410 U.S. 113 (1973).
67. Steven Puro, "Presidential Relationships with the Solicitor Generals of the United States: Political Science Research at Presidential Libraries" (Paper delivered at the 1978 annual meeting of the Missouri and Kansas Political Science Associations).
68. *Brown v. Board of Education,* 347 U.S. 483 (1954).
69. John Ehrlichman, *Witness to Power: The Nixon Years* (New York: Simon and Schuster, 1983), 133.
70. *Hepburn v. Griswold,* 8 Wallace 603 (1870).
71. Robert Jackson, *The Struggle for Judicial Supremacy: A Study of a Crisis in American Power Politics* (New York: Knopf, 1941), 196.
72. *Ex parte McCardle,* 7 Wallace 506 (1869).
73. Recently a number of conservatives in Congress, led by Sen. Jesse Helms of North Carolina, unhappy with recent Supreme Court rulings on controversial issues such as abortion and prayer in public schools, have proposed legislation that would deny the Court jurisdiction over cases involving such

issues. Should the legislation be passed (it was defeated in the Senate in 1982 through the use of the filibuster), President Reagan would face a difficult choice: his own views on these issues might incline him to approve the legislation; but because of concern that such laws—like Franklin Roosevelt's court-packing proposal—might be considered a political attack on an independent judiciary and may even be unconstitutional, he could decide to veto them.

74. In addition to regular legislation, Congress can affect the operation of the Supreme Court by proposing amendments to the Constitution. The president's veto power, however, does not extend to constitutional amendments.
75. *Ex parte Merryman*, 17 Fed. Cases 144 (1861).
76. *Youngstown Sheet and Tube Co. v. Sawyer*, 343 U.S. 579 (1952).
77. *United States v. Nixon*, 418 U.S. 683 (1974).
78. *Marbury v. Madison*, 1 Cranch 137 (1803).
79. Chief Justice Marshall should have disqualified himself from hearing the case since he was the one who failed to deliver the commission when he was secretary of state.
80. *Dred Scott v. Sandford*, 19 Howard 393 (1857).
81. William Howard Taft, *Our Chief Magistrate and His Powers* (New York: Columbia University Press, 1916), 144.
82. Clinton Rossiter, *Alexander Hamilton and the Constitution* (New York: Harcourt, Brace, and World, 1964), 248.
83. Theodore Roosevelt, *An Autobiography*, ed. Wayne Andrews (New York: Scribner's, 1958), pp. 197-98.
84. John Locke, *Two Treatises of Civil Government* (New York: Dutton, 1924), 199.
85. *Ex parte Milligan*, 4 Wallace 2, 121 (1866).
86. *Panama Refining Co. v. Ryan*, 293 U.S. 338 (1935); *Schechter Poultry Corp. v. United States*, 295 U.S. 495 (1935). Although both cases invalidated legislation passed by Congress, they are included here because they affected presidential actions taken under the authority of the legislation.
87. *Humphrey's Executor v. United States*, 295 U.S. 602 (1935).
88. *Myers v. United States*, 272 U.S. 52 (1926).
89. *Youngstown Sheet and Tube Co. v. Sawyer*, 343 U.S. 579 (1952).
90. *New York Times v. United States*, 403 U.S. 713 (1971).
91. *United States v. United States District Court for the Eastern District of Michigan*, 407 U.S. 297 (1972).
92. *United States v. Nixon*, 418 U.S. 683 (1974).
93. *Train v. City of New York*, 420 U.S. 35 (1975).
94. *Nixon v. Administrator, General Services Administration*, 433 U.S. 425 (1977).
95. *Prize Cases*, 2 Black 635 (1863).
96. *Schenck v. United States*, 249 U.S. 47 (1919); *Abrams v. United States*, 250 U.S. 616 (1919); and *Pierce v. United States*, 252 U.S. 239 (1920).
97. *Korematsu v. United States*, 323 U.S. 214 (1944); *Ex parte Quirin*, 317 U.S. 1 (1942).
98. *Ex parte Endo*, 323 U.S. 283 (1944).

99. *Duncan v. Kahanamoku,* 327 U.S. 304 (1946).
100. Elder Witt, ed. *Guide to the U.S. Supreme Court* (Washington, D.C.: Congressional Quarterly Inc., 1979), 200.
101. *Foster v. Neilson,* 2 Pet. 253 (1829); *Holtzman v. Schlesinger,* 484 F. 2d 1307 (1973).
102. From 1961 to 1966, the Kennedy and Johnson administrations filed 77 amicus briefs; from 1981 to 1986, the Reagan administration filed 206 amicus briefs ("Reagan Crusade before Court Unprecedented in Intensity," *Congressional Quarterly Weekly Report,* March 15, 1986, 616, citing Steven Puro as source of information).

Selected Readings

Abraham, Henry. *Justices and Presidents: A Political History of Appointments to the Supreme Court.* 2d ed. New York: Oxford University Press, 1985.

Baum, Lawrence. *The Supreme Court.* 2d ed. Washington, D.C.: CQ Press, 1985.

Carp, Robert, and Ronald Stidham. *The Federal Courts.* Washington, D.C.: CQ Press, 1985.

Chase, Harold. *Federal Judges: The Appointing Process.* Minneapolis: University of Minnesota Press, 1972.

Grossman, Joel. *Lawyers and Judges: The ABA and the Politics of Judicial Selection.* New York: Wiley, 1965.

Jackson, Robert. *The Struggle for Judicial Supremacy: A Study of a Crisis in American Power Politics.* New York: Knopf, 1941.

Neff, Alan. *The United States District Judge Nominating Commissions: Their Members, Procedures, and Candidates.* Chicago: American Judicature Society, 1981.

Scigliano, Robert. *The Supreme Court and the Presidency.* New York: Free Press, 1971.

Witt, Elder. *A Different Justice.* Washington, D.C.: Congressional Quarterly, 1986.

PART THREE

The President and Public Policy

The president's relations with Congress and the judiciary and his efforts to manage and direct the executive branch are important primarily as means to achieve specific policy objectives. That is, they are instrumental in nature. Not all policies are of equal importance, and presidents have tended to devote most of their energy to two policy areas, national security and economic management. John Kessel has characterized national security—his phrase is "international involvement"—and economic management as imperative policy areas because presidents feel that they *must* respond to issues and problems such as nuclear arms control and unemployment and inflation. The several remaining policy areas are usually lumped together and designated as domestic policy. Included in domestic policy are such broad policy areas as social welfare, civil rights, agriculture, and natural resources.

Previously noted was Aaron Wildavsky's concept of the "two presidencies," one for foreign and defense policy and the other for domestic policy. The rise in the importance of economic management issues since 1970 has elevated economic policy to the status of an imperative policy area. It will therefore be examined separately from national security policy and domestic policy. Separate treatment of the three principal areas of presidential policy involvement is somewhat artificial in that they are interrelated. What happens in one policy area affects what happens and what can be done in the others. An economic recession, for example, triggers increases in social welfare spending to compensate for the effects of unemployment. Or a military buildup to meet an external threat affects fiscal policy. Moreover, as the U.S. economy has become increasingly dependent on external sources of raw materials, the relationships between the three primary areas of presidential policy involvement have strengthened.

The reason for examining each of the three areas separately is analytical convenience and advantage. Each area has its own pattern of politics and its own time cycles. Separate organizational structures and operating procedures

365

have developed within the presidency to support presidential activities in each area.

Presidents are drawn to national security policy and to economic policy because developments in those areas can more strongly affect their support than most domestic policy developments. In addition, presidents are subject to fewer internal political constraints in dealing with national security policy. Still, presidents cannot avoid coming to grips with domestic policy, for powerful local, regional, and group interests continually exert pressure upon them both directly and indirectly through members of Congress. Also, domestic policy demands some presidential attention if for no other reason than that almost every action the president takes, or decides not to take, is divisive, causing some loss in popular support. Although domestic policy tends to be more sharply focused than economic management policy or foreign and defense policy, its aggregate impact is extensive. Few, if any, Americans are unaffected by it. Presidents can ignore domestic policy issues and problems only at risk to their popular support and their standing among other key participants in national policy-making processes.

Part Three, comprising Chapters 9, 10, and 11, examines how modern presidents have responded to challenges in domestic, economic, and national security policy.

The food stamp program, administered by the Department of Agriculture's Food and Nutrition Service, provides coupons to welfare recipients for use in buying groceries.

CHAPTER NINE

The Politics of Domestic Policy

Within the broad realm of domestic policy, presidents encounter different patterns of politics based on the type of policies with which they must deal. They also confront a congested agenda that results from the interrelatedness, overlapping, and layering of issues.[1]

Political scientists have classified public policy for analytical purposes. The most widely used classification scheme, or typology, is Theodore Lowi's division of policies into distributive, regulatory, and redistributive categories.[2] He based his categories on the extent to which their effects can be disaggregated, or broken down, and the likelihood of coercion. *Distributive* policies have the most diffused impact. They affect specific groups of people and provide individualized benefits. They have low visibility, produce little conflict, and are not likely to require the application of coercion. Examples of distributive policies include agricultural price supports, public works projects, and research and development programs. *Regulatory* policies affect large segments of society and involve the application of coercion. Although regulatory issues tend to be highly technical, they often are quite visible and controversial. Examples include pollution control, antitrust, and occupational safety and health. *Redistributive* policies have the broadest impact on society. They involve the transfer of resources (wealth and income) from some groups to others. They require coercion, are highly visible, and usually are accompanied by social or class conflict. Examples of redistributive policies include civil rights, social security, and tax reform.

Lowi argued that the type of policy determines the focus and behavior of political actors. Thus, distributive policy politics involve limited presidential and extensive congressional participation and decision making that relies heavily on logrolling—the mutual exchange of support for legislation. Regulatory policy politics produce moderate presidential and substantial congressional interest and involvement, with frequent conflict between the president and Congress. Redistributive policy politics are often fraught with ideological disputes and presidential-congressional conflict. Presidents tend to be most heavily involved with redistributive policy issues. This is the case whether the government is seeking to expand or contract the scope of its activities.

Steven Shull has used Lowi's policy typology to examine presidential and congressional roles in domestic policy formation.[3] He found that there were "some differences in presidential and congressional behavior . . . along lines anticipated by the 'theory,' " [4] and that "modest empirical distinctions" exist among the three policy categories.[5] The principal problem encountered in using Lowi's typology is the difficulty in operationalizing it for purposes of measurement. The problem arises because an issue may change its designation over time, starting out, for example, as a redistributive issue and becoming distributive. This is what happened to Title I of the Elementary and Secondary Education Act of 1965, a program of federal assistance to local school districts for economically disadvantaged children. Initially, the program had redistributive effects and sparked great controversy, but over time it became a routinized distribution of federal funds that was part of the established structure of school finance. In other words, Lowi's categories are not mutually exclusive. Shull concluded that Lowi's typology is not as useful as substantive classification based on policy content.

John Kessel has broken down domestic policy into areas involving social benefits, civil liberties, agriculture, and natural resources.[6] Each area entails a specific type of politics and its own temporal pattern, both of which have implications for presidential participation. The politics of social benefits are allocative (there is a strong similarity here to Lowi's distributive and redistributive categories). Presidents use the distribution of social benefits to build public support; thus, they tend to pay most attention to social benefits as they approach reelection, after which (if they are successful) they are much less concerned. Civil rights involves a pattern of politics that is highly sensitive and regulatory, because of different conceptions of fairness. Presidents are most likely to act on civil rights issues immediately after their election, both because these issues are highly controversial and because campaign promises must be fulfilled. The politics of natural resources are primarily regulatory, and agriculture mostly involves allocation. The temporal patterns in natural resource and agricultural policy politics are a function of long-range developments and entail limited presidential participation.

Whether one approaches domestic policy using Lowi's analytical typology or Kessel's substantive classifications, it is clear that presidents can become fully involved with only a small number of problems and issues. Both the Lowi and Kessel approaches suggest that in domestic policy, presidents will tend to focus on matters such as maintaining the financial integrity of the social security system, reforming welfare, and advancing civil rights proposals. They will not take up all major redistributive, social benefit, and civil rights issues and may consciously avoid some, such as national health insurance, which has enormous financial costs. They are unlikely to become bogged down with routine distributive policies or with the technicalities of economic and social regulation. Jimmy Carter, however, became entangled in a politically damaging controversy with Congress over eighteen water projects that he regarded as unnecessary. Other presidents have been content to leave the distribution of "pork barrel" projects to Congress.

The range and complexity of domestic problems and issues produces a policy congestion that makes coordination the essential presidential function in this area. Coordination has been complicated, however, by the interrelatedness of domestic, economic, and national security policy. If presidents attempt to coordinate policies through simplification, say, by proposals to balance the budget or reorganize the bureaucracy, they encounter the opposition of powerful forces mobilized around policy issues, programs, and administrative agencies. (Ronald Reagan's proposals to move toward a balanced budget by reducing social security cost-of-living allowances is an excellent example. Opposition from the "gray lobby" and most members of Congress have stymied the idea.) The proliferation and professionalization of interest groups and the expansion of their financial and electoral power have been accompanied by a decline in the policy influence of political parties. Parties no longer play the role of broad-based organizations with which presidents can bargain to bring coherence to domestic policies and thus resolve policy congestion. Nor are parties a centripetal counterweight to the centrifugal tendencies of organized group interests.

Chapter 9 examines the president's involvement in domestic policy politics. (Economic policy politics and national security policy politics are the subjects of Chapters 10 and 11, respectively.) This chapter first analyzes the process by which the president's agenda is set and presented to Congress. It next explores the domestic policy environment within which the president must operate. The conclusion is a description of the domestic policy apparatus, that is, the institutional arrangements that have been developed to assist the president in dealing with domestic policy.

The Domestic Policy Process

The domestic policy process has formal and informal dimensions, both of which affect the presidency. The formal dimension consists of actions that culminate in the development and presentation of legislative proposals to Congress, the issuance of executive orders, and the preparation and submission of annual budgets. There is a cyclical regularity to much of the formal policy process, for annual events, such as the State of the Union, budget, and economic messages, define the broad outlines of the president's program.[7] (Although these events occur at approximately the same time each year, the full cycles last longer than a year. The budget for the fiscal year that began on October 1, 1986, for example, had its origins in the budget review process conducted in the spring of 1984.) The formal policy cycles are preceded by and merge with an informal process that sets the president's agenda.

Policy Streams

The process of setting the president's domestic policy agenda can be understood as the convergence in the White House of three tributary streams: the first identifies problems and issues requiring attention; the second produces proposed solutions to the problems; and the third carries the political factors that establish the context for policy making.[8] According to John Kingdon, the three streams operate largely, but not absolutely, independently of one another. Problems and solutions develop separately and may or may not be joined, and political factors may change regardless of whether policy makers have recognized a problem or whether a potential solution is available. In Paul Light's model, the streams are brought together by two "filters"—resources and opportunities. In reality, he argues, presidents keep the flow of problems and solutions under control by having the White House staff (including the domestic policy apparatus) make the "filtering decisions." Successful policy leadership results from combining appropriate problems and solutions under favorable political circumstances.

Problems and Issues.　Problems and issues move onto the president's domestic policy agenda either because their seriousness and high visibility make it impossible to avoid them or because of presidential discretion. Recent unavoidable problems have included the energy shortages of the 1970s, double-digit rates of inflation and unemployment, the emergence of acquired immune deficiency syndrome (AIDS) as a major threat to public health, and the sharp drop in farm income accompanied by a shrinkage of agricultural credit.

Problems and issues stand a good chance of gaining a place on the agenda when enough important people, inside and outside the government, begin to think that something should be done about them.[9] This may happen as a consequence of changes in economic and social indicators, such as rates of inflation, unemployment, infant mortality, and scores on Scholastic Aptitude Tests. Key decision makers in the presidency, the bureaucracy, Congress, the private sector, and state and local governments routinely monitor changes in a large array of indicators. Whether the various indicators amount to a problem is a matter of interpretation. That interpretation takes place in the context of the symbolic significance of the matter, the personal experiences of the president and the other decision makers with it, and the relationship of the subject to other problems and issues.

The president and other key decision makers may be moved to recognize a condition as a compelling problem because of a "focusing event," such as a disaster or a crisis. For example, the near meltdown of a reactor at the Three

Mile Island power plant in March 1979 thrust the issue of nuclear safety to the forefront of the domestic agenda after its proponents had struggled for years with little success to gain recognition for it.

In addition, the president on occasion has no choice but to deal with a problem, even though he may strongly prefer not to do so. In 1986, for instance, President Reagan had to confront demands from some U.S. industries and their workers for protection from foreign competition when the House of Representatives passed a bill restricting textile and apparel imports. Reagan announced his opposition to the bill and pledged to work against Senate passage. His commitment to free trade was stronger than his aversion to facing a difficult issue.

Some problems and issues remain on the agenda through successive presidential administrations. Feasible solutions may not have been found, solutions may have been tried unsuccessfully, or the problem may have been "solved" only to reemerge in a different form. Education exemplifies such an issue. President Dwight D. Eisenhower turned to it reluctantly in 1958 as an appropriate response to the Soviet satellite *Sputnik*. Efforts of Presidents John F. Kennedy and Lyndon B. Johnson combined to spark the enactment of legislation establishing a wide range of federal programs that were expected to solve the problems of American education. President Carter brought education back to the agenda to fulfill a campaign promise to establish a cabinet-level department for the various programs. President Reagan took office publicly committed to abolish the newly created Department of Education. However, after several reports raised the issue of the falling quality of education, he called for improvement in the effectiveness of federal education programs (although with less funding) and dropped his proposal to abolish the department. Education remained on the domestic agenda even though Reagan would have liked to remove it. To have ignored it would have been a bad move symbolically.

Not all problems and issues, however, can command a place on the president's agenda. Presidents have broad discretion to determine which problems they will emphasize. The reason presidents place certain problems and not others on their agendas is that they see these problems as instrumental to the achievement of their goals. According to Paul Light, three goals affect presidents' selection of problems and issues for their agenda: reelection (for a first-term president); historical achievement; and a desire to shape public policy in accordance with their beliefs.[10] Presidents vary in the emphasis they place on these goals. President Richard Nixon's willingness to propose innovative policies for welfare reform and revenue sharing, even at the expense of alienating some of his conservative supporters, reflects his concern with historical achievement.[11] President Reagan has consistently defined domestic policy in terms of his conservative ideology, even at the risk of electoral disadvantage. President Carter shifted from initially making agenda decisions on the basis of his beliefs to making them increasingly on the basis of politics as he approached his reelection campaign. Variations in presidential goals help one to understand why abortion and school prayer have been important symbolic issues for Reagan but not for Ford and Carter, who were strongly committed to ratification of the Equal Rights Amendment.

Solutions. Once a problem or an issue has been recognized, the availability of a solution becomes an important determinant of whether it will rise to a high position on the president's agenda.[12] Rarely do presidents attempt to find new solutions; the incentives to do so are few.[13] Solutions take several forms, ranging from direct actions (such as legislative proposals or executive orders), to symbolic actions (such as appointment of a study commission or a task force), to no action at all. Problems can have several solutions, and a solution can be applied to more than one problem. Solutions attach themselves to a problem, or they may be consciously selected from among competing alternatives.

Most solutions that are coupled with problems on the president's agenda come from ideas generated outside the presidency. This is because the presidency is a small institution relative to its external environment, which contains an enormous number of potential sources of ideas. Also, there is not sufficient time for the presidency independently to analyze problems and issues and to evaluate alternative solutions to them. The principal external sources of ideas are Congress, the bureaucracy, interest groups, universities, research institutes, and state and local governments. Within the presidency, the president's campaign promises are a source of policy proposals and a benchmark for evaluating externally generated ideas.[14] Occasionally, the president's domestic policy staff may develop new ideas.

Many of the ideas that emerge as proposed solutions to problems on the president's agenda have been circulating among members of "issue networks" that develop around clusters of related problems and issues. (See the discussion in Chapter 7.) Individual policy entrepreneurs in Congress, government agencies, research organizations, universities, and state and local governments promote specific ideas and proposals, such as welfare reform and tax reform. These advocates are motivated by a desire to advance their personal and organizational interests and to influence public policy in accordance with their values. They study, analyze, and discuss problems and solutions among themselves, and they attempt to inform and influence key decision makers in the government, the most important of whom is the president.

The process by which ideas develop, advance, and either succeed or fail to gain acceptance in an issue network is often lengthy and generally diffused. John Kingdon describes it as a "policy primeval soup" in which ideas are continually bumping into one another, with some of them surviving, dying, combining, or emerging into new forms.[15] Those that manage to become incorporated in policy proposals that the president accepts are evaluated using three criteria: economic, political, and technical feasibility.

The budgetary cost of a potential solution is especially important, as demands for federal expenditures far outweigh the government's capacity to fund them. Few proposals for major new spending programs are likely to survive in an era of resource constraints. Proposals to restrain or reduce spending are more attractive to a president struggling to control the budget deficit. A proposal's political feasibility is determined initially by its compatibility with the values and interests of other key decision makers, particularly in Congress. Ultimately, a proposal must gain the acquiescence, if not the acceptance, of the mass public. The technical feasibility of a proposal—the question of its workability—does not receive as much attention as its economic and political costs. Some ideas—such as proposals for welfare reform that maintain reasonably high payments, reduce inequities between recipients in different states and between recipients and the working poor, and do not increase the cost to the government—are economically and politically very attractive but unworkable in practice. Presidents Nixon and Carter made this discovery, much to their dismay, after major efforts to achieve welfare reform.[16] Such conflict between the three criteria is always present. Budget costs may rule out a proposal that is politically and technically feasible, such as rapid cleanup of toxic waste sites. Or political costs may prevent acceptance of a workable proposal that is compatible with a tight budget, such as freezing social security cost-of-living increases. Eventually, a short list of presidential proposals emerges from a multitude of potential solutions.

Political Factors.   The third major component of the presidential policy stream is the tributary that carries political factors.[17] It flows independently of the problems and issues streams, but it strongly affects the setting and implementation of the president's agenda. The principal political factors are the national mood, the balance of political forces, and events within the government.

The national mood is a somewhat amorphous phenomenon that is difficult to define. It is not identical with public opinion, nor can it be ascertained through survey research. It is perhaps best described as the perception among important decision makers that a consensus exists or is building in the country among various attentive publics and political activists for specific governmental policies. Politicians sense the national mood in suggestions, requests, and other communications from interest groups, state and local government officials, corporate executives, and politically active citizens; in news media coverage of events; and in editorial commentary. The national mood also reflects the influence of social movements such as civil rights, environmentalism, and consumerism. Without a favorable national mood, major new policies, such as the deregulation of air transportation in 1978 or the military buildup since 1981, are not likely to be adopted. The national mood is, then, a reflection of the politically relevant climate or temper of the times.

Considerably more concrete than the national mood is the extent of consensus and conflict among organized political forces. The prospects for adoption of a proposed policy change depend strongly on the balance of organized interests and other forces. The assessment of the balance on an issue is largely a matter of informed guesswork. The complex pattern of pluralistic political forces and the fragmentation of government authority combine to provide a strong advantage to the *opponents* of policy change. Often, heavy political costs are associated with even raising an issue for consideration, let alone obtaining adoption of a proposal. This is particularly the case with existing government programs, most of which have powerful clientele groups that stand ready to defend their programs. Clientele interests, in triangular subgovernmental alliances with agencies that administer "their" programs and with congressional subcommittees with jurisdiction over those programs, engage in bargaining and logrolling to maintain and enhance the programs. To overcome the natural inertia of the government, a strong constituency for political change must be mobilized; otherwise, a proposal will encounter much difficulty. For example, the Carter administration's efforts to enact a national energy policy were unsuccessful despite widespread shortages of fuels, until compromises made the proposal acceptable to the oil industry and consumer interests.

Events in government itself are the third major political factor that shapes the president's policy agenda. Election outcomes that result in a change in personnel from the president down through the executive branch and in Congress can produce fundamental changes in the agenda. The Republican victory in 1980, which brought Ronald Reagan to the presidency and control of the Senate for the first time in a quarter of a century, was such an event. An ideologically defined, conservative agenda replaced the liberal agenda that had been in effect since the New Deal. Even the change of a single key official, such as the appointment of Donald Regan as White House chief of staff in February 1985, can have a substantial effect on the formulation and content of the agenda. Under Regan, the domestic issue agenda was determined increasingly by a few aggressive cabinet members—Attorney General Edwin Meese III and Treasury Secretary James A. Baker III—rather than by several cabinet committees, as in Reagan's first term.[18]

Jurisdictional matters are another intragovernmental development that may affect agenda setting. Disputes over bureaucratic and committee turf often delay or prevent action, although jurisdictional competition occasionally may accelerate consideration of a popular issue. Also, a proposal may be structured so that it will be handled by a committee or agency that is favorably disposed to it.

In sum, the most significant domestic policy action is likely to occur when the national mood and election outcomes combine to overcome the normal inertia produced by the balance of political forces and the fragmentation of government authority among numerous bureaucratic and congressional fiefdoms. Once items begin to rise on the agenda, however, organized political forces attempt to shape policy proposals to their advantage or to defeat them outright.

Resources and Opportunities

The convergence of specific problems and solutions under favorable circumstances creates a strong probability of a place on the president's agenda. Not all problems and solutions, however, can receive the president's attention and consideration. Because agenda space is limited, presidents must establish priorities.[19] This is accomplished through what Light calls a "filtering process" that maintains an orderly flow of problems and solutions to the president and merges them to produce policy proposals. The objectives of the process are to control the flow of items so that important problems, issues, and alternatives receive attention without overloading the president and to ensure that policy proposals have been formulated with due regard to relevant political factors. There are two filters through which problems and solutions pass as they are melded into presidential decisions: resources and opportunities.

Presidents cannot place all policy proposals that they receive on their agenda. Some proposals are not compatible with their overall objectives and their ideologies, but many otherwise acceptable proposals never reach the agenda because limitations on their resources impose constraints on the choices open to presidents. When President Reagan took office, a lengthy list of conservative policy goals awaited action. He decided to focus on the goals of reducing the scope of domestic programs, increasing military preparedness, and reducing taxes. He accomplished most of this agenda during his first year in office. He disappointed many of his supporters, however, by not moving forward with equally strong support for proposals that would end abortion, restore prayer in public schools, and provide financial aid to parents of children enrolled in private schools. Reagan and his staff recognized that his resources, although substantial, were limited and that successful policy leadership requires the careful use of them.

The president's principal policy resources are time, energy, information, expertise, political capital, and material wherewithal (that is, money, people, supplies, equipment, and land). The president must decide how to allocate these resources among the policy proposals competing for his attention and a place on the agenda. Time and energy impose limits on all human activity. If presidents tend to be preoccupied with national security policy and economic policy, as most modern presidents have been, domestic policy matters frequently are neglected or are handled by staff. Presidents usually have greater access to information and expertise than other decision makers, but solutions to some problems may not exist, or they may be based on questionable assumptions. Most presidents have had to learn on the job, acquiring information and developing expertise as their terms progress.

"Political capital" is the reservoir of popular and congressional support with which newly elected presidents begin their terms. As they make controversial decisions, they "spend" some of their capital, which they seldom are able to replenish. They must decide which proposals merit the expenditure of political capital and in what amounts. Reagan, for example, has been willing to spend his capital heavily on reducing the role of the federal government, cutting taxes, and reforming the income tax code, but not on antiabortion or school prayer amendments to the Constitution. Material resources determine which proposals for new programs can be advanced and the emphasis to be placed on existing programs. Reagan's commitments to strengthen national defense and maintain social security meant that his costly proposal to provide income tax credits to parents of children attending private schools had little prospect of being adopted.

Opportunities are often described metaphorically as windows: they open for a while, and then they close. They may be scheduled or unscheduled. Scheduled opportunities occur in conjunction with the annual cycle of presidential messages to Congress (State of the Union, budget, and economic report), the congressional calendar, and action-forcing deadlines, such as renewals of program authorizations. The president's greatest opportunity to set the agenda occurs during January and February, when Congress convenes and he delivers his messages, and in August and September, when Congress returns from recess and earlier proposals can be replaced or modified.[20] Unscheduled opportunities occur as the result of focusing events or changes in political conditions. Both scheduled and unscheduled windows of opportunity eventually close, some sooner than others. An opportunity is more likely to be seized and an issue given a high place on the president's agenda when problems, solutions, and political factors come together.[21] Without a viable solution and in the absence of favorable political conditions, a problem has limited chance of moving up on the agenda. For instance, popular support for biomedical research is substantial, but the slow pace of development of treatments and cures for cancer limits presidential attention to the issue.

Opportunities also fluctuate as a presidential term progresses. In a president's first year in office, Congress and the public have high expectations of policy change based on campaign promises and the election mandate. Opportunities tend to be at their peak during the so-called honeymoon period. In the second and fourth years of a president's term, concern focuses increasingly on the forthcoming election campaign, and policy opportunities decline. The third year is frequently regarded as crucial, for the administration is by then experienced, mature, removed from immediate electoral pressures, and anxious to make its mark.[22] Opportunities are most likely to be exploited effectively then and in the first year of a president's second term, assuming he is reelected. Once it appears that a president will not continue in office beyond his current term, his "lame-duck" status tends to restrict further his policy opportunities. The effects of lame-duck status on presidential initiatives are especially notable following the midterm election in a president's second term.

There are conflicting patterns in the progression of a president's opportunities as he moves through his term. On the one hand, as presidents acquire experience and expertise, they become more effective and thus increase their policy opportunities. On the other hand, as their congressional and popular support declines through the term, they lose opportunities. Light describes these patterns as cycles of increasing effectiveness and declining influence.[23] It is ironic that as presidents become more skilled at finding opportunities, they become less able to exploit them.

The Domestic Policy Environment

The most outstanding characteristic of the domestic policy environment is its complexity. A myriad of actors—individuals, groups, and other government institutions and agencies—each pursues a seemingly incalculable range of objectives and protects countless interests. Although the president's power is limited,[24] he is better situated than anyone else to give direction and bring some degree of coordination to the domestic policies of the U.S. government.

The fragmentation of political power and influence that is the hallmark of the U.S. political system is the product of a heterogeneous and pluralistic society and of constitutional arrangements designed to produce deliberate rather than expeditious governmental decision making. Nowhere is the fragmentation of power more apparent and more profound than in the domestic policy environment.

Outside the government, thousands of interest groups constantly seek to influence policy. They range from organizations that are concerned with the full range of the government's activities, such as Americans for Democratic Action, to those that focus sharply on a single issue, such as the National Rifle Association (NRA), which is dedicated to preventing the adoption of strict gun control legislation. (In early 1986, the NRA succeeded in getting Congress to relax restrictions on the ownership of hand guns.) Interest groups are concerned not only with virtually every government program that distributes benefits to individuals and organizations and regulates their conduct but also with possibilities for new programs. Simply stated, the objectives of interest groups are to secure the adoption of policies that are beneficial to their members and to prevent the adoption of policies that they view as harmful to them. Interest groups operate in all sectors of domestic policy— agriculture, civil rights, social welfare, and natural resources. They include organizations that represent business, labor, the professions, consumers, state and local governments and their subdivisions, public officials, social groupings based on age, sex, race, religion, shared attitudes and experiences, and groups that present themselves as protectors of the unorganized public interest.

Within the national government, interest groups attempt to exert influence directly on Congress, the bureaucracy, the courts, and the presidency. Presidents beginning with Lyndon Johnson have responded in two principal ways to the proliferation of interest groups, the apparent rise of group influence, and efforts of groups to influence them. First, they assigned to individual White House aides responsibility for maintaining liaison with interest groups in key policy areas such as civil rights, education, and health. Second, when a few individual aides were unable to manage the function of interest group liaison, as increasing numbers of groups sought access to the presidency, the Public Liaison Office was established in the White House as a counterpart to the Congressional Liaison Office. (The Public Liaison and Congressional Liaison offices are discussed further in Chapters 4 and 6, respectively.) Interest groups have attempted to exert influence indirectly, principally by endorsing and making campaign contributions to presidential and congressional candidates and by urging their members to bring pressure to bear on the White House and on their representatives in Congress.

It is difficult to measure the effectiveness of interest group influence on public policy because there are multiple points of access to government decision makers, numerous groups usually seek to influence a particular policy or set of related policies, and powerful forces other than interest groups are also at work. Nonetheless, there is widespread belief that the growth in interest group activity since 1965 contributed substantially to the rise of federal spending on domestic programs and the expansion of federal regulation into noneconomic areas, such as consumer protection, product safety, and occupational safety and health.[25] Since 1965, previously unorganized groups—for example, consumer groups, public interest groups, and groups representing various minorities and the poor—have successfully demanded federal benefits and regulatory intervention in behalf of their members. These demands, often asserted as a matter of "right" and defended on grounds of values such as fairness or improving the quality of life, placed severe stress on the fiscal capacity of the federal government and created new conflicts in society.

Mancur Olson, an economist, has argued that societies with large numbers of powerful "distributional coalitions" (his term for interest groups) have experienced unsupportably high public spending and little or no economic growth as a consequence of the political influence of such groups. The groups press for public benefits for their members even though the result may be disadvantageous to the entire community. According to Olson, unless an interest group encompasses most of the population, there is "no constraint on the social cost such an organization will find it expedient to impose on the society in the cause of obtaining a larger share of the social output for itself." [26] To a substantial extent, domestic policy politics have become the pursuit of narrow group interests, even at the expense of the general public interest, which is usually unorganized, unarticulated, and difficult to identify or define. The president is better situated, in terms of political resources, than anyone else to define, enhance, and defend the public interest. That is his principal challenge in the domestic policy area. President Truman was fond of saying that his job was to act as a lobbyist for the American people, most of whom are not represented by lobbyists.

The pattern of interest group activity traditionally has been described as "policy subgovernments," mutually beneficial triangular relationships between interest groups, administrative agencies, and congressional subcommittees. Subgovernments, and the more open and amorphous "issue networks" that cut across and intersect with them, contribute to the fragmentation of power and influence in the domestic policy environment. (See Chapter 7.)

That fragmentation is enhanced by constitutional arrangements that divide power among the branches of government and between the national and state governments and also by the internal structures of Congress and the federal bureaucracy. The constitutional design was created to prevent the abuse of power through the establishment of a system of "separated institutions sharing power." [27]

The Framers invented federalism as a means of resolving the seemingly insoluble conflict between advocates of a consolidated system of government and the proponents of state sovereignty. Their ingenious compromise, which artfully avoided establishing a precise boundary between national and state powers, has been adapted to the needs of the times by successive generations of political leaders. The current system of centralized federalism still leaves primary responsibility for most basic government services in the hands of the states and their local subdivisions. These services include public education, public and mental health, public safety, and construction and maintenance of streets, roads, and highways. The federal government has programs that help finance state and local activities in these and other areas, and it exerts a substantial degree of influence on them by virtue of its grant and regulatory programs. Still, most of its domestic policy activity does not entail direct federal administration.

The president's leadership role in domestic policy requires that he persuade, bargain, and cooperate with Congress, federal administrators, and state and local officials. In these relationships he has limited power to command. Rather, he must rely on his skills as a political leader—principally persuasion and bargaining—to achieve his goals.

The structure of authority in Congress is highly decentralized, providing members with extensive opportunities to influence policy. Consequently, Congress finds it very difficult to give direction to public policy, and presidents encounter problems in their relations with Congress. (See Chapter 6.) In today's political environment, unlike that of the late 1950s and early 1960s, presidents cannot negotiate agreements with top party leaders and one or two key committee chairs in each house and be confident that those agreements will prevail in floor voting. Rather, contemporary presidents must deal separately, in each house, with several committee chairs, subcommittee chairs, and party leaders. In addition, they must remain attentive to the positions of party caucuses and subcaucuses. Agreements reached at one stage in the legislative process often come undone later on; such reverses frequently happened during the 1980s as President Reagan and Congress struggled to reduce budgetary deficits. There is also increasing conflict within Congress between committees resulting from initiation of the practice of referring bills to more than one committee and from the establishment of the congressional budget process in 1974. The functions of the newly established budget committees have encroached upon the powers of the appropriations and authorization (legislative) committees.

The effects of Congress's extensive fragmentation on the president's involvement in domestic policy are mixed. On the one hand, Congress is unable to counterbalance the presidency by providing alternative policy leadership. On the other hand, presidents have found it increasingly difficult to lead Congress. Congressional influence is extensive because of its inertia and its ability to resist presidential direction.

Fragmentation of a different sort characterizes the federal bureaucracy. As noted in Chapter 7, an independent power exists in the bureaucracy that is based in career civil servants who constitute a permanent government. The members of the permanent government have professional and agency loyalties and close ties to the interest groups who constitute their clientele and to the congressional subcommittees with jurisdiction over their appropriations and the legislation that authorizes their programs. Subgovernments and issue networks comprise members of the permanent government and complicate presidential control of policy development and implementation in the bureaucracy. Also, the fragmentation resulting from the size and complexity of the federal bureaucracy creates enormous problems of management and policy coordination for the president.

The Domestic Policy Apparatus

The need for presidential coordination in domestic policy has been recognized for some time. The principal effort to enable presidents to provide the necessary coordination was the development of a domestic policy staff apparatus in the Executive Office of the President. The domestic policy staff evolved slowly, in conjunction with the development of the president's legislative role. (See Chapter 6.) This was an evolutionary process that relied initially on the Bureau of the Budget (BOB) and later saw the establishment of a separate staff to formulate and implement domestic policy.

BOB: Central Clearance and Legislative Program Planning

From the early nineteenth century until the creation of BOB in 1921, the president's role in domestic policy formulation was ad hoc and unorganized.[28] In its first year of operation, BOB required that all agency legislative proposals for the expenditure of federal funds be submitted to it before being sent to Congress. Those proposals that BOB determined were not in accord with the president's financial program were not sent to Congress, and agencies were to inform Congress if pending legislation had been found not in accord. This procedure, known as "central clearance," was expanded during Franklin D. Roosevelt's administration to cover the substantive content of proposed legislation. Its original function was to ensure that legislative proposals of various departments and agencies were compatible with the president's overall program goals.[29] Over time, central clearance acquired additional functions, including supervising and coordinating executive branch legislative initiatives, providing a clear indication to congressional committees of the president's position on proposed legislation, and making various administrative units aware of one another's goals and activities.

Beginning in 1947, BOB's domestic policy role expanded to include participation in developing the president's legislative program.[30] Its Legislative Reference Division worked directly with the White House staff in reviewing agency recommendations and integrating them in a comprehensive legislative program. The addition of responsibilities to formulate policy involved BOB personnel in the pursuit of the president's political goals, a development that may later have resulted in questions about its ability to provide professional staff services to the president. Moreover, in the 1960s, as BOB became deeply involved in program planning, White House staff played an increasing role in the clearance process, and the line between clearance and legislative program planning became more and more blurred.[31]

Although President Eisenhower was initially unprepared to submit a legislative program to Congress, he quickly recognized that he was expected to do so. The centralized clearance and planning processes lodged in BOB were quite compatible with Eisenhower's penchant for systematic staff operations, and he continued to employ them throughout his administration. The principal distinction between him and his predecessor in this regard was that Eisenhower attached a lower priority to new domestic policy proposals. Central to the process of legislative programming as it had developed by 1960 were annual submissions of legislative proposals by departments and agencies. Items that were not enacted in one year were introduced in the next. The result was a highly routinized process that was nearly impervious to new ideas. This system was quite suitable for Eisenhower's limited domestic policy initiatives.

Task Forces and Study Commissions

The activist Democratic presidents of the 1960s, John Kennedy and Lyndon Johnson, overcame the rigidities and bureaucratic domination of the BOB-based program planning process by obtaining ideas and suggestions from nongovernment sources.[32] The mechanism used for this purpose was the task force. Before his inauguration, Kennedy appointed several study groups, or task forces, of experts from inside and outside the government to advise him on the major issues and problems facing the new administration. The reports of these task forces, and of a number of others appointed after Kennedy took office, provided the basis for much of his New Frontier program.[33]

Although Kennedy remained eager for new ideas and suggestions, he did not rely heavily on outside sources of advice after the initial round of task forces. Instead, he turned primarily to his cabinet for suggestions. Johnson appointed a set of task forces in the spring of 1964 with the specific mission of developing a distinctive program for his administration. The Johnson task forces comprised outsiders, and they operated in secret. He was so pleased with their reports, which furnished much of the form and substance of his Great Society program, that he made task forces a regular part of his program development process. The White House staff coordinated the task force operations, and BOB integrated the proposals into the annual legislative program.

Johnson favored the task force process because it largely avoided the tortuous task of bargaining with departments and agencies and because it was not adulterated by bureaucratic, congressional, and interest group pressures.[34] He used the task force device so extensively, however—in 1967 alone at least fifty task forces were preparing reports—that it became routinized and lost the informality and flexibility that had made it so valuable for developing new proposals. Moreover, later in his presidency, Johnson's emphasis shifted from domestic to foreign and military policy as the nation became heavily embroiled in the Vietnam War and the need for new ideas declined.

The presidents who followed Johnson made little use of task forces. (Nixon appointed fourteen task forces during his campaign, but their suggestions did not figure prominently in his initial legislative proposals.) Instead, they have relied on more formal advisory bodies, such as commissions and White House conferences, to study issues and problems and to gather outside recommendations. Presidential commissions are broadly represen-tative bodies that often are appointed to defuse highly sensitive issues. In September 1981, for example, President Reagan appointed the National Commission on Social Security Reform to develop a solution to a crisis in so-cial security funding. (Although the commission did not solve the social security crisis, it provided "cover" under which the principals, President Reagan and House Speaker Thomas P. O'Neill, worked out a compromise solution.)[35]

Because of the representative character of presidential commissions, their reports often blur critical issues. This occurs in consequence of their efforts to obtain consensus. Or, commissions may make findings and suggestions that embarrass the president, as did the 1970 report of the Scranton commission, which blamed campus disorders on President Nixon.

White House conferences bring together groups of experts and distinguished citizens for public forums held under presidential auspices. Their principal function is to build support among experts, political leaders, and relevant interests for presidential leadership to deal with the problems at issue. Neither White House conferences nor presidential commissions have served as the basis for major legislative proposals, but they have given legitimacy to certain presidential undertakings.

Domestic Policy Staffs

President Johnson's successors have not regularly employed task forces in developing their legislative programs, nor have they relied almost entirely on agency submissions, as did Truman and Eisenhower. Instead, they have used domestic policy staffs in the Executive Office of the President and a more politicized Office of Management and Budget (OMB).

President Nixon established the Domestic Council in 1970 as part of a reorganization of the presidency, in which the Bureau of the Budget was redesignated as the Office of Management and Budget.[36] The Domestic Council comprised the president, the vice president, the attorney general, and the secretaries of agriculture, commerce, housing and urban development, interior, labor, transportation, treasury, and health, education and welfare, as well as the director and deputy director of OMB. Initially, it was envisioned that the Domestic Council would be a top-level forum for discussion, debate, and determination of policy analogous to the National Security Council (NSC). (See Chapter 11.) Like the NSC, the Domestic Council had a staff of professionals and support personnel. Headed by John Ehrlichman, the presidential assistant for domestic policy, the staff dominated Nixon's domestic policy-making process during the last two years of his first term, 1971-1972.[37]

The Domestic Council conducted its activity through work groups headed by one of six assistant directors. These groups prepared working papers for the president, evaluated departmental proposals for legislation, and participated in drafting presidential messages to Congress and preparing supportive materials for specific legislative proposals. In addition to assisting the president in formulating policy proposals, the Domestic Council also advocated, monitored, and evaluated policy.[38] This arrangement, in effect, made Ehrlichman the president's general agent for domestic policy. The Domestic Council under Ehrlichman centralized control over domestic policy in the White House. The president's interests, as defined and expressed by Ehrlichman, took precedence over the interests of departments and agencies as conveyed by cabinet members and agency heads.

The Domestic Council's domination of domestic policy did not survive Ehrlichman's departure from the White House in April 1973.[39] The influence of the staff was clearly a function of Ehrlichman's status with the president. Under Ehrlichman's successor, Kenneth Cole, the Domestic

Council became more of a service unit, and OMB resumed many of the functions of planning legislative programs.

In addition to the development of a presidential staff for domestic policy, Nixon also effected a major transformation in OMB by using it for his own political purposes. The director of OMB became indistinguishable from other high-level presidential assistants, and a layer of political appointees, called "program assistant directors," was placed above OMB's career staff. The politicization of OMB by Nixon reduced its capacity to serve the institutional needs of the presidency as an impartial professional staff agency.

President Ford used OMB to facilitate the unusual transfer of power from Nixon to himself, and he relied on it to help plan and coordinate programs in a more traditional and less partisan manner than did his predecessor. Initially, Ford intended to give the Domestic Council a major planning role by making Vice President Nelson Rockefeller its chair. However, Rockefeller never became Ford's general agent for domestic policy. The long delay in congressional confirmation of Rockefeller's appointment and his conflict with White House chief of staff Donald Rumsfeld appear to have prevented such a development.[40] The council's staff director, James Cannon, a Rockefeller appointee, never gained influence with Ford, who sought advice from a wide range of sources including OMB, several cabinet members, and the Economic Policy Board, which was established in 1974 as a result of Ford's concern with economic policy problems. (See Chapter 10.) That emphasis partly explains why Ford seldom used the Domestic Council for policy planning. Indeed, Stephen Wayne reports that by the fall of 1976 the council no longer participated in legislative programming, and the staff was engaged in such diverse activities as answering presidential mail, preparing policy option memoranda, drafting presidential statements on legislation, and helping to explain the president's program to Congress.[41]

President Carter abolished the Domestic Council shortly after taking office, but he retained a domestic policy staff headed by one of his top aides, Stuart Eizenstat. In some respects Eizenstat and his staff acquired a policy-making role that resembled that of Ehrlichman and the Domestic Council in the Nixon administration. Margaret Wyszomirski concludes, however, that Eizenstat and the domestic policy staff did not dominate the domestic policy process and that they functioned more in the role of "effective administrator and of contributing advisor." [42] Lester Salamon believes that Ford and Carter brought about a "significant de-institutionalization" of the White House domestic policy role through the use of interagency policy task forces chaired by department or agency heads.[43] He further maintains that during the Carter administration these task forces produced undesirable effects, including interagency rivalry, lack of timeliness and coherence in decisions, and a disorderly process that bypassed career personnel in the Executive Office of the President.

According, however, to *National Journal* correspondent Dom Bonafede, a veteran observer of the presidency, Eizenstat was deeply involved in domestic policy making:

> He helps select presidential priorities, reviews prospective initiatives with top-level Administration officials, coordinates interdepartmental proposals, drafts options available to the President, offers personal recommendations, supervises his staff in the refinement of policy, maintains liaison with members of Congress to effect mutually acceptable solutions and frequently briefs the press and other interested groups on Administration positions.[44]

Not surprisingly, the concentration of such authority in a presidential policy staff led to questions of whether the staff was overextended and whether it had "accumulated too much power at the expense of the Cabinet." [45] Like his predecessors, Carter had moved from initial expressions of support for the cabinet as a primary source of advice and ideas to the centralization of domestic policy making in the White House.

Perhaps pressures on Eizenstat and the domestic policy staff were excessive, for by early 1980 Vice President Walter Mondale was chairing a committee charged with preparing the president's legislative program.[46] The committee, staffed by Mondale's office, reviewed proposals, consulted with OMB or the domestic policy staff about them, winnowed out those proposals requiring presidential support, and prepared memoranda on them for the president's approval. The domestic policy staff then prepared the president's messages. It was not clear whether this change was merely a shift in the workload from an overburdened domestic policy staff or constituted a substantial diminution in its role. It is significant that President Carter's major policy concerns and initiatives during his fourth year in office were with foreign and military policy—the Iranian hostage crisis, the Soviet invasion of Afghanistan, increased defense spending in the 1981 budget, and his proposal to institute selective service registration.

Ronald Reagan, who came to office with a set, ideologically defined policy agenda and a strong commitment to cabinet government, created a new policy apparatus. The principal units were the Office of Policy Development (OPD), seven cabinet councils, and OMB. OMB's domestic policy involvement was especially crucial during Reagan's first year in office (1981) when the prime objective of drastically reducing the role of the federal government was linked to a budget reduction strategy that was implemented through use of the congressional budget process. (See Chapter 10.) OMB director David Stockman was the principal architect of the first substantial rollback of the government's domestic programs since the New Deal. OPD was the Reagan equivalent of Carter's domestic policy staff. Headed by a presidential assistant for policy development, OPD worked through cabinet councils, which had jurisdiction over the following areas: economic affairs, commerce and trade, human resources, natural resources and environment, food and agriculture, legal policy, and management and administration.[47] The councils' members included appropriate cabinet and subcabinet officers and personnel from

OMB and the White House staff. Each council had a secretariat composed of department and agency representatives and used working groups to provide expertise and to analyze issues.

OPD and the councils did not, however, become the directing force for domestic policy; other factors, particularly the president's long-range objectives and budgetary pressures, determined the agenda from the beginning of the administration. According to Chester Newland, President Reagan's domestic policy apparatus worked out "details secondary to the president's fixed view of government." [48] In other words, it performed an administrative rather than an advisory role.

To the extent that Reagan required domestic policy advice, he obtained it from a small group of top aides, each with his own base of influence and with independent access to the president. Included among Reagan's principal domestic advisors were presidential counselor Edwin Meese, White House Chief of Staff James Baker, budget director David Stockman, and Treasury Secretary Donald Regan. In spite of frequent conflicts among this group, it managed to give direction to domestic policy actions within the limits imposed by the president's ideology. Newland maintains that because the Reagan administration defined domestic policy goals in ideological terms and proceeded to structure and staff the domestic policy apparatus accordingly, its "imprint will endure only as long as it remains in office." [49] Certainly the role of the Reagan domestic policy staff and its director has been smaller than at any time since its creation in 1970.

Developments in the first year of Reagan's second term resulted in a further diminution of the OPD/cabinet council system. Early in 1985 Baker and Regan changed jobs, and Meese became attorney general. Stockman returned to private life in August 1985. As chief of staff, Regan moved quickly to bring the three major policy areas—economics, national security, and domestic policy— under his control. The number of cabinet councils was reduced from seven to two, Economic Affairs and Domestic Policy. (The National Security Council, a statutory body, remained as it was.) Baker and Meese chaired the economic and domestic policy councils, respectively. OPD was reduced in size, and its director reported to Regan. In addition to simplifying and reducing the size of the OPD/cabinet council system, Regan centralized authority over domestic policy in his office. However, the two remaining cabinet council chairs, Meese and Baker, enjoyed substantial autonomy to pursue policy projects of their own choosing. By early 1986 Regan had gained control of all access to the president with respect to domestic policy not under the purview of the two cabinet councils. The competition between Meese, Baker, Stockman, and Regan to influence domestic policy had all but disappeared.

The diminished domestic policy apparatus of Reagan's second term reflected a shift in the administration's orientation from changing policies to defending them. Having accomplished most of his initial domestic policy agenda, principally curtailment of the growth of federal programs and a reduction in spending on them, Reagan concentrated his energies on national security and economic policy objectives. The domestic policy apparatus under Reagan has been at least partially deinstitutionalized. Its future role will depend, in large part, on the policy goals and operating styles of Reagan's successors. Presidents who seek major policy changes and those who rely extensively on staff analyses for policy-making support will require a more elaborate domestic policy apparatus than that inherited from the Reagan administration.

Modern Presidents and Domestic Policy

Modern presidents have varied greatly in the extent of their interest and involvement in domestic policy. Franklin Roosevelt was preoccupied with domestic policy during his first two terms (1933-1941) as he orchestrated the development, enactment, and implementation of the New Deal. The New Deal encompassed the most extensive set of social and economic reforms in the history of the United States. Its immediate stimulus was the Great Depression, but it was also a response to the effects of urbanization and industrialization.

Roosevelt's approach to domestic policy was very pragmatic. He tried a wide range of policies. Those that did not work were quickly discarded. Those that were successful were incorporated in a greatly expanded role for the federal government, which assumed positive responsibilities for individual, corporate, and general welfare that went far beyond the traditional negative functions of safeguarding public health, safety, and morals. Among the most prominent legacies of the New Deal are the social security system, unemployment compensation, support of agricultural prices, insurance of bank deposits, extensive public works projects such as the Grand Coulee dam, the Tennessee Valley Authority, and federal regulation of securities exchanges, communications, and energy. During his final years in office (1941-1945), FDR devoted himself almost exclusively to national security policy, as "Dr. Win-the-War" took over from "Dr. New Deal."

Roosevelt's successor, Harry Truman, was heavily involved with national security from the start of his presidency even though his interests and experience lay in the area of domestic policy. In his first term (1945-1949), Truman offered few domestic policy initiatives, for he was occupied with the transition from war to peace and with difficulties in dealing with America's wartime ally the Soviet Union. Following his upset reelection victory in 1948, Truman proposed a comprehensive set of domestic policy reforms called the Fair Deal. The Fair Deal agenda included national health insurance, federal aid to education, and expanded agricultural price supports. Little of the Fair Deal was implemented, however, as the Cold War intensified and the United States became involved in the Korean War (1950-1953).

Truman's successor, Gen. Dwight Eisenhower, a World War II hero, was a conservative who had no desire to expand the federal government's role in the life of the nation. He did not, however, attempt to repeal any of the New Deal reforms. His administration (1953-1961) was marked by economic expansion, punctuated by recessions in 1954 and 1958, and by stabilization in international affairs. Among Eisenhower's major domestic policy accomplishments were the passage of the National Defense Education Act in 1958, a direct response to the Soviet success in launching the first earth satellite, and limited civil rights bills in 1957 and 1960.

Domestic policy innovation and expansion of federal programs were a central objective of Presidents John Kennedy (1961-1963) and Lyndon Johnson (1963-1969). Kennedy developed and submitted to Congress an extensive domestic policy agenda labeled the New Frontier. It included most of the unfinished agenda of the Fair Deal plus proposals for expanded civil rights legislation.

At the time of Kennedy's assassination, in November 1963, Congress was considering several pieces of New Frontier legislation. President Johnson moved quickly and effectively in 1964 to secure passage of much of the Kennedy agenda; for example, the Vocational Education Act, the Higher Education Act, and the Civil Rights Act of 1964. In addition, he launched the War on Poverty, featuring the Economic Opportunity Act of 1964, which established the Office of Economic Opportunity. In his 1964 election campaign, Johnson proposed additional domestic reforms under the rubric the Great Society. The year 1965 witnessed the largest outpouring of new domestic policy legislation since the New Deal. Congress passed the Elementary and Secondary Education Act, the Voting Rights Act, and legislation authorizing medicare, medicaid, and the model cities program. New departments of Housing and Urban Development and of Transportation were established. Hundreds of new federal grant-in-aid programs for state and local governments were implemented. Johnson's zealous pursuit of domestic policy goals gave way, however, to international concerns. His attention in his last two years in office (1967 and 1968) was taken up by the Vietnam War. Funding for Great Society programs was restricted before many of them could be fully implemented as the costs of the war consumed an increasing portion of the federal budget. Opposition to the war in the United States and from abroad led Johnson to retire from public life rather than seek reelection.

President Richard Nixon, who succeeded Johnson in 1969, was primarily interested in national security policy. However, he did offer an innovative proposal to reform the welfare system, which Congress ultimately rejected. He also considered a variety of innovative suggestions for reforming the financing of public education. Perhaps his principal domestic policy accomplishment was the establishment of federal revenue-sharing with state and local governments. Nixon's major achievements, however, were in the realm of national security policy.

Nixon's successor, Gerald Ford, was a conservative who had no strong commitments to domestic policy innovation. Although Ford had a substantial domestic policy background, he was essentially a passive president in the area.

President Jimmy Carter, a moderate in a largely liberal party, presented a wide range of domestic policy proposals during his administration. He struggled extensively with Congress over a national energy policy. The legislation that eventually passed was a watered-down compromise. He was unable to obtain passage of his proposal for welfare reform, and he temporized at length before proposing a national health insurance plan. Carter was an active president in domestic policy, but he achieved few of his major objectives.

Ronald Reagan campaigned successfully for the presidency in 1980 with the most radical and conservative proposals for domestic policy since the New Deal. Reagan's stated purpose was no less than to institute a "new American Revolution." The essentials of that revolution in domestic policy were defined in terms of Reagan's conservative ideology. The role of the federal government would be drastically curtailed, except for the armed forces and support for law enforcement. There would be a massive devolution of federal programs to state and local governments. The reduction in federal spending for domestic programs would provide the resources for an overdue military buildup, made necessary by the threat posed by the Soviet Union, and for a substantial cut in income taxes. Reagan further believed that the tax cut would stimulate an economic expansion that would generate enough revenue to bring the federal budget into balance. Finally, Reagan was firmly committed to reducing drastically federal regulation of the economy, the environment, and the work place.

The foundation of Reagan's domestic policy goals was an unswerving belief in the viability of a free market as the means of rationally and efficiently allocating resources and maximizing productivity. This would increase material well-being and enhance individual freedom. Reagan's domestic policy objectives were long-range. He was not, nor did he ever become, interested in the details of specific programs. What was to be done in domestic policy had to be compatible with the long-range goals that flowed from his ideological frame of reference. Pragmatic adjustments and compromises with individuals and interests who did not share his ideology were to be avoided at all costs. In this respect he stood in sharp contrast to his predecessors from FDR to Carter.

Conclusion

Presidents approach the task of making domestic policy with variable amounts of resources and differing policy opportunities. Their domestic policy leadership depends to a large extent on their effectiveness in using the available resources to exploit existing opportunities and create new ones.

They are most apt to do this effectively when the three components of the policy stream—problems, solutions, and politics—converge. A president's ability to bring these three tributary streams together is one indication of effective policy leadership.

Successful policy leadership requires careful expenditure of presidential resources and skillful exploitation of opportunities. To do so further requires that presidents pay particular attention to four strategic factors: goals, priorities, timing, and costs and benefits.

Modest, flexible goals usually are easier to achieve than those that are extensive and ideologically derived. So too, are goals that enjoy substantial support among the public and policy-making elites. In establishing their goals, presidents take such considerations into account along with their values and beliefs. A primarily pragmatic set of objectives tends to be easier to accomplish than one that is ideologically derived. It is less likely, however, to have an impact on society than is a more visionary and comprehensive set of objectives. In some circumstances ideological goals may be highly appropriate. For example, President Reagan initially struck a responsive note in Congress and the public with his unabashedly conservative domestic program. Presidents are free to be as pragmatic or as ideological as they wish in establishing their goals. However they decide, the mix they choose affects their policy leadership.

Closely related to goals, priorities also affect policy leadership. Presidents who clearly define their priorities have generally been more successful than those who have not done so, because the policy process can handle only a few major issues at a time even though many contend for attention. If a president does not indicate his preferences, other participants will pursue their own objectives, possibly to the detriment of the president's. Nor is it realistic for presidents to expect that all of their goals will receive consideration to the exclusion of those of other participants. In this respect a comparison between Presidents Carter and Reagan is instructive. Carter developed a lengthy domestic agenda and insisted that all of his goals were vitally important to the nation and deserving of enactment. Congress responded by taking its time in dealing with Carter's program and by pursuing many of its own objectives. Key Carter goals, such as welfare reform and national health insurance, were never adopted; others, such as a national energy policy, were passed in greatly modified form after extensive delay and bargaining. Many congressional Democrats complained that Carter failed to provide them with direction and guidance for his domestic proposals. In contrast, Reagan made his priorities clear at the beginning of his administration, and he continued to do so. Congress had little doubt about which goals Reagan considered vital and on which he would spend political capital and those that were less important to him. Cutting domestic spending, strengthening national defense, and reducing and reforming taxes have taken precedence over balancing the federal budget, ending abortion, and restoring school prayer.

Timing, the third strategic consideration in successful policy leadership, is crucial to effective exploitation of opportunities. If opportunities are missed, they may be lost indefinitely. Good timing also involves taking advantage of the regular policy and electoral cycles. Proposals submitted at appropriate times in those cycles have greater likelihood of adoption. Proposals can also be withheld until conditions are ripe for their submission. A potential proposal that has limited support can be moved to the top of the agenda and pushed successfully as the result of a disaster, crisis, or other focusing event. Presidents who are able to time the presentation of proposals to coincide with favorable events and conditions are more likely to be effective policy leaders than those who lack such a sense of timing. Two presidents whose timing of domestic proposals was effective were Franklin Roosevelt during the First 100 Days of the New Deal, when the Great Depression provided the rationale for a comprehensive set of economic recovery and reform laws, and Lyndon Johnson, who in early 1964 used the shock of the Kennedy assassination to secure passage of the Civil Rights Act.

Finally, successful policy leadership requires that presidents be attentive to the costs and benefits of raising problems for consideration and proposing solutions to them. As presidents decide which problems and issues to emphasize, they focus on potential benefits. They select agenda items according to the prospective electoral, historical, and programmatic benefits of the items.[50] When presidents select solutions for problems they are addressing, their emphasis is on costs.[51] Political costs, assessed in terms of congressional, electoral, bureaucratic, and interest group support, enter their calculations at each stage of the process.[52] Economic costs have sharply limited the alternatives in recent years as budgetary pressures have mounted. They force hard choices on presidents, such as whether to support new programs and which existing programs to emphasize, maintain, or reduce. Technical costs and questions of workability also enter the selection of policy alternatives.

No prescription or formula can guarantee that a president will provide successful domestic policy leadership. In part this is because some problems, such as the high unemployment rate among teenaged black males, are unsolvable, or solutions do not exist for them. Another reason for the absence of a workable formula is that conditions, like the protean character of the institutional presidency, constantly change. Some problems may be solved only to reemerge in a new form; others may decline in importance. Solutions that are viable today may not be so a few years hence, or solutions may have unanticipated consequences or side effects that become problems in their own right. Political conditions, such as the popular mood or control of Congress, are in flux, so strategies may have to be modified frequently. Thus, many of the requirements of successful policy leadership, like the presidency itself, are protean in nature. They are not fixed. What worked well for one president may be only partially useful to his successors.

Even presidents who come to office committed to concentrate their energies on domestic policy encounter extensive frustrations. They may enjoy some initial successes, as did Reagan; but the difficulties of accomplishing additional objectives eventually increase, and the sharing of power with Congress, the bureaucracy, and organized interests becomes ever more burdensome. The natural tendency is for presidents to turn their attention to national security and economic policy. In these policy areas, the challenges are more immediately threatening to the general welfare; the constraints on their ability to act, although very real, are not as frustrating; and successful policy leadership appears less elusive.

Notes

1. The concept of "issue congestion" was developed by Hugh Heclo, "One Executive Branch or Many?" in *Both Ends of the Avenue*, ed. Anthony King (Washington, D.C.: American Enterprise Institute, 1983), 26-58.
2. Theodore J. Lowi, "American Business, Public Policy, Case Studies, and Political Theory," *World Politics* (July 1964): 677-715.
3. Steven A. Shull, *Domestic Policy Formation: Presidential-Congressional Partnership?* (Westport, Conn.: Greenwood Press, 1983); and Steven A. Shull, "Change in Presidential Policy Initiatives," *Western Political Quarterly* (September 1983): 491-498.
4. Shull, *Domestic Policy Formation*, 155.
5. Shull, "Change in Presidential Policy Initiatives," 497.
6. John H. Kessel, *Presidential Politics* (Homewood, Ill.: Dorsey, 1984), 112-115.
7. Ibid., 68-69.
8. The policy stream metaphor borrows from Paul Light, "The Presidential Policy Stream," in *The Presidency and the Political System*, ed. Michael Nelson (Washington, D.C.: CQ Press, 1984), 423-448; and John W. Kingdon, *Agendas, Alternatives, and Public Policies* (Boston: Little, Brown, 1984), 92-94.
9. This discussion follows Kingdon, *Agendas, Alternatives, and Public Policies*, chap. 5.
10. Paul Light, *The President's Agenda: Domestic Policy Choice from Kennedy to Carter* (Baltimore: Johns Hopkins University Press, 1983), chap. 3; and Light, "The Presidential Policy Stream," 427-428.
11. Ironically, Nixon's preoccupation with the judgment of history helped to cut short his presidency. He has consistently explained the installation of the secret taping system in the Oval Office as motivated by his desire to have a complete and accurate record for use by historians. That record provided the "smoking gun," which led the House Judiciary Committee to vote the impeachment charges that prompted his resignation in August 1974.
12. Kingdon, *Agendas, Alternatives, and Public Policies*, 150.

13. Light, *The President's Agenda*, 149.
14. Jeff Fishel, *Presidents and Promises: From Campaign Pledge to Presidential Performance* (Washington, D.C.: CQ Press, 1984).
15. Kingdon, *Agendas, Alternatives, and Public Policies*, 138.
16. Vincent J. Burke and Vee Burke, *Nixon's Good Deed: Welfare Reform* (New York: Columbia University Press, 1974); Laurence E. Lynn, Jr., and David deF. Whitman, *The President as Policymaker: Jimmy Carter and Welfare Reform* (Philadelphia: Temple University Press, 1981).
17. This discussion is based on Kingdon, *Agendas, Alternatives, and Public Policies*, chap. 7.
18. Ronald Brownstein and Dick Kirschten, "Cabinet Power," *National Journal*, June 28, 1986, 1589.
19. This discussion follows Light, "The Presidential Policy Stream," 440-446.
20. Ibid., 444-445.
21. Kingdon, *Agendas, Alternatives, and Public Policies*, 204.
22. Kessel, *Presidential Parties*, 60.
23. Light, *The President's Agenda*, 36-38.
24. Richard E. Neustadt, *Presidential Power: The Politics of Leadership from FDR to Carter* (New York: Wiley, 1980).
25. Harold Wolman and Fred Tietlebaum, "Interest Groups and the Reagan Presidency," in *The Reagan Presidency and the Governing of America*, ed. Lester M. Salamon and Michael S. Lund (Washington, D.C.: Urban Institute Press, 1984), 299-301.
26. Mancur Olson *The Rise and Decline of Nations* (New Haven: Yale University Press, 1982), 44.
27. Neustadt, *Presidential Power*, 26.
28. Lester M. Salamon, "The Presidency and Domestic Policy Formulation," in *The Illusion of Presidential Government*, ed. Hugh Heclo and Lester M. Salamon (Boulder: Westview, 1981), 179.
29. Richard E. Neustadt, "The Presidency and Legislation: The Growth of Central Clearance," *American Political Science Review* (September 1954): 641-670; Robert S. Gilmour, "Central Clearance: A Revised Perspective," *Public Administration Review* (March/April 1971): 150-158.
30. Richard E. Neustadt, "The Presidency and Legislation: Planning the President's Program," *American Political Science Review* (December 1955): 980-1018; Larry Berman, *The Office of Management and Budget and the Presidency* (Princeton: Princeton University Press, 1979), 42-43; Stephen J. Wayne, *The Legislative Presidency* (New York: Harper and Row, 1978), 103-105.
31. Gilmour, "Central Clearance: A Revised Perspective"; Berman, *Office of Management and Budget*.
32. Norman C. Thomas and Harold L. Wolman, "The Presidency and Policy Formation: The Task Force Device," *Public Administration Review* (September/October 1969): 459-471.
33. Texts of the reports were published in *New Frontiers of the Kennedy Administration* (Washington, D.C.: Public Affairs Press, 1961).
34. Lyndon B. Johnson, *The Vantage Point* (New York: Holt, Rinehart and Winston, 1971), 326.

35. Paul Light, *Artful Work: The Politics of Social Security Reform* (New York: Random House, 1985), 232.
36. Berman, *Office of Management and Budget,* 106-113.
37. Raymond J. Waldman, "The Domestic Council: Innovation in Presidential Government," *Public Administration Review* (May/June 1976): 260.
38. Margaret Jane Wyszomirski, "The Roles of a Presidential Office for Domestic Policy: Three Models and Four Cases," in *The Presidency and Policy Making,* ed. George C. Edwards, Steven A. Shull, and Norman C. Thomas (Pittsburgh: University of Pittsburgh Press, 1985), 134.
39. John Helmer and Louis Maisel, "Analytical Problems in the Study of Presidential Advice: The Domestic Council Staff in Flux," *Presidential Studies Quarterly* (Winter 1978): 52-53.
40. Wyszomirski, "Roles of a Presidential Office," 136-137.
41. Stephen J. Wayne, *The Legislative Presidency* (New York: Harper and Row, 1978), 123.
42. Wyszomirski, "Roles of a Presidential Office," 140.
43. Salamon, "The Presidency and Domestic Policy Formulation," 184.
44. Dom Bonafede, "Eizenstat and Staff at Hub of Policy," *National Journal,* June 6, 1979, 945.
45. Ibid.
46. Dick Kirschten, "Carter Charts Cautious Course for 1980," *National Journal,* February 16, 1980, 267.
47. For an extended description of the OPD/cabinet council system, see Chester A. Newland, "Executive Office Policy Apparatus: Enforcing the Reagan Agenda," in *The Reagan Presidency and the Governing of America,* ed. Salamon and Lund, 153-159.
48. Ibid., 160.
49. Ibid.
50. Light, *The President's Agenda,* 71.
51. Ibid., 134-136.
52. President Kennedy, for example, did not move initially to propose civil rights legislation because of his slender electoral margin and because he needed the support of southern members of Congress for other important proposals, such as his reciprocal trade program.

Selected Readings

Derthick, Martha. *Policymaking for Social Security.* Washington, D.C.: Brookings, 1979.
Fishel, Jeff. *Presidents and Promises: From Campaign Pledge to Presidential Performance.* Washington, D.C.: CQ Press, 1984.
Kessel, John H. *Presidential Politics.* Homewood, Ill.: Dorsey, 1984.
Kingdon, John W. *Agendas, Alternatives, and Public Policies.* Boston: Little, Brown, 1984.

Light, Paul C. *The President's Agenda: Domestic Policy Choice from Kennedy to Carter.* Baltimore: Johns Hopkins University Press, 1982.

———. *Artful Work: The Politics of Social Security Reform.* New York: Random House, 1985.

Lynn, Laurence E., Jr., and David deF. Whitman. *The President As Policymaker: Jimmy Carter and Welfare Reform.* Philadelphia: Temple University Press, 1981.

Palmer, John L., and Isabell V. Sawhill, eds. *The Reagan Experiment.* Washington, D.C.: Urban Institute Press, 1982.

———, eds. *The Reagan Record.* Washington, D.C.: Urban Institute Press, 1984.

Shull, Steven A. *Domestic Policy Formation: Presidential-Congressional Partnership?* Westport, Conn.: Greenwood Press, 1983.

Sundquist, James L. *Politics and Policy: The Eisenhower, Kennedy, and Johnson Years.* Washington, D.C.: Brookings, 1968.

After a nationally televised address from the Oval Office, May 28, 1985, President Ronald Reagan displays a copy of his plan for overhauling the federal income tax laws.

CHAPTER TEN

The Politics of Economic Policy

Since the early years of the Republic, presidents have been concerned over the condition of the economy. Presidents who confronted serious economic adversity, such as Martin Van Buren (in 1837), Ulysses S. Grant (in 1873), Grover Cleveland (in 1893), Theodore Roosevelt (1907), and Warren G. Harding (1921), did little more than ride out the storm. Voters, however, reacted negatively on occasion by, for example, denying reelection to Van Buren and inflicting sizable losses on the president's party in the midterm congressional elections of 1838, 1874, and 1894. In fact, the existence of a relationship between business cycles and election results was known long before Edward Tufte's precise empirical analysis of the phenomenon.[1] Only since the early 1930s, however, have presidents attempted to control business cycles through public policy, and the public has come to expect them to do so.

This chapter examines the president's economic policy activities and responsibilities. It begins by distinguishing between actions designed to manage the entire economy (macroeconomic policy) and to control specific aspects of the economy (microeconomic policy). The primary focus of the chapter is on macroeconomic policy. It reviews presidential efforts to manage the economy from 1933 to 1986 and then describes the politics of macroeconomic policy making. Next, the chapter analyzes how the presidency functions in making economic policy and the ways in which presidents since Dwight D. Eisenhower have handled the problem of coordinating economic policy. The chapter concludes with an assessment of the congressional role in macroeconomic policy making.

Macroeconomic Policy

Management of the economy by the government is known as macroeconomic policy. There are two principal tools of macroeconomic policy: fiscal policy and monetary policy. Fiscal policy refers to the government's efforts to regulate the level of the nation's economic activity by varying taxes and public expenditures. Fiscal policy seeks to expand the economy by increasing spending and reducing taxes or to contract it by decreasing spending and increasing taxes. Thus, a budget deficit is expansionary whereas a budget surplus is deflationary. Monetary policy refers to the government's efforts, through its central bank (in the United States, the Federal Reserve System), to regulate economic activity by controlling the supply of money. The president and Congress jointly make fiscal policy. They determine expenditures through budgeting and appropriations, and they establish taxes through legislation. An independent agency, the Board of Governors of the Federal Reserve System, makes monetary policy.

The goals of macroeconomic policy have remained constant since the Great Depression of the 1930s: to hold down the rate of inflation, establish and maintain full employment, and achieve a steady rate of economic growth. There are, however, alternative theories that have guided makers of macroeconomic policy in their pursuit of these goals: classical conservative economics, Keynesianism, monetarism, and supply-side economics.

Conservative economic theory prevailed as orthodox doctrine before the Great Depression and still has its adherents today. Conservative thinking regards a balanced budget as the key to a healthy economy and views deficits as dangerously inflationary and destructive of confidence in the monetary system. When confronted with an economic downturn, conservative theory prescribes reduced spending to balance the budget. Restoration of economic activity, which will follow the demonstration of fiscal integrity, will then produce expanded revenues, which will allow expenses to increase and taxes to be cut.

Conservative economic theory lost credibility during the Great Depression, and the budget-balancing efforts of the administrations of Herbert Hoover and, early on, of Franklin D. Roosevelt failed to restore confidence to the economy and produce the desired upturn. FDR quickly discovered that emergency spending and loan programs did provide relief and did produce a measure of recovery.

The ideas of John Maynard Keynes, a British economist whom Roosevelt met in 1934, offered an explanation of the phenomenon of economic response to fiscal stimulus and eventually provided a rationale for deficit spending. Keynes argued that the cause of an economic decline was a drop in private demand for goods and services. Government could stimulate demand by increasing its expenditures or by reducing its revenues. The temporary deficits created by fiscal stimulation would be financed by government borrowing and repaid during periods of hyperactivity in the economy. FDR did not fully accept Keynesian ideas until a sharp recession followed his attempt to return to a balanced budget in 1937. Eventually, the recovery of the economy as a result of mobilization during World War II provided most economists with empirical validation of Keynes's basic theories. Conservative economics, however, retained its hold on many political leaders, such as President Eisenhower, who made balanced budgets their goal and regarded fiscal stimulation of lagging demand as an emergency measure.

When Keynesianism was establishing itself as the new orthodoxy, another theory emerged to challenge it. The monetarists, under the leadership of Milton Friedman, a University of Chicago economist, held that the key to maintaining economic stability lay not in the stimulation of demand but in limiting the growth rate of the money supply to no more than the actual growth rate of the economy. Inflation occurs, monetarists claim, when the money supply expands too rapidly. The only remedy for inflation is thus a painful contraction in the money supply. Fiscal policy and the size of budget deficits are held to be subordinate to the basic means of managing the economy.

Monetarism gained adherents as the limitations of Keynesianism became apparent during the 1970s. A primary defect of Keynesian theory as the basis for macroeconomic policy was its inflationary bias. Decisions on taxing and spending are made by politicians concerned with reelection—the president and members of Congress—and not by professional economists. Consequently, it has proved easier in practice to increase spending and cut taxes, the Keynesian prescription for expansion, than to cut spending and raise taxes, the remedy for inflation. In the 1970s, when inflation became the nation's leading economic problem, the Keynesian solution was ineffective because political decision makers were unwilling to impose it. They feared the electoral consequences of reducing government spending and raising taxes when their constituents were struggling to make ends meet. Although the inflationary bias of Keynesianism is a political defect rather than a weakness in the theory itself, the effect has been its reduced attractiveness as a guide to policy.

Monetarism, whatever its theoretical merits and limitations, offered the prospect of controlling inflation in a politically less painful manner by having the autonomous Federal Reserve Board (known as "the Fed") contract the money supply. Opposition to the consequences of monetary contractions, such as high interest rates and rising unemployment, can be deflected by political officeholders to the Fed and its amorphous supporters: "Wall Street" and the banks. The attempt to compensate for the lack of fiscal discipline by monetary contraction during the 1970s eventually proved so painful that monetarism also became politically unattractive. By the early 1980s a new theoretical approach, supply-side economics, had emerged and was embraced by President Ronald Reagan.

Essentially, supply-side economics is an amalgam of Keynesianism and monetarism.[2] Supply-siders endorse strict monetary restraint as the means to control inflation, but they reject the monetarist reluctance to use fiscal policy to achieve macroeconomic policy objectives. The supply-siders maintain, however, that the Keynesian focus on stimulating demand is misdirected. Instead, they advocate tax cuts designed to provide incentives that will stimulate investments and lead to a growth in productivity and real disposable income. Supply-siders are not disturbed by budget deficits resulting from tax-cut incentives. The stimulative effect of the tax cuts will, they argue, create enough additional savings to finance the added deficits without an inflationary expansion of the money supply, and an expanded economy eventually will generate enough revenues at lower rates of taxation to balance the budget.

Supply-side economics draws sharp criticism, on the one hand, from liberals who charge that it is but another version of the discredited "trickle down" approach to economic policy under which tax advantages for the affluent are justified on the grounds that they eventually lead to prosperity for all. On the other hand, conservatives fear that supply-side tolerance of budget deficits will lead to excessive rates of inflation and erosion of confidence in the monetary system. Both Keynesian liberals and conservatives doubt the validity of the assumptions on which supply-side economics rests. Although they hope it will work, they do not believe that it can. Experience since 1981 with a massive cut in federal income taxes, based on supply-side reasoning, supports their pessimism. Although the economy has expanded, revenues have not risen sufficiently to reduce, let alone balance, the federal budget. (See the discussion of the budget deficit under "The Congressional Role in Macroeconomic Policy.")

Microeconomic Policy

Macroeconomic policy should not be confused with microeconomic policy, a term used to describe government regulation of specific economic activities and antitrust policy. Microeconomic policies focus on specific industries or on economic practices in several industries. They are designed to affect directly the infrastructure of the economy and only indirectly its performance. Modern presidents generally have paid less attention to microeconomic than to macroeconomic policy, largely because its impact is so much more sharply focused. Most presidents, however, have on occasion endorsed specific microeconomic policies or used microeconomic policy tools to achieve macroeconomic or other policy goals. President Reagan, for example, strongly supported deregulation and privatization as a means of reducing the role of government and strengthening the free market. Greater reliance on the market, he believed, would lead to a more productive economy.

Earlier in the nation's history, presidents were involved only with microeconomic policy and did not regard overall management of the economy as a primary policy responsibility. To preserve competition in the market, Theodore Roosevelt and William Howard Taft vigorously enforced the Sherman Anti-Trust Act of 1890—Roosevelt with great fanfare and Taft with quiet effectiveness. Woodrow Wilson persuaded Congress to establish an independent regulatory agency, the Federal Trade Commission, with extensive authority to regulate anticompetitive and unfair business practices. Roosevelt, Taft, and Wilson believed that the federal government should act to correct imperfections in the operations of the free market economy.

During the New Deal, Franklin Roosevelt endorsed legislation that established additional independent regulatory agencies: the Securities and Exchange Commission (SEC), the Federal Power Commission (FPC), the Federal Communications Commission (FCC), the Civil Aeronautics Board (CAB), and the National Labor Relations Board (NLRB). These agencies received broad grants of authority to regulate the interstate aspects of specific industries, such as trade in stocks and bonds (SEC), electric power and natural gas (FPC), broadcasting and wire communications (FCC), and air transportation (CAB), as well as economy-wide activities such as labor-management relations (NLRB). In addition, Roosevelt experimented with a form of government-sponsored industrial self-government in the National Industrial Recovery Act as a means of mitigating the effects of destructive competition. Later in 1937 he ordered an intensified enforcement of the antitrust laws, charging that anticompetitive practices were responsible for the continuation of the Depression. FDR's use of microeconomic policy was characterized by a pragmatic search for techniques of government intervention that would improve the operation of certain economic sectors or lead to an improvement in the overall health of the economy. Policies that worked were retained; those that failed were abandoned.

FDR's successors varied in their use of microeconomic policies. Presidents Harry S Truman, Dwight Eisenhower, John F. Kennedy, and Lyndon B. Johnson appeared to accept the legitimacy of the pattern of government regulation of economic activity that had been established by 1940, including antitrust policy. They differed mainly in the intensity of enforcement and their willingness to use certain microeconomic policy tools.

Beginning in the late 1960s and continuing into the 1970s, Congress passed a new set of statutes expanding federal regulation of economic activity as a means of achieving noneconomic goals, such as a cleaner physical environment, safer automobiles and other consumer products, and a higher degree of occupational safety and health. Presidents initially approved the new regulatory activities, but as the economic costs of the new regulations became apparent, Presidents Richard Nixon and Gerald R. Ford raised questions about the appropriateness of federal regulation in general. A deregulatory movement gained support, and Presidents Gerald Ford and Jimmy Carter endorsed it. Ford assigned overall responsibility for deregulation to a member of the Council of Economic Advisers (CEA) and issued an order that required agencies to analyze the impact of their actions on inflation. Carter established a Regulatory Analysis Review Group, chaired by a CEA member, with responsibility for reviewing new rules and regulations with potential economic costs of $100 million or more. There is little evidence, however, that these actions reduced the volume of new regulations or the economic impact of regulation on industry.[3] Carter also gave his support to legislation that provided for deregulation of the airline and trucking industries. (The CAB ceased to function at the end of 1984, but the Interstate Commerce Commission continued to regulate railroads.)

Reagan promised in his 1980 election campaign to reduce substantially the amount of federal regulation and argued that regulation was a primary cause of the decline in the productivity of the economy. He established a Task Force on Regulatory Relief to analyze the economic effects of existing and proposed regulation. As a matter of principle, he was strongly opposed to regulation. Although rhetorical opposition to regulation did not translate quickly into sweeping deregulatory actions, the Reagan administration employed a three-pronged administrative strategy that substantially reduced the effectiveness of regulation.[4] First, the review procedures of the Office of Management and Budget (OMB) were used to kill or to slow the issuance of regulations. Second, the intensity of regulatory enforcement was reduced. Third, Reagan appointees changed their agencies' orientation from confrontation to cooperation as a means of achieving compliance.

In all modern presidential administrations, microeconomic policies have been secondary to macroeconomic policy. Microeconomic policies, such as vigorous antitrust enforcement or support for deregulation, can be used to supplement macroeconomic policy goals and to highlight the theoretical rationale for administration policy, but microeconomic policies cannot replace fiscal and monetary policies as the primary means by which presidents discharge their responsibility for the health of the nation's economy.

Presidents and the Economy: 1933-1986

The modern era of macroeconomic policy and the president's role as manager of the economy date from President Franklin Roosevelt's New Deal. One of the hallmarks of the New Deal was its commitment to make positive use of the federal government's power to bring about recovery from the Great Depression. The most significant theoretical achievement of the New Deal for economic policy was not the adoption of a comprehensive ideology for the development of a welfare state but the discovery of Keynesian economics and its prescription of increased government spending to compensate for inadequate private spending for investment and consumption.

Ultimately, it was not the New Deal reforms and recovery programs that ended the Depression but the huge increase in government spending during World War II. All of the nation's unused productive capacity—capital facilities and human resources—were mobilized to achieve victory, and government borrowing financed much of that mobilization. After the war Congress passed the Employment Act of 1946, a statute that committed the U.S. government to maintain "maximum employment, production, and purchasing power."

The Employment Act translated into law the widespread expectation that had developed during the Roosevelt administration that the government would guarantee to the fullest extent possible a prosperous economy. It also made the president primarily responsible for providing economic policy leadership, although it furnished him with few new tools for the task. It did give him a Council of Economic Advisers and an accompanying staff, and it required him to report annually to Congress on the condition of the economy and to offer his proposals for improving or maintaining its health. Ultimate power over the president's economic proposals, however, has remained with Congress.

From the end of World War II until the late 1960s, presidents and Congress fought with each other over economic policy. President Truman struggled unsuccessfully with Congress over its desire to reduce wartime taxes. He was somewhat more effective in controlling the inflation that resulted from spending for the Korean War. President Eisenhower's conservative policies tended to prevail over the plans of a Democratically controlled Congress to increase domestic spending. The Eisenhower administration was marked by two recessions, in 1954 and 1958, interspersed by a period of expansion. The Kennedy-Johnson administration fully embraced Keynesian theory, and a 1964 income tax cut had the desired effect of expanding the economy and increasing revenues. It was thought that economic forecasting and management of the economy had developed to the point where fine-tuning of unemployment and the inflation rate was possible.[5]

In 1966, however, economic conditions began to change as Vietnam War expenditures rose rapidly, the deficit increased, and President Johnson shifted his focus from economic expansion to economic restraint. Congress resisted Johnson's requests for higher excise taxes, and for political reasons he refrained from asking for income tax increases. (He feared that Congress would refuse the request and that in the course of congressional debate embarrassing questions would be raised about the war and its cost. With a congressional election scheduled in 1966, he was unwilling to risk debate and defeat.) By the time Johnson did request additional income taxes and Congress responded (it approved a temporary 10 percent surtax), the economy had begun a prolonged inflationary period in which the conditions that had been relatively stable since 1946 began to change drastically. (An inflation rate of approximately 3 percent a year, an unemployment variance between 4 and 8 percent, and sustained growth in the gross national product characterized the first twenty-five years of the post-World War II period.)

Presidents since Johnson have had to contend with a changing and increasingly less manageable economy. Inflation rates crept upward into double digits in the early 1980s before declining; unemployment has remained high by postwar standards; and the federal budget has run a deficit in every year since 1970. (See Figures 10-1 and 10-2, which depict trends in inflation and unemployment, and Table 10-1, which shows federal receipts and outlays from 1969 to 1987.) Underlying these developments have been systemic factors beyond the control of the government: the increased dependence of the economy on foreign sources of raw materials, especially oil; the growing interdependence of the U.S. economy with those of other industrial democracies; the declining productivity of the U.S. economy relative to foreign competition; the growth and maturation of domestic social welfare programs based on statutory entitlements; and a commitment to improve the quality of the physical environment even at substantial cost to economic growth and productivity.

Perhaps the most perplexing phenomenon for economists to explain and for economic policy makers to handle was the condition called "stagflation," in which economic stagnation was accompanied by high inflation rates. The comforting inverse relationship between unemployment and inflation (known as the "Phillips curve"), which had been a fixed star for policy makers until the 1970s, disappeared. It was no longer possible to calculate the trade-off between unemployment and inflation. Toleration of a specific rise in the inflation rate could not be relied upon to produce a predicted drop in unemployment. Nor could unemployment be brought down to a target level with the knowledge that the action would cause a predetermined increase in the rate of inflation. The U.S. economy contains many intractable problems and unpredictable trends that complicate the task of the president as its principal economic policy maker.

Richard Nixon was the first president to encounter the changing economic environment of the United States. His response was two-pronged. He consistently pursued the classical conservative course of attempting to counter inflation by pushing Congress for reductions in federal spending in order to balance the budget. In addition, Nixon took the extraordinary step, for a conservative Republican, of freezing prices and wages in August 1971. (See Chapter 7.) The imposition of wage and price controls is an extreme measure, for through it the president suspends the normal operation of market forces. Although Roosevelt and Truman imposed controls during World War II and the Korean War, Nixon is the only president to have resorted to them in peacetime. He acted under authority that Congress delegated to the president in the Economic Stabilization Act of 1970, which it passed over his strong objections.

A rapid rise in the rate of inflation led Nixon to implement a phased program of controls. In Phase I, wages, prices, and rents were frozen for ninety days. Then, during Phase II a pay board administered mandatory wage controls, and a price commission had jurisdiction over prices and rents. The objective was to limit the annual rate of inflation to 3 percent and to keep wage increases below 5.5 percent. The program of controls proved highly unpopular with both business and labor, and Nixon replaced it in January 1973 with Phase III. Under Phase III a Cost of Living Council supplanted the pay board, and the price commission and mandatory controls were replaced by employer-administered "standards." The standards lasted until July 1973, when they gave way under Phase IV to commitments from firms in various sectors of the economy to limit price hikes for a year. Congress did not renew the president's price control authority when it expired in April 1974.

President Nixon's experiment with peacetime price and wage controls was initially popular, for inflation slowed dramatically. However, the public quickly lost interest in it, and opposition mounted from business and labor, each of whom charged that they were having to make greater sacrifices than the other. The pay board and the price commission responded to criticism by granting exemptions, which led to more charges of unfairness and increased pressure for exemptions. These actions undermined the effectiveness of the controls in combating inflation and lessened public support for them. The 1971-1973 experience suggests that peacetime wage and price controls are at best a temporary means of curbing inflation and that they can quickly become a political liability unless their impact is moderated.

President Ford assumed, upon taking office in August 1974, that the principal economic problem confronting the United States was inflation, and he pushed to cut federal spending. Almost before his anti-inflation campaign was launched, however, economic conditions changed, and Ford spent his last year as president combating a recession that contributed to his electoral defeat in 1976. Ford's successor, Jimmy Carter, fared little better. Carter initiated an antirecession program of increased federal spending and tax cuts to stimulate business investment. The economy responded almost too quickly, and Carter soon confronted surging inflation rates that reached double digits during his last year in office.

Perhaps Carter's most important decision affecting the economy was the appointment in 1979 of Paul Volcker as chairperson of the Federal Reserve Board. Volcker's appointment reflected Carter's disenchantment with the ability of Keynesian theory to provide solutions to stagflation. Essentially a monetarist, Volcker moved quickly to curb inflation by restraining the growth of the money supply. He subsequently became regarded as one of the strongest chairpersons the Fed has ever had.

Figure 10-1 Consumer Prices and Inflation, 1970–1984

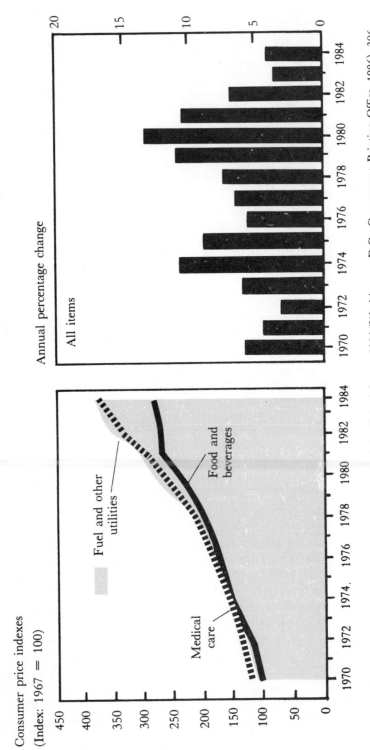

Consumer price indexes
(Index: 1967 = 100)

Annual percentage change

Source: U.S. Bureau of the Census, *Statistical Abstract of the United States: 1986* (Washington, D.C.: Government Printing Office, 1986), 306.

Figure 10-2 Trends in the Labor Force, 1950-1984

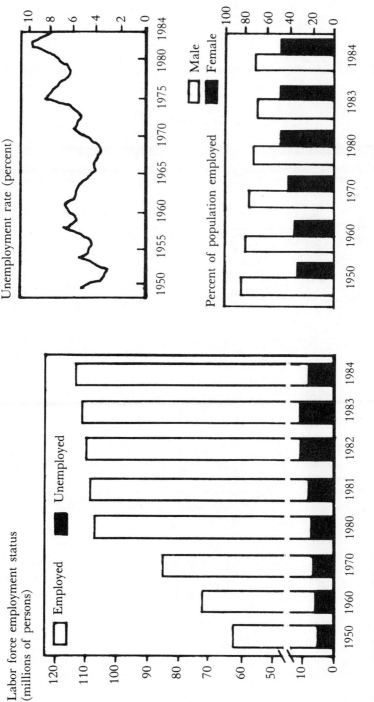

Source: U.S. Bureau of the Census, *Statistical Abstract of the United States: 1986* (Washington, D.C.: Government Printing Office, 1986), 386.

Table 10-1 Federal Budget Receipts and Outlays, 1969-1987
(Billions of Dollars)

Year	Receipts	Outlays	Surplus or Deficit (−)
1969	187.8	184.5	3.2
1970	193.7	196.6	−2.8
1971	188.4	211.4	−23.0
1972	208.6	232.0	−23.4
1973	232.2	247.1	−14.8
1974	264.9	269.6	−4.7
1975	281.0	326.2	−45.1
1976	300.0	366.4	−66.4
1976 TQ [a]	81.7	97.4	−15.7
1977	357.8	402.7	−45.0
1978	402.0	450.8	−48.8
1979	465.9	493.7	−27.7
1980	520.0	579.6	−59.6
1981	599.3	657.2	−57.9
1982	617.8	728.4	−110.6
1983	600.6	796.0	−195.4
1984	666.5	851.8	−185.3
1985	734.1	946.3	−212.3
1986	769.1	989.8	−220.7
1987 [b]	842.4	1,015.6	−173.2

Sources: For 1969-1979, *Statistical Abstract of the United States, 1980* (Washington, D.C.: Government Printing Office), 258; for 1980, *Congressional Quarterly Weekly Report*, March 14, 1981, 443; for 1981, ibid., February 12, 1982, 225; for 1982, ibid., February 5, 1983, 245; for 1983, ibid., February 4, 1984, 171; for 1984, ibid., February 9, 1985, 217; for 1985, ibid., February 8, 1986, 219; for 1986 and the 1987 estimate, ibid., January 10, 1987, 44.

[a] In 1976 the beginning of the fiscal year was changed from July 1 to October 1. Thus, there was a transition quarter (TQ), July 1-September 30, 1976, that belonged to neither fiscal 1976 nor 1977.
[b] Estimated.

Although Carter did not fully abandon Keynesianism, he gave monetarism a prominent role in macroeconomic policy making for the first time.

The rate of inflation did not respond quickly to Volcker's efforts to tighten the money supply, but interest rates rose sharply. These developments undoubtedly contributed to Carter's defeat by Ronald Reagan in the 1980 election. One of Reagan's campaign pledges was to restore vitality to the economy through a revolutionary program of major reductions in taxing and spending. Congress responded positively to Reagan's initiatives in 1981 by enacting the largest income tax cut in U.S. history and by sharply reducing domestic spending in nonentitlement programs. (As observed in Chapter 9, Reagan implemented a major change in domestic policies through budgetary politics rather than the enactment of an extensive legislative program.) Congress also supported Reagan's proposals for a major defense buildup, projected over five years from 1981 through 1986.

The results of the Reagan administration's macroeconomic policies have been mixed. The major accomplishment—credit for which must also be given to the Fed—has been the curtailment of inflation, which has been at an annual rate of between 3 and 4 percent since 1983. Also, in 1983 the economy began a sustained period of growth that has lasted well into 1987. Before that growth spurt, however, the United States experienced the most severe recession in the post-World War II period with unemployment rising to 10.75 percent in the fourth quarter of 1982. In spite of the prosperity achieved since that recession, unemployment has not dropped much below 7 percent. Without question, the major problem resulting from the Reagan administration's macroeconomic policies has been massive federal budget deficits. (See Table 10-1.)

The deficits grew rapidly as a result of the recession of 1982, when revenues fell, automatic countercyclical spending (such as unemployment compensation) rose, and the tax cuts and increased defense spending authorized in 1981 became effective. The latter created a large structural, or permanent, deficit as the increases in federal revenues promised by supply-side advocates failed to materialize, and sizable additional cuts in nondefense spending could not be obtained from Congress.

The deficits proved embarrassing to President Reagan because they are contradictory to traditional conservative values of fiscal restraint. But the deficits also brought political advantage to the Reagan administration. They served as the basis for the sustained recovery from the 1981-1982 recession. That recovery was a key factor in Reagan's 1984 reelection victory, for voters concluded that his economic policies had worked quite well. That Reagan had become a practitioner of Keynesian demand management on a grand scale was immaterial to him and his supporters. The deficits also provided Reagan with an effective short-run rationale for restraining the growth of nondefense spending.

The Politics of Macroeconomic Policy Making

Presidents do not make macroeconomic policy in a vacuum solely according to economic theories. Their decisions in this crucial area are intensely political and are affected by consideration of other policy goals (including microeconomic policy), electoral politics, interest group politics, and bureaucratic politics among institutional participants in the policy-making process. In a very real sense the United States has a political economy, and it is an economic polity. The president is the focal point of the relationships involved in both of these entities.

Policy Politics

The achievement of macroeconomic policy goals is affected by, and has an effect on, other policy goals. National security policy objectives, for example, often have a profound impact on economic policy. Recently, the widely held consensus that U.S. military strength had declined compared with that of the Soviet Union resulted in substantial increases in defense spending beginning in fiscal year 1982. These increases, however, were a major obstacle to efforts to balance the budget. Moreover, the added deficit resulting from increased military expenditures contributed to upward pressure on interest rates, which in turn impeded the ability of tax-cut incentives to stimulate productivity.

Similarly, budget-balancing efforts in domestic program areas conflicted with commitments made to social security beneficiaries, welfare recipients, and numerous other groups served by federal programs. In another area, the macroeconomic goals of economic growth, increased productivity, and full employment are often at odds with regulatory policies designed to improve environmental quality, enhance occupational safety and health, increase the safety of automobiles and other consumer products, and protect consumers against a variety of unfair business practices.

Foreign policy also intrudes on macroeconomic policy. For example, foreign military and economic assistance and the stationing of U.S. forces overseas contribute to the nation's balance-of-payments deficit, which in turn undercuts confidence in the dollar and reduces economic stability. These illustrations should be sufficient to demonstrate the interrelationship of macroeconomic policy goals with those of other policies. As Chapter 11, on the politics of national security policy, will show, a major component of successful presidential leadership is the capacity to manage the contradictions between policies.

Electoral Politics

A second dimension of the politics of macroeconomic policy is its relationship to electoral politics. It is widely recognized that presidential administrations and congressional majorities have long manipulated economic policy to produce short-run improvements in economic conditions that will enhance their party's election prospects. Both the timing and location of benefits may be adjusted to achieve this end. Tufte maintains that economic improvement is greatest in presidential election years.[6] He has discovered two electoral-economic cycles that have operated between 1948 and 1976, in each administration except Eisenhower's. One is a two-year cycle, geared to congressional elections, in which real disposable income per capita rises in even-numbered years and falls in the odd ones. Tax cuts and increases in social security and other benefits are often used to boost real disposable income. The other cycle, which occurs over four years in conjunction with presidential elections, involves a drop in unemployment in the months before the election and an increase in it from twelve to eighteen months afterward.[7]

Presidents do not, however, attempt to change the underlying structure of the economy for short-run political advantage. Rather, they seek to make marginal adjustments in the rates of inflation and unemployment or in disposable income. Because of electoral politics, however, what is economically optimal is either not done or is substantially modified as a result of the pressures. Political influence on economic policy can have substantial costs, including "a lurching, stop-and-go economy," a preference for policies that contain "highly visible benefits and deferred hidden costs," and responsiveness of "coalition-building politicians" to special interests.[8] In such a politically sensitive environment, long-range economic planning is most difficult.

Few presidents can resist the pressures of party and special constituencies to seek short-run political gain even at the expense of longer-range economic stability and efficiency. President Reagan, however, during his first six years in office, remained firm in his commitment to the income tax cut of supply-side theory, even though it meant proposing and defending budget deficits that fluctuated around $200 billion. Several leading congressional Republicans as well as much of the nation's financial community continually pressed him to reconsider his stand against raising taxes or to retreat from his insistence on a big military buildup. Reagan consistently resisted such entreaties. Out of ideological firmness he was less willing than other modern presidents to sacrifice what he regarded as long-run economic well-being for short-run electoral benefits in making economic policy.

Interest Group Politics

Presidents also are subjected to pressures from several important groupings of interests. These interest group constituencies include business, labor, agriculture, the financial community, state and local governments, and foreign governments. Their effect on policy varies according to the issues and to current economic conditions in the United States and elsewhere.

Business interests include the full array of private corporations engaged in producing goods and services, except those involved in financial affairs (which will be considered separately). Businesses attempt to exert influence collectively through umbrella organizations, such as the Chamber of Commerce of the United States and the National Association of Manufacturers, and through industry-based trade associations, such as the Automobile Manufacturers Association and the American Gas Association. Individual firms, especially large corporations, also try to shape policy to their liking. Businesses usually concentrate their lobbying on microeconomic policies that specifically affect their operations. To the extent that business influences macroeconomic policy, it does so by expressing support for balanced budgets, tax-cut incentives, and monetary restraint to control inflation. The economic policy stance of business is, then, conservative and traditional. A few corporations are exceptions to this general statement, but presidents and their economic advisers know that conservative fiscal and monetary policies normally will receive strong business support.

Labor encompasses the giant AFL-CIO and a host of independent unions. Its position on macroeconomic policy issues is usually in sharp contrast to that of business. Labor supports fiscal stimulation of the economy in periods of recession and opposes the use of monetary restraints to curb inflation. It is not unduly disturbed by budget deficits. As a rule, labor is much more worried by unemployment than by inflation. Labor takes great interest in microeconomic policy, including regulation of labor-management relations and regulations in behalf of occupational safety and health.

Four large organizations represent agriculture. The American Farm Bureau Federation and the National Grange support conservative policies; the National Farmers Union and the National Farmers Organization take a much more liberal stance. Regardless of their ideology, farm organizations tend to oppose monetary policies that result in high interest rates, because the use of credit is an essential feature of farm management.

The financial community consists of two principal components, the securities exchanges, or Wall Street, and banks and other financial institutions. Both Wall Street and financial institutions buy and sell government and private financial obligations, called "paper," and longer-term securities, called "bonds." The reaction of Wall Street to monetary and fiscal policies is registered in the price of corporate stocks traded on the major stock exchanges. Movements of stock market indicators, such as the Dow Jones Index of thirty leading industrial stocks, often reflect the degree of investor confidence in administration policies. Bond prices move upward or downward inversely with interest rates and thus reflect monetary policy shifts. The interest paid on short-term government and commercial paper varies directly with monetary policy.

An administration's main interest in the financial community is that its policies be favorably received by Wall Street. It also seeks the approval of major banks and other leading financial institutions. A vote of "no confidence" by the financial community in the government's economic policies makes the administration vulnerable to criticism by political opponents and weakens its popular support. Like their brethren in the broader business world, members of the financial community tend to support conservative fiscal policies and monetary restraint to control inflation. They fear large deficits, whether due to high spending levels or sizable tax cuts. Since 1981 many leading securities traders, major bankers, and private economic analysts have been skeptical of the Reagan administration's economic policies ("Reaganomics"), especially the large and growing budget deficits. Reagan's failure to overcome Wall Street skepticism of his economic policies cast a cloud over them and made their ultimate effectiveness more problematic than they otherwise would have been.

With the advent of the Great Society domestic programs in the mid-1960s, state and local governments became vitally interested in macroeconomic policy. The federal government is a source of funding for a wide range of state and local programs in areas such as education, welfare and social services, housing and urban development, transportation, and health care. In addition, states and their local subdivisions received unrestricted revenue-sharing funds from 1972 through 1987. Consequently, many state and local governments, both through national associations, such as the U.S. Conference of Mayors, and individually through efforts of members of Congress, have exerted pressure to maintain the flow of federal funds, even though this could be accomplished only at the expense of larger and potentially inflationary budget deficits.

Reagan's successful effort in 1981 to reduce federal funding for many state and local activities and his subsequent proposals for further reductions were an essential part of his long-term objective of balancing the budget. Although some state and local officials backed Reagan, the responses of most such officials ranged from cautious skepticism to strong opposition. His objective of a major reordering of federal fiscal functions was not accomplished,[9] although revenue sharing ended in fiscal 1987 as pressures to reduce the deficit increased dramatically under the stimulus of the Gramm-Rudman-Hollings balanced budget act. (This act is discussed further in the section "The Congressional Role in Macroeconomic Policy.")

Perhaps the most important aspect of Reagan's approach to intergovernmental financial relations is that he seized the initiative. Instead of responding to the requests of state and local officials for ever-increasing support, he sought to direct state and local governments into a posture of reduced dependence on federal funding. This innovative attempt to restructure fiscal federalism in a way that served macroeconomic policy objectives may provide a model for Reagan's successors.

Foreign governments are another important constituency with an interest in macroeconomic policy. Friendly governments—the European Community, Japan, and Saudi Arabia—are especially significant. They support a dollar that is neither overvalued nor undervalued and a healthy U.S. economy with full employment and a low inflation rate. If the dollar is weak, the value of much of their international currency reserves declines, and their goods are less competitive in U.S. markets. If the dollar is too strong, their investment capital migrates to the United States, and the high competitiveness of their products in U.S. markets threatens to provoke trade restrictions. If unemployment in the United States rises, the major market for their goods declines. If interest rates are higher in the United States than in Europe or Japan, investment capital moves to the United States. Consequently, foreign governments press U.S. administrations to keep the exchange value of the dollar from fluctuating widely and to hold down interest rates.

Foreign governments feel less free to influence fiscal policies designed to stimulate the economy because these entail essentially domestic decisions. Presidents and their administrations are constrained to some degree, however, by the effect of economic policy decisions on the economies of other countries.

Presidents do not respond to all interest group constituencies, and the constituencies whose support they do seek vary in importance to the president. In no case, however, do presidents make macroeconomic policy decisions without regard to some of them, for interest groups are a major feature in the politics of economic policy making.

Bureaucratic Politics

The president's economic policies also reflect the organizational interests of the institutions involved in the policy-making process—the Council of Economic Advisers, the Office of Management and Budget, the Treasury Department, and the Federal Reserve Board—and the beliefs of the officials whom he has appointed to manage them. The next section describes the functions and organizational perspectives of those agencies and the nature of their relationship with the president.

The Economic Subpresidency

The president's macroeconomic policy-making role entails discharging statutory duties and responsibilities and meeting popular and elite expectations that his actions will result in a prosperous economy. In his role as economic manager, the president must develop and implement policies and build support for those policies in the public and within the Washington community. To accomplish this complex and demanding task, he needs information, advice, and administrative assistance to focus energy on major issues, to integrate the policies of his administration, to take account of all important interests, and to maintain the cohesion of his administration. This advice and assistance is provided by certain organizations and processes, located in the presidency and within the executive branch, which James Anderson and Jared Hazleton call "the economic subpresidency." The use of the economic subpresidency varies among presidents and with economic conditions, but it is central to policy making and presidential management of the economy.

According to Anderson and Hazleton, the economic subpresidency comprises all those who are engaged in making, defining, communicating, and implementing economic policy decisions, "whether they act personally or as part of an institution." [10] Activities of the economic subpresidency include direct advisory relationships with the president and interaction between other advisers with respect to economic policy. The economic subpresidency consists of four major administrative units—the CEA, OMB, the Treasury Department, and the Fed—and various intragovernmental committees and councils, presidential assistants, and other advisers.

The Council of Economic Advisers

The CEA comprises three members appointed by the president and subject to Senate confirmation, plus a small staff of approximately thirty-five persons divided evenly between professional economists and support personnel. Traditionally, most CEA members and professional staffers have had extensive experience in business or government. The CEA's chairperson is its dominant figure and is responsible for administration of the council, hiring staff, representing it on other government councils and committees, and reporting to the president. He or she establishes the council's orientation according to the president's overall objectives. The chairperson's relationship with the president largely determines the CEA's influence in shaping economic policy.

The CEA has no operational responsibility but serves entirely in a staff capacity. Its principal functions are to gather information, make economic forecasts, analyze economic issues, and prepare the president's annual economic report to Congress. Its primary role has been to provide the president with expert economic advice. On occasion CEA members have acted as public spokespersons for the president. The council usually has not performed coordinating or brokerage functions, although its members tend to reflect the theories and policy views of professional economists who share the president's perspectives. In general, Democratic presidents have had Keynesian CEA members, and Republicans have selected classical conservative and monetarist economists. Reagan, for example, appointed a conservative economist to chair the CEA at the start of his presidency and added a monetarist and a supply-sider. All three were committed to limited federal intervention in the economy, free trade, reduced government spending, and a balanced federal budget. In his second term, Reagan selected a monetarist to chair the CEA.

The CEA's relationship with the president is a function of how he perceives his need for economic expertise. If he feels such a need—and most presidents have when confronted with the seriousness and complexity of economic issues—and if he and the CEA members share basic interests and values, then the council will play an important role in economic policy making. Its expertise enhances presidential policies, and its analyses and forecasts acquire political significance through association with the presidency. However, the council can do only what the president asks and allows it to do.

The relationship of Presidents Carter and Reagan to the CEA illustrates the range of uses that can be made of the council and of its influence on policy. The chairperson of Carter's CEA was Charles Schultze, who had served as director of the budget in the Johnson administration. Schultze played a dominant role in shaping the Carter administration's economic policies, and the CEA was very much at the center of the economic subpresidency. In contrast, the two CEA chairpersons in Reagan's first term, Murray

Weidenbaum and Martin Feldstein, were overshadowed by budget director David Stockman and Treasury Secretary Donald Regan, neither of whom were economists. Weidenbaum's influence was primarily in regulatory policy. Feldstein, a distinguished academician, quickly fell out of favor with the president and the White House because of his dire predictions of the probable consequences of administration policies. The CEA was at the periphery of the economic subpresidency during Reagan's first term. Indeed, when Feldstein returned to Harvard in July 1984, the president delayed appointing a successor for almost a year. The council's professional staff shrank in size, and rumors circulated in Washington that Reagan wanted to abolish the unit. He finally named a new chairperson in April 1985, Beryl Sprinkel, an economist who had served for four years as undersecretary of the treasury for monetary affairs and who was well known to him and to White House chief of staff Donald Regan. Sprinkel rebuilt the council's staff and moved it back into the mainstream of the economic subpresidency.[11]

The council's forecasts help to set the boundaries of the president's legislative program and budget proposals. It is to the president's advantage for the council to approach its advisory task deductively, fitting program pieces together within the framework of his overall objectives. As former CEA chairperson Paul McCracken has observed, "An economic adviser does his most effective work when he is positioned to look at the general interest." [12] The council's contribution to policy making is, then, primarily conceptual and not in the realm of implementation or coordination. As Edward Flash has aptly put it, the council's forecasts and analyses "feed much of the argument and negotiation on which debate of the alternatives is based, for they provide the criteria for judging specifics within policy choices." [13] Thus, the council is influential in the early stages of policy formulation, where its expertise is "the dominant body of relevant knowledge," many alternatives are under consideration, institutional positions are not fixed, and decisions reflect "general objectives and plans" rather than "operating commitments." [14] Even after an administration sets a policy course, however, the need for economic policy advice continues; conditions are anything but static, new problems emerge as old ones are brought under control, and the next election draws ever nearer. Presidents may, as did Ronald Reagan, look elsewhere in the economic subpresidency for advice than to the CEA.

The Office of Management and Budget

Presidents receive economic advice of a different sort from the Office of Management and Budget. Whereas the CEA's primary concern is with controlling the business cycle and achieving sustained economic growth, OMB's major focus is on the allocation of resources to administrative agencies and their programs through the annual preparation of the president's budget. Its institutional bias is toward holding down spending. It is the principal instrument through which the president fashions the expenditure component of fiscal policy. In addition, OMB provides economic forecasts to the president and acts as a "legislative and regulatory gatekeeper" by conducting detailed policy analysis of proposed bills and agency rules.[15]

OMB was originally a presidential staff agency comprising an elite group of government careerists devoted to serving the presidency and the president. Since President Nixon reorganized OMB in 1970, it has been more actively involved in serving the political needs of the president. Beginning in the Nixon administration, OMB directors have actively participated in developing presidential policies and in building support for them. The budget has become as much a political weapon as a managerial tool or an instrument of fiscal policy.

The politicization of OMB and the political utilization of the budget were never more apparent than in the Reagan administration during David Stockman's tenure as budget director (1981-1985). Stockman designed and imposed a system of top-down budgeting that made the budget the means of implementing Reagan's domestic policy priorities. He also served the administration as its principal fiscal policy spokesperson in Congress, where he explained and defended proposed budgets with a dazzling array of data based on OMB's forecasts. Stockman candidly admitted, however, first in a series of luncheon conversations during 1981 with journalist William Greider and later in a memoir he wrote after leaving the administration, that the assumptions underlying OMB projections of modest deficits in fiscal 1982 and a balanced budget in fiscal 1984 were erroneous.[16] Stockman conceded that he had defended the projections before congressional committees while convinced that they were not viable. His political commitment to the president conflicted with an institutional role that called for fiscal restraint. Although Stockman knew that the budget deficit would be enormous because of the magnitude of the tax cut and increases in defense spending, he was unable to convince the president. Publicly, he continued to express optimism and support for the budget while privately he conveyed his dismay to Greider, his journalistic confidant, who described Stockman as having a "mixture of tactical cynicism and intellectual honesty." [17]

When publication of Greider's article revealed Stockman's apostasy, congressional demands arose for his resignation, and the president administered a mild reprimand. However, Stockman remained at his post because his detailed knowledge of the budget and his ability to manage its preparation and presentation to Congress were essential to Reagan's determination to cut domestic program spending. According to Stockman, he stayed on in the hope that he could reverse the president's resistance to additional taxes, which were needed, given the commitment to defense and the inability substantially to cut domestic spending below the initial amounts achieved in 1981.[18] Stockman left the government in May 1985, having concluded that fiscal stability could not be achieved as long as the American people supported an extensive welfare state and the president willfully misunderstood the deficit problem.

Stockman dominated federal budgeting in a manner unknown before him. He centralized the executive budget process in OMB and involved himself extensively in the congressional budget process through direct negotiations and bargaining with congressional committees. Hugh Heclo has identified four major characteristics of Stockman's system of budget management.[19] First, he dealt with the total budget rather than with incremental choices at the margins. This forced political decisions on all factors affecting spending with the terms of debate framed by the White House. Second, Stockman reinforced the top-down approach by continually readdressing the deficit. Successive searches for spending cuts went to the core of domestic programs, the previously sacrosanct budgetary base. This led to the third element of Stockman's approach to managing the budget, which was to "move the debate from program particulars to general politico-economic justifications." [20] The final aspect of Stockman's system was to adopt a single budgetary strategy of cutting back domestic spending wherever politically possible. That strategy was continually strengthened by the pressure of ever-increasing deficits. Stockman also made less extensive use of OMB's career staff than his predecessors did. Stockman further politicized OMB, and he also personalized it. Heclo concludes that although OMB's political power increased, OMB was weakened institutionally.[21] Under Stockman's successor, economist James C. Miller III, OMB continued to serve Reagan's political interests, but much less visibly. The budget remained the primary instrument for the achievement of the president's goals, and Miller continued Stockman's role as a spokesperson to Congress. Miller, however, was not as intimately involved in shaping economic strategy and in direct negotiations with Congress as his predecessor had been, nor was OMB as weighty a participant in the economic subpresidency. The Stockman experience suggests that neither OMB, the presidency, nor the incumbent president are well served by a budget director who, with the president's blessing, becomes a master sales agent for presidential decisions.

The Treasury Department

The third institutional participant in the economic subpresidency is the Treasury Department. It is responsible for collecting taxes, managing the national debt, controlling the currency, collecting customs, and handling international monetary affairs, including management of the balance of payments and the value of the dollar relative to other currencies. It is the primary governmental source of information on revenues, the tax system, and financial markets. It also takes the lead in developing tax bills and steering them through Congress.[22]

The primary concerns of the Treasury Department traditionally have been the adequacy of revenues, the soundness of the dollar, and the cost of financing the debt. To finance the debt, the department has advocated either low interest rates or a balanced budget. Since 1951, it has not advocated easy credit, however, and usually has acted as a restraint on expansionary fiscal policies. Before the Reagan administration, a situation in which high interest rates accompanied a large deficit was an anathema to the institutional interests of the Treasury. Its position altered substantially under President Reagan and Donald Regan, secretary of the treasury during Reagan's first term. An avowed believer in supply-side economics, Regan argued that temporary deficits resulting from tax-cut incentives would lead ultimately to economic growth, expanded revenues, and balanced budgets. He opposed efforts to reduce the deficit by raising taxes. His concern was much more with the supply of money in the domestic economy than with the exchange value of the dollar. Regan's successor at Treasury, James A. Baker III, concentrated heavily on exchange rate problems.

Organizationally, the Treasury Department is divided between large units with major line responsibilities, such as the Internal Revenue Service, and policy-related units, such as the office of the undersecretary for monetary affairs. The policy-related units, located in the office of the secretary, have never provided coordination of economic policy for an administration, although the potential to do so exists.[23]

The Federal Reserve Board

The Federal Reserve Board is formally an independent agency charged with responsibility for regulating the money supply and the banking system. Its seven members are appointed by the president to fourteen-year terms with the consent of the Senate. The president designates one member of the board to act as its chairperson for a four-year term. The Fed has three means by which it controls the money supply: the rediscount rate, reserve requirements, and open-market operations.

The rediscount rate is the interest rate charged commercial banks to borrow from the Federal Reserve. An increase in the rediscount rate tightens the availability of credit because it forces banks to charge more to their borrowers.

Reserves are balances that commercial banks belonging to the Federal Reserve System must maintain with it. Reserve requirements are expressed as percentages of a commercial bank's deposits, usually 10 to 20 percent. A reduction in reserve requirements increases the availability of credit.

Open-market operations are the major instrument through which the Fed manages the money supply, through the purchase and sale of U.S. government securities by regional Federal Reserve Banks. When the Fed wants to expand the supply of money, it orders its regional banks to buy government securities on the money market. The regional Reserve Banks pay for the securities by drawing checks on themselves. The checks are cashed by the Treasury at commercial banks, and as a result the Treasury's account balances are increased. The commercial banks present the checks to regional Reserve Banks on which they were drawn for redemption. The regional

Reserve Banks credit the checks to the commercial banks' reserve accounts with the Federal Reserve. The commercial banks may then lend money at the reserve requirement ratio. If the ratio is, say, 10 percent, the banks can lend to private borrowers ten times the original amount of the securities purchased. Conversely, sale of government securities by the Federal Reserve in the open market contracts the money supply in a similar manner.[24]

Although neither the president nor Congress can tell the Fed how to conduct monetary policy, the board has traditionally been responsive to political pressures. According to Robert Shapiro, the Fed has shown far greater responsiveness to political timing than to cyclical fluctuations in the economy.[25] He maintains that the formal independence of the Fed is a myth and that its policies are designed primarily to maintain its internal cohesion and reduce its external vulnerability.

As a government agency the Fed is involved in bureaucratic politics, and its decisions must, to some degree, reflect political considerations. Monetary policy has political as well as economic consequences. A restrictive monetary policy tends to slow down economic activity and thus increase unemployment. An expansionary monetary policy removes constraints on prices and wages, promotes economic activity, and increases employment. These outcomes can have profound political consequences. Monetary policy also affects fiscal policy by making it easier or more difficult for the Treasury to fund budget deficits and refinance existing securities as they mature. High interest rates and "tight" money act as a restraint on deficit financing and on the growth of government spending. In making monetary policy, the Fed can hardly be unmindful of its political ramifications. Nevertheless, recent Fed chairpersons, such as William McChesney Martin (1951-1970), Arthur Burns (1970-1978), and Paul Volcker (1979-1987), repeatedly clashed with presidents over the effect of their actions on fiscal policy. Only William Miller, who served briefly as chairperson in 1978-1979, worked closely with the president to coordinate monetary and fiscal policy.

In some respects the independence of the Fed has political value to the president and Congress. It serves as a frequent and convenient scapegoat for adverse economic conditions. Traditionally, expansionary monetary policy has been attacked as a major cause of inflation, and restrictive policy has drawn fire for contributing to economic stagnation and unemployment. In 1981-1982 presidential and congressional frustration over efforts to improve the economy resulted in criticism from the White House and Capitol Hill that ultra-high interest rates were: (1) causing unemployment, (2) pushing up prices, and (3) increasing the size of the budget deficit. After 1982, the sharp drop in inflation and the prolonged recovery from the 1981-1982 recession enabled the Fed to lower interest rates. Political attacks on the Fed largely ceased as it gauged the money supply to the needs of an expanding economy not plagued by inflation. Also, as Reagan appointees began to serve on the board (by 1986 they were a majority), the White House criticized the Fed less often.

Although the short-run results of its discretionary actions have often led to attacks on the Fed, in the long run—since 1945—it appears to have served the major policy objectives of the nation's elected leaders. The Fed has been the instrument of creation of the enormous, permanent national debt; and the debt has helped finance both U.S. military power, which has preserved national security in a precarious international environment, and social welfare programs, the nation's response to urbanization and industrialization. As Shapiro observes, the Fed's "political authority over the American money system has helped create the political space within which the national leadership, legislative and executive, has been able to pursue its own understanding of the nation's interest abroad and of the nation's collective responsibilities at home." [26]

Presidents and Economic Policy Coordination

The independence of the Fed, the operational needs and organizational interests of the Treasury, and the institutional perspectives of other departments and agencies have led presidents to seek various ways of coordinating economic policy. For reasons explained in Chapter 7, the cabinet has not been a satisfactory vehicle for collective leadership. Instead, presidents have developed a variety of intragovernmental councils and committees designed to provide a cohesive macroeconomic policy and to integrate it with other policy objectives. Most of these entities failed to survive the administrations of their creators, for subsequent presidents sought mechanisms more compatible with their own operating styles. However, a review of these undertakings reveals common patterns in their approaches and indicates the essential requirements for a minimal amount of coordination.

Eisenhower

President Eisenhower displayed a preference for sharply focused groups including the Advisory Board on Economic Growth and Stability, the Council on Foreign Economic Policy, the Cabinet Committee on Small Business, the Trade Policy Committee, the Cabinet Committee on Price Stability for Economic Growth, and the Interdepartmental Committee to Coordinate Federal Urban Area Assistance Programs. Although these bodies met regularly, they were too numerous to bring about effective coordination.

Kennedy

In keeping with his preference for a less formal structure in policy-making processes, President Kennedy abolished the Advisory Board on Economic Growth and Stability and the Council on Foreign Economic Policy as well as several lesser bodies. Kennedy preferred to work with ad hoc groups created to address specific problems, such as housing credit, small business, and labor-management relations. He did, however, establish the Interdepartmental

Committee of Under-Secretaries on Foreign Economic Policy. It dealt with a wide range of issues except for international monetary affairs.

The most significant development for macroeconomic policy making during the Kennedy administration was the creation in 1961 of the "troika," an informal committee consisting of the chairperson of the CEA, the secretary of the treasury, and the director of the budget. The troika's original purpose was to coordinate economic forecasting, but it quickly became a mechanism for developing cooperation within the economic subpresidency in formulating fiscal policy and, when joined by the chairperson of the Fed, for coordinating monetary policy. (When the troika members were joined by the chairperson of the Fed, the group was known as the "quadriad.")

Working with staff support from the CEA, the Treasury, OMB, and on occasion the Fed, the troika/quadriad has helped presidents formulate macroeconomic policy in a rapid and adaptive manner with some measure of shielding from political and bureaucratic pressures. Not all presidents have made extensive use of the troika, but it is a natural institutional grouping that continues to operate, with the Treasury assuming responsibility for revenue estimates, OMB generating estimates of federal expenditures, the CEA forecasting economic trends, and the Fed (when involved) projecting money supply requirements.

Johnson

Under President Johnson, the troika operation became regularized, and it emerged as the principal mechanism for the development of fiscal policy advice and alternatives.[27] The troika's proposals, arrived at through discussion and debate, usually resulted in a consensus, which Johnson accepted. He had other sources of advice, but most of them were informal. He listened to other cabinet members and a wide variety of outsiders. The loosely structured informality of the troika operation and the use of informal channels of advice were characteristic of Johnson's ad hoc approach to policy formulation generally.

Nixon

President Nixon preferred a more formally structured approach to policy making and, on taking office, established the Cabinet Committee on Economic Policy, which he chaired. The council also included the vice president, the secretaries of treasury, agriculture, commerce, labor, and housing and urban development, the director of the budget, the chairperson of the CEA, the deputy secretary of state for economic affairs, and the two counselors to the president (economist Arthur Burns and political scientist Daniel Patrick Moynihan). In addition, Nixon created councils on urban affairs and rural affairs and, in January 1971, a council on international economic policy.

Nixon was uncomfortable, however, with these attempts to make policy by cabinet-level committees. In early 1971 he designated Secretary of the

Treasury John Connally as his economic "czar" with the responsibility for making major decisions. Connally worked through the troika, which he dominated. His successor as treasury secretary, George Shultz, inherited Connally's title but operated in a more collegial manner. At the start of his second term, in January 1973, Nixon made Shultz assistant to the president for economic affairs and named him to chair a new cabinet-level coordinating body, the Council on Economic Policy. Shultz soon became the dominant figure in making and expounding economic policy for the Nixon administration. He worked primarily through interdepartmental committees focused on specific problems rather than through the Council on Economic Policy.

Following Shultz's departure in May 1974, Nixon appointed Kenneth Rush, deputy secretary of state for economic affairs, as his counselor for economic affairs. Rush was overshadowed by two powerful rivals, OMB director Roy Ash and Treasury Secretary William Simon. Although he chaired most formal interagency economic policy committees, Rush worked primarily through an informal "economic group" based in the Executive Office of the President. It consisted of a Treasury representative, the OMB director, the chairperson of the CEA, the executive director of the Council on International Economic Policy, and the administrator of the Federal Energy Agency. Before Rush could consolidate his authority over economic policy, Nixon had resigned the presidency. Toward the end of his administration, as he struggled to remain in office, Nixon had little interest in economic policy, which was made primarily by a small group of officials and advisers in a largely ad hoc fashion.

Ford

President Ford moved quickly to replace the Nixon machinery with a more formal and structured process that would operate openly and comprehensively and reflect Ford's intense interest in economic affairs. In September 1974 Ford established the Economic Policy Board (EPB) and assigned it responsibility for coordinating domestic and foreign economic policy. The secretary of the treasury chaired the EPB, which also included the secretaries of labor, commerce, and state, the chairperson of the CEA, the director of OMB, and the assistant to the president for economic affairs (who directed the small EPB staff, housed in the Executive Office of the President). Departments and agencies provided information, analysis, and expertise.

Roger Porter, who served as executive secretary to the EPB throughout its existence, has described it as providing systematic advice to the president by exposing him to competing arguments "in a group discussion that permitted exchange and argument among the advocates before the president." [28] The president acted as a magistrate, hearing arguments, considering analyses and evidence, and deciding on a course of action. The EPB process was designed to provide the president with options, not to reach a consensus. Its underlying assumption was that the best method of developing policy was a systematic, orderly, and balanced competition of ideas and views. The assistant to the president for economic affairs, L. William Seidman, a Michigan businessman and longtime political associate of Ford's, managed the EPB process, playing the role of an honest broker. Perhaps the most important aspect of the EPB was that it served only the president; it was his "exclusive instrument."

Porter concludes that the EPB successfully performed functions such as identifying issues and problems meriting presidential consideration, confining the president's attention to major issues, presenting information and analysis, ensuring adequate consideration of interests affected by an issue, developing a full range of options and identifying their costs and benefits, aiding in the implementation of presidential decisions, and evaluating policy outcomes. The major limitations of the EPB process were political insensitivity, the domination of a single (conservative) ideology, and insufficient attention to long-range planning.

Porter suggests that the EPB experience demonstrates that presidents can best achieve economic policy integration and coordination through the use of a cabinet-level council managed by a senior presidential assistant who functions as an honest broker. Ben Heineman and Curtis Hessler, in their prescriptive advice to presidents for the management of domestic affairs in the 1980s, cite the EPB as the "proper model" for an "objective, procedurally oriented coordinating staff" for economic policy.[29] They note favorably the attachment of the EPB staff to the presidency. Ford's successors, however, have not adopted the EPB model or its approach.

Carter

President Carter replaced the EPB with the Economic Policy Group (EPG), cochaired by the secretary of the treasury and the chairperson of the CEA. The Economic Policy Group was a large and unwieldy body. It had no staff, was accessible to a wide range of interested officials, and was not organized as a formal advisory body to the president. Attempts to focus its work led to the creation of a steering committee, chaired by the secretary of the treasury and including the chairperson of the CEA, the director of the budget, and the presidential assistants for domestic affairs and for national security affairs. Its operations were so unstructured that it was unable to coordinate even major policy initiatives.[30]

Perhaps the most significant influence on economic policy within the presidency during the Carter administration belonged to domestic policy assistant Stuart Eizenstat, CEA chairperson Charles Schultze, and special trade representative Robert Strauss. According to Colin Campbell, Eizenstat effectively defended domestic program interests in EPG steering committee deliberations, Schultze dominated policies designed to protect the exchange value of the dollar, and Strauss played the lead role in trade policy, a major concern of Carter's.[31] Carter did not appoint an assistant for economic affairs, nor did he rely heavily on any one person to make policy recommendations. Throughout his administration he made the decisions and was very much in charge of economic policy. He did name an inflation adviser (first politico Robert Strauss, who served before being appointed special trade representative, and later economist Alfred Kahn), who also chaired the Council on Wage and Price Stability. Still, neither those persons nor Eizenstat nor Schultze managed an advisory or coordinating process. Also, under Carter, the role of the secretary of the treasury and of the Treasury Department was substantially diminished.[32]

Aside from the activities of the troika in coordinating economic forecasting, Carter managed macroeconomic policy with limited staff assistance. Although the results—the performance of the economy—were not especially salutary, they were not appreciably worse (or better) than those achieved by Ford.

Reagan

President Reagan replaced the Economic Policy Group with the Cabinet Council on Economic Affairs (CCEA). Like its predecessor in the Nixon administration, the CCEA was a forum for discussion of issues and alternatives. Roger Porter served as its secretary and informally coordinated its operations. The council was an active means of establishing consensus within the administration. In addition to the council, the troika met regularly to coordinate economic forecasting.

Against the backdrop of the relatively smooth operation of the CCEA, economic policy making during Reagan's first term involved a struggle for influence within the economic subpresidency. The major participants were Secretary of the Treasury Donald Regan, OMB Director David Stockman, and presidential assistants James Baker and Edwin Meese. The administration had clearly defined macroeconomic policy goals: to reduce the role of the federal government in the U.S. economy, thus reducing taxes and spending, and to increase productivity, savings, and investment, thus ensuring vigorous and sustained economic growth and full employment. There was, however, sharp conflict over the choice of means to that end. That conflict reflected competition among classical conservative, monetarist, and supply-side theories and focused on the significance of federal budget deficits. According to Stockman's memoir, the winners in the conflict were Regan and Meese. He (Stockman) was the principal loser. The reasons for that outcome, as seen by Stockman, were his own political naiveté, Regan's Iago-like cultivation of the president, Meese's political expediency, and Reagan's stubborn refusal to abandon the ideological principles that he brought with him when he took office (for example, a commitment to supply-side economics and opposition to taxes).[33]

Whatever the validity of Stockman's judgments, the dominance of Donald Regan over economic policy emerged in Reagan's second term.

(Treasury Secretary James Baker did play the leading role in the development and passage of the Tax Reform Act of 1986 and in international economic policy.) The CCEA was replaced by the Economic Policy Council; Stockman, Baker, and Meese left the White House; and Regan dominated economic policy from his position as chief of staff. One of Regan's former subordinates at Treasury, Beryl Sprinkel, became chairperson of the CEA; and Stockman's successor at OMB, James Miller, was acceptable to Regan. Interestingly, however, the content of macroeconomic policy changed very little. This absence of change suggests that a carefully managed economic policy process, designed along the lines of Ford's Economic Policy Board, would not have made much difference in Reagan's economic policy decisions, which were based more on an unyielding commitment to a theory (supply-side economics) than on carefully reasoned analysis or on accurate economic forecasts.

As in other areas of policy, the nation is heavily dependent on presidents' attitudes, values, and operating styles for economic leadership. Congressionally established advisory mechanisms, such as the CEA, are helpful, and presidents can take other measures to assist them in identifying issues and achieving policy coordination; but there is no guarantee that the president will adopt effective policies or achieve his objectives. There is, moreover, an important check on his economic policy making—the powers of Congress over taxing, spending, and the monetary system.

The Congressional Role in Macroeconomic Policy

Most of the executive branch agencies and processes that involve macroeconomic policy and the president's economic role are founded in statutes: the Federal Reserve Act of 1914, the Budget and Accounting Act of 1921, and the Employment Act of 1946. Traditionally, Congress has dealt with economic policy through separate consideration of tax legislation and annual appropriations. Tax bills have entailed redistributive issues, that is, questions of who bears the burdens, and efforts of special interests to secure favorable provisions, or "loopholes." The congressional tax-writing committees (House Ways and Means and Senate Finance) have jealously guarded their powers and been unwilling to propose new tax legislation that did not accommodate special interests. The 1986 tax reform act departed substantially from traditional revenue legislation that contains numerous advantages and benefits for a wide range of interests. The two tax-writing committees, under the strong-willed leadership of their chairpersons (Sen. Bob Packwood, R-Ore., and Rep. Dan Rostenkowski, D-Ill.), responded positively to Reagan's call for simplification and reform of the federal tax code. (However, the initiative for tax reform came from Sen. Bill Bradley, D-N.J.; Rep. Richard A. Gephardt, D-Mo.; and Rep. Jack F. Kemp, R-N.Y.)

Appropriations decision making, centered in the House and Senate Appropriations committees, has, until recently, focused primarily on incremental changes in budget requests of departments and agencies. The politics of the budgetary process were a highly stylized game in which the institutional participants played specific roles. The primary consideration in Congress was the amount of increase or decrease in each agency's base, which was the previous year's appropriation. The total level of expenditures was the sum of the thirteen major appropriations bills.

Neither through its taxing nor its spending legislation did Congress attempt consciously to shape fiscal policy. Rather, its money decisions were the product of its fragmented structure of authority, as reflected in the multiplicity of powerful committees and subcommittees, the weakness of its party organizations, and the strong constituency orientation of its members because of their constant concern with reelection.

Although the Budget and Accounting Act of 1921 required the president to prepare an annual budget, which has been a comprehensive plan for spending, and the Employment Act of 1946 required an annual economic report that projected revenues and expenditures in light of economic forecasts, Congress imposed no such requirements on itself. Fiscal policy was whatever remained of the president's program after it emerged from "a piecemeal and haphazard legislative process." [34] Consequently, presidents and their economic advisers lacked the capacity to predict accurately the economic impact of the federal government. The inability of Congress to participate rationally on an equal basis with the presidency in shaping fiscal policy led to sharp conflict during the Nixon administration when federal spending became a politically significant issue. Spending grew rapidly in response to previously enacted statutory "entitlements" that could not be disregarded without revising the original authorizing legislation. (Entitlements include automatic increases in social security benefits and in federal retirement payments due to inflation, farm price support payments, welfare payments, and contractual obligations.) Presidents struggled to control spending as Congress continued to commit the government to future outlays through the passage of legislation. The problem was compounded by "off-budget" spending through loan guarantees and tax credits.

Nixon challenged Congress to act responsibly on fiscal issues by curbing spending; when it did not do so, he frequently vetoed spending bills and made extensive use of impoundment. The primary response of Congress to this controversy with Nixon and to frustration over its inability to shape policy was the Budget and Impoundment Control Act of 1974, which created a procedure for handling impoundments. (See Chapter 7.) More important, that statute established a congressional budget process, created House and Senate Budget committees, and provided Congress with independent staff support for macroeconomic forecasting and budget analysis in the form of the Congressional Budget Office.

The central feature of the budget process is two budget resolutions that Congress must pass each year. The first resolution, which must be adopted by May 15, sets targets for the forthcoming fiscal year for revenues, total spending, and the thirteen appropriations bills. These targets can be exceeded only by revising them upward in the second budget resolution, which Congress must adopt by September 15. In contrast to the first resolution, which serves as a guide, the second one is binding. (Congress failed to adopt second resolutions for fiscal years 1984 through 1987, which made the first resolutions binding.)

The House and Senate Budget committees play a key role in the process as authors of the resolutions, which embody congressionally determined fiscal policy. They must persuade the revenue and appropriations committees to consider the effects of their actions on the fiscal goals in the binding budget resolution. They derive their strength from the realization of most members that the success of the budget process is essential to congressional parity with the presidency in making fiscal policy.

The creation of the budget process did not, however, "significantly alter the established process in Congress for raising and spending money." [35] Nor did it enable Congress to solve the problem of uncontrollable spending arising from entitlement programs and statutory obligations. There is available in the process a technique, the "reconciliation" procedure, for addressing the problem. Reconciliation involves incorporating in one of the budget resolutions instructions to specific committees to recommend statutory changes that will achieve the spending or revenue levels set in the resolution. The committees' recommendations are subsequently enacted in a reconciliation bill. Congress used reconciliation to accomplish modest budgetary savings ($8.3 billion) in 1980 and extensive expenditure cutbacks ($35.2 billion) in more than two hundred domestic programs in July 1981.

The sweeping scope of the reductions, which carried over through fiscal year 1984 and were made without extensive committee hearings or detailed floor debate, prompted complaints that Congress had abandoned its independent control of spending and created a process whereby the president can obtain approval of his entire package in a single vote. Allen Schick has observed that "overreaching in 1981 poisoned the well for expansive use of the reconciliation process in subsequent years." [36] Since then, savings achieved through reconciliation have been small by comparison, but the process remains available for use by a congressional majority determined to make major cutbacks.

The principal effect of the congressional budget process has been a change in executive-legislative budget relationships.[37] The increased centralization of budgetary decision making in Congress has enhanced its ability to influence presidential budget policies while providing the president with greater leverage over congressional budget decisions. Congress and the president have, as Schick puts it, become "more interdependent: each is more vulnerable than before to having its budget preferences blocked or modified by the other." [38]

The budget process has not made Congress more fiscally responsible. Nor has it prevailed over the political and economic forces that have, since 1982, produced record deficits. (The deficit increased, as a percentage of gross national product, from 2 percent in fiscal 1981 to 5 percent in 1984.)[39] The primary causes of the growth in the deficit have been the increased cost of financing the rapidly growing national debt, the defense buildup begun in 1981, and the 1981 tax cuts. Although discretionary nondefense spending has declined since 1981, increases in expenditures for defense and entitlement programs have caused total federal spending to grow, as a percentage of GNP, from 22.4 percent in fiscal 1980 to 24 percent in 1985.[40]

Concern over the record deficits and frustration over its inability to control their growth led Congress, in December 1985, to pass the Balanced Budget and Emergency Deficit Control Act, known as the Gramm-Rudman-Hollings bill after the senators who sponsored it (Phil Gramm, R-Texas; Warren B. Rudman, R-N.H.; and Ernest F. Hollings, D-S.C.). Gramm-Rudman-Hollings established an automatic deficit reduction process designed to bring the budget into balance by 1991.[41] The key feature of Gramm-Rudman-Hollings was the automatic spending reduction device, the mandatory sequester order. The rationale behind Gramm-Rudman-Hollings was that the cuts would be so unacceptable that both the president and Congress would compromise their budgetary differences to avoid them. Before the device could be used, however, the Supreme Court ruled that it was unconstitutional on the grounds that it violated the separation of powers between the legislative and executive branches.[42] For the Court, the fatal flaw was the granting of executive-type powers to the comptroller general, an agent of Congress who can be removed only by Congress. Gramm-Rudman-Hollings contained a fallback procedure for imposing the sequester order, passage of a joint resolution. However, the fallback requires passage by Congress and is subject to a presidential veto; hence, it lacks the automatic spending-cut feature that was the heart of the process.

Even though the Gramm-Rudman-Hollings targets, restrictions, and obligations remain in effect, it appears unlikely that the act will ever accomplish its objective. The Supreme Court's ruling thwarted a desperate attempt of Congress and the president to impose fiscal discipline automatically and indiscriminately by surrendering legislative and executive discretion over future spending.

Congress did pass a deficit measure for fiscal 1987 that met the Gramm-Rudman-Hollings targets.[43] (The projected deficit of $151 billion was within $10 billion of the $144 billion target and substantially below the actual $220.7 billion deficit for fiscal 1986.) Congress accomplished the reductions in the projected deficit through a combination of asset sales, user fees, a first-year windfall of $11 billion from the 1986 tax reform act, changes in health program charges, the decision to move the final military payday of fiscal 1987 into 1988 thus "saving" $2.9 billion, and assorted spending cuts including elimination of the politically popular federal revenue sharing program. The bulk of the reductions were one-time savings that did not contribute to long-term deficit reduction and merely papered over the budget gap. Also, the assumptions about economic growth in the economic forecast were very optimistic. Indeed, by January 1987 the Congressional Budget Office was estimating a deficit of $175 billion for the fiscal year.[44] With the deficit overshooting the target by more than $30 billion, it will be extremely difficult to hit the fiscal 1988 target of $108 billion. In its first year at least, Gramm-Rudman-Hollings tended to favor short-run, politically based fixes over the long-run economic stability it was designed to achieve.

The congressional budget process is neither a success nor a failure. A committed majority can use it, as events in 1980 and 1981 demonstrated, to exert substantial control over fiscal policy, but only at the expense of the capacity to act primarily, if not solely, in response to interest group and constituency pressures. Since 1981, Congress has been locked in protracted conflict with President Reagan over fiscal policy and the deficit.

Meanwhile, there has developed what Paul Peterson calls a "new politics of deficits."[45] The taming of inflation through monetary policy targeted on the money supply has undermined the traditional belief that large budget deficits cause inflation. Insofar as the business cycle is the outcome of monetary policy, it is possible for politicians to ignore the short-run effects of deficits. Politicians continue to make ritualistic denunciations of deficits, but few of them are willing to cut popular or strongly supported programs, such as social security and defense, or to raise taxes to reduce or eliminate them. As President Reagan's experiences have demonstrated, there is little payoff, in support from public opinion or the voters, for efforts to curtail popular programs or to raise taxes. The budget deficit is not a winning political issue.

Only in the long run are deficits now regarded as dangerous, because they eventually will reduce private investment by diverting capital into public sector spending.[46] This will slow the rate of growth in economic output and productivity. Peterson argues that the new politics of deficits will continue until the next major recession, at which time even more massive increases in annual deficits and the public debt will lead to the general belief that "the cause of economic and political turmoil is the growing public debt."[47]

Continuing large deficits present another serious problem in that they remove much presidential and congressional discretion from fiscal policy. The protracted stalemate between Reagan and Congress over spending priorities and the need for additional taxes locked the nation in what Jonathan Rauch colorfully described as a "fiscal ice age," characterized by a "frozen mass of spending priorities that no one has really chosen and no one really likes."[48] With no consensus on the level of spending for defense, entitlements, and other domestic programs, there is no agreement on the appropriations base on which budgetary planning, bargaining, and choices have traditionally rested.[49] Until budgetary consensus is reestablished, fiscal policy will remain largely directionless.

Conclusion

Can the president bring order and cohesion to macroeconomic policy? Can the presidency serve as the instrument for effective management of the economy? Such questions have become increasingly important since 1970 as the U.S. economy has matured, interdependence with other economies has increased, and the ability to increase productivity, sustain economic growth, and keep inflation and unemployment at acceptably low levels has faltered from time to time. Clearly, the challenge to presidents posed by their economic policy role is of continuing importance. Presidents face formidable obstacles and problems as they respond to that challenge. There are, however, encouraging factors indicating that the task, although difficult, is not impossible.

Three major obstacles confront presidents in the performance of their economic policy role: expectations are inordinately and unrealistically high; they have limited authority to meet those expectations; and the base of knowledge on which they act is often limited and unreliable. The problem of unrealistic expectations is not peculiar to macroeconomic policy. Modern presidents have tended to make sweeping promises in order to be elected, and the American people have developed a deep faith that a strong, capable president can provide solutions to their most pressing problems. Although this belief in the efficacy of strong executive leadership acting through the federal government temporarily abated in the disillusionment resulting from the Vietnam War and Watergate, it regained its former vitality by the 1980 election. Candidate Ronald Reagan asked the American people if they were better off after four years of the Carter presidency than they had been at the start of it. The implication and the promise contained in the question were clear: things, including the condition of the economy, had worsened under Carter's stewardship, but a President Reagan would set them right. Reagan's overwhelming victory was ample evidence that Carter had failed to meet popular expectations. Reagan's promise of an economic resurgence helped to create sweeping expectations for his own presidency.

As presidents attempt to develop policies that will produce outcomes that meet popular expectations, they encounter problems. The public is impatient for tangible results, and the pressure for actions that can provide a "quick fix" is great. Approaching elections heighten the search for measures that will produce short-run improvements in conditions. Also, fulfillment of one set of expectations, such as curbing inflation, may lead to consequences, such as increased unemployment and high interest rates, that dampen others. Pressure for action is usually great, and the popular bias against inaction runs deep; yet inaction may be the most prudent course to follow. In short, exaggerated popular expectations that the president will manage the economy effectively may limit his capacity to do so.

In striving to meet the unrealistic expectations of a public eager to place its trust in executive leadership, presidents discover that their authority to act is quite limited. In the area of macroeconomic policy three factors restrict presidential ability to act: congressional prerogatives, the independence of the Federal Reserve Board, and the absence of coordinating power within the executive branch. Presidents must collaborate with Congress in making fiscal policy. Their success depends on congressional responsiveness to their leadership, to their effectiveness as communicators and persuaders. They do not have independent authority to increase or reduce taxes or spending.

Although fiscal policy leadership is a difficult task because of congressional prerogatives, monetary policy is even more confining because of the independence of the Fed. The only resources the president has available to influence the Fed are persuasion and the periodic opportunity to appoint new members to the board and to designate its chairperson. Although presidents have regularly exerted pressure on the Fed, and it has taken political factors into consideration, there is no assurance that monetary policy will be compatible with fiscal policy or that it will not impede the achievement of other policy objectives. Presidents lack the authority to coordinate fiscal and monetary policy. They must rely instead on persuasion and on ad hoc committees to coordinate their economic policies and to integrate economic policy goals with those of other policies.

Presidents also discover that economics provides a rather shaky foundation for recommending policies that directly affect the operation of the entire economy. Economic forecasting is an inexact science and is subject to considerable margins of error. The validity of the projections of the Council of Economic Advisers, the Office of Management and Budget, the Treasury, and the Federal Reserve Board depends on the assumptions that underlie them and on the quality and quantity of information available. The assumptions vary with the institutional orientation of the agency making the forecast, the theories of the economists on the agency's staff, and political pressures on the agency. The Fed's assumptions, for example, currently reflect the influence of monetarism; OMB's, a traditional concern with budget balancing. As David Stockman's account of his tenure as OMB director indicates, there is also pressure on forecasters to resolve budgetary problems by adopting best-case or "rosy" scenarios of economic performance.[50] If the assumptions underlying a forecast prove wrong, then policies based on the forecast may lead to unanticipated outcomes. For example, the record deficits incurred during his administration initially caught President Reagan by surprise because he enthusiastically accepted OMB's rosy scenario.

In spite of the formidable obstacles to effective presidential management of the economy, some encouraging factors suggest that the task is not hopeless.

First, the CEA, throughout most of its existence, has provided presidents with expert economic analysis; and presidents, for the most part, have been receptive to that advice. Perhaps the most positive feature of the CEA's performance is that it has remained a staff agency, and its members have not assumed operational responsibilities. Consequently, it has not expanded to the point where it has become a large, unwieldy bureaucracy. Nor have its chairpersons emerged as challengers to other top officials—such as the secretary of the treasury or the director of OMB—for primacy within the economic subpresidency. The CEA has not always produced sound advice, nor has it always been able to persuade presidents to follow its advice (as was true during most of Reagan's first term); but it has made available to presidents the professional competence of economists—common analytical frameworks and methodologies and a core of theoretical agreement about economic behavior. If presidents have occasionally acted out of economic ignorance, it is not because expert professional advice was unavailable to them, but because they lacked the good judgment to avail themselves of it.

A second encouraging feature of the economic subpresidency is the sustained and successful operation of the troika since its inception during the Kennedy administration. The informal coordination of economic forecasts and projections has been a major force for policy cohesion within the government. Although presidents have continued to make final decisions, the troika (and occasionally the quadriad) has helped to enable administrations to avoid contradictory statements and actions. The resolution of differences arising from the institutional perspectives of the Treasury, OMB, the CEA, and the Fed is not likely ever to be fully accomplished, but the troika has achieved substantial progress toward that end. That the chairperson of the Fed has occasionally participated in the quadriad operation is an additional positive move toward coordination and policy cohesion. The negative consequences of the Fed's independence have been at least partly offset by its involvement in efforts to coordinate monetary and fiscal policy.

The final encouraging factor in macroeconomic policy making is the development of the capacity for (if not the assumption of) fiscal responsibility in Congress. Through the creation of the congressional budget process and the establishment of the Congressional Budget Office, Congress has acquired the capability for independent economic analysis and forecasting and required itself to consider the aggregate consequences of its individual taxing and spending decisions. At the very least, the fiscal decisions of Congress have been made less capricious. The budget process also has increased congressional-presidential interdependence in making fiscal policy. The failure of the budget process to produce fiscal responsibility in the 1980s is due to political factors—the absence of a committed congressional majority and the presence of an ideologically committed and highly popular president—and not to inherent defects in the process itself. The Gramm-Rudman-Hollings act of 1985 is a manifestation of congressional frustration with those political factors.

The protean character of the presidency is apparent in the realm of economic policy in a substantive but not a procedural sense. The nation has moved from a conservative consensus on economic policy in the 1920s and early 1930s to a Keynesian consensus in the 1950s and 1960s to a lack of consensus in the 1980s. Policies have shifted sharply from President Nixon's imposition of wage and price controls to President Reagan's embrace of supply-side theory. Nonetheless, presidents have consistently lacked the capacity to control the economy even though rapidly changing economic conditions, in the United States and elsewhere, would seem to require a maximum amount of adaptiveness in the presidency. The president's ability to respond to new situations, such as a sudden, large increase in the price of oil, is very limited. Institutional arrangements, both statutory and constitutional, restrict the president's actions and dictate that he rely primarily on persuasion to accomplish his objectives. Moreover, experience with different processes for economic policy making and coordination in the Ford and Carter administrations suggests that the internal structure of the presidency has little effect on policy outcomes in this area. Beyond economic conditions, over which the president has little control, the factors that appear to affect economic policy making and outcomes most substantially are the president's ideology and leadership.

Notes

1. Edward R. Tufte, *Political Control of the Economy* (Princeton: Princeton University Press, 1978).
2. James A. Reichley, "A Change in Direction," in *Setting National Priorities: The 1982 Budget,* ed. Joseph A. Pechman (Washington, D.C.: Brookings, 1981), 236-240.
3. Alan Stone, *Regulation and Its Alternatives* (Washington, D.C.: CQ Press, 1982), 262.
4. Lester M. Salamon and Alan J. Abramson, "Governance: The Politics of Retrenchment," in *The Reagan Record,* ed. John L. Palmer and Isabell V. Sawhill (Washington, D.C.: Urban Institute Press, 1984), 47.
5. Walter W. Heller, *New Dimensions in Political Economy* (New York: Norton, 1966).
6. Tufte, *Political Control of the Economy,* 24.
7. Ibid., 27.
8. Ibid., 143.
9. David R. Beam, "New Federalism, Old Realities: The Reagan Administration and Intergovernmental Reform," in *The Reagan Presidency and the Governing of America,* ed. Lester M. Salamon and Michael S. Lund (Washington, D.C.: Urban Institute Press, 1984), 440.
10. James E. Anderson and Jared E. Hazleton, *Managing Macroeconomic*

Policy: The Johnson Presidency (Austin: University of Texas Press, 1986), 14.

11. Dick Kirschten, "Sprinkel Finds a Better Market for Advice in Second Reagan Term," *National Journal,* March 22, 1986, 714-715.

12. Paul W. McCracken, "Reflections on Economic Advising" (Paper delivered at the Princeton University Conference on Advising the President, Princeton, N.J., October 31, 1975), 4.

13. Edward S. Flash, "Macro-Economics for Macro-Policy," *The Annals of the American Academy of Political and Social Science* (March 1971): 51.

14. Ibid., 51.

15. Joseph A. Davis, "Policy and Regulatory Review: Growth in Legislative Role Sparks Concern in Congress," *Congressional Quarterly Weekly Report,* September 14, 1985, 1809.

16. William Greider, "The Education of David Stockman," *Atlantic Monthly,* December 1981, 27-54; David A. Stockman, *The Triumph of Politics: Why the Reagan Revolution Failed* (New York: Harper and Row, 1986).

17. Greider, "Education of David Stockman," 51.

18. Stockman, *Triumph of Politics,* chap. 2.

19. Hugh Heclo, "Executive Budget Making," in *Federal Budget Policy in the 1980s,* ed. Gregory B. Mills and John L. Palmer (Washington, D.C.: Urban Institute Press, 1984), 266-267.

20. Ibid., 291.

21. Ibid.

22. Anderson and Hazleton, *Managing Macroeconomic Policy,* 27.

23. Colin Campbell, *Managing the Presidency: Carter, Reagan and the Search for Executive Harmony* (Pittsburgh: University of Pittsburgh Press, 1986), 123-135.

24. Robert J. Shapiro, "Politics and the Federal Reserve," *The Public Interest* 66 (Winter 1982): 122.

25. Ibid., 120.

26. Ibid., 136.

27. Anderson and Hazleton, *Managing Macroeconomic Policy,* 83.

28. Roger B. Porter, *Presidential Decision Making: The Economic Policy Board* (New York: Cambridge University Press, 1980), 176.

29. Ben W. Heineman, Jr., and Curtis A. Hessler, *Memorandum for the President* (New York: Random House, 1980), 223.

30. Campbell, *Managing the Presidency,* 138.

31. Ibid., 139.

32. Ibid., 139-140.

33. Stockman, *The Triumph of Politics.*

34. James L. Sundquist, *The Decline and Resurgence of Congress* (Washington, D.C.: Brookings, 1981), 199.

35. Allen Schick, "The Evolution of Congressional Budgeting," in *Crisis in the Budget Process: Exercising Political Choice,* ed. Allen Schick (Washington, D.C.: American Enterprise Institute, 1986), 8.

36. Ibid., 29.

37. Ibid., 15.

38. Ibid.

39. Ibid., 26.

40. Ibid., 53.

41. The statute set annual targets, beginning in fiscal 1986, that would reduce the deficit to zero by 1991. Each year, in August, the Congressional Budget Office and the Office of Management and Budget estimate the amount by which spending must be reduced to meet the target. Using these estimates, the General Accounting Office develops its estimate of the deficit. If the GAO predicts that the deficit will exceed the target by more than $10 billion, and if it sees no recession in prospect, it determines the percentage that programs must be cut to meet the target. Half of the cuts must come from defense and half from eligible domestic programs. (Exemptions are granted for interest on the debt, social security, medicaid, and partly for medicare.) On September 1, the president must issue a "sequestering order" making the cuts determined by the comptroller general, who is the head of GAO. The order becomes effective on October 15 unless, in the interim, Congress and the president enact other cuts or tax increases sufficient to hit the target.

    The cuts apply across the board and do not distinguish between expenditures for equipment, personnel, or services to beneficiaries. Neither the president nor Congress may alter or modify the percentages determined by GAO; the process is automatic.

42. Elizabeth Wehr, "Court Strikes Down Core of Gramm-Rudman," *Congressional Quarterly Weekly Report,* July 12, 1986, 1559-1563.

43. Stephen Gettinger, "Budget Measure Helps Congress Hit Deficit Goal," *Congressional Quarterly Weekly Report,* October 25, 1986, 2709.

44. Jonathan Rauch, "The FY 88 Budget: Round One," *National Journal,* January 10, 1987, 82.

45. Paul E. Peterson, "The New Politics of Deficits," in *The New Direction in American Politics,* ed. Paul E. Peterson and John E. Chubb (Washington, D.C.: Brookings, 1985), 365-397.

46. Herbert Stein, *Presidential Economics: The Making of Economic Policy from Roosevelt to Reagan and Beyond* (New York: Simon and Schuster, 1984), 347.

47. Peterson, "The New Politics of Deficits," 39.

48. Jonathan Rauch, "The Fiscal Ice Age," *National Journal,* January 10, 1987, 58.

49. Aaron Wildavsky, *The Politics of the Budgetary Process* 4th ed. (Boston: Little, Brown, 1984).

50. Stockman, *The Triumph of Politics,* 97-98, 329-332.

Selected Readings

Aaron, Henry J., et al. *Economic Choices 1987.* Washington, D.C.: Brookings, 1986.

Anderson, James E., and Jared E. Hazleton. *Managing Macroeconomic*

Policy: The Johnson Presidency. Austin: University of Texas Press, 1986.

Fisher, Louis. *Presidential Spending Power.* Princeton: Princeton University Press, 1975.

Mills, Gregory B., and John L. Palmer, eds. *Federal Budget Policy in the 1980s.* Washington, D.C.: Urban Institute Press, 1984.

Pfiffner, James P., ed. *The President and Economic Policy.* Philadelphia: Institute for the Study of Human Issues, 1986.

Porter, Roger B. *Presidential Decision Making: The Economic Policy Board.* New York: Cambridge University Press, 1980.

Schick, Allen, ed. *Crisis in the Budget Process: Exercising Political Choice.* Washington, D.C.: American Enterprise Institute, 1986.

Stein, Herbert. *Presidential Economics: The Making of Economic Policy from Roosevelt to Reagan and Beyond.* New York: Simon and Schuster, 1984.

Stockman, David A. *The Triumph of Politics: Why the Reagan Revolution Failed.* New York: Harper and Row, 1986.

Tufte, Edward R. *Political Control of the Economy.* Princeton: Princeton University Press, 1978.

Wildavsky, Aaron. *The Politics of the Budgetary Process.* 4th ed. Boston: Little, Brown, 1984.

President Jimmy Carter and Soviet president Leonid Brezhnev shake hands at the first meeting of the SALT II negotiations in Vienna, Austria, June 15, 1979.

CHAPTER ELEVEN

The Politics of National Security Policy

Modern presidents since Franklin D. Roosevelt have been drawn almost irresistibly to concentrate on foreign and military policy rather than domestic policy. (In this chapter, foreign and military policy will be called collectively *national security policy*.) Even presidents who were not strongly oriented toward national security issues when they took office, such as Ronald Reagan and Jimmy Carter, devoted much of their energy and resources to foreign and military affairs. The reasons for the domination of national security in presidential policy-making politics are at least twofold: first, the crucial importance of the United States in the international community; second, the political advantages that presidents derive from devoting much of their energy to national security.

This chapter examines the president's role as the dominant figure in making and directing national security policy. It reviews the major concepts and issues that have dominated national security policy since World War II. It then defines the national security policy-making problem as one in which the president is both the solution and the problem. It explains this situation by analyzing (1) the relationship between the president and Congress with respect to national security and (2) attempts by modern presidents to organize an effective policy-making system for national security and the ways they have approached the task of managing national security policy making.

The President's Interest in National Security Policy

Since the end of World War II the United States has been one of the two dominant nations in world affairs. It and the Soviet Union have been cast in the role of adversaries, leading two armed camps of nations—one democratically governed, the other ruled by Communist party dictatorships. The industrial democracies and the Communist bloc have coexisted in an uneasy peace, maintained in part by the threat of mutual nuclear annihilation. At the same time, each power grouping has actively courted the support of the "uncommitted" nations of the so-called third world. These countries, many of which face enormous economic and social problems, have varied in their orientations toward Washington and Moscow.

Superimposed on the basic pattern of U.S.-Soviet superpower competition is the twentieth-century technological revolution in communications, transportation, and weaponry, which has shrunk the effective dimensions of the world. This shrinking has made the risks of military confrontation much greater than they have ever been. In addition, the United States has become increasingly dependent economically on other countries, especially suppliers of basic raw materials, such as oil. In an environment characterized by military precariousness and economic interdependence, foreign and military policy necessarily assert a high-priority claim on the president's attention. No president, however much he may be so inclined, can focus primarily and indefinitely on domestic policy. Sooner or later, presidents find themselves caught up with national security issues.

Although presidential preoccupation with national security policy abated somewhat during the 1970s as a consequence of public and congressional reactions against U.S. involvement in the Vietnam War and abuses of power by Presidents Lyndon B. Johnson and Richard Nixon, it has by no means disappeared. Presidents Gerald R. Ford, Jimmy Carter, and Ronald Reagan all found that Congress and the public expect presidential leadership in this area. They also discovered, as had many of their predecessors, that foreign policy activity could detract public attention from sticky domestic problems. Furthermore, such activity need not even be successful. President Carter, for example, enjoyed high popular approval ratings for several months during the Iranian hostage crisis of 1979-1980 and used the crisis to his advantage during his campaign for renomination. Public patience is not unlimited, however, and Carter's failure to secure release of the hostages before the election undoubtedly contributed to his defeat.

Presidents have been vitally involved in national security policy not only because of the tremendous stakes and political responsibilities that stem from the superpower role of the United States but also because of their own political self-interest. It is the role of U.S. presidents in national security policy that "has allowed them to establish the primacy of their office, their reputation for leadership and for the effective stewardship of the nation's affairs."[1] Whereas domestic policy leadership is fraught with opposition within Congress and from interest groups, presidents find they have much greater autonomy and freedom of action in national security policy. Although public support is more freely given and congressional deference is greater than in domestic affairs, the issues that presidents face in the national security realm are no less difficult and intractable than those they encounter in domestic affairs.

Issues and Conflicts in National Security Policy

From the end of World War II until March 1968, when the North Vietnamese Tet offensive precipitated President Johnson's decision to end the escalation of American involvement in the Vietnam War, U.S. national security policy rested on a single overarching concept or doctrine, which was supported by a broad consensus: the necessity for military containment of Communism. That goal was pursued consistently, and differences of opinion within the policy-making elite and in the mass public were accommodated by compromises. Bipartisan support for the consensus in Congress gave presidents a free hand in formulating and implementing foreign and military policies. The only effective constraints imposed on presidential actions were the boundaries of the consensus. For example, the consensus did not include acceptance of the risk of war with the Soviet Union, nor did it allow countries such as South Korea or South Vietnam to fall to Communism. The consensus began to break up in 1968 when it became apparent that containment could be preserved only through an indefinite, limited war in Vietnam or greatly expanded U.S. involvement that carried risks of conflict with the Soviet Union.

In a systematic study of U.S. involvement in Vietnam, Leslie H. Gelb concludes that presidents would do well to avoid the temptation to cast national security policy in the framework of an overall doctrine supported by consensus.[2] The problem with policy doctrines such as containment, Gelb argues, is that they create a "framework of necessity" in which "anything that becomes necessary to do in the first place becomes virtually impossible to undo thereafter."[3] Overarching policy concepts or doctrines also stifle dissent and lead to operational rigidity.

Nevertheless, even after the United States failed to "contain" Communism in Vietnam, presidents have continued to employ single, overall concepts to build domestic political support for their national security policies. They have found, as James Chace put it, that "selling programs to Congress and the American people in the postwar era was always made easier if they could be clothed in one garment."[4] In 1972 and 1973 President Nixon told the American people that a policy of détente would ease if not end the precarious Soviet-American tensions of the cold war era. Détente was to be implemented through such actions as cultural exchanges, increased trade between the two countries, and negotiations to limit strategic nuclear weapons. Established attitudes and behavior patterns are not easy to change, however, and Nixon and his successor, Gerald Ford, found it convenient to seek support for their policies by citing threatening Soviet actions in various parts of the world, such as Africa, Latin America, and the Middle East.

President Carter proclaimed at the outset of his administration that morality, manifested in universal commitment to the defense of human rights, would be the cornerstone of U.S. foreign policy. Carter's human rights focus failed to provide the basis for a new consensus because it could not be consistently applied. The United States found it easier to protest and threaten to take action against human rights violations in countries not vital to its interests, like the Soviet Union and its allies, than in those that were vital, like South Korea and South Africa. Indeed, misguided application of the human rights doctrine hastened the downfall of the shah's friendly but authoritarian government in Iran and contributed to the establishment of the equally oppressive, but virulently anti-American, Islamic republic of Ayatollah Ruhollah Khomeini.

Carter's inability to establish a new foreign policy consensus based on human rights illustrates the contradictions that have become inherent in the international environment of the United States. From an American perspective, that environment has become more and more unmanageable because of the decline in the relative economic power of the United States, which stems from increased dependence on imported oil and from economic interdependence with other industrial democracies. In addition to the contradiction between the commitment to human rights and the need for stable allies, serious dilemmas for the United States are embodied in many key issues: devotion to Israel versus the need for Arab oil; the desire for military strength sufficient to deter aggression and protect vital U.S. interests versus domestic political and economic pressures for a balanced budget; a commitment to free trade versus a desire to protect from foreign competition U.S. industries such as steel, automobile manufacturing, and textiles; and strategic and tactical imperatives involving national security interests versus domestic political pressures (for example, Congress's imposition of an embargo on arms sales to Turkey, a vital ally, following the Cyprus crisis of 1974). This list is by no means exhaustive, but it is sufficient to reveal the complexity of the problems that the president faces in attempting to provide cohesive and consistent leadership in national security policy.

The intermingling of new international issues, predominantly economic ones, with domestic social and macroeconomic policy issues further complicates the president's efforts to present national security policy in terms of an overarching framework. These new issues include the leverage exerted on the United States by foreign producers of oil and other natural resources, the management of the international monetary system, international sales of U.S. agricultural products, and international trade policy. These issues have immediate and powerful effects on important domestic constituencies and must be dealt with through negotiations. In addressing such issues presidents do not enjoy the discretion or broad support that traditionally has been accorded them in foreign and military policy.

The Reagan administration's handling of national security policy from 1981 through 1987 exemplifies the new issues and conflicts presidents face in this area of policy making. During his first year in office, Reagan chose to concentrate primarily on the issue that underlay his election mandate:

improvement of the domestic economy. Consequently, he refrained from making a sweeping statement of his administration's foreign policy until he had been in office for several months. Except for a few spontaneous remarks, he left national security policy pronouncements to Secretary of State Alexander Haig, Secretary of Defense Caspar Weinberger, and presidential counselor Edwin Meese III. These officials, and other members of the national security policy-making elite, often contradicted one another, which led to criticism by journalists and opposition Democrats that the new administration lacked a coherent foreign policy. When Reagan did speak out, in November 1981, it was to reinforce what had become increasingly apparent: if his administration had a conceptual framework for national security policy, it was continued opposition to and competition with the Soviet Union. But Reagan's November 1981 foreign policy speech was a far cry from the strident ideological anti-Communism that had characterized his public statements before becoming president.

In practice, Reagan's anti-Soviet stance has been less than doctrinaire. In April 1981, over the strong opposition of Secretary of State Haig, Reagan lifted the embargo on grain sales to the Soviet Union that President Carter had imposed in retaliation for the December 1979 invasion of Afghanistan by the Soviets. Reagan was under strong pressure from Secretary of Agriculture John Block and domestic farm interests to remove the embargo, while Haig objected on the grounds that it would send signals of weakness to the Soviet leaders. In November 1981, facing a growing peace movement in Western Europe, Reagan offered to cancel plans to place additional land-based intermediate-range missiles in West Germany and in several other North Atlantic Treaty Organization (NATO) countries in exchange for the withdrawal of comparable Soviet SS-20 missiles from Eastern Europe and the western part of Russia. The Reagan administration's response to the imposition of martial law in Poland in December 1981 was notably lacking in forceful action. Although the United States asserted that it held the Soviet Union responsible for the events in Poland, its actions—restriction of trade in high-technology items, denial of landing rights in the United States to Aeroflot (the Soviet civilian airline), postponement of negotiations on pending agreements on grain sales and maritime relations, and review of scientific and cultural exchange programs—failed to match the rhetoric of the president and other officials before the Polish crackdown.

The pattern of strong anti-Soviet rhetoric and restrained conduct continued through the Reagan administration. The president, however, who throughout his political career had steadfastly proclaimed opposition to accommodating the Soviet Union, found it difficult to build a successful national security policy on that position. For example, negotiations to limit nuclear weapons and curtail the arms race, although unsuccessful through 1986, were seriously pursued.[5] In November 1985, Reagan held a summit meeting with the new Soviet leader, Mikhail Gorbachev, in an effort to reduce tensions between the two superpowers. In October 1986 Reagan and Gorbachev held a hastily called summit in Iceland at which they almost reached an agreement to phase out all nuclear weapons over a ten-year period. (Inability to resolve the issue of the Strategic Defense Initiative was the principal stumbling block.) Also, in August 1986, Reagan approved the sale of federally subsidized grain to the Soviet Union in an effort to help debt-ridden U.S. farmers.

Reagan found that he had to deal with crucial issues case by case; for example, the Marxist influence in Central America and the August 1986 arrest on espionage charges of an American journalist in the Soviet Union. Repeatedly, the Reagan administration sought support for its foreign and military policies by coalition building among discrete domestic constituencies. Chace's 1978 prediction that the United States "may simply have to learn to conduct foreign policy for a very long time without a single underlying theme on which to base a broad national consensus" appears to have applied to the Reagan administration.[6]

The Reagan administration kept its foreign policy difficulties under control until late in its sixth year. During the first term, critics raised general questions about the direction and goals of foreign policy, but these concerns were not a major problem for the president. Among the more serious incidents were strains with Western European allies over the use of American technology to construct a natural gas pipeline to the Soviet Union and the car-bombing of a U.S. Marine barracks in Beirut, Lebanon, that killed 242 servicemen. In these and other situations the president quickly rallied popular support and defused questions about his stewardship of foreign policy. He enjoyed favor, in the United States and abroad, as the president who had restored lost respect for the nation. In April 1985 Reagan's decision to visit a military cemetery at Bitburg, Germany, in which members of Hitler's notorious SS were buried, resulted in sharp criticism and questions about his sensitivity to the Holocaust. However, his explanation of the visit as a gesture intended to symbolize the healing of the breach between Germany and its former enemies put the matter quickly to rest.

In August 1986 a series of seemingly unrelated foreign policy misadventures began that culminated with revelations that the United States had secretly sold arms to Iran in an apparent exchange for U.S. citizens held hostage in Lebanon and that profits from the sales had been diverted to contra rebels in Nicaragua. The Iran-contra affair precipitated a sharp drop in public support for President Reagan and raised questions about the content of his administration's foreign policy and the process through which it was made and implemented.

The first disquieting event was the seizure in Moscow on espionage charges of Nicholas Daniloff, an American correspondent for *U.S. News & World Report*. Daniloff's arrest occurred shortly after the Federal Bureau of Investigation arrested in New York on charges of spying a member of the Soviet mission to the United Nations (UN). The U.S. government protested vigorously that Daniloff had been framed and asserted that it would not be blackmailed into exchanging a bona fide spy for him. After high-level diplomatic negotiations, however, Daniloff was released, and the Soviet diplomat was allowed to return home after a perfunctory court appearance. Both conservative and liberal critics of the administration's foreign policy attacked the apparent swap, but the president and Secretary of State George Shultz insisted that there had been no deal. Reagan's continued high popularity and the quick disappearance of the story from the news indicated that the public accepted the administration's version of the matter.

In early October 1986, three additional unsettling events occurred. First, a private transport plane carrying supplies to contra rebels was shot down in Nicaragua, and one of the crew members, U.S. citizen Eugene Hasenfus, was captured. The U.S. government denied any knowledge of or involvement with the aircraft, but Hasenfus (who subsequently was tried on charges of "terrorism," convicted, sentenced, and pardoned) stated that he believed the Central Intelligence Agency (CIA) was behind the operation.

The second event concerned a series of stories, published in late August 1986 in the *Wall Street Journal,* asserting that Libya was planning a renewal of its terrorist activities against the United States and other Western countries. At approximately the same time as the Hasenfus incident, it was revealed that these stories had been part of a government "disinformation" campaign designed to disrupt Libyan leader Muammar Qaddafi.

The third and most critical event was Reagan's agreement, on short notice, to the Iceland summit meeting with Gorbachev. The ostensible purpose of the meeting was to prepare for a formal visit to the United States by Gorbachev. Several foreign policy experts outside the administration, such as former national security advisers Henry Kissinger and Zbigniew Brzezinski, warned against going to a summit without careful preparation, but the Reagan administration was undeterred. The meeting appeared to end in failure when an agreement to phase out nuclear weapons fell apart over the Strategic Defense Initiative (SDI, or "Star Wars"). The Soviet Union charged that only President Reagan's intransigence had prevented an historic agreement. Reagan and administration spokespersons, however, stressed how close they had come to a major breakthrough on arms control. Reaction to the summit was decidedly negative among America's European allies who were angered that they had not been consulted over such a fundamental change in Western defense strategy.

During these four events journalists and political critics questioned the administration's interpretation and explanation of its actions, but the president experienced little or no damage to his popular support. The critics also raised questions about the president's knowledge of the details of the events and the role of the State Department, the CIA, and the National Security Council (NSC) and its staff in handling them. The president's popularity and his effectiveness in explaining and justifying apparent mistakes to the public accounted for the reluctance of most critics to press the matters.

That reluctance ended abruptly with the disclosure of the Iran-contra affair. In early November a Lebanese faction with ties to the government of Iran released David Jacobsen, an American whom it had been holding hostage. Shortly afterward, a Lebanese newspaper reported that sources in Iran contended that Jacobsen and two other American hostages who had been released previously had been exchanged for shipments of arms from the United States. The administration acknowledged that it had sent arms to Iran, but stated that only a small amount of obsolete weapons had been involved. It maintained that the shipments were designed to establish contact with and encourage moderate elements in Iran. Reagan refused to acknowledge that selling arms to Iran had been an error, and he vigorously denied that there had been any explicit exchange of arms for hostages, although each hostage's release had been preceded by an arms shipment. Unlike previous instances when his actions were questioned, the president was unable to convince the public and many members of Congress that he was telling the truth. The seriousness and complexity of the affair increased in late November when the president acknowledged, through Attorney General Edwin Meese, that profits from the arms sales ($10-30 million) had apparently been diverted to the Nicaraguan contras through a numbered Swiss bank account. Contra leaders asserted, however, that they had never received such funds. Allegations later arose that some of the missing money had been used to finance the campaigns of candidates in the 1986 congressional elections who favored U.S. support of the contras.

The Iran-contra affair raised issues about the content of the policies involved, the appropriateness and even legality of certain actions by the president and members of his staff, and the president's credibility and competence. The selling of arms to Iran in apparent exchange for American hostages called into question the commitment of the United States to resisting terrorism and isolating countries, such as Iran, that support terrorism. It also undermined the U.S. position of neutrality in the seven-year war between Iran and Iraq and damaged its relations with moderate Arab states such as Saudi Arabia. Several members of Congress charged that the arms sales apparently violated laws requiring "the administration to report on covert operations and other diplomatic and military operations overseas." [7] (The president exempted himself from the legislation and the embargo against arms sales to Iran that had been in effect since the hostage crisis began in November 1979 by formally making a finding that the sales were necessary to national security.)

After the affair was revealed, Secretary of State Shultz and Secretary of Defense Weinberger publicly distanced themselves from the arms transfer. Both apparently had been aware of its general outlines but had objected to its implementation. Shultz learned in December 1986 that the U.S. ambassador to Lebanon had been involved in the matter upon instructions from NSC staff but had been directed not to report his actions to the State Department. The NSC staff provided the impetus for the arms transfer, and one of its members, Marine Lt. Col. Oliver North, directed its implementation with CIA assistance. North also apparently initiated and implemented the diversion of profits from the sales to the contras. These actions were in direct conflict with the decision of Congress not to authorize military aid to the contras in 1986. To the surprise of many observers, when Reagan disclosed that funds had secretly been diverted to the contras, he stated that he had not been fully informed about the matter. In dismissing North and accepting the resignation of National Security Adviser Vice Adm. John Poindexter, Reagan praised their service. (His admiration for them later diminished when they invoked their constitutional rights against self-incrimination and refused to testify before congressional committees. Their initial silence prevented the full dimensions of the Iran-contra affair from becoming known and undoubtedly contributed to continuing congressional and media pursuit of the matter.)

Questions about the president's competence in managing foreign policy focused on his detached administrative style, which entailed extensive delegation and a disdain for factual details. His supporters explained that he took care of "the big picture" and left the rest to subordinates. Until late 1986 this approach seemed to serve him quite effectively. The Iran-contra affair emboldened critics to point out that regardless of how little Reagan may have known, he was accountable for the actions of his administration. Journalist Elizabeth Drew charged Reagan with intellectual laziness and opined that "he did not understand the nature of the trouble he was in." [8] The operation of the foreign policy process, especially the NSC staff, contributed a great deal to Reagan's political difficulties and did little to protect him from foreign policy mistakes. Part of the difficulty resided in its personnel and part in its functions (which will be examined later in this chapter).

As this is written, neither the full details nor the ultimate effects of the Iran-contra affair are known. Observers agree that it is an important event, with implications for President Reagan's performance in the remainder of his term and for the role of the president and Congress in making and implementing U.S. foreign policy. At a minimum both Reagan's leadership and the direction and conduct of U.S. foreign policy have been damaged. On the one hand it is possible that Reagan's remarkable resilience and persuasive powers will at least partly restore his popular support and professional reputation. On the other hand, he may continue to falter in his efforts to persuade the public that he did nothing wrong and that no harm was done to the presidency or to U.S. foreign policy. Regardless of the success of these efforts, the Reagan administration's foreign policy as it moved through its seventh year seemed to be based more on ad hoc, opportunistic initiatives than on careful actions taken in pursuit of integrated, strategic concepts.

The National Security Policy-making Problem

Since a national security policy built on a broad consensus appears to be beyond reach both at present and in the foreseeable future, and bipartisan congressional support for administration policies was one of the casualties of the Vietnam War, the need for effective international leadership in the United States is all the more critical. The governmental structure established in the Constitution—separate institutions sharing powers—creates continuing tension between the president and Congress over the control of national security policy. Edward S. Corwin observed that the Constitution "is an invitation to struggle" between the two branches "for the privilege of directing American foreign policy." [9] Although the struggle continues, and power over foreign policy is divided, the president has played the dominant role in shaping national security policy through most of the nation's history and even more so in recent years. As I. M. Destler has noted, "Americans are unavoidably dependent on their presidents for foreign and defense policy leadership." [10]

Dependence on presidential leadership carries risks, however. The idiosyncrasies of individual presidents' operating styles and personalities can be sources of uncertainty and lack of cohesiveness in policy and can reinforce the institutional tensions between Congress and the president. (To some extent this happened in consequence of the Iran-contra affair.) The nation needs in its national security policy "institutions that provide continuity" and "structures and processes that promote coherence." [11] The problem is that if institutions, structures, and procedures respond to the short-run needs and whims of individual presidents, discontinuity in policy is likely to multiply. Presidents tend to object, however, to making the national security policy apparatus responsive to other needs and concerns in order to achieve continuity and consistency. National security policy making presents the United States with a circular and seemingly inescapable problem: the country's dependence on the president for central policy leadership, born of constitutional arrangements and operational imperatives, leads to discontinuity in policy and a lack of cohesiveness that result from a policy-making system geared to presidential domination. The president is, then, "both solution and problem." [12]

The President, Congress, and National Security

The powers of the United States in international affairs are "inherent, plenary, and exclusive." [13] They are not granted expressly by the Constitution; rather they derive from the nation's existence as a sovereign entity in the international community. To say that the national power over international affairs is inherent means that it does not depend on an affirmative grant of power in the Constitution. The exclusive and plenary character of that power means that it cannot be exercised by the states or anyone else and that its exercise is not limited by the reserve powers of the states.

John Locke, writing in the late seventeenth century, characterized a government's "powers of war and peace, leagues and alliances, and the transactions with all persons and communities without the commonwealth" as "federative" powers.[14] According to Locke, for practical reasons it is necessary that the federative and executive powers, which involve management of external and internal security, be placed in the same hands.

Although the Founders were familiar with Locke, the Constitution is ambiguous in its assignment of the power to control foreign relations. That both the president and Congress have formal constitutional powers in that sphere indicates that the Founders intended control to be shared. In a 1793 debate with Madison in the *Gazette of the United States*, Hamilton argued that direction of the nation's foreign policy is inherently an executive function.[15] Madison's position—that since the power to declare war is vested in Congress, presidential powers in this regard are merely instrumental—has not been borne out by subsequent events. Longstanding usages and the practical aspects of the conduct of foreign relations have combined to make the president the sole organ of the United States in the conduct of its external affairs. Negotiations and communications with other governments have been from the early years of the Republic a presidential monopoly.

Congress, however, has retained considerable ability to influence the substantive content of the foreign and defense policies that the president implements. Policies formulated by the president cannot remain viable for long without congressional support in the form of implementing legislation and appropriations. Nevertheless, throughout most of U.S. history the president has been and is today the "most important single factor in the determination of American foreign policy." [16] The reasons can be understood, at least in part, through examination of the powers of the president and Congress in national security matters.

The Powers of the President

In addition to the inherent powers of the executive, which are similar to Locke's federative power, derived from the involvement of the United States in the international community, the president's powers over national security stem from two sources: formal powers granted by or implied from specific constitutional provisions and powers delegated to the executive branch by Congress.

The specific constitutional provisions on which the president's dominant national security policy role is based include the power to receive ambassadors and ministers, the power to negotiate treaties, the clause designating him as commander in chief of the armed forces, the general grant of executive power, and the clause enjoining him to "take care that the laws be faithfully executed." Operationally, these provisions result in four major areas of presidential authority over national security: recognition and nonrecognition of other governments; making, implementing, and terminating international agreements; the appointment of key personnel to conduct foreign and military policy; and the use of military force as a means of achieving policy goals.

Recognition and Nonrecognition of Foreign Governments.   The president's power, granted in Article II, Section 3, of the Constitution, to "receive Ambassadors and other public Ministers" is the source of the power of recognition and nonrecognition of foreign governments. Since foreign diplomats are accredited to the president, the decision whether to receive them and thus recognize their governments is exclusively his. Congress may formally pressure the president to grant or refuse recognition, but it has no direct involvement in the decision. Because the president can grant recognition, by implication he can also refuse to grant it or withdraw it.

Traditionally, under international law, governments grant recognition to other governments provided they are stable, have effectively established their authority, and are meeting their international obligations. The United States, at least since Woodrow Wilson's administration, has used recognition as an instrument of its foreign policy by refusing to grant it to governments that may lack popular support, violate the rights of their citizens, or fail to conduct themselves in accordance with international law. The United States has expressed its approval or disapproval of foreign regimes through recognition and nonrecognition. This is a particularly effective weapon when exercised by a nation as powerful and influential as the United States. Nonrecognition by the United States connotes a lack of respectability, if not a lack of legitimacy, in the international community. The prospect of U.S. recognition and the threat of its withdrawal can be used to influence the conduct of another nation. Although the leverage gained through use of the recognition power is limited, its considerable symbolic significance makes it an important instrument.

Several key instances involving use of the recognition power illustrate its value as well as its limitations. After the Russian revolution in 1917-1918, the United States refused to recognize the Communist government of the Soviet Union on the grounds that it had obtained power illegally, expropriated foreign-owned property without compensation, and oppressed its own citizens. Although the disapproval of the Soviet regime implied through nonrecognition did not end, President Franklin Roosevelt established diplomatic relations with the Soviet Union in 1933; he believed that practical considerations made recognition advantageous to the United States. In contrast, immediately following the proclamation of the new Israeli state in 1948, President Harry S Truman granted recognition; the support of the United States has been vital to the survival of Israel under precarious conditions.

When a Communist regime took power in China in 1949 after a

revolutionary struggle, the United States refused to recognize it and persisted in regarding the Nationalist government on the island of Taiwan as the legitimate government of China. Not until 1979 did the United States establish diplomatic relations with the People's Republic of China (Communist China). The process leading to this action began with Henry Kissinger, the special assistant to the president for national security, who conducted delicate negotiations on behalf of President Nixon, and it was concluded by President Carter and Secretary of State Cyrus Vance. Recognition of the People's Republic of China symbolized a resumption of the historic friendship between the two countries. It was made possible by a relaxation of ideological rigidity by the Chinese regime, U.S. acceptance of the regime as the legitimate government of China, and mutual awareness of the policy and economic advantages that would accrue to each nation. At the same time, however, the United States did not recognize Chinese sovereignty over Taiwan.

U.S. relations with one of its closest neighbors, the Republic of Cuba, also involve the recognition power. In protest against certain actions of the Communist government of Premier Fidel Castro, especially the expropriation of U.S. property, President Dwight D. Eisenhower broke diplomatic relations with Cuba in January 1960. Subsequently, some presidents have, through informal soundings and suggestions, offered to reestablish diplomatic relations if the Castro government would agree to cease its support of revolutionary movements in other Latin American countries. So far, Cuba has refused the bait and remains a major national security problem for the United States.

The United States broke diplomatic relations with the Islamic Republic of Iran in December 1979 because of that regime's support of the seizure of the U.S. embassy by radicals in November of that year. The damage to U.S.-Iranian relations resulting from the hostage crisis that ensued and the virulent anti-Americanism of the Islamic regime make it unlikely that a U.S. president will resume diplomatic relations until conditions change. Reagan's approval of limited arms sales as a means of establishing contact with moderate elements in Iran to improve the climate between the two countries has not provided the basis for diplomatic ties.

In the above instances, and in other cases involving the recognition power, presidents are legally free to act without regard to Congress. However, congressional views and public opinion effectively limit the range of presidential discretion. Nonrecognition of Communist China, for example, had outlived its usefulness for some time before the first tentative steps were taken in 1971 to normalize relations. Still, it was not until China had broken with the Soviet Union and the excesses of the Chinese regime began to moderate that President Nixon, whose credentials as an unrelenting opponent of Communism were impeccable, felt free to move. Today it would be quite costly in domestic political support for a president to extend recognition to Cuba without substantial changes in Cuban foreign policy and an abatement of the repressiveness of the Castro regime. Yet a strong case can be made that the interests of the United States in Latin America and the Caribbean could be advanced more effectively and Cuban conduct moderated if the two countries conducted normal diplomatic and commercial intercourse. Public and congressional shock in reaction to Reagan's Iranian initiative suggests that it was premature and that resumption of diplomatic relations with Iran is some distance in the future.

Recognition or nonrecognition is an effective presidential instrument in international politics, but it is not to be taken lightly. Once recognition is granted or relations are broken, much of the leverage that the power provides is lost.

International Agreements.   The Constitution provides a second influential presidential power in foreign affairs: the authority to negotiate agreements with other nations that result in treaties or binding executive agreements. The constitutional basis for the treaty-making power is found in Article II, Section 2, which declares that the president "shall have the power, by and with the advice and consent of the Senate, to make treaties, provided two-thirds of the Senators present concur." The authority to make executive agreements is not mentioned explicitly but may be inferred from the president's executive function as the nation's sole organ for the conduct of foreign relations, the power to receive ambassadors from other countries, the commander-in-chief power, and the "take care" clause of the Constitution. In addition, executive agreements may be concluded pursuant to provisions of valid treaties and of existing legislation.

The principal distinction between treaties and executive agreements is that senatorial approval is required for treaties. The Senate's role in the treaty-making process has been limited by a precedent established in 1789, when the Senate refused George Washington's request to meet with it to obtain advice on provisions of a treaty under negotiation. The Senate may, however, amend or attach reservations to treaties submitted for its approval. Amendments change the content of a treaty and thus require additional negotiations; reservations merely clarify the Senate's understanding of the treaty's provisions. The requirement of a two-thirds vote for approval gives the Senate substantial leverage over the executive in the treaty-making process.[17]

As an alternative to the formal treaty process, modern presidents have relied extensively on executive agreements to conclude understandings with other governments. Since World War II approximately 95 percent of the agreements that the United States has entered with other countries have been executive agreements.[18] The distinction between treaties and executive agreements is unclear since the latter are not specifically mentioned in the Constitution. In practice, any international agreement that the president submits to the Senate for approval as a treaty is a treaty. All other agreements are executive agreements. Congress has repeatedly expressed its disapproval of the use of executive agreements in lieu of treaties, but the only limitation it has imposed is to require, in the Case Act of 1972, that it be notified of all such agreements.

Presidents have continued to submit international agreements for Senate approval as treaties because of domestic political considerations. Approval by the Senate gives an international agreement a degree of legitimacy that would otherwise be lacking. For instance, President Carter chose to submit to the Senate as a treaty the agreement providing for gradual termination of U.S. control of the Panama Canal. Carter apparently knew that such action would be difficult to defend publicly in any case, and avoidance of Senate approval could impose unacceptable political costs on his administration. Carter also submitted the second Strategic Arms Limitation Talks agreement to the Senate as a treaty even though approval was highly doubtful.

On several occasions, however, modern presidents have taken important action through executive agreements: in 1940 Franklin Roosevelt exchanged fifty "overage" destroyers for ninety-nine-year leases on bases in British possessions in the Western hemisphere; toward the end of World War II, Roosevelt, British Prime Minister Winston Churchill, and Soviet leader Joseph Stalin entered into extensive agreements on the occupation of Germany and the restoration of civil government in Eastern Europe; in 1973 the United States and North Vietnam ended hostilities and exchanged prisoners of war through an executive agreement; and in 1981 the United States and Israel negotiated an agreement for strategic cooperation in the Middle East.

Not all important international agreements are submitted to the Senate as treaties, nor would it be practical to do so. The decision to designate an international agreement as a treaty is the president's. Such a decision is a political and not a legal one. Regardless of that decision, Congress is not without influence, especially if the agreement is not self-executing. That is, if a treaty or an executive agreement requires legislation or an appropriation for its implementation, Congress is in a position to require the executive to take note of its views. Congress has no constitutional duty to implement a treaty or an executive agreement.[19] Moreover, even though treaties and executive agreements have the force of law, they cannot contravene specific provisions of the Constitution.

Although the president's power to negotiate international agreements is subject to political and constitutional limitations, the power to terminate such agreements is not. Clearly, the president can terminate an agreement that did not receive Senate approval. The Constitution is silent, however, about whether approval of the Senate is required to terminate a treaty. The Supreme Court ruled in 1979 that the president can unilaterally abrogate a treaty.[20] At issue was a defense treaty with Taiwan that President Carter terminated as part of the agreements whereby diplomatic relations were established between the United States and the People's Republic of China.

The power to negotiate international agreements is a key aspect of the president's role in foreign affairs. It has a firm constitutional basis and as a practical matter is solely an executive function. However, the constitutional role of the Senate in the treaty approval process and the necessity for congressional action to implement most international agreements ensure that congressional influence will be felt in the making and implementation of such agreements.

Appointments.   As noted in Chapter 7, the power to appoint subordinates is an important aspect of presidential control over policy. It is a power that the president shares with the Senate, however, in naming high-ranking officials. Although the general considerations affecting presidential appointments also apply to national security policy makers, specific concerns in this sphere warrant attention here.

The most important appointments affecting national security are the positions of secretary of state, secretary of defense, and the assistant to the president for national security. In addition, the president must fill subcabinet posts in the State and Defense departments, name the heads of agencies concerned with national security, such as the Central Intelligence Agency and the Agency for International Development, select the secretaries of the three armed services and their principal assistants, and designate the military officers who will serve on the joint chiefs of staff. Finally, he must appoint ambassadors, the most important of whom represents the United States in the United Nations.

By his appointments, the president emphasizes the direction and orientation of the foreign and military policy of his administration. The appointment of the secretary of state is highly significant for procedural and substantive reasons. The choice of a widely known figure with definite policy views, such as the selection of Gen. George C. Marshall by President Truman, John Foster Dulles by President Eisenhower, or Gen. Alexander Haig by President Reagan, reflected presidential intention to rely heavily on the secretary for advice and guidance. The choice of a relatively unknown individual, such as President John F. Kennedy's designation of Dean Rusk or President Nixon's selection of William Rogers, indicates that the president himself intends to play the dominant role in foreign policy formulation and to relegate the secretary to management of the foreign affairs bureaucracy. The president can change his procedural role, however, as Nixon did at the start of his second term when he replaced Rogers with Henry Kissinger. By selecting a secretary with prominent policy views, such as Dulles or Kissinger, the president indicates his own policy preferences.

Similarly, the appointment of the secretary of defense can have substantial significance. President Kennedy's choice of Ford Motor Company president Robert S. McNamara signified his determination to make the armed forces more efficient through application of modern management techniques. President Nixon's selection of Rep. Melvin Laird of Wisconsin, a powerful Republican leader, symbolized his intention to give greater weight to congressional views in the operation of the department. In contrast, President Reagan's appointment of Caspar Weinberger, who earned a reputation through service in the Nixon administration as a budget cutter (he was called "Cap the Knife"), created confusion because Reagan was publicly committed to sharp increases in defense spending. Weinberger's principal qualifications were administrative ability and a longstanding political association with the president. In his long tenure as defense secretary, Weinberger quickly cleared up any confusion by establishing himself as a loyal and effective exponent of presidential priorities.

Presidents have generally left the appointment of subcabinet officials in the State and Defense departments to the discretion of the secretaries. On occasion, however, such appointments have been used to signify a particular policy focus, to balance the policy orientation of the secretary, or to reward a political supporter. President Kennedy's appointment of Chester Bowles as undersecretary of state at the outset of his administration served to include in the national security policy elite a prominent liberal Democrat who favored a softer approach to relations with the Soviet Union than the president took in his initial statements and actions. President Carter's nomination of Theodore Sorensen to head the Central Intelligence Agency reflected Carter's criticism of the excesses of the agency during the Nixon administration. Sorensen's previous sharp criticism of the agency aroused extensive opposition in the Senate, however, and the nomination had to be withdrawn. President Reagan's designation of Ernest LeFever as assistant secretary of state for human rights, a choice that symbolized his rejection of President Carter's primary foreign policy emphasis, also resulted in Senate opposition. The Senate Foreign Relations Committee rejected the nomination, and it was withdrawn before the full chamber voted on it.

Appointments of ambassadors and special envoys have similar and other uses. By making Jeane Kirkpatrick ambassador to the United Nations, President Reagan served notice that the United States would react much more vigorously to anti-American actions of third world countries in that international body. In contrast, the Carter administration's UN ambassador, Andrew Young, had actively courted third world favor and rarely responded to sharp and even scurrilous attacks on the United States. Other ambassadorial appointments reflect a combination of operational and patronage concerns. Appointees to sensitive positions, such as ambassador to the Soviet Union, tend to be either senior career diplomats or seasoned politicos with substantial knowledge or experience relevant to the post. Important political supporters of the president or his party often are appointed as ambassadors to major friendly nations. In selecting an ambassador, the president must weigh the advantages of having an experienced professional in the position against the political gains of a patronage appointment.

When the United States established diplomatic relations with the People's Republic of China in 1979, President Carter appointed the head of the United Automobile Workers (UAW), Leonard Woodcock, to serve as ambassador. Woodcock had no diplomatic experience, but he had a long-standing interest in China and, as a union leader, was an experienced labor negotiator. In addition, the UAW is an important ally of the Democratic party. When Carter named former senator Mike Mansfield ambassador to Japan, he combined professional expertise and political gain. Mansfield, who had just retired from the Senate, where he had served as majority leader for sixteen years, was trained as a Far Eastern historian. The appointment proved so successful that Reagan asked Mansfield to remain in the post in his Republican administration.

In making high-level executive and diplomatic appointments, the president must be attentive to senatorial attitudes and concerns. The Senate normally defers to presidential choices even in the face of doubts about the competence of the nominee. Reagan's nomination of a longtime political associate, California Supreme Court Justice William P. Clark, as deputy secretary of state brought strong criticism from the press and several senators when Clark revealed a dreadful lack of knowledge of foreign affairs during his confirmation hearing before the Foreign Relations Committee. Nevertheless, the committee recommended Clark's approval and the Senate complied.[21] Reagan experienced much more sustained and frustrating opposition to many of his State Department and diplomatic appointments from North Carolina senator Jesse Helms, a senior Republican member of the Foreign Relations Committee. Throughout the Reagan administration, Helms delayed presidential appointees on the grounds that they were too liberal and did not represent the president's own foreign policy views. The committee eventually would approve the appointments, but Helms made painfully clear, to the White House and the Senate, his objections to the appointees and the direction of administration policy. Had Helms been joined by other members of the committee, his influence over appointments and policy would have been substantial. The Senate's resistance to nominees such as Sorensen and LeFever and the opposition of Senator Helms indicate the limits to the scope of presidential choice.

One of the most important national security appointments, that of the national security adviser, is not subject to Senate approval. (The role of that official in the national security policy process is examined later in this chapter.) The president is also free to designate personal representatives to conduct negotiations or perform specific missions without the requirement of confirmation. President Carter used distinguished career diplomats Ellsworth Bunker and Sol Linowitz to negotiate with the governments of Panama and several Middle Eastern countries, respectively. W. Averell Harriman, a prominent Democratic statesman, served as a roving ambassador without portfolio under several presidents beginning with FDR.

The appointment power is essential to presidential control of the direction and implementation of foreign and military policy. It is a means whereby the president can shape both the conduct and the content of policy. He enjoys wide latitude in exercising the power, but he must be sensitive to the limits imposed by international and domestic politics and by the Senate.

The Use of Military Force. The Constitution states that "the President shall be the Commander-in-Chief of the Army and Navy of the United States" and of the state militia when they are called into federal service (Article II, Section 2). It does not, however, define the nature of the president's powers and duties as commander in chief. In fact, extensive powers pertaining to the use of military force are found in Article I, the legislative article. Most important, Congress is empowered to declare war. Constitutionally, then, the power to use military force is shared between Congress and the president. Historical practice, however, has resulted in a vast expansion of presidential authority to use force at the expense of the powers of Congress. The dominance of the president in this regard has been almost total in wartime; in times of peace Congress has partially reclaimed the ground that it lost. Nonetheless, the result has been the continual aggrandizement of presidential power.[22] Indeed, the resurgence of Congress during the 1970s in the wake of presidential war making in Vietnam has already abated.

The war powers of the president are sweeping and have their basis in the Constitution, in statutory delegations of authority by Congress, and in judicial interpretations. The constitutional foundation of the president's war powers was laid early in the Civil War when Abraham Lincoln married the commander-in-chief clause to the "take care" clause.[23] He used the resulting war powers to justify a wide range of actions to suppress the rebellion. These included activation of state militias, expenditure of appropriated funds for unauthorized purposes, suspension of the writ of *habeas corpus* in militarily insecure areas, and the imposition of a naval blockade of Confederate ports. The Supreme Court upheld the legality of the blockade in the *Prize Cases*,[24] in which it declared that the president had a duty to defend the nation by appropriate means, including military action. The refusal of the Court to overturn any of Lincoln's actions until after the war set a precedent of judicial deference that would be followed in future wars.

Lincoln's actions demonstrated that the war powers of the president extend far beyond mere military command. During World War II the president's powers as commander in chief expanded exponentially under FDR. Among other things, Roosevelt ordered the internment of all persons of Japanese ancestry, including both naturalized and native-born U.S. citizens, who were residing in the Pacific Coast states. The Supreme Court acquiesced in this massive deprivation of basic civil liberties.[25] Roosevelt also created by executive order emergency agencies, such as the War Labor Board, and endowed them with sweeping regulatory powers and accompanying sanctions. In his most dramatic assertion of the war power, FDR demanded in a message to Congress September 7, 1942, that it repeal certain sections of the Emergency Price Control Act of 1942. If Congress did not act by October 1, he threatened to act on his own authority:

> In the event that the Congress should fail to act, and act adequately, I shall accept the responsibility, and I will act.
>
> At the same time that farm prices are stabilized, wages can and will be stabilized also. This I will do.
>
> The President has the powers, under the Constitution and under congressional acts, to take measures necessary to avert a disaster which would interfere with the winning of the war. . . .
>
> The American people can be sure that I will use my powers with a full sense of my responsibility to the Constitution and to my country. The American people can also be sure that I shall not hesitate to use any power vested in me to accomplish the defeat of our enemies. . . .
>
> When the War is won, the powers under which I act will automatically revert to the people—to whom they belong.[26]

Congress responded by acting as the president wished, thus avoiding a constitutional showdown.

Congress further contributed to the development of the president's war powers through extensive statutory delegations in the two world wars. During World War I statutes were enacted that authorized the president to regulate, requisition, and purchase a wide range of materials and products, to prohibit exports, to license trade, to censor international communications, to regulate enemy aliens in the United States, and to seize and operate the railroads. These powers were expanded during World War II through passage of legislation such as the Lend-Lease Act, which authorized the procurement and leasing of war materials to countries regarded as vital to the defense of the United States; the Emergency Price Control Act, which established the Office of Price Administration and authorized it to fix prices and ration a wide range of goods and services; and a host of other statutes. Many congressional delegations of authority to the president were open-ended and were not revised or withdrawn until passage of the National Emergencies Act of 1976.

In short, presidential powers in periods of declared war are vast. To ensure national survival, whatever the president declares must be done is done without regard to constitutional considerations and with the acquiescence, if not full approval, of the Supreme Court and Congress. Some leading constitutional scholars have charged that the Constitution is suspended in wartime and the president becomes a de facto dictator.[27]

The president's power to use military force in peacetime, or even in periods of undeclared war, is less clear-cut. The Supreme Court has been reluctant to resolve questions in this area, and Congress has been more assertive of its prerogatives; however, the president still has substantial responsibilities and concomitant powers to protect American lives and property abroad, discharge international obligations, and preserve national security. Constitutional language is vague, and statutory enactments are an incomplete guide to the exercise of this authority. The critical issue involving the president's military powers in situations other than declared wars is "whether he has independent power to use military forces not only to protect the nation from attack but to further the nation's interests—as he perceives those interests." [28]

Between the two world wars Congress sharply circumscribed the president's military powers through enactment of the Neutrality Acts. However, the failure of the congressional attempt to declare and implement a foreign policy of isolation from world conflicts became manifest in the 1930s when Germany, Italy, and Japan aggressively expanded their territorial holdings and began a war into which the United States inevitably was drawn. Following World War II successive presidents fashioned an internationalist foreign policy, with bipartisan congressional support, based on the military containment of Communism. Presidents were expected to take the initiative, and Congress reviewed their actions through the passage of necessary legislation and appropriations. [29] The most sensitive issue during this period, which ended in 1968 when the failure of U.S. military involvement in Vietnam became apparent, was the authority of the president to commit U.S. troops to fight abroad.

On several occasions between 1945 and 1965, presidents sent U.S. forces into combat or placed them in situations that could easily result in combat. [30] These included the Korean War, the dispatch of four divisions to Western Europe as a permanent commitment to NATO, President Eisenhower's responses to Chinese pressures on Taiwan and to increased tensions in the Middle East, the 1965 intervention in the Dominican Republic, and the Vietnam War.

In June 1950 President Truman decided to intervene in Korea without consulting Congress, although congressional leaders were informed before the public announcement. This action, undertaken to help South Korea resist invasion by Communist North Korea, received strong bipartisan support in Congress. The assertion by a prominent Republican senator, Robert A. Taft of Ohio, that there was no constitutional basis for the unilateral presidential commitment of U.S. forces to combat went largely unheeded. In effect, Congress ratified Truman's actions by extending the draft and voting appropriations to support the conduct of the "police action" in Korea.

Senator Taft's views on the issue received a full hearing in early 1951 when the Senate conducted a "Great Debate" over Truman's decision to send four divisions to Western Europe as a commitment to NATO military forces. After extensive committee hearings and floor debate, the Senate adopted, by a vote of 69 to 31, a nonbinding resolution calling for congressional approval of the dispatch of troops. However, the House refused to approve the resolution.

The consequences of the Senate's action were unclear. The president's authority to commit forces without the approval of Congress had been questioned, and the Senate formally expressed the view that such approval should be obtained; but no restrictions were placed on the commitment to NATO, and Congress did not attempt to make foreign policy by statute.

President Eisenhower, apparently believing that Truman had been politically unwise not to have consulted Congress before committing forces, sought and obtained authorizing resolutions on two occasions: in 1955 when Communist China threatened the islands of Quemoy and Matsu, which were controlled by Taiwan, and in 1957 when the Soviet Union began to extend its influence into the Middle East, an area that was left highly unstable as a result of the abortive attempt of Great Britain and France to prevent nationalization of the Suez Canal by Egypt. Eisenhower made no commitment of forces under the authority of the resolutions, and when he briefly sent marines into Lebanon to protect U.S. citizens during a domestic crisis there, he was not challenged.

The Vietnam War produced the most extensive and controversial instances of presidential war making in the post-World War II era. Beginning with Truman, presidents made commitments of military aid and provided military advisers to the government of South Vietnam. By the end of 1963, more than 16,000 military advisers were in that country, many of them actively participating in combat although not formally authorized to do so. In August 1964, following a confrontation in the Gulf of Tonkin between a North Vietnamese gunboat and a U.S. destroyer, Congress passed, at President Johnson's request, the Gulf of Tonkin Resolution authorizing the president to "take all necessary steps including use of armed force" to assist nations belonging to the Southeast Asia Treaty Organization (to which the United States was a signatory) in defense of their freedom. Only two negative votes were cast against the resolution, both in the Senate. The resolution did not distinguish between powers the president already possessed and newly delegated authority. On the authority of the Constitution, the Southeast Asia Treaty, and the Gulf of Tonkin Resolution, President Johnson proceeded to order a vast increase in the strength of U.S. forces in Vietnam, so that by late 1967 they exceeded 500,000. He also authorized military commanders to conduct air raids against military targets in North Vietnam.[31] President Nixon extended the scope of military operations even while trying to negotiate an end to U.S. involvement in the war. In 1970 he ordered a covert invasion of Cambodia to destroy enemy supply and staging areas, and in December 1972 he authorized the bombing of the North Vietnamese capital city of Hanoi and the major port city of Haiphong. These actions were taken without consulting Congress.

Initially, Congress was highly supportive of efforts to contain Communism in Southeast Asia through the use of military force. As the war dragged on in spite of escalating U.S. participation, however, popular support began to wane, a widespread domestic protest movement developed, and opposition to U.S. policy developed abroad from its allies and from third world nations. Many members of Congress questioned the wisdom and the legality of placing the decision to use military force entirely in the president's hands. As long as presidential use of force appeared to be successful, congressional opposition was minimal; but when the use of force appeared to be failing, or the risks increased and the costs in popular support became too great, Congress reasserted its constitutional authority to participate as an equal partner with the president in determining where and under what conditions the United States would wage war.

The Reassertion of Congressional Powers

Congress has substantial constitutional powers that enable it to claim parity with the president in shaping national security policy. As noted in the discussion of the president's powers, the Senate is directly involved in the treaty approval process and the confirmation of appointments; congressional action in the form of authorizations and appropriations is necessary to implement all presidential decisions that are not self-executing; and the power to declare war rests solely with Congress and implies a congressional prerogative over the use of military force. However, operational realities and a bipartisan foreign policy consensus led to presidential domination of national security policy during the cold war with the Soviet Union that followed World War II.

The failure of the Vietnam War—which was, essentially, the presidents' war—ended, at least temporarily, Congress's deference to presidential domination of national security policy. During the 1970s Congress limited presidents' ability to wage undeclared war, reduced unrestrained use of executive agreements, restored the treaty as the principal means of making international agreements, reassessed its sweeping delegations of authority to presidents in past wars and emergencies, and curbed secrecy and covert activities in the conduct of foreign and military affairs.

The most important congressional attempt to reclaim powers lost or given to the executive was the War Powers Resolution of 1973. Passed over President Nixon's veto, House Joint Resolution 542 provided that the president may commit the armed forces to combat only in the event of a declaration of war, specific statutory authorization, or a national emergency created by an attack on the United States or its armed forces. The resolution urged the president to consult with Congress in "every possible instance" before committing forces to combat abroad, and it required consultation after such commitment. Specifically, it required a written report to Congress within forty-eight hours of a commitment and required ending of the commitment within sixty days unless authorized by Congress. The commitment could be extended for thirty additional days if the president certified to Congress that military conditions required continued use of the forces to ensure their safety. Finally, it stated that, through use of a concurrent resolution that would not be subject to presidential veto, Congress may order the disengagement of U.S. forces before the end of the first sixty days.

The effectiveness of the War Powers Resolution as a congressional means of controlling presidentially initiated military action is unclear. Presidents from Nixon through Reagan have not conceded the constitutionality of the statute, although Ford, Carter, and Reagan have all filed reports of military actions with Congress. Ford filed four reports in 1975: three involved the withdrawal of U.S. forces from South Vietnam; the other, the rescue of the *Mayaguez*, a merchant ship that had been seized by Cambodian gunboats. Carter's sole filing occurred after the abortive attempt to rescue the American hostages in Iran in April 1980. Reagan sent troops into Lebanon in 1982 as part of a peace-keeping force. He informed Congress of the action "consistent with the War Powers Resolution," but based the move on his constitutional authority as commander in chief. Congress responded by authorizing the troops to remain in Lebanon for eighteen months, through the 1984 election. Following the bombing of a U.S. Marine barracks near Beirut in October 1983, Reagan removed all ground forces from Lebanon in early 1984. In October 1983, Reagan filed a report with Congress of the invasion of Grenada "consistent with the War Powers Resolution." His use of the wording "consistent with" rather than "under the authority of" followed the practice of Ford and Carter and was designed to avoid conceding the constitutionality of the resolution.[32] Although some members of Congress believed that Reagan's handling of the Lebanon and Grenada incidents did not conform with the resolution, Congress took no action to enforce compliance with it.[33] The Reagan administration also was criticized for its failure to consult congressional leaders before the invasion. Interestingly, disputes over handling of the Grenada invasion focused on procedures rather than on the substantive merits of the action.

In addition to presidents' refusals to accept the constitutionality of the War Powers Resolution, its effectiveness is further threatened by uncertainty regarding the implications of the *Chadha* decision,[34] which outlawed the legislative veto. The Reagan administration and some legal scholars argue that *Chadha* rendered invalid section 5(c) of the resolution, which requires the president to withdraw troops from hostilities if directed to do so by congressional passage of a concurrent resolution.[35]

The effect of the War Powers Resolution on the constitutional roles of the president and Congress in making decisions about war and peace is unclear. At the very least, the legislation was a symbolic victory for Congress, serving notice that sustained military commitments outside the country could no longer be made by presidential fiat but required congressional approval and, by implication, popular support. As Destler has observed, "It is hard to conceive of a formula better crafted to balance the need for presidential capacity to respond quickly to foreign emergencies and the need—as a matter of right *and* effective policy—for democratic judgment on the deployment of troops in combat." [36]

Presidents have maintained that the resolution is unconstitutional, but no legal challenge to it has been sustained. Some critics of the resolution have asserted that it imposes potentially damaging shackles on the ability of the executive to provide effective national security leadership, while others have charged that it amounts to a ninety-day blank check. The ambiguities surrounding the resolution could be clarified by tightening its language and subjecting it to Supreme Court interpretation, but neither Congress nor the president has so far been willing to take such action, perhaps because the outcome is uncertain. Citing as precedent the history of presidential war making, the Court could sustain the resolution. Or, noting that since it was forced on the presidency at a time of institutional weakness, it "undercuts the legitimacy of the executive branch," the Court might choose to overturn it.[37]

Increased congressional participation in national security decision making may not be constitutionally mandatory, but it is increasingly necessary on practical political grounds. The impact of international issues on domestic politics and the entry of domestic political interests, such as the Israel lobby and the Greek lobby, into the policy-making process force presidents to seek congressional support in order to protect their own political positions. As Douglas J. Bennett, Jr., assistant secretary of state for congressional affairs during the Carter administration put it:

> Presidents and Congresses of the future will find themselves thrust into a tar-baby embrace on the central international issues of the times, each unable to abdicate its responsibilities to the other, each compelled to justify itself to an impatient public, and each constrained to seek the other's support. Each will need all the legitimacy the other can convey.[38]

It is somewhat ironic, however, that increased congressional desire to share in making national security policy and increased knowledge and competence on the part of individual members and expanded committee staffs have not been accompanied by congressional capability to assume the added responsibility.[39] Congressional reforms during the 1970s, especially in the House, have further fragmented power and made it more difficult for Congress to speak authoritatively with one voice. The proliferation of subcommittees and the growing interdependence of domestic and foreign policy issues have increased the number of congressional participants in national security policy matters. Congressional staffs have grown in size and influence so that they, too, are drawn into negotiations between the branches. These developments, along with expanded pressures from interest groups and other domestic constituencies, make the achievement of interbranch consensus much more difficult.

The difficulty that Congress currently faces in assuming a more active and constructive role in national security policy should not obscure the positive contributions that it has made in recent years. Among other things, it has curbed unrestrained presidential war making; it has forced reconsideration of extensive if not excessive overseas commitments and imposed caution on assuming new ones; it has broadened the popular base of U.S. foreign policy; and it has instituted more careful scrutiny of agencies involved in national security. Following the revelation of the Iran-contra affair, Congress moved through its relevant committees to find the facts so that responsibility could be affixed and recommendations made for changes in procedures. In sum, Congress has expanded the base of legitimacy for foreign and military policy.

The constitutional "invitation to struggle" is still present. Congress confronts alternative approaches to developing its national security policy role in the complex international environment of the 1980s. At times it will be tempted to revert to the pattern of acquiescence in presidential domination that prevailed from World War II until 1973. On other occasions it will be tempted to take matters into its own hands, because of either popular pressures or distrust of the presidents' policies and capabilities. A third path, and one that would be most beneficial to the nation, is that of collaboration tempered by a sense of constitutional and political responsibility to be constructively critical. Although the president must provide leadership, and only the executive branch can conduct and implement national security policy, Congress has a vital role to play in refining, legitimating, and reviewing all policies.

Organizing and Managing National Security

Beyond dealing with the constitutional issues and political considerations involved in national security policy, the president also confronts a formidable administrative task: organizing the presidency and the executive branch for the formulation and implementation of policy and managing the processes that have been established. The organizational task entails establishing and changing structures and processes. The management task entails the use of processes to establish policies and put them into effect. The president is more intimately and actively involved in the management task, but organization is important in that it can affect management styles and practices. Moreover, most presidents have made organizational changes according to their approaches to management.

National Security Organization

One of the soundest responses to the frequently asked question whether organization really matters was that of the Commission on the Organization of the Government for the Conduct of Foreign Policy (the Murphy Commission). It opened its 1975 report with the observation that "good organization does not insure successful policy, nor does poor organization preclude it." [40] The commission went on to assert, however, that organizational arrangements do have a continuing and powerful impact on the content of public policy and the effectiveness with which it is implemented. Organization determines the level of government (national, state, or local) and the agency that will deal with a problem. Governmental organization performs three primary functions: it "creates capabilities" for performing tasks that are beyond the reach of individuals; it "vests and weighs particular interests and perspectives" by increasing or reducing the probability of their inclusion in decision making; and it "legitimates decisions" by ensuring that relevant parties are consulted and that decisions are made by proper authorities.[41]

Although there is no specific model to which national security organization must conform, two considerations are paramount: it must be capable of adapting to changing events and conditions, and it must be able to accommodate the operating style of the president whose constitutional roles make him the focal point of the policy-making process. Congress has enacted legislation, such as the National Security Act of 1947, establishing organizational units to aid the president in the conduct of national security policy. The principal such units are the National Security Council and its staff, the departments of State and Defense, the joint chiefs of staff, and the Central Intelligence Agency. Congress cannot, however, effectively prescribe how the president shall use those units or the processes by which the president will develop broad policy goals and strategies for carrying them out; nor can it prescribe how he will manage and coordinate the complex and far-reaching activities of the military establishment, the foreign policy bureaucracy, and the intelligence community. The president needs help to discharge these responsibilities, and he has the authority to obtain it. Specifically, he needs staff assistance, mechanisms and procedures for the discharge of his responsibilities, and support and effective performance by cabinet departments and independent agencies. How he obtains that assistance is the essence of his management of national security.

Presidential Management of National Security

Although the National Security Council, which is the basic structure for the management of national security affairs, has remained substantially unchanged since its creation in 1947, presidents have employed it in various ways. Congress established the council in response to the pressures of the cold war and in reaction, at least in part, to the administrative chaos that characterized President Franklin Roosevelt's freewheeling approach to management. FDR enjoyed the rough-and-tumble of conflict and competition between cabinet members and administrative units. He consciously used organizational ambiguity to increase his control over his administration. By late 1944, however, the difficulties of coordinating military operations, economic activity, and the ongoing functions of civil government led to the establishment of the State-War-Navy Coordinating Committee to improve communications.[42] Two senior wartime leaders, Army Chief of Staff George

Marshall and Secretary of the Navy James P. Forrestal, actively advocated the creation of permanent machinery for coordinating national security policy.

The Truman Administration.   President Truman endorsed Marshall's proposal for unification of the armed forces in a single service. Congress responded by passing the National Security Act of 1947, which unified the army, navy, and air forces (established in the act as a separate service) within the framework of a new Department of Defense. The legislation also created the NSC as an advisory body to the president, but it did not prescribe any duties for the council or delegate powers to it. Beyond the statutory listing of its members (the president, vice president, and the secretaries of state and defense), the act was silent, and the pattern of the council's operations and its staffing arrangements were left to the discretion of the president.

Initially, Truman was somewhat suspicious of a legislatively mandated advisory body that to some extent reflected Congress's lack of confidence in his ability to conduct foreign and military policy. However, he moved quickly to establish his authority over the NSC by integrating it fully into the Executive Office of the President and ensuring that it would be dominated by the State Department rather than by the new Department of Defense. Forrestal, who had become the first secretary of defense, proposed that the council be lodged in the Defense Department and that it rely on the department for staff support. Truman, however, designated the secretary of state to chair council meetings in his absence and relied on the State Department for the preparation of analytical papers and other staff support. After the outbreak of the Korean War, Truman used the council as an advisory forum to aid in coordinating the administration's political and military responses to what was perceived as the challenge of international Communism. The council's role was limited to advice and coordination once decisions were made. Control over policy formulation and the selection of appropriate means of implementation remained firmly with the president and his principal adviser, Secretary of State Dean Acheson.

The Eisenhower Administration.   President Eisenhower continued to use the NSC as a major advisory forum, but he consulted it far more frequently than Truman had done. More important, Eisenhower expanded the council's role as the key component in a highly structured, comprehensive process of policy analysis and coordination. He established a Planning Board and an Operations Coordinating Board.

The Eisenhower NSC process concentrated on developing general policies that would guide ongoing operations. It imposed a comprehensive framework of order on national security affairs. Its critics charged that the process was so ponderous that it could not guide responses to emergencies or develop new policy initiatives. Moreover, they asserted that its emphasis on consensual agreement within the NSC suppressed hard choices and resulted in ambiguity rather than flexibility. Its defenders responded that the process guaranteed that the president would be made aware of all relevant issues and viewpoints and that it provided rational coordination of policy formulation and implementation.

To some degree, debate over the formal NSC process under Eisenhower was beside the point because the council did not decide the most important national security issues. Eisenhower relied heavily on Secretary of State Dulles for advice, and the State Department dominated the foreign policy advisory process. More important to the development of the NSC as a primary instrument of presidential leadership for national security was Eisenhower's expansion of the role of its staff, which was enlarged and given responsibility for analyzing and reviewing agency positions. Of particular significance for later developments was the creation in 1953 of the position of special assistant for national security. Eisenhower's special assistant, Robert Cutler, functioned primarily as a staff coordinator, but in subsequent administrations the position took on added dimensions.

The Kennedy Administration. President Kennedy disdained the formal approach to managing national security that characterized the Eisenhower presidency and to some extent that of Truman. Kennedy dismantled most of the Eisenhower process for obtaining systematic national security policy advice so that all that remained was the statutory council and a small staff headed by the special assistant for national security affairs, historian McGeorge Bundy, former dean of the Harvard faculty. Kennedy consulted frequently with the members of the NSC and with the two statutory advisers added in 1949, the chairperson of the joint chiefs of staff and the director of the CIA, but he seldom used the council as a forum for obtaining policy advice. He did employ an ad hoc group of senior officials as an advisory body during the Cuban missile crisis of October 1962. This group, called the Executive Committee of the National Security Council, met both with and without the president in attendance to examine alternatives for dealing with the situation. The group reflected Kennedy's collegial approach to managing national security.

The most significant development in presidential management of national security that occurred during the Kennedy administration involved the council neither as an advisory and decisional body nor as the focal point of a formal process for the analysis, development, and coordination of policy. Rather, it entailed an enhancement of the role of the special assistant and the NSC staff. Under Bundy, the special assistant became a principal policy adviser to the president with responsibility for managing day-to-day national security affairs on his behalf.[43] Bundy recruited a small (twelve person), but highly talented staff and through it coordinated interagency decision making. The NSC staff also became a major source of information for the president.

Although Bundy functioned primarily as a facilitator and did not monopolize policy-making activity, the position of special assistant and the NSC staff gained enormous influence over policy at the expense of the secretary of state and his department. The NSC staff and the special assistant became a major presidential instrument for managing foreign policy, a development that complemented Kennedy's preference for an informal and flexible policy-making process.

The Johnson Administration.   Bundy continued to serve as special assistant following the abrupt transition to the Johnson administration. Johnson relied heavily on Bundy to help acclimate him to dealing with national security affairs. He sent Bundy on missions to Vietnam and the Dominican Republic as his personal emissary and used him to rebut criticism by having him appear in public forums such as "Meet the Press."

After Bundy's departure in 1966, Johnson sought to reduce his dependence on the special assistant and the NSC staff by relying more heavily on the State Department for policy coordination. Although the NSC staff continued to generate information and analytical papers, it no longer served to identify issues and manage them centrally. Johnson seldom used the NSC as an advisory forum or decision-making vehicle. Rather, he employed special assistant Walt W. Rostow and the NSC staff as a focal point for directing foreign policy and for interagency coordination.[44] In sum, Johnson continued and did not significantly modify the NSC's role as a high-level presidential policy instrument. Rostow wielded less influence under Johnson than Bundy had under Kennedy, partly because Johnson wished to demonstrate his independence and partly because Rostow was more oriented toward ideas and policy content than toward process. A central element of Bundy's strength had resided in his control of the process to serve the needs of the president.

The Nixon-Ford Administration.   It remained for President Richard Nixon and Henry Kissinger, his special assistant for national security affairs, to establish a highly formal, White House-centered system for management of national security policy making and coordination. Kissinger directed a formal planning process in which a newly created National Security Council Review Group, chaired by Kissinger, screened analytical studies initiated by Kissinger and conducted by an NSC staff directed by Kissinger. The purpose of the process was to generate options for the president's decision. At the same time, Kissinger managed the ongoing national security business of the president.[45] In the course of Nixon's first term in office, Kissinger also assumed operational responsibilities. He became the president's personal envoy and conducted secret negotiations with the Soviet Union and the People's Republic of China that led to détente and to Nixon's historic visit to Peking. Kissinger actively advocated particular policies and campaigned against others within the highest circles of the administration, and he became its primary foreign policy spokesperson.

The result of the Nixon-Kissinger system was to convert what had originally been a staff position, the special assistant, into a major line operator. The special assistant became a major competitor of the secretary of state for primacy in advising the president on foreign policy. Also, the NSC staff assumed many functions involving policy implementation and inter-agency coordination formerly performed by the State Department. (The displacement of that department and its secretary was more severe than was the case with the Defense Department, primarily because of the technical nature of military operations compared with the more general character of foreign affairs.) From Nixon's perspective, the advantage of centering the national security policy system in the White House, under the direction of the special assistant, was that it enhanced his control over issues that he chose to manage. The Nixon-Kissinger system also discouraged departments and agencies from developing independent analytical capabilities. The result was that senior officials outside the White House, mainly cabinet members and agency heads, found it difficult to function as forceful, independent sources of policy advice.

Matters that necessarily had to be managed by the departments, however, often resulted in bureaucratic stalemate and lack of continuity and cohesion in policy. The advantages of professional expertise and institutional memory that a departmentally based policy system can provide, and the accompanying enhancement of policy continuity and cohesion, are largely forgone if the president opts to center the system in the White House.

The controversy over having the foreign policy system centered in the White House as opposed to the State Department abated in 1973, when Kissinger became secretary of state while retaining the special assistant's portfolio. At that point his domination was made manifest and he employed the resources of both the NSC staff and the State Department to fashion national security policy in accordance with his and the president's views. Even after President Ford appointed Kissinger's deputy, Gen. Brent Scowcroft, to the special assistant's post in November 1975, Kissinger continued to be the dominant figure in the national security policy system. Interestingly, the State Department did not recapture lost power under Kissinger, who had little concern for its organizational interests and who continued his highly personalized approach to policy. Scowcroft, as special assistant, shunned publicity and avoided conflict with Kissinger. He was content to act as a coordinator and facilitator.

The Carter Administration. President Carter came to office deter-mined to avoid both the centralization of policy making in the White House and public competition between the national security assistant and the secretary of state. A believer in cabinet government, Carter conceived of himself as the hub of a policy-making wheel in which he would be the principal initiator and manager.[46] He allowed other officials and advisers to have frequent and direct contact with him, and he involved himself at a fairly early stage in the process. However, Carter also instituted a formally structured NSC policy process that relied heavily on the special assistant, Zbigniew Brzezinski, and the council staff for analytical studies. A primary Carter objective was to have Secretary of State Vance act as his principal foreign policy adviser and to limit Brzezinski to a staff role.[47] Brzezinski actively advocated his own views, however, and did not confine himself to the tasks of policy analysis and coordination. Although Brzezinski never dominated the national security policy system as Kissinger had done under Nixon, he did assume certain operational responsibilities and speak publicly for the president on policy matters.

Carter's attempt to manage national security policy through an approach that combined elements of formal and collegial decision making proved unsuccessful. The substance of foreign policy and the process for making it appeared to be fragmented and incoherent.[48] By 1978, Vance and Brzezinski were publicly at odds with each other, particularly over how to deal with the Soviet Union. Carter often complicated the situation by taking major policy initiatives without adequate preparation or consultation, leaving it to Vance and Brzezinski to provide explanations, rationales, and policy adaptations. Disagreements between the two officials became publicly identified as a conflict between the State Department and the White House for control of foreign policy. Carter's inability or unwillingness to settle the conflict resulted in a foreign policy that appeared to lack direction and a fragmented policy-making process that the president did not control. Eventually, Carter relied on Brzezinski to impose control over foreign policy issues, but in doing so he undermined Vance's position as secretary of state.[49] Vance finally left the administration in May 1980 following the failure of the military effort to rescue the U.S. hostages in Iran. The decision to attempt the rescue was made during Vance's absence from Washington, but with full knowledge of his opposition to the mission. Vance's successor, former senator Edmund Muskie (D-Maine), also found himself outflanked by Brzezinski and complained about being omitted from discussions on a major change in nuclear strategy.

The weaknesses of Carter's management of national security policy appear to have been due to the following factors: his personal style of operation, which was characterized as hyperactive pursuit of many goals in a short period of time and a tendency to initiate policies without sufficient consultation and analysis; his inability to recognize the contradictions between important policies; and the inescapable pressures on presidents who centralize the management of the national security policy system in the White House. The advantage, from a president's perspective, of a system centered in the White House is that his senior advisers are close at hand and have no competing institutional or political loyalties, as do cabinet members and the joint chiefs of staff.

The Reagan Administration.   Like other recent presidents, including Carter, Reagan took office determined to avoid the mistakes of his predecessor. He announced his commitment to cabinet government and stated his preference for a national security policy system in which the secretaries of state and defense would play dominant roles. He named two experienced, highly skilled veterans of the Nixon administration, Alexander Haig and Caspar Weinberger, to head the departments of State and Defense. The NSC staff was downgraded, as its director, National Security Assistant Richard Allen, was denied direct access to the president. Allen's appointment signified a reduced role for the NSC staff. He was neither a close Reagan associate nor a leading Republican spokesperson with an independent power base. Allen reported to the president through presidential counselor Edwin Meese. Meese, along with Chief of Staff James Baker and Deputy Chief of Staff Michael Deaver, constituted a "troika" that advised the president on crucial issues. Meese had special responsibility for resolving policy disagreements among advisers and for coordinating the development of major policy options for staff consideration.

Reagan's initial system for national security policy failed to produce coherent policies or smoothly functioning collegial decisions. The president rejected an early attempt by Secretary of State Haig to establish himself as the principal adviser to the president and spokesperson for the new administration. Anonymous "White House sources" complained to reporters that Haig's imperious conduct was damaging the president's ability to achieve his other policy goals. Haig also feuded publicly with Defense Secretary Weinberger and National Security Assistant Allen. Policy disagreements between Haig and Weinberger created confusion in Washington and abroad over the administration's objectives. Also, charges were made, in Congress and in the press, that there was no identifiable foreign policy and that the system for managing national security was not working as designed.

Perhaps the most important reason for the apparent failure of Reagan's initial system for national security policy was his lack of experience in the area and his primary interest in domestic and economic policy. His top priority during his first year in office was to put his economic program, with its tax and spending cuts, in place. He was also determined to increase defense spending sharply. Except for Haig and Weinberger, who were often at odds with each other, none of his key national security advisers was sensitive to the pragmatic compromises that are often required to make policy acceptable abroad and defensible at home. In addition, Reagan's closest policy adviser, Meese, lacked the ability to manage conflicts between national security policy goals and the objectives of domestic and economic policy. Meese's primary objective was to protect the president's political interests.

Reagan's disdain for careful study of issues and his lack of interest in the implementation of policy further contributed to the appearance of disarray. Finally, Richard Allen's lack of access to Reagan and the deliberate downgrading of the NSC staff and its policy process ruled out a coordinating or facilitating role for the national security assistant. Allen's departure in early 1982 and his replacement by William Clark helped to strengthen national security staffing. Nonetheless, as Reagan entered his second year in office, there was no clear indication that he had settled on a White House-centered national security system.

At the same time, however, Secretary of State Haig had not achieved his goal of dominating national security policy. This failure was due primarily to objections from Reagan's top aides, mainly Meese, Baker, and Weinberger, and not to the president's unwillingness to have Haig do so. Interestingly, Reagan was largely uninvolved in the struggle for control of the national security policy system among Haig, Weinberger, and his top White House aides. His interest in national security appeared limited to insistence on the overarching commitment to oppose the spread of Soviet influence. Issues involving tactical implementation of that strategic objective seemed to be more of an annoyance than a major concern to him.

Haig's inability to control his personal relations with other high-ranking administration officials and his policy disagreements with them eventually led to his resignation.[50] Journalist Dom Bonafede suggested that Haig decided to resign when he realized "that he alone could not control U.S. foreign policy." [51] Similarly, political scientist Kevin Mulcahy has observed that "Haig forgot the fundamental tenet of successful secretarial-presidential relations in foreign policy making: it is the president who makes policy and he is free to consult whomever he wishes and to establish what structural processes he deems necessary." [52] Haig failed to recognize that his attempt to take command of foreign policy would be regarded by Reagan's aides as an attempt to upstage the president, which, if successful, would damage him politically.

Haig's departure may have been made inevitable when William Clark became national security assistant. Although Clark had served effectively as Haig's deputy at the State Department and had a high regard for him, Clark's primary loyalty was to the president. Clark apparently regarded Haig's conception of his role as secretary and the discord that Haig created as threats to the president. The appointment of George Shultz as Haig's successor lends credence to this interpretation. Shultz—who had served in the Nixon administration as director of the Office of Management and Budget, Secretary of Labor, and Secretary of the Treasury—had a reputation as a team player who would neither publicize his disagreements with other administration officials nor upstage the president by attempting to dominate foreign policy. Shultz's performance during most of his long tenure as secretary confirms this assessment.

The national security policy system that developed after Haig's resignation does not fit either the White House-centered or State Department-centered model. Clark and his two successors, Robert McFarlane and John Poindexter, appeared to work closely with Shultz. There was no public competition between the secretary and the national security assistant for preeminent influence with the president. Sharp conflict frequently has erupted between Shultz and Defense Secretary Weinberger, with Shultz prevailing more often than not, thanks to support from key White House aides, including the national security assistant. Shultz's apparent emergence, by the beginning of Reagan's second term, as the administration's principal foreign policy maker appeared to have been due to three factors: his skill as a bureaucratic infighter; his reluctance to seek the limelight as the architect of administration foreign policy; and a close alliance with the White House. Shultz prevailed where the more flamboyant and assertive Haig had failed.

Beginning with Clark, the role of the national security assistant increased in importance. Clark regained direct access to the president and assumed the role of a facilitator and broker. Robert McFarlane assumed an enhanced role as a special envoy for the president in conjunction with the Iranian arms sales and as a policy advocate. McFarlane's deputy, John Poindexter, helped to plan the sale of arms to Iran and the capture of the terrorists who had hijacked the liner *Achille Lauro* in late 1985. It was also during McFarlane's tenure that Oliver North (who was deputy director of the NSC's political-military affairs staff) either received authorization to conduct or began on his own to conduct covert operations. One of the puzzles of the Iran-contra affair was the basis on which North acted and the extent to which the president and Chief of Staff Donald Regan were aware of his activities.

As national security adviser, Poindexter continued to be involved in planning covert operations and to function as an advocate of specific policies, such as arms sales to Iran. He operated so secretively that most top officials in the Pentagon, the State Department, and the White House itself were often unaware of important developments. According to news reports, Poindexter's tenure "was marked by turmoil on the N.S.C. staff [and] distrust on Capitol Hill," and he lacked an understanding of "the hard politics of the situation." [53] He also lacked skill in dealing with the media and Congress and he had a low standing with Shultz and Weinberger.

After Poindexter's resignation in November 1986, Reagan appointed a veteran bureaucrat, Frank Carlucci, to the national security adviser's post. Carlucci's immediate task was to restore order to the NSC process and remove the NSC staff from an operational role. Key cabinet officials and members of Congress required reassurance that their views would be heard and that foreign and defense policies would be coordinated.

By Reagan's second term, the administration had developed a national security policy system characterized by instability in the relationship between the State Department and the White House. Secretary Shultz was the principal foreign policy spokesperson, but he was not privy to some of the covert operations conducted by North and other members of the NSC staff, and his views on the arms sales to Iran were rejected. The national security assistant acted as a policy advocate rather than as an honest broker coordinating policy making by departments and agencies, and McFarlane even carried out special missions for the president. The task of White House Chief of Staff Regan was to protect the president's political interests. He failed utterly to do so with respect to the Iran-contra affair. That unfortunate incident strongly indicated that the system was not providing the president with good advice. Mulcahy describes the system as a "collegial arrangement for the management of foreign affairs with the White House acting as umpire," [54] which it may well have been; but it could not keep the president from making a major blunder. An unanswered question is whether any conceivable system for managing foreign policy could have overcome Reagan's "laid back" style of administrative leadership and his tendency to respond instinctively to foreign policy challenges and opportunities rather than deliberately, that is, according to a strategic design.

Although Reagan avoided making an organizational choice, between centering management of the national security policy system in the White House or the State Department, and he did not actively involve himself in the development of policy, his stewardship of U.S. foreign policy before the Iran-contra affair was generally regarded as quite successful.[55] Until then, the Reagan experience appeared to contradict the analyses of experts, such as Destler and Alexander George, who insist that the president must adopt an operational strategy for managing national security policy or face dire consequences.[56] The affair suggests that the president would have done well to be more attentive to the management of national security.

It is important, however, to place the Iran-contra affair in perspective when evaluating the Reagan administration's national security policy performance. A major blunder can seriously damage a president, but it does not necessarily negate his accomplishments. Moreover, it should be recognized that the criteria for judging the success or failure of an administration's foreign policy are not universally agreed upon. By one obvious criterion, achievements, the Reagan administration has not been very successful: there has been no measurable progress toward peace in the Middle East; after six years U.S. and Soviet negotiators have not reached an arms control agreement; the Communist threat in Central America has not been removed; and terrorism is still an international plague. However, using the obverse criterion, avoidance of major setbacks, one could conclude that the administration has been successful. Only the peace-keeping mission in Lebanon and Iran-contra affair stand as significant failures. By two other measures of success, international standing and avoidance of war, the Reagan administration has done quite well. The power and prestige of the United States have improved noticeably since 1981, and there has been no sustained military conflict involving U.S. armed forces.

At least three factors have contributed to Reagan's national security policy successes (however they are evaluated), none of which involves organizational structures and processes: good luck, statecraft, and understanding and use of national power. Reagan has had the good fortune to be in office at a time when the American people have not demanded concrete policy achievements. Rather, they have wanted reassurance of America's strength and goodness. Reagan has provided it to them. He has benefited from internal difficulties in the Soviet Union and the collapse of the Organization of Petroleum Exporting Countries. Most of the time, as foreign policy analyst Michael Mandelbaum has observed, "Mr. Reagan has been in the right place at the right time." [57]

In addition, he has exhibited key elements of statecraft, such as a good sense of timing and a sharp awareness of where to draw the line between principles and stubbornness. He handled potential crises, such as the Soviet destruction of a Korean airliner in 1983 and the Beirut hijacking of a TWA airliner in 1985, with a combination of forceful rhetoric and restrained response. When he has used force, in Grenada in 1983 and in the 1986 air strike against Libya, the situations have been ones not likely to escalate into wider conflict. He has demonstrated flexibility while maintaining a principled stance. His policies, maintains Mandelbaum, "have been informed by a sense of proportion, of limits, of how far they could be pressed without taxing the prudence of other countries and exhausting the goodwill of the American public." [58] Those boundaries appear to have been crossed only in the Iran-contra affair.

Perhaps equally important to Reagan's reputation as a competent leader, somewhat more so at home than abroad, has been his approach to and handling of national power. He rejected the thesis of Nixon and Carter that the decline in U.S. power in the 1970s resulted from long-term historical and economic forces; he espoused instead the proposition that the decline had resulted from "misguided American actions that can and must be reversed." [59] The means of restoring U.S. power were simple and within national capabilities: (1) strengthen the economy by reducing the involvement of government and by increasing incentives for investment and (2) build up military forces. Reagan used his conservative ideology to support these power-restoring actions.

According to Terry Deibel, Reagan has used the restored national power more to project psychological images of strength than to achieve policy objectives by coercion. Deibel warns, however, that regardless of how successful projections of power appear to be, there is a "point beyond which demonstrations of American power cannot stretch." [60] And foreign policy success is provisional, not permanent; for political and economic conditions, at home and abroad, are constantly in flux.

Conclusion

National security is the most important substantive policy responsibility of the president; it presents him with major and complex problems of leadership and management. For the nation, the effectiveness of foreign and military policy in preserving and protecting its sovereignty and independence is the paramount interest. That interest stands or falls to a large extent on the president's performance. He must interpret and exercise his powers within constitutional and statutory limits. He finds it imperative to consult with Congress, and to be effective he must have congressional cooperation. Yet, operational realities—the advanced state of weaponry and the unrelenting persistence and patience of international adversaries who are not bound by the constraints of constitutional democracy—require that he be accorded ample latitude to act independently and often secretly. Tensions inevitably arise between Congress and the president over national security policy. The tasks involved are predominantly executive in nature, but the Constitution provides an important role for Congress.

The development and evolution of the war power of the president and the efforts of Congress to curb presidential war making illustrate once again the protean character of the presidency. What Arthur Schlesinger described in 1973 as an imperial presidency became, in the words of Gerald Ford, an imperiled presidency by 1980. The constitutional roles of the president and Congress with respect to national security policy require continual adjustment to events and conditions that reflects a shifting balance between the values of national survival and democratic freedoms.

Presidents also discover that resolution of national security issues must be coordinated with the handling of domestic and economic issues. Increasingly, major issues tend to overlap and solutions cannot be compartmentalized. Presidents no longer can fashion national security policies without regard to domestic political and economic pressures. Such pressures in turn lead presidents to seek ways of managing national security policy that provide them with flexibility in action and that protect their personal political stakes.

The principal institutional means that modern presidents have employed to manage national security—a White House-centered national security system directed by a national security assistant heading a professional NSC staff—has served this purpose, but at the expense of long-range continuity and cohesion in policy. The alternative organizational strategy—a State Department-centered system with the secretary of state playing a dominant policy-making and advisory role—has attracted support from students of national security policy and from political outsiders as a means of obtaining the desired degree of continuity and integration. Presidents since Eisenhower, however, have found such an arrangement unsuitable to their style of operation. President Reagan's approach to managing national security has been eclectic. At first, he enhanced the role of the secretary without strengthening the State Department, and he downgraded the position of the national security assistant and the NSC staff. When that arrangement resulted in conflict within the administration, criticism from without, and confusion everywhere, Reagan adopted a more collegial system centered neither in the State Department nor in the White House and dominated by neither the secretary of state nor the national security assistant. That system served him fairly well until the Iran-contra affair erupted. Yet it is not clear whether Reagan would have avoided that fiasco had he made the organizational choice that analysts assumed was inescapable. The changing roles and structures within Reagan's national security system are another manifestation of the protean presidency.

The Reagan presidency also demonstrates once again how dependent the nation is, in the critical area of national security policy, on the personality, operating style, and policy preferences of individual presidents. Reagan's major foreign policy blunder as well as his substantial successes appear due to personal factors, such as a disdain for facts, a penchant for delegation, adept statecraft, and his approach to and handling of national power. The Reagan experience does not provide an answer, however, to the question of the extent to which organizational arrangements can contribute to effective management of national security.

Notes

1. John Spanier, "Introduction—Congress and the Presidency: The Weakest Link in the Policy Process," in *Congress, the Presidency and American Foreign Policy*, ed. John Spanier and Joseph Nogee (New York: Pergamon, 1981), xx.
2. Leslie H. Gelb, *The Irony of Vietnam: The System Worked* (Washington, D.C.: Brookings, 1979).
3. Ibid., 362-363.
4. James Chace, "Is a Foreign Policy Consensus Possible?" *Foreign Affairs* 57 (Fall 1978): 3.
5. A major obstacle to an agreement was President Reagan's insistence on excluding from the discussions the Strategic Defense Initiative (SDI, or "Star Wars"), a missile defense system based on laser technology. The Soviet Union made restrictions on development and testing of SDI a condition for an agreement to reduce intermediate and strategic weapons. The sudden Soviet offer, in spring 1987, to remove intermediate- and short-range U.S. and Soviet missiles from Europe caught the Reagan administration unprepared and created confusion and dissension within the NATO alliance.
6. Chace, "Is a Foreign Policy Consensus Possible?" 16.
7. John Felton, "Secret Weapons Sale Stirs Up Legal Questions," *Congres-*

sional Quarterly Weekly Report, November 22, 1986, 2929.

8. Elizabeth Drew, "Letter From Washington," *The New Yorker,* December 19, 1986, 86.

9. Edward S. Corwin, *The President: Office and Powers,* 4th ed. (New York: New York University Press, 1957), 171.

10. I. M. Destler, "National Security Management: What Presidents Have Wrought," *Political Science Quarterly* (Winter 1980-1981): 574.

11. Ibid., 574.

12. Ibid., 588.

13. Joseph E. Kallenbach, *The American Chief Executive* (New York: Harper and Row, 1966), 485.

14. John Locke, *Of Civil Government* (New York: Everyman's Library, Dutton, 1924), 151.

15. Corwin, *The President: Office and Powers,* 179.

16. Ibid., 185.

17. The treaty-making process entails three distinct stages: negotiation, Senate approval, and ratification by the president. Contrary to popular understanding, the Senate does not ratify a treaty; it approves the treaty negotiated by the president. The president may refuse to sign, that is, to ratify, a treaty approved by the Senate, either because of amendments or reservations or because his administration did not negotiate it.

18. Cecil V. Crabb, Jr., and Pat M. Holt, *Invitation to Struggle: Congress, the President and Foreign Policy,* 2d ed. (Washington, D.C.: CQ Press, 1984) 16.

19. Arthur S. Miller, *Presidential Power in a Nutshell* (St. Paul, Minn.: West, 1977), 154-155.

20. *Goldwater v. Carter,* 444 U.S. 996 (1979).

21. Clark subsequently proved to be a quick learner and a person of great administrative ability. In less than a year he was receiving praise from many of his former critics.

22. Corwin, *The President: Office and Powers,* chap. 6; Arthur M. Schlesinger, Jr., *The Imperial Presidency* (Boston: Houghton Mifflin, 1973), chaps. 1-7.

23. Corwin, *The President: Office and Powers,* 229.

24. *Prize Cases,* 67 U.S. (2 Black) 635 (1863).

25. *Korematsu v. United States,* 323 U.S. 214 (1944).

26. Quoted in Miller, *Presidential Power in a Nutshell,* 183.

27. Clinton Rossiter, *Constitutional Dictatorship: Crisis Government in Modern Democracies* (New York: Harcourt, Brace and World, 1963).

28. Miller, *Presidential Power in a Nutshell,* 191.

29. James L. Sundquist, *The Decline and Rusurgence of Congress* (Washington, D.C.: Brookings, 1981), 107.

30. Such actions have numerous precedents, including Jefferson's dispatch of the Navy to stop the Barbary pirates from seizing U.S. merchant ships and holding their crews for ransom and Theodore Roosevelt's contribution of U.S. Marines to the international expeditionary force that put down the Boxer Rebellion in China in 1904.

31. Larry Berman, *Planning a Tragedy: The Americanization of the War in Vietnam* (New York: Norton, 1982).

32. Michael Rubner, "The Reagan Administration, the 1973 War Powers Resolution, and the Invasion of Grenada," *Political Science Quarterly* (Winter 1985-1986): 637.
33. Ibid., 642.
34. *Immigration and Naturalization Service v. Chadha,* 462 U.S. 919, 952 (1983).
35. Rubner, "The Reagan Administration," 629.
36. I. M. Destler, "The Constitution and Foreign Affairs," *News for Teachers of Political Science,* Spring 1985, 16.
37. Ibid., 15.
38. Douglas J. Bennett, Jr., "Congress in Foreign Policy: Who Needs It?" *Foreign Affairs* (1978): 43.
39. Sundquist, *The Decline and Resurgence of Congress,* 270; Edward A. Kolodziej, "Formulating Foreign Policy," in *The Power to Govern: Assessing Reform in the United States,* ed. Richard M. Pious (New York: Academy of Political Science, 1981), 186-189.
40. *Report of the U.S. Commission on the Organization of the Government for the Conduct of Foreign Policy* (Washington, D.C.: Government Printing Office, 1975), 1.
41. Graham T. Allison and Peter Szanton, "Organizing for the Decade Ahead," in *Setting National Priorities: The Next Ten Years,* ed. Henry Owen and Charles Schultze (Washington, D.C.: Brookings, 1976), 232-233.
42. Anna Kasten Nelson, "National Security I: Inventing a Process (1945-1960)," in *The Illusion of Presidential Government,* ed. Hugh Heclo and Lester M. Salamon (Boulder: Westview, 1981), 231.
43. Destler, "National Security Management," 578-579.
44. I. M. Destler, "National Security II: The Rise of the Special Assistant," in *The Illusion of Presidential Government,* ed. Heclo and Salamon, 270.
45. I. M. Destler, "National Security Management: Some Lessons from Thirty Years," *World Politics* (January 1977): 158.
46. Destler, "National Security II," 272; Colin Campbell, *Managing the Presidency: Carter, Reagan, and the Search for Executive Harmony* (Pittsburgh: University of Pittsburgh Press, 1986), 82-85.
47. Kevin V. Mulcahy, "The Secretary of State and the National Security Adviser: Foreign Policymaking in the Carter and Reagan Administrations," *Presidential Studies Quarterly* (Spring 1986): 281.
48. Alexander L. George, *Presidential Decision-Making in Foreign Policy: The Effective Use of Information and Advice* (Boulder: Westview, 1980), 161.
49. Mulcahy, "The Secretary of State," 286.
50. Haig encountered substantial opposition to: his attempt to negotiate a settlement to the Falkland Islands dispute between Argentina and Great Britain; his recommendation that the United States not oppose the construction of a natural gas pipeline from the Soviet Union to Western Europe; and his support of the Israeli invasion of Lebanon to destroy the Palestine Liberation Organization.
51. Dom Bonafede, "A Dean, Not a Vicar," *National Journal,* July 3, 1982, 1184.

52. Mulcahy, "The Secretary of State," 289-290.
53. Keith Schneider, "Poindexter at the Security Council: A Quick Rise and a Troubled Reign," *New York Times*, January 12, 1987, 4.
54. Mulcahy, "The Secretary of State," 296.
55. Michael Mandelbaum, "The Luck of the President," *Foreign Affairs: America and the World 1985* 3 (1986): 393; Terry L. Deibel, "Why Reagan Is Strong," *Foreign Policy* (Spring 1986): 108.
56. George, *Presidential Decision-Making in Foreign Policy;* Destler, "National Security Policy Management."
57. Mandelbaum, "The Luck of the President," 397.
58. Ibid., 399.
59. Deibel, "Why Reagan Is Strong," 111.
60. Ibid., 121.

Selected Readings

Berman, Larry. *Planning a Tragedy: The Americanization of the War in Vietnam*. New York: Norton, 1982.

Crabb, Cecil V., Jr., and Pat M. Holt. *Invitation to Struggle: Congress, the President and Foreign Policy*. 2d ed. Washington, D.C.: CQ Press, 1984.

Destler, I. M. *Presidents, Bureaucrats, and Foreign Policy: The Politics of Organizational Reform*. Princeton, N.J.: Princeton University Press, 1974.

Gelb, Leslie H. *The Irony of Vietnam: The System Worked*. Washington, D.C.: Brookings, 1979.

George, Alexander L. *Presidential Decisionmaking in Foreign Policy: The Effective Use of Information and Advice*. Boulder: Westview, 1980.

Halperin, Morton M. *Bureaucratic Politics and Foreign Policy*. Washington, D.C.: Brookings, 1974.

Janis, Irving. *Groupthink*. 2d ed. Boston: Houghton Mifflin, 1982.

Plischke, Elmer. *Diplomat in Chief*. New York: Praeger, 1986.

President's Special Review Board (Tower Commission). *Report of the President's Special Review Board*. Washington, D.C.: Government Printing Office, 1987.

Schlesinger, Arthur M., Jr. *The Imperial Presidency*. Boston: Houghton Mifflin, 1973.

Spanier, John, and Joseph Nogee, eds. *Congress, the Presidency and American Foreign Policy*. New York: Pergamon, 1981.

CONCLUSION

Assessment and Reform of the Protean Presidency

In Parts One, Two, and Three, we examined a broad variety of topics pertaining to the presidency. Included were the selection process, the kinds of persons it produces, and the president's relationship with the American people between elections; the development of the presidential and vice-presidential offices, and the president's association with the Congress, other executive branch officials, and the courts; and, finally, the president's role in formulating and implementing domestic, economic, and national security policies. This analysis has sought to be objective in reporting and integrating the views of a wide range of students of the presidency.

The Conclusion differs from the preceding chapters in two respects. First, we attempt here to give an overall picture of the presidency, returning to the basic considerations raised in the Introduction of this book. Second, we assess and evaluate—that is, give our personal, subjective views on—the matters under discussion.

The first part of this chapter focuses on our assessment of the current state of the protean presidency. The latter part analyzes possible reforms of that presidency, those pertaining both to the selection of the president and to the office itself.

Assessment

Several recent developments have changed the the U.S. presidency. These developments have not occurred primarily in the presidential office itself; rather, they have occurred mostly in the environment in which the president must operate.

One significant area of change for the chief executive is that of public politics. Not so many years ago, individual incumbents benefited from the generally positive attitude of most Americans toward the nation, its constitutional system, and its chief political officer, the president. However, two major

483

debacles of the 1960s and 1970s—the Vietnam War and the Watergate scandals, which threatened the domestic underpinnings of the constitutional order—combined to make the public increasingly skeptical of the national government and of the presidency as an institution. As a result, unlike many of their predecessors, recent presidents have not been able to draw so readily upon the innate trust and confidence of the American people to support and sustain them in difficult times.

Although Vietnam and Watergate sensitized Americans to the potential abuse of presidential power, a permanent, major scaling down of the presidency has not taken place. Presidents Gerald R. Ford and Jimmy Carter consciously reduced the dimensions of the office in response to the apparent demand of the public for more restrained leadership, but by 1980 an electoral majority clearly indicated through its choice of Ronald Reagan that the United States is inescapably dependent on vigorous presidential leadership to cope with the complex and often intractable problems it faces. President Reagan has not restored the imperial presidency that fell into disrepute a decade earlier, but he has moved forcefully to establish a predominant leadership role for himself in domestic and international affairs.

The relationship between the president and the mass media also has changed. It is doubtful that even presidents as skillful in handling the media as Franklin D. Roosevelt and John F. Kennedy would fare as well with today's assertive representatives of the press, television, and radio, who employ the tenets of investigative and adversary journalism. It is significant that John Kennedy, first as a presidential candidate and then as incumbent of the office, was able to charm and deflect the criticisms of most members of the media, but his younger brother Edward M. Kennedy was not. No less personally appealing and in some ways a more skillful legislator and politician than JFK, Ted Kennedy was the subject of vigorous questioning from generally sympathetic reporters, such as Roger Mudd, out to prove that the media were not soft on political liberals in general and on the Kennedys in particular. Presidents have found the media to be both a means of building support for themselves and their programs and a potential threat to their popularity. On the one hand, the media, especially television, afford presidents the opportunity to preempt the center of the political stage and make direct appeals to millions of citizens. Presidents with the ability to communicate effectively via television, such as Ronald Reagan, enjoy an enormous advantage over their political opponents. On the other hand, presidents who do not have such skills, such as Lyndon B. Johnson, may project a negative image on television that undercuts their support. Moreover, all presidents run the risk of overexposure via television and the other mass media. They therefore must use the media selectively, that is, only on the occasions and in the format most likely to be effective for them.

Presidential dealings with other informal groups linking the American people to their government also have become very difficult. The decline in the influence of U.S. political parties means that the president cannot count on his own party to help him rally majorities to support his administration and his policies. Instead, he must face an increasingly broad array of assertive interest groups—economic, social, and cultural—that pressure him to support their particular concerns and, especially in the case of many single-issue groups, that judge his performance in office almost entirely by that support.

Presidential leadership also has been hindered by recent developments within the governmental structure itself, particularly in the legislative and executive branches. The devolution of power within the Congress from senior chamber leaders and committee chairpersons down to subcommittees chaired and populated by very junior members means that the president must garner support for his legislative program from a broad range of independent members of Congress who can no longer be counted on to follow the lead of their more experienced elders. Moreover, the sheer number of executive branch employees and the proliferation of "issue networks" and "iron triangles"—comprising interest group representatives, committee and subcommittee chairpersons, and department heads and bureau chiefs—bedevil presidents who try to control what is supposed to be their own branch of government.

The substantive problems U.S. presidents face also have become more complex. No longer the chief executive of the dominant nation in the world, the president of the United States today must contend with the equal military force of the Soviet Union and the restored, and in some respects superior, economic power of Japan and Western European countries. Moreover, less influential countries, such as those of the third world, and even allies such as Israel are able to frustrate the president in his role as major protector of U.S. national security. Developments abroad also affect the U.S. domestic economy, over which the president is supposed to preside, forcing him to ask for large sums of money to safeguard the nation's military and economic interests. These expenditures, coupled with domestic entitlement programs—such as social security, medicare, and medicaid—dominate the nation's budget and leave little room for outlays for other programs pressed upon the president by an ever-increasing number of aggressive interest groups.

The U.S. president today must contend with a wide variety of autonomous, and often uncooperative, political actors in a highly factional environment. At the same time, he faces increasingly complex substantive problems that require concerted action from those individuals and groups with whom he shares the governance of the nation. Complicating the situation still further are recent developments in the presidential selection process that have tended to elevate to the presidency persons such as Jimmy Carter and Ronald Reagan who have limited experience dealing with prominent political officials or the salient issues of national politics.

This combination of developments has led to some very pessimistic assessments of the presidency. As indicated in the Introduction, the terms "impotent" and "imperiled" presidency have been used to characterize the office in recent years. Columnist David Broder has gone even further in asking whether the United States is now in the era of the "mission impossible" presidency.

Although such terms are in some respects applicable to the presidency, they appear to us to be somewhat exaggerated. The presidency has always been considered a very difficult office, one known to some observers as a "splendid misery." The conditions described in the preceding paragraphs differ from those of the past only in degree. Chief executives since George Washington have felt themselves under attack by members of the press. With the exception of Thomas Jefferson, Andrew Jackson, and Woodrow Wilson, none has been a successful leader of his political party; and only Jefferson, Wilson, Franklin Roosevelt, and Lyndon Johnson have managed to steer a broad legislative program through Congress. Moreover, few if any chief executives have managed to tame the federal bureaucracy over which they supposedly preside. Finally, difficult substantive problems are not new to U.S. presidents: during his administration Franklin Roosevelt faced first a worldwide depression and then a war that spanned several continents.

The major paradox of today's presidency is that, on the one hand, because the U.S. political system has become more and more fragmented, incumbents find it difficult to build a governing coalition to deal with the mounting foreign and domestic problems. On the other hand, the divided state of the American polity, with its complex issues, forces individuals and groups to turn to the president as the only person who is in a position to focus national attention on major problems and to propose ways of dealing with them.

Events that followed the election of Ronald Reagan in 1980 graphically illustrate this latter tendency. Immediately upon assuming office he proposed a bold new program of deep cuts in both taxes and domestic expenditures and steered these innovative proposals through Congress. The following year the new Republican president had more difficulties with the national legislators but still managed to persuade them not to eliminate the third year of his scheduled income tax cuts (and instead to raise certain other taxes) and to make even greater reductions in domestic social programs. All the while, he was able to retain most of his projected major increases in defense expenditures and to persuade Congress to accept the greatest budgetary deficit in U.S. peacetime history. The president accomplished all this while public opinion polls were showing that most Americans preferred to decrease expenditures for defense rather than those for social programs and were willing to forgo the scheduled third-year income tax cut in order to help balance the budget. The president's priorities on taxes and expenditures (with some modifications by Congress) continued to guide public policy making during the first two years of his second term in office.

In the mid-1980s a new concern emerged among some scholars. According to Samuel Kernell, the nation's highest office has become a "public" presidency;[1] to Theodore Lowi, it has become a "plebiscitary" one.[2] They argue that the modern presidency is a highly personal office in which the chief executive governs not by building coalitions with other political elites, such as congressional and party leaders, but by using the media to manipulate the public by persuasive rhetoric. The dangers of this situation are said to be that the president will dominate policy making and that such rhetoric will raise unrealistic public expectations of what the president can accomplish. These expectations, in turn, will lead to public disillusionment with the presidency.

Although there is no question that direct contact between the president and the American people has become closer because of the development of the broadcast media, especially television, it is less clear that this factor has radically changed public policy making in the United States. Tax reform, which emerged as one of the principal domestic issues in Reagan's second term, did not follow the script of the public or the plebiscitary presidency. As previously noted, the initiative on that issue came not from the president but from congressional leaders—Sen. Bill Bradley (D-N.J.), Rep. Richard A. Gephardt (D-Mo.), and Rep. Jack F. Kemp (R-N.Y.). Although Reagan did join these members of Congress in pushing the issue, he was never able to stir up genuine public support, despite his best rhetorical efforts. Tax reform occurred in 1986 as a result of the kind of coalition building between the president and congressional elites that was thought to be a product of the past. Moreover, it was successful despite the efforts of many interest groups, thereby confounding current political wisdom that interest groups unduly control public policy making in the United States.

Another major issue in the mid-1980s that casts doubts on the accuracy of the concept of the public or plebiscitary presidency is the imposition of sanctions against South Africa because of its policy of apartheid. Despite the fact that presidents are supposed to be particularly influential on foreign policy issues, and despite the best rhetorical efforts of a highly persuasive leader, Reagan was not able to change public attitudes favoring sanctions. He was not even able to win the support of congressional leaders of his own political party, including the chairperson of the Foreign Relations Committee, Sen. Richard G. Lugar (R-Ind.). Moreover, both houses of Congress overrode his veto of the congressional legislation imposing sanctions. These events hardly support the thesis of a public or plebiscitary presidency.

In our view, the difficulties of American society are not attributable to the presidential form of government. There is little evidence that other democratic nations with parliamentary systems are having greater success in dealing with the complexities of the modern world. The major problem of U.S. presidents, like that of other chief executives, is not one of persuading other decision makers with whom they share the governance of the nation to accept their proposals. Rather, it is one of knowing what those proposals should be, that is, having the wit and imagination to recognize the ideas and programs that will work.

It is difficult to make reliable generalizations about the American presidency. Recent history has contradicted Clinton Rossiter's sanguine observation in 1960 that "the vast power of this office . . . has elevated often and corrupted never, chiefly because those who held it recognized the true source of the power and were ennobled by the knowledge." [3] However, recent events also have contradicted George Reedy's gloomy analysis just a decade later that as an institution, the presidency's "prospects [of survival] are dim." [4]

As suggested in the Introduction, such observations are too time-bound; that is, they take the circumstances of the moment and project them into the future. Yet, if one lesson can be gleaned from studying the presidency, it is that the office is a *protean* institution, one that is exceedingly variable because it is shaped by developments in the other formal and informal institutions in American society, by the types of problems with which the president must contend, and by the kind of person who holds the office at a particular time. As these factors change, so does the character of the presidency.

Our own vision of the future of the American presidency is closer to Rossiter's than to Reedy's. We see it as being "long and exciting" [5] (although not as bright as Rossiter suggests) rather than as being in its "twilight" years, as Reedy predicts.[6] The reason for our cautious optimism is that the presidency is an institution capable of responding to changes in U.S. society and that the American people, in the long run, have no alternative but to place their hope and trust in the continued success of the only office and incumbent in a position to take the leadership in meeting the nation's needs.

We recognize that there are risks in having a political system depend so heavily on the performance of a single person—on the values, leadership style, character, and persuasive talents of the president. Even in parliamentary systems, however, the success of the nation in meeting its problems depends to a great extent upon the perception and skills of the prime minister (Winston Churchill, Jawaharlal Nehru, or Charles de Gaulle), who dominates the cabinet and the legislature as well. Moreover, the United States, under strong and vigorous presidential leadership, has dealt effectively with the principal challenges and crises it has faced in two hundred years of operation under the Constitution. The presidential form of government has been, over time, much more a source of strength than weakness.

Although our assessment of the American presidency is generally favorable, we nonetheless contend that there are some problems that need to be discussed and possible reforms of the presidency that at least should be considered. It is to those subjects that we now turn.

Reforming the Selection of the President

The process of choosing the president encompasses the nomination and the election stages, through which voters pass judgment on the competing candidates. The nomination process has already undergone numerous reforms; the election process—in particular, the electoral college—has been the object of several reform proposals; and ways of predicting presidential performance are of interest to both voters and students of the presidency.

The Nomination Process

As indicated in Chapter 1, the method of choosing delegates to the national convention has undergone major changes in recent years, particularly in the Democratic party. In 1984, about half the states used the presidential primary to select their delegates; the other half used the caucus-convention system. In addition, the Democratic convention now includes a contingent of "super-delegates," made up of Democratic governors, members of the Democratic National Committee, and 80 percent of the Democratic members of Congress.

In our opinion this mixed nomination system is a desirable one. It provides a judicious blend of political amateurs, primarily concerned with the candidates' stands on issues, and party professionals, who bring distinctive "peer" perspectives to bear on the candidates' ability to work effectively with other public officials with whom they must share the governance of the nation. Professionals also consider how successful candidates are likely to be in helping to compromise the differences that exist among the many increasingly assertive groups in U.S. society. At the same time, the presidential primaries place a premium on candidates who possess the personality and communications skills needed to attract the support of rank-and-file voters.

The sequence of state contests in 1988 probably again will give Iowa and New Hampshire too much influence simply because they are likely to hold their caucus convention and primary sooner than any of the other states. It now appears, however, that a "Super-Tuesday" in early March 1988 will include even more southern states than in 1984 and that several midwestern states will hold their state contests on a common date soon after that. It remains to be seen just what the final schedule will be and what effect the Iowa and New Hampshire contests will have on the fortunes of the candidates in later contests. These developments offer the distinct possibility, however, that presidential hopefuls will be required to establish early on their political appeal in a broad range of states rather than in only small and somewhat unrepresentative ones, such as Iowa and New Hampshire. Thus, a pattern of regional contests, long advocated by many critics of the presidential nomination process, has resulted from decisions made at the state level without the necessity of a national law on the matter.

Finally, problems still exist in the way the mass media cover the nomination process. The media continue to concentrate on the "horse race" aspect of the campaign and devote little effort to giving in-depth information on the issues of the campaign or the records of candidates in their previous offices. One mitigating factor is the recent development of debates among the competing candidates, the Republicans in 1980 and the Democrats in 1984. Such encounters enable the voters to judge the candidates' ability to think on their feet and to see how the participants handle common questions (in regular campaign speeches, the candidates frequently talk past one another).

Thus, although the nomination process is far from ideal, it has undergone some change for the better, particularly in the 1980s. Moreover, there is little one can do about some of the problems, such as the way the media in a free society choose to cover the campaign. Finally, as the recent record of the Democratic party demonstrates, there is real danger in constantly revising the rules of the game: unintended and unfortunate consequences often result from such changes. Everyone involved would benefit from a needed hiatus in the quest for perfection in the presidential nomination process.

The Election Process

The most serious problem pertaining to the election of the president continues to be the electoral college. It was devised as a means of allowing knowledgeable elites in the states to choose a "continental" character, but its essential form remains for an entirely different purpose—to enable rank-and-file voters to select their major public officials in a nationwide popular election. As a result of this perversion, a number of abuses have developed in the presidential election system.

The electoral college as it operates today violates some of the major tenets of political equality. Each person's vote does not count equally: the influence one has in the election of the president depends on the political situation in one's particular state. For many Americans who support a losing candidate in their state, it is as though they had not voted at all, since under the general-ticket system all the electoral votes of a state go to the candidate who wins a plurality of its popular votes. Other citizens who live in populous, politically competitive states have a premium placed on their vote because they are in a position to affect how large blocs of electoral votes are cast. Nor does the electoral college ensure that the candidate who receives the most popular votes will win the presidency: John Quincy Adams in 1824, Rutherford B. Hayes in 1876, and Benjamin Harrison in 1888 went to the White House even though they trailed their respective political opponents, Andrew Jackson, Samuel Tilden, and Grover Cleveland. In 1976 Jimmy Carter almost suffered the same fate as Jackson, Tilden, and Cleveland: if some nine thousand voters in Hawaii and Ohio had shifted their ballots to President Ford, Ford would have edged out Carter in the electoral college, 270-268.

The requirement that a candidate win a majority of the electoral votes or have the election decided by the House of Representatives also violates the idea of political equality. In 1948 Harry S Truman defeated Thomas Dewey by more than two million popular votes, but if some twelve thousand people in California and Ohio had voted for Dewey rather than the president, the election would have been thrown into the House of Representatives for a decision. The same thing could have happened in 1960 if some nine thousand people in Illinois and Missouri had voted for Richard Nixon instead of Kennedy, and again in 1968 if about forty-two thousand people in Missouri, New Jersey, and Alaska had cast their ballots for Hubert Humphrey rather than President Nixon.[7] Permitting the House of Representatives, voting by states, to select the president of the United States is not consistent with the "one person, one vote" principle.

The 1968 election also illustrates another danger of the electoral college system: an elector need not cast his or her ballot for the candidate who wins the plurality of votes in the elector's state. Had Nixon failed to win a majority of the electoral votes, third-party candidate George Wallace would have been in a position to bargain with him. Wallace could have asked his forty-five electors to cast their ballots for Nixon, which would have given Nixon enough electoral votes to prevent the election from going into the House.[8] Although Wallace's forty-five electoral votes would not have been enough to give Humphrey a majority of the electoral votes (even if Humphrey had carried Missouri, New Jersey, and Alaska), the Alabama governor could have tried to bargain with him by offering to influence southern members of the House of Representatives to chose Humphrey over Nixon.

Over the years these problems have created a great deal of dissatisfaction with the electoral college. The sentiment for changing it has increased recently, particularly after the elections of 1948, 1960, 1968, and 1976, in which a switch in votes of a relatively few people in key states would have sent the selection of the president into the House or immediately changed the result. Although agreement on the need to change the electoral college is widespread, there is marked disagreement over what form that change should take. Five plans have been suggested as substitutes for the present system.

The first, known as the *automatic plan*, which would change the present system least, would eliminate the possibility of "faithless electors" by abolishing that office and automatically casting a state's electoral votes for the popular-vote winner in that state. If no candidate received a majority of the electoral votes, a joint session of Congress would choose the winner, and each representative and senator would have one vote.

The second, known as the *district plan*, proposes a return to the method the states used early in the nation's history (and that was recently reinstated by Maine), under which the presidential candidate who wins the plurality vote in each House district would receive its electoral vote, with the remaining two electoral votes going to the statewide popular winner. If no candidate received a majority of the electoral votes, senators and representatives, sitting jointly and voting as individuals, would choose the president from the three candidates having the highest number of electoral votes. This plan's major supporters have been members of Congress and private groups from rural areas, such as the American Farm Bureau. If the plan were adopted, the crucial areas would be the politically competitive congressional districts where the two major parties traditionally divide the vote 55 to 45 percent.

A third proposal, known as the *proportional plan*, would divide each state's electoral votes in proportion to the division of the popular vote: a candidate receiving 60 percent of the popular vote in a state would receive 60 percent of its electoral votes. A plan of this nature, introduced by Republican senator Henry Cabot Lodge of Massachusetts and Democratic representative Ed Gossett of Texas, passed the Senate in 1950 but failed to be enacted by the House. The plan would eliminate the present advantage of the large states in being able to throw all their electoral votes to one candidate and has therefore been opposed by many of their legislators, including John Kennedy when he was a senator from Massachusetts. One possible consequence of a proportional division of the electoral votes would be a fairly even split between the two major candidates so that neither would receive a majority; hence, there would be a greater likelihood of elections being thrown into the House for decision.[9]

The fourth plan, *direct popular election* of the president, has picked up major support in recent years, especially since its recommendation in 1967 by a special commission of the American Bar Association. In addition, it has been endorsed by politically disparate groups such as the Chamber of Commerce of the United States and the AFL-CIO. In 1969 the House passed a constitutional amendment providing that the president (and vice president) be elected by a minimum of 40 percent of the popular vote and, if no candidate received so large a vote, that a runoff be held between the two front-runners. The Senate failed to pass the amendment, however, despite the efforts of its major sponsor, Birch Bayh (D-Ind.). After Carter's narrow electoral college victory, Bayh introduced the same measure in 1977, but it failed to clear the Congress that year. No such proposal subsequently has been enacted.

A fifth proposal, recently advanced by the Twentieth Century Fund, a research group, is known as the *national bonus plan*.[10] It would award the nationwide popular winner, 102 "bonus" votes (2 for each state plus 2 for the District of Columbia), which would be added to the electoral votes received under the present state-by-state system. To win the election a candidate would have to receive 321 votes, that is, a majority of 640, the new total number of the electoral votes (538, the former total, plus the 102 bonus votes). If no one received a majority of the electoral votes, a runoff would be held between the two front-runners. Thus, the proposal retains the electoral college system but makes the total electoral vote better reflect the nationwide popular vote. It also allows the voters rather than the House of Representatives to make the final choice of the president if no candidate receives a majority of the electoral votes.

In our judgment, the first three plans have serious defects. The automatic plan meets only the problem of the faithless elector and ignores several others: the undue influence of the very small and very large states; the winner-take-all principle by which all the electoral votes of a state go to the candidate who wins a plurality of the popular votes, no matter how narrow that margin may be; and the possibility of a person's winning the presidency even though he trails his opponent in the nationwide popular vote. The district plan would incorporate into the selection of the president the gerrymandering abuses present in elections to the House of Representatives— manipulation of district boundaries to favor particular political interests. The proportional plan would eliminate the winner-take-all advantage now enjoyed by the large states but would retain the small-state benefit, because all states, regardless of size, would receive two electoral votes representing their two senators. It also would not prevent the possibility of a minority-vote president.

The last two plans, the direct popular election of the president and the national bonus plan, provide the most promising prospects for reform. Direct popular election ensures what none of the other plans can: that the person receiving the largest number of nationwide popular votes will be elected president. The national bonus plan makes it much more likely than does the present system that the popular-vote winner will also obtain a majority of the electoral votes but *does not guarantee it.* By retaining elements of the present state-by-state electoral system, however, the bonus plan incorporates features of federalism that are not present under the direct popular election plan.

In our judgment, either direct popular election or the national bonus plan would be far superior to the present system. Of the two, we prefer direct popular election because it guarantees that the national popular-vote winner will be chosen as president. Although the national bonus system does retain the state-by-state feature of the present system, we think that sufficient elements of federalism already are contained in the U.S. political system through the equal representation of the states in the Senate and in the arrangement of separate state powers and political institutions whose independence is guaranteed from national encroachment by the Constitution. We see no reason why federalism should also require that states be represented as electoral units in the selection of the only major national official.

Arguments can be made against the direct popular election of the president. Some analysts contend that it will jeopardize the two-party system, a fear based on two separate considerations. The first is that, since the election will depend on a nationwide instead of a state-by-state vote, candidates will no longer need to deal with state political leaders. This change would weaken these leaders, who have traditionally played a vital role in American political parties. The second concern, expressed by Alexander Bickel, is that direct popular election of the president would encourage minor political parties, freed of the necessity of actually winning state electoral votes, to run and support enough candidates to prevent either major party nominee from winning the necessary 40 percent of the nationwide popular vote.[11] These minor parties would then be in a bargaining position to determine which of the two leading candidates would win in the runoff election.

We believe these fears are unfounded. State party leaders would continue to play a role in presidential nominations. It is even possible that they would become more active in the general election under a popular election system, since all votes that they could muster would count in their candidate's nationwide total. We also think it highly improbable that the winning party candidate would not be able to win 40 percent of the popular vote. As Lawrence Longley and Alan Braun point out,[12] in the presidential elections held since 1824, only Abraham Lincoln in 1860 failed to achieve that proportion (he won 39.8 percent of the vote).[13] If anything, the electoral college system is more vulnerable to minor parties than is the popular election system, because in the United States such parties tend to be regional and thus are best able to affect the distribution of electoral votes of individual states. A case in point occurred in New York in 1976. Many observers maintain that if independent candidate Eugene J. McCarthy had been on the ballot in New York, he would have drained away enough popular votes from Carter to allow Ford to carry the state and, with it, enough electoral votes (forty-one) to win the presidential election.

Another significant problem of the direct election system is the effect that its adoption might have on the nomination process.[14] As Austin Ranney suggests, most of the arguments made against the electoral college and in favor of direct national election can also be made against national party conventions and in favor of a direct national primary.[15] Both the electoral college and the national conventions violate the one-person, one-vote rule, make it possible to choose a candidate preferred by a minority, and place artificial barriers between the people and their choice of candidates. Although Ranney does not make the point explicitly, it might well be argued that the adoption of the direct election of the president would lead in time to enactment of a national primary law; for historically, the number of a state's electoral votes has affected the size of its delegation to national conventions. In this way, the selection and nomination processes have been linked, and tampering with one might influence the other.

The last possibility gives us the greatest cause for concern since we do not favor the adoption of a national primary that could further diminish the influence of political leaders in the nomination process. We do think, however, that the two processes are distinct, and changing one does not necessarily mean altering the other. Moving from the electoral college system to a direct popular election of the president would not be nearly so radical a change as abandoning the convention system for a national presidential primary. Direct popular election would not significantly change the method of selection or the people participating in the election of the president; it merely would change *how the votes are counted*. A change in the presidential nominating system, however, would impose a whole new method of selection and bring into the process people who are not now eligible to vote in presidential primaries. Such a change also would require a new means of choosing vice-presidential candidates and of adopting the party platform. It would, it is hoped, be much more difficult to persuade political decision makers to adopt a national primary than to adopt direct popular election of the president. A diverse range of groups favors direct election of the president, but the idea of a national primary has no broad support. Moreover, the House has approved direct election, but Congress has not given serious consideration to a national primary.

The known defects of the present electoral college system must be weighed against the possible dangers that the direct election of the president might bring, particularly its potential effect on the nomination process. Still, we would be willing to take the gamble of a change. We cannot see the wisdom of perpetuating an electoral system that in 1976 almost permitted an appointed chief executive, who lost his only presidential election by almost 2 million votes, to remain in office another term. The U.S. political system, already subject to a great deal of cynicism by the American people, should not have to bear that additional threat to its legitimacy.

Predicting Presidential Performance

In addition to the nomination and election process, a basic matter affecting the selection of the president is the ability of the voters to make good judgments in choosing among the contending candidates. In doing so, they are, in effect, predicting which of the candidates will do the best job once in office. It therefore becomes important to determine the information that is most helpful in making such a prediction.

James David Barber maintains that the reasons political leaders give for their actions are of limited value to voters in understanding why they behave as they do in high political office.[16] Nor have presidents' ideologies been of much help in explaining what they do in office. Rather, the key to determining how persons will behave in the presidency is their character, which is determined in their early childhood. By analyzing two features of that character—whether they are "active" or "passive" (invest much or little energy in political activities) and whether they are "positive" or "negative" (seem to enjoy these activities or engage in them out of a sense of compulsion)—one can predict how they will perform in the presidency.

Barber's 1972 study, discussed in Chapter 3, in which he first set forth this bold proposition, contained few predictions.[17] Rather, with the exception of Richard Nixon, then the incumbent, all the presidents whose character Barber analyzed had already completed their terms. Thus, Barber's assessments of twentieth-century presidents were primarily *retrospective* judgments, not *prospective* ones.

Most impressive about Barber's 1972 study, however, was the judgment it contained about Nixon's character. Writing considerably before the development of the Watergate scandals, Barber predicted that if anything ever severely threatened Nixon's "power and sense of virtue," he could be expected to respond by adopting a rigid course of action to meet that threat.[18] When Nixon later responded to the Watergate scandals in much the way Barber had envisioned, people began to take seriously his proposition that one can use character analysis to predict presidential performance.

Since 1972, Barber has predicted the type of president each of those chosen for the office would turn out to be. He contended that Gerald Ford and Jimmy Carter would be active-positive presidents.[19] Barber's assessment of Ronald Reagan, made before the 1980 election, was that he would be a passive-positive chief executive.[20]

Barber's categorization of Ford, Carter, and Reagan is questionable. Although Ford was positive in his attitude, he hardly qualifies as an activist president in the mold of Franklin Roosevelt, Harry Truman, or John Kennedy, who charted new directions in public policy. Carter's compulsive work habits and preoccupation with the "malaise" of the American people seem to be more negative than positive. Nor does Ronald Reagan fit the categorization of passive-positive. In his first year in office he successfully courted Congress and the American people in behalf of an ambitious program of major tax cuts, reductions in domestic social programs, and massive increases in military expenditures. He subsequently took an active leadership role in securing aid for the contras fighting in Nicaragua, for research on the Strategic Defense Initiative ("Star Wars"), and for Senate approval of his nominations of William Rehnquist as chief justice and for Antonin Scalia to fill Rehnquist's seat.[21]

There is even some question how accurately Barber has categorized the presidents who served in office before publication of his 1972 edition, that is, those whom he was judging retrospectively. In his biography of Dwight D. Eisenhower, Fred Greenstein does not characterize Ike as the passive chief executive Barber maintains he was.[22] Rather, Greenstein refers to the Eisenhower administration as "the hidden-hand presidency," meaning that Ike exerted strong political leadership from behind the scenes. Describing the president's leadership style, Greenstein states that Eisenhower managed

> to be vague and folksy in public yet precise and analytic in private, to exude an apolitical aura while constantly devising political strategies and accurately appraising political personalities and practices, to view his immediate associates and other political actors with analytic detachment while conveying easy openness in working with them, and to pour intense energy into his efforts while appearing in public to be reasonably relaxed.[23]

Alexander George points out several major problems in trying to categorize presidents by Barber's character types.[24] Perhaps the principal problem is whether persons can be described as either "active" or "passive," "positive" or "negative." George suggests that their tendencies in these directions instead may be located on a continuum with no clear cutoff points.[25] There is also the question whether Barber's categories adequately allow for alterations in a person's behavior as his moods and behavior change over time and with circumstances.

Barber does acknowledge the influence of external circumstances on presidential performance—the "power situation" the president faces with the Congress, the courts, interest groups, and political parties, and the "climate of expectations" regarding the public's need at a particular time for progress, reassurance, or legitimacy in the presidency. Still, he clearly emphasizes character as the key to understanding presidents' performance in office. It would seem, however, that external circumstances are as important as character to understanding presidential behavior. If this is indeed the case, then one must be able to assess accurately not only a person's character but also *the situation he will face when he becomes president*—no easy task in today's rapidly changing world.

The presidencies of Richard Nixon and Lyndon Johnson both illustrate this latter point. Had Watergate not occurred, it is entirely possible that Nixon's presidency would be viewed not as tragic but as successful, one in which progress was made in foreign affairs, particularly in improving U.S. relations with China and the Soviet Union. Similarly, had Johnson not been faced with Vietnam, a war he did not really understand, he may well have gone down in history as another Franklin Roosevelt, known for his demonstrated ability to handle domestic problems. Presidential performance is shaped not only by an incumbent's general character traits but also by how those traits relate to the particular problems he faces while in office.

George also suggests that Barber overemphasizes a president's personal character compared with his "world view," or basic political beliefs. It is entirely possible that Herbert Hoover persisted in his opposition to a relief program during the Great Depression not because of a negative, rigid attitude triggered by threats to his sense of self-worth, but because he genuinely believed that such relief was inconsistent with the competitive free enterprise system. Similarly, Reagan's decision in his second year in office to continue with his economic program in the face of a recession seemed to be motivated by the conservative beliefs he had espoused for many years. In any event, Reagan's decision cannot be attributed to his negative tendencies, since Barber himself identified Reagan as positive in his orientation toward life.

We see other inadequacies in Barber's attempt to categorize presidents. His criteria for determining whether a president is active or passive—namely, how much or little personal energy he invests in the job—presents problems. According to Greenstein, Eisenhower poured intense energy into his efforts but appeared in public to be reasonably relaxed. Therefore, to look at matters from the outside (as most students of the presidency do) may not provide an accurate picture of presidential activity. Also, that activity may be sporadic. Although one hardly can characterize Reagan as a "workaholic," at a crucial stage in a major political battle, he would engage in concerted efforts to win the support of wavering members of Congress, interest group representatives, and the American public in general. Finally, whether a president is active or passive should not be determined by effort alone; the *results* of that activity should also be taken into account. The Reagan administration has succeeded in dominating the nation's political agenda since its inception; it has also succeeded in having most of its major economic proposals enacted (many of which slowed down or reversed liberal programs established over the years). Characterizing these activities and accomplishments as the work of a passive president is questionable.

Barber's categorizations of presidents has little to do with the *substance of their public policy preferences.* Placing Franklin Roosevelt and Gerald Ford in the same active-positive category (as Barber does) provides little perspective on the kinds of administrations over which they presided. The same is true of active-negative presidents Woodrow Wilson and Richard Nixon.

In his book on specifically this issue—that is, what voters should be looking for in evaluating presidential candidates—Bruce Buchanan takes essentially the same position as Barber.[26] He argues that assessing candidates by either their policy stands or their previous "track records" is not helpful to voters. The first criterion is not satisfactory because voters cannot be expected to find the time to acquaint themselves with the policy options provided by the competing candidates; and even if they did, there is no assurance that candidates will try to carry out their campaign promises. The second potential criterion for choice is not valid because only the presidency itself serves as an adequate training ground for that unique office. Like Barber, Buchanan considers the candidate's character or personality the best indicator of what he will do once in office.

Buchanan identifies three characteristics as the most relevant for determining how the candidate will handle the job of president. The first is the ability to establish and maintain a successful relationship with the American people. This factor involves the candidate's self-presentation and can be gauged by the reactions of the public to his character and personal style. The second is the way he combines his own skills and limitations with those of others to accomplish his policy goals, described as a candidate's "management style." The third characteristic for assessing presidential candidates is how they will handle the psychological pressures of the presidency.[27]

Buchanan uses the records of Carter and Reagan to support his arguments. Although Carter had the ability to establish a rapport with certain kinds of audiences, such as blacks, children, and the elderly, he lacked Reagan's ability to relate effectively to all kinds of Americans, those with and without social and economic advantages. Carter's management style combined a mastery of detail—setting an example of hard work for his subordinates—

with reliance on a small group of longtime associates whom he trusted (including his wife). Reagan's management style, in contrast, entails extensive delegating of authority to subordinates, distancing himself from many decisions, and reserving to himself the task of selling the generalities of programs to the American people. Finally, Buchanan argues that Carter handled the psychological pressures of the presidency by facing problems head-on and taking full responsibility for what occurred in his administration; in contrast, Reagan deals with such pressures by distancing himself from unpopular events and outcomes, by rationalizing inconsistent actions as being consistent with his principles, and by denying facts that are at variance with his beliefs and preferences.

Buchanan's analysis presents many of the same problems as Barber's. As in Barber's first edition of *The Presidential Character*, Buchanan's evaluation is *retrospective* rather than *prospective*. Moreover, it fails to take into account the particular situations a president faces while in office. Reagan's managerial style and method of dealing with the psychological pressures of the office generally served him well in his first administration. However, the lesser abilities of his subordinates in his second term, together with the particular problems presented by the Iran-contra affair, made his techniques of extensive delegation, distancing himself from controversies, and rationalizing and denying inconsistencies in his policies (such as taking a strong stand against dealing with terrorists while selling them arms) less appropriate, both for his own well-being and that of the nation. Finally, Buchanan's analysis places inordinate demands on voters: he argues that they cannot be expected to find time to acquaint themselves with the policy stands of the presidential candidates, but he expects them to be able to comprehend the imprecise nature and complex applications of psychobiography.

We disagree with Barber's and Buchanan's assertions that one cannot rely on politicians' statements to understand what they do or will do in office. As discussed in Chapter 4, presidents do act on the promises they make in their campaigns, and they have a considerable degree of success in seeing that those promises are enacted either by Congress or through executive orders.[28] It therefore behooves voters to listen to what presidential candidates say during their campaigns because that information provides a basis for predicting what kind of policies they will try to formulate and implement if they become president.

Having recognized these problems, we nonetheless feel that Barber and Buchanan perform a valuable service in sensitizing observers of the presidency to the influence of character in shaping a president's performance in office. Character may not be as important as they suggest, but it does need to be taken into account along with basic political beliefs, public policy preferences, experience in other political offices, and the political circumstances of the time, in assessing how various candidates will perform if elected president. More attention also should be paid to the close associates, campaign managers, and aides of presidential candidates (such as H. R. Haldeman, Hamilton Jordan, and Edwin Meese III) since such people typically end up in key administrative and policy positions if their candidate wins the presidency. The vice-presidential candidates also should receive close scrutiny since one of them may succeed to the presidential office. The mass media could provide a valuable public service if they gave more attention to informing the American people about such vital matters rather than focusing so much of their efforts on the horse race aspects of presidential campaigns.

Reforming Governmental Structure

The recurrent pattern of conflict and deadlock between the president and Congress, punctuated by occasional frenetic periods of legislative output in response to crises and strong presidential leadership, has produced a variety of proposals for changes in the structure of governmental institutions and processes.[29] The two most sweeping reform proposals are the adoption of parliamentary government and revitalization of the party system. A parliamentary government would eliminate the separation of powers and the idea of a balanced constitution. It would fuse executive and legislative leadership. The main arguments for parliamentary government are: (1) it would increase the responsiveness of elected officials and make them more accountable; (2) it would enhance the legitimacy of the government by strengthening the link between public opinion and public policy; and (3) it would improve political control of the bureaucracy.

We believe that the arguments against parliamentary government are more persuasive. First, it would reduce the direct accountability of the president and other executive officials to the public. Second, it would eliminate the restraining influence of checks and balances on governmental action. Third, and most important, the fusion of executive and legislative leadership is no guarantee against stalemate and governmental instability. An American parliamentary system would probably be accompanied by a multiparty system reflecting the pluralism of the society. In all likelihood it would be very difficult to establish a legislative majority. Government by unstable coalitions, such as those that have characterized the Italian republic since 1946, would probably be the rule.

Another reform proposal, which received serious attention in the mid-1970s, is the adoption of a congressional vote of no-confidence in the president followed by new elections. This suggestion retains the separation-of-powers structure while grafting onto it a key feature of parliamentary government. This proposal entails several possibilities, including requiring the president to face a new election or to run against his record. Conceivably, Congress could be dissolved and its members required to face a new election also. The major argument for the no-confidence scheme is that it would force the president to maintain the confidence of Congress through much closer consultation with its leaders and members. This, in turn, would reduce the likelihood of deadlock and stalemate.

We believe that the argument against the no-confidence proposal is the stronger one. Its principal defect is that it would severely cripple the presidency without overcoming the weaknesses of Congress. It would also be likely to result in manipulation to secure short-run political gains. We strongly suspect that it would have highly destabilizing consequences.

A third proposal for improving presidential-congressional relations and strengthening national policy leadership is to limit the president to a single six-year term. The arguments for the six-year term are that it would remove partisan political considerations and preoccupation with the next election from presidential policy leadership and thus result in more objective and rational decisions. Also, many contend that four years is an insufficient time for a president to develop a program, steer it through Congress, and direct its implementation.

We feel that the six-year term proposal is seriously flawed. Conceptually, it assumes that partisan politics is a major cause of the inability of American governmental institutions to provide cohesive leadership and coherent policies. Our position is that the major cause of that limitation is the weakness of political parties in the United States. Since the Progressive era in the early twentieth century, parties have been a primary target of reform proposals that have sought to weaken them. The suggestion for a six-year term is in keeping with that reform tradition. We regard parties as essential to the establishment and maintenance of responsible government and democratic accountability. If parties are weak, the health of the democratic process is threatened.

The six-year term also has serious defects operationally. Because the president would be ineligible for reelection, he would have reduced leverage over other politicians. (We view the Twenty-second Amendment limiting the president to two four-year terms as similarly but less deficient.) The president would have fewer resources for bargaining and coalition building in Congress than he would have if he could succeed himself. A second serious defect of the single six-year term is that it assumes the viability of presidential policies and the competence of the president. If the voters elect an incompetent president who proposes disastrous policies, he will remain in office two additional years before he can be replaced. Furthermore, if the president cannot accomplish his objectives in four years, it is unlikely that two additional ones will make much difference.

We do not believe that improvement of presidential-congressional relations can be accomplished through structural reforms, such as those discussed here. Unless there is a total collapse of the political system, it is most unlikely that the American people will abandon their dedication to the separation-of-powers doctrine in favor of parliamentary government. Nor will they experiment with parliamentary devices such as no-confidence resolutions and dissolution. The commitment to the basic structural design established in the Constitution has remained inviolate since 1789. State governments also have preserved that commitment. Presumably, if there were any tendencies toward parliamentary government, they would have manifested themselves in some of the more venturesome and progressive states.

The six-year term is a less radical reform, but it would upset the normal rhythm of the two- and four-year election cycle and for this reason alone could be expected to draw strong opposition. Moreover, all of these changes would necessitate constitutional amendments. The amending process is slow, cumbersome, and highly public; and to be used successfully, it requires overwhelming majorities. The kind of demand that would produce changes in the basic structures and processes of government does not exist at present, nor does it appear likely to do so in the foreseeable future.

A second major prescription, beyond adoption of parliamentary government, for reformers bent on overcoming the inherent weaknesses of the constitutional structure and improving the presidential-congressional relationship is to strengthen the political party system. These analysts look to the model of responsible party government provided by Great Britain and to periods in U.S. history when strong presidents, such as Andrew Jackson and Franklin Roosevelt, used their political parties to bridge the gap between the executive and legislative branches. Strengthening the party system could be accomplished, it is argued, through legislation and through actions by the parties themselves and would not require constitutional amendments.

The substance of proposals to improve party government are beyond the scope of our discussion here. The problem with such proposals is not their content, but the generally low regard in which the American public holds political parties. The public tends to regard partisan politics as self-serving if not openly corrupt and as antithetical to the common good. The parties have been declining since the mid-1930s, and voter independence, as opposed to party affiliation, has been on the rise since the early 1960s. For reasons we have already discussed, national party conventions now meet to ratify the selection of a candidate chosen in a series of primary elections. The successful candidate, if he should become president, owes little to the party whose standard he carried, and it has little control over him.

A further element of party weakness lies in the lack of control that national party organizations have over congressional nominations. That weakness afflicts leaders of congressional parties as well. They cannot discipline or command the votes of their members. The only instrument the parties have for defining policy goals and outlining means to achieve them is the platform adopted at the quadrennial nominating convention. None of the party's national officeholders, however, is obligated to support the policies stated in the platform. They are free to act independently according to their own attitudes and beliefs and in response to the interests of their constituencies, and many members of Congress do.

Nevertheless, most political scientists accept the proposition that parties are the most effective means of overcoming the disunity and dispersion created by American governmental institutions. That point of view is not widely held among the public, however. Experience with divided control of the government in twenty of the thirty-four years from 1953 through 1986 has contributed further to popular disenchantment with political parties. During those years of divided government, stalemate and maneuvering for partisan advantage by presidents and congressional leaders have been commonplace. Even the high degree of comity between Reagan and the Democratic House of Representatives that characterized the first year of his presidency gave way to a predominant pattern of conflict and bickering in subsequent years. Increasingly, the public seems to regard political parties in a less favorable light and tends to blame the parties and their leaders for government's inability to function effectively and responsibly.

As James Sundquist has observed, "The revitalization of political parties cannot be willed." [30] That event will happen only if the people are moved, in response to a major challenge or crisis, to use political parties as a means to achieve their ends. Efforts of reformers to use parties to overcome structural problems in the government will not succeed until then.

How, then, can government be made to function effectively if structural change in the Constitution and party revitalization are out of reach as ways for overcoming governmental disunity and improving the presidential-congressional relationship? One is left with the hope that presidents and members of Congress will gain greater understanding of the forces that increase conflict between them and of the need for cooperation between them. For the president, the key is to maintain his support among the people. If he is unable to do so, no amount of legislative skill or rhetorical polish will induce Congress to pass his proposals. For Congress, the question is whether it can overcome the localism of its members and its internal fragmentation of authority so as to develop cohesive institutional policies. Only then can it look forward to participating with the president as a responsible partner in the process of governing. It is also quite likely, if experience is any guide, that important changes in the presidential-congressional relationship will continue to occur in response to changes in the political environment. That is partly what we mean when we refer to the protean character of the presidency. We cannot, however, predict accurately the nature or the effects of such changes. Nor can we offer any specific institutional reforms or prescriptive actions for presidents and members of Congress that will guarantee collaboration and cooperation. Such improvements will require patience and constant effort by them as well as understanding on the part of the public. Disappointments and frustrations with governmental performance are the price Americans must pay for the constitutional system to which they are devoted.

Notes

1. Samuel Kernell, *Going Public: New Strategies of Presidential Leadership* (Washington, D.C.: CQ Press, 1986).
2. Theodore Lowi, *The Personal President: Power Invested, Promise Unfilled* (Ithaca, N.Y.: Cornell University Press, 1985).
3. Clinton Rossiter, *The American Presidency* (New York: Harcourt, Brace, 1960), 262.
4. George Reedy, *The Twilight of the Presidency* (New York: New American Library, 1970), 194.
5. Rossiter, *The American Presidency,* 237.
6. Reedy, *Twilight of the Presidency,* 194.
7. In each of these elections, persons other than the two major party candidates received electoral votes. The losing candidates, Dewey, Nixon, and Humphrey, therefore could have carried the key states named in the text and still not have had a majority of the electoral votes.
8. Although Wallace actually earned forty-five electoral votes, he received forty-six because one elector in North Carolina (which went for Nixon) cast his vote for the Alabama governor. In 1960, 1972, and 1976, single electors in Oklahoma, Virginia, and Washington also did not cast their ballots for the candidate receiving the popular-vote plurality in their state.
9. Most of the proportional plans have suggested lowering the winning electoral-vote requirement from a majority to 40 or even 35 percent to avoid the possibility of having the election go to the House. They have also proposed that, if no candidate receives the requisite proportion of electoral votes, the two houses, meeting jointly and voting as individuals, choose the president.
10. *Winner-Take-All: Report of the Twentieth Century Task Force on Reform of the Presidential Election Process* (New York: Holmes and Meier, 1978), 4-6.
11. Alexander Bickel, *The New Age of Political Reform: The Electoral College, The Convention, and the Party System* (New York: Harper and Row, 1968), 14-16.
12. Lawrence Longley and Alan Braun, *The Politics of Electoral College Reform* (New Haven: Yale University Press, 1975), chap. 2.
13. Neal Peirce, *The People's President: The Electoral College in American History and the Direct-Vote Alternative* (New York: Simon and Schuster, 1968), 295, also cites figures compiled by Donald Stokes showing that in 170 gubernatorial elections occurring in the thirty most competitive states between 1952 and 1964 (these contests, of course, were based on a direct popular vote), the winning candidate never received less than 40 percent of the popular vote.
14. We do not find significant the argument that the electoral college is desirable because it presently amplifies close popular election outcomes (Martin Diamond, *The Electoral College and the American Idea of Democracy* [Washington, D.C.: American Enterprise Institute, 1977], 16). The same is true of the contention that direct popular election would increase the possibility of vote fraud (Judith Best, *The Case against the Direct Election of*

the President: A Defense of the Electoral College [Ithaca, N.Y.: Cornell University Press, 1975], chap. 6). Justifying a distortion of the actual election results to create a false mandate seems curious. Moreover, the effects of vote fraud are more likely to be felt at the state than the national level; in 1976, nine thousand false ballots in Hawaii and Ohio could have reversed Carter's electoral victory, but it would have taken almost one hundred times that number to have eliminated his 1.7 million nationwide popular plurality.

15. Austin Ranney, *The Federalization of Presidential Primaries* (Washington, D.C.: American Enterprise Institute, 1978), 4.

16. James David Barber, "Strategies for Understanding Politicians," *American Journal of Political Science* (May 1974): 463-464.

17. James David Barber, *The Presidential Character: Predicting Performance in the White House* (Englewood Cliffs, N.J.: Prentice-Hall, 1972).

18. Ibid., 441-442.

19. Barber's prediction about Ford, which he cites in his third edition (James David Barber, *The Presidential Character: Predicting Performance in the White House*, 3d ed. [Englewood Cliffs, N.J.: Prentice-Hall, 1985], 555), first appeared in *U.S. News & World Report*, September 2, 1974, 23-25. Barber's prediction about Carter, made shortly before his inauguration, is contained in his second edition (James David Barber, *The Presidential Character: Predicting Performance in the White House*, 2d ed. [Englewood Cliffs, N.J.: Prentice-Hall, 1977], chaps. 14, 15).

20. *New York Times,* September 8, 1980, A19.

21. Two biographies on Reagan written by journalists are Lou Cannon, *Reagan* (New York: Putnam's, 1982), and Lawrence Barrett, *Gambling with History: Reagan in the White House* (Garden City, N.Y.: Doubleday, 1983). However, both cover only through the early years of Reagan's first term in office. For an assessment written in the second year of his second term, see "Yankee Doodle Magic," *Time,* July 7, 1986, 12-16.

22. Fred Greenstein, *The Hidden-Hand Presidency: Eisenhower as Leader* (New York: Basic Books, 1982).

23. Ibid., 233.

24. Alexander George "Assessing Presidential Character," *World Politics* (January 1974): 234-282.

25. In fairness to Barber, it should be noted that he himself recognizes that his categories are "pure" ones and that no individual fits entirely into one category. He feels that it is possible, however, to judge people on the basis of their dominant characteristics. See Barber, *The Presidential Character,* 3d ed., 524.

26. Bruce Buchanan, *The Citizen's Presidency: Standards of Choice and Judgment* (Washington, D.C.: CQ Press, 1987), esp. chap. 6.

27. Recall from the Introduction that Buchanan expressed a similar concern with psychological pressures on the president in a previous book: Bruce Buchanan, *The Presidential Experience: What the Office Does to the Man* (Englewood Cliffs, N.J.: Prentice-Hall, 1978).

28. Jeff Fishel, *Presidents and Promises: From Campaign Pledge to Presidential Performance* (Washington, D.C.: CQ Press, 1985); Arnold Muller, "Public

Policy and the Presidential Election Process: A Study of Promise and Performance" (Ph.D. diss., University of Missouri-Columbia, 1986); and Fred Grogan, "Candidate Promises and Presidential Performance" (Paper delivered at the annual meeting of the Midwest Political Science Association, Chicago, April 21-23, 1977).

29. Norman C. Thomas, "Reforming the Presidency: Problems and Prospects," in *The Presidency Reappraised,* ed. Thomas E. Cronin and Rexford G. Tugwell (New York: Praeger, 1977).

30. James L. Sundquist, *The Decline and Resurgence of Congress* (Washington, D.C.: Brookings, 1981), 477.

Selected Readings

Barber, James David. *The Presidential Character: Predicting Performance in the White House.* 3d ed. Englewood Cliffs, N.J.: Prentice-Hall, 1985.

Greenstein, Fred. *The Hidden-Hand Presidency: Eisenhower as Leader.* New York: Basic Books, 1982.

Longley, Lawrence, and Alan Braun. *The Politics of Electoral Reform.* New Haven: Yale University Press, 1975.

Lowi, Theodore. *The Personal President: Power Invested, Power Unfilled.* Ithaca, N.Y.: Cornell University Press, 1985.

Sundquist, James L. *Constitutional Reform and Effective Government.* Washington, D.C.: Brookings, 1986.

Appendixes

Results of Presidential Contests, 1912-1984

Year	Republican nominee (in *italics*) and other major candidates	Democratic nominee (in *italics*) and other major candidates	Election winner	Division of popular vote[a] (percent)	Division of electoral vote[b]
1912	*William Howard Taft* (incumbent president) Theodore Roosevelt[c] (former president)	*Woodrow Wilson* (governor of New Jersey) James Champ Clark (representative from Missouri and Speaker of the House)	Wilson (D)	42-23	435-8
1916	*Charles Evans Hughes* (justice, U.S. Supreme Court) Elihu Root (former secretary of state)	*Woodrow Wilson* (incumbent president) None	Wilson (D)	49-46	277-254
1920	*Warren G. Harding* (senator from Ohio) Leonard Wood (general) Frank Lowden (governor of Illinois) Hiram Johnson (senator from California)	*James Cox* (governor of Ohio) William McAdoo (former secretary of the treasury) A. Mitchell Palmer (attorney general)	Harding (R)	60-34	404-127
1924	*Calvin Coolidge* (incumbent president) Hiram Johnson (senator from California)	*John W. Davis* (former solicitor general) Alfred Smith (governor of New York) William McAdoo	Coolidge (R)	54-29	382-136

Year	Candidates	Winner	Popular vote	Electoral vote
1928	*Herbert Hoover* (former secretary of commerce) Frank Lowden (governor of Illinois) (former secretary of the treasury) *Alfred Smith* (governor of New York) James Reed (senator from Missouri) Cordell Hull (representative from Tennessee)	Hoover (R)	58-41	444-87
1932	*Herbert Hoover* (incumbent president) Joseph France (former senator from Missouri) *Franklin D. Roosevelt* (governor of New York) Alfred Smith (former governor of New York) John Garner (representative from Texas and Speaker of the House)	Roosevelt (D)	57-40	472-59
1936	*Alfred Landon* (governor of Kansas) William Borah (senator from Idaho) *Franklin D. Roosevelt* (incumbent president) None	Roosevelt (D)	61-37	523-8
1940	*Wendell Willkie* (Indiana lawyer and public utility executive) Thomas E. Dewey (U.S. district attorney for New York) Robert Taft (senator from Ohio) *Franklin D. Roosevelt* (incumbent president) None	Roosevelt (D)	55-45	449-82

Year	Republican nominee (in *italics*) and other major candidates	Democratic nominee (in *italics*) and other major candidates	Election winner	Division of popular vote[a] (percent)	Division of electoral vote[b]
1944	*Thomas E. Dewey* (governor of New York) Wendell Willkie (previous Republican presidential nominee)	*Franklin D. Roosevelt* (incumbent president) Harry Byrd (senator from Virginia)	Roosevelt (D)	53-46	432-99
1948	*Thomas E. Dewey* (governor of New York) Harold Stassen (former governor of Minnesota) Robert Taft (senator from Ohio)	*Harry S Truman* (incumbent president) Richard Russell (senator from Georgia)	Truman (D)	50-45	303-189
1952	*Dwight D. Eisenhower* (general) Robert Taft (senator from Ohio)	*Adlai Stevenson* (governor of Illinois) Estes Kefauver (senator from Tennessee) Richard Russell (senator from Georgia)	Eisenhower (R)	55-44	442-89
1956	*Dwight D. Eisenhower* (incumbent president) None	*Adlai Stevenson* (previous Democratic presidential nominee) Averell Harriman (governor of New York)	Eisenhower (R)	57-42	457-73

Year				Popular vote	Electoral vote
1960	*Richard Nixon* (vice president) None	*John F. Kennedy* (senator from Massachusetts) Hubert Humphrey (senator from Minnesota) Lyndon B. Johnson (senator from Texas)	Kennedy (D)	49.7-49.5	303-219
1964	*Barry Goldwater* (senator from Arizona) Nelson Rockefeller (governor of New York)	*Lyndon B. Johnson* (incumbent president) None	Johnson (D)	61-39	486-52
1968	*Richard Nixon* (former Republican presidential nominee) Ronald Reagan (governor of California)	*Hubert Humphrey* (incumbent vice president) Robert F. Kennedy (senator from New York) Eugene McCarthy (senator from Minnesota)	Nixon (R)	43.4-42.7	301-191
1972	*Richard Nixon* (incumbent president) None	*George McGovern* (senator from South Dakota) Hubert Humphrey (senator from Minnesota) George Wallace (governor of Alabama)	Nixon (R)	61-38	520-17
1976	*Gerald R. Ford* (incumbent president) Ronald Reagan (former governor of California)	*Jimmy Carter* (former governor of Georgia) Edmund Brown, Jr. (governor of California) George Wallace (governor of Alabama)	Carter (D)	50-48	297-240

Year	Republican nominee (in *italics*) and other major candidates	Democratic nominee (in *italics*) and other major candidates	Election winner	Division of popular vote[a] (percent)	Division of electoral vote[b]
1980	*Ronald Reagan* (former governor of California) George Bush (former director of Central Intelligence Agency) John Anderson (representative from Illinois)	*Jimmy Carter* (incumbent president) Edward M. Kennedy (senator from Massachusetts)	Reagan (R)	51-41	489-49
1984	*Ronald Reagan* (incumbent president) None	*Walter F. Mondale* (former vice president) Gary Hart (senator from Colorado)	Reagan (R)	59-41	525-13

Note: The table begins with the year 1912 because presidential primaries were first held that year.

[a] Division of popular vote is between the Republican and Democratic nominees.

[b] Division of electoral votes is between the Republican and Democratic nominees.

[c] When the Republican convention failed to choose him as its nominee (selecting instead the incumbent president, William Howard Taft), former president Theodore Roosevelt withdrew from the party and created the Progressive party. As the Progressive party nominee, Roosevelt received 27 percent of the popular vote and 88 electoral votes.

APPENDIX B

Personal Backgrounds
of U.S. Presidents

President	Age at first political office	First political office	Last political office[a]	Age at becoming president	State of residence[b]	Father's occupation	Higher education[c]	Occupation
1. Washington (1789-1797)	17	County surveyor	Commander in chief	57	Va.	Farmer	None	Farmer, surveyor
2. Adams, J. (1797-1801)	39	Surveyor of highways	Vice president	61	Mass.	Farmer	Harvard	Farmer, lawyer
3. Jefferson (1801-1809)	26	State legislator	Vice president	58	Va.	Farmer	William and Mary	Farmer, lawyer
4. Madison (1809-1817)	25	State legislator	Secretary of state	58	Va.	Farmer	Princeton	Farmer
5. Monroe (1817-1825)	24	State legislator	Secretary of state	59	Va.	Farmer	William and Mary	Lawyer, farmer
6. Adams, J. Q. (1825-1829)	27	Minister to Netherlands	Secretary of state	58	Mass.	Farmer, lawyer	Harvard	Lawyer
7. Jackson (1829-1837)	21	Prosecuting attorney	U.S. Senate	62	Tenn.	Dirt farmer	None	Lawyer
8. Van Buren (1837-1841)	30	Surrogate of county	Vice president	55	N.Y.	Tavern keeper	None	Lawyer
9. Harrison, W. H. (1841)	26	Territorial delegate to Congress	Minister to Colombia	68	Ind.	Farmer	Hampden-Sydney	Military
10. Tyler (1841-1845)	21	State legislator	Vice president	51	Va.	Planter, lawyer	William and Mary	Lawyer
11. Polk (1845-1849)	28	State legislator	Governor	50	Tenn.	Surveyor	U. of North Carolina	Lawyer

12. Taylor (1849-1850)	None	None	a	65	Ky.	Collector of internal revenue	None	Military
13. Fillmore (1850-1853)	28	State legislator	Vice president	50	N.Y.	Dirt farmer	None	Lawyer
14. Pierce (1853-1857)	25	State legislator	U.S. district attorney	48	N.H.	General	Bowdoin	Lawyer
15. Buchanan (1857-1861)	22	Assistant county prosecutor	Minister to Great Britain	65	Pa.	Dirt farmer	Dickinson	Lawyer
16. Lincoln (1861-1865)	25	State legislator	U.S. House of Representatives	52	Ill.	Dirt farmer, carpenter	None	Lawyer
17. Johnson, A. (1865-1869)	20	City alderman	Vice president	57	Tenn.	Janitor-porter	None	Tailor
18. Grant (1869-1877)	None	None	a	47	Ohio	Tanner	West Point	Military
19. Hayes (1877-1881)	36	City solicitor	Governor	55	Ohio	Dirt farmer	Kenyon	Lawyer
20. Garfield (1881)	28	State legislator	U.S. Senate	50	Ohio	Canal worker	Williams	Educator, lawyer
21. Arthur (1881-1885)	31	State engineer	Vice president	51	N.Y.	Minister	Union	Lawyer
22. Cleveland (1885-1889) 24. (1893-1897)	26	Assistant district attorney	Governor	48	N.Y.	Minister	None	Lawyer
23. Harrison, B. (1889-1893)	24	City attorney	U.S. Senate	56	Ind.	Military	Miami of Ohio	Lawyer
25. McKinley (1897-1901)	26	Prosecuting attorney	Governor	54	Ohio	Ironmonger	Allegheny	Lawyer

President	Age at first political office	First political office	Last political office[a]	Age at becoming president	State of residence[b]	Father's occupation	Higher education[c]	Occupation
26. Roosevelt, T. (1901-1909)	24	State legislator	Vice president	43	N.Y.	Businessman	Harvard	Lawyer, author
27. Taft (1909-1913)	24	Assistant prosecuting attorney	Secretary of war	52	Ohio	Lawyer	Yale	Lawyer
28. Wilson (1913-1921)	54	Governor	Governor	56	N.J.	Minister	Princeton	Educator
29. Harding (1921-1923)	35	State legislator	U.S. Senate	56	Ohio	Physician, editor	Ohio Central	Newspaper editor
30. Coolidge (1923-1929)	26	City councilman	Vice president	51	Mass.	Storekeeper	Amherst	Lawyer
31. Hoover (1929-1933)	43	Relief and food administrator	Secretary of commerce	55	Calif.	Blacksmith	Stanford	Mining engineer
32. Roosevelt, F. (1933-1945)	28	State legislator	Governor	49	N.Y.	Businessman, landowner	Harvard	Lawyer
33. Truman (1945-1953)	38	County judge (commissioner)	Vice president	61	Mo.	Farmer, livestock	None	Clerk, store owner
34. Eisenhower (1953-1961)	None	None	[a]	63	Kan.	Mechanic	West Point	Military
35. Kennedy (1961-1963)	29	U.S. House of Representatives	U.S. Senate	43	Mass.	Businessman	Harvard	Newspaper reporter
36. Johnson, L. (1963-1969)	23	Assistant to member, U.S. House of Representatives	Vice president	55	Texas	Farmer, real estate	Southwest Texas State Teacher's College	Educator

37. Nixon (1969-1974)	29	Office of Price Administration	Vice president	56	Calif.	Streetcar conductor	Whittier	Lawyer
38. Ford (1974-1977)	36	U.S. House of Representatives	Vice president	61	Mich.	Businessman	U. of Michigan	Lawyer
39. Carter (1977-1981)	38	County Board of Education	Governor	52	Ga.	Farmer, businessman	U.S. Naval Academy	Farmer, businessman
40. Reagan (1981-)	55	Governor	Governor	69	Calif.	Shoe salesman	Eureka	Entertainer

a This category refers to the last civilian office held before the presidency. Taylor, Grant, and Eisenhower had served as generals before becoming president.
b The state is where the president spent his important adult years, not necessarily where he was born.
c Refers to undergraduate education.

APPENDIX C

The Constitution on the Presidency

Article I

Section 3. ... The Vice President of the United States shall be President of the Senate, but shall have no Vote, unless they be equally divided.

The Senate shall chuse their other Officers, and also a President pro tempore, in the Absence of the Vice President, or when he shall exercise the Office of President of the United States.

The Senate shall have the sole Power to try all Impeachments. When sitting for that Purpose, they shall be on Oath or Affirmation. When the President of the United States is tried the Chief Justice shall preside: And no Person shall be convicted without the Concurrence of two thirds of the Members present.

Judgment in Cases of Impeachment shall not extend further than to removal from Office, and disqualification to hold and enjoy any Office of honor, Trust or Profit under the United States: but the Party convicted shall nevertheless be liable and subject to Indictment, Trial, Judgment and Punishment, according to Law.

Section 7. ... Every Bill which shall have passed the House of Representatives and the Senate, shall, before it become a Law, be presented to the President of the United States; If he approve he shall sign it, but if not he shall return it, with his Objections to that House in which it shall have originated, who shall enter the Objections at large on their Journal, and proceed to reconsider it. If after such Reconsideration two thirds of that House shall agree to pass the Bill, it shall be sent, together with the Objections, to the other House, by which it shall likewise be reconsidered, and if approved by two thirds of that House, it shall become a Law. But in all such Cases the Votes of both Houses shall be determined by yeas and Nays, and the Names of the Persons voting for and against the Bill shall be entered on the Journal of each House respectively. If any Bill shall not be returned by the President within ten Days (Sundays excepted) after it shall have been presented to him, the Same shall be a Law, in like Manner as if he had signed it, unless the Congress by their Adjournment prevent its Return, in which Case it shall not be a Law.

Every Order, Resolution, or Vote to which the Concurrence of the Senate and House of Representatives may be necessary (except on a question of Adjournment) shall be presented to the President of the United States; and before the Same shall take Effect, shall be approved by him, or being disapproved by him, shall be repassed by two thirds of the Senate and House of Representatives, according to the Rules and Limitations prescribed in the Case of a Bill.

Article II

Section 1.   The executive Power shall be vested in a President of the United States of America. He shall hold his Office during the Term of four Years, and, together with the Vice President, chosen for the same Term, be elected, as follows.

Each State shall appoint, in such Manner as the Legislature thereof may direct, a Number of Electors, equal to the whole Number of Senators and Representatives to which the State may be entitled in the Congress: but no Senator or Representative, or Person holding an Office of Trust or Profit under the United States, shall be appointed an Elector.

[The Electors shall meet in their respective States, and vote by Ballot for two Persons, of whom one at least shall not be an Inhabitant of the same State with themselves. And they shall make a List of all the Persons voted for, and of the Number of Votes for each; which List they shall sign and certify, and transmit sealed to the Seat of the Government of the United States, directed to the President of the Senate. The President of the Senate shall, in the Presence of the Senate and House of Representatives, open all the Certificates, and the Votes shall then be counted. The Person having the greatest Number of Votes shall be the President, if such Number be a Majority of the whole Number of Electors appointed; and if there be more than one who have such Majority, and have an equal Number of Votes, then the House of Representatives shall immediately chuse by Ballot one of them for President; and if no Person have a Majority, then from the five highest on the list the said House shall in like Manner chuse the President. But in chusing the President, the Votes shall be taken by States, the Representation from each State having one Vote; a quorum for this Purpose shall consist of a Member or Members from two thirds of the States, and a Majority of all the States shall be necessary to a Choice. In every Case, after the Choice of the President, the Person having the greatest Number of Votes of the Electors shall be the Vice President. But if there should remain two or more who have equal Votes, the Senate shall chuse from them by Ballot the Vice President.][1]

The Congress may determine the Time of chusing the Electors, and the Day on which they shall give their Votes; which Day shall be the same throughout the United States.

No Person except a natural born Citizen, or a Citizen of the United States, at the time of the Adoption of this Constitution, shall be eligible to the Office of President; neither shall any Person be eligible to that Office who shall not have attained to the Age of thirty five Years, and been fourteen Years a Resident within the United States.

In Case of the Removal of the President from Office, or of his Death, Resignation, or Inability to discharge the Powers and Duties of the said Office,[2] the Same shall devolve on the Vice President, and the Congress may by Law provide for the Case of Removal, Death, Resignation or Inability, both of the President and Vice President, declaring what Officer shall then act as President, and such Officer shall act accordingly, until the Disability be removed, or a President shall be elected.

The President shall, at stated Times, receive for his Services, a Compensation, which shall neither be encreased nor diminished during the Period for which he shall have been elected, and he shall not receive within that Period any other Emolument from the United States, or any of them.

Before he enter on the Execution of his Office, he shall take the following Oath or Affirmation: — "I do solemnly swear (or affirm) that I will faithfully execute the Office of President of the United States, and will to the best of my Ability, preserve, protect and defend the Constitution of the United States."

Section 2.   The President shall be Commander in Chief of the Army and Navy of the United States, and of the Militia of the several States, when called into the actual Service of the United States; he may require the Opinion, in writing, of the principal Officer in each of the executive Departments, upon any Subject relating to the Duties of their respective Offices, and he shall have Power to grant Reprieves and Pardons for Offenses against the United States, except in Cases of Impeachment.

He shall have Power, by and with the Advice and Consent of the Senate, to make Treaties, provided two thirds of the Senators present concur; and he shall nominate, and by and with the Advice and Consent of the Senate, shall appoint Ambassadors, other public Ministers and Consuls, Judges of the supreme Court, and all other Officers of the United States, whose Appointments are not herein otherwise provided for, and which shall be established by Law: but the Congress may by Law vest the Appointment of such inferior Officers, as they think proper, in the President alone, in the Courts of Law, or in the Heads of Departments.

The President shall have Power to fill up all Vacancies that may happen during the Recess of the Senate, by granting Commissions which shall expire at the End of their next Session.

Section 3.   He shall from time to time give to the Congress Information of the State of the Union, and recommend to their Consideration such Measures as he shall judge necessary and expedient; he may, on extraordinary Occasions, convene both Houses, or either of them, and in Case of Disagreement between them, with Respect to the Time of Adjournment, he may adjourn them to such Time as he shall think proper; he shall receive Ambassadors and other public Ministers; he shall take Care that the Laws be faithfully executed, and shall Commission all the Officers of the United States.

Section 4.   The President, Vice President and all Civil Officers of the United States, shall be removed from office on Impeachment for, and Conviction of, Treason, Bribery, or other high Crimes and Misdemeanors.

Article VI
    . . . This Constitution, and the Laws of the United States which shall be made in Pursuance thereof; and all Treaties made, or which shall be made, under the Authority of the United States, shall be the supreme Law of the Land; and the Judges in every State shall be bound thereby, any Thing in the Constitution or Laws of any State to the Contrary notwithstanding.

    The Senators and Representatives before mentioned, and the Members of the several State Legislatures, and all executive and judicial Officers, both of the United States and of the several States, shall be bound by Oath or Affirmation, to support this Constitution; but no religious Test shall ever be required as a Qualification to any Office or public Trust under the United States.

Amendment XII *(Ratified June 15, 1804)*
    The Electors shall meet in their respective states and vote by ballot for President and Vice-President, one of whom, at least, shall not be an inhabitant of the same state with themselves; they shall name in their ballots the person voted for as President, and in distinct ballots the person voted for as Vice-President, and they shall make distinct lists of all persons voted for as President, and of all persons voted for as Vice-President, and of the number of votes for each, which lists they shall sign and certify, and transmit sealed to the seat of the government of the United States, directed to the President of the Senate; — The President of the Senate shall, in the presence of the Senate and House of Representatives, open all the certificates and the votes shall then be counted; — The person having the greatest number of votes for President, shall be the President, if such number be a majority of the whole number of

Electors appointed; and if no person have such majority, then from the persons having the highest numbers not exceeding three on the list of those voted for as President, the House of Representatives shall choose immediately, by ballot, the President. But in choosing the President, the votes shall be taken by states, the representation from each state having one vote; a quorum for this purpose shall consist of a member or members from two-thirds of the states, and a majority of all the states shall be necessary to a choice. [And if the House of Representatives shall not choose a President whenever the right of choice shall devolve upon them, before the fourth day of March next following, then the Vice-President shall act as President, as in the case of the death or other constitutional disability of the President —][3] The person having the greatest number of votes as Vice-President, shall be the Vice-President, if such number be a majority of the whole number of Electors appointed, and if no person have a majority, then from the two highest numbers on the list, the Senate shall choose the Vice-President; a quorum for the purpose shall consist of two-thirds of the whole number of Senators, and a majority of the whole number shall be necessary to a choice. But no person constitutionally ineligible to the office of President shall be eligible to that of Vice-President of the United States.

Amendment XX *(Ratified Jan. 23, 1933)*

Section 1.   The terms of the President and Vice President shall end at noon on the 20th day of January, and the terms of Senators and Representatives at noon on the 3d day of January, of the years in which such terms would have ended if this article had not been ratified; and the terms of their successors shall then begin.

Section 2.   The Congress shall assemble at least once in every year, and such meeting shall begin at noon on the 3d day of January, unless they shall by law appoint a different day.

Section 3.[4]   If, at the time fixed for the beginning of the term of the President, the President elect shall have died, the Vice President elect shall become President. If a President shall not have been chosen before the time fixed for the beginning of his term, or if the President elect shall have failed to qualify, then the Vice President elect shall act as President until a President shall have qualified; and the Congress may by law provide for the case wherein neither a President elect nor a Vice President elect shall have qualified, declaring who shall then act as President, or the manner in which one who is to act shall be selected, and such person shall act accordingly until a President or Vice President shall have qualified.

Section 4.   The Congress may by law provide for the case of the death of any of the persons from whom the House of Representatives may choose a

President whenever the right of choice shall have devolved upon them, and for the case of the death of any of the persons from whom the Senate may choose a Vice President whenever the right of choice shall have devolved upon them.

Section 5.   Sections 1 and 2 shall take effect on the 15th day of October following the ratification of this article.

Section 6.   This article shall be inoperative unless it shall have been ratified as an amendment to the Constitution by the legislatures of three-fourths of the several States within seven years from the date of its submission.

Amendment XXII *(Ratified Feb. 27, 1951)*

Section 1.   No person shall be elected to the office of the President more than twice, and no person who has held the office of President, or acted as President, for more than two years of a term to which some other person was elected President shall be elected to the office of the President more than once. But this Article shall not apply to any person holding the office of President when this Article was proposed by the Congress, and shall not prevent any person who may be holding the office of President, or acting as President, during the term within which this Article become operative from holding the office of President or acting as President during the remainder of such term.

Section 2.   This Article shall be inoperative unless it shall have been ratified as an amendment to the Constitution by the legislatures of three-fourths of the several States within seven years from the date of its submission to the States by the Congress.

Amendment XXIII *(Ratified March 29, 1961)*

Section 1.   The District constituting the seat of Government of the United States shall appoint in such manner as the Congress may direct:

A number of electors of President and Vice President equal to the whole number of Senators and Representatives in Congress to which the District would be entitled if it were a State, but in no event more than the least populous State; they shall be in addition to those appointed by the States, but they shall be considered, for the purposes of the election of President and Vice President, to be electors appointed by a State; and they shall meet in the District and perform such duties as provided by the twelfth article of amendment.

Section 2.   The Congress shall have power to enforce this article by appropriate legislation.

Amendment XXV *(Ratified Feb. 10, 1967)*

Section 1.   In case of the removal of the President from office or of his death or resignation, the Vice President shall become President.

Section 2.   Whenever there is a vacancy in the office of the Vice President, the President shall nominate a Vice President who shall take office upon confirmation by a majority vote of both Houses of Congress.

Section 3.   Whenever the President transmits to the President pro tempore of the Senate and the Speaker of the House of Representatives his written declaration that he is unable to discharge the powers and duties of his office, and until he transmits to them a written declaration to the contrary, such powers and duties shall be discharged by the Vice President as Acting President.

Section 4.   Whenever the Vice President and a majority of either the principal officers of the executive departments or of such other body as Congress may by law provide, transmit to the President pro tempore of the Senate and the Speaker of the House of Representatives their written declaration that the President is unable to discharge the powers and duties of his office, the Vice President shall immediately assume the powers and duties of the office as Acting President.

Thereafter, when the President transmits to the President pro tempore of the Senate and the Speaker of the House of Representatives his written declaration that no inability exists, he shall resume the powers and duties of his office unless the Vice President and a majority of either the principal officers of the executive department or of such other body as Congress may by law provide, transmit within four days to the President pro tempore of the Senate and the Speaker of the House of Representatives their written declaration that the President is unable to discharge the powers and duties of his office. Thereupon Congress shall decide the issue, assembling within forty-eight hours for that purpose if not in session. If the Congress, within twenty-one days after receipt of the latter written declaration, or, if Congress is not in session, within twenty-one days after Congress is required to assemble, determines by two-thirds vote of both houses that the President is unable to discharge the powers and duties of his office, the Vice President shall continue to discharge the same as Acting President; otherwise, the President shall resume the powers and duties of his office.

Notes

1. The material in brackets has been superseded by the Twelfth Amendment.
2. This provision has been affected by the Twenty-fifth Amendment.
3. The part in brackets has been superseded by Section 3 of the Twentieth Amendment.
4. See the Twenty-fifth Amendment.

Index